FAMILIES
OF
BEAVER COUNTY
PENNSYLVANIA

Excerpted from
History of Beaver County, Pennsylvania

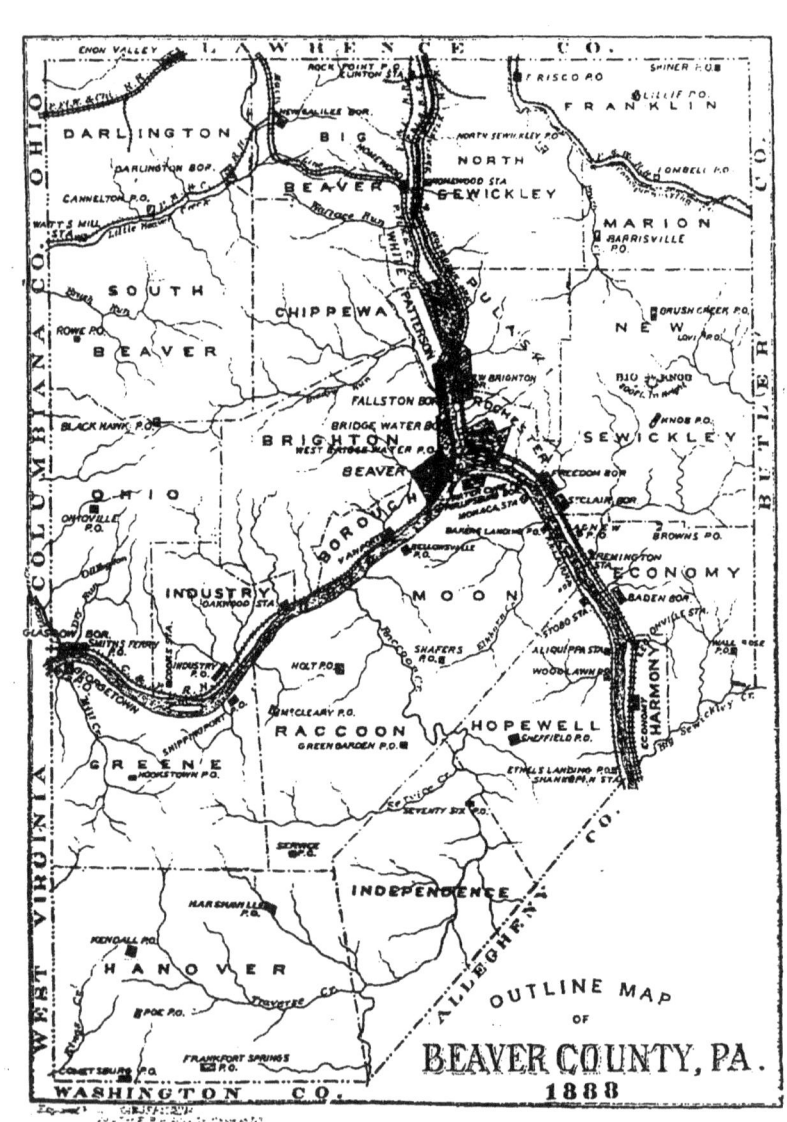

FAMILIES

OF

BEAVER COUNTY

PENNSYLVANIA

Compiled by
J. Fraise Richard, et al.

Excerpted from
History of Beaver County, Pennsylvania

CLEARFIELD

Originally published as pages 609–908
of *History of Beaver County, Pennsylvania* (1888).

Reprinted for
Clearfield Company, Inc. by
Genealogical Publishing Co., Inc.
Baltimore, Maryland
1997

International Standard Book Number: 0-8063-4724-4

Made in the United States of America

CHAPTER XXVI.

BIOGRAPHIES—WEST SIDE.

O. E. ABER, merchant, P. O. Industry, was born in Allegheny county, Pa., in 1852. The family came from Germany at an early day. John Aber, grandfather of O. E., was a native of Allegheny county, Pa., and a farmer. He had twelve children, of whom John, the eldest, was born and remained on the farm until he was twenty-four years of age. For a time John was engaged in school-teaching, and, later, in mercantile business, which he followed until his death. He married Marie Katz, who bore him three sons and three daughters, of whom O. E. is the youngest. Coming to Beaver county in 1861, the father located at Industry, where he became a prominent merchant up to the day of his death. He was succeeded by his eldest son and son-in-law, our subject being engaged as clerk, and finally becoming sole proprietor. He (O. E.) was married in 1873 to Eliza, daughter of Richard Walton, of this county, and one child, Cora Bell (now deceased), was born to them. Mr. Aber has eighty acres of well cultivated land and thirty-three cows, whose milk is daily shipped to Pittsburgh. He and his wife are members of the Presbyterian church. In politics he is a Republican.

J. E. ACKISON, JR., dealer in boots and shoes, Beaver Falls, was born in Washington, Pa., Nov. 25, 1856, and is a son of William and Mary (Knight) Ackison, of Washington county. His paternal grandfather was William Ackison, and maternal grandfather Joseph Knight, natives of England and pioneers of Washington county. Our subject was reared in his native county, and at the age of fifteen entered the store of William Semple, of Allegheny City, as an entry clerk, where he was employed five years. In 1878 he entered the employ of R. Hay, of Pittsburgh, and from 1882 until 1885 was with the wholesale shoe firm of Albree & Co., of Pittsburgh. In November, 1885, he embarked in the retail boot and shoe trade at Beaver Falls. He is a gentleman of enterprise and business experience, and is building up a large and lucrative trade.

JOHN J. AGGEMAN, glass presser, Beaver Falls, was born in Pittsburgh, Feb. 7, 1853, and is a son of John and Elizabeth Aggeman. He was reared and educated in his native city, where he learned his trade. He located in Beaver Falls in 1879, and was one of the organizers of the Coöperative Flint Glass Works, of which he has since been a stockholder, and was employed there until June 1, 1887. He served two years as a member of the board of directors of this company. He married, in 1882, Sadie Wright, of Walrose, Pa., by whom he has had three children: Katie A., John Thomas (deceased) and Eloy J. He is a member of St. Mary's Catholic church, and the Catholic Mutual Benefit Association. Politically he is a Democrat.

DANIEL AGNEW. The outbreak of the rebellion found the supreme court of the United States, most of the state supreme courts, and by far the larger number of the lower courts, federal and state, in the hands of those whose political training inclined them to excuse, if not to approve, the cause of those who were seeking to betray the Union to its destruction. The Pennsylvania bench was no exception to this rule. The majority of its supreme court was as little able as President Buchanan then seemed to be, to find any law or precedent to justify national self-preservation or to authorize the suppression of a gigantic rebellion. One of this majority, Judge George W. Woodward, when the dissolution of the Union seemed imminent in 1861, declared, "If the Union is to be divided, I want the line of separation to run north of Pennsylvania." Later, this same judge was very properly chosen to formulate the decision of the Democratic majori y of the court which disfranchised the Pennsylvania soldiers in the field. These and kindred acts so highly recommended Judge Woodward to his party that in the critical days of 1863, when the cause of the Union was trembling in the balance, he was selected to contest the re-election of Governor Andrew G. Curtin. Chief-Justice Lowrie, who was in entire accord with his colleague on the bench, Judge Woodward, and the author of a then recent decision of the state supreme court, declaring the national draft law unconstitutional, was a candidate for re-election. In selecting a candidate to run against Chief-Justice Lowrie, the Republicans or Union men looked for a jurist of high legal attainments, who was firm in his convictions and of approved loyalty. All this and much more they found in Judge Agnew, of the Seventeenth Judicial District, whose services to the Union cause had made his name well known throughout the state. The ticket thus composed of Andrew G. Curtin for governor and Daniel Agnew for supreme judge proved too strong for the opposition, and carried the state, in October, by 15,000 majority. By virtue of this popular decision Pennsylvania's great War governor was retained in the position he had filled so worthily and well, and the state supreme court received an infusion of fresh blood, new thought, intense energy, and high patriotic impulse, which at that time it sadly needed. Judge Agnew's accession brought that court into harmony with the Union sentiment of the state and added immediately and in a marked degree to its strength and influence as a judicial body.

Judge Agnew is a Pennsylvanian only by adoption and a life-long residence He was born in Trenton, N. J., Jan. 5, 1809, and while yet a lad his parents came to Western Pennsylvania, on their way to the state of Mississippi, and after a brief sojourn in Butler county, settled in Pittsburgh. There young Daniel lived, increasing in wisdom and stature until the dawning period of manhood, when he left the parental roof to go a little farther west and grow up with Beaver county. His father, James Agnew, M. D., was a native of Princeton, N. J., and graduated at its college in 1795. He studied medicine with Dr. McLean, the father of President McLean; took his degree in medicine at the University of Pennsylvania in 1800, and remained a year in Philadelphia under Dr. Benjamin Rush. His mother, Sarah B. Howell, was the eldest daughter of Governor Richard Howell, of New Jersey, who was a major of the New Jersey Continental line in the army of the Revolution. His paternal grandfather, Daniel Agnew, came from the County Antrim, in the north of Ireland, in the year 1764, and settled in New Jersey. On his mother s side he belonged to the Howells, of Caerfille. in Wales. The father of the future chief-justice was for a time uncertain where he should permanently pitch his tent. The century was just opening; a new country was all before him where to choose, and he was embarrassed by this wide range of choice. He first practised his profession for several years in Trenton, New Jersey, and then went to Mississippi in 1810. He returned in 1813, riding on horseback all the way from Natchez to Princeton, through the Indian country then known as the "wilderness." In the following October he started on his return journey to Mississippi with his family, intending to remain during the winter at the house of John L. Glaser, the owner of a furnace in Butler county, whose wife was a sister of Mrs. Agnew. But Mrs. Agnew, becoming alarmed at the wildness of the West and the dangers of navigation, then made in arks or flat-boats, declined to make the voyage down the Ohio and Mississippi, and the whole party came to a halt in Butler county. It was through this circumstance that Mississippi lost and Pennsylvania gained Daniel Agnew as one of its citizens. The family were not unrepresented in Mississippi, however. Mrs. Agnew's brother established himself there, and her niece, Varina Howell, Judge Agnew's first cousin, is the present wife of the ex-Confederate chieftain, Mr. Jefferson Davis.

Daniel Agnew was educated at the Western University, in Pittsburgh, and studied law under Henry Baldwin and W. W. Fetterman. He was admitted to practice in the spring of 1829, and opened an office in Pittsburgh. Not succeeding as he wished, he went to Beaver in the summer of the same year, intending to return in a year or two. He soon created a practice, however, which once gained by a young lawyer is not lightly to be given up, and this fact, in connection with another, decided him to remain in Beaver permanently. The other potent influence on his decision was a Miss Elizabeth Moore, daughter of General Robert Moore, a leading lawyer and representative in congress, who had lately died. In the abundant leisure afforded by a law practice still in the future, he wooed, won and married in July, 1831, this lady, who has now shared his joys and sorrows, his honors and his cares, for fifty years, and still lives, no less hale and hearty than the Judge himself, rejoicing in the more constant companionship which the termination of her husband's long engrossing public duties now brings to her. Land titles were unsettled in that western country, and in the extensive litigation growing out of this circumstance, young Agnew early had a chance to show what he was made of, and he was prompt to improve it. He soon gained a high standing as a land lawyer, and with it a large practice. His first service to the state at large was in 1837, as a member of the constitutional convention which in that and the year following sat in Harrisburg and Philadelphia, forming a series of amendments to the constitution of 1790, and which subsequently became a part of it. Mr. Agnew drew up the amendment offered by his colleague, John Dickey, as to the appointment and tenure of the judiciary, known as Dickey's Amendment, afterwards modified by the amendment of 1850.

It is proper to correct here a false charge brought against Judge Agnew by political enemies: that he voted in the convention to insert the word "white" in the article upon elections. On the question of *insertion*, he voted always against it; but after failing in that, voted for the section as a whole, on account of other most important amendments intended to prevent fraudulent voting.

In June, 1851, he was appointed by Governor Johnston President Judge of the Seventeenth District, then composed of Beaver, Butler, Mercer and Lawrence counties. In the following October the people confirmed the appointment, electing him for a term of ten years. In 1861 he was reëlected without opposition at the call of the members of the bar of all parties. He did not, however, consider that his duties as judge superseded his duties as a citizen, and when the rebellion broke out, he became known at once as an ardent and active supporter of the Union cause. The Virginia Pan-Handle made Beaver a border county, and brought the atmosphere and spirit of secession into its very midst. A committee of public safety of one hundred members was appointed, and Judge Agnew made its chairman. Later he was a zealous participant in the formation and maintenance of the Christian Commission. As a judge, all his energies were bent to preserve peace and order, and to check the budding treason which had the temerity to show its head in the Seventeenth Judicial District. Other judges, even such as were in sympathy with the Lincoln administration, were in doubt and perplexity as to their proper course in regard to the new issue which was suddenly sprung upon them. Judge Agnew, however, never hesitated. In him sound learning and sound sense went hand in hand; and he found no difficulty in making the eternal principles which underlie all law apply to every time and every emergency. He was the first of the state judges to take cognizance of the aiders and abettors of rebellion around him, and enforce the necessity of obedience and the paramount duty of loyalty to the government. In May, 1861, more than four years before President Johnson talked of making treason odious, Judge Agnew, instructed the grand jurors of Lawrence country that treason was a crime, and all who had any part or lot in it were criminals before the law. In this charge he combated with overwhelming conclusiveness the doctrines held by the Northern allies of rebellion, that aid to the enemies of the United States, which the constitution defines to be treason, meant foreign enemies only. He instructed the grand jury that where a body of men were actually assembled for the purpose of effecting by force of treasonable purpose, all those who perform a part, however minute or however remote from the scene of action, were actually leagued in the general conspiracy, and were to be considered traitors.

These were words fitly spoken and nobly spoken, at a time when treason was noisy and aggressive, and our leading public men were still under the delusion that it might be put down by soft words and gentle dalliance. Had other Northern judges everywhere displayed the same spirit, the progress of our arms would not have been so often obstructed and the war prolonged by a disheartening and demoralizing fire in the rear. In answer to those who denied the power of the government to maintain itself against domestic assaults, he wrote and delivered a careful and elaborate address on the "National Constitution in its Adaptation to a State of War." This address was so timely and so strong, breathing such a lofty spirit of patriotism, and evidently drawn from such rich stores of legal knowledge, that it at once invited public attention to its author, whose fame had been before confined to Western Pennsylvania. By special request of the members of the Legislature Judge Agnew repeated this address in Harrisburg in February, 1863. Secretary Stanton called for a copy of it, and the Union League, of this city, determined to scatter it free-handed. Two large editions of it were published by the league, and when Chief-Justice Lowrie's term in the supreme court was about to expire, the author of the address, while absent in the West, and without an effort on his part, was nominated by the Republicans to succeed him, and elected in October, 1863.

As a member of the supreme court of Pennsylvania, Judge Agnew was early called to make a practical application of the doctrines, of which, as a citizen and judge of a lower court, he had been a zealous advocate. A majority of the bench, consisting of Chief-Justice Lowrie and Judges Thompson and Woodward, had pronounced against the constitutionality of the draft law. Judges Strong and Reed dissented. The question came up again immediately after Judge Agnew's accession to the bench, and, as the senior members of the court were evenly divided, it devolved upon this new judge to decide the question, and his first opinion as supreme judge was in affirmation of the constitutionality of the draft law (see 9th Wright, 306). He thoroughly believed in the right of the government to suppress insurrection and to enforce obedience to its laws.

Soon after the question of the constitutionality of the draft acts of congress had been decided, an important question of marine insurance came up, involving the true *status* of the seceding states. It grew out of the capture of the merchant vessel "John Welsh" by the Confederate privateer "Jeff Davis." The question was whether the letters of marque of the "Jeff Davis," and the nature of the service in which she was engaged, divested her capture of its piratical character. Woodward, then chief-justice, in an elaborate opinion, sustained the capture as an *act of war* by a *de facto* government, and on that ground held it to be within an exception in the policy. The effect of this *status* of the rebel government was too important to be suffered to go out as the doctrine of the supreme court of Pennsylvania, was combated, therefore, by Judge Agnew in a vigorous opinion. He held that secession and confederation were nullities—that the United States was the supreme government both *de jure* and *de facto*, not displaced—its functions temporarily suspended in certain districts, but its actual existence continued everywhere within its rightful jurisdiction; coupled with actual possession of important posts in every seceding state, and necessarily excluding all other sovereignties. That a rebellion or attempted revolution by a portion of a people, taking the form of a government, but leaving the true government *in esse*, actively and successfully asserting its rightful authority, with important possessions, does not constitute a *de facto* government, for the reason that it in no sense represents a nation in fact, nor exercises its sovereignty. He, therefore, denied Judge Woodward's conclusions of an accomplished revolution—the position of an independent power *de facto*—and the abrogation of the constitution in the seceded states, leaving them under the laws of war and of nations alone.

Pennsylvania was the third state in which the constitutionality of the act of congress, authorizing the issue of treasury notes and making them lawful money and a legal tender for debts was called in question. The court of appeals of New York and the supreme court of California sustained the act, and Judges Agnew, Strong and Reed, overruling Chief-Justice Woodward and Judge Thompson, brought, in turn, the Pennsylvania supreme court into line. Judge Agnew differed from his colleagues in holding that a specific contract for payment in coin was not payable in treasury notes, but that the latter were receivable only for debts payable in lawful money. Judge Agnew had, however, ruled the same question, sustaining the legal tender clause, while in the common pleas of Butler county, as early as the summer of 1863, in the case of Crocker *vs.* Wolford (Pittsburgh *Legal Journal*, Sept. 14, 1863).

The war of the rebellion brought into existence immense armies. While the constitutional power of the government to draft men into service was supported as essential to the safety of the nation, it yet fell heavily upon the people, and the distribution of its burdens was exceedingly unequal. The necessity as well as the hearts of the people demanded these rigors of the system to be relieved as far as possible. This led to a system of bounties paid by the counties, towns, and townships of the state, to induce those who could be better spared, to enter into the service as substitutes for the drafted men. It was opposed, however, by those whose sympathies were not with the cause of the Union; and the right to raise money by taxation to pay these bounties was strongly denied on constitutional grounds. The question came up to the supreme court in Speer *vs.* Blairsville (14th Wright), and was argued in opposition to the power to tax by ex-Chief-Justices Black and Lowrie. It was settled conclusively in favor of the power in an opinion by Judge Agnew, both able and eloquent, which placed it beyond future cavil. Another phase of the war arose in the question of the right of deserters from military service to vote at state elections. Two cases came before the supreme court, Huber *vs.* Reilly (3d Smith) and McCafferty *vs.* Guyer (9th Smith). In the first case a majority of the court held that the electoral franchise of a deserter from military service could not be taken away by an act of congress without a conviction of desertion by a court-martial, and that a board of election officers was'incompetent to try the fact. Justice Strong, who wrote the opinion, put the decision on this ground, conceding that the act of congress was not an *ex post facto* law, and that congress had power to pass it. Judge Agnew, in an elaborate opinion, not then published, maintained that the question before the election board was in no sense a trial for a penalty, but an inquiry into a personal privilege claimed by one offering to exercise it, and the real question was one of fact only, desertion, triable as any other fact, in relation to citizenship, by the election board; the consequence being declared by congress, whose right to declare it was not denied by Justice Strong. In McCafferty *vs.* Guyer the question came up under a state law, authorizing the board of election officers to try the fact of desertion. Justice Agnew took the ground that the whole question was resolved into a single one: Is a deserter, proscribed by act of congress, a *freeman* under the election article of the constitution? In a most elaborate and convincing opinion he traced the origin of the term "freeman" from the earliest period into the constitutions of 1790 and 1838, and proved that a proscribed deserter was not a freeman within the meaning of the term in the constitution, and the election board, being authorized by statute to determine the fact, McCafferty was rightfully denied a right to vote. In all these war questions Judge Agnew stood resolutely by his country. The effect of adverse decisions will be seen if we note the influence they would have had on the ability of the government to carry on the war to suppress insurrection. Without the power to draft the military arm of government would be powerless. Without money to carry on the war it would be ineffectual. Without the power to pay bounties the hardships of war would fall on classes least able to be spared. With a *de facto* standing of the confederate government, it would have been entitled to recognition by European powers; its prize-court decisions would be recognized as a valid source of title; its ports would be opened by foreign powers, and various obstacles thrown in the way of the United States to prosecute its lawful authority. With a right to vote by deserters the whole policy of the state might be changed and its safety endangered.

An important question upon the status of negroes in Pennsylvania arose before the adoption of the *post bellum* amendments of the constitution of the United States and before the passage of the Pennsylvania act of 1867, making it an offense for a railroad company to discriminate between passengers on account of race or color. A considerable time elapsed before the case was reached in the supreme court in 1867, and public opinion then ran high in favor of the rights of colored persons. The court below decided against the right of the railroad company to direct a negro woman to take another seat; but "one in all respects as comfortable, safe, and convenient, and one not inferior to the one she left." This was a written point. Judge Agnew, whose courage is equal to his convictions, stood with two of his brethren, Woodward and Thompson, for reversal. He saw that as the *constitution* and *judicial precedents* stood when the case arose, it was impossible to deny with honesty that the *legal status* of the negro, both civil and political, differed from that of the white man; and that the social status was even more dissonant—that the rights of carriers and the repugnance of races necessarily involved a reasonable power of *separation* of passengers as a part of the carriers' duty, in the preservation of the public peace and the proper performance of his public obligations. His opinion (found in 6th Smith, 211) is as unanswerable in argument as it was faithful to duty; though at the time of its delivery (in 1867) the progress of public opinion, after the close of the war, led many who were ignorant of the time and circumstances under which the case arose, to suppose he was wrong. Of all the judges who heard the argument, Judge Reed alone dissented, and Judge Strong, who was absent at the argument, afterward told Judge Agnew that he agreed with him—that his opinion was right.

A great question arose after Judge Agnew became chief-justice, perhaps the most important of the many arising during his term of office. A majority of the convention called to propose amendments to the constitution, to be voted upon by the people, conceived that its powers were not restricted by the call under which it was convened; and claiming absolute sovereignty, undertook to displace the existing election laws in the city of Philadelphia, by an ordinance, without any previous submission of the new constitution to the people, as required by the laws under which the convention was called and authorized. The case came before the supreme court on a proceeding to enjoin the convention appointees from interfering with the lawful election officers. After the hearing an eminent member of the court thought it better to dismiss the bill on the ground of want of jurisdiction. But the effect of this would have been to leave the ordinance in force, and to countenance the exercise of an unlimited power not conferred by the people, and which might in future cases be dangerous to their liberties. Finally, however, the court unanimously agreed to meet the question on its merits, and enjoin the appointees of the convention from interfering. The opinion was written during the night following the argument, and, considering time and circumstances, was perhaps the most able delivered by Judge Agnew during his term. It was supplemented by an opinion in Wood's Appeal by Judge Agnew, in which the claim of absolute sovereignty was discussed upon fundamental principles, and the same conclusion reached. The two cases, Wells *vs.* Bain and Wood's Appeal, are found in 25 P. F. Smith, 40 and 49.

The ruling of Judge Cox as to the qualifications of jurors in the Guiteau case, recalls the fact that Judge Agnew was the first judge in Pennsylvania to modify the rule which excluded jurors who had formed opinions in capital cases, and admit them if their opinions were not so fixed but that they could still try the prisoner on the evidence, freed from the influence of previous impressions. This he ruled when judge of the Seventeenth District. Afterwards on the supreme bench he rendered several decisions to the same effect. In the Ortwein murder case, decided in Pittsburgh in 1874, Chief-Justice Agnew considered at length the plea of insanity as a defense in murder trials, and laid down some rules which would have been ill-relished by Guiteau, if made to apply in his case In his opinion Judge Agnew said: "The danger to society from acquittals on the ground of a doubtful insanity demands a strict rule. Mere doubtful evidence of insanity would till the land with acquitted criminals. To doubt one's sanity is not necessary to be convinced of his insanity. A person charged with crime must be judged to be a reasonable being until a want of reason positively appears. Insanity as a defense must be so great as to have controlled the will and taken away the freedom of moral action. When the killing is admitted, and insanity is alleged as an excuse, the defendant must satisfy the jury that insanity actually existed at the time of the act; a doubt as to the sanity will not justify the jury in acquitting."

To give any adequate idea of the impress which Judge Agnew made through his decisions upon the law of Pennsylvannia is beyond the scope of this sketch. Every Monday morning during the sessions of the supreme court brought a full budget of his decisions, and every day of his vacation was spent in preparing opinions in knotty cases reserved for that time of greater leisure for careful elaboration. Until 1874 the supreme court consisted of but five judges, while it had all the work which was afterward found sufficient for seven. Ill health prevented Judge Williams from assuming his share of the labor of the bench, and disinclination for work was an impediment in other quarters, so that before the reorganization of the court the labor incident to its duties fell almost entirely on two or three of its members. The reports of that period, as well as for the entire fifteen years Judge Agnew was on the bench, bear testimony to his prodigious industry. They show him also to be one of those broad-minded judges who have regard to the meaning and spirit of a law rather than its letter. The whole body of his opinions as therein recorded illustrate at every step the keenness of his intellect, the soundness of his judgment, and the extent and precision of his legal learning. He became chief-justice in 1873, and continued until January, 1879. In permitting him to retire from the bench in that year, the state lost from its supreme court one of the strongest members and best judicial minds that body ever possessed.

Perhaps the most marked characteristics of his judicial career was his determined support of the sacredness of the fundamental rights of persons, as declared and maintained in the constitution. His opposition to all infringments upon these rights was constant and unwavering. This may be seen in many opinions and addresses. He held that the maintenance and protection of these rights were the true end of all good government, and nothing short of a real public necessity should be permitted to override them. Another leading characteristic is the rapidity with which he writes. Besides the case of Wells *vs.* Bain, another example may be seen in the contested election cases in 15 P. F. Smith, 20, the opinion being written during the night after the argument.

Judge Agnew never was a politician in its ordinary sense, and never filled a political office. He avoided both the legislature and congress, preferring to sit as an independent judge, acknowledging no political favor, and returning a full equivalent for office by his services on the bench. In early life he was a national republican, supporting the American system of Henry Clay, especially the tariff, of which his preceptor, Judge Baldwin, was an eminent advocate. He joined the Whig party at its formation in 1832–33, and remained a Whig until its extinction in 1854. He advocated on the stump the election of Harrison in 1840, Clay in 1844, and in 1848 he was an elector on the Taylor and Fillmore ticket, and canvassed Western Pennsylvania zealously in its support. After his election to the bench in 1851, he withdrew from active participation in politics, except as events of unusual importance called him out. He openly opposed the Know-Nothing movement in 1854, and two years later he assisted at the formation of the Republican party in the convention in Lafayette Hall, in Pittsburgh.

Judge Agnew's original intention was to retire from the supreme bench at the end of his fifteen years' term. The continued absence from home, which its duties necessitated, had all along been exceedingly unwelcomed to his wife. His life, too, had been a busy and laborious one, and, though still in the full vigor of his powers, he thought that at the age of seventy he was entitled to a rest. He made known to some of his political friends his intention not to be a candidate for re-election, but was induced by them to remain silent, and was subsequently brought out by them as a candidate, seemingly with the intention of using his name to head off other candidates, and then sacrificing him in turn. The double dealing and cross purposes of this period are all laid bare in Judge Agnew's open letter, published a few days before the election of 1878, and it is unnecessary to recapitulate them here. It is enough that he changed his purpose and resolved to go into the convention, if he did not have ten votes. In that body, with all the regular party machinery against him, he developed an unexpected strength, but the bosses had decided to put him aside, and from their decree there was no appeal.

Representatives of the National party, knowing that Judge Agnew could command a large personal following independent of any party, requested permission to propose his name for supreme judge in their convention, but this he refused. Subsequently he was, without his consent, put in nomination by the state committee of the National party. Of the nomination he never received official notification, nor was it designed that he should. He was not in sympathy with the economic teachings of that party. He believed only in a coin currency, or one based on coin, having an undoubted representative value, and his thorough republicanism was unquestioned and unquestionable. This the National leaders knew, but they thought his name would aid their ticket, and they placed it on it without troubling themselves further about his consent. A similar proposal, made by the temperance convention of that year, Judge Agnew expressly declined in a letter to its chairman, on the ground that having been an "ostensible" candidate before the Republican convention, he could not honorably put himself in the front of another party. He determined to hold himself free from any entanglement, and it was a fear of such a charge being made after the election which brought out his open letter before it. During the canvass he was offered the attorney-generalship in writing, under the incoming Republican administration, on condition of withdrawing from the National ticket. Through his son he declined this proffer expressly on the ground that he was nominated without his participation, had not accepted, and had nothing to decline.

Judge Agnew is still in the full enjoyment of physical health and activity, and of mental vigor. Since his retirement he has lived a quiet and comparatively uneventful life among his old friends and neighbors, of Beaver. Great changes have occurred in state and nation since that stripling lawyer went there prospecting for litigation fifty-two years ago, but the essential features of that staid old county-seat remain unchanged. Six children have been born to Judge and Mrs. Agnew, two of whom, their eldest son and eldest daughter, are dead. The latter was the wife of Col. John M. Sullivan, of Allegheny City, and died in 1874. Of the others, there are two sons, both lawyers; the elder, F. H. Agnew, now in the senate of Pennsylvania, is practicing in Beaver, and the younger, Robert M. Agnew, in Lancaster, Pa. One of his daughters is the wife of Hon. Henry Hice, of Beaver, late President-Judge of the court Judge Agnew formerly presided over. The other daughter is the wife of Rev. Walter Brown, of Cadiz, Ohio,

The degree of Doctor of Laws has been twice conferred on Judge Agnew, first by Washington College and then by Dickinson. Occasionally he indulges in writing or speaking on legal and public subjects to keep from rusting out. On General Grant's return from his tour around the world, Judge Agnew was selected to deliver the address in Pittsburgh, and in the succeeding canvass for nomination he favored that of General Grant for the presidency as best calculated to produce national unity. He was employed by Allegheny county in the riot cases, wrote the address to the legislature, and argued the question of the county's liability before the state supreme court. He recently argued the case of Kelly vs. The City of Pittsburgh in the United States supreme court. His brief is an elaborate statement of the purpose of the fourteenth amendment, and a vindication of individual fundamental right, and the jurisdiction of the court in a case of unlawful taxation, infringing upon the right of property without due process of law.

In the senatorial contest of last winter Judge Agnew's name figured somewhat in the scattering vote. The state would do itself a high honor if it should select such a man to represent it at Washington, or to be its chief executive. Judge Agnew's numerously published addresses, to which, for lack of space, scarcely any allusion has been made, and his opinions, involving great public questions, as recorded in the state reports, show that he is no mere lawyer, but has all the grasp of mind and breadth of view of the true statesman. As United States senator he would take rank at the outset with the ablest and most influential members of that body; as governor of the Commonwealth he would be a grateful and wholesome relief from the dead level of mediocrity, which has had monopoly of that office for many years. But the Boss is still supreme in Pennsylvania politics, and such political honors as he does not retain for himself or his lieutenants, he takes care to secure for some one of the great anonymous. Under the regime the post of honor is the private station, and it is there, with rare exceptions, that we find our men of most distinguished ability and recognized worth.

For a short time after Judge Agnew left the Bench, he practiced law. He was engaged in several important causes, especially those of the county of Allegheny, growing out of the great riots at the Union Depot of the Pennsylvania Railroad, in Pittsburgh, in 1877. He, with his associates, drew up and presented to the legislature the address for legislation to relieve the county from the onerous liability growing out of the act making a few counties liable for injuries done by rioters.

He also argued before the supreme court of Pennsylvania the cases growing out of the same law, to show that the law did not survive the former constitution of the State, and was not continued in force by the schedule of the new constitution. The argument was deemed unanswerable by impartial minds, but the great interests of Philadelphia and the railroad company, the city itself being a large stockholder, carried the case against the county of Allegheny. He also argued before the supreme court of the United States the important question of the power of Pittsburgh to tax outlying rural districts within the corporate limits, for the special city purposes of police, fire, etc.

Finding that professional business was encroaching largely on his time and labor, and curtailing the relief he expected on retiring from the Bench, he, in the course of two or three years ceased to take cases or to be employed professionally, though many inviting offers came to him. In the year 1880, being strongly impressed with the necessity of curbing the evils of drunkenness, from which, as a judge and lawyer, his observation taught him that four-fifths of the crime and pauperism of the state arose, he became the president of the Constitutional Prohibition Amendment Association. In this work he performed great labor, writing and speaking in most of the principal places in the state. The effect of the efforts of this association, and others engaged in the temperance cause, was to carry a large majority of prohibitionists into the house of representatives in 1881. The constitutional amendment was carried in the house by a vote of nearly two to one. These efforts continued brought a majority also into the house in the session of 1883. Before this house, Judge Agnew delivered an elaborate address on prohibition. He contended in that address, and in other arguments, against the doctrine of compensation, a position since fully sustained by the supreme court of the United States. These efforts have been crowned with final success by the passage of the proposed amendment by the assembly of 1887.

His pen has also been employed in other work than legal. He has been called to deliver numerous addresses, in and out of the state, before colleges, seminaries of learning, and public audiences, civil and military. Notably he delivered the address of welcome at the convention of the bankers of the United States in Pittsburgh, and an address to them on the general banking law of the nation. In the canvass of 1880, for Garfield's election, he also delivered two very elaborate addresses on the past and present relations of the northern and southern sections of the United States.*

He yet, in 1888, enjoys good health and strength and a vigorous intellect.

HON. FRANKLIN H. AGNEW, attorney, P. O., Beaver, was born in that place April 6, 1842, and is a son of Hon. Daniel Agnew. He was reared in Beaver, and received his earliest education in the old Beaver Academy. He afterwards attended Jefferson College, from which he was graduated in 1862. After his graduation he taught in the Beaver Academy, then in Washington county. Being desirous of obtaining a thorough knowledge of book-keeping, he attended the Iron City Business College, where he took a thorough course, and was afterward a teacher in the same institution. Returning to Beaver, he became principal of the old Beaver Academy. He then went on the the United States Coast Survey, which he resigned in 1871. In 1872 he began the study of law in his father's office, and, after his admission to the bar, he formed a partnership with John M. Buchanan, which continued till 1887. He was elected state

---

* He delivered also the address on the completion of the Chanoine Dam at Davis Island, six miles below Pittsburgh, in 1885.

senator in 1882, and served one term.   July 16, 1885, he was married to Miss Nan K., daughter of Rev. W. H. Lauch. Her parents were of Scotch and German origin. Mr. and Mrs. Agnew have one child, Elizabeth. They are members of the Methodist church, in which he is a steward. Politically he is a Republican.

FESTUS ALLEN, retired, Beaver Falls, was born in county Galway, Ireland, March 7, 1832, and is a son of Richard and Fanny (Kelly) Allen. He was reared in his native county, where he began the trade of shoemaker. He came to America in 1850 and worked at his trade as a journeyman in New York and New Jersey cities three years. In 1853 he located in Pittsburgh and followed his trade there and in Allegheny City up to 1864, when he settled in New Brighton, this county. In 1867 he located in Beaver Falls, where he has since resided, working at his trade until 1885. In the latter year he erected one of the finest brick stores on Seventh Avenue. He married, in 1862, Keziah Goodwin, of Somerset, Jefferson county, Ohio, daughter of Jesse Goodwin, a soldier of the Mexican war. By this union there are five children living: Thomas R., Festus W., Clara, Lizzie and Albert. Mr. Allen is a member of the I. O. O. F. and the K. of L. Politically he is a Democrat.

EDWARD JAMES ALLISON, assistant cashier of the First National Bank, at Rochester, Pa., Beaver, was born in Bridgewater, Beaver county, Feb. 8, 1852, and is a son of Thomas and Emily (Logan) Allison, natives of Pennsylvania, of English and Scotch-Irish descent. The father was a merchant. Our subject is a grandson of the late Hon. James Allison, who settled in Beaver county in 1804, and subsequently served two terms as a member of congress. His uncle, the late Hon. John Allison, served two terms in the legislature, and two in congress, and was register of the United States treasury, under General Grant, for six years. Edward J. is the only child of his parents, and has spent his life in Beaver county. Early in life he clerked in a store. In 1883 he became a clerk in the First National Bank, of Rochester, and after 1886 was assistant cashier; has resigned his position in the First National Bank of Rochester, Pa., to accept the cashiership of the First National Bank of Beaver, Pa. In politics he is a Republican. He is a member of the Presbyterian church, at Beaver, and a trustee.

SANFORD ALMY, oil producer, P. O., Ohioville, son of Pardon and Mary (Cook) Almy, was born, Feb. 17, 1830, at Little Compton, R. I. His father, a son of Sanford and Lydia (Gray) Almy, was born June 18, 1792, at same place, and died in October, 1864. His mother, who was born June 5, 1799, a daughter of Samuel and Lydia Cook, who were of Scotch descent, died in February, 1856. His grandfather was a son of John and Hannah (Cook) Almy, natives of Portsmouth, R. I. His father was a son of Job and Bridget (Sanford) Almy, also of Portsmouth. He in turn was a son of Job Almy, Sr., who was a son of William Almy, who came from England about the year 1600, and settled in Jersey, but subsequently moved to Rhode Island. Our subject, when about fifteen years of age, moved to New Bedford, Mass., where he clerked in a general furnishing store nights and mornings, and finished his education at the high school, from which he graduated in 1850. He then continued to clerk in the furnishing store until 1858, when he bought out the establishment and continued the business until 1861, in April of which year he enlisted in the first call for troops, and served as paymaster of the Third Regiment three months. He then enlisted in the Eighteenth Massachusetts Infantry, as regimental quartermaster, and served until mustered out in August, 1864. He next embarked in the oil business, at Wellsville, Ohio, where he put down one well; he then moved to his present location at Island Run Oil Regions. Sept. 4, 1878, Mr. Almy married Catherine J. Wright, born Aug. 5, 1846, daughter of Nathan and Eliza (Potts) Wright; and two children have been born to them, Mary E. and Sanford E. Mr. and Mrs. Almy are members of the Methodist Episcopal Church, at Ohioville. He is a Republican, and has served four terms as justice of the peace; was notary public and also school director for some time.

GEORGE W. ALTSMAN, painter, P. O. Beaver Falls, of the firm of Altsman Brothers, was born in Pike county, Ohio, Feb. 20, 1856, a son of James and Elizabeth (Cave) Altsman, and of English and German descent. His father, a painter by trade, settled in Beaver Falls in 1867, where George W. was educated in the public schools, and learned his trade with his father, with whom he embarked in business in 1876, under the firm name of Jas. Altsman & Son. In 1878, our subject formed a partnership with his brother William, under the name of Altsman Brothers, which partnership still exists. They are one of the leading firms in their line in Beaver county, and do an extensive business. George W. Altsman has been twice married; first in 1881, to Belle Hutchinson, of Mt. Pleasant, Pa., by whom he had one child, Roy H.; and, second, Jan. 21, 1886, to Lou A. Blaze, of Pittsburgh, by whom he has one child, Ira B. Mr. Altsman is a member and trustee of the Methodist Episcopal church, and is a member of the Y. M. C. A. In politics he is a Republican.

ALEX. H. ANDERSON, farmer, P. O. New Galilee, was born in Hanover township in 1833. His grandfather, William Anderson, came to America from Ireland at an early day, and settled in Beaver county, where he purchased a tract of land of four or five hundred acres, part of which is still owned by his descendants. His early life was full of hardships and dangers, His son, Thomas Anderson, born in Hanover township in 1782, was a farmer, and died in 1857. By his second wife, Jane Patten, he had three children, of whom Alexander H. is the youngest. Our subject remained at home until 1860, when he bought and removed to a farm in Darlington township, where he now lives. This farm contains 120 acres in a high state of cultivation. Mr. Anderson was married in 1862, to Rebecca, daughter of Samuel Reed, Esq., and by her has had seven children, six of whom are living: William T., Jennie E., Madge F., Martie M., Laura L. and Frank R. Mr. Anderson has held the positions of school director and trustee of Greersburg Academy, and is greatly esteemed in the community. He is a member of the Presbyterian church; politically a Republican.

A. T. ANDERSON, dealer in real estate, Beaver, was born in Independence township, Beaver county, Pa., July 11, 1842. His parents, Benoni and Jane (Thompson) Anderson, were natives of this county and of Scotch-Irish descent. His father, who was a merchant in early life and afterward a farmer, had two children: A. T., and Mary E., wife of John M. Springer, of Ohio. Our subject was reared in Hanover township, and received his education in the common schools. Early in life he was clerk in his father's store, and then embarked in that business for himself. He has bought and sold many stores, has also dealt extensively in real estate, and has succeeded well in business. In politics he is a Democrat; he is a Master Mason. Mr. Anderson was married in Washington county, in 1868, to Sue C., daughter of John Duncan, and of Scotch descent. They have three children: Lillie L., Harry D. and Laura. Mrs. Anderson is a member of the Presbyterian church.

JOSEPH L. ANDERSON, printer, was born in Beaver, Beaver county, and is a son of Joseph (a farmer), and Mary (Eakin) Anderson. His parents were natives of Pennsylvania, and of Scotch-Irish origin. His father had four children, of whom Joseph L., the youngest, was reared in Beaver borough, and attended the common schools and the old Beaver Academy. At an early age he entered the office of the old *Argus*, where he learned printing, a business he followed until he became a partner in the paper. In 1867 he was appointed transcribing clerk in the Pennsylvania Senate, and served two years. At the present time he holds the position of foreman of the *Evening Chronicle-Telegraph*, of Pittsburgh. He was married in 1861, to Margaret, daughter of Joseph and Matilda (Crooks) Hall, of English and Scotch-Irish origin. Her father was born in Allegheny county in 1807, but has spent most of his life in Beaver county. He was a ship carpenter, and spent his early life on the Ohio river working at his trade. Mrs. Anderson's mother now resides in Beaver. Mr. and Mrs. Anderson have been blessed with three children: James Paul, Stanley and Mary Olive, who graduated in Beaver College in 1886. The boys are in the railroad business. Mrs. Anderson is president of the Woman's Christian Temperance Union and of the Children's Aid Society, of Beaver.

SAMUEL ANDERSON, farmer, P. O. Black Hawk, was born in Beaver county in 1834. His grandfather, James, came to America about 1784, and settled in Washington county, where he was extensively engaged in farming. He had two sons and five daughters. Bernard, the eldest son, was born in Ireland, and came with his parents to America when three years of age. James purchased about 120 acres of land in Beaver county in 1808, his son Bernard settling upon same. Bernard married Elizabeth Hill, by whom he had six sons and three daughters, Samuel being the second youngest. Bernard died in 1860, aged seventy-six years, and his wife in 1865, aged seventy-two years. Samuel was reared on a farm and remained with his father until 1860, when he married Elizabeth, daughter of Wilson and Catherine (Barnes) Elliott, of New York state. They have had six children (five of whom are living): Virginia Catherine, Wilson, McClain, James Hill, William B. C. (deceased), and Olive Josephine. In 1883 Mr. Anderson purchased his present farm of 56 acres, nearly all of which is under cultivation. He is an elder in the United Presbyterian church; in politics a Republican.

JAMES ANDERTON, brewer, Beaver Falls, was born in Streetbridge, Lancashire, England, June 26, 1830, and is a son of James and Sarah (Morris) Anderton, who came to America in 1856 and settled in Fallston in September of the same year. They had three children: John, James and Joseph, all now residents of Beaver county. James settled in Beaver county in 1856, and in 1867 moved to Beaver Falls where he embarked in the hotel business. In 1869 he commenced the erection of the Spring Water Brewery, making his first brewing of ale in November of the same year. His business is increasing every year. In August, 1852, he married Betty, daughter of Joseph and Mary Greenwood, by whom he has three children living: Jonathan, Mary (Mrs. W. C. Rohrcaste) and William H. Mr. Anderton is a F. and A. M., and a member of the I. O. O. F., K. of P., and A. O. U. W.; in politics he is a Democrat.

HUGO ANDRIESSEN, druggist and apothecary, Beaver, was born June 14, 1843, at Steele, on the Ruhr, Rhenish Prussia, Germany. His father, Frederick Andriessen, was born at Crefeld, Prussia, July 19, 1802, and died at Beaver, Pa., Oct. 14, 1869. By his first wife he had a family of five children, of whom one son and two daughters are yet living. After the death of his first wife Frederick married Louise, born at Cologne, Prussia, Oct. 17, 1819, and now a resident of Columbus, Ohio. Their children, living, are Hugo, Arthur, Richard, Lilly and Rosa; three are dead. Frederick Andriessen was a civil engineer by profession, and constructed many railroads in Germany, Austria, Russia and Portugal, including the first railroad which was built in Germany. He was also a very fine landscape painter and a man of many talents. He came to the United States in 1861, and located in Pittsburgh, Pa. Hugo received his education in high schools and gymnasiums in Germany and Austria, and on account of the many positions in different countries of Europe which his father filled, he studied many languages. He always had an especial love for the study of natural history. After clerking in different prominent drug stores in Pittsburgh, he finally, in October, 1869, settled in Beaver, where he has the best equipped and largest pharmacy in the county, the well-known "Beaver Drug Store." May 12, 1870, Mr. Andriessen married Miss Lou, daughter of Thomas and Harriet McKinley, who formerly lived at Darlington, Beaver county, where she was born Aug. 4, 1847. Their children are Belle, born April 6, 1871; Fritz, born Sept. 7. 1873; Edith, born Sept. 1, 1875. In religion and philosophy Mr. Andriessen quotes Professor Huxley, who says: "Some twenty years ago or thereabouts, I invented the word 'agnostic,' to denote people who, like myself, confess themselves to be hopelessly ignorant concerning a variety of matters about which metaphysicians and theologians, both orthodox and heterodox, dogmatize with the utmost confidence. Agnosticism is the essence of science, whether ancient or modern. It simply means that a man shall not say he knows or believes that which he has no grounds for professing to know or believe. Agnosticism simply says that we know nothing of what may be beyond phenomena." In politics Mr. Andriessen is a radical. He is a member of the American Pharmaceutical Association and the Western Pennsylvania Botanical Society. He is a contributor to several scientific and philosophical journals and German literary publications. [For sketch of Mr. Andriessen's museum, see page 580.]

JOHN ARMSTRONG, formerly oil and lumber dealer and farmer, P. O. Beaver, was born in this county, Aug. 27, 1831, and has been an active, successful business man. He is now living a retired life on his handsome and well-improved farm in Brighton township. His parents, John and Nellie (Dillon) Armstrong, were natives of Pennsylvania, and of Irish descent, the former of whom was a farmer all his life. The family consisted of two sons and three daughters. John, the third child, was reared on the farm, attended the common schools, and chose lumbering as a business. He also dealt in oil, and finally engaged in farming. When he first concluded to engage in agricultural pursuits he bought 225 acres of land. He was married in Warren county, to Belle M., daughter of John and Janet Adams, and their children are—Cancie A., Nettie N., wife of Prof. John J. Allen, Anna M., J. Burt and Vinnie B. The family are members of the Methodist church, of which Mr. Armstrong is a trustee.

WILLIAM PERRY BADDERS, teacher, P. O. Black Hawk, was born in South Beaver township in 1847. His great grandfather, George Badders, was a soldier in the British army during the Revolution, and at the close of the war settled in York county, where he engaged in farming and milling. He married Deborah Huston, of Irish parentage, by whom he had nine children, seven of whom grew to maturity. He died in his seventy-seventh year. James, the second son, who came to Beaver county about 1816, and was by occupation a distiller, held a commission from the government of Ohio as captain of state militia. He settled on the land now owned by William P., his purchase consisting of 375 acres. He married Christiana Frey (by whom were born two daughters and nine sons), and died in January, 1869, aged eighty years. George, the eldest son, born Aug. 18, 1811, married Lucinda, daughter of Benjamin Todd, of Maryland, and had four sons and one daughter. William Perry, the eldest son, received his education at the common schools and at Beaver College. In 1876 he married Olivia, daughter of Samuel and Margaret Shrodes, of Hopewell township, this county. They have four children: Grace, George, Maggie and William. Since 1868, with the exception of five years, Mr. Badders has been engaged in teaching. He owns a part of the farm purchased by his grandfather. He and his wife are members of the Methodist church; politically he is a Democrat, and is strictly temperate in principle and practice.

GEORGE BAKER, farmer, P. O. Rock Point, was born in Big Beaver township in 1823. About 1795, his father, Robert Baker, at the age of nine years, came to America with his brother-in-law, James McKay, and at the age of eighteen years purchased a tract of 400 acres in Big Beaver township. He married Rachel, daughter of Thomas Williams, and by her had ten children, George being the youngest. Robert Baker died at the age of ninety-five years. George was educated in the common schools, and in 1844 married Jane, daughter of Matthew Mitchell, of Allegheny county. The had six children, five of whom are living: Robert A., George H., Meralda, Emeline and Sophenia. The mother of these children died in 1866, and in 1873 Mr. Baker married Elmira, daughter of James McCoy. By her he has one son, William. Mr. Baker has a valuable farm of 170 acres, which is a part of the tract purchased by his father. It is underlaid with rich coal veins and a clay bank nine feet in depth. The clay is valuable for fine potter's work. Mr. Baker is a Democrat and a member of the school board.

JOHN BALZER, glass worker, Beaver Falls, was born in Germany, Dec. 18, 1823, and is a son of Conrad and Clara Balzer. He came to America in 1852 and located in Pittsburgh, where he was employed in the glass works until 1879. He then located in Beaver Falls, and was one of the organizers of the Coöperative Flint Glass Works, of which he is a stockholder, and where he has since been employed. In 1852 he married Margaretta, daughter of Conrad and Margaretta (Fischer) Balzer, and has five children living: Mary, John, Charles, Andrew and Martina. Mr. Blazer and wife are members of the St. Mary's Catholic church, of Beaver Falls. In politics he is a Democrat.

FRANCIS L. BANKS, foreman hardening room, Western File Works, Beaver Falls, was born in New York City, July 19, 1825, and is a son of Francis and Maria (Burden) Banks, and of English and German descent. He was reared in New York city, where he learned his trade of file hardener with Evans, Davidson & Lound, serving an apprenticeship of seven years. He worked at his trade as a journeyman in different sections of the country thirty-five years prior to coming to Beaver Falls, where he located in 1869 and began in his present position in the Western File Works. He is a member of the T. of H., G. T., R. A., and A. O. U. W. He was grand templar, state of Pennsylvania in 1884. He is a member and one of the vestrymen of the Episcopal church of Beaver Falls. In politics he is a Republican.

JEREMIAH BANNON, a native of Tipperary, Ireland, emigrated to this country at the age of sixteen years. He was a soldier in the Revolution, enlisting Nov. 20, 1776, and was discharged in April, 1783. His wife's maiden name was Nancy Dawson. The couple, after marriage, settled on the Seven-mile Island, in the Ohio, near Pittsburgh, where sixteen children were born to them. They subsequently removed to the locality of Mt. Jackson, then in Beaver county. Mr. Brannon died in 1832, and was buried in Westfield cemetery.

HARRY T. BARKER, civil engineer, Beaver Falls, was born in New Brighton, Aug. 28, 1849, and is a son of Thomas A. and Eliza (Oakley) Barker. His paternal grandfather was Abner Barker, of England, a pioneer of Pittsburgh. His maternal grandfather was Milton Oakley, a large ship owner of Baltimore, and a pioneer of Butler county. His wife was a daughter of Isaac Wilson, a pioneer of Harmony, Butler county, and later of New Brighton. He was one of the original projectors of the iron industry of Beaver county, and his furnaces were located on the ground now occupied by the cutlery works in Beaver Falls. Thomas A. Barker was a native of Pittsburgh, but resided in New Brighton many years, where he was engaged in mercantile pursuits, and died in 1859. He had three children: Frank A. (deceased), Harry T. and Nellie (Mrs. Harry Brown), of Pittsburgh. Harry T. was educated in the public schools, and at Myers Academy, Westchester, Pa., and at the Cooper Institute, N. Y., where he was graduated in his profession in 1879. Since then he has been located in Beaver Falls. In 1873 he married Anna, daughter of Capt. George C. and Sarah (Thompson) McLean, of Philadelphia.

PETER BATES, farmer, P. O. Beaver, was born in Allegheny City, Pa., Aug. 27, 1835, and is a son of Peter and Elizabeth (Silcox) Bates, natives of England, and who settled at Pittsburgh in 1828. They had eight children, of whom Peter, the fifth, was reared in Allegheny City, where he received his education. He learned the carpenter and machinist trade, which he followed until he took charge of the water works at Allegheny City as chief engineer, a position he held for nine years. He came to Beaver county in 1875, and has since devoted his time to agricultural pursuits. He was married, in 1857 to Nancy, daughter of Thomas C. and Jane Hall, who were born in Maryland, of English descent. The children of this marriage are Edwin P., clerk in the Valley railroad office; J. W. H., at home, farming; Milton B., a bookkeeper in Allegheny City; John E., cashier of a store at Allegheny City. Mr. and Mrs. Bates and children are members of the Methodist Episcopal Church. He is a Republican in politics, and has been school director six years. He is a Master Mason.

ALBERT M. BEANER, fish and oyster market, Beaver Falls, was born in Bridgewater, March 30, 1849, and is a son of Joseph and Mary (Jenkinson) Beaner, of Westmoreland county, Pa., who settled in Bridgewater in 1847. His father was a tanner, and carried on his trade many years in this and Westmoreland counties. He had seven children: James, Nancy J. (Mrs. C. D. Renouf), Maggie (Mrs. S. G. Bliss), Joseph S., Albert M., John W. and Mary E. (Mrs. Robert Mitchell). Albert M. is a painter by trade, which he followed for sixteen years. In 1883 he located in Beaver Falls and embarked in his present business. His wife was Elsie A., a daughter of Capt. A. B. Lee, of Sullivan, Ill., by whom he has four children : Oris B., Jessie E., Hattie M. and Joseph C. Mr. Beaner is a member of the M. E. Church and E. A. A. U.; in politics he is a Republican.

REV. JAMES BEATTY, P. O. Black Hawk, was born in Columbiana county, Ohio, Feb. 12, 1818. William Beatty, his father, came from County Tyrone, Ireland, to America, in 1806, and worked at his trade, that of a weaver, in the east until

1814, when he moved to Columbiana county, Ohio, where he resided until his death. He married in this country Letticia Orr, also of County Tyrone, Ireland, and they had twelve children, of whom six are living. He eventually became a farmer, purchasing first 160 acres, to which he added by subsequent purchases until he owned 480 acres at his death. James was educated at the common schools, and at the age of thirty-one attended Allegheny College, a Methodist Theological institution, for one year. He was married in 1849 to Elizabeth A. R., daughter of Isaac and Catherine (Eaton) Garrett, and they had three children: Victoria A. C. A., Antoinette I. Z., Leonidas L. J. H. (deceased). The mother died in 1875, aged forty-six years. After leaving the theological seminary Mr. Beatty became a licensed minister, and since 1850 has been engaged in this work. He owns 100 acres of land in South Beaver township, Beaver county, Pa., and a farm in Columbiana county, Ohio, of 160 acres. He has always taken an active part in politics, and received the nomination of the Democratic party for the office of prothonotary, and trustee of Beaver Academy, but on account of the great Republican majority in the county was defeated. He is a F. & A. M. and a member of the I. O. O. F. Mr. Beatty adds: "I do not regret the steps I have taken, in the country, in the church, or the orders, to which my name is attached. I only regret my unfaithfulness. I am a Democrat from principle, and will remain such while I have a country, a constitution to govern it, the stars and stripes to honor us as an independent government. *Strength in union, weakness in division."*

WILLIAM BEATTY, farmer, P. O. Homewood, was born in Big Beaver township in 1832, and is the only living member of a family of eleven children born to Jonathan and Margaret (McClure) Beatty. Jonathan Beatty came to this county at an early day, with a brother, from Westmoreland county, and took up 400 acres of land, where he remained until his death. William resides on the homestead farm where he was born and reared, and has always followed farming. He owns 160 acres. He was married, in 1852, to Sidney. daughter of Richard Baker, and they have five children living: Richard James, William George, Phalysta Alice, Laura Emma, and Mary Lamia. In close proximity to the Pittsburgh & Lake Erie railroad Mr. Beatty owns a fine and profitable quarry of sandstone. In politics he is a Republican.

LOUIS BERORD, axe-maker, Beaver Falls, was born in the district of Montreal, Canada, July 12, 1843, and is a son of Joseph and Charlotte (Beausoleli) Berord. He was reared in Canada, where he learned the carpenter's trade. In 1862 he located in East Douglass, Mass., where he worked three years at axe-making, and in 1865 removed to Allegheny City, where he worked six years in the axe factory of Joseph Graff, Esq. In 1871 he came to Beaver Falls, where, with the exception of one year, he has since resided, working at his trade for Joseph Graff and Hubbard & Co., and has accumulated a fine property. In 1864 he married Sarah Demess, of the district of Montreal, by whom he has had nine children: Charles (deceased), Harry (deceased), John (deceased), George, Vincent, Charley, Bessie, Bella (deceased), and an infant daughter. Mr. Berord is a member of the Catholic church, and A. O. U. W. He is a Democrat.

CHARLES BEVINGTON (deceased), was born in Beaver county, Pa., in October, 1796. He was the son of Thomas and Elizabeth Johnston, who were among the earliest settlers of Beaver county. Our subject's father was a soldier in the Revolutionary war, serving three years as a spy, and was also three years in the Indian war. The male members of the family had usually been tillers of the soil. Our subject's parents spent many years of their lives on the farm in Ohio township, where they were married. There Charles was born, reared and lived until he was thirty-six years old, when he moved to Brighton township, Beaver county, Pa., and settled on a farm. He attended the common schools and served six years in wars. He reared a family of eleven children. At his death he had a farm of 126 acres of land, where his two daughters now reside.

ELLIS N. BIGGER, attorney at law, Beaver, a member of the firm of Bigger & Henry; of Beaver and New Brighton, was born in Hanover township, Washington county, Pa. His parents were Thomas and Mary (Nicholson) Bigger, the latter a daughter of Hon. Thomas Nicholson, who served several terms as a member of the legislature. Thomas Bigger was a farmer all his life. Ellis N. was the eldest of three children, and was reared in this county, his parents having moved here when he was a child. He attended the common schools and the Frankfort Academy, and engaged in teaching, first in the district schools, and afterward as assistant principal of Frankfort Academy. He studied law with S. B. Wilson, was admitted to the bar June 2, 1879, and began practice Nov. 14, 1881, in company with the late Frank Wilson, of the Beaver bar. Since 1883 he has been associated with Thomas M. Henry, Esq. Mr. Bigger was married, in 1882, to Della, daughter of John Caughey, of Scotch-Irish origin, and they have had one child, John Caughey. Mrs. Bigger died March 16, 1885. She was a member of the Presbyterian church, to which Mr. Bigger also belongs. In politics he is a Republican, and has served as a member of the council of Beaver borough.

FRANK R. BIRNER, tailor, P. O. Beaver Falls, was born in Hirschberg, Austria, March 3, 1855, son of Rudolph and Elizabeth (Huk) Birner. He was reared in his native town, where he learned his trade, at which he served an apprenticeship of three years, after which he worked as journeyman in the principal cities of Germany for six years. In 1878 he entered the Austrian army as second lieutenant of his company, and served three years. In 1881 he was a merchant tailor in Hirschberg. In 1882 he sailed for America, and located in Beaver township where he has since worked at his trade as a journeyman. In 1883 Mr. Birner married Antonia Welzger, a native of Munchengratz, Austria. He is a member of the Catholic church, Turners and Druids.

SAMUEL BLAIR, farmer, P. O. Homewood, was born where he now resides, Dec. 27, 1826. His grandfather, Samuel, removed from Chartiers to the location our subject now occupies, in 1797. He secured a large parcel of land. His family numbered several children, including only one son, Samuel. The latter married Isabella, daughter of John Stockman, who came from Chester county, Pa., and settled near Mr. Blair in 1801. The Stockman family, according to tradition, was of Irish and the Blair family of Scotch origin. All were connected with the Presbyterian church as are their descendants to the present day. They never sought political preferment, although they always supported the Republican party. Samuel Blair died in 1858, aged sixty-five years, and his wife in 1877, being about eighty-one years old. Of their eleven children five sons and three daughters grew to maturity. Moses died at home unmarried; John was killed at the battle of Cold Harbor; Robert resides in New Chillicothe, Kan.; Samuel, our subject; Silas died in hospital from a wound received at the battle of Fair Oaks; Eliza, unmarried, resides in Big Beaver township; Isabella married John F. Hillman, of Big Beaver township, and after her death, the younger sister, Martha Ann, became his wife. Samuel Blair has a farm of 200 acres, and enjoys a fine home. He is also interested in a royalty in a coal bank in Lawrence county. He married Margaret, daughter of John and Hester (Cochran) Stratton, all of Irish descent. Mrs. Blair was born in Chippewa township, this county, Dec. 24, 1836. She is the mother of ten children, of whom six are living; all at home. Their names in order of birth are as follows: John C., Hettie, Isabella, Resetta, Frank P. and Edmund Bates.

J. C. BOYLE, county commissioner, P. O. Beaver Falls, was born in what is now Beaver Falls, Nov. 22, 1819, and is a son of David and Rhoda (Hendrickson) Boyle. His paternal grandfather, Henry Boyle, of Irish descent, was a blacksmith by trade, also a furnaceman, and was a veteran of the war of 1812. He was a pioneer of what is now Beaver Falls, and later removed to Yellow Creek, Ohio, where he died. His children were—Alexander, Henry, John, William, David, Ellen, Nancy, Mary and Jane. The grandmother was taken a prisoner by the Indians in pioneer times while gathering greens. Her husband went to the rescue and killed one redskin, cut the bands which bound his wife, grabbed his children, and they made their escape. While running away he received three bullets in his body, which he carried to his grave. The maternal grandfather of our subject was Daniel Hendrickson, a pioneer of what is now Lawrence county, in early times a part of Beaver. David Boyle, father of J. C., was a blacksmith by trade, and worked in the first furnace in what is now Beaver Falls. In later life he engaged in farming in Chippewa township, on the farm now owned and occupied by our subject, and died there. He was a soldier of the war of 1812, and was on the brig "Niagara" when it was disabled by the British on Lake Erie. His children were ten in number: Jackson, John C., Daniel, Milo, Henry, Christopher, Sabina, Mary, Sarah and Eliza. J. C. was reared in Beaver Falls, where he learned the blacksmith's trade, which he followed for several years. He then went on the canal and was one of the first captains to take a boat from Pittsburgh to Cleveland. He followed the canal twelve years, and then engaged with James Wood & Co. as manager of their furnaces in Ohio and Pennsylvania. In 1858 he located in New Brighton and was postmaster there nine years. Since 1883 he has lived in Chippewa township. He has been married twice. His first wife was Eleanor Loomis, of Beaver county, by whom he had two children, Milo and David, both of whom were in the war of the rebellion, the former being killed at the battle of Chancellorsville. Mr. Boyle's present wife was Nancy M. Foster. He is one of the prominent substantial citizens of the county, and was elected county commissioner in 1884 for a term of three years; he is a Republican.

JOHN R. BRADEN, teacher, Beaver Falls, was born in Huntingdon county, Pa., Oct. 1, 1821. His parents, Joseph and Margaret (Rankin) Braden, settled in Beaver county in 1832, locating in Little Beaver township (now Lawrence county), and lived and died there. Their children were Elizabeth (Mrs. Thomas Middleton), Anna M. (Mrs. John Wilson), Margaret (Mrs. John McCotton), Matilda (Mrs. Joseph Consolus), Belle (Mrs. Augustus Corey) and John R. The latter began teaching at the age of sixteen years, which he has followed continuously as a profession since 1837. He is said to be the oldest teacher in Beaver county. He was three times wedded: In 1838, he married Jemima Cochran, of Chippewa township, this county. His second wife was Nancy, daughter of John B. Wallace, of Alleghany county, and by her he had six children: Wallace (who served three and one-half years in the war of the rebellion, having enlisted in Company E, 14th Pennsylvania Volunteers; was promoted to sergeant and sergeant-major of second battalion, and received an honorable discharge at the expiration of service); William, Joseph, John, Margaret (Mrs. Samuel McQuiston), and James W. Mr. Braden's third wife was Mrs. Jane Freed. Mr. Braden is a member of the Presbyterian church, and the I. O. O. F. In politics he is a Republican.

M. M. BRADEN, liveryman, Beaver Falls, was born in Raccoon township Jan. 24, 1842, and is a son of John A. and Arabella (Elliott) Braden. His paternal grandfather was John Braden, a farmer of Raccoon township and a son of James Braden, of Welsh descent, who at one time owned 1,000 acres of land in the southern part of the county, where he settled about 1795. He was driven away by the Indians, but returned and spent the rest of his life in Raccoon township. He had one son, John, who also lived in Raccoon township. He had five children: James, John A., William, Margaret (Mrs. Robert Potter), and Rebecca (Mrs. John Porter). Of these John A. was a farmer, and lived on the homestead farm on the Ohio river. He had five children by his first wife: John, Margaret (Mrs. William Elliott), Willie, James R., and Montrose M. By his second wife, Rebecca (Alcom), he had the following children: Mary A. (Mrs. Joseph Allen), Robert H., Oliver C. and Armida. Mr. Braden's maternal grandfather, William Elliott, settled in Moon township in 1825. Our subject located in Beaver Falls in October, 1873, and embarked in the livery business with his brother, James R., in which they have been very successful. In 1873 he married Harriet daughter of Reason and Mary J. (Rambo) Barnes, by whom he has two children living: Meda C. and Howard.

ARTHUR B. BRADFORD, farmer, P. O. Enon Valley, was born in Reading, Pa., March 28, 1810, and is a son of Ebenezer G. and Ruth Bradford. His paternal grandfather was Rev. Ebenezer Bradford, of Massachusetts, a descendant in the fifth generation from William Bradford, who came over in the "Mayflower" in 1620. Mr. Bradford was educated at the Northumberland academy, and at the Milton academy under the Rev. David Kirkpatrick, receiving the honorary degree of A.M. from Union College, Schenectady, N. Y. He was married in 1836 to Elizabeth, daughter of Captain Benjamin Wickes, of Philadelphia. The children of this marriage are Oliver B., Mary

Elizabeth, Ruth Anna B., Isabella Graham, Josephine Frazer, Arthur B., Margaret Ann and Samuel Winchester. Mr. Bradford came from New Jersey in 1838 to Darlington, Beaver county, Pa., in the capacity of a Presbyterian minister, and during the next year became pastor of the church of Mount Pleasant, near that village. He remained such for sixteen years. In 1847 he took part with a number of other clergymen of the Old and New School Presbyterian churches, in forming the Free Presbyterian church, consisting of several Presbyteries, and whose only point of difference from the organization they left was, that the Free church was decidedly anti-slavery in character, and refused to hold church communion with slave holders. In 1854 Mr. Bradford removed to New Castle, Pa., and became pastor of the Free Presbyterian church which had been organized in that town, and so continued to be until the civil war broke out. In 1861 he accepted the appointment, offered him by President Lincoln, of United States consul to the city of Amoy, one of the five open ports of China; but the climate of that latitude being unfriendly to his health, which had been previously broken down, he returned home and resumed his pastoral duties at New Castle. After the war ended in the triumph of the Union and the Constitution, and slavery had been abolished by the proclamation of the President, the Free church disbanded, and the ministers and congregations which had composed the body found such ecclesiastical connections as they pleased. Having, during his voyage and residence abroad, made the acquaintance of all the five different races into which the human family is divided, and having discovered that the sentiments of justice, honor, chastity, benevolence, self-respect, etc., were the same among the so-called "heathen" as they were among his countrymen at home, he began to suspect that his religion, which consigned them all to eternal perdition, because, for no fault of their own, they were ignorant of the Bible, was a theological system deficient in truth, justice and mercy. This suspicion strengthened with further observation and reflection, and finally led to such an examination of the evidences of Christianity as he had never before given the subject; because, when a student enters a theological seminary in this country, as he had done, he takes for granted the truth of Christianity and of his sectarian creed, and his sole object is,—not to study the subject of religion as a topic in the science of man; and whether Christianity is true and all other religions false,—but to qualify himself to become a preacher in the sect to which he belongs, and in whose creed he has been educated. He only takes, and that necessarily, an *ex parte*, or profile view of the subject. This fact explains how it comes to pass that a clergyman, after preaching his religion for years, may undergo a thorough revolution in his opinions without being justly charged with previous hypocrisy in preaching what he did not believe, since he may have been all the time living up to the light he had, entirely ignorant of the merits of the other side of the question. Hence, a person wonders how his intelligent and good neighbors can be, the one a Catholic, the second a Methodist, the third a Baptist, and the fourth a Unitarian, while each one of them wonders how he can be a Presbyterian. Such antagonisms of opinion are not visible among the students and professors of physical science, because their department is one of inquiry, in which the dogmas of authority have no sway; and this fact shows that in the first case there has been no investigation of both sides of the questions so diametrically at issue, but each party holds his creed to be true, because he has been educated to believe so, while the scientist accepts nothing but what, after the most careful examination, *pro* and *con.*, is demonstrated to be true. Mr. Bradford's investigations extended through several years, with his prejudices all the time in favor of his religion; but the force of what appeared to him to be the truth was so great, that it resulted in a radical change of opinion, and he felt it his duty as an honest man to withdraw from the church and ministry entirely. This he accordingly did, and retired to his farm, where he was living in the seventy-eighth year of his age at the time of this writing, laboring through the medium of the press to prevent other people from being involved in the same cloud of darkness out of which it had cost him so much to emerge.

JACOB S. BRADLEY, steamboat steward, P. O. Vanport, was born in York county, Pa., Dec. 1, 1826, and is a son of John and Catherine (Miller) Bradley, of Dutch and Irish descent, former by trade a carpenter. The family consisted of five children, of whom Jacob S., the fourth, was reared in Allegheny City, attended school there and has been engaged as steward for many years. He was married at Cincinnati, Ohio, to May, daughter of Thomas and Mary (Duffy) Ryan, and their children were—John, who died at the age of twenty-two years; Anna, wife of Matthew Brookmyre, of Vanport; Willie, who died at seven years of age; Joseph, a boatman on the Ohio river; George, also a boatman on the Ohio river, and Frank, a telegraph operator on the Lake Erie railroad. Mr. Bradley is a member of the Catholic church. In politics he is a Democrat.

J. PHILLIS BRADSHAW, farmer, P. O. Darlington, was born in 1829, and is the eldest son of Robert Bradshaw, a farmer by occupation, who died in 1874, aged seventy-five years; his widow is yet living at the age of eighty-five years. Robert Bradshaw, grandfather of our subject, came from Westmoreland county, about 1796, and bought 250 acres of land in South Beaver township. He married Sarah Wood, who bore him two sons, Thomas and Robert, and four daughters. J. Phillis Bradshaw was reared on the farm and received a common-school education. He was married, in 1859, to Elizabeth, daughter of John and Elizabeth (Thompson) Cuthbertson, and they have had seven children: Robert, Maggie, John, Joseph, Evalina, William S. and Tamar Mabel. The family are members of the Reformed Presbyterian church. Mr. Bradshaw is a Republican.

B. F. BRADSHAW, farmer, P. O. Darlington, was born in South Beaver township in 1846, and is a son of Robert and Margaret Bradshaw. He received a common-school education, and has always followed farming. He was married in 1877 to Jennie A., daughter of John Reed, of this county, and they had five children, of whom four are living: John Reed, Sadie Hunter, Jessie Garfield and Mary Ellen Vance. Mr. Bradshaw has always lived in this county, with the exception of six years spent in Iowa, Illinois and Kansas. In 1883 he purchased his present farm of 123 acres. He and his wife are members of the Reformed Presbyterian church of Darlington. He is a Republican.

MILO BRADSHAW, farmer, P. O. Darlington, was born in South Beaver township in 1833, and is a grandson of Robert and Sarah (Wood) Bradshaw, who settled in South Beaver township about 1796. The Bradshaws were originally from Ireland. Thomas Bradshaw, father of Milo, was born in 1787 and died in 1869. He married, in 1810, Martha Barclay, who bore him nine children, seven of whom grew to maturity, Milo being the youngest. The mother died in 1875 aged eighty-five years. Milo Bradshaw was married, in 1861, to Jennie Hunter, born in Ohio township in 1836, daughter of John and Jane (Johnson) Hunter. Five children have been born to this union, as follows: Ella Martha, born in 1863; Minnie Belle, in 1864; Jennie Blanche, in 1868; George C. S., in 1870, and Birdie Viola, in 1875. Mr. Bradshaw is a member of the Reformed Presbyterian church. Politically he is a Republican.

WILLIAM H. BRICKER, register and recorder, Beaver, was born in Cumberland county, Pa., Aug. 6, 1837. He is a son of John and Eliza (House) Bricker, natives of Pennsylvania and of Swiss and German descent. His father was a farmer and the father of six children, all of whom were boys, William H. being the second. Our subject grew to manhood in Cumberland county, receiving his education in the common schools, and chose farming as a business. When the civil war broke out he promptly enlisted in Company H., Third Pennsylvania Volunteer cavalry, was promoted to the office of second lieutenant and assigned to Company B. In that capacity he served until 1863, when he was captured in Virginia; was a prisoner for sixteen months, eight and a half months of that time in Libby prison. He managed to escape, but after twelve days was re-captured and returned to prison. His regiment was discharged and returned to Cumberland county five months before his release; he arrived home on Christmas Eve. He again engaged in farming, and in 1870 was appointed United States storekeeper, which office he held until 1876, when he resigned and removed to Beaver Falls, where he was engaged in the mercantile trade until 1883. In 1884 he was elected to his present position by 1595 majority. He is a member of Post No. 35, G. A. R.; in politics he is a

628   HISTORY OF BEAVER COUNTY.

Republican. Mr. Bricker married in 1868 Frances E., daughter of John and Susannah (Raber) Fishburn, who were of German descent. Mr. and Mrs. Bricker are members of the Presbyterian Church. He has held the office of register and recorder for three years, and during that time he has filled the position with credit to himself and to the entire satisfaction of the people. In 1887 he was reëlected by 1804 majority, which led the entire ticket.

FRANK F. BRIERLY, hardware merchant, Beaver Falls, was born in Enfield, Mass., in February, 1848, and is a son of Samuel and Orilla (Kendrick) Brierly, who settled in Lawrence county, Pa., in 1849, and in 1859 located in New Brighton, this county, where our subject was reared and educated. He learned the carpenter's trade, which he followed as an occupation six years. In 1871 he located in Beaver Falls and embarked in the general hardware business, which he has successfully continued since. He has occupied the present double store on the corner of Seventh avenue and Sixth street since 1874. The store room is 40 by 75 feet, and an addition in the rear is 20 by 45. The business comprises hardware, tinware, stoves, lime and cement, paints and oils and general building material, and is the largest and leading establishment of the kind in the county. Mr. Brierly is one of the stockholders and treasurer of the Coöperative Stove Company. He is also a stockholder in the Beaver Falls Glass Company, and a member of the firm of Knott, Harker & Co., manufacturers of grates and mantels. He is one of the live, enterprising citizens of Beaver Falls, a member of the Y. M. C. A. and Methodist Protestant church: in politics he is a Republican.

W. H. BRIGGS, proprietor of hotel, P. O. Industry. Soon after the landing of the Pilgrim Fathers on the shores of Massachusetts, three families, named respectively Briggs, Goodwin and Austin, came from England and settled in that state, the Briggs' being blacksmiths by trade. Henry Briggs, a descendant of this pioneer family, and the second son born to his parents, left his native state with his family in 1838, and took up a quarter-section of land in South Beaver township, this county, where he followed blacksmithing and hotel keeping. Moving to Youngstown, Ohio, he remained there a short time and then returned to the farm known then as "Black Hawk Postoffice." He married Mary Weascott, whose ancestors came from Massachusetts, and six children were given them. W. H., the eldest son was born in 1823, near the old "Stamping Ground" occupied by his early ancestors. The father died at the age of eighty-four years, his widow at the age of eighty-nine. Our subject learned the trade of his forefathers, which he has followed, together with other pursuits, to the present time, and for the past thirty years he has been engaged in steamboat engineering. During the war he carried supplies for northern soldiers, operating in the south. For the past twenty-two years his present place has been his home, and in his absence the "River View Hotel" is conducted by Mrs. Briggs. He was married in 1846 to Deborah, daughter of Joseph, and sister of Captain Stockdale, of Allegheny county. Their children are Joseph S., Elizabeth A. (now Mrs. Johnson), Flora B. (in Des Moines, Iowa), and George E. The family are members of the Christian church. Mr. Briggs is a Republican.

R. J. BRITTAIN, physician, New Galilee, was born in Beaver (now Lawrence) county, in 1838. James, his father, a farmer by occupation, was born in this county in 1805 and died in 1848; he married Jane McChesney, by whom he had four children, our subject being the second son. The grandfather, Jeremiah, who was Scotch-Irish, located in this county in 1797, and purchased land. Dr. Brittain was educated at private schools and at the Darlington and Beaver academies. He was married in 1864 to Mary E. daughter of George Grier. He was next married to Kizzie O'Brien, a sister of his first wife, and by her had four children born: Elmer E., in 1868; Amelia L., in 1871; Estella E. and Cordelia E. (twins), in 1873. Our subject began the study of medicine in 1854 with Drs. Hezlop and Meigs. He entered Jefferson Medical College in 1860, and was graduated in March, 1863. For two years thereafter he practiced in Philadelphia, and in 1865 came to New Galilee, where he has since remained. He enjoys an extensive and lucrative practice. During the war he was a member of the volunteer corps of surgeons. He is a member of the Presbyterian church. In politics an independent Republican.

WILLIAM BROMAN, glass-presser, Beaver Falls, was born in Allegheny City, Pa., Aug. 11, 1849. His parents, Henry and Lena (Rosafield) Broman, were natives of Alsace, France (now Germany), and came to America about 1840, settling in Allegheny City, where our subject was reared and educated. He began his trade at Pittsburgh in 1859, and has worked at it ever since. He located in Beaver Falls in 1879, and was one of the organizers and stockholders of the Coöperative Flint Glass Works, where he has since been employed. His wife was Sarah Iseley, of Pittsburgh, by whom he has two children living, Charlie and Sarah. Mr. Broman is a member of the A. O. U. W. and of the German Lutheran church. In politics he is a Democrat.

HARVEY BROWN, merchant, Bridgewater, was born in Beaver county April 23, 1842, and is a son of John and Margaret (Hart) Brown, natives of Beaver county. His paternal ancestors came from Ireland. His mother was a descendant of John Hart, a signer of the Declaration of Independence. Our subject's grandparents settled on the south side of Beaver county, and followed agricultural pursuits. His father was a boat builder by trade, and in later life was engaged in selling stoves in Allegheny City. His family consisted of five children, four now living. Harvey, the second in the family was reared in Bridgewater, where he was educated in the common schools. He also attended Duff's college, in Pittsburgh. In 1863 he began clerking for A. S. Harvey, and remained with him until 1867, when he embarked in his present business. He deals in glass, wooden, willow and queen's ware and hardware. In 1862 he enlisted in the Beaver Infantry, Company F, 140th Regiment, under Colonel Roberts, and was discharged Feb. 6, 1863. He is a member of the G. A. R., also of the K. of P. and of the I. O. O. F. He is a director of the first building association of Rochester, also of West Bridgewater Association, and is a F. & A. M. Mr. Brown was married March 21, 1871, to Mrs. Martha Elizabeth Ady, a native of Wheeling, W. Va., and of English descent. Their children are Ella and James L. The family are members of the Methodist Episcopal church. Mr. Brown has been a member and treasurer of the official board for eleven years, and at present is superintendent of the Sabbath-school.

JOHN E. BRYER, glass-blower, Beaver Falls, was born in Pittsburgh, Pa., May 11, 1844, and is a son of John and Susan (Gailey) Bryer, of Pennsylvania. He was reared and educated in his native city, where he learned his trade. He located in Bridgewater in 1863, and worked at his trade until 1869; then removed to Pittsburgh and was in the employ of Brice Bros. nine years. In 1878 he came to Beaver Falls, and was the projector of the Coöperative Flint Glass Works, of which he is now a stockholder, and where he has since been employed. His wife was Kate, a daughter of Daniel Torrance, of Bridgewater, by whom he has three children: William D., Oliver J. and Lillie May. Mr. Bryer is one of the stockholders of the Citizens' Gas Co., is a member of the K. of P., and the Methodist Protestant church. Politically he is a Republican.

JOHN M. BUCHANAN, attorney at law, Beaver, is a son of Thomas C. and Eliza (Mayhew) Buchanan, the former of whom died when his son was but an infant. John M. (with the exception of the first five years of his life spent in and near Florence, Washington county, Pa., where his forefathers had resided since 1791, and two years spent in Fairview, W. Va.), was reared in the home of an uncle, Joseph K. Buchanan, in Hanover township, Beaver county, Pa. He was prepared for college by the Hon. Thomas Nicholson and Rev. J. P. Moore, chiefly by recitations made during winter evenings, and was graduated at Washington and Jefferson College in the class of 1869. Immediately after graduation he was entered as a student of law in the office of the Hon. Samuel B. Wilson, and reaching the requisite legal age, was admitted to the bar on motion of Edward B. Daugherty, Esq., Sept. 2, 1872, having supported himself in the meanwhile by teaching. In 1874 he was elected district attorney, as a Democrat, by a majority of 94 and was reëlected in 1877 by 303 majority. Mr. Buchanan very soon after his admission placed himself in point of ability and success among the leading attorneys of the county, and has since been largely identified with its most important litigation.

630   HISTORY OF BEAVER COUNTY.

GEORGE BURHENN, glass presser, Beaver Falls, was born in Hesse Cassell, Germany, March 1, 1851, and is a son of Ewald and Elizabeth Burhenn, who came to America in 1854 and settled in Pittsburgh, Pa., where the father, who was a nailsmith by trade, resided until his death. George was reared and educated in Pittsburgh, and there learned his trade, which he has followed since 1862. He located in Beaver Falls in 1879, and was one of the organizers and stockholders of the Coöperative Flint Glass Works, in which he has since been interested. In 1879 he married Clara, daughter of Christopher Chobert, of Pittsburgh. By her he has four children : Henry, Peter E , John and George H. Mr. Burhenn is a member of the I. O. O. F., K. of H. and Turner Society. Politically, he is independent.

JACOB BURHENN, glass presser, Beaver Falls, was born in Pittsburgh, Pa., Aug. 8, 1860, and is a son of Ewald and Elizabeth Burhenn, who came to America in 1854 and settled in Pittsburgh, Pa., where the father, who was a nailsmith by trade, resided until his death. Jacob was reared, educated and learned his trade in Pittsburgh. July 1, 1887, he located in Beaver Falls, where he has since been in the employ of the Coöperative Flint Glass Works. July 18, 1886, he married Lizzie, daughter of Jonas Batz, of Pittsburgh, by whom he has one child, Edward. He is a member of the Glass Workers' Union, and in politics is a Republican.

JOHN CAIN, farmer, P. O. Darlington, was born in Lancaster county in 1814, and came to Beaver county in 1841. His father, James Cain, came from Ireland at an early day, locating in Marietta, Pa., and was by occupation a "nailer." He married Jane, daughter of Samuel Getty, also of Ireland. Born to James Cain and his wife were seven children, of whom John is the eldest. He had but few opportunities in youth for receiving an education, his father having died when he (John) was comparatively young. His mother came to Allegheny county in 1841, and soon after moved to Darlington township, where since that date he has resided. Mr. Cain has been a farmer since he was thirteen years of age. He followed tanning for three years, but never learned the trade. He was married, in 1836, to Sarah, daughter of James Mahan, of Allegheny county, and thirteen children were born to them. Those living are James, John, Eliza, Franklin, Ella, Harry, William, Ida, Homer and Delight. Mr. Cain has held many township offices, and has always been regarded, by those who know him, as an upright and honest man, much respected. He is a F. & A. M.; in politics, a Democrat.

LEANDER CAIRNS, retired, P. O. New Brighton, was born in this county in 1828, and is a son of William and Edna (Morrow) Cairns (the latter a native of Philadelphia), the parents of nine children, seven now living, Leander being the only surviving son. The father was born in Westmoreland county, Pa., in 1793, and in 1800 was brought by his parents to Beaver county. Here he followed farming until he was eighteen years of age, and then learned carpentering and cabinet making. He was prominently identified, politically, in Beaver county, and was elected sheriff in 1833, also associate judge, as well as to other positions of trust. For many years he carried on boat-building and the saw and grist milling business. Leander chiefly remained at home, assisting his father in his various industries, and was for some time engaged in the gunboat service on the Mississippi river under Commodore Davis, but was compelled, on account of ill-health, to retire from the same. Mr. Cairns and a sister now make Industry their home, where they live in quiet retirement.

JOHN H. CALER, blacksmith, P. O. Fallston, was born in Big Beaver township, Beaver county, in August, 1833, and is a son of Michael Caler and Susanna (Nicolson) Caler, natives of Beaver county and of German and English origin. The father was a riverman, and in later life bought timber land and sold cord wood, also worked a stone quarry on his land. The family consisted of nine children. John H., the eldest son, was reared in Big Beaver township, and attended school three months in winter. Early in life he learned the blacksmith's trade, but has preferred to work at the more difficult departments of the trade, and is well known in larger cities. Most of his work comes from outside of Beaver county. Since 1861 he has been manufacturing oil tools. Mr. Caler was married in Beaver county to Miss Mary I., daughter of William

BIOGRAPHIES—WEST SIDE. 631

Moore, and their children are William, Ira and John, blacksmiths, Lewis, Elva and Edith. In politics Mr. Caler is a Republican. He is a member of the town council and president of the school board. Mrs. Caler is a member of the Methodist church.

STEPHEN CALVIN, farmer, P. O. Black Hawk, was born in this county in 1807, and is one of the oldest citizens now living in South Beaver township. He is the eldest of thirteen children born to James and Elizabeth (Grosscross) Calvin. James Calvin died in 1835, aged fifty years. He came to Beaver county from Allegheny county about 1794, and with a brother purchased 400 acres of land on Brush Run. He continued farming until his death. Six of his children are living. Stephen has been engaged in various pursuits. In early life he was a carpenter, and was for some time employed in milling. In 1836 he purchased his present farm of 160 acres. In 1842 he was married to Jane, daughter of Andrew Graham, and they had ten children, eight of whom are living: James, Robert, Mary Jane (Mrs. May), Elizabeth, Stephen, William L., Emeline and Martha A. (Mrs. Funkhouser). The mother died in 1861, aged forty-one years. Mr. Calvin is a Democrat.

WILLIAM CAMPBELL (deceased) was born in county Tyrone, Ireland, in 1819, and died in 1885. He came to America about 1842, landing in Philadelphia. In 1848 he moved to Beaver county, and was for four years employed in a woolen factory. He then purchased 125 acres of land, which he successfully tilled for a number of years. At his death he owned 200 acres. He married Mary, daughter of William and Margaret (Graham) McKey, of this county. She bore him seven children (of whom six are living): David, Matilda, Margaret, Annie (Mrs. Moore, deceased), Jennie P., James A. and Mary E. The mother died in 1881. The surviving children are all living on the homestead, and none are married. They are members of the Presbyterian church.

JESSE W. CAROTHERS, farmer, P. O. Beaver, was born in Patterson township, this county, Dec. 20, 1826. He is a son of John and Nancy (White) Carothers, natives of Pennsylvania, the mother of Irish parentage, and the father born in the Cumberland valley. John Carothers, who was a farmer, came to Beaver county in 1814, and settled in Patterson township. His family consisted of nine children, seven of them now in Beaver county. Jesse W., the fourth, was reared in Patterson township, on the farm, attended the district school and chose farming as a business, which he has followed all his life. He was married in Beaver county, in 1851, to Sarah, daughter of Joseph Mitchell, and of Irish descent. They have three children now living: Anna Agnes (wife of Thomas Purdy), Eliza Elma (wife of Frank Dunkin), and Sarah Luella. Mr. and Mrs Carothers are members of the Presbyterian church. He is a Democrat, and has served for ten years as school director and four years as justice of the peace. He is the owner of a farm of nearly 200 acres of well-improved land.

WILLIAM CARTER (deceased) was born in Westmoreland County, Va., Dec. 2, 1802, and was a son of Charles and Jane (Anderson) Carter; former, born in the same county in 1760, and latter in Washington county, Md., in 1778. His paternal grandfather was Charles B. Carter, a son of Robert Carter, who was a son of King Carter, a gentleman of immense wealth, who emigrated to Virginia from England in 1704. The family, who are well and favorably known in Virginia, are principally engaged in agricultural pursuits, though one or two are connected with the United States navy. Charles B Carter, paternal grandfather of our subject, was a large planter in Virginia, and died in Berkeley county in 1807. Charles Carter, father of William, was an iron master; he was an officer in the Revolutionary war, and was present at the surrender of Cornwallis at Yorktown. He made a settlement at what is now Beaver Falls in 1797, remaining but a short time. In 1802 he returned and built a furnace at old Brighton (now Beaver Falls), in which he forged the first piece of iron made in the county. He died near Mount Etna Furnace, Butler county, in 1829. His wife was a niece of Gen. Carlisle, of Revolutionary fame. They had eight children: John (a soldier of the war of 1812), George, William, Charles (a major-general of the Pennsylvania line, who participated in several Indian wars, and who was in the government service until 1861); David A. (in the war of 1812); James A. (who served in the Mexican war under Gen. Taylor); Jane C. (Mrs. Hiram Reed) and Elizabeth (Mrs. Horatio M. Large). William Carter was a teacher by profession, but in later years followed engineering. He was justice of the peace for many years, and died in New Brighton, June 30, 1876. His wife, Valeria, was a daughter of Daniel and Margaret (Steen) Reeves. They had eight children, four of whom are living: Charles, Addie V. (Mrs. John Scott), Margaretta and Elizabeth (Mrs. Lewis Graham).

JOHN CHANEY, farmer, P. O. Ohioville, son of William and Elizabeth (Christler) Chaney, was born Jan. 22, 1852, near Ohioville, this county, where he spent the days of his youth and received his education. His father was born Oct. 4, 1821, in Columbiana county, Ohio, and died Oct. 3, 1886. His mother was born on the old homestead near Ohioville. John's grandfather, Johnson Chaney, was born at Pittsburgh, Pa., and his father, John, was one of the first settlers at Pittsburgh. Mr. Chaney's grandfather, on his mother's side, George Christler's father, immigrated to this country, settled near Shippingport, Pa., and was one of the first settlers of this place. Our subject was married Sept. 26, 1876, to Ella Amelia Lyan, daughter of Alfred and Ellen (Fowler) Lyan, born Dec. 16, 1856. near Ohioville, Beaver county, Pa. Four children have been born to this union: Raymond C., Nellie, Leroy and Charles W. Mr. and Mrs. Chaney are members of the Reformed Presbyterian church. Mr. Chaney's father was an elder in the same church, and after his death Mr. Chaney assumed the same office.

JOHN W. M. CHILDS, machinery dealer, Smith's Ferry, a son of Lorenzo and Ann Caroline (Marshall) Childs, was born in Brooklyn, N. Y., Jan. 1, 1838. His father was born in August, 1810, at Vershire, Vt.; his mother was a native of Brooklyn, and died March 20, 1841. Lorenzo Childs spent his youth at the place of his birth, and, when a young man, went to New York City, where he learned the machinery business. He married, April 30, 1833, in the Episcopal church, Jamaica, L. I., and shortly after came to Cleveland and thence moved to Pittsburgh. Later he moved to Fallston, and subsequently started a shop for himself at New Brighton, afterward taking in David McConnell as partner, under name of Childs & McConnel. After doing business in New Brighton, as the firm of Childs & McConnell, for some time, they removed their machine shop to Fallston, purchased new site with good water power, they then took in new partner. The firm name was then changed to Childs, McConnell & Darragh, doing quite an extensive business up to the time of Mr. Child's selling his interest out of the machine business. About the year 1859 he came to Smith's Ferry, built a mill, which was operated for some time by him and Mr. Smith. They afterward closed out the mill and engaged in the oil business. He died at Bridgewater, Aug. 19, 1864. The subject of this sketch came to Pennsylvania with his parents about 1843, and received his schooling in Beaver county. He learned the machinist's trade at his father's shop at New Brighton and at Fallston. In 1859 he came to Smith's Ferry with his father and engaged in setting up machinery; in 1867 he began to sell machinery, and by hard work and attention has been successful; he is the owner of good buildings and a fine residence, and has a large trade in machinery, carrying a heavy stock. Most of his trade, however, is foreign, since the decline of the oil trade here. Mr. Childs married at Pittsburgh, Sept. 30, 1869, Agnes B., daughter of Ralph and Margaret (Alman) Ecoff, born at Rochester, Pa., Jan. 23, 1848. Her father was a carpenter and contractor, a native of this county, born Sept. 9, 1818, and died of small pox at Rochester, Jan. 14, 1855. Her mother was also a native of this county, born June 15, 1822, and died April 18, 1854. Three girls and one boy were born to Mr. and Mrs. Childs: John W. M., now clerk for his father; Grace Mary, attending school at Beaver; Agnes Gertrude and Blanche Margaret, at home. Mr. Child's family are members of the Presbyterian church.

JOHN COALMAN came from New Jersey and settled at the mouth of Little Beaver at an early day. In 1803 he moved near the town of Mt. Jackson, then in Beaver county. In 1807 he started on a journey to Philadelphia with saddle and pack-horses, carrying with him $300 worth of furs. After disposing of the above articles he started home.

When about one hundred miles from the city he was beset by highwaymen, robbed of money and horses, and threatened with death if he attempted to return to Philadelphia. Thus situated, with nothing but gun and ammunition, he began a weary journey of three hundred miles on foot, living by the way on wild game, roots, etc. He returned safely, however, and ever after lived on his farm, where he died at the age of ninety-nine years. His wife was Mary Mahen, by whom he had eleven children, eight girls and three boys.

JOHN COLEMAN, blacksmith, Bridgewater, was born in County Antrim, Ireland, in January, 1843, and is a son of Thomas and Eleanore (Shaw) Coleman. His father, a blacksmith, came to America in 1866, living only three weeks after his arrival, and leaving three sons and three daughters. John, the eldest son, received his education in the old country, where he also learned the blacksmith's trade with his father, and has followed his trade twenty-four years in Beaver county. He worked for the railroad company before they built the shops. He was married in Ireland, in 1862, to Mary A. Russell, and their children are Thomas, a mould maker; William, a blacksmith; Robert John; Anna R.; Elenore, and Mary Jane. The mother died March 10, 1887, a member of the Presbyterian church. Mr. Coleman is an elder and trustee of same church, and has taught in the Sabbath-school. He is a member of the school board, and in politics is a Republican.

JAMES M. CONKLE, pattern maker, Beaver Falls, was born in Greene township, this county, Sept. 10, 1832, son of John and Catherine (Persley) Conkle. His paternal grandfather was Henry Conkle, a pioneer of Beaver county, and an Indian scout for a number of years. He was also in the war of 1812, and was a noted hunter and expert shot in his day. He finally settled in Greene township, this county, and engaged in farming, residing there until his death in about 1840. His children were John, George, Jacob, Samuel, Sally, Betsey, Ann and Polly. John, the eldest, was a native of Greene township, and lived and died there. He was a carpenter by trade, which he followed in early life, but later engaged in farming. His children were Henry, Mary A., Margaret, Jacob, John, James M., Robert, William, Milton and Vincent. James M. was reared in Greene township, this county, where he learned the millwright's trade, which he has followed as a business, off and on, to the present time. For the past two years he has been engaged principally in pattern making. He located in Beaver Falls in 1867, where he has since resided. In 1866 he married Mary, daughter of Robert and Hannah (Ruth) McKeage, who settled in Beaver county in 1847, and by this union there are three children living: Charlie, Walter and Roy. Mr. Conkle is a member of the I. O. O. F. and K. of P. In politics he is a Democrat.

ROBERT CONKEL, carpenter, P. O. McCleary, was born in Greene township, this county, Nov. 26. 1834, and is a son of John and Catherine (Persley) Conkel. His paternal grandfather was Henry Conkel, a pioneer of Beaver county, a noted Indian scout and hunter, and a soldier in the war of 1812. He was a farmer by occupation, and lived and died in Greene township. He had eight children, of whom John, the father of our subject, was the eldest. He was a carpenter by trade and was born and reared in Greene township, where he resided until his death. Robert was reared in Greene township, where he learned the carpenter's trade. In 1854 he located in Missouri and later in Illinois, where he worked at his trade as a journeyman, and did considerable business as a contractor and builder. In 1862 he enlisted in the 76th Illinois Infantry, and participated in the siege of Vicksburg, battles of Fort Blakely and Spanish Fort, as well as other engagements, and was honorably discharged at Galveston, Tex., in August, 1865. In 1866 he located in Hookstown, this county, and in 1868 in Beaver Falls, remaining there until 1884, when he removed to Raccoon township, where he now resides. In 1867 Mr. Conkel married Mary J., daughter of David and Mary Glenn, of Greene township, this county, and has nine children : Marilda, Frank, William and Dora (twins), Alma, John A., Thomas, Henry and Emma J. He is a member of the G. A. R.; in politics a Republican.

THOMAS B. CONWAY, Vanport, was born in New Brighton, this county, Jan. 6, 1831, and is a son of John and Fannie (Barchus) Conway, natives of Pennsylvania and of Irish descent. His father died when he was but two years of age. Our subject attended the common schools and acquired a fair education. At the age of seventeen he went forth into the world to do for himself. In 1846 he had charge of a construction train as conductor, which occupation he followed for nine years; being also a foreman of construction of the Cleveland & Pittsburgh R. R. when it was built. He married Mary, daughter of James H. and Margaret (Caldwell) Douds, in the year 1856. His wife was born in Beaver county, and is of Scotch descent. In the year he was married, he came to Vanport, and has made that his home since, being the possessor of two residences there. He has followed the lime business since his marriage, and is well known throughout the county as a manufacturer of the Beaver county gray lime. He has three children living : Fannie B. (wife of W. H. Gordon, a merchant of Vanport), John D. (a telegraph operator, employed in the master of machinery's department P. & L. E. R. R., Chartiers), May, youngest daughter, at home. Mr. and Mrs. Conway are prominent members of the Presbyterian church, Bridgewater. In politics, he is a staunch Republican, and has held various positions on the school board of this place.

GEORGE W. COOK, ticket and express agent, C. & P. R. R., at Cook station, P. O. Industry, was born in Princeton, N. J., Sept. 13, 1816. His parents, William and Ruthie (Drummons) Cook, were natives of New Jersey, where they were married and died. They had three children. George W., the only survivor, was married March 5, 1839, to Margaret Fuhr, a native of Philadelphia, born in 1822, a daughter of Major George Fuhr (deceased). To this union have been born eight children, six now living: William, Amanda, Ernest, Sarah I., Bertha and Clara; Caroline and Deborah are deceased. The mother died May 30, 1874. Mr. Cook is by trade a willow-basket maker, which business he was followed since his thirteenth year; has also been ticket agent for the C. & P. R. R. for a period of twenty-nine years. He has been a resident of Beaver county since 1853, and own his residence, as well as the ferry which bears his name. He is a Democrat, and has filled several township offices.

HENRY COPMANN, teamster, Beaver Falls, was born in Hanover, Germany, Oct. 15, 1845, and is a son of Fred and Henrietta Copmann, who came to America in 1879, and settled in Allegheny City. Our subject was reared and educated in his native town. He came to America in 1866, and located in Beaver Falls in 1872, where he has since resided. He embarked in business there as a teamster, which vocation he still follows. Beginning without a dollar, he has accumulated a fine property, of which he justly feels proud. He does the hauling and teaming for several of the largest manufacturing concerns in Beaver Falls. besides considerable outside work. Mr. Copmann married, in 1869, Mary Wickman, of Allegheny City, by whom he has seven children: John, Mary, Carrie, Emma, Harry, Annie and Maggie. He is a member of the German Lutheran church and the Society of Druids; in politics he is a Democrat.

JOHN CORBUS, superintendent of car works, Beaver Falls, was born in Fallston, this county. Oct. 13, 1831, and is a son of John S. and Eliza (Reeves) Corbus, the former a native of Muskingum county, Ohio, and the latter of Beaver county. Pa. The father came to Beaver county about 1824, and served an apprenticeship in Fallston at scythe making, which he followed there for several years. He then learned the trade of wire drawer with Robert Townsend. Esq., in whose employ and that of his son, William P. Townsend, he has passed upwards of fifty years. His children were seven in number: Mary J. (Mrs. Hugh Irwin), John, Thankful (Mrs. Dr. Louis Jack), Elizabeth (deceased), Margaret (Mrs. Richard Irwin), Daniel R. and Jesse M. John was reared in Beaver county, and for many years was engaged in merchandising in New Brighton. In 1879 he accepted the position he now holds in the Beaver Falls car works. He has twice married; first to Mary, daughter of David and Eleanor (Daly) Blair, of Pittsburgh, and by her he had three children; Curtis B., Harold H. and Clarence H. His second wife was Elsie, daughter of Dr. Isaac and Eliza (Sheets) Winans, of Mahoning county, Ohio, and by her he had six children: Lila W., Howard L., May E., Helen and Louis (twins), and Edward T. Mr. Corbus is a member of the Presbyterian church and the Royal Arcanum; he is a R. A. M.; politically a Republican.

A. M. CRAWFORD, dealer in general merchandise, Darlington, Pa., was born in Darlington, this county, Aug. 13, 1839. His father was John M. Crawford, who, in company with his brother Peter, came from New Jersey to Beaver county, when both were quite young men. He married Miss Catherine Miller, of Belmont, Pa., and to them were born two children, of whom A. M. is the elder. His education was attained at Greersburg Academy. He was married in 1864 to Miss Malissa M. McMinn, daughter of Robert McMinn, Jr., whose grandfather, Robert McMinn, Sr., was one of the oldest residents of the county and who died at nearly one hundred years of age. To Mr. and Mrs. Crawford were born five children: Lena D., Nellie A., Fred C., Ira F. and Alice M. Mr. Crawford has for over thirty years been engaged in business in Darlington, and has been identified in many ways with the interests of the town in which he lives. Politically he is a Republican. In his religious belief he clings to the Presbyterian faith.

SAMUEL CREESE, contractor and builder, Beaver Falls, was born in Allegheny county, March 25, 1850, and is a son of Philip and Jane (Skiles) Creese, natives of Allegheny county, and residents of Beaver Falls since 1879. Samuel Creese learned the carpenter's trade, which he followed for fourteen years. He located in Beaver Falls in 1879, and in 1881 embarked in business as a contractor and builder. He is a thorough mechanic and a careful and competent builder. He is a member of the Presbyterian church, National Union and Knights of the Maccabees; in politics he is a Democrat.

JOHN CRUMP, retired merchant, Beaver, was born in Virginia, October 7, 1807, and is a son of Stephen and Nancy (Sisson) Crump, natives of Virginia and of Welsh origin. His father, who was a carpenter, lived to the advanced age of ninety-three, and died in West Virginia. John Crump's elder brother, who died at the age of ninety-two, was a soldier in the war of 1812. John is the fifth of eight children, four sons and four daughters. He was reared in West Virginia, attended the common schools, learned the carriage maker's trade, and carried on business in Virginia twenty-five years. He then embarked in the dry goods business in Virginia. In 1864 he went to Ohio, where he was in the mercantile business until 1867, when he came to this county, bought a place on the banks of the Ohio, and retired from business. He was married in 1829 to Ruth, daughter of John Robinson, and their children were Stephen S., a coal merchant; John R., who was a physician; George, a dealer in agricultural implements in Missouri; William H., in the foundry business at Chicago; and L. Wesley and James S. (deceased). Mrs. Crump died in 1886. She and her husband were members of the Methodist Episcopal church for more than half a century. Mr. Crump has been steward and class leader. In political preferment he is a Republican.

G. A CUBBISON, jeweler, Beaver Falls, was born in Harrisville, Butler county, Sept.16, 1863, and is a son of George and Mary A. (Milner) Cubbison. He was reared and educated in Mercer county, and served an apprenticeship of four years at the jeweler's trade in Butler, Pa. with D. L. Cleeland. In 1880–82, he worked at his trade as a journeyman in Mercer, Pa. In March, 1883, he located in Beaver Falls where he was employed in a jewelry store one year, and in October, 1885, he embarked in business for himself in Beaver Falls, where he has already built up a large and lucrative business, which is steadily increasing. He has also a first-class gents' furnishing store.

JOHN CUNNING, dealer in real estate, Beaver Falls,was born in Maryland,June 15,1839; a son of George and Maria (Williams) Cunning, and of Irish and English descent. His parents settled in Independence township, this county, in 1842, where his father engaged in farming and resided nineteen years. He then removed to Lawrence county, Pa., residing there until his death. His children were John, Hugh, Mary J. (Mrs. Frank Callahan), Sarah (Mrs. James McKelvy), Daniel, Anna (deceased) and Robert. John was reared in Independence township where he received a common-school education. In 1861 he married Martha, daughter of Andrew and Sarah McKindley, of Independence township, who settled there about 1840. By this union there are five children living: Eva E. (Mrs. Robert S. Frazier) John E., Charles, Mary E. and George G. Mr. Cunning located in Beaver Falls in 1868, and embarked in mercantile trade, in which he was engaged two years. He then engaged in the real estate business, which he has followed more or less since, with the exception of two years. He has kept a hotel and restaurant for the past twelve years, and has owned the Merchant's hotel, one of the principal hostelries of Beaver Falls, since 1882. He is a member of the Catholic church; in politics, independent.

JAMES HAMILTON CUNNINGHAM, attorney, Beaver, is of Scotch and Irish ancestry, and was born Dec. 12, 1846, in Beaver, Beaver county, Pa. At the age of seven years he became a resident of Industry township, where much of his early youth was passed as a pupil in the common schools and in farm labor. In 1864 he enlisted in Company F, 140th Regiment P. V., and served until the close of the civil war, participating in the battles of the Wilderness, Todd's Tavern, Corbin's Bridge, Spottsylvania, North Ann, Cold Harbor, and other engagements of less importance. At Cold Harbor he was wounded, captured and confined for six months in the prison at Andersonville, Ga., from which he was paroled and subsequently exchanged. Rejoining his regiment he participated in all the engagements from March, 1865, to the surrender of Gen. Lee at Appomatox. On his return from the service he resumed his studies, receiving private instructions from Prof. M. L. Knight, then, as now, one of the leading teachers of the county, and from others; meanwhile defraying the expenses by farm labor and in teaching. April 5, 1870, he entered the office of E. P. Kuhn, of Beaver, then a rising and brilliant young lawyer, and was admitted to the bar July 31, 1872. In the fall of the same year he entered into partnership with his preceptor, and on the death of the latter, the following year, continued the practice of his profession alone. Mr. Cunningham, by his energy, and by methodical habits of business, soon won success and a patronage which is yearly increasing in proportion. He has devoted himself assiduously to his profession, and avoided all such diversions as would lead him from its legitimate pursuit. May 11, 1875, Mr. Cunningham married Miss Nellie I., daughter of Captain S. A. Reno, of Rochester. Their children are Charles S., Carrie May, Annie R. and James H., Jr.

DRS. OLIVER AND SMITH CUNNINGHAM, two physicians, who were cousins, came to Beaver prior to 1832, and established themselves in the practice of their profession. Oliver had been a skiff builder in Pittsburgh prior to his advent here. Smith and his brother came from Ohio. Oliver was two or three years the earlier settler, and also the senior in age. Dr. Smith Cunningham was followed by his brothers Robert, Thomas and Nathaniel. Robert studied medicine and practiced in North Sewickley township. Thomas and Nathaniel studied law with John R. Shannon, and the former was admitted to the bar of Beaver county about 1834. Nathaniel was admitted afterward, either in Beaver or Mercer county, and subsequently studied medicine with his brother Robert, and practiced for a time in this county. He removed to some place in Ohio, where he died. Drs. Oliver and Smith died in Beaver many years since. Oliver died childless, but the others, except Nathaniel, left descendants, some of whom are still in the county. Thomas was appointed by President Buchanan governor of one of the Western territories, but after a brief administration he returned and resumed the practice of his profession. Thomas was a lawyer of more than ordinary ability, and Drs. Oliver, Smith and Robert were considered respectable practitioners.

MILO CUNNINGHAM, clerk, P. O. New Galilee, was born in 1850. The Cunninghams are among the oldest families in this township. Archibald came from County Donegal, Ireland, and settled in Beaver township in 1800. He purchased 250 acres of land, on which he lived until his death. He married Nancy King, who bore him seven children. Of these Archibald was born in 1810 and died April 10, 1887. He was reared a farmer, and at his death owned the land purchased by his father. In 1838 he was married to Isabella, daughter of Robert and Margaret (Stephenson) Russell, of Lawrence county, Pa., and by her had ten children, of whom six are living: Alvin, Leander, Milo, James, Alice (Mrs. Marshall) and Lizzie (Mrs. Davidson). Milo was reared on the farm and was educated in the common schools. He was married in 1876 to Mary E., daughter of Captain Samuel and Celisia (Whan) Miller, of this county, and two sons, Herbert and Horace, were born to them. Since 1878 Mr. Cunningham has been employed as baggage clerk, by the P. F. W. & C. R. R. Co. He is a carpenter by trade. He is a member of the United Presbyterian church; politically a Republican.

SAMUEL CUNNINGHAM was born at Squirrel Hill, Allegheny county, Pa., in the year 1784. At the age of eighteen years he came to Beaver county and settled in Chippewa township. He became the father of eleven children, six of whom, Mrs. Mary A. Warren, of Darlington; James Cunningham, of Chippewa township; John Cunningham, of New Brighton; Joseph Cunningham, of Edinburgh, Lawrence county; William Cunningham, of Darlington, and Wilson Cunningham. of Beaver Falls, are yet living. He died in March, 1857, at the age of seventy-three years.

SMITH CURTIS, P. O. Beaver, member of the firm of Curtis & Bliss, editors and publishers of the *Rochester Daily Argus and Radical*, was born in Sherburne, Chenango county, N. Y., Dec. 21, 1834. His parents were John and Elsie (Jones) Curtis, the former a native of New York and the latter of Connecticut. His father was a miller and a tanner, and was also engaged in the manufacture of boots and shoes. His family consisted of ten children, of whom Smith is the fifth. He attended common school in his native county until he was sixteen years old, worked in the mill and tannery and went to New York, where he clerked in a store two years; then returned to his native county to prepare for college. He attended an academy in Franklin county one year; then entered Hamilton College, New York, where he spent three years. He then entered Union College, Schenectady county, N. Y., and was graduated in 1858 with honor. He was a diligent and successful student and was frequently chosen as a representative of the college in literary contests. He received a prize for an essay while in Hamilton College. After his graduation he commenced the study of theology and spent one year at the seminary at Princeton, N. J. He then entered the Union Theological Seminary at New York, from which institution he was graduated in 1861. He then went to Toledo, Ohio. In 1861 he was ordained a minister, by the Congregational Association, of Ohio, at Columbus, to be elegible to election as chaplain for the 62d Regiment Ohio Vols. From there he went to Fostoria, in the same state, where he took charge of the Presbyterian church for three years. He then resigned and opened an academy there, which he continued two years, when he was appointed chaplain of a regiment belonging to General Butler's command. The war soon closed, and he did not join his regiment. In 1862 he was elected chaplain of the 62d Pennsylvania Volunteers, but through the rascality of the colonel of the regiment he was not permitted to serve. He came to Pennsylvania in 1865 and was married March 1, that year, to Isidore, daughter of Capt. Richard and Elizabeth (McCurdy) Calhoun. Five children have been born to Mr. and Mrs. Curtis, three of whom are now living : John Richard, Dora E. and Elizabeth M. Mrs. Curtis is a consistent member of the Presbyterian Church. Mr. Curtis was principal of the public school of Beaver borough in 1868 and 1869. He is an active member of the Republican party, and served as secretary of the county committee from 1866 till 1872. He succeeded M. S. Quay as editor of the *Beaver Radical*, and continued its publication until the consolidation of the paper with the *Beaver Argus* in the fall of 1873. In 1879 he purchased from the Hon. James S. Rutan a half interest in the consolidated papers, and has since been connected with it as publisher and editor.

SCUDDER HART DARRAGH, manufacturer, P. O. Beaver, was born in Bridgewater, Pa., Feb. 27, 1817, and is a son of Hon. Robert and Deborah (Hart) Darragh. His father was state senator in 1849. His mother was a granddaughter of John Hart, of New Jersey, one of the signers of the Declaration of Independence. She was born near Trenton, N. J., and was of German origin. His father was born in Ireland, and early in life came to America and settled at Bridgewater, Pa., that place being then called Sharon. He was one of the early hotel keepers of this county. He afterward embarked in the mercantile trade in Sharon, which was then a shipping point, and did a large and successful business. His family consisted of eight children, seven of whom grew to maturity, six of them now living, and of whom our subject is the youngest. Hart died in 1885 from injuries received in the oil works. He was then in his seventy-third year.

The family are remarkable for longevity. S. H. was reared in Bridgewater, and attended the common school and the Beaver academy. His first work was as a clerk in a bank in Beaver. He then went on the river and ran a keel boat and steamboat. In 1849 he moved to California and remained two years. He then returned and continued the machine and foundry business, which he had established before going to California. The books of the machine shops and foundry are kept by S. H. Darragh. The title of the business at Bridgewater is M. & S. H. Darragh. The other is at Fallston, where the firm name is M. Darragh & Co. They are extensively engaged in the manufacture of machinery for wire works, and of iron bridges. They employ fifteen men the year round. Mr. Darragh was married Aug. 23, 1865, to Catherine Weyand, daughter of Hon. Daniel Weyand, ex-state senator and attorney, of Somerset, Pa. She is of German and English descent. They have had five children: Susan D., Mary H., Robert W., Daniel W., and Herbert S. (deceased). Mrs. Darragh is a member of the Methodist church. Mr. Darragh is a member of the town council, and has been school director; has also been a bank director. In politics he is a Republican.

FRED DAUBER, butcher, Beaver, was born in Baden, Germany, March 20, 1832, and is a son of Jacob and Philipina (Faus) Dauber, natives of Germany. His father was a farmer during his entire life. His family consisted of seven children. Fred, the second, was reared in Germany and attended the common schools there. He came to this country in 1852, and first settled in Wheeling, W. Va. He then went to Ohio, where he remained three years and learned the butchering business. He came to Beaver in 1858, and has carried on that business here ever since. He was married, in 1866, to Nancy, daughter of Archie Smith, and of Scotch descent. Their children are Lewis, Minnie, Charles and Anna. Mrs. Dauber is a member of the Methodist Episcopal church. In politics Mr. Dauber votes for the man and not for the party. He is energetic and industrious, and has made what he owns by his own exertions. He is the owner of real-estate in Beaver.

EDWARD B. DAUGHERTY, attorney, was born in New Sewickley township, in this county, and is a son of Daniel and Elizabeth (Black) Daugherty. His mother was born in Beaver county on the farm where she now resides and where she has lived all her life. She is the daughter of John Black, and was born Jan. 15, 1805. Daniel Daugherty, father of Edward B., was born in Londonderry, Ireland, in 1790; came to America in 1796, locating in Delaware county, Pa. In 1801 he came to this county with his father, Edward, who settled on a farm in the wilderness, in New Sewickley township. He had four children, two of whom are living; Edward B. and a daughter, Mary, who is the wife of P. H. Coyle, a farmer of this county. The early life of Edward was spent on the farm with his parents and attending the common schools and Beaver Academy. He studied civil engineering and surveying at which business he worked for a time, and also taught school. Finally choosing the law as a profession he studied with S. B. Wilson, was admitted to the bar in 1860, and began practice in New Brighton, where he remained until 1869, since when he has practiced in Beaver. He was married, May 5, 1870, to Mary Cunningham, whose parents were born in Ireland. Their children are Samuel Wilson and Mary. The family are members of the Catholic church. In politics Mr. Daugherty is a Democrat.

JAMES DAVIDSON, farmer, P. O. Black Hawk, was born in Middleton township, Ohio, Dec. 25, 1814. His father, James, was a native of Maryland, and in early life a shoemaker, and afterward a farmer. He was one of the first settlers on Little Beaver creek, coming there the year after the state line was run. He was married to Mary Johnson, had ten children, and died in 1828, aged sixty-three. Our subject has resided within a mile and a half of his present place for over seventy-three years, and remembers the time when bears, wolves and deer were numerous. He owns 150 acres of land. He was married in 1838 to Matilda J., daughter of Benjamin Pancake. By her he had eight children, seven of whom are living : Elizabeth, Sarah, Benjamin, George, Amy Ann, Mary and James E. Mr. Davidson owns 320 acres of land in Missouri. In politics he is a Republican.

J. J. DAVIDSON, oil producer, Beaver, is a son of Daniel R. Davidson (deceased), who was born in Fayette county, Pa., Jan. 12, 1820, a son of William and Sarah (Rogers) Davidson, natives of Pennsylvania and of Scotch-Irish origin. The father of Daniel R., Hon. William Davidson, was born in Carlisle, Cumberland county, Feb. 14, 1783. He served as a member of the State Legislature, also as State Senator and Speaker of the House. Daniel R. was reared in Fayette county and attended the select schools. His business relations were varied and extensive. He dealt largely in coke and coal and owned valuable mines. He was an influential railroad official for many years. At the time of his death he was president of the Commercial National Bank of Pittsburgh. He was also one of the board of directors of the National Bank of Commerce at Pittsburgh. He was the owner of two plants in coke regions, and was president of the Love Manufacturing Company of Rochester, Pa. In politics he was a Republican. He was married in Fayette county, in 1846, to Margaret C., daughter of Alexander Johnston, and of Scotch-Irish origin. Their children are Charles, Sarah, William J., Elizabeth, George, James J., Louis and Frederick. Mr. Davidson died March 18, 1884.

AMOS DAWSON, proprietor of Shady Lane Farm, P. O. Ohioville, is a son of Nicholas and Elizabeth (Harvy) Dawson, and was born Aug. 21, 1848, in the same house which he now occupies. His parents were natives of Maryland; his grandfather of Ireland, and his grandmother (one of the first settlers here) of Scotland. Amos was reared on the farm and received his education at home and at Mount Union, Ohio. Dec. 23, 1875, he was united in marriage with Marie Harker, daughter of Benjamin and Susan (Warrick) Harker, of East Liverpool, where she was born Dec. 26, 1852. Her mother was also a native of East Liverpool, Ohio. Her father was born at Tipton, Staffordshire, England, came to this country in 1837, and for a short time lived at Pittsburgh, but in 1839 moved to East Liverpool, Ohio, where he engaged in the pottery business, and only ceased active connection with the same in September before his death, which occurred Dec. 25, 1881. In 1840 Mr. Harker erected the Etruria Pottery, which he carried on for over forty years. In 1876 he retired from the firm of George S. Harker & Co., erected the Wedgewood Pottery under the firm name of Benjamin Harker & Sons, and manufactured the C. C. ware. He was a practical potter, having a knowledge of the ceramic art in all its intricacies and supposed secrets; was possessed of fine business ability and respected by all who knew him. To Mr. and Mrs. Dawson have been born one child, George Anna. Mrs. Dawson is a member of the Methodist Episcopal church. Mr. Dawson is a Royal Arch Mason and a Knight Templar, of Allegheny City. He makes a specialty of horses and Shetland ponies, and has some registered Jersey cattle.

BENJAMIN DAWSON, farmer, P. O. Smith's Ferry, son of Amos and Rebecca (Dawson) Dawson, was born about one mile from Smith's Ferry, July 20, 1825. Benjamin was reared on a farm and educated at the schools of Smith's Ferry, and is now a prosperous farmer just across the Little Beaver from that place. He was married Jan. 31, 1860, to Susan Hughs, daughter of Peter and Margaret (Laughlin) Hughs; she was born at Philadelphia June 5, 1837, and emigrated to this place when she was about twelve years old, with her mother and the other children, after her father's death. Mrs. Dawson's mother was born May 3, 1805, and died Feb. 14, 1885. She was the daughter of John and Margaret Laughlin, who were born in 1771 and 1773, respectively. Five children were born to Mr. and Mrs. Dawson: Jennie, Letitia, Minnie, Amos and Mary, all at home.

ROBERT D. DAWSON (deceased), one of Ohio township's prominent men and early settlers, was born at Ohioville July 30, 1801; a son of Benoni and Catharine Dawson. His father was a native of Maryland, and was one of the first settlers of Ohioville. Robert D. was married, Feb. 9, 1826, to Miss Elizabeth, daughter of Ruel and Mary Ann (Debolt) Reed, who was born Feb. 12, 1803. Ten children blessed this union: Mary Ann, Catharine, Benoni, Ruel Reed, James M., Rebecca, Benjamin, Robert D., Daniel Debolt and William McKennon. Mary Ann and Catharine live at the old homestead; Benoni and Daniel D. live in the west part of the township; Ruel R. in Kansas; Robert D. in Delaware; Rebecca died Oct. 29, 1864; James M., Benjamin and William McK.

are also dead. Mr. Dawson moved on his farm north of Ohioville in 1839, where he spent a long and useful life. His wife died Oct. 22, 1864, and he followed her to his final resting place Dec. 2, 1882.

WILLIAM DEHAVEN, farmer, P. O. Black Hawk, was born in 1822. It was some time previous to 1774 that one William Deh&ven came from Maryland (where he had recently landed in company with two brothers, sailors from England) to Beaver county, Pa., the journey being made in a sledge drawn by oxen. He was a distiller by trade. Soon after coming to Beaver county, he took up 400 acres of land, on which he erected a house and distillery, the former of which was still standing a few years since. He married Catherine Cooper, of Raccoon township, and had six children; Nathan, Abraham and William being the sons. William died in 1829, his widow surviving until 1859, when she died, aged eighty-nine years. William and Abraham purchased 200 acres of land, which was half of the tract occupied by their father. They afterward made additional purchases, and William, the only surviving brother, now owns 450 acres in South Beaver and Brighton townships. Abraham died in 1877, aged sixty-one. By his own efforts, Mr. Dehaven has accumulated a great deal of property. He is a member of the Episcopal church; in politics, independent.

JOHN B. DICKEY, merchant, Fallston, was born in Armstrong county, Pa., Dec. 30, 1857, and is a son of S. A. and Diana (Wolf) Dickey, natives of Pennsylvania and of German and English descent. His father, who was a civil engineer employed in government works, spent many years of his life in Fallston; his family consisted of eight children, of whom John B. is the eldest. Our subject was reared in Beaver county, attended the common schools at Fallston and the academy at Beaver. After a seven years' clerkship in a grocery, he, in company with his brother, bought the Handle Works at Fallston, and they have since conducted them. In April, 1887, he established a general store in Fallston. Mr. Dickey was married Nov. 27, 1883, to Miss M. L., daughter of R. G. Phillips, of Beaver. She is a member of the Methodist church. Mr. Dickey is a Republican; a member of the I. O. O. F.

WILLIAM A. DICKEY, postmaster at Bridgewater (name of office being West Bridgewater), was born in Bridgewater, Pa., July 26, 1858, and is a son of John S. and Sarah (Allison) Dickey. His father was born in Lawrence county, Pa., and his mother in Beaver county. She was a daughter of Hon. James Allison, and of Scotch-Irish descent. The father was an owner of steamboats, and spent many years on the water; he owned the steamboats "Lake Erie" and "Cleveland." He served nine years as steamboat inspector at Pittsburgh. In later life he sold out all his interest on the river, and engaged in mercantile trade in Bridgewater. He was an active Democrat. His family consisted of eight children, of whom William A., the youngest, was reared in Bridgewater. He studied civil engineering, and was first employed on the Pittsburgh & McKeesport and Allegheny railroads, where he spent two and one-half years. He also worked at surveying in Beaver county. In 1887 he was appointed postmaster at Bridgewater. He is a member of the Junior Order of American Mechanics.

JAMES DILLON, farmer, P. O. New Galilee, was born in Big Beaver township, this county, in 1818. The progenitor of the family in this country came from Ireland some time previous to the Revolutionary war. Matthew Dillon, a native of New York state, came, in 1796, from Washington county and purchased 300 acres of land in Big Beaver township. He married Mary Cooper, and by her had five sons and three daughters. Matthew died at the age of eighty years, and for fifty years previous to his death he was totally blind. James, the second child, was born in New Jersey in 1784, and when two years of age came with his parents to Washington county. He married Catherine, daughter of Barnard Naugle, of Germany, who took part in the Revolution. Nine children were born to James and Catherine Dillon, two of whom are now living. The father died in 1865, aged eighty-one, and the mother in 1862, aged seventy-eight years. James, our subject, was born and reared on the farm. He was married in 1846 to Barbara Ann, daughter of Joseph Smith, and they have had thirteen children, of whom are living Catherine (Mrs. Thompson), Joseph Smith, Price Cooper, James, J. M.,

BIOGRAPHIES—WEST SIDE. 641

Margaret, Beulah Ann, Elizabeth (Mrs. Sechrist), Sarah Lucinda and John Wesley. Mr. Dillon has followed farming principally, but like his father is a natural mechanic. He now owns 100 acres. He is a Republican, and has held several township offices, including that of school director. He is a member of the Methodist church.

JAMES P. DILLWORTH, retired, P. O. Enon Valley, Pa., was born in this county Oct. 15, 1805. Benjamin Dillworth came from Scotland to America at an early date. He was a farmer by occupation and settled in Westmoreland county, Pa. He married Mary McMinn, who bore him five sons and three daughters. Of these sons George was reared in Westmoreland county, and as early as 1796, came to Beaver county, where he purchased 400 acres of land, and remained until his death. His wife, Margaret (Kees,) of Irish descent, and who died in October, 1839, aged seventy-four, bore him eight children, of whom James was the youngest. George Dillworth died in 1840, aged seventy-five years. James P. was born and reared on the farm where he has always lived. He now owns 300 acres, part of the original tract. He was married, in 1851, to Mary, daughter of Joshua and Margaret (Hatfield) Newell, of Westmoreland county, and four children have been born to them: Maggie K., born July 5, 1852; George H., born April 5, 1855; Wilbert J., born January 22, 1857; Mary Eunice (deceased), born June 30, 1861. Mr. Dillworth has retired from active business, and the work of the farm is successfully carried on by his sons. He has been a member of the Presbyterian church for many years; politically he is a Republican.

JOHN A. DODDS, miller, P. O. New Galilee, was born in Allegheny county in 1831. Among the most prominent flouring mills in Beaver county is the "Upper Ten," owned by John A. Dodds. This mill is a frame structure, three stories high, 35 by 40 feet, with basement, and contains the latest and most improved machinery for the manufacture of flour, feed, etc. An engine of fifty-horse power is used, and ten sets of rolls. John Dodds, grandfather of John A., was born in County Monaghan, Ireland, in 1779, and was reared a farmer. At the age of twenty-two he was ordained an elder in the Secession church for the purpose of holding him in the Secession church. Shortly after, however, he united with the Reformed Presbyterian church. In 1803 he was married to Elizabeth McKee. He had ten children, of whom Robert was the oldest. John came to America in 1820, landing at St. John, New Brunswick. He went to Philadelphia, and thence to Freeport, Pa., and thence to Middlesex, Butler county, Pa., where he died in 1852 at the age of seventy-four. Robert, father of John A., was for thirty years a merchant, and later in life a farmer. He was born in 1804, and is still living in Allegheny county. He married Lettie Rowen, and had twelve children. John A. received a liberal education and learned the blacksmith trade, which he followed six years, subsequently engaging in mercantile business for ten years. In 1864 he enlisted in Company D, Sixth P. H. A., and served until the close of the war. In 1867 he began milling in Butler county. In 1875 he purchased a one-half interest in his present mill, and in 1877 bought out the other half. Mr. Dodds was married, in 1852, to Margaret, daughter of Maj. John Fife, of Allegheny county, and by her has had eleven children, ten of whom are living: Elzina Irene (Mrs. Dr. Balph), now a missionary in Asia Minor; R. M. J., an engineer; Lettie B. (Mrs. Quay); Miss Willia A. S., also a missionary in Asia Minor; Margaret B., a teacher; R. T. F., a miller with his father; Mary, a music teacher; Z. Z., a student at Geneva College; Lizzie B. and Ethan Ira. Mr. Dodds is a ruling elder in the Reformed Presbyterian church. In politics he is a Prohibitionist.

HENRY DONALDSON, manufacturer of kegs, New Galilee, was born in New York City in 1816, and is a son of Frederick and Mary (Hyatt) Donaldson. Frederick was also a keg manufacturer in New York City. He had nine children. Henry received a common-school education, and early engaged in manufacturing kegs in New York City. In 1863 he came to New Galilee, where he has since resided. He has been twice married; first, in 1836, to Mary Ann Bayles, and second, in 1837, to Ann Proctor. By the latter wife he has had five children: Henry M., Edwin M., William M., Jane A. and Emma F. Mr. Donaldson gives employment to about ten hands, and turns out about one thousand kegs per week. They are mostly sold to the paint works at Pittsburgh. An engine of six-horse power and the latest and most improved machinery are used. Mr. Donaldson is a member of the Presbyterian church; politically a Republican.

CAPTAIN DANIEL M. DONEHOO, postmaster at Beaver, was born in Washington county, Pa., March 30, 1825. His parents were John and Isabella (McElheny) Donehoo, natives of Pennsylvania and of Scotch-Irish descent. His paternal and maternal ancestors were among the early settlers of Pennsylvania. His grandparents arrived at Fort Pitt, in 1801, and soon afterward moved to Washington county. His father was first a farmer, then during the last thirty years of his life a school teacher. His family consisted of ten children, of whom Daniel M. is the third. He grew up in Allegheny county, and early in life learned the trade of a millwright, and engaged in building mills. He followed that business until 1862, when he resolved to enlist in the army. He took an active part in raising the 17th Cavalry, and on the organization of the regiment was elected colonel, but the order was to commission regular soldiers only as colonels of cavalry, so he accepted the rank of captain. He was soon afterward injured while trying to capture a deserter, and resigned and returned home. He had two brothers in the army: Henry M., now a hotel keeper at New Brighton, and Frank M., who died in the army. In 1864 Captain Donehoo engaged in the oil producing business, which he continued until 1866. He was engaged in the construction of railroads for four years. He is a Master Mason, and has always been an active Democrat. He was appointed postmaster in 1887. He was the Democratic candidate for the state senate in 1862, and was defeated although he ran largely ahead of his ticket. He was census marshal in Beaver county in 1860, and again in 1880. He has been many times a representative in Democratic state conventions, and once in the national convention. He has been twice married; first in 1848, and had two children by this marriage: Clara J., wife of Prof. Briggs, of Pittsburgh; and Gertrude, wife of John King, superintendent of the New Brighton water works. The children by his second marraige are Cora B., W. Edwin, Lulu A. (wife of Eugene H. Rider, railroad ticket agent at Wheeling, W. Va.), Claire, Sarah M., Effie and Miriam.

THOMAS DONOVAN, farmer, P. O. Black Hawk, was born in South Beaver township, in 1840. His parents, Cornelius and Mary (Hindman) Donovan, had twelve children, five of whom are now living, Thomas D. being the seventh child. Cornelius was a farmer and settled on the farm now owned by Thomas and Samuel H. Donovan in 1829, the farm then containing 189 acres. Cornelius died in 1874, aged sixty-eight years. Thomas, grandfather, of our subject, came from Ireland and settled in West Virginia. He had eleven children, of whom Cornelius was the second son. Thomas, our subject, received a good education, and chose agricultural pursuits as an occupation. He was married, in 1867, to Anna E., daughter of John and Sarah (McCormick) Wylie, and they have had four children, only one of whom, Laura M., is now living. Mrs. Donovan died in 1873, aged twenty-seven years. Mr. Donovan now owns ninety-four acres of land purchased by his grandfather, nearly all of which is under cultivation. He is a member of the United Presbyterian church at Four Mile ; politically a Republican. He enlisted in 1863, and served three months in Company I, 56th Pennsylvania Regiment. In 1864 he re-enlisted in Company H, 5th P. H. A., and served until the close of the war.

JAMES I. DOUDS, farmer and stock grower, thresher and sawyer, P. O. Beaver. was born in this county July 19, 1836. His parents, B. D. and Mary (Irons) Douds, were also natives of this country, and of German and Irish descent. His father and grandfather were farmers ; his great grandfather was a soldier in the Revolutionary war, and was killed in battle. The grandfather was in the war of 1812. He spent his life as a farmer. The father of our subject had five children, of whom four are now living. The second son was killed in the war of the Union at the battle of Spottsylvania. James was reared on the farm until he was twenty-four years old, attending the common school. He is the owner of eighty-five acres of land where he now resides in Brighton township, and forty in Hopewell township. He was married, in 1863, to Eliza, daughter of Archibald McCoy, and they have five children: Rosanna, wife of

George Barckley; Ada M., wife of John Gillespie; Mary A., Archibald D., and John W. The family are members of the United Presbyterian church. He is a Republican in politics, and is serving his third year as county auditor. He has been school director for ten years, has also served as supervisor, and has held all the other township offices.

JOSEPH DOUTHITT was born in 1764. When quite a young man he married Miss Mary Loutzenhiser, by whom he had thirteen children: Thomas, Peter, Barbara, Danie., Robert, Jonathan, Joseph, Duncan, Henry, Anthony, Eliza, Mary H. and John, the last two of whom, as also Robert, are still living. Robert, the father of S. N. Douthitt, one of the proprietors of the Beaver Falls Plaining Mill, is eighty-six years old. Joseph Douthitt, Sr., removed from Carlisle, Pa., in 1796, and settled in Beaver county, thus becoming one of its early pioneers. He died nearly forty-one years ago.

JOSEPH DOUTHITT, farmer, P. O. Darlington, was born in Darlington township, this county, in 1841. This family were among the earliest who settled in Beaver county. Jonathan Douthitt was born in this county, and married Sarah, daughter of James Cannon, of Lawrence county, Pa. They had ten children, of whom Joseph is the second son. Jonathan was a farmer. Joseph received his education at the common schools in the county, and since early childhood has worked on a farm. In 1873 he purchased his present farm of 120 acres, which is beautifully situated, and of rich soil. He was married, in 1863, to Mary L.. daughter of John and Mary (Black) McClure, of Washington county, who came to Darlington township and lived there the remainder of their lives. Mr. and Mrs. Douthitt have one son, Harry E., at home. The grandfather, Joseph, a farmer, came from the East to this county at an early period. Our subject is a member of the Presbyterian church; in politics a Democrat.

SHIPMAN N. DOUTHITT, manufacturer, Beaver Falls, was born in Big Beaver township May 8, 1835, and is a son of Robert and Phebe (Newkirk) Douthitt. His paternal grandfather was Joseph Douthitt, of Carlisle, Pa., who settled in Chippewa township in 1796. His children were Thomas, Barbara (Mrs. Henry Veon), Peter, Robert, Daniel, Eliza (Mrs. Samuel Conn), Duncan, Jonathan, Henry, Anthony, Mary (Mrs. Francis Gilkey), and John. His maternal grandfather was Henry Newkirk, a pioneer of Big Beaver township. Robert Douthitt was born in Chippewa township, where he resided for many years. He was a blacksmith; also carried on a farm and kept tavern in Chippewa township. He retired when the Fort Wayne railroad was built, and since 1885 has been a resident of Mercer county. He reared a family of five children: Anthony W., Mary E. (deceased), Shipman N., Robert J. and Rebecca A. (Mrs. T. B. Satterfield). Shipman N. was reared in Chippewa township. He enlisted in August, 1861, in Company D, 100th P. V. I., and was at the battles of James Island, second Bull Run, South Mountain, Antietam, Fredericksburg, Fall of Vicksburg, and through the Wilderness campaign to Petersburg. He was promoted first sergeant, and honorably discharged in September, 1864. He then engaged in farming in Chippewa township until 1870, when he located in Beaver Falls, and for nine months was engaged in the grocery business. In 1872 he embarked in the lumber business in Michigan and Beaver Falls, in which he is still engaged, and is a member of the Beaver Falls Planing Mill Company, with which he has been identified for twelve years. Mr. Douthitt was married, in 1864, to Sarah C., daughter of Major W. H. and Tabitha (Bowles) Powers, of Big Beaver township, by whom he had one daughter, Carrie (now Mrs. William Raymer). Mr. Douthitt is a member of the I. O. O. F., A. O. U. W., G. A. R and U. V. L. Politically, he is a Democrat

AMOS DOUTT, lime burner, Vanport, was born in Northumberland county, Pa., July 7, 1817. His parents, John and Catherine (Good) Doutt, were of English and German descent, the former a farmer and tanner. Amos, the third in a family of seven children, was reared in Harmony township, Butler county, receiving his education in the common schools. His father being a man of limited means, Amos was obliged to begin work early in life. He has followed the business of lime burning for many years. He was married, Nov. 9, 1847, to Sarah McNaughton, of Irish descent, and they have four children: Irvin W., Henry A., Agnes (wife of Joseph Courtney), and Katie. Mr. and Mrs.

Doutt are members of the Presbyterian church. In politics he is a Democrat, and has been school director, supervisor and assessor, and has filled nearly all the offices within the gift of the township.

JOHN F. DRAVO, member of the legislature from Beaver county, was born in West Newton, Westmoreland county, Pa., Oct. 29, 1819. His parents were Michael and Mary (Fleming) Dravo, natives of Pennsylvania and of French and Irish origin, former a coal merchant at McKeesport, Pa. They had ten children, of whom John F. is the eldest. He was reared in Allegheny county, attending schools in his native town and the high school in Pittsburgh. He also attended Allegheny College, at Meadville, Pa. He learned the coal business in his father's office, and embarked in trade for himself about 1845, with a partner. He carried on the business in Pittsburgh until 1880, and met with marked success. In 1864 he bought a handsome place on the banks of the Ohio in the borough of Beaver, and has ever since been identified with the advancement of the borough. He still retains large business interests in Pittsburgh. From 1868 to 1883 he was interested in an extensive stock company, which dealt largely in coke, and in which he was the principal stockholder. His charities are extensive. Those who know him best say he has given away more than he has lost and more than he now owns. He retired from business in 1883. He has held many positions in business and official circles, and was a delegate to the convention that nominated Abraham Lincoln to the presidency in 1860. He was formerly a Whig, and has been an active member of the Republican party since its formation; has stumped Western Pennsylvania for all presidential candidates of his party from Fremont to Harrison, and is a very forcible speaker. In 1887 he had the honor of nominating Hon. M. S. Quay for the United States senate. He is a strong advocate of temperance, and introduced the constitutional prohibitory amendment, which passed the legislature of 1887. He was appointed surveyor of the port of Pittsburgh by President Garfield, May 23, 1881. He served several years as president of the Pittsburgh chamber of commerce, and was one of the charter members; served four years as director and vice-president of the Pennsylvania Reformed School; is a director of the Tradesmen's National Bank of Pittsburgh, and served as general manager of the Pittsburgh Gas, Coal and Coke Company. In educational matters he has also taken a deep interest. He is a trustee of the Allegheny College, and president of the board of trustees of Beaver College and Musical Institute, to which latter institution he gave at one time $15,000 and at another $5,000. Mr. Dravo was married, Nov. 23, 1843, to Eliza J., daughter of Robert and Margaret Clark, and they have had nine children, five of whom are now living: Margaret, widow of Robert Wilson; Josephine, wife of J. H. McCreery; John S., a merchant in Pittsburgh, in company with his sister, Mrs. Wilson; Lida and Ettie, at home. The family are all members of the Methodist church. Mr. Dravo has been a member of the church since he was eighteen years old. He has been a local preacher for many years, and has been Sabbath-school superintendent.

JOHN C. DUFF, farmer, P. O. Darlington, was born in Little Beaver township in 1823. His ancestors came from Westmoreland county, Pa. James, his father, married Mary Kennedy, by whom five sons and three daughters were born, John C. being the fourth child. The father, James Duff, was a blacksmith by trade, and afterward a farmer; he died at the age of seventy-five years. John C. was born and reared on the farm and received a common school education. He engaged in mercantile business early in life, and followed it for twenty-three years. At one time he had three stores, one each at Darlington, East Palestine and Beaver Falls. Mr. Duff was married, in 1849, to Marie, daughter of Samuel Caughey, of this county. By her he had two sons and two daughters: Agnew Alexander, Samuel Addison, Nancy Jane, and Emma A. (deceased). Mr. Duff has, since his retirement from mercantile pursuits, been actively engaged in various business enterprises. For three years he gave his attention to oil drilling. He afterward purchased a 125-acre tract of land, and now owns some 200 acres, nearly all under cultivation, underlaid with rich veins of coal and iron ore, and containing a superior quality of clay. Mr. Duff has been among the most active spirits in his section of Beaver county, having taken a prominent financial part in erecting the United Presbyterian church edifice, of which the people of Darlington can well feel proud. He is a Republican.

SAMUEL C. DUFF, farmer, P. O. East Palestine, Ohio. a descendant of one of the oldest families in this county, was born in 1822. He was married, April 28, 1874. to Emma C., daughter of Robert Wilson, of Muskingum county, Ohio, who bore him three children: William James, Mary Jane and Esther Anna Olive, all of whom are living. His father, William Duff, was born in Westmoreland county, came to Beaver county in 1798, and lived with his father, Oliver, who owned a 408-acre farm in Darlington township, until he purchased a farm of 117 acres of his own. William married Esther Caughey, who bore him six children, of whom Samuel C., the only son, is the third. Our subject was given a common-school education, and has, since leaving school, been a farmer, possessing 200 acres of land. He belongs to the United Presbyterian church; politically he is a Republican. Mr. Duff has two sisters older than himself: Sarah Ann, now Mrs. Wallace, and Eleanor C., now Mrs. A. McNair; and three younger—Mary, E. J. and Esther P., the latter of whom resides in Woodson county, Kan., the wife of J. F. Bayless, and has five children, one son and four daughters.

THOMAS DUNLAP, eldest son of John Dunlap, was born in a tavern in Lancaster county, Pa. In early life he immigrated to McKeesport, Pa., where he married, Feb. 20, 1794, Miss E. Fowler. Early in March, 1796, he moved to Chippewa township, Beaver county, where he located on the farm at present owned by his descendants. He served in Wayne's war with the Indians, and received for his services 160 acres of land. He commanded in the blockhouses of Logstown, Raccoon, Georgetown and New Brighton, under Capt. James Sample, at each of which places he had to appear weekly for eighteen months. He was the father of nine children: John, Robert, James, Nancy, Thomas, Eliza, Joseph, David and Cynthia. He died Feb. 7, 1839, aged seventy-five years, eight months and twenty-six days.

WILLIAM DUNLAP, farmer, P. O. Black Hawk, was born in South Beaver township in 1830. He was educated in the common schools, and later was a student in the Curry Institute at Pittsburgh, during which time he was also engaged in teaching. In 1855 he married Matilda J., daughter of Robert Kennedy, of Allegheny county. She bore him two children, of whom one is living: Annie M. (now Mrs. Groetzinger). Aug. 5, 1862, Mr. Dunlap enlisted in Company F, 139th Regiment, and served until the close of the war. He was engaged in many battles, including Bull Run, Antietam, Fredericksburg, the Wilderness, Spottsylvania and Petersburg, and was several times wounded. He was severely wounded at Cedar Creek, Oct. 19, 1864, being first sergeant of Company F at the time. After the war he returned to Allegheny county, and in 1881 came to South Beaver township, where he purchased eighty acres of land. He now owns 180 acres, the management of which he superintends, having been in ill health since the war. He is a member of and an elder in the Presbyterian church, having joined the church during the war. Politically he is a Republican.

JOHN R. EAKIN is a manufacturer of ranges and stoves at Rochester, Pa. He was born in Beaver borough July 20, 1829, and is a son of James and Mary (Quaill) Eakin, the former born in Ireland and the latter in Washington county, Pa., of Scotch-Irish descent. The father came to Beaver in 1822. He was a teacher in early life, having taught school in the old Academy at Beaver, also in Allegheny county, and was afterward a merchant. He died in 1847. He was justice of the peace and burgess of Beaver borough. The family consisted of seven daughters and two sons. John R., the eldest son, was reared in Beaver. He went on the Ohio river, first as clerk on a steamboat and subsequently as captain. He followed the river for twelve years; then clerked in the office of the county commissioner of this county; was also deputy county treasurer for one term; then engaged in the manufacture of glass at Beaver Falls for five years. In 1875 he was elected county treasurer, and served one term. In 1879 he embarked in his present business at Rochester, Pa. He has full charge, being secretary, treasurer and general manager. From twenty-five to thirty hands are employed. The success of the business is largely due to the personal efforts of Mr. Eakin. The union of Mr. and Mrs. Eakin has been blessed with the following named children: Anna, wife of J. Rankin; Martin, district attorney of Beaver county; Emma and Joseph M. Mrs. Eakin is a member of the Presbyterian church. Mr. Eakin is a F. & A. M.; politically a Republican.

NATHAN EAKIN, farmer, P. O. Enon Valley, was born in 1821, in Columbiana county, Ohio. His father, William, was a native of Ireland, and came to America when but nine years of age, He married Miss Mary Patton, who bore him eight children, of whom Nathan is the youngest son. His grandfather (also a native of Erin) and father were both farmers. Nathan received a common-school education and learned chair making, which he followed for three years. In 1851 he married Elizabeth Edgar, daughter of Samuel and Elizabeth Edgar, to whom were born ten children, of whom eight are living: Mary E. (now Mrs. McAllister), Samuel Edgar, William Patton, Ellen Jane (now Mrs. Newell), Maggie L., Phoebe M., John Christie and Sarah Mirilda. Mr. Eakin came to Beaver county in 1843 and settled in Darlington, where he remained in the chair making business one year; then was engaged in mercantile business nine years; and after that settled upon his 200-acre farm, where he has since remained. He has been school director and supervisor, and has identified himself with the Republican party. He is a member of the United Presbyterian church of Darlington.

RICHEY EAKIN (deceased), one of the honored and respected citizens of Brighton township, was born in Allegheny county, Pa., Jan. 22, 1809, son of David and Margaret (Gray) Eakin, who were of Irish descent. His father and grandfather James Eakin were farmers, the latter a man of great force of character. David Eakin moved to Brighton township in 1814. Here Richey was reared attending school in the old log schoolhouse. He was married, in 1833, to Louisa Anderson, born in 1813, daughter of John Anderson, a farmer, and they had twelve children: John, a farmer; David, a teacher; James, William and Joseph, farmers; the rest being deceased. Few men were more highly respected or more missed than Mr. Richey Eakin, who departed this life in 1869. He was a successful farmer, and at the time of his death was the owner of 350 acres of good land; in politics he was a Republican.

JOHN A. EAKIN, farmer and stock raiser, P. O. Beaver, was born in Brighton township, this county, July 3, 1834, and is a son of Richey and Louisa (Anderson) Eakin. The parents were natives of Pennsylvania and of Irish descent, the father a farmer. They had fourteen children, John A. being the eldest. He was reared on the farm and attended the common schools. He is the owner of a well improved farm, where he now resides, in Brighton township. He has been twice married; first, in 1861, to Miss Delila Richardson, who died in 1881. This union was blessed with eight children, five of them now living. His present wife is Henrietta, a native of Ireland, daughter of William Noonhan. By her he has two children. Mr. Eakin is a Republican.

GILBERT L. EBERHART. The ancestors of Mr. Eberhart emigrated from Germany in 1754 and settled in Eastern Pennsylvania, Adam Eberhart, his great grandfather, finally locating in Washington county, in the same state. His son John, born in the latter county May 9, 1761, died Nov. 10, 1831. He had two sons, Andrew and John, the latter of whom was born in Beaver county, where his father was engaged in farming, on the 28th of June 1792, and died Jan. 19, 1858. Much of his life was spent in the above county, either as a cabinet maker or a prosperous merchant. He married Sarah, daughter of Gen. Samuel Power, and had five children: Wilford A. P., Albert Gallatin, Emeline E., Eleanor M. and Gilbert Leander. The last named, and youngest of these children, was born in North Sewickley township, Beaver county, Jan. 15, 1830, and with a brief interval has spent his life in the county of his birth. His education was received at the Mercer Academy and Washington College, in Washington county, Pa. He then engaged in civil engineering and teaching until the outbreak of the rebellion, when in April, 1861, he entered the army, and was later made Quartermaster of the 8th Regiment Pennsylvania Volunteers, serving in 1862 on the staff of Gen.

BIOGRAPHIES—WEST SIDE. 647

George G. Meade. After active service in the field, he received his discharge in May, 1864. In September he was appointed by Gen. Saxton, superintendent of education for the state of Georgia in connection with the Freedman's Bureau. He was admitted to the bar of Beaver county in 1870, and has since that time continued in active practice. Mr. Eberhart was, in 1852, married to Maria, daughter of Dr. Peter Smith, of San Franciso, and latterly of London, England. Their only surviving child is a daughter, Georgiana, wife of Dr. H. S. McConnel, of New Brighton. Mr. Eberhart, as a Republican has been an influential factor in local politics. He was superintendent of schools for Mercer county in the years 1856-57; member of the State House of representatives for 1877-78, and has twice been elected mayor of New Brighton. He is an Episcopalian in his religious belief, and a member of the church of that denomination in New Brighton.

JOHN EBNER, general merchant, Beaver Falls, was born in Bavaria, Germany, Feb. 19, 1826, and is a son of Peter and Margaret Ebner. He was educated in Bavaria and served an apprenticeship of eight years at the printer's trade. He came to America in 1854, locating in Pittsburgh, where he worked four years as a printer. He then engaged in butchering, which he followed for twenty years, and was also in the grocery business in Braddock three years. In 1868 he came to Beaver Falls, and carried on butchering four years. He then opened a coal bank in Pulaski township, and carried his coal across Big Beaver Creek to Beaver Falls by cable. Four years later he went to Braddock and conducted a general store eight years. In 1887 he returned to Beaver Falls and embarked in his present business. He married Magdalena Carl, by whom he has four children: Joseph L., Mary, Louisa and Katie. Mr. Ebner was one of the founders of the German Catholic church of Beaver Falls. Politically he is independent.

ELIHU ECKLER, owner and builder of flatboats, Vanport, was born in Moon township, this county, March 6, 1833, a son of John and Nancy (Weigle) Eckler. His mother was born in Moon township, Beaver county. His father was born in Lancaster, Pa., east of the mountains. He was a blacksmith. Elihu, the fourth in a family of seven children, was reared in Moon township and attended the common schools. The early part of his life was spent on the farm, and when fifteen years old he went on the Ohio river as cook on a steamboat; then he served as second mate and mate on a passenger boat for several years. He is now a dealer in boats. He was married, in 1862, to Sophia E., the fifth of nine children born to Joseph and Margaret (Small) Conrad. Her father was a steamboat pilot and captain, and in later life a merchant in Beaver, and one of the first settlers of Vanport. He was a large landholder in the town and surrounding country. Mrs. Eckler is of German extraction, and has spent just fifty years in this place. Their children are—Frank L., a printer in Knowles & Co.'s decorating shop, East Liverpool, Ohio; Alfred S., a river pilot on coal packets running from Pittsbourgh to Louisville; Maggie S., James S. Mr. and Mrs. Eckler and two eldest boys are members of the Presbyterian church at Beaver. He has been school director for fifteen years, and is a Republican; as are also Frank L. and Alfred S.

PERRY ECOFF, clerk, Bridgewater, was born Aug. 25, 1867, and is a son of Samuel and Margaret (Arbuckle) Ecoff. The father, Samuel Ecoff (now deceased), was born in Maryland, June 13, 1813, but spent most of his life in Bridgewater. He learned the carpenter's trade, and made that the main business of his life. He built many handsome structures, which are still standing, in Beaver county and elsewhere. His reputation for honest work was well known, and secured for him all the contracts he cared to undertake. In later life he dealt largely in real estate in Bridgewater. He was a progressive man. In the spring of 1849 he went to California to seek his fortune in the gold mines, and worked there for more than four years, when he returned to his family at Bridgewater and spent the remaining portion of his life here. He was in the grist and saw mill business in Bridgewater in company with Mr. Darragh for a time, and was engaged in various enterprizes, usually with marked success. He was a Whig and a Republican, and was a member of the council of Bridgewater; also tax collector. He was an active member of the Methodist Episcopal church, and for many years trustee. He was three times married; first to Miss Martha Small, and the second time to Margaret Arbuckle, both of whom are buried in Beaver cemetery; and third to Margaret May.

648   HISTORY OF BEAVER COUNTY.

W. J. EISENBROWN, harness-maker, Beaver Falls, was born in New Sewickley township, this county, July 28, 1864. His parents, Daniel and Barbara (Bown) Eisenbrown, natives of Germany, settled in New Sewickley township about 1855, where they now reside. W. J. was reared in his native township, and learned his trade in Freedom. He embarked in business for himself in Beaver Falls in 1884, and gives employment to three hands. He has the only store of the kind in the place, and has a thriving, constantly increasing trade. He is a member of the Lutheran church; politically he is independent.

JOHN S. ELDER (deceased) was a native of this county, born in 1837. His father, William Elder, came from the "Emerald Isle" in 1835, and soon after located in Beaver county, where he followed milling for a brief period. Subsequently he purchased 150 acres of land and engaged in farming. At his death he owned 600 acres of as good land as could be found in South Beaver township. He married Sarah Stewart, who bore him four children. He died in 1862, aged sixty-two years; his widow is still living at the age of eighty-three. John S. was the oldest son. He was a youth of unusual ability and was educated for the ministry, graduating from Westminster College with first honors. On account of ill health he was obliged to give up his studies, and engaged in farming. In 1864 he married Sarah E., daughter of James and Mary (McKenzie) Stewart, the former a prominent merchant of Wellsville, Ohio. They had four children: William S. (deceased), James, Robert Boyd and William Carle. Mrs. Elder is a graduate of Washington Seminary (1860), and a member of the Seceder's church. Mr. Elder died in 1886.

MATTHEW ELDER (deceased), whose portrait appears elsewhere in this volume, was born in the parish of Finvoy, County Antrim, Ireland, in January, 1788. In 1812 he came to America, and after working as a weaver in a woolen mill at Wilmington, Del., went to Columbiana county, Ohio. On the 15th of September, 1815, he was married, at New Lisbon, to Mary, daughter of Thomas Frederick. The latter was carried off by Indians from Eastern Pennsylvania in childhood, and remained with them until he had nearly lost all knowledge of the language and customs of the whites. On his return to his home he had some difficulty in establishing his identity, and was only recognized by a scar on the back of his neck, which was familiar to his mother. At the time of his marriage Mr. Elder was operating a woolen mill in New Lisbon, and so continued until the mill was destroyed by fire in 1820. The next year he built a factory on Little Beaver Creek, in Darlington township, two miles below Cannelton; and while the factory was being built he ran a set of cards in the mill half a mile above the factory. This was in what was then called Little Beaver township. At that time they had to go to what is now called Old Enon to vote, and the nearest postoffice, Greersburg, was five miles away. The name of the town was changed to Darlington on account of letters addressed to Greersburg going to Greensburg. Then the township was divided and called Darlington, and what was left of Little Beaver township went into Lawrence county when that was formed. Mr. Elder did an extensive business and bought nearly all the wool grown in Beaver, Lawrence and Washington counties, Pa., and Columbiana county, Ohio. He possessed a considerable tract of land about the mill at one time. Between the years 1830 and 1840 he owned, remodeled and enlarged the grist mill and oil mill and bought wheat and flaxseed, which was a great advantage to the farmers at that time. Between the years 1841 and 1843 he dug a tail race three-quarters of a mile long, walled the same with stone on both sides. It was to gain a fall so that he could remodel and put in an overshot wheel; the cost of this was $10,000 or over. In 1844 he built a large brick store and dwelling, and in 1845 opened a store of general merchandise, which had the most extensive line of custom of any store in the country. He was a great admirer of fine horses, a passion which is characteristic of his descendants. His grandsons are now engaged in breeding Clydesdale and coach horses, and also fine cattle and swine. In 1851 Mr. Elder again suffered from the fire-fiend, his mill being swept away. He at once rebuilt and continued to operate it until his death, which occurred in 1863. His faithful helpmate also passed away during the same year. Mrs.

Elder was born Aug. 25, 1797. Mr. Elder was universally regarded as a very useful citizen. He attended strictly to his own business which was beneficial to the community, and gave little attention to public affairs, his only service in that line having been to serve as judge or inspector of election in the township, which he could not avoid; he served as a director of the old United States Bank of Beaver county in New Brighton, before the administration of Andrew Jackson. He adhered, as do his descendants, to the Presbyterian faith, Associate branch, and voted with the Whig party and its Republican successor. He was noted for his benevolence and hospitality, and was a benefactor to the poor and laboring. None ever sought work but got it if possible; if not and had not the means to travel further, he was provided with means. Neither man or beast ever went hungry away. In the busy season the table was rarely uncovered from noon until night, and more meals were served and horses fed than at a large majority of the hotels. He gave a home in his family to an old man named John McConnell, a distant relative from the same part of Ireland that Mr. Elder came from, and fed and clothed him for thirty years, and buried him. He also gave a home to a boy named Joseph Green, whom the poor board brought to him; he was of weak intellect, but Mr. Elder kept him also until his death, which occurred a few years before his own. Of his twelve children eight reached maturity. The eldest, John R., now resides in Pulaski county, Mo.; Margaret Ann, widow of John Taggart, resides in Palestine, Ohio; Thomas F., [see sketch below]; Matilda, widow of William Sterling, resides in Leetonia, Ohio; Mary Jane was the wife of Daniel H. Wallace, and died at her home in New Castle, Pa.; Elizabeth Catharine, wife of Walter D. Sprout, died in Darlington township; Hannah died unmarried; Rebecca, widow of Calvin F. Chamberlin, resides at Palestine; Mary, Matthew and Henry (twins) all died in childhood, as did also a son named Matthew Henry.

THOMAS F. ELDER, farmer, P. O. Cannelton, is the third child of Matthew Elder, whose biography and portrait appear in this work, and was born in New Lisbon, Ohio, July 27, 1820. He assisted his father in the woolen mill, and finished his education in Greersburg Academy, in Darlington. For three years he kept a store in that borough, and was connected with the operation of the mill until the sale of the latter after his father's death. In 1857 he purchased his present farm of 159 acres, in South Beaver, about a mile from the site of the mill. The latter was destroyed by fire after passing into the hands of a stock company. Mr. Elder has a fine brick residence and an excellent farm, which is underlaid with coal. In 1844 he married Euphemia L. Scroggs, daughter of Rev. E. M. and Margaret Scroggs, of Columbiana county, Ohio. She was the mother of one child, Margaret Elzarune, who died when about eight months old of brain disease, its mother died six months later. His second wife is Mary A., daughter of Richard and Jemima (Pierce) Parrett. Mrs. Elder was born in Pittsburgh in 1828, and her parents were natives of Ireland and Philadelphia, respectively. In her youth she was engaged in teaching, as is her daughter now. Like his father, Mr. Elder adhered to the Republican party in politics and has served as town supervisor, judge and inspector of elections, and has also been solicited to run for county offices, but declined. The family is connected with the Associate Presbyterian church, and includes three sons and one daughter: Harry Clifford and Matthew Richard, at home, extensively engaged in breeding fine horses and other stock; Thomas Frank, in Atchison, Kan., and Nettie Euphemia, with her parents.

S. R. ELDER, farmer, P. O. Darlington, was born in 1841, the youngest son of William Elder, who came from Ireland in 1834, and located in Beaver county. He (the father of our subject) was married in 1837 to Sarah, daughter of John and Martha Stewart, and by her had four children—three sons, J. S., Robert B. and S. R. Elder, and one daughter, Mattie J. Elder (Creighton). About 1838 he, in connection with his brother Matthew, built quite a large flouring mill on Little Beaver creek, intending to grind and ship flour east, some lots going as far east as Philadelphia. Not proving a successful enterprise he sold his interest and located on a farm in South Beaver township. At his death, which occurred in 1862, he owned some 600 acres. The subject of this sketch was born and reared in South Beaver township, and received an academical education. At the age of twenty he was left in charge of his father's farm of 600 acres, of which he now owns 200 acres. He is the only living male member of his father's family. A brother enlisted in 1861, in Company D, 100th Regiment, the famous "Round Head," and died at Beaufort, S. C., in February, 1862, of coast fever. Mr. Elder was married, in 1863, to Mary, daughter of James and Jane (McCreery) Cook, by whom he has three children: Jennie K., William B. and James F. S. Mr. Elder resides on the 200-acre farm which was formerly the property of Andrew Johnson. He is a member of the Seceder's church, and politically a Republican.

JAMES L. ELLIOTT, farmer, P. O. Darlington, was born in Butler county, in 1855. Dr. F. Elliott, now a practicing physician of Ohio township, and a resident of Beaver county for sixty years, married Catherine Flick, who became the mother of seven children, two of whom are deceased, James L. being the eldest son living. He was reared to farming, an occupation he has followed principally through life, and received a good common-school education. He was married, in 1878, to Annie E., daughter of George and Permelia (McMillin) Wilson, of this county, and they have three children: George C., Florence Gertrude and Raymond Carlton. Mr. and Mrs. Elliott are members of the Presbyterian church. Mr. Elliott is a Democrat.

JAMES S. ELLIOTT, Beaver Falls, physician, was born in Trumbull county, Ohio, in 1823, and is a son of William and Margaret (Patterson) Elliott, who settled in Moon township in 1826. They had ten children: Jane (Mrs. Robert Keenan), Nancy (Mrs. William Davidson), Arabella (Mrs. John A. Braden), Ellen (Mrs. James Braden), John M., William P., Susan, Rachel (Mrs. James Johnson), James S. and Thomas. James S. was reared in Moon township, and educated in the schools of Beaver. He began the study of medicine in 1847 with Dr. Cunningham, entered Starling Medical College, Columbus, Ohio, in 1848, and was graduated in 1851. From 1852 until 1869 he practiced in Moon township, after which he located in Beaver Falls. His eldest son, Washington F., began the study of medicine in 1883, entered Jefferson Medical College, Philadelphia, in 1885, and was graduated in 1887. He is now associated with his father. Dr. Elliott was twice married, his first wife being Maria, daughter of David and Mary (Witherspoon) Ramsey, of Lawrence county, Pa., by whom he had four children: Washington F., Istie, Charles and Thomas M. His second wife was Jennie, daughter of Samuel and Martha (Moody) Witherspoon, of Beaver county, by whom he had four children: Charles M., Etta, Bertie and Harry. Dr. Elliott is a member of the Beaver County Medical Society.

WILLIAM ELLIOTT, lumberman, P. O. Beaver Falls, was born in Cumberland, W. Va., July 17, 1835, a son of John and Rachel (Farnsworth) Elliott, and of Scotch-Irish descent. He was reared and educated in his native county, and in 1857 located in Raccoon township, this county, where he was engaged in farming for seven years. He then located in Greene township, this county, and embarked in mercantile trade, in which he continued thirteen years. In 1878-79 he was engaged in the manufacture of salt in Raccoon township, after which he embarked in the lumber business, in various parts of the county, in which he is still interested. He married, in 1857, Margaret P., daughter of John A. and Mary (Elliott) Braden, of Raccoon township, and of an old pioneer family of Beaver county. By this union he has seven children living: Rebecca (Mrs. George Bisphim), Arabel (Mrs. James Ridell), John A., Ada, Charles M., Idona and Jessie. Mr. Elliott is a member of the Methodist church; in politics a Prohibitionist.

JAMES E. EMERSON. Ezekiel Emerson, the great grandfather of the subject of this biography, was for a period of thirty years a Congregational preacher in the town of Norridgewock, Me. His son Ezekiel, a native of the above place, was by occupation a farmer and devoted the winter months to fur-hunting. He married Mary Chadwick, whose children were three sons, Ezekiel, Luther and Jothan, and three daughters. Ezekiel, the eldest of these, was born at Norridgewock, and left fatherless at the early age of eight years. Removing in 1826 to Bangor in the same state, his life was devoted to the labors of a husbandman. He was united in marriage to Amanda, daughter of

David Leeman, of Augusta, Me., and had nine children: James E., David, Simon, John (killed during the late war at Galveston Harbor, Texas), Phebe, Amanda, Mary (deceased), Sarah and Elizabeth. James E. Emerson, the eldest of these children, was born Nov. 2, 1823, in Norridgewock, and in early youth removed to Bangor. Here he received such education as the schools of the time afforded, the winter months being devoted to study and the summer to labor on the farm. Intelligent reading and a thoughtful habit of mind compensated in a measure for the want of early scholastic training. At the age of twenty-one, being left free to choose a pursuit in life, he became proficient in the trade of a house carpenter, and continued thus occupied in his native state until 1853, building, in 1850, by contract, the first three blocks of houses in Lewiston Falls, Me., for the Lewiston Falls Water Power Company. He then emigrated to California and established himself as a manufacturing carpenter, introducing machinery to a great extent in the construction of buildings. For five years he carried on an extensive lumbering business, and while operating a circular saw-mill at Oroville, Cal., invented his first inserted tooth circular saw, and placed it in successful operation. Selling the interest in his mill he devoted some time to travel for the purpose of inserting teeth in saws, and general repairing of the same. Mr. Emerson later located in Sacramento, where he established a similar business, which was soon extended to San Francisco. Selling his entire interest in 1859 to Mr. N. W. Spaulding, who continued its successful management, he removed to Trenton, N. J., and during the Civil War manufactured over one hundred thousand cavalry sabres for the government, as also many officers' swords of fine quality. He at a later period organized the American Saw Company, still in active operation in the latter city. Returning from an extended tour in Europe, Mr. Emerson made Beaver Falls his home and established the company of which he is the head, known as the Emerson Saw Works. He is a recognized authority in his special department of mechanics, and undoubtedly the pioneer inventor of inserted tooth saws. Mr. Emerson was, in 1847. married to Mary P. Shepard, of Bangor, and their children are Florence Eldorado (Mrs. Martell, of Beaver Falls), Leanora A. (Mrs. Rabe, of Oakland, Cal.), Hattie L. (Mrs. Midgley, of Beaver Falls), Alena G.. and Charles M. (located as a saw repairer in Bay City, Mich.).

JOSEPH ENGLE, fruit-grower, P. O. Industry, was born on the farm where he now resides, in 1837. He is a son of George and Amy (Dannals) Engle, the former a native of Pennsylvania and the latter of New Jersey. They had nine sons and one daughter: George, Henry, Stacy, Jemima, John, David, Washington, Franklin, Joseph and Enoch. Joseph was educated in the common schools of his native county, and was reared to farm life. In 1860 he married Mary A., daughter of John Crum, and to this union were born three children: Charles, Audie and Eva May. Soon after marriage Mr. Engle moved to near Fostoria, Seneca county, Ohio, where he followed farming for three years; then returned to Beaver county and settled on his present farm, part of the old homestead. He was the first shipper of cultivated fruit (grown on his own place) from this part of the country. He and family are members of the United Brethren church.

J. J. EWING, gas-fitter, Beaver Falls, is a native of Beaver county, and was born Nov. 16, 1844. He is a son of Joseph Ewing, whose ancestors were among the early settlers of Industry township, this county. He located in Beaver Falls in 1879, where he has since followed his occupation of gas-fitter. He married, Nov. 13, 1866, Alice, daughter of William and Nancy (Irwin) McDonald, of Moon township, Beaver county. Mrs. Ewing's paternal grandfather was John McDonald, an old steamboat captain on the Ohio river, and her maternal grandfather was William Irwin, both prominent citizens and pioneers of Beaver county; the former was an early settler of Hopewell township and the latter of Moon township. In 1880 Mrs. Ewing opened the only exclusive music store in Beaver county at Beaver Falls, dealing only in pianos and organs, and has conducted a large and successful business since. Mrs. Ewing is a member of the Methodist Protestant church. Mr. Ewing is a member of the Mystic Circle; in politics he is a Republican.

JOHN F. FERGUSON, contractor and ice dealer, Beaver Falls, was born in North Sewickley township Dec. 8, 1850, and is a son of John and Janiza (Elliott) Ferguson. His paternal grandfather was John Ferguson, of Ireland, who settled in North Sewickley township about 1809. His maternal grandfather was Thomas Elliott, a pioneer of Marion township. John F. was reared in his native town, located in Beaver Falls in 1880 and engaged in livery and teaming business, now running nine teams. He embarked in the ice business in 1884, has full control of the business in Beaver Falls and also does a good trade in New Brighton. He has been engaged as a contractor since 1883. Mr. Ferguson is a stirring business man; in politics he is a Democrat.

S. W. FIELDS, farmer, P. O. Darlington, was born in 1845, in that part of Beaver county now included in Lawrence county. David Fields married Sarah, the first child born to William Kyle (of Ireland) after he came to America. Two children were born to David and his wife, S. W. being the youngest. David was born in Lawrence county and is now seventy years of age. He was a carpenter, but is now retired from business. S. W. has always been a farmer. He came to South Beaver township in 1872, and purchased 186 acres of land, comprising his present farm. He was married in 1875 to Nancy, daughter of Smiley Rhodes, of this county, and they have six children: John F., David S., Otis A., Sarah T., Maggie Myrtle and Lydia Laura. Mr. Fields is a member of the Reformed Presbyterian church; politically a Republican.

GEORGE FISHER, farmer, P. O. Ohioville, was born June 6, 1832, in Columbiana county, Ohio, a son of Michael and Elizabeth (Dawson) Fisher. The former was born Feb. 14, 1800, and died in January, 1885. George spent his early youth at the place of his birth, and received his education at the district school. He assisted his father on the farm until his marriage, which occurred Dec. 25, 1866, and soon after moved to Ohioville, locating upon his present farm of 158 acres. Mrs. Fisher was Sarah, daughter of William and Nancy (Reed) George; she was born in 1886 in this county, but moved to Iowa with her parents, where all her people reside. Her father was born in Columbiana county, Ohio, in January, 1814. Her mother was born in Beaver county, Nov. 3, 1815, her father being one of the early settlers of the county. William George was a son of Thomas and Sarah (Ganzales) George. His wife, Nancy (Reed), was a daughter of Ruel and Mary Ann (Tebalt) Reed, former of whom was a native of Ohio towns..ip, born Aug. 4, 1769. Two children have been born to Mr. and Mrs. Fisher: Benjamin P. and Laura D., both of whom attended school in the vicinity.

O. H. FRANKLIN, D.D.S., Beaver Falls, was born in Industry township, Feb. 3, 1858, and is a son of Benjamin and Martha (Reed) Franklin. His father has been a resident of Beaver county for over thirty-five years, and was county superintendent of schools, six years. His mother is a daughter of Milo Reed, of Industry township. O. H. Franklin was reared in Fallston, and in 1878 began the study of dentistry with Dr. A. M. Whisler, of New Brighton. In 1879 he entered the Pennsylvania Dental College, of Philadelphia, and was graduated Feb. 25, 1882. In April he located in New Brighton, where he practiced until April, 1884, when he established himself in Beaver Falls. In 1885 he married Lucy, daughter of John and Martha (Mitchell) Thornley, of New Brighton. Dr. Franklin is a successful dentist, a member of the Dental Society of Western Pennsylvania. He belongs to the Presbyterian church; in politics he is a Republican.

JOHN T. FRAZIER, farmer, P. O. Industry, was born near Wellsville, Columbiana county, Ohio, Sept. 9, 1847, and is a son of William and Mary (Burk) Frazier. The father is a native of near Canfield, Ohio, born Aug. 25, 1825, and at present carries on farming in Wood county, W. Va., near Parkersburg. He enlisted Aug. 2, 1862, in Company I, 140th Regiment, P. V., and participated in several hard-fought battles, among them, Gettysburg (where he was wounded in the left leg, and taken prisoner, though owing to his injuries he was soon afterward paroled), Chancellorsville, Wilderness and Sailor's creek, near Richmond, Va., where he lost his right leg. He was honorably discharged June 27, 1865, and on his return home located in Brighton township, this county, until 1872, when he removed to his present home. John T. Frazier en-

BIOGRAPHIES—WEST SIDE. 653

listed Feb. 21, 1865, in Company G, 78th P. V. V., stationed at Nashville, Tenn., and was honorably discharged Sept. 11, same year. He married March 23, 1871, Sarah, daughter of William Morrow, and by her has five children, all at home: Mary Bell, William M., Ida Alice, Sadie Clare and John. Mr. Frazier has resided on his present farm of 123 acres for the past five years. He has held the office of supervisor two years, and is now school director. In politics he is a Republican. He and his wife are members of the Methodist church.

HERMAN J. FRIELING, Pastor St. Mary's Catholic church, Beaver Falls, was born in Hanover, Germany, Sept. 26, 1860, and is a son of Henry and Margaret (Usselman) Frieling. He was reared in his native town of Osnabruck, where he received his early education, and afterward attended school at Ankum, where he studied the higher branches, including Latin, Hebrew and French, for three years. In 1877 he came to America and was a student at St. Vincent's College, Westmoreland county, Pa., until 1884, when he was ordained and appointed assistant pastor of St. Joseph's church, Pittsburgh. He remained there until August, 1886, when he was appointed pastor of St. Mary's parish, Beaver Falls.

W. S. FULKMAN, P. O. Beaver Falls. A publication styled *Spray of the Falls* was established in Beaver Falls in September, 1887. It is a seven-column quarto sheet, containing fifty-six well filled columns of reading matter well illustrated. *The Spray* is issued the first of each month from No. 802 Seventh Avenue (Musser Building), and from its first appearance has been well received by the people of Beaver county. It combines several new features in journalism, giving to the country readers the advantages possessed by their more fortunate city friends, in the way of an abundant supply of pure, wholesome and interesting selections, general news and home news, all of which is made more attractive by the free use of the engraver's art. *The Spray*, although started as a monthly, is designed to become a weekly journal as it grows older and stronger, and now bids fair to rival its time-honored competitors and settle down into the race for existence as one of the fixed institutions of the valley. Its projector and manager, Wilson Stanley Fulkman, is a native of Allegheny county, Pa., having been born on the banks of the Ohio river, nine miles west of Pittsburgh, Dec. 7, 1854. His parents were named Abram S. and Rebecca S. Fulkman, both of whom were natives of the United States, the former now residing in Virginia, the latter having died March 20, 1879. W. S. Fulkman located in New Brighton Oct. 15, 1879, where he still resides. Although a practical printer, he did not commence to learn his trade until in his twenty-second year; since locating in Beaver county he has been connected with the press thereof in numerous capacities, the first work he did in the county being for the *Beaver Valley News*, of New Brighton, as solicitor; he afterward served on the Beaver Falls *Globe*, and prior to engaging in the publication of *The Spray* Mr. Fulkman was engaged with the *Daily Tribune*, of Beaver Falls, for two years, the latter part of his engagement serving as local editor, in which position he proved himself an able and trustworthy newsgatherer. Mr. Fulkman was married, Dec. 26, 1878, to Ruth Emma McDanel, eldest daughter of Thomas C. and Margaret A. McDanel, of North Sewickley township, this county. Unto them have been born three children, one son and two daughters, named, respectively, Reid, Ethel and Margie.

JOHN GASTON, foreman file cutting department, Western File Works, Beaver Falls, was born in County Antrim, Ireland, Nov. 29, 1855, and is a son of Daniel and Anna (McFarland) Gaston, who came to America in 1868 and located in Beaver Falls. The father was a miller by occupation, and died in 1870. John is a miller and file cutter by trade. He worked at milling two years in his native land, and learned the trade of file cutter in the Western File Works of Beaver Falls, where he worked as a journeyman fifteen years. In 1885 he was appointed foreman of the file cutting department, which position he still occupies. He is a member of the I. O. O. F.; in politics he is independent.

GEORGE HENRY GERBER, merchant tailor, Beaver Falls, was born in Baden, Germany, July 6, 1847. He served four years' apprenticeship at the tailor's trade in his native town, and in 1866 emigrated to this country, settling in Pittsburgh, where he worked as a journeyman for nineteen months. He then came to New Brighton, where he worked seven years as a journeyman and four years as a cutter. In 1879, he came to Beaver Falls, and was in the employ of Harry Goldsmith for five years. January 1, 1884, he embarked in business for himself, and has now a large and successful trade.

HARRY GOLDSMITH, clothier, merchant tailor and dealer in gents' furnishing goods, Beaver Falls, was born in London, England, in 1840, and came to America in 1863. In 1865 he located in Pittsburgh, where he was engaged in the clothing business until 1872. He then located in Beaver Falls and embarked in his present business, in which he has built up a large trade, occupying three stores, one for each department of his business. He has been a member of the Beaver Falls Building and Loan Association since 1879; is a member of Beaver Valley Lodge, No. 478, A. Y. M.; is Past H. P. of the Royal Arch Chapter, 206; a member of the I. O. O. F., A. O. U. W., K. of P., Royal Arcanum, Heptasophs, Mystic Circle and Encampment, and is president of the Beaver Falls School Board. He was one of the Executive Committee of Beaver county in the Garfield campaign, and is at present occupying the same position. Politically he is a Republican.

. . J. M. GORMLY, justice of the peace and engineer, P. O. Industry, was born in Industry township in 1838, and is a son of Samuel and Rachel (Marker) Gormly, the former a native of this county, a printer by trade in his youth, but in later life a boat builder. He was a justice of the peace in Industry township for ten years, and, from the first opening of the Cleveland & Pittsburgh Railway till within two years of his death, was ticket agent for that company. Our subject learned steam-boat engineering when about twenty-one years of age, and has since followed that business, chiefly on the Missouri and Yellowstone rivers. He was married in 1859 to Maggie, daughter of Joseph Allen, and by her has had five children, two now living: Ivy M. and Josie F. Mr. Gormly was elected in 1885 to the office of justice of the peace. In politics he is a Republican.

JOHN GRAEBING, retired, P. O. New Galilee, was born near Frankfort, Germany, in January, 1820, and in 1833 came with his parents, Sigfried and Elizabeth (Haydt) Graebing, to America, landing in Baltimore, Md. Sigfried was a chairmaker, a trade he followed during life. He located permanently in Pittsburgh, and was at one time a captain of militia in that city. He died in 1860, aged eighty-four years. Few citizens of Beaver county are better known than John Graebing. He was educated in the common schools of his native country. In the month of December, 1833, with his parents and two brothers and two sisters he started on foot from Baltimore to Pittsburgh. That winter was remarkable for cold weather and heavy snows. The family suffered much during the journey, being obliged for a time to live on frozen apples. Mr. Graebing has been engaged in various pursuits. He was twelve years on the canal, two years teaming over the Allegheny mountains, three years butchering, and for a number of years a conductor on the P., Ft. W. & C. Ry. In 1857 he purchased the Union Hotel at New Galilee, and until 1882 was its owner and proprietor. He was married in 1841 to Fredericka Hartze, by whom he had the following named children: John, Albert, Christian, William, Henry, Edward and Emma. His wife died in 1881. Mr. Graebing was in 1861 elected to the office of sheriff by the Democratic party.

· ALEXANDER GRAHAM, liveryman, Beaver Falls, was born in Venango county, Pa., Dec. 12, 1840, and is a son of John and Sarah (Stevenson) Graham, of English and Irish descent. His parents settled in Rochester, this county, in 1847, and died there. Their children were Robert, Henry, Mary, Alexander, David, Perry and John. Alexander was reared in Rochester and vicinity from seven years of age. He was engaged in various occupations after reaching his majority up to 1871, when he located in Beaver Falls and embarked in the livery business, in which he has been successfully engaged up to the present time. July 2, 1861, he married Elizabeth, daughter of Nicholas and Elizabeth (Gehring) Phillips, of an old family of Beaver county, and has four children living: Mary (Mrs. Robert Todd), John, Wesley and Stella. Mr. Graham is a F. & A. M., a member of the I. O. O. F., A. O. U. W. and K. of P. Politically he is a Democrat.

BIOGRAPHIES—WEST SIDE. 655

WILLIAM GRAHAM, farmer, P. O. Black Hawk, was born in South Beaver township in 1824. Andrew, his father, came to Beaver county at an early age from Ireland and purchased fifty acres of land in Beaver township. He married Mary, daughter of Robert McCloy, of Beaver county. To this couple twelve children were born, three of whom are living. Andrew, at his death in 1868, owned 157 acres of land; he was eighty years of age. His wife died in 1870 aged eighty-five years. William now owns the homestead, where he has always lived. He is not married. In politics he votes the Democratic ticket.

GRAY BROTHERS, merchant tailors, Beaver Falls, are natives of New Brighton, this county, sons of St. Clair and Mary A. (Betout) Gray. Their paternal grandfather was John Gray, a native of Lancaster county, Pa., and a tailor by trade, who settled in New Brighton, this county, about 1812, where he resided until his death. His children were John, Barton, Samuel, Eliza and St. Clair. The latter was a tailor by trade and carried on business in New Brighton for forty years. His children were Samuel B., Mary A., Ellen, Franklin P., Wilbur F., James S., Frederick (deceased), Emma (deceased), George W. and Pink E. The subjects of this sketch were reared in New Brighton and educated in the public schools. They learned the tailor trade in their father's shop, and embarked in business in Beaver Falls in 1875, where they have built up a large and profitable trade. Franklin P., the senior member of the firm, was born Aug. 8, 1852, and married, in 1872, Carrie M., daughter of Hiram Cole, of Alexandria, N. Y. He has four children living: Frank L., Roy S., Claude M. and Muriel. The junior member of the firm, James S., was born Jan. 21, 1856, and married, in 1876, Katie L., daughter of Phillip Dimond, of Beaver Falls. He has two children: Clara P. and Anna. Both gentlemen are members of the Royal Arcanum, and are Republicans.

THOMAS GREENLEE, steamboat captain, P. O. Vanport, is of Scotch-Irish descent, born Oct. 8, 1809, and is a son of Thomas and Mary (Quinn) Greenlee, natives of Allegheny county, former by occupation a farmer. Our subject was only two years old when his father was killed at the raising of a log building. Thomas was the youngest of eight children. Thomas and Nancy (Greenlee) Shane are the only ones now living. He was reared in Allegheny county, and attended the common schools and an academy in Allegheny county; he went on the river when quite young, and has followed it most of his business life; he was forty years on the Ohio and Mississippi in different capacities, and has run as pilot and captain for many years; he was married in Allegheny county, in 1828, to Susan, daughter of Peter and Mary (Kintner) Onstott, of German descent. The children of Capt. and Mrs. Greenlee are Nancy, wife of John R. Large, an attorney at Pittsburgh; Robert, steam-boat pilot, married to Frances Johnston; Lucinda, wife of James Mitchell; Anna H., wife of Henry Large, Jr.; Virginia E., wife of George W. Johnston; Arminda V. and Alvin L., twins (Arminda V. is the wife of James M. Cornelius. Alvin L. enlisted Aug. 6, 1862, in the 140th Regt. Co. F, Col. R. P. Roberts commanding; was wounded at Gettysburg, July 2, 1863; had a limb amputated and died from the effects Aug. 3, 1863); Estella J., wife of J. P. Ross. The family belong to the Presbyterian church. In politics Captain Greenlee is a Republican.

GEORGE H. GRIER, farmer, P. O. New Galilee, was born in Darlington township in 1853, and is a descendant of one of the oldest settlers in this section. His grandfather laid out the present town of Darlington, and in his honor it was named Greersburg. George Grier, father of our subject, married Margaret Holmes. Eight children were born to this couple, George H. being the only son. George Grier was a prominent farmer in his day. He died in 1883. George H. was educated in the common schools, and at the death of his father came into possession of the homestead where he now lives. Besides managing the work of the farm he is also engaged in the lumber business. In politics he is a Republican.

WILLIAM H. GRIM, physician, Beaver Falls, was born in New Sewickley township, Oct. 20, 1833, and is a son of Michael and Martha (Shearrer) Grim. His grandfather, Philip L. Grim, of German descent and a native of York county, Pa., moved to Beaver county in 1800, settling in New Sewickly township, where he cleared and improved a farm. He erected a two-story residence, which is now occupied by Sampson Pearsall. He had four sons and four daughters, the sons being John, George, Philip and Michael, the last named a soldier of the War of 1812. He cleared and improved a farm in his native township, and died there. His wife was a daughter of John and Mary Shearrer, pioneers of Butler and Beaver counties. They had eight children: Philip L., John, George, Conrad, David, William H., Joseph and Esther (Mrs. George Hartje). His second wife was Susan Nye, by whom he had one son, Benjamin. William H. Grim was reared in Beaver county, taught school for six years, and later studied medicine. He took his first course of lectures in the Medical College of Ohio at Cincinnati, and was graduated from Jefferson Medical College of Philadelphia in 1869. He located in Beaver Falls, where he now has a large practice. He was twice married; first to Lucinda, daughter of Levi and Leah (Tice) Spangler, of Lebanon county, Pa., by whom he has one son, William Simpson, now a student of medicine. His second wife was Amelia A., daughter of Archibald and Ann R. (Baker) Robertson, of Beaver Falls. Dr. Grim has served officially in the school board of Beaver Falls for many years. He is a member of the Beaver County Medical Society; is a F. & A. M., and a member of the A. O. U. W.; politically he is a Jeffersonian Democrat.

ABRAM S. HALL, carriage manufacturer, Beaver Falls, was born in Beaver, Nov. 11, 1840, and is a son of John L. and Eliza (Shockey) Hall. His father was a native of Kittanning, Pa., and with three brothers, David, Solomon and Richard, came to Beaver county about 1817, where he followed the occupation of a tailor for most of his life. His wife was a daughter of Abraham Shockey, formerly of Hollidaysburg, Pa., and a pioneer tailor of Beaver county. Mr. Hall had ten children who grew to maturity: Mary J., Catherine, Eliza, Matilda, Amelia, Abram S., Richard, Dallas, Frank and John. Abram S. was reared in Beaver, learned his trade with C. West & Co. of Pittsburgh, and worked as a journeyman several years. He was in business at New Brighton three years, located in Beaver Falls in 1874, and with his brother Richard embarked in their present business. They are said to be the only carriage manufacturers in Beaver county who have continued successfully in the business for any length of time. In 1873 Mr. Hall married Ellen Nippert, of New Brighton, by whom he has three children living: Florence, Ellen and Lillie.

JOHN A. HALLER, contractor and builder, Beaver Falls, was born in Butler county, Pa., July 30, 1852, and is a son of Adam and Elizabeth (Martsolf) Haller. He was reared in his native county, and learned carpentering in Pittsburgh. In 1877 he located in Beaver Falls, where he worked at his trade until the fall of 1882, when he embarked in business as a contractor and builder with Jacob D. Martsolf, which partnership expired Jan. 1, 1887, since which time he has been in the same business on his own account. He has built a large number of first-class buildings in Beaver Falls and elsewhere, and his reputation for first-class work is firmly established. He is a member of the Lutheran church, and the Royal Arcanum; in politics he is a Democrat.

JAMES HAMILTON and his brother Thomas were both natives of Ireland. The former resided in the territory now known as South Beaver township. He was shot and killed by men lying in ambush, as he was riding on horseback along with a party of land agents, United States marshals and others, who were dispossessing settlers of their lands.

J. Q. HAMILTON, station agent and telegraph operator, Beaver, was born in Beaver Nov. 12, 1855. He is a son of G. W. and Eliza Jane (Todd) Hamilton, natives of Pennsylvania and of English descent. His father started in life as a steamboat engineer, which occupation he followed for over twenty-five years. During the civil war he was appointed United States revenue collector for Beaver, Lawrence and Washington counties, and held that office until his death, which occurred in 1885. He served for several years as a director of the First National Bank of New Brighton. His family consisted of four sons : Samuel T., a captain in the regular army; G. W., a machinist at Rochester; William, a station agent on the Lake Erie railroad; and J. Q., who was reared in Beaver, attended the Beaver Seminary and early in life learned telegraphing. His first position was on the C. P. R. R. as operator from 1872 to 1879. When the Lake Erie railroad was built to Beaver he came to this place and took charge of Beaver station, where he has been ever since. Mr. Hamilton was married, in 1881, to Lizzie, daughter of David Patton, and of English descent. They have one child,.Mabel Virginia. Mr. and Mrs. Hamilton are members of the Presbyterian church. In politics he is a Republican.

WILLIAM D. HAMILTON, farmer and stock grower, P. O. Beaver Falls, was born in Pittsburgh, Pa., April 5, 1828, and is a son of James and Nancy (Dinsmore) Hamilton, natives of Ireland, who came to America when they were both children. His father grew up in Pittsburgh, learned the machinist's trade and spent most of his life in that occupation; he died in 1859; his family consisted of eight children, William D. being the youngest and only one now living. His brother, Hon. John S. Hamilton, served two terms in the legislature from Pittsburgh, and also served a term from Iowa. He was a Democrat, and was elected in districts strongly Republican. William D. was reared in Pittsburgh, attended the graded schools, and early learned the carpenter's trade, which he followed until he came to Brighton township and bought his present farm. He was married in Allegheny county to Miss Amanda Hall, a lady of Pennsylvanian origin. Her father was a manufacturer of plows. Mr. and Mrs. Hamilton have five children now living: James H., Carrie R., William D., Robert C. and John S. Our subject is a member of the Presbyterian church. He is a Democrat, and was a member of the council seven years at Pittsburgh. He is a Master Mason.

ROBERT HARBISON (deceased), whose portrait appears elsewhere in this volume, was born in South Beaver township, about 1795. At the time of his death, in 1887, he was probably the oldest native of the county resident in it. His grandfather was a merchant in Belfast, Ireland, of which city our subject's parents were also natives. They came and settled in South Beaver township two years before the birth of our subject, and reared a family of six sons and five daughters under the teachings of the Presbyterian church. Elizabeth married James McMillin, and lived and died in South Beaver; Mary married Isaac Warrick, and lived in Ohio township; Robert was the third child; Adam died in Enon Valley; Jane married John McMillin, and died at their home in South Beaver; Ann married Ezariah Inman, and lived in Chippewa township; John's home was near Beaver Falls; James dwelt in South Beaver, and died near Newcastle, this state; Sarah married George Powers and dwelt in Big Beaver; Samuel and Matthew remained in South Beaver, and the latter never married. Matthew died in 1833, aged sixty-five years, and his remains were deposited in New Salem cemetery, Ohio township. Robert Harbison had very limited educational privileges, but his native shrewdness made him a very successful man. By judicious investments in real estate he realized a competence, and his only loss occurred in the Savings Bank of Allegheny, where he sunk six thousand dollars. He was at one time a stockholder in the P., Ft. W. & C. Ry, whose tracks crossed his farm. When his brethren of the Free Presbyterian church objected to this holding he withdrew from that body, and for a time associated with the Methodist Episcopal church, but he was not satisfied with this connection, and at the time of his death was a member of the United Presbyterian church. Politically he associated with the Free-Soil party, but afterward joined the Democrats. He was first married when thirty-five years of age, and three times after that. His first wife, Mary Johnson, died in 1847, aged forty-eight years; she bore him one daughter, Mary Eliza, wife of John Glass. His second wife was Jane D., widow of Dr. James W. Johnson; she died in 1852, aged thirty years; her two children, Robert P. and Andrew died young. Mr. Harbison's third wife was Mrs. J. Anderson, who died without issue in 1883, aged seventy-eight years. His fourth wife was Mrs. Lichau, whom he married in 1885. She is now living in Beaver Falls. Mary Eliza Harbison was married in 1858, to John H. Glass, of whom more particular mention is here appropriate. He was born in Ohio township, Nov. 11, 1826. His parents moved to Ohio and afterward settled at Ossian, Ind., where he was brought up. Here he kept a store for some time and also dealt in live stock. In 1861 he moved to Allegheny City and made that place and Pittsburgh his headquarters until his death, which occurred on the 27th of July, 1877. At that time he was a member of the firm of Holmes, Lafferty & Co., extensive dealers in stock, and enjoyed a reputation for integrity and fair dealing, and a thorough judgment of the merits and value of animals. His son, Robert Harbison Glass, is a resident of Allegheny. Jeanetta Josephine, the eldest child, is the wife of B. F. Pyle, whose biography will be found in this volume. John Drummond, third child of Mr. and Mrs. Glass, died at the age of eleven years. Mrs. Glass was born in South Beaver Dec. 9, 1838, and died in November, 1882.

JAMES L. HARBISON, contractor and builder, Beaver Falls, was born in Allegheny City, Sept. 22, 1841, and is a son of Adam and Jane (Lowry) Harbison. He was reared and educated in his native city, where he served an apprenticeship of three years at the brick-layer's trade. He worked as a journeyman until 1869, when he located in Beaver Falls, and in 1870 became associated with H. T. Howe as a contractor and builder. He married Mary E., daughter of William and Ellen (Hockenberry) Graham, of Butler county, Pa., and has two children—Ida J. and William. He is a member of the I. O. O. F.; politically he is a Republican.

JAMES HARPER, county surveyor, P. O. Beaver, was born in Hanover township, this county, June 1, 1828. His parents, James and Elizabeth (Hay) Harper, were natives of this state, his mother being born in Washington county and his father in York county. They were of Scotch descent. His grandfather came from York county to Beaver county in 1800, when his father was only eight years old, and settled in Hanover township. He was a miller and built the Harper Mills in Hanover township. His son, James, was also a miller. His family consisted of eight children, six of whom lived to adult age. Our subject is the eldest son, and the only surviving member of the family now living in this county. He attended the district schools of Hanover township, Frankfort Academy and the academy at Hookstown. He very naturally chose the occupation of his father and grandfather, and learned the miller's trade in the old Harper Mills, which had been in the possession of the family for three generations. He worked at surveying for forty-one years, twenty years of that time in connection with milling in Hanover township. Since 1866 he has made surveying his only business. In 1859 he was elected county surveyor, and served one term. He was again elected in 1874, and has held the office ever since except during two years. In politics he was first a Whig and then a Republican. He held many offices in Hanover township, serving nine years as school director. He was married in September, 1850, to Alice Ann, daughter of William Carothers, a member of one of the earliest families of this county. He was of Irish descent. They have had five children : Mary, James (a machinist), Clementine (deceased), William (a glass cutter), and Elizabeth. They are members of the United Presbyterian church, of which Mr. Harper is an elder.

J. R. HARRAH, attorney, Beaver, was born in this county March 25, 1848. His parents, William and Eliza (Fleming) Harrah, were natives of Allegheny county and of Scotch-Irish origin. His father was a miller by trade, which he made the business of his life. He had seven sons and four daughters. Our subject, who is the fourth child, was reared on the farm and worked in the mill with his father. He received his education in the district school, and early in life began teaching, an occupation he followed until March 9, 1862, when he enlisted in Company F, 140th Regiment, P. V. I. He served as orderly sergeant until the close of the war, except when he was on detached service. He was in the Fourth Army Corps under General Hancock, and was with his regiment when it stood directly in front of Pickett's great charge. He was with his company when they fought over what is now so well known as the wheat field at the battle of Gettysburg; also participated in the battle of Chancellorsville. Soon after the battle of Gettysburg he was appointed recruiting officer, and was sent to Pittsburgh. He was then detailed in the quartermaster's department, subsequently returned to his regiment, and was again put on detached service in the Quartermaster General's department. After the close of the war he began the study of law in the office of S. B. Wilson, of Beaver, and in 1866 began practice in Beaver. He is an active member of the Republican party, and has been one of the prime movers in getting pavements and gas and water works in the borough. He has been a member of the council of Beaver and of

BIOGRAPHIES—WEST SIDE.   659

the school board. As a lawyer Mr. Harrah has been successful. He was married, in 1875, to Mary A., daughter of William B. and Elizabeth J. (Kennedy) McGaffick, and is of Irish descent. Mr. and Mrs. Harrah have one child : Matthew S. They are members of the Presbyterian church.

SIMON HARROLD. The great-great-grandfather of the subject of this biographical sketch was a soldier of the Revolution. His son Peter, who resided in Eastern Pennsylvania, was the father of David Harrold, one of the pioneer settlers in Ohio. To his wife, formerly Miss Bear, were born twelve children. Samuel, of this number, whose birth occurred Aug. 16, 1816, in Columbiana county, Ohio, still resides in his native county. He married Susanna Crumbaker, also descended from Revolutionary stock. Their children were twelve in number, all of whom with one exception survive. Their son, Simon Harrold, was born Nov. 3, 1840, in Columbiana county, Ohio, where he remained until his majority was attained. Becoming a pupil of the common and select schools he later spent four years in acquiring a knowledge of the carpenter's and builder's trade, and in 1866 chose Beaver Falls as a favorable point of settlement. Here an extended field awaited him. He erected the second new dwelling in the place, which his family occupied. He then built a planing mill, and embarked in the business of a lumber merchant and contractor. These departments of industry he still conducts, and has during his residence in the town erected most of the factories and important buildings besides its churches, school-houses and hotels. He has also constructed two court houses in Ohio, and done much important work in other parts of Pennsylvania. He is a director of the First National Bank of Beaver Falls, and is connected with various manufacturing enterprises. Mr. Harrold was in January, 1866, married to Louisa, daughter of Jacob Schauweker, of Columbiana county, Ohio. Their children were : Edward R. (deceased), Julia C., Alberta S., Irvin C., Mary E., Isadore L., Katherine Maud, Alfred E. A staunch Republican, Mr. Harrold has never been an active worker in the field of politics. He is a member of the Methodist Protestant church of Beaver Falls, and connected with Echo Lodge, F. & A. M., that borough.

ROBERT HARSHA, dealer in musical instruments and sewing machines, Beaver, is a native of this county, born in Hanover township June 17, 1824. His parents, John and Mary (Moore) Harsha, were natives of this state and of Irish and German descent. His father started in life as a school-teacher and a surveyor. He was a college graduate, and a man of high literary attainments. He served for a time as justice of the peace, and was a member of the legislature for Beaver county in 1836-37-38. He had eleven children, of whom Robert, who is the ninth, is the only survivor. He was reared in Hanover township, attended the common schools, and followed farming until 1869, when he came to Beaver and engaged in traveling and selling farming implements for a time. He then embarked in his present business, which he has since followed with success. In this business his son, J. W., is a partner. He was married, in 1857, to Miss E. A., daughter of John and Nancy (Charles) McCauley, natives of Beaver county and of Irish descent, former of whom, a farmer, was born in 1805. Mr. and Mrs. Harsha have had ten children, nine now living. They are members of the United Presbyterian Church, of which Mr. Harsha has been an elder for twenty years. He also acted as Sabbath school superintendent for about fifteen years. He held most of the local offices in Hanover township. In politics he is a Republican.

HENRY WATERS HARTMAN. Mr. Hartman, one of the most prominent representatives of the manufacturing interests of the county, is descended from German stock. His grandfather, Peter Hartman, emigrated from Germany and joined the Revolutionary army under Gen. Anthony Wayne. Settling after his discharge in Chester county, Pa., he subsequently removed to Perry county in the same state and engaged in farming. His three children were Benjamin, Frederick, and a daughter who became Mrs. Shoemaker, the mother of Prof. Shoemaker, Ph. D., of Blairstown, N. J. Benjamin Hartman was born in Perry county, afterward resided for twenty years in Huntingdon county, and ultimately removed to Blair county, in the same state, where he remained until his death; he married Penina M. Wilson, of Huntingdon county, and had children:

Eldon W., Henry Waters, Jesse L., Frank R. and Mary E. (Mrs. J. A. Marvin). Henry Waters, the second son, was born Dec. 21, 1850, in Huntingdon county, and in 1860 bècame a resident of Blair county. His education was limited to the common schools, with two additional terms at Academia Academy, in Juniata county, Pa.; after which he devoted some time to labor on the farm, and later began a more active business career as clerk in a store at Hollidaysburg, from whence he was promoted to a position in the office of the Hollidaysburg Iron & Nail Company. Two years after he was placed in charge of the rolling mill and nail factory, and for three years acceptably filled that position. Mr. Hartman then removed to Pottstown, in connection with the Pottstown Iron Company, remaining two years with this company prior to accepting the assistant superintendency of the Gautier Steel Works, at Johnstown, Pa. In 1882, two and a half years later, Mr. Hartman came to Beaver Falls and organized the Hartman Steel Company, limited, of which he is chairman. From small beginnings this company has increased in capacity and importance until it now employs eleven hundred men in the manufacture of steel wire, wire nails of every variety, and many specialties, such as wire mats, picket and woven fence, cold die-rolled steel, etc. Mr. Hartman is also director of the Bridgewater Gas Company, of which the Hartman Steel Company are the principal owners, His business interests engross his entire attention and preclude active participation in matters of more general import. Aside from keeping well informed on the public questions of the day he gives no time to party or political measures. Mr. Hartman was, in October, 1876, married to Mary, daughter of A. L. Holliday, of Hollidaysburg, and has two children.

JOHN E. HARTON, builder, Beaver, was born in Beaver borough in November, 1835, and is a son of James and Eliza (Elliott) Harton, latter a native of Ireland.' They were married in Beaver. James Harton, who was of Irish descent, was born in Chester county, Pa.; he was a mason by trade, and resided in Beaver county from 1850 until his death; his family consisted of three sons and five daughters. John E. attended the common schools in his native town, and early in life learned the mason's trade, at which he worked for a time. After he reached his majority he learned the carpenter's trade, and since 1867 has been engaged in contracting; he is a member of the firm of Harton & Tallon in Beaver. Mr. Harton was married, in June, 1862, to Mary, daughter of William and Ellen (Edwards) Moore, natives of Beaver county and of German descent. Her father was born in 1806, and died at her home in Beaver in 1887. Mr. and Mrs. Harton have four children: William E., Ella A., Harry M. and Stanford N. In politics Mr. Harton is a Republican, and has served as school director and president of the school board in Beaver for two terms, and one term as county auditor. He is a member of the I. O. O. F. lodge and encampment, and has served two terms as representative of the Grand Lodge. He enlisted in 1862 in the 140th Regiment, P. V., Company I; was in many battles, including Gettysburg, Chancellorsville, the Wilderness, and was discharged at the close of the war; he is a member of Post No. 473, G. A. R.; he has worked at railroad bridge building.

JOHN HARTSHORN, retired farmer, P. O. East Palestine, Ohio, was born in Darlington township in 1812. This family were among the original settlers of the county. Thomas Hartshorn came from Maryland to Westmoreland county, and from there to Beaver about 1796. He purchased 200 acres of land in Darlington township, where he remained until his death; he died in 1833, aged sixty-five years. He married Jane, daughter of Oliver Duff, also an early settler in this county, and they had five sons and two daughters, John being the second son. Our subject left home in 1837 and purchased 150 acres of land, where he has since resided; now owns about 300 acres of valuable farming and timber land. He was married July 20, 1837, to Lucinda, daughter of George McKein, of this county, and they have had four children, two of whom are living: Thomas, and Mary Jane (Mrs. Maginnis). The mother died in 1881, aged sixty-six years. Thomas has always remained on the farm with his father, and is unmarried. In 1864 he enlisted in Company H, 205th Heavy Artillery, and served until the close of the war. Mr. John Hartshorn has been an industrious farmer. He is a member of the United Presbyterian church; politically he is a Republican.

D. W. HARTSHORN, farmer, P. O. East Palestine, Ohio, is the third son of Thomas and Jane (Duff) Hartshorn. He was born in 1815, on the farm he now owns, which is the original tract purchased by his father. Mr. Hartshorn has always lived on his present farm. He received his education at the "old log schoolhouse." He was married, in 1851, to Martha Jane, daughter of William and Matilda (Robinson) Hasson, and they have seven children: Matilda Jane, Sarah Emma, Mary E., Thomas Wallace, William, Robert C. and Lucy S., Mr. Hartshorn has for many years been a member of the United Presbyterian church; he is a Republican, and has filled the offices of school director and tax collector, and has held other positions of trust.

HARRY F. HAWKINS, agent Adams Express Company, Beaver Falls, was born in Indiana county, Pa., June 6, 1861, and is a son of S. M. and Margaret A. (Fleming) Hawkins. His paternal grandfather was Matthew Hawkins, a farmer of Westmoreland county, Pa., and his maternal grandfather was Alexander Fleming, of Maryland, a resident of Beaver county since 1870. S. M. Hawkins was reared in Westmoreland county, and settled in Beaver Falls in 1867, where he was in business as a merchant tailor for ten years. During the war of the rebellion he served nine months in Company D., 135th P. V. and was honorably discharged. He was a prominent F. & A. M., and served several years as a member of the Board of Education of Beaver Falls, of which he was treasurer at the time of his death, Jan. 14, 1887. Harry F. Hawkins was reared in Beaver Falls from his seventh year. He was employed in the saw works of Emerson, Smith & Co. for several years; was mail agent on the Pittsburgh, Fort Wayne and Chicago Railway for some time, and has held his present position since July, 1886.

JOSEPH G. HAYS, driller of gas and artesian wells, is a son of Charles H. and Margaret (Grove) Hays, and was born at Augusta, Carroll county, Ohio, Oct. 7, 1837. Charles H. Hays was a native of Ireland, born in 1796. In 1846 he moved his family from Augusta to Industry, Beaver county, Pa., where is wife, Margaret, died in May, 1871, and where only a few months later, in November of the same year, he followed her to his last resting place. At Industry, the subject of this sketch received his education and resided until 1872, when he moved to Ohioville, his present location. May 15. 1861, he enlisted in Company F, Tenth Regiment, P. R. C., and fought in the battles of Dranesville, Mercersville, Gaines' Mill, White Oak Swamp, Malvern Hill, Bull Run, South Mountain, Fredericksburg, Gettysburg, Mine Run, Wilderness, Bethesda Church and others; was wounded at the Battle of Gaines'- Mill in the leg by a ball, which he still carries, and was compelled to enter the hospital, where he remained two months As soon as the doctor's consent was obtained he again resumed his place in the field. At Pittsburgh, Pa., June 11, 1864, he was mustered out of service. Mr. Hays was united in marriage, Dec. 6, 1866, with Miss Margaret, daughter of Jacob and Elizabeth (Stewart) Penebaker, who was born March 29, 1839. Her father died Jan. 17, 1871. Her mother still resides in Greene township. Four children have been born to Mr. and Mrs. Hays, three of whom are at home, and nearly grown to manhood and womanhood, named respectively—Joseph, Eula and Austin Stanley. George, the youngest, died at the age of eleven years. Mr. and Mrs. Hays and Eula are members of the Methodist Episcopal church at Ohioville. Mr. Hays is a F. & A. M.; a member of the G. A. R. Post 328, and of the A. O U. W.; he is a Republican.

THOMAS HENRY was born in Ireland May 16, 1781. William Henry, his father, emigrated to the United States in the year 1783, about the close of the Revolutionary war, and first settled in Maryland, not far from Havre de Grace. He removed thence to Beaver (then Allegheny) county, in the year 1796, and commenced an actual settlement on the easterly side of the Big Beaver. The country was then a wilderness. The treaty of peace, concluded with the Indians by Gen. Wayne, at Fort Greenville, Aug. 3, 1795, ratified in the following December, having opened the way, the tide of emigration from the back settlements set in in the year 1796. Judge Henry was then in his sixteenth year. He was therefore identified with all the hardships, privations, interests and feelings of the early settlers and pioneers of the county. In the year 1802 he came to the town of Beaver to engage in working at his trade with his elder brother. Possessing naturally a vigorous mind and a bold and energetic disposition, he soon began to take part in political affairs. On the 24th of December, 1808, he was appointed a justice of the peace by Simon Snyder; in 1810 he was elected a county commissioner; in the fall of 1814 he was elected captain of one of the companies drafted from this county to protect the shores of Lake Erie against an invasion of the British, supposed to be intended to be made during the following winter. He marched with his company and wintered near the lake shore. Here his company suffered much from sickness and the severity of the cold ; and he himself labored under a severe and lingering attack of typhus fever. It was during this campaign Judge Henry laid the foundation of many warm friendships, as lasting as the lives of those who became his friends, and some still are living who will ever remember him with deep regard. In 1815 he was elected a member of the legislature, and in 1816 appointed prothonotary and clerk of the several courts of the county, which post he retained until the fall of 1821, when elected sheriff by the people. In the year 1825 he became the proprietor and editor of the *Western Argus*, a newspaper established originally by James Logan, Esq. He continued in this vocation until the year 1831, when the paper passed into the hands of his son, the present editor, William Henry. [See chapter on the Press.] In 1828 and 1829 he filled the office of treasurer of the county ; in 1831 he was appointed by Gov. Wolf associate judge. This office he filled with much credit and an independence seldom exhibited by associates ; not hesitating on proper occasions to maintain his opinions with decision and firmness and with a knowledge and understanding ripened by a familiar acquaintance with judicial business. Upon his nomination to congress, he resigned his judicial commission, and in the fall of 1836 was elected to a seat in that body by a handsome majority over a gentleman of acknowledged worth and great popularity. He was reëlected in 1838, and again in 1840, in each instance by flattering majorities, though opposed by popular candidates.

With the close of his congressional term in 1843, ended the active duties of his public life ; but he continued to afford useful and often efficient aid to his friends in the political field. As a public officer he performed his duty with a fidelity, correctness, and honesty of purpose which won the confidence of the community. If his firmness was ever supposed to border on obstinacy, it was still characterized by manifest singleness of heart and desire to be right that obtained the respect of those who might have believed him in error. As a politician, for such it must be conceded he was for most of his long and useful life, he always occupied open and well-known ground. Never trimming to the popular breeze, his energy of character, fearlessness, boldness of action and independence of thought caused him rather to lead than to follow public opinion. While the prominence of his public life seems naturally to fill the foreground of description, the virtues which adorned his private character (if it may be so distinguished) can not pass unnoticed. They, too, occupy a large portion of the picture. Pursuing the faith of his forefathers he became a follower of Christ, and as early perhaps as the year 1816 connected himself with the Presbyterian church. In 1825 he was chosen an elder. In this position, as in all others of his life, he exerted a marked influence. At his house the minister of God always found a welcome and a home, while his time, his services and his substance were freely devoted to aid the church of his choice and build up the interests of religion. It is true, in ecclesiastical as in secular affairs, while on one hand holding firmly many fast friends, he was not without his opponents. But it was the result of these traits which secured to him his influence, to wit: his firmness, his independence and fearlessness. In this relation his opponents always acknowledged his upright honesty, while they may have deprecated his supposed errors.

The great and leading trait of his character was honesty of purpose, to which he added excellent judgment and strong common sense. Hence his counsel and advice were much sought for by his fellow citizens of every portion of the county. Few men enjoyed a more extensive acquaintance, or stood higher in the estimation of the public. The same traits of character often led him to be chosen to offices of private trust, in which the interests committed to his charge were always managed with great success and scrupulous fidelity. He has left behind him many who remember his services with gratitude and none who can say of him they suffered from neglected duty, erroneous judgment, or voluntary dereliction. As a neighbor he was obliging and kind, as a friend constant and unwavering, as a citizen useful, as a Christian exemplary, and in his domestic relations, the attachment of his family furnishes the strongest proof of how much he was loved and respected. He died July 20, 1849.

WILLIAM HENRY, born in the town of Beaver June 28, 1808, was the eldest son of Hon. Thomas Henry. His education was such as the schools of the village afforded. At the age of sixteen he entered his father's printing office as an apprentice, and was connected with the paper, as boy and man, for twenty-seven years. At the age of twenty-three he became sole editor and proprietor, by purchase of the paper, then known as the *Western Argus*. He was married, April 18, 1833, to Eliza S. Hamilton, and continued as editor of the *Argus* until Nov. 26, 1851, when in a valedictory, reviewing the moral, political, manufacturing and agricultural condition of the county, he took a final leave of the subscribers of the paper. During the time he occupied the editorial chair, questions of great public moment were ably and fully discussed. The Nullification movement, U. S. Bank, Tariff Currency, the acquisition of Texas and the Mexican War, the Compromise measure of 1850, were subjects upon which the readers of the paper were fully informed. His style of writing was terse, nervous and vigorous, compact and concise and aggressive to the last degree, in political discussions. He was an untiring friend and advocate of any measure tending to improve and develop the resources of the county. The Erie Canal, from the Ohio to Lake Erie, was a subject upon which his pen was early and often employed. The Beaver & Conneaut railroad, of which a survey was made in 1836, starting from "The Point," and going up the west bank of the Beaver to Conneaut Harbor, was also a favorite enterprise, but the crash of 1837 brought everything to a standstill. The ground is now occupied by the Pittsburg & Lake Erie railroad. Mr. Henry was an early and constant advocate of the building of the Ohio & Pennsylvania railroad, now the Ft. Wayne; and in fact every public enterprise, found in him a ready, active, and inspiring advocate. He was treasurer of Beaver county in 1857-58, and after leaving the office, he was appointed secret agent of the county to buy up the bonds issued in the construction of the Cleveland & Pittsburg railroad; the $100,000 subscription being taken up by the payment of about $71,000. He was a member of the Legislature in 1861-62-63. Mr. Henry died July 4, 1875.

SAMUEL HENRY, merchant, Darlington, was born in Armstrong county, in 1839. Thirty years later he removed to Beaver county. His father, Wilson Henry, a native of Westmoreland county, married Eliza Garvin of Armstrong county, and to them were born eleven children, of whom Samuel is the eldest. Wilson was a farmer by occupation, and is now living in Allegheny county. His grandfather, Samuel, came from Ireland. He was a descendant of the famous Matthew Henry, and was also a farmer. Mr. Henry was married in 1866 to Miss M. A., daughter of Francis Beatty, of Allegheny county, and became the father of seven children, three of whom, Alice, Fannie and Nettie, are yet living. Mr. Henry enlisted at the breaking out of the rebellion in Company B, 63d Regiment, P. V. I., and served in the famous Kearney's division, his term of service being three years. Since the war he has been engaged in general merchandising, having located successfully in Rochester, Cannelton, Beaver county, and in Darlington, in which latter place he is still engaged in business under the firm name of Henry & Mansfield. Mr. Henry has been prominent in local circles in which he moves; he has been school director; is a prominent member of the G. A. R. and of the U. V. L., and also of the Presbyterian church. In politics he is a Republican.

THOMAS M. HENRY, attorney, Beaver, of the firm of Bigger & Henry, of Beaver and New Brighton, was born in Beaver, April 22, 1858, within a few rods of the site of the courthouse; he is the eldest son of Evan James and Lucy M. (Rigg) Henry, latter born in Kirkudbrightshire, Scotland. His father, who is a native of Beaver, of Welsh and Irish descent, studied law with Hon. Daniel Agnew, and was admitted to the bar

Sept. 3, 1839; he practiced here for a time, then went to Cincinnati, Ohio, and practiced there for ten years. About 1858 he retired and has since lived in Princeton, N. J. Thomas M. first attended school in Princeton; then went with his parents to Europe, and remained abroad for four years, attending school most of the time while there. After his parents' return to America in 1873, he was under private instructions for two years. In 1875 he entered Princeton College, and was graduated in 1879. He then entered Columbia Law School in New York, was graduated in 1881, and admitted to practice in the state of New York. In the following November he came to Beaver, and in 1882 was admitted to the bar in Beaver county. His grandfather, Thomas Henry, was a captain in the war of 1812, and went with his company from Beaver county. Captain Henry's brother, William, was the first sheriff of Beaver county, and was associate judge in Southern Ohio, whence he moved soon after the war of 1812. The Henry family may truly be called one of the pioneer families of Beaver county.

ROBERT HERRON settled in Chippewa township in 1798. He was of Scotch-Irish parentage, and was born in York county, Pa., June 17, 1765. In very early boyhood he removed to Cumberland county, Pa., where he attained his majority. He was married, in 1794, to Miss Agnes Crawford, a native of Lancaster county, and in the following year removed to the "Forts of Yough," two years later taking up his residence in "White Oak Flats," Beaver county. One year later he entered Chippewa township, living for twelve months near what is now known as the Dunlap school district. In 1799 he removed to the farm of which he became owner, and which is yet occupied by his grandchildren. It is located on the south side of the township, near Brady's Run. Here he resided until his death, Aug. 17, 1838. He held the office of justice of the peace for nineteen consecutive years immediately preceding his decease, and was during the latter part of his life an elder in the Associate Presbyterian Church of Darlington, and afterward in the Four Mile Church. He left four sons and two daughters: William, Joseph C., John S., Margaret, Mary O. and David. All lived, and are identified with the history of Chippewa township. William was a soldier in the war of 1812; Joseph C. was a coroner of the county one term, about 1828; John S. was justice of the peace three years, holding the appointment at time of his death, he was also an elder in the Four Mile Church, and, later, of the United Presbyterian Church, of Beaver Falls; David died in childhood; Margaret became the wife of Joseph Niblock; Mary O. is yet residing, an unmarried lady, in Beaver.

JAMES HERRON, an older and unmarried brother of Robert, served as a scout with Capt. Samuel Brady in the Beaver valley and elsewhere, and engaged in numerous hand-to-hand conflicts with the Indians, from which he had many remarkable escapes. He was present at St. Clair's defeat, Nov. 4, 1791; served during the war of 1812, and was present at the battle of New Orleans, under Gen. Jackson. The date of his death is not known.

JOHN HERRON, dairyman, Fallston, was born in Chippewa township, this county, April 29, 1824. His parents, William (a farmer) and Sarah (Alexander) Herron, were of Irish origin. The mother was born in Mifflin county, and the father in Allegheny county. Their grandparents came from County Down, Ireland. John, who is the seventh in a family of fourteen children, was reared on a farm in Chippewa township and attended the schools of his native township. Early in life he learned the carpenter's trade and followed it for thirty years. He subsequently worked in a bucket factory at Fallston for a time, then bought the flouring mills at that place, and conducted them for seventeen years; he then sold out and embarked in his present business; he was married, in Brighton township, March 27, 1851, to Sarah Ann, daughter of David and Mary (Lawrence) Kennedy, of Irish descent, the father at one time a commissioner of Beaver county. Mr. and Mrs. Herron have had ten children, nine of whom are living: David K., now in Washington Territory; Mary, wife of Henry Moore; William, employed in a keg factory at Fallston; Frank, in a flouring mill here; Sarah, wife of William Moore; Walter and Elmer in the factory; Maggie J. and Clara. The mother died April 5, 1882, and Mr. Herron married, in 1884, Elazan, daughter of Joseph C.

Herron. Mr. and Mrs. Herron are members of the United Presbyterian Church, of which he has been deacon and trustee. In politics he is a Republican.

HENRY HICE. Judge Hice is of German parentage; his grandfather, Henry Hice, was one of the pioneers of the Legonier Valley, Indiana county, Pa., and among the earliest to till the soil of that region. He was twice married; William, a son by the first union, born in 1793, in the above county, having in 1823 removed to Allegheny county, Pa., where he engaged in the pursuits of a farmer. He married Hannah Eacbal, of Beaver county, and became a resident of Hopewell township, in that county, in 1828. His children were Mary Ann, Catherine, Eliza, Sarah, Hannah, William and Henry, of whom Mary A. and Catherine are deceased. Henry, of this number, was born in Hopewell township on the 24th of January, 1834, and with the exception of two years has spent his life in the county of his birth. After preliminary instruction at the common schools he received an academic education, and in 1857 began the study of law with the late Col. Richard P. Roberts, of Beaver. Immediately after his admission in June, 1859, he became associated with his preceptor as partner, and continued this relation until the death of the latter, at Gettysburg, during the late war, since which date Judge Hice has continued in the practice of his profession. During the interval between 1871 and 1877 he resided at Beaver Falls, but in the latter year returned to his former home, having been appointed judge of the courts of the 36th Judicial District of Pennsylvania, which office he held until January, 1885. when his practice was resumed. While evincing a commendable interest in local and public affairs this is the only office he has accepted. Judge Hice was, on the 3d of April, 1860, married to Ruth Ann Ralston, granddaughter of John Roberts, of the same county, and has four children. Mrs. Hice died in 1872, and he afterward married, July 25, 1877, Mrs. Sarah H. Minis, daughter of Chief-Justice Agnew.

J. F. HILLMAN, farmer, P. O. Rock Point, was born in Allegheny county, Sept. 24, 1833. Frederick Hillman, his father, was born in Allegheny county, in 1801, removed to Beaver county in 1852, and purchased a farm of 130 acres. He was a well-to-do farmer, and died in 1861; his wife Hannah (Wiley) bore him three children, two of whom are living. J. F., the second one, was reared a farmer, and has always followed this business. He purchased, in 1878, the farm of 135 acres where he lives. He also owns a fine farm in Lawrence county. Mr. Hillman was married, in 1860, to Isabella, daughter of Samuel Blair, and they had four children: Ann Eliza (Mrs. Wilson), Martha Jane (Mrs. Hoffman), William F. and Samuel (deceased). Mr. Hillman is a prosperous farmer, and has an extensive dairy. He is a member of the Presbyterian church; politically, he is a Republican.

SMILEY HITES, farmer, P. O. Darlington, was born in South Beaver township, in 1818. His father, Anthony Hites, came from Germany, first locating in Washington county, and soon after coming to Beaver county he bought fifty acres of land. He married Hester, daughter of Moses Dillon, and Smiley is the youngest of their eight children. The father died at the age of fifty years. Smiley has always been a farmer. In 1852 he purchased his present farm of fifty acres, all of which is under cultivation. He was married, in 1845, to Elizabeth, daughter of Henry Veon, of this county, and they have had ten children, five of whom are living: Hiram, Milton, Anthony, Robert and Mary Josephine (Mrs. Neal). Mr. Hites now superintends the work on his farm, Robert, the youngest son, doing the work. Mr. Hites is a member of the Methodist church; in politics, a Democrat.

THOMAS HOGAN, farmer and fruit grower, P. O. Beaver, was born in Ireland, in 1827, the eldest of the three children of Michael Hogan, who was a farmer in Ireland. He was reared on the farm in Ireland, and when eighteen years old came to America. After working on the railroad in Vermont and in Pittsburgh, he came, in 1857, to Beaver county, and was section boss on the railroad until 1870, since when he has been engaged in agricultural pursuits. His farm consists of seventy-three acres of land, where he now resides. He was married, in 1855, to Hanora, daughter of John Mullins. She is a native of Ireland. Their children are Anna, Mary, Hannah, John, Thomas, James.

and Rettie. The family are all members of the Catholic church. In politics Mr. Hogan is a Democrat.

WILLIAM H. HOON, tin, copper and sheet iron manufacturer, Beaver Falls, was born in Butler county, Pa., Oct. 20, 1843, and is a son of James and Sarah (Bateman) Hoon. His paternal grandfather was Philip Hoon, of Easton, a pioneer of Beaver Falls; he removed to Mercer county and died there; he reared a family of twelve children: William, John, Samuel, Wesley, Stewart, Hiram, Eliza, Sophronia, James, Philip, Margaret and Mary. Of these, James was born in Beaver Falls in 1807. He was a shoemaker, and worked at his trade for many years at Zelienople, Butler county. He was justice of the peace there fifteen years, returned to Beaver Falls in 1872, and died there March 3, 1881. He had twelve children: John W., Elizabeth, George W., David H., Thomas J., Sarah J., James M., Ellen, William H., Margaret A., Joseph S., and Charles A. William H. was reared in Butler county, learned his trade in Peekskill, N. Y., and established his present business in 1867. He has secured an extensive trade in this and adjoining counties. In 1863 he married Louisa, daughter of Captain Bennett Gilbert, of Peekskill, N. Y., by whom he has four children: W. Sherman, Lois P., Charles M. and Franklin H. Mr. Hoon is a F. & A. M., and a member of the I. O. O. F. and K. of P. Politically he is a Republican.

CHARLES A. HOON, grocer, P. O. Beaver Falls, was born in Zelienople, Butler county, Pa., Oct. 5, 1850, and is a son of James and Sarah (Bateman) Hoon. His paternal grandfather was Philip Hoon, a native of Eastern Pennsylvania and a pioneer of what is now Beaver Falls. He reared a family of twelve children, of whom James, father of our subject, was the ninth child and seventh son. He was a native of Beaver Falls. In early manhood he moved to Butler county, Pa., and was justice of the peace at Zelienople for fifteen years. He returned to Beaver Falls in 1872, where he died March 3, 1881. He had twelve children, of whom Charles A. is the youngest. Our subject was reared and educated in Butler county. He located in Beaver Falls in 1867, and worked as a tinsmith for twelve years. Oct. 16, 1879, he embarked in the grocery business in Beaver Falls, in which he has since successfully continued, being one of the leading grocers of the place. Oct. 6, 1874, he married Mary E. daughter of Thomas and Catherine (Morrison) Leslie, of Beaver Falls, and has two children, Carrie and Howard. He is a member of the Methodist Protestant church; in politics a Republican.

CHARLES HOSMER, D. D. S., Beaver Falls, is a native of Worcester, Mass., and a son of Benjamin G. and Maria (Stearns) Hosmer, of English-Irish descent. He came with his parents to Beaver Falls in 1869, and in 1874 began the study of dentistry with Dr. A. M. Whisler, of New Brighton, with whom he remained two years. He passed the state board of examination in 1878. In 1876 he began the practice of his profession in Beaver Falls, where he has since been located, and by his scientific skill has built up a large and lucrative practice, which is steadily increasing. When Dr. Hosmer located in Beaver Falls there were nine dentists there; now there are but five, of whom he is one of the principal, if not the leader in the profession. He believes in keeping up with the times, and has all the modern appliances used in his profession, including the new Richel Vulcanizer, for making artificial teeth in one-third less time than by any other process; and also extracts teeth without pain by any anæsthetic desired. By strict attention to business, Dr. Hosmer has made many friends in Beaver Falls and vicinity, and is considered one of the leading practitioners in Western Pennsylvania. He is an active F. & A. M., member of the I. O. O. F. and Heptasophs; politically he is a Republican.

J. V. HOUK, hatter, Beaver Falls, was born near Wurtemberg, Lawrence county, Pa., Feb. 20, 1858, and is a son of John C. and Elizabeth (Butler) Houk, who settled in New Brighton in 1867, where they now reside. Mr. Houk was reared and educated in New Brighton from twelve years of age. In 1874 he entered the store of E. Autenreith as clerk, where he remained four years; then went to Allegheny City and entered the store of E. Semple, where he served in the same capacity until 1880. He then returned to Beaver county, and for four years was clerk in the store of Blumenthal & Co.

BIOGRAPHIES—WEST SIDE.   667

Jan. 20, 1887, Mr. Houk embarked in his present business, and though established but a short time, he has a large and constantly increasing trade.

J. T. HOWARTH, proprietor of billiard parlors, Beaver Falls, was born in Oldham, Lancashire, England, July 29, 1858. His parents James and Martha (Holland) Howarth, came to America in 1859 and located in Fallston, this county. Our subject was reared and educated in Beaver county, and for eight years was in the employ of the Western File Works. He has been engaged in his present business four years in Beaver Falls, opening the elegant parlors he now occupies Sept. 1, 1887.

HENRY F. HOWE, contractor and builder, Beaver Falls, was born in Fallston Feb. 24, 1837, and is a son of Joseph and Belle (Williams) Howe. His paternal grandfather, John Howe, a native of England and a bricklayer by trade, settled in Beaver Falls in 1830; he had six children: Joseph, Margaret (Mrs. William Horner), Ellis, Jane (Mrs. John Douthitt), Richard and Ann (Mrs. James Scofield). Joseph Howe was also a bricklayer, and for many years a resident of Fallston and Bridgewater. He erected many of the early brick buildings of Beaver Falls and New Brighton. His children were Henry F., John, Carrie (Mrs. Henry F. Williams) and Joseph. Henry F. was reared in Fallston, and learned the bricklayer's trade in Cincinnati, Ohio. He worked as a journeyman until the breaking out of the war of the rebellion, when June 7, 1861, he enlisted in Company G, 6th O. V. I.; was promoted to sergeant and honorably discharged June 22, 1864. In 1866 he located in Beaver Falls, where he has since followed his trade. In 1867 he became a contractor and builder, and in 1870 became associated with J. L. Harbison, under the firm name of Howe & Harbison. He married Sarah J., daughter of Adam Frazier, and has three children: Charles W., Richard C. and Elizabeth. Mr. Howe is a member of St. Mary's Episcopal Church, the I. O. O. F., G. A. R., A. O. U. W, and Veterans' Legion. Politically he is a Democrat.

JASON HOYT, farmer and fruit grower, P. O. Industry, was born in Columbiana county, Ohio, April 18, 1835, son of John and Sophia (Stevens) Hoyt. Mrs. Hoyt's father was a native of Maryland, where she also was born, and where her grandfather and great-grandfather were slaveholders. Thomas Hoyt, the paternal grandfather of Jason, was a native of Lancaster county, Pa., and moved from there to Beaver county about 1790. He married Mary Fitzsimmons. Mr. and Mrs. John Hoyt had thirteen children, three of whom survive: Caroline, Jason and Jasper Jason was educated in the common schools, and since 1864 has resided on his present farm of seventy acres, where he makes a specialty of growing small fruits. He was married in 1862 to Lizzie, daughter of Nicholas and Isabel (Jamison) Beighey, and by her had seven children, four now living: Franklin, in Kansas; William, in Humboldt county, Cal.; Marshall and Flora, at home. Those deceased are Ella, Lizzie and Freeman (latter died in infancy). Mr. Hoyt has held several township offices, among them those of supervisor, school director and assessor. In politics he is a Republican. He and his wife are members of the United Brethren church, present pastor, Rev. Fulton.

JOHN HULMES, coal merchant, Beaver Falls, was born in Lancashire, England, March 31, 1829, and is a son of John and Anna (Mort) Hulmes. He came to America in 1869 and located in Beaver Falls, where he began work as a coal miner in the mines of H. C. Patterson. He shortly afterward opened a coal bank for White & Shoemaker, which he operated for them until 1873, when he became sole proprietor and operated on his own account seven years, mining on an average 15,000 bushels per year. He opened since three coal banks in Beaver Falls borough, which he sold in 1884. Mr. Hulmes came to Beaver Falls without a dollar, but by energy and perseverance has accumulated a competence. He has made fifteen voyages across the Atlantic, six since 1869. His mother came to this country in 1880, aged eighty years, and is now a resident of Beaver Falls. His father was killed in England, in a coal pit, Aug. 30, 1873. Mr. Hulmes is a member of the Episcopal Church; was elected a member of the Board of Education in November, 1886; politically he is a Republican.

J. WESTON HUM, proprietor of the St. Cloud hotel, Bridgewater, was born Feb. 9, 1865, a son of J. W. and Margaret (Briggs) Hum. The mother was born in Massachusetts. The father was born in Ohio, and was alone in the world from the time he was ten years old. He came to Beaver county and soon found steady employment on a steamboat. He learned the carpenter's trade and was employed at that work on the boat for ten years, following the Ohio until 1849. He then commenced to sell lightning rods, and met with great success. He was the principal mover in forming the North American Lightning Rod Company, at Philadelphia, in 1851. This company, which consists of four members, does all the manufacturing of lightning rods in the country. Our subject's father has full charge of the department at Pittsburgh, where he has carried on business for many years. He was married in Beaver county, and has five sons and two daughters. J. Weston, the fourth child, was reared in Bridgewater. At the age of fourteen he began to learn the blacksmith's trade, serving a regular apprenticeship, but has never worked at the trade since. He went on the road as foreman of a gang of men in his father's employ in the lightning rod business. In 1887 he bought the St. Cloud hotel. Mr. Hum was married, Dec. 29, 1885, to Tillie, daughter of John Hindman, a prominent farmer of Beaver county, and they have one child, Ed. In politics Mr. Hum is a Democrat. He is a prominent member of the Bridgewater Fishing Club.

F. C. HUM is the fifth of the seven children of J. W. and Margaret (Briggs) Hum. The former was a native of Ohio, and the latter of Massachusetts. He was born on the 9th of January, 1867, and was reared in Beaver county, where he attended school. He subsequently attended the Beaver High School, then Iron City College, where he graduated in 1885. He is employed as a bookkeeper in the city of Pittsburgh, but still makes his home in Beaver county.

WILLIAM C. HUNTER, farmer and stock grower, P. O. Beaver, was born in Brighton township, this county, July 14, 1831. His parents, William and Mary (Givan) Hunter, were natives of Ireland. The father was a farmer and one of the early settlers in Brighton township. He was an orderly sergeant in the war of 1812. William C., the fifth of ten children and the eldest son, was reared on the farm and attended the common schools. His grandfather, John Hunter, Sr., came to Brighton township about 1800. Our subject has made farming his business, and has only been off the farm five years, when he lived in Bridgewater. He is the owner of 100 acres of land, where he now resides. He was married, in 1860, to Mira, daughter of Joseph Moorhead, and born in this county. They have one child, Edna Dell. Mr. and Mrs. Hunter are members of the Presbyterian church, in which he is ruling elder. In politics he is a Republican, and has been school director and county auditor.

JOHN G. HUNTER, merchant, Beaver Falls, was born in Brighton township, this county, June 13, 1833, and is a son of William and Mary (Given) Hunter. His paternal grandfather was John Hunter, a native of County Down, Ireland, who settled in Ohio township, this county, in 1803, where he lived and died. He had a family of nine children. William, after his marriage, settled in Brighton township, this county, engaged in farming, and resided there until his death. His children were Nancy, Jane, Maria, Lucinda, William C., John G., Thomas B. and Margaret. John G. was reared in Brighton township and resided there until 1869, when he located in Beaver Falls and embarked in the mercantile business, which he has since successfully conducted. July 2, 1863, he married Sarah M., daughter of Joseph and Martha (Johnson) Lawrence, of South Beaver township, this county, and has two children living: Joseph L., a clergyman of the Presbyterian church, and John R. Mr. Hunter is a member of the Presbyterian church, the Royal Arcanum and A. O. U. W., and is a staunch Prohibitionist.

THOMAS B. HUNTER, farmer and stock-grower, P. O. Beaver, was born on the farm which he now owns in Brighton, March 22, 1836, and is a son of William and Mary (Given) Hunter. His father was a farmer, and spent most of his life on the farm where Thomas B. now resides. Our subject was reared in Brighton township, attending the common schools. He has made farming his business, and is the owner of 150 acres of land. He was married in 1869, to Sarah J., daughter of John and Mary Ann (Laughlan) Johnston, and they have five children: John C., William P., Mary A., Jennie

Maud and Pearl. They are members of the Presbyterian church. Mr. Hunter is a Republican in politics, and has held most of the township offices, he was elected county commissioner in 1887. He enlisted in Company I, 140th Pennsylvania V. I., and became a non-commissioned officer; was in thirty-one regular battles, including Gettysburg, Spottsylvania, Chancellorsville and the battle of the Wilderness, and was wounded at Petersburg. He is a member of the G. A. R.

CHARLES B. HURST, late insurance agent, had an office at Beaver and one at Rochester, Pa. He was born in England, and was a son of William and Amelia (Parsons) Hurst. His father, who was a merchant, came to America in 1839 and settled in Beaver county, where he spent the remainder of his life. Charles B., the eldest of seven children, was reared in Bridgewater and attended boarding schools. His first employment was as a clerk in the forwarding commission office at Rochester, where he remained until 1862 when he obtained a position as clerk of a steamboat. He was on the water in different capacities for twenty-one years, the last eight years as captain of a steamboat. In 1862, he embarked in the insurance business in which he successfully engaged till his death He represented some of the oldest and best known companies in the world, such as the Ætna and Phœnix, of Hartford, the Royal, of London, and many others. His residence was at Rochester, where he died Nov. 19, 1887. He was married at Rochester, in May, 1850, to Anna M., daughter of John S. and Mary (Lyons) Darragh. Her grandfather Lyons was captured by the Indians, and was kept in captivity for several years. Mr. and Mrs. Hurst had seven children: Charles, who is now in the insurance business and has an office at Rochester; William; Mary, wife of John Moulds; Henry and Alfred, living, and John and Robert, deceased. Mr. and Mrs. Hurst were members of the Episcopal church, of the vestry of which he had been a member. In politics he was a Democrat, and served as a member of the council in Rochester. He was a member of the I. O. O. F., of the K. of P. and was a Sir Knight Templar.

ALFRED C. HURST. William Hurst, the father of the subject of this biographical sketch, born Nov. 27, 1804, emigrated from England in 1840, and located in Bridgewater, Beaver county. Here he established himself as a merchant, and until his death in 1879 was a resident of the place. He married, Dec. 18, 1828, Amelia Parsons, born Aug. 11, 1807, who resided in the suburbs of London, England, and had children: Charles B., John P., Amelia P. (Mrs. John Blake), Alfred C., Ellen (deceased), Henry (who was killed during the civil war at the battle of Fair Oaks), N. Fetterman, and Sarah F. Mrs. Hurst still resides in Bridgewater, and in her eightieth year enjoys exceptional health. Alfred C. Hurst was born Feb. 3, 1838, at Kingswood Hill, near Bristol, England, and came with his parents to America at the age of four years. His whole life since that event has been passed in Bridgewater, where he first attended the common schools of the place, and finished his education at Coulter's Academy, Richmond, Ohio. His first business experience was in connection with a clerkship on the steamers "Convoy" and "Rocket," plying between Pittsburgh and other points on the Ohio river. Later he entered his father's store, of which he in 1863 became sole proprietor, and has since that time been extensively engaged in the retail dry goods and carpet trade. He is largely identified with the interests of the county of his residence, and is director of the First National Banks of Rochester and of Beaver, director of the Rochester Pottery Company, limited; of the Union Street Railway Company; president of the Equitable Building and Loan Association Number Two; director of the Equitable Building and Loan Association Number One; and of the Bridgewater Building Association. Mr. Hurst was married, Oct. 23, 1867, to Mary O., daughter of David Greer, of Pittsburgh, and their children were Vida, Alfred C., Jr., Frank L., Cory May (deceased), Harry H., Oliver, Eugene, Lawrence B. and William R. Mr. Hurst has been for several years school director and councilman, and since 1875 treasurer of the school board of Bridgewater. He is an active Mason and member of Rochester Lodge No. 229 of that order and of Eureka Chapter No. 167, of Rochester.

JAMES MILTON IMBRIE, son of Rev. David Imbrie, was born near Greersburg, Beaver county, March 9, 1816. His grandfather, James Imbrie, was a native of Glasgow,

HISTORY OF BEAVER COUNTY.

Scotland, and emigrated to America about 1760, landing in New York. There he remained several years; was married and engaged in business as a merchant in New York and Philadelphia. During the revolutionary war he was arrested by British spies or officers for having an American gun or rifle among his stock of goods' and was imprisoned. His wife appealed to Gen. Howe, whose sympathies she won, and obtained her husband's release. In 1787 he returned to his native country, Scotland, and there remained about ten years. He returned to America and located in Philadelphia, where he was engaged in commercial trade. He was then quite wealthy, but the loss of some vessels at sea injured his fortune; fortunately, however, he had money enough left to continue business. Not being able to compete successfully with others after his losses, he sold out and removed to Fayette county, Pa., and from there to Frankfort Springs, Beaver county, where he engaged in business as a drover. He died at the age of seventy years, leaving a family of fourteen children. Three of his sons settled in Beaver county, where some of their descendants still remain. David, his eldest son; was born in New York in 1777, and received a classical education at Glasgow University. He studied theology under Dr. John Anderson, of Frankfort Springs, and was licensed by the Associate church when twenty-seven years of age. In 1805 he settled in Big Beaver township, then a thinly settled region, covered with dense forests, near the town of Greersburg (now Darlington), and here, for forty years, was engaged in the work of the ministry. He married Jane Reed, daughter of David Reed, of Cannonsburgh, Washington county, Pa. He had three sons and four daughters. On the 12th of June, 1842, while on his way to church, he had a stroke of apoplexy, of which he died, aged sixty-five years. James Milton, the youngest son, was born on the farm where he now resides, and, with the exception of three years, has always lived there. He received his education at the Greersburg Academy. Mr. Imbrie has a farm of 100 acres, where he resides, the greater part of which he cleared with his own hands. He also owns one in Darlington township. He has been very successful as a farmer; starting with nothing, he has by industry and economy accumulated a farmer's fortune. His farms are always kept in good repair. For a number of years he has been engaged in wool growing, and so successful has he been in this, that his wool is known far and near to be the best grown in that section of country. He married Clarinda, daughter of Samuel Jackson, of Darlington, and he has three children, one daughter and two sons. He gave his family a good education, his sons being both graduates of Washington and Jefferson college. The youngest son, Addison M., is an attorney at law, a partner of the firm of Marshalls & Imbrie, counselors at law, Pittsburgh, Pa. The other, William J., is at home assisting his father keeping up the farms and taking care of the sheep. Both sons have the industrious habits of their father, and are well respected by their neighbors. Mr. Imbrie is now in his seventy-second year, and enjoys good health. He is a member of the Reformed Presbyterian church; in politics a Republican.

R. S. IMBRIE, real estate and insurance agent, Beaver, was born in Big Beaver township, this county, Aug. 12, 1831, and is a son of John and Nancy (Rankin) Imbrie, natives of Pennsylvania and of Scotch descent, former of whom was a farmer and tanner. John Imbrie's family consisted of ten children, six of whom are living, R. S. being the third. Our subject was reared in Big Beaver township, on the farm, and attended the Darlington Academy, his earliest life being spent in agricultural pursuits. He subsequently taught school, and afterwards embarked in mercantile business in Franklin county, Pa. In 1861 he removed to Darlington, where he remained until 1865, when he came to Beaver, where he has since resided. The first twelve years spent in Beaver he was engaged in the sewing machine business, most of the time as a general agent. In this he met with financial success, starting in 1865, when the profits to agents were almost as much as the price of a machine now. He was married in Beaver county in 1859, to Nannie E., daughter of William Scott, and of Scotch-Irish descent. She is a sister of John M. Scott, clerk of the courts of Beaver county. Mr. and Mrs. Imbrie's children are J. Maurice, Nannie S., Nettie, Mabel, Grace and Jessie. They are members of the United Presbyterian church. Mr. Imbrie has been an elder and assistant

Sabbath-school superintendent; is now teacher of the Bible class, and is at present superintendent of the Sunday-school in the U. P. church. He is a Republican.

JOHN W. INMAN, merchant, Cannelton, was born in this county in 1840. His grandfather, Henry Inman, came from east of the Allegheny mountains, and was one of the first to settle west of the Ohio river. He died at the age of ninety years. He had three sons and two daughters. The eldest son, Abraham, married Elizabeth Thatcher, and by her had seven children, of whom John W. is the eldest son. Abraham was reared to agricultural pursuits, was a cabinet maker by trade, and afterward a farmer. He died on his farm of 175 acres near the headwaters of Brady's run, aged seventy-six years. John W. was reared on the home farm, and remained there until twenty-two years of age. He was married in 1862 to Hannah Y., daughter of William Edwards, and they have seven children: William G., Elizabeth, Clyde Maud, William Henry, Harrie, Raymond and Leland. Mr. Inman learned the carpenter's trade, which he followed for thirty-two years. Since 1885 he has been a merchant at Cannelton, where he is also postmaster. He is a member of the Baptist church; politically a Democrat.

NELSON INMAN, carpenter and painter, Fallston, was born in Chippewa township. His parents, Abraham and Elizabeth (Thacker) Inman, were natives of Beaver county and of English and German origin. The father and grandfather were farmers, the latter a soldier in the war of 1812 in Captain Henry's Company. The family were among the earliest settlers of Beaver county, and were here when the Indians were numerous in the vicinity. Our subject's uncle was killed by the Indians in that township. Nelson, who is the sixth in a family of eight children, was reared in Chippewa township, and early in life learned the carpenter's trade, afterward taking up painting. He now works at both trades and resides in the borough of Fallston, where he has a neat and substantial residence. In 1861 he enlisted in the 134th Regiment P. V., in Company I. He was in several battles, among them being Fredericksburg, Chancellorsville and Antietam, and was honorably discharged at the close of the war. Returning home he went to the oil regions of Pennsylvania and Virginia, and engaged in drilling wells for six years. For five years he was at Burning Springs, W. Va. Returning to Beaver county he followed farming for a time, and since 1872 has worked at his trade. He was married, in 1867, to Elizabeth Jane, daughter of Thomas and Nancy (Ayers) Small. Mr. Inman is a Democrat in politics and has served as school director. He is a member of the I. O. O. F. lodge and encampment.

JOHN D. IRONS, sheriff, Beaver, was born in Hopewell township, this county, Feb. 21, 1840, and is a son of William and Hannah (Dickson) Irons, natives of Lowellville, Ohio, and of Scotch-Irish descent. The father was born in 1814, is a farmer, and resides in Hopewell township. The grandfather, Solomon Irons, came to Beaver county in 1807, and settled in Hopewell township. He was also a tiller of the soil. John D., the second in the family, was reared on the farm, received his education in the district school, and chose agriculture as his occupation. Aug. 17, 1862, he enlisted in Company A, Pennsylvania Cavalry, serving as commissary sergeant and sergeant-major for several months; was in the battle of Gettysburg, and served until the close of the war. On his return home he resumed farming, which he continued until 1884, when he was elected sheriff of Beaver county, which office he still holds. He was married, in 1861, to Josephine H., daughter of George and Eliza Ann (Harper) Nevin, who are of Scotch-Irish descent. Mr. and Mrs. Irons have four children: Eva, Georgia M., William H. and Samuel C. The family are members of the United Presbyterian church. Mr. Irons is a comrade in the G. A. R.; in politics he is a Republican.

WILLIAM J. JACKSON, contractor and builder, Beaver Falls, was born in Moon township, April 9, 1851, and is a son of Thomas and Melinda (Alcorn) Jackson. His paternal grandfather, James Jackson, a native of Ireland, settled in Industry township about 1810. He was a farmer by occupation and served in the war of 1812. He resided in North Sewickley township for several years, and died there at the age of eighty-two. His children were Robert, James, Thomas, Orville, Sharp and Margaret J. Mr. Jackson's maternal grandfather, William Alcorn, was a farmer of Moon township.

Thomas Jackson is a farmer, and resides in Moon township. His children are William J., Lizzie, John O. and Thomas S. William J. was reared in Moon township, learned the carpenter's trade, and located in Beaver Falls in 1879, where he worked at his trade until 1883, when he commenced his present business. In 1875 he married Maggie E., daughter of James and Nellie (Nelson) Stone, of Slipperyrock township, Lawrence county, Pa., and they have four children: Lizzie L., Maggie V., Robert S. and Mary Adell. Mr. Jackson is a member of the I. O. O. F.; in politics a Democrat.

JOHN S. JACKSON, physician, Beaver Falls, was born in North Sewickley township, April 15, 1853, and is a son of James and Esther (Aiken) Jackson. His paternal grandfather was James Jackson, a farmer of North Sewickley township, and a son of James Jackson, a pioneer of that township. Mr. Jackson's mother was a native of Ireland, her father being one of the early settlers of North Sewickley. John S. was educated in the North Sewickley Academy, and Mt. Union College, Ohio. He began the study of medicine in 1879 with Dr. Joseph Rhodes, of Lawrence county, Pa., entered the medical department of the Baltimore University in 1883, and was graduated in 1886. He passed examination the same year at Jefferson Medical College and located in Beaver Falls, where he began the practice of his profession. Though but recently established, ne has a large practice. He was married, May 12, 1887, to Zelie, daughter of Henry Mentz, of Zelienople, Butler county, Pa. Mr. Jackson is a member of the I. O. O. F.

DAVID JOHNSON, county commissioner, Fallston, was born in Butler county, Pa., April 26, 1819, and is a son of Thomas and Elizabeth (Shanor) Johnson, former born in Maryland and latter in Pennsylvania. The father came to Beaver county in 1826. He was a manufacturer and dealer in sawed lumber in Fallston. David is the fourth in a family of eight children. He attended school in his native town and in Fallston, and also John English's select school in Beaver. Early in life he entered a saw-mill and worked from 1833 until 1844; then went into a bucket shop at Fallston as foreman and continued until 1866, from which year till 1882 he was foreman for Miner & Co.'s sawmill at Fallston, and then was elected county commissioner, which office he has since held. He has been a member of the Republican party since its inception; served as justice of the peace six years, has been school director and a member of the council of Fallston. Mr. Johnson was married, Dec. 23, 1843, to a daughter of Jacob and Sarah Covert, which union has been blessed with the following named children: Jacob M.; Sarah J., wife of J. H. Dean, of Ohio; Rufus P.; Thomas F.; Lydia E., wife of J. S. Mitchell, of Beaver Falls; Charles F.; George Albert; D. R., now in the government printing office at Washington, D. C.; H. W., in Ohio; Mary Ida, the wife of John W. Pontifract, of Pittsburgh, Pa., and Edwin L. There has been as yet no death in the family. Mr. and Mrs. Johnson are members of the Methodist Episcopal church, of which he is class leader. He is a member of the I. O. O. F., and has been through all the chairs, and served as district deputy to the Grand Lodge. He is the oldest member of Lodge 450.

ANDREW JOHNSON, farmer, P. O. Darlington, was born in 1824, in the township of South Beaver. Among the earliest settlers of South Beaver township was Andrew Johnson, who came from Westmoreland county, Pa., in 1790. He was extensively engaged in farming and the purchase and sale of land, having at one time 1,000 acres. He married a Calgore, who bore him ten children. He died in 1849, having lived to a ripe old age. Francis, the fourth child born to Andrew and his wife, died in 1840, aged forty-seven, and his wife in 1879, aged seventy-one. Andrew, our subject, was reared on the farm purchased by his grandfather, and has always been a farmer. He purchased his present home in 1850, consisting of 114 acres. He was married, in 1861, to Ruth Newill, daughter of John and Sarah Newill, of Ohio, and they have had four children: Llewellyn (deceased), Estella, Ora N. and Minerva. Mr. Johnson has been successful in his chosen occupation, having one of the finest homes in South Beaver township. He is a Democrat.

CAPT. JAMES H. JOHNSON, miller, P. O. Ohioville, was born near Ohioville. Beaver county, Pa., Sept. 26, 1840, the fourth of seven children of Matthew and Elizabeth

(Laughlin) Johnson. His father, a son of James Johnson, who was a native of Pennsylvania and one of the early settlers of this county, was born in this county, in 1806, where he followed farming and for several years was engaged in shipbuilding. His mother was a native of Lancaster, Pa., born in 1810. Matthew Johnson was the second eldest of a family of three sons and three daughters, of whom two, Rebecca and John, live in Ohio township, Beaver county; Ann and Samuel live at Meadville, Pa.; Eliza is deceased. He died in 1879; his widow is still living. The subject of this sketch spent his youth and school days in Ohio township, and at the age of nineteen went to Jackson county, Ind., where he taught school until April 18, 1861, at which time he enlisted in Company H, 6th Regiment Indiana Infantry, and was at once engaged in the battles of Laurel Hill and Carrick's Ford, W. Va.; was discharged Aug. 13, and re-enlisted Oct. 7, 1861, in Company K, 50th Regiment Indiana Infantry. Aug. 20, 1862, he was taken prisoner by Gen. Morgan at Gallatin, Tenn.; was exchanged in November, and sent to Jackson, Tenn. Dec. 31, 1862, he was in the battle of Parker's Cross Roads. In June, 1863, he was promoted to second lieutenant, and soon after was sent to Helena, Ark., and placed in the Seventh Army Corps under Maj.-Gen. Fred Steele. On the 10th of September, 1863, this corps captured Little Rock, Ark., and soon after went into winter quarters at Louisburg. In the spring of 1864 he was in the Red River campaign, and for twenty days, from April 1st, they fought nearly every day; April 26th they made a retreat from Camden, Ark., but were overtaken, and fought the battle of Jenkin's Ferry, where Brig.-Gen. S. A. Rice, the captain of Company K, Richard McCowick and our subject, were among the many wounded. The captain returned home and Mr. Johnson remained in charge of the company although unfit to be on duty. Notwithstanding their condition and limited supply of food they began the march to Little Rock, and were seven days without food. In December, 1864, Mr. Johnson was promoted to captain and assigned to Company C, 50th Regiment Ind. Veterans; afterward went to New Orleans, crossed the Gulf of Mexico, and on March 27, 1865, to April 9, fought day and night at the siege of Spanish Fort, Ala. In May, 1865, at Montgomery, Ala., the regiment was consolidated with the 52d Regiment of Veterans: discharged Sept. 10 at Montgomery, Ala., and mustered out Sept. 19, 1865, at Indianapolis, Ind., making a service of over four years and two months, when our subject returned to Beaver county. In the fall of 1869 he went to Mason county, W. Va., where he taught school until the fall of 1879, when he returned to Ohio township, and erected a saw and grist mill, which he has since operated. He is also proprietor of the Gas-Light Poultry Yards, where he is engaged in breeding high classed poultry. While in West Virginia, about 1876, he was licensed to preach by the Mission Baptist church, of which he and his wife are members. In May, 1871, he returned to Indiana and married Mary Storey, daughter of Stephen and Elizabeth (Brewer) Storey, born Feb. 19, 1853. Three children resulted from this union: Elizabeth Jane, Olivia Ann and Charles Matthew, all at home. Mr. Johnson has been elected by the Republican party to the offices of assessor, constable and collector, and now holds the last named offices.

F. A. JUDD, teacher, Darlington, was born in Cleveland, Ohio, Oct. 14, 1849, and is a son of Albert S. and Jennette Pope Judd; his ancestors were of Scotch origin. He was educated at the Rectory school, Camden, Conn., and at Clark's Academy, Canandaigua, N. Y. He was married, in 1870, to Alice, daughter of Thomas C. Floyd, of Cleveland, Ohio, and their children were Albert F., William P., Thomas E. (deceased), Howard L. and Louisa J. Mr. Judd began the study of law with Hon. W. C. McFarland, of Cleveland, Ohio, in 1867, and was admitted to the bar in 1870. He came to Beaver county in 1872; he has taught in the public schools eight terms. From 1884 to 1886 he was assistant teacher in the academy, and in December of the latter year he was elected principal. He is a member of the Presbyterian church; in political preference a Republican.

JACOB KELLER, glass mould maker, Beaver Falls, was born in Pittsburgh, July 15, 1850, and is a son of Jacob and Dora (Ammon) Keller, who came from Germany in 1843, and settled in Pittsburgh. Jacob was reared in that city, and served an apprenticeship of four years (1865–1869) at his trade with Andrew Thompson, after which he worked for McKee Bros., for ten years. In 1879 he located in Beaver Falls, and became one of the founders of the Coöperative Flint Glass Company, where he has since been employed. In 1874 he married Minnie, daughter of John Heil, of Pittsburgh, by whom he has four children: William, Lillie, Florence and Albert. He is a member of the board of directors of the Coöperative Flint Glass Works Company; politically he is a Democrat.

R. S. KENNEDY, editor of the *Star*, Beaver, was born in this county April 7, 1841, a son of William A. and Rosa (Shannon) Kennedy, natives of Pennsylvania and of Scotch-Irish descent. His father, who is a prominent farmer residing in Independence township, this county, had one son and one daughter, R. S. being the eldest. Our subject was reared on the farm in Independence township, and attended the common schools and Beaver Academy. He studied medicine, graduated from Jefferson Medical College, Philadelphia, in 1856, and was engaged in the practice of his profession in Beaver county for ten years. Afterward he carried on the drug business in New Brighton for one year, and Oct. 5, 1877, he engaged in his present business, in which he has been very successful. April 7, 1874, he was married to Mary A., daughter of David Patton, of English descent, and two children have been born to them: Owen and Ola. Mrs. Kennedy is a member of the Presbyterian church. In politics Mr. Kennedy is a Democrat.

WILLIAM W. KERR, bookkeeper, Beaver Falls, was born in Freedom, this county, June 23, 1833, and is a son of Thomas G. and Grizzy H. (McCurdy) Kerr. His paternal grandfather was Nathaniel Kerr, of Scotch-Irish descent, a soldier of the war of 1812 and a pioneer farmer of this county; he reared a family of three children: Thomas G., Mary A. (Mrs. Thomas Crooks), and Nathaniel P. Of these Thomas G., a blacksmith by trade, lived and died in this county. He had three children who grew to maturity: William W., Rev. Nathaniel P. and Mary (Mrs. George McCaskey). The maternal grandfather of our subject was William McCurdy, a pioneer of Brighton township, this county. William W. was reared and educated in Freedom, where he learned the trade of ship carpenter, which he followed from 1849 until 1877. Since then he has been a bookkeeper. He located in 1886 in Beaver Falls, where he has since resided. In 1856 he married Nancy J., daughter of Thomas and Abigail Devenney, of New Brighton, this county, and by her has four children: Thomas C., Olive S., Mary M. and Myra E. Mr. Kerr is a member of the Methodist Episcopal church; he is a F. & A. M.; in politics a Republican.

JOHN KIRKPATRICK, farmer and stock grower, was born on the farm where he now resides, in Brighton township, Oct. 20, 1888, and is a son of Alexander and Jenney (Noss) Kirkpatrick, former a native of County Antrim, Ireland, latter of Pennsylvania. Alexander Kirkpatrick commenced farming in 1823, when he first came from Ireland, in Maryland, and the next year moved to Beaver county. In early life he studied engineering and surveying. He was married in 1833 in Beaver county, and died in 1838, three months before John was born. John attended the common schools, and chose farming for his occupation. In early life he taught school for three winters. His sisters, Eliza J., and Mary, are both at home and attend to keeping the house. Mr. Kirkpatrick is a Republican; he has been constable and assessor five years, and township treasurer and clerk nine years.

JACOB KLEIN, dealer in flour, feed, and farming implements, Beaver Falls, was born in Marion township, Beaver county, March 9, 1860, and is a son of Jacob and Elizabeth (Blinn) Klein, natives of Germany, and residents of Beaver county for over thirty years. They now reside in Pulaski township and have three children: Jacob, Charles, and Mary. Jacob came to Beaver Falls in 1884, and engaged in butchering one year. In 1885 he embarked in his present business, and is having a large and successful trade. In February, 1886, he married Annie, daughter of Conrad Zahn, of Pulaski, and has one child, Charles Theodore. Mr. Klein is a member of the Junior Order United American Mechanics; politically he is a Democrat.

AMOS KNIGHT, farmer, P. O. Industry, was born on the farm where he now resides, Feb. 15, 1828, and is a son of David and Elizabeth (Mason) Knight, natives of Pennsylvania, former of whom was a son of John Knight, of German descent. Mrs. Elizabeth Knight's father, George Mason, was a native of Pennsylvania, and he and John Knight were among the first settlers of Beaver county. David and Elizabeth Knight had thirteen children, six of whom yet survive: Louis (in Industry township), Amos, Emanuel, Cynthia, Elmira and Elizabeth. Amos was married April 30, 1863, to Matilda, daughter of Michael and Ella Mason, and they have had five children, three now living: Thomas J., David J., and Mary V., all at home. Mr. Knight was educated in the common schools of his native township, and has been a successful farmer. He owns 173 acres of well-improved land. In politics he is a Democrat. Mrs. Knight is a member of the United Brethren church.

MARTIN L. KNIGHT, superintendent of schools, Beaver Falls, was born in Industry township Sept. 22, 1837, and is a son of Richard and Elizabeth (Ewing) Knight, former a native of Adams county, and latter of Huntingdon county, Pa. His paternal grandfather was John Knight, who settled in Industry (then Ohio) township in 1809. His children were Mary (Mrs. Archibald Seabrooks), Jacob, John, Daniel, Richard, David, Catherine (Mrs. Charles Bevington), Elizabeth (Mrs. Samuel Biddle), Susan (Mrs. John McLaughlin) and Rebecca (Mrs. Simeon Mason). Mr Knight's maternal grandfather, Samuel Ewing, a native of Ireland, settled in Industry (then Ohio) township in 1803. Richard Knight was a pioneer of Industry township, where he resided until his death in 1868. He was a soldier of the war of 1812. His wife died in 1879 at Beaver Falls. The children who grew to maturity were Nancy (Mrs. George Rich), Maria (Mrs. James Alcorn), Lucinda (Mrs. Mason Bevington) and Martin L. The latter was educated in the public and select schools of his native town and Beaver Academy. From 1856 until 1863 he taught in common schools, and in 1863 was elected principal of the Bridgewater public school, remaining one year. From 1867 until 1873 he taught in the graded school of Industry township, and in 1873 was elected county superintendent of schools for a term of three years. In August, 1877, he located in Beaver Falls, where he has been principal of the public schools until the present time (1888). In 1881 he was elected borough superintendent of schools for a term of three years; re-elected in 1884, and again in 1887. Mr. Knight was married Oct. 1, 1863, to Virginia C., daughter of Jeremiah and Elizabeth (Fawcett) Gardner, of Industry township, and by her he has two children: Lulu N. and Byrd C. Mr. Knight was one of the projectors of the Beaver Valley Street Railway Company, of which he has been President since Sept. 17, 1884.

JOHN KOESSLER, blacksmith, Beaver Falls, was born in France, March 23, 1841, and is a son of John and Catherine Koessler, who came to America in 1844 and settled in Pittsburgh, where John was reared and learned his trade. He has worked in a glass house since he was ten years of age, with the exception of three years that he was in the army. He enlisted in 1861, in Co. L., P. V. I. under Col. Gary, being afterward transferred to the 147th P. V., and was honorably discharged at the expiration of his service. In 1879 he located in Beaver Falls, and was one of the organizers of the Co-operative Glass Company, in which he has since been interested as a stockholder, and served one year on the board of directors. His wife was Elizabeth, a daughter of Frank Pates of Pittsburgh, by whom he has five sons: John, Edward, George, Henry, and Frank. Mr. Koessler is a member of the Catholic church; in politics he is independent.

LAWRENCE KONKEL and his brother Michael Konkel settled in South Beaver township, Beaver county, in the year 1797, on a 400 acre tract of land, and divided it between them equally. They came from Westmoreland county, Pa., and were of German descent. A family of children were born to Michael, among the eldest being John, a farmer, who married Mary, daughter of John Cline, of Ohio. Eleven children were born to this couple, Michael being among the youngest. John died in 1862, aged sixty-seven years. Michael was born and reared on the farm he now owns, and contains 165 acres, nearly all of which is under cultivation. He received a common-school education. In 1853 he married Margaret, daughter of Andrew Ferney, of Ohio, and three children were born to them, one only surviving, J. E., who was born on his grandfather's farm and has always lived there. He was married in 1879 to Miss M. E. Badders, daughter of George Badders, of this county, and has one child, William H. Michael has always taken a special interest in farming, but has given way to his son, J. E., who successfully superintends the work. He is a member of the Presbyterian church.

PHILIP KUCKERT, glass packer, Beaver Falls, was born in Germany May 1, 1843, and is a son of Peter and Kate Kuckert, who came to America in 1846 and settled in Pittsburgh. Philip was reared in that city, came to Beaver Falls in 1879, and became one of the organizers of the Coöperative Flint Glass Works, of which he is a stockholder, and where he has since been employed; his wife was Sarah, daughter of Lewis Wiegel, of Pittsburgh, and by her he has four children: Emma, Laura Albert and Charles. Mr. Kuckert is a member of the A. O. U. W; in politics he is a Republican.

HENRY KURTZ, iron moulder, Beaver Falls, was born in Germany March 9, 1850, and is a son of Adam and Anna (Bittner) Kurtz, also natives of Germany, who came to America in 1849, locating in Westmoreland county, and later moving to Allegheny county, Pa., where they now reside. Henry was reared and educated in Allegheny City, and learned his trade with Alexander Bradley, of Pittsburgh, where he served an apprenticeship of three years. Since 1869 he has worked as a journeyman in various sections of the country, in the meantime serving as manager of the A. F. Wolf Stove Foundry, Beaver Falls, three years, and manager of Martin's Ferry, Ohio, Stove Works eighteen months. He has been a resident of Beaver Falls since 1880, and is now in the employ of the Howard Stove Company as journeyman iron moulder. He is liberal in religious views, is a member of the Iron Moulder's Union, Royal Arcanum and Improved Order Red Men. In politics he is a Republican.

GENERAL ABNER LACOCK. Concerning a once prominent man in Pennsylvania Charles Lauman, in his *Biographical Annals of the Civil Government of the United States,* says, in 1876; "ABNER LACOCK. Born in Virginia in 1770. Without the advantage of much early education, he raised himself by his talents to eminence as a legislator, statesman and civilian. He filled various public stations for a period of nearly forty years; was a representative in congress from Pennsylvania from 1811 to 1813, and United States Senator from 1813 to 1819. He died in Beaver county, Pennsylvania, April 12, 1837." This brief paragraph contains the germ of a biography rich with important lessons and fraught with hopeful encouragement to the struggling genius of this, a more highly favored age.

The subject of this sketch, known in his day as General Abner Lacock, was born on Cub Run, near Alexandria, Va., July 9, 1770, his father being English, his mother French. When Abner was quite young he removed with his father and settled upon a farm in Washington county, Pa., but in 1796 he became a citizen and one of the early settlers of what is now the town of Beaver. Sept. 19, 1796, he received from Governor Thomas Mifflin, a commission as justice of the peace for Pitt township, Allegheny county, and thus was the first justice in what afterward became Beaver county. The signal ability and natural justice, exhibited by him in this office, commended him to his fellow citizens, who, in 1801, elected him the first representative to the state legislature. This position he held until 1803, when he was, at the organization of the county, selected as one of the associate judges.* In this capacity he served but a year when his constituents calling him to serve them in the house of representatives of his adopted state for four consecutive sessions. In 1808 he was chosen to represent the counties of Allegheny, Beaver and Butler in the state senate, a position he filled with ability and credit and to the satisfaction of the people. But a higher sphere of usefulness was to open to him. Hon. William Henry in an able article on Gen. Abner Lacock, published in the *Western Argus* for April 19, 1837, says:

---

*The first court held in Beaver county, commencing Feb. 6, 1804, was held at the house of Abner Lacock, at that time one of the innkeepers of Beaver.

BIOGRAPHIES—WEST SIDE. 677

"In 1810 the question of a war with Great Britain agitated the country in every quarter, and the strong feeling of indignation in the minds of the people against the usurpations of that government, the repeated insults she had cast upon our flag, impressing our seamen, and crippling our commerce, brought many men of high character and talent into the national councils, and among them was Abner Lacock. The people of his district called him out as the *War Candidate*, and secured his election by a triumphant majority. His friends were not deceived in their expectations. In congress he took a bold stand for war measures, and in that period of gloom and despondency, stood firmly by the Democratic administration of James Madison in the noble effort to sustain the character and independence of the Republic, and the rights of our citizens. While in the house he took part in the proceedings on most questions of public policy, and at all times showed forth with good effect the natural sound sense and statesmanlike views of his strong and vigorous mind. In that body he possessed great influence, and with the chief magistrate to an extraordinary degree. So honorably had he acquitted himself in the house, that in the spring of 1813, the legislature of Pennsylvania, with great unanimity, elected him a senator of the United States, which station he filled with credit and ability for six years. During all this time, when not called from home in the public service, with true Republican plainness, like Cincinnatus of old, he followed the plow, and tilled the soil with laborious assiduity, attending steadily to all the duties of an American farmer; at the same time endeavoring by observation and extensive reading to make up for the want of an early education."

General Lacock served in the National House of Representatives during the Twelfth Congress, and in the National Senate during the Thirteenth, Fourteenth and Fifteenth Congresses. His friendship for Madison and Monroe was as strong as his dislike for Andrew Jackson was intense. During the closing year of his senatorial career he was a member of the committee which investigated General Jackson's conduct in the Seminole war, and was the author of the report which severely criticised the hero of Orleans. It is said that General Jackson felt the rebuke so keenly that he declared he would, the first opportunity he had, *cut Lacock's ears off*. General Lacock tarried in Washington several days for the purpose of giving the irate Indian fighter an opportunity to execute his threat, but was not disturbed, being permitted to leave with his ears of natural size.

General Lacock was a favorite with men of national character. On one occasion Henry Clay called him to occupy the speaker's chair during the discussion of an important question, a worthy compliment to a "new member." When Mr. Clay was passing down the Ohio in 1847, he stopped at Beaver Point, where he made a brief address in which he stated that he had long known Beaver county through its representatives in Congress. Said he: "I remember well Abner Lacock, who stood shoulder to shoulder with me and others before and during the late war with Great Britain, than whom Pennsylvania never produced a better and very few abler men."

He was specially active in all movements that looked toward internal improvements. Shortly after his retirement from the United States senate, he entered actively into a scheme for joining the waters of the Delaware and the Ohio by a state line of canals and railroads. On the 11th of April, 1825, five commissioners were chosen to make this preliminary survey, consisting of as follows: John Sergeant, William Darlington, David Scott, Robert M. Patterson and Abner Lacock. The latter, a member of the Board of Commissioners, was chosen to supervise the construction of the west division of the canal from Pittsburgh to Johnstown. Under his direction, mainly, this division was built, and as a compliment, the first canal boat west of the Allegheny mountains was called the "General Abner Lacock." He was subsequently chosen a commissioner to survey and construct the Pennsylvania and Ohio Canal, generally known as the "Cross Cut Canal," joining the Erie Division of the Pennsylvania Canal with the Portsmouth and Ohio Canal. This occurred in 1836, the year prior to his death. General Lacock's devotion to common-school education was so sincere and earnest, that he is justly ranked as standing on an equal footing as a champion of popular education with Governor Wolf and Thaddeus Stevens.

General Lacock was of average height, compactly built and well proportioned. He was was strong and athletic. With brown hair, blue eyes and ruddy complexion, he was a man who strongly impressed those with whom he mingled. His social life was pleasant and happy, his wife being gifted with strong intelligence and great business tact. She ably managed his affairs in his absence. The death of General Lacock occurred April 12, 1837, at the age of sixty-five years, nine months and three days. He was one of Beaver county's most noted and highly respected citizens, whose impress upon the destiny of the county was most marked. His family was as follows: Bethsheba (Lacock) Pentland, wife of Judge Ephraim Pentland; Atlas E. Lacock; Minerva (Lacock) Reno, a widow in her ninety-first year, still living in Rochester and receiving a pension of the war 1812 (she and the widow of Atlas E. Lacock are the only pensioners of the war of 1812 receiving their stipends from the government through the office of T. M. Taylor, Esq., Rochester); Caroline (Lacock) Bousman; Adelaide (Lacock) Linton; and Abner P. Lacock, who died April 20, 1888. One of the sons died a cadet at West Point, on the 15th of October, 1818.

W. A. LAIRD, contractor, P. O. Beaver, was born in Brighton township, this county, May 27, 1823, and is a son of Josiah and Jane (Anderson) Laird, former a native of Washington county, latter of Chester county, and both of Scotch-Irish descent. His grandfather, William, and father came to Beaver county in 1810, and settled in Brighton. His father died in 1855. He had five children, of whom W. A. is the third. Our subject was reared in Beaver borough; his educational advantages being limited, and early in life he began to learn the trade of a house plasterer. He served an apprenticeship of four years. He was then ready to start for himself, but had not a dollar in the world. He took a contract to plaster a house and was to take his pay all out of the store. He made arrangements with the man he was boarding with to take part of the goods, and has followed the business of contracting ever since, sometimes employing twenty and twenty-five men. The college and county house at Beaver are among the buildings he contracted for. He owns valuable property in Beaver, where he has resided most of his life. He is a Republican in politics, but never held any office except court crier eight years. He was married in 1850 to Nancy, daughter of William McCallister. She is of Scotch-Irish origin. Her father served as register and recorder of Beaver county. Their children are Josiah, a merchant at Beaver Falls; William, of Kansas City (he chose his father's trade and is a contractor); Richard R., in business in New York City; F. H., a lawyer, who studied with H. Hice, ex-judge of Beaver county, and was admitted to the bar in 1884; Albert G., a clerk in New York City; and Anna G. and Matthew M., at home. Mr. and Mrs. Laird were formerly members of the United Presbyterian church, of which he was thirty years an elder. In 1887 they moved their membership to the Presbyterian church in Beaver.

JOSIAH LAIRD, grocer, Beaver Falls, was born in Brighton township, Sept. 21, 1851, and is a son of W. A. and Eleanor (Green) Laird. His paternal grandparents were Josiah and Jeannette (Anderson) Laird, pioneers of this county. His maternal grandfather was William McAllister, a pioneer of Bridgewater, where he kept a general store for a time, though he was a surveyor by occupation, and in the early days an official of the county. W. A. Laird is a contractor and plasterer by trade. He has eight children living: Josiah, William M., Richard R., Frank H., Jeannette A., Anna G., Albert N. and Matthew M. Josiah was reared in Beaver, and by trade is a plasterer, an occupation he followed eight years. Since locating in Beaver Falls in 1883, he has been successfully engaged in the grocery business. Politically he is a Republican.

HORATIO M. LARGE (deceased) was born in Philadelphia May 28, 1816, and was a son of Daniel and Mary Large, of England, former of whom settled in what is now Beaver Falls in 1828, and with James Patterson purchased 600 acres of land. Daniel Large was interested in the first flour and saw mill in the place, and with his brother Christopher built the first cotton mill in the place. His children were Daniel, Christopher, William, Horatio M., Eliza (Mrs. James Patterson), Ann and Ellen (Mrs. Leonard Krouse). Horatio M. was reared in Beaver Falls from twelve years of age. He learned the cabinet maker's trade with John Sims, and followed it for several years; then engaged in carpenter work until 1880, when he retired. In 1860 he erected a planing mill, which he conducted about ten years. He married Elizabeth, daughter of Charles and Jane Carter, pioneers of this county, former of whom was forger in the first furnace built in Beaver county, and made the first iron in the county. Seven of the children of Mr. Large are living: Charles, Christopher, Daniel, William, Ella (Mrs. George Liscomb), Elizabeth and Hannah.

MILTON LAWRENCE was born in Beaver, Pa., in November, 1801. He was the eldest child of Samuel Lawrence, for many years prothonotary of Beaver county, and the cashier of the Bank of Beaver, established in 1816. His early life was spent in his native place, where he was educated. He studied medicine under Dr. Milo Adams, a well known physician of that day, and in 1826 settled in Hookstown in the southern part of the county, where he soon acquired a large practice. He early acquired a taste for politics, as the average boy reared in Beaver does, and in 1839, as a Whig, was elected prothonotary of the county over Samuel W. Sprott, the Democratic candidate, by 59 majority. He was reëlected in 1842 and again in 1845, holding the office until 1848, and was then succeeded by John Collins. His duties completed in the prothonotary's office he at once returned to Hookstown and resumed the practice of his profession. He was a candidate for congress in 1850, but was beaten by one vote by John Allison, afterwards register of the treasury of the United States for many years. In the election following Greene township gave a majority of votes for Mr. Allison's opponent, something quite unusual in that day and since. Hon. John Scott, one of the associate judges of Beaver county, having deceased, on March 11, 1862, Governor Curtin commissioned Dr. Lawrence to fill the vacancy until the ensuing election when, Oct. 14, 1862, he was elected a Republican, beating that incorruptible and noble old Democrat, Robert Potter, of Raccoon by 480 votes; on the 8th of October, 1867, he was reëlected, and again October 13, 1872, serving continuously till November 6, 1877, a period of fifteen years and eight months, and so well was he acquainted with the duties of his office that in March term, 1873, when Judge Acheson, who was presiding, was called home suddenly, Judge Lawrence presided during the quarter sessions week with marked ability. In the year 1854, when Know-Nothingism was sweeping over the county, Judge Lawrence, with Agnew, Collins and others, was unflinching in his denunciation of its aims and tendencies.

Judge Lawrence was a clear headed, bright man, strong in his likes and dislikes, a born politician possessed of unbounded influence throughout Greene and Hanover, and of a strong influence over the county, and although he was inclined to reward his friends and punish his enemies, he was kind hearted as a child, even to those who deserved nothing from him. Although he always had a large practice yet he collected so little of his money that he died comparatively a poor man. In 1872 he removed to Beaver. While on a visit to his daughter, Mrs. Lizzie McKissock at Altona. Ill., he was taken ill and died on Sabbath, Oct. 2, 1880. His remains were brought back to Beaver, and laid in their final resting place in the cemetery of that place. There they laid him on a calm October evening, a fit emblem of a peaceful close of a busy, useful life, its working days ended, its Sabbath entered on—the rest that remaineth for the soul.

WILL H. LEIGH. artist and photographer, Beaver Falls, was born in East Liverpool, Ohio, June 3, 1856, and is a son of Peter and Emma (Whitton) Leigh, of Derbyshire, England. His father served in the war of the rebellion in the 3d Ohio Battery, and was killed in a railroad accident in Tennessee in 1863, while engaged in the line of duty. Mr. Leigh was reared in Beaver county, located in Pittsburgh, and in 1879 entered the gallery of H. Bowen as a student in photography, remaining nearly two years. He then took a course of portrait painting under Henry Wagner, of Pittsburgh. Mr. Leigh located in Beaver Falls in 1883, where he has one of the best arranged photographic art establishments in this section. He is an artist not only in name, but in education; one who understands the art principles of lighting and posing his subjects, wherein lie the true merits of a portrait.

CHARLES LEVI, baker and grocer, Beaver Falls, is a native of Würtemberg, Germany, where he was reared and educated. He came to America in 1866, located in

Beaver Falls in 1868 and opened a bakery, which, with the exception of two years, he has since continued, being the pioneer baker of Beaver Falls. In 1885 he added a line of groceries in connection with his other interests, and is among the prominent and successful business men of the place. He is a member of the I. O. O. F.; in politics a Republican.

DR. JOHN C. LEVIS, in his lifetime one of the well-known and most skillful surgeons and physicians of Beaver county, was born in Zelienople, Butler county, Jan. 3, 1830, and died July 26, 1887, at his home in Bridgewater, Beaver county, in his fifty-eighth year. His father was the late Hon. John Levis, who, for several years subsequent to 1848, represented the Allegheny-Butler district in the state senate. Our subject attended school at Harmony, Butler county, where he acquired the rudiments of a classical education, and his preliminary studies completed, he read medicine with Dr. Lusk, of Zelienople, subsequently attending lectures at the Western Reserve Medical College at Cleveland, from which he graduated in 1851. His first practice began at Columbiana, Ohio, in April, 1853, and continued at that place one year. Meantime, Nov. 2, 1853, he married Miss Catherine Dehoff, of the same town. Only one child, a daughter, blessed this union; she died at the age of two and a half years. In April, 1854, Dr. Levis changed his location to Darlington, Beaver county, Pa., and practiced his profession there until January, 1857, when he removed to Bridgewater, where he resided, except the interruptions of army life, until the day of his death. When the war of the rebellion broke out, the Doctor's patriotic impulses constrained him to enter the army. He was mustered as assistant surgeon of the 85th P. V. on the 23d of October, 1861, at Uniontown, and served in the Peninsular campaign of McClellan; promoted to be surgeon of the 101st Regiment Sept. 15, 1862, but two days prior to the battle of Antietam, having been assigned to the charge of the hospital at Chambersburg, Pa., Sept. 25, he was captured by Gen. J. E. B. Stewart, on Oct. 10, and signed the parole of his fellow-prisoners; ordered to Jefferson Barracks, St. Louis, Mo., Dec. 22, and remained on duty until the following June, when he was assigned to duty on the U. S. Hospital steamer, "R. C. Wood," then running between Vicksburg and Memphis. In this capacity he served during Grant's siege and capture of Vicksburg. In November, 1863, he was ordered to Pittsburgh to be surgeon of the post, and remained about nineteen months. Of his arduous labors there, a city paper said:

"Dr. John C. Levis, examining surgeon of this Post, Girard House, during the year ending Dec. 1, 1864, examined 10,964 recruits, and visited 1,024 sick and wounded soldiers at their houses in the two cities and boroughs, besides attending to all who have been able to visit him at his office. The Doctor has also performed a large number of surgical operations with success, some of the latter being of a difficult and complicated character."

President Grant, in recognition of the Doctor's services during the war, proffered him a consulship to Mexico. Precarious health, however, forced him to decline the honor. He was a member of Rochester Post, No. 183, G. A. R., and an unswerving advocate of the principles of the Republican party. He was noted for taking an unusual interest in the collection of antiquated papers and books. He was kind and generous, a foe to sham and mere pretense, and an ardent supporter of every enterprise which looked to the mental elevation and amelioration of the people. He is survived by his devoted wife, who shared with him many of the trials and inconveniences of army life, and by four brothers: O. D., Henry M., Robert S. and Isaac N., and one sister, Miss Elizabeth H.

NEWTON LEYDA, merchant, Beaver Falls, was born in Lancaster county, Pa., Aug. 29, 1866, and is a son of J. N. and Mary A. (Jeffries) Leyda. He was reared and educated in Allegheny City, and came to Beaver Falls in 1885, where he was a clerk in a shoe store ten months. In October, 1886, he embarked in the boot and shoe business, and by strict attention to business and courteous treatment of all is securing a large and growing trade.

FRANK LINDEMAN, glass presser, Beaver Falls, was born near Berlin, Germany, May

27, 1862, and is a son of Charles and Emily (Groth) Lindeman, who came to America in 1872, located in Allegheny City, and in 1877 removed to Beaver Falls, where they now reside. His father was a glass worker and a member of the Coöperative Flint Glass Company of Beaver Falls, of which he was one of the organizers in 1879. Mr. Lindeman's mother is an artist in the making of fruit wreaths, and received a medal for the finest display at the Beaver County Fair in 1888. Our subject was educated in the public schools of Allegheny City, and graduated from the Iron City Commercial College Sept. 13, 1884. He was in mercantile trade in Beaver Falls in 1884 and 1885, and is a stockholder and one of the organizers of the New Brighton Glass Company, established in 1886, where he has since been employed as a glass presser. He is a member of the German Lutheran church, has served one term as county committeeman of the fifth ward, Beaver Falls, and in politics is a Republican.

GEN. JOHN SMITH LITTELL comes of a martial family, and is the only native of Beaver county who rose to the rank of general during the war of the rebellion. His grandfather, William, came to this country from Belfast, Ireland, prior to the Revolution, and served as a clerk in the colonial forces, in which his brother James was a private. After the close of that struggle William settled in Hanover township, this county. His wife, Elizabeth (Walker) Littell, often spent the night with her children in treetops to avoid surprises by hostile Indians, and her brother, Robert Walker, was killed by the savages near Toledo in 1813. William Littell died about 1820, and was supposed to be about eighty years of age at the time. His wife was the daughter of a former sweetheart of his, and must have been many years his junior. They had ten children, nine of whom grew to maturity: James died in Calcutta, Ohio; Betsey married John Reed, and died in Pittsburgh; Jane married Joseph Calhoon, and died in Greene township; David lived on the old homestead, which is still in possession of his heirs; Mary married James Todd, and died at Beaver Falls; Thomas was last heard of in Oregon; Alice, wife of William Sharp, died at Mechanicstown, Ohio; Agnes, the youngest of the family (married Bennet Libby, who died in Rochester, this county), now resides in Pittsburgh. William, fourth child of William and Elizabeth Littell, was born in Hanover township, in 1794, and his wife, Cynthia, daughter of John Smith, of Gettysburg, was born near Pittsburgh, in 1801. William was an American soldier during the war of 1812. He reared his family under the religious instruction of Rev. John Anderson, of the Seceder's church, who founded a theological seminary, probably the first west of the Alleghany Mountains, from which grew the present institution located at Xenia, Ohio. Cynthia Littell died in 1853, and her husband a year later. They had twelve children: Gen. John S.; Eliza (Mrs. G. L. Robertson) resides at Mechanicsburg, this county; Rebecca Ann (Mrs. John Calhoun), in Raccoon township; Maria (Mrs. J. P. Ewing), in Raccoon township; Nancy (Mrs. John Ewing), in Lawrence, Kan.; Cynthia Jane (Mrs. John McHenry), in Raccoon township; Washington, in Creston, Ohio; William M., in Corydon, Iowa; David, in Lawrence, Kan.; James M. died at Rolla, Mo., in 1862, from disease contracted in the Union army; and Henry C., died at Beaver, in 1867, from the same cause; Morgan died when one year old; William M., whose second name is McElwee, after Rev. Wm. M. McElwee, was a captain in the 23d Iowa Infantry, and James was a private in the same regiment; Washington and Henry served in the 16th Ohio Infantry. John Smith Littell was born in Hanover Oct. 22, 1822, and was educated in the common schools. He developed a strong mathematical talent, but gave his attention chiefly to agriculture until diverted by military affairs. In 1845 he married Mary Calhoon, who was born in Raccoon township, in 1821, a daughter of Richard and Sarah (Moffet) Calhoon, the former a native of Beaver county, the latter of Ireland. In 1866 Gen. Littell was elected sheriff of Beaver county, on the Republican ticket, and made an excellent record in that office. On the expiration of his term in 1869, he retired to the farm which he now occupies, in Big Beaver township, and which he purchased in 1867. This property is located three miles south of New Galilee (his postoffice address), and contains 223 acres of valuable land, rich in fine clay and coal. All the members of the family attend the United Presbyterian Church, in which the General is

HISTORY OF BEAVER COUNTY.

an elder. All the seven children reside near the paternal home: Richard W. served three and one fourth years during the civil war in the 76th Pennsylvania Regiment, going as a drummer in his father's company, and is now on the home farm; William P. served twenty months in the 6th Ohio Cavalry, and is now on a farm in Chippewa township; Robert C. is a street car conductor in Allegheny City; Isadore S. is the wife of B. B. White, and resides in Cannelton; Harriet Frances, Joseph M. and Ina Belle reside with their parents. Of the General's military service Bates' *Martial Deeds of Pennsylvania* says:

"He early joined a militia company and in 1853 was elected captain, and afterward brigade inspector of the nineteenth division. He recruited a company for the 76th Pennsylvania Regiment, of which he was captain. Soon after its organization it was ordered to the Department of the South, where it was engaged with the enemy at the capture of Fort Pulaski, and in the battles of Pocotaligo, James Island, Morris Island, and in the first and second assaults on Fort Wagner, in all of which he lead his company with a steadiness and devotion which characterized his entire service. At Morris Island, on the 10th of July, he was slightly wounded, but kept the field. On the following morning he was again hit, receiving a flesh wound in the right arm and side. The assault on Fort Wagner proved very disastrous to the regiment, the loss being nearly half its entire strength. In the summer of 1864 it was taken to Virginia and attached to the army of the James. On the 31st of May Captain Littell was promoted to the rank of lieutenant-colonel, and on the following day, in the action of Cold Harbor, received a severe wound, the missile entering the right thigh, tearing quite through both limbs and emerging from the left After lying in the hospital for a time he was taken to his home, but his wound was slow in healing and his recovery was protracted. On the 17th of August following he was promoted to colonel. In January he sailed with the expeditions, first under Gens. Butler and Weitzel, and finally under Gen. Terry, for the reduction of Fort Fisher, commanding the approaches to Wilmington, N. C. Col. Littell was of Pennepacker's brigade, and followed that gallant officer in the desperate assault upon this stronghold. In the midst of the struggle, and while leading on his regiment in the face of a destructive fire. he was struck by a minie-ball in the left thigh, which passed through, penetrating a pocket-book containing a roll of bank notes, and finally lodging in the body. It was an ever memorable day for the armies of the Union, and though experiencing intense suffering, he still had spirit to rejoice over the glorious victory achieved. He was removed to Fortress Monroe, after having the ball extracted, and, when sufficiently recovered, to his home. As a merited recognition of his valor on this field upon the recommendation of Gen. Terry, he was breveted brigadier-general."

While recovering from the wounds received at Cold Harbor some of Col. Littell's inferior officers tried to secure his discharge thinking to thus make better their own chances of promotion, but he returned to duty while his wounds were yet running, and those who "digged a pit" for him in his absence afterward fell therein.

JAMES LUKE, retired farmer, P. O. Enon Valley, came from Ireland in 1821 and settled in Beaver (now Lawrence) county. David Luke came from Ireland (County Antrim) about 1810. Some time after his arrival, or about 1815, he moved to Beaver county and purchased a farm of fifty acres near where the town of Bridgewater stands. He married Sarah, daughter of Patrick and Elnor Wallace, also of Ireland. Of their three children James is the eldest. He was born and reared on the farm, and resides on the property purchased by his father in 1820, consisting of 100 acres. He died at the age of eighty five years, and his wife at the age of ninety-three. James was married Dec. 28, 1846, to Margaret, youngest daughter of James and Susannah McAnlis, natives of Ireland. They have had ten children, of whom seven are living: David Wallace, William John, Robert James, Susan Elizabeth (Mrs. Watt), Martin Kirk, Emma (Mrs. Long), and Delmer Johnson. Mr. Luke is a member of the Covenanter church; in politics a Republican.

JOSEPH E. MCCABE, grocer, P. O. Beaver Falls, was born in Bridgewater, this county, Jan. 6, 1841. His parents, Robert and Mahala (Lee) McCabe, natives of Washington county, Pa., and of Scotch descent, settled in Bridgewater, this county, about 1825. After the flood of 1832 Robert, who was a carpenter and boat-builder, rebuilt the first dwelling in that place. He died in 1840. His children were William, James,

BIOGRAPHIES—WEST SIDE. 683

Leander, Robert, Samuel, John, Eliza (Mrs. Levi Booth), Mary A. (deceased), Margaret (deceased) and Joseph E. Our subject was reared in Bridgewater, and followed the river until 1855, first as cabin boy and afterward as steward. He learned the carriage painter's trade in Ravenna, Ohio, where he remained six years, then spent one year in Wooster, Ohio, and returned to Beaver county in 1862. Sept. 6 of that same year he enlisted as a private in Company A, 17th Cavalry, and participated in the battles of Chancellorsville, Gettysburg, Boonesborough, Brandy Station (three engagements), Rappahannock, Kilpatrick's raid to Richmond, Cold Harbor, Winchester, Appomatox, Five Forks, and many other engagements. Nov. 1, 1862, he was promoted to sergeant, and was duty sergeant commanding a scouting party under General Sheridan until the close of the war. He was mustered out June 16, 1865, returned home and shortly after went to St. Louis, Mo., where he remained one year. He then located in Allegheny City, Pa., where he was engaged as foreman in the painting department of one of the largest carriage shops in that city until 1871. He then came to Bridgewater, this county, where he superintended the erection of several buildings for manufacturing purposes. In 1873 he embarked in the grocery business in Bridgewater, which he continued until the fall of 1882, when he was elected a member of the General Assembly by 304 majority over his opponent, in a strong Republican county. In 1883 he came to Beaver Falls and embarked in the grocery business. In 1862 he married Tillie, daughter of William Read, of Beaver, by whom he has three daughters: Maggie, Edith and Stella. Mr. McCabe is a member of the G. A. R. and I. O. O. F.; has passed all the chairs of the subordinate lodges of the latter order, has served as inside guardian of the Grand Lodge of Pennsylvania, also of the Grand Encampment of Pennsylvania; was elected Grand Junior Warden, afterward Grand Senior Warden, Grand High Priest and Grand Patriarch of Pennsylvania, the highest branch of the order. During his residence in Bridgewater he served twelve years on the school board. In 1881 he was elected captain of Company E, 10th Regiment N. G., which he resigned in 1886. He is a member of the Methodist Episcopal church; politically he is a Democrat.

W. F. McCague, liveryman, Beaver, was born in Independence township, this county, June 17, 1861, son of William and Lucinda (Thomson) McCague, natives of this county and of Scotch-Irish descent, former of whom is a farmer in Independence township. They have two children, of whom Anna is at home. Our subject attended the common schools, and in 1885 he came to Beaver, where he embarked in the livery business. His stable is on Third street, in the business center of the borough. He keeps eight horses, and first-class carriages, and his business is steadily increasing. He was married June 8, 1885, to Ida, daughter of Thomas Brunton, of Salem, Ill. She is of Scotch-Irish descent. They have one child, William Elden. Mrs. McCague is a member of the Presbyterian church. In politics Mr. McCague is a Republican.

Joseph D. McCarter, physician, Beaver Falls, was born in Chippewa township, Feb. 16, 1856, and is a son of John and Emeline (Douthitt) McCarter. His paternal grandfather was Daniel McCarter, of Scotch parentage, a pioneer of Darlington, where he reared a family of eight children: John, Alexander, William, George, Daniel, Elizabeth (Mrs. John Young), Ann (Mrs. Moore) and Jane (Mrs. Alexander Anderson). His maternal grandfather was Joseph Douthitt, whose father was a pioneer of Beaver county. His maternal great-grandmother, whose maiden name was McMinn, was said to be the first white woman who crossed the Ohio river at Beaver. John McCarter was a farmer of Chippewa township, and died there in 1873, aged fifty-two years. He had twelve children: Joseph D., Mary J. (Mrs. Robert McCaughtry), an infant son deceased, John E., Robert M., George C., William W., Frank S., Charles H., Clement B., Laura E. and Olive L. Joseph D. began the study of medicine in 1879 in the office of James Scroggs, Jr., of Beaver; entered Jefferson Medical College at Philadelphia in 1881, and was graduated in 1883. He located in Beaver Falls, where he has a large and growing practice. Oct. 28, 1885, he married Anna, daughter of Henry and Sarah Chandley, of Beaver Falls, and has one daughter, Lucy E.

John McCaughtry, farmer, P. O. Enon Valley, Pa., was born in Northampton county, Pa., in 1808. His parents, John and Elizabeth (Gabel) McCaughtry, had four children, of whom our subject is the only son. The father was a farmer and shoemaker by trade. John, our subject, who has always been a farmer, purchased his present farm of 92 acres in 1836. He was married in 1848 to Margaret Braden, daughter of Joseph and Margaret (Rankin) Braden, and they have had ten children, nine of whom are living: William John, Joseph, James Harper, Robert, Mary, Elmer, Elsie, Frank and Floyd. Mr. McCaughtry has retired from active work on the farm, which is successfully managed by his sons. He joined the Presbyterian church at the age of eighteen; politically he is a Democrat.

S. S. McCLURE, farmer, P. O. Enon Valley, Pa., was born in Beaver county in 1838. This family on account of persecution were compelled to leave their native land, Scotland, and came to America in the seventeenth century. William McClure located in Lancaster county, Pa., and to this pioneer were born five sons, among whom was one James. He came to Gettysburg, Adams county and engaged in farming. He was married to Elizabeth Lemond, who bore him three sons. John, the youngest, who was born in 1810, was married to Mary Jane Black, of Allegheny county, and to them were born six children. He was a farmer by occupation; came to Beaver county in 1833, where he settled on a farm which he afterward purchased. He died in 1874. Samuel S. McClure, the third child born to John and Mary Jane (Black) McClure, received a liberal education, and was reared on the farm which he now owns. He married, in 1865, Ella, daughter of James McGeorge of this county, and two sons, John Kirk and Everett Lemond, were the result of this union. Mr. McClure enlisted in 1861 in Company D, 100th Regiment, known as the "Round Head Regiment," and was in active service three years. He was wounded, taken prisoner and confined in Libby prison five months. He is a member of the G. A. R.; in politics he is a Republican. He has been an elder in the United Presbyterian church for several years.

WILLIAM JAMES McCLURE, P. O. New Galilee, was born on the farm where he now resides. His father, William, was a son of John McClure, who was of Scotch-Irish parentage and resided in Lancaster county, where he died. William came from Lancaster county to this county in 1822, traveling the entire distance on foot and carrying his possessions in a knapsack. On coming here he purchased 250 acres of land, which he afterward increased to 300 acres. He died in 1877 at the age of eighty-three years; his wife, Mary (McChesney), daughter of Richard McChesney, of Lancaster county, died at the age of thirty-two years. They had five children: John (deceased), Sarah Jane (deceased), Martha L. (deceased), William James, and Mary Ann (deceased). Our subject was the fourth child and is the only surviving member of the family. He was educated at the common-schools, and has always resided on the homestead. He has been engaged in farming and stock dealing and now owns 400 acres of land, nearly all of which is under cultivation. He attends the United Presbyterian church; politically he is a Republican.

WILLIAM McCLURG, retired farmer, P. O. New Galilee, was born in Mercer county, Pa., in 1808. His grandfather, John McClurg, came originally from Ireland and purchased a farm in Washington county, Pa. His father, James, was born in Mercer county, and bought a farm in Ohio, on which he lived. His mother was Nancy, daughter of William McClurg, also a native of Ireland. Our subject is the second son and had six brothers and four sisters. He was born and reared on the farm, came to Beaver county in 1828 and married, in the following year, Sarah, daughter of Joseph and Sarah (Hartshorn) Marshall. To them were born nine children, of whom four are living: Lucy (now Mrs. Raney); Mary (now Mrs. James); Eliza (now Mrs. King); and Nancy (Mrs. Crawford). Mr. McClurg bought the farm on which he now lives in 1850. It consists of ninety-six acres, and has been under his cultivation ever since his purchase. He is a member of the United Presbyterian church; politically he is a Republican. Two of his sons, James and John, died during the war, the latter in Andersonville prison.

WILLIAM H. McCONNELL, carpenter, P. O. Negley, was born in South Beaver township, Beaver county, Pa., in 1855, and is the eldest of four children of William P. and Ellen

BIOGRAPHIES—WEST SIDE. 685

(McMillin) McConnell, former of whom died in 1879, aged sixty-six years. John, the grandfather of our subject, came from County Down, Ireland, about 1795, and in 1798 located in Beaver county, where he purchased 100 acres of land. He married Dorotha, daughter of ex-Judge Wright, and had ten children. He died in 1852, aged eighty years. William P. was reared a farmer, and at his death owned 137 acres of land. William H. has always followed farming until the past few years, during which he has been working at carpentering. He was married in 1882 to Alice, daughter of Isaac Dever, of this county, and they have two children: H. Dever and Ada Clara. Mr. McConnell is a member of the Reformed Presbyterian church; in politics he is a Republican.

JOHN MCCOWIN (deceased) was born in Beaver county in 1810. His parents, James and Margaret (Allen) McCowin, had ten children. James came to this county in 1798 from Maryland. John received a common-school education, and learned the trade of carpenter and mason. He was married in 1836 to Jane Wiley. She died, and in 1843 he married Juliet, daughter of Alexander Anderson. He had six children, all of whom are deceased. From 1834 to 1885 Mr. McCowin was prominently engaged in building and contracting. He was one of the principal managers in the building of the Darlington & Cannel Coal Railroad; was secretary and superintendent of that road for a time, and also a prominent stockholder. He was a member of the Methodist church; in politics a Republican.

BENJAMIN MCFARLAND, farmer, P. O. Black Hawk, was born in Chippewa township, Beaver county, in 1824. His father, Robert, married Catherine Pence, and had ten children, of whom five are living. Benjamin is the fifth. Robert was a shoemaker by trade and followed that business through life. He came to this county from Westmoreland in 1812. He died in 1862, aged eighty-four years; his wife died in 1860, aged sixty-six years. Benjamin followed the trade of a stone-mason for twenty-five years. He came to South Beaver township in 1844, and purchased his present farm of sixty-four acres. He was married, in 1856, to Mary, daughter of Cornelius Donevan. By her he has six children: Mary Ellen, Catherine (Mrs. Porter), John, Arthur Benjamin, Sarah Jane (Mrs. Potter) and Elizabeth, at home. Mrs. McFarland died in 1866, aged thirty-two. Mr. McFarland started in life poor, but by industry and perseverance has achieved success. He is a member of the Reformed Presbyterian church; politically, he is a Republican.

SAMUEL S. MCFERRAN, postmaster, Beaver Falls, was born in Hookstown, Oct. 16, 1829, and is a son of Robert and Mary (Scott) McFerran. His paternal grandfather, Joseph McFerran, of Scotch Irish descent, settled in Adams county, and removed to Butler county, Pa., about 1790, and married a lady named Stewart, soon thereafter settling in Beaver. He was a teacher, and did the clerical work for the Harmony Society in the early days of the county. He reared four children: Joseph, Robert, Sarah (Mrs. Dr. Milton Lawrence) and Samuel. The maternal grandfather of Mr. McFerran was Rev. George M. Scott, who was born in Bucks county, Nov. 14, 1759, and served in the revolution. In 1787 he began the study of theology, entered the University of Pennsylvania, at Philadelphia, and was graduated in 1793. In 1797 he was licensed to preach by the presbytery of New Brunswick, N. J. May 17, 1798, he married Anna, daughter of Samuel Rea, of Mt. Bethel, and the same year filled vacancies in the presbytery of Washington county, Pa. He was ordained in 1798, at New Brunswick, and in 1799 took charge of the Mill Creek Congregation, in Beaver county, and the Flatts Congregation, of Brooke county, Va. In 1826 he resigned the latter, but continued to preach to the Mill Creek Congregation until 1838. He died at Hookstown in 1847. Robert McFerran, the father of our subject, was a cabinet maker and surveyor. He served as justice of the peace of Greene township for twenty-seven years, and always took an active part in public affairs. He had seven children, who grew to maturity: Sarah (Mrs. Hugh McKissock), George, Samuel S., Jane (Mrs. Joshua Wright), John S., Mary S. (Mrs. John Munnell) and Milton L. Samuel S. was reared in Beaver county. He engaged in mercantile business at Hookstown, which he continued for twenty-three years in various parts of the country. In 1874 he located in Beaver Falls, and was

38

superintendent of the gas works until 1881. He was then appointed postmaster of Beaver Falls, which position he still holds. In 1858 he married Louisa, daughter of Samuel and Agnes (Lask) Edgar, of Fallston, by whom he has one daughter, Ada; his son, Percy Edgar, died in 1883. Mr. McFerran is a member of the A. O. U. W.; politically he is a Republican.

JAMES MCGEORGE, farmer, P. O. New Galilee, was born in Darlington township in 1833. His grandfather, William McGeorge, came to America from Scotland about 1790, and soon after his arrival settled in Allegheny county. He came to Beaver county finally and purchased 400 acres of land, which he owned at the time of his death. William, a son of this pioneer, was born in 1790, and followed farming all his life. He married Nancy Young, of Allegheny county, Pa., and by her had six children, James being the only son. William received from his father 200 acres of the original tract, and died on the farm in 1854. James was born and reared on the same farm; he still owns it. He was educated in the common schools and Greersburg Academy. He was married, in 1864, to Fannie, daughter of Thomas and Margaret (Gettis) Craig, of Pittsburgh, Pa., and they have had seven children, of whom six are living: Margaret Blanche, William Clifton, Minerva Craig, Thomas Hamilton, Bessie and Edward Glenn. The family are members of the Reformed Presbyterian church.

REV. JOHN K. MCKALLIP, pastor of the Presbyterian church at Beaver, was born in Westmoreland county, this state, Sept. 19, 1847. His parents, Henry K. and Mary (Keely) McKallip, are natives of Pennsylvania, the father of Scotch-Irish and the mother of Dutch descent. His father was a successful merchant in Shearersburg and Leechburg. Our subject is the seventh of eleven children, and was reared in the counties of Westmoreland and Armstrong. He graduated from Washington and Jefferson College in 1868, and the Western Theological Seminary, at Allegheny, in 1871. His first charge was at Elizabethtown, Ky., where he remained two years. He relieved the congregation of a heavy debt by an Eastern trip in soliciting financial aid. His next settlement was at Uhrichsville, Ohio, where he labored for nearly eight years, building up a large congregation. The church edifice was also entirely remodeled. In 1882 he undertook the pastoral charge of the First church of Bellaire, Ohio, and succeeded in the removal of a large church debt there. In 1887 he accepted a call to the Beaver Presbyterian church. His ministry here has already borne a large fruitage, and is full of promise. He is a preacher of no small accomplishments and of great popularity. He was married, in 1871, to Marion, the youngest daughter of the late Rev. Benjamin J. Wallace, D.D., and six children blessed this union, three of whom survive : Mary, Harry K. and John K. Mrs. McKallip died in April, 1884.

D. A. MCKEAN, farmer, P. O. Enon Valley, was born April 13, 1828, in Beaver county, where he has always lived. His grandfather, George, came from Westmoreland county, and his great-grandfather from Scotland. The latter settled in Westmoreland county and opened an inn, now known as McKean's hotel. Here George was born and reared, and took part in the "Whisky Insurrection." He came to Beaver county in 1795, purchased 500 acres of land, farmed it and afterward built upon it a tannery which he managed for fifty years. He married Mary Johnson, and had six sons and four daughters. His second wife was Elizabeth Smith, who bore him seven children. Johnson, father of our subject, was the second son; he worked at tanning until he was twenty-three years of age, when he was given 100 acres of land, upon which he lived until his death; he died in 1877, at the age of seventy-six years. He was married to Margaret Adams, daughter of Daniel and Mary (McCurdy) Adams, former of whom came from Ireland, latter born east of the mountains, in Pennsylvania, and was the father of three sons and seven daughters, six of whom are now living. D. A., the second son, was reared on the land originally purchased by his grandfather, but now owned by him. He received a common-school education, and has since been a farmer. He was married, Jan. 26, 1860, to Mary L., daughter of Joseph and Lizzie (Patterson) Marshall, who bore him seven children (six of whom are living): Johnson, William A., Elizabeth Anna, John W. (of Allegheny), Robert (deceased), Emma Clara and Charles Alvin. Mr. McKean in religion is a Presbyterian; in politics a Democrat.

LEWIS and JOHN MCKIM, farmers, P. O. Homewood, are grandsons of James McKim who came from Ireland previous to the revolutionary war, and settled in Beaver county as early as 1801. He married Hannah Lewis, who bore him nine children. William, his second son, born in 1791, was a farmer, and at his death in 1856 owned 160 acres of land. He was twice married, and by his first wife, Lucretia (Miller) he had four children:- Robert M., Hannah, Lewis and James. The mother died in 1828. Lewis, the second son, was born Jan. 26, 1823, received a common-school education, has always followed farming, and now owns fifty acres of land; he has never married. The second wife of William McKim was Margaret, daughter of Francis and Mary Gilky; she bore him five children: F. W., John C., William A., Mary Jane and Harvey, all of whom are living. John C., the second son, was born in 1835. He was reared on the farm, and at an early age learned the carpenter's trade, which he has followed for twenty-eight years. In 1864 he married Rufina, daughter of William and Margaret (Crawford) Miller, and by her has one son, William M. Mr. McKim now resides on the farm owned by his father-in-law, Mr. Miller. He served four months in the civil war, in Company E, 13th Regiment. He is a Republican.

WILLIAM H. MCLAUGHLIN, farmer, P. O. Ohioville, son of William and Harriet (Cairns) McLaughlin, was born at Mansfield, Ohio, Sept. 16, 1858. His grandfather, Neal McLaughlin, emigrated here from Ireland in 1792, and purchased from the government 400 acres of land in what was then called Pittsburgh township, Allegheny county, but now Ohio township. He subsequently added 200 acres more to the farm, nearly all of which has always remained in the name of his descendants. He was one of the very earliest settlers of this county, and was married to Isabella Carr, a native of Carlisle, Pa. Six children were born to them, viz.: William, Sarah, John, Elizabeth, Thomas and an infant, all of whom are now deceased. Neal McLaughlin died Sept. 3, 1838, at the age of sixty-seven years. All of his children, except William, died without having married, and were buried on his farm. John, born in 1806, survived the others, and at his death, Oct. 12, 1836, he left most of the estate to William H. (our subject). Thomas was born March 31, 1809, and died Jan. 25, 1875. Sarah, born in 1804, died Dec. 9, 1885. The subject of this sketch spent his youth and received his education at Mansfield, Ohio. In 1877 he came to Ohio township, Pa., and has since lived on the McLaughlin farm. Of the original farm, 100 acres were sold, 100 acres belong to William's three sisters, and the remainder to him. William H. was married, in 1884, to Lollie B., daughter of George and Martha (Morse) Christian, born Nov. 11, 1859, in Pittsburgh. Her father was born April 4, 1827, in Ireland, and her mother, born Aug. 17, 1830, is a native of Pittsburgh. Two children have been born to Mr. and Mrs. McLaughlin—William H. and Marie. Mrs. McLaughlin is a member of the Methodist Episcopal church.

GEN. WILLIAM MCLAUGHLIN (deceased), father of the above, was born in Ohio township, in February, 1802. He studied law at Beaver, Pa., and in 1827 moved to Mansfield, Ohio. He was a soldier in the Mexican and civil wars, and won considerable fame. His wife, Mrs. Harriet (Cairns) McLaughlin, is well-known in Mansfield, and is one of the oldest residents there. Patriotism was the distinct and distinguishing attribute of his character and life. He was a soldier naturally, and returning from the service after Bull Run, he was authorized by the president to raise a squadron of cavalry, to be named in honor of himself. With this he again took the field, but the physical man gave way, and the senator, speaker and soldier died in August, 1862.

RALSTON A. MCMILLIN, SR., retired, P. O. Achor, Ohio, is a descendant of Jas. McMillin, the pioneer of the name, who came from Ireland at an early day with other emigrants, and purchased a large tract of land in Brush Run, Beaver county. He was a farmer, and had daughters and three sons. John, his oldest son, married Rebecca Arbuckle, who bore him nine children. At his death he owned some 500 acres of land. Ralston A. was born in 1811, the youngest of five sons, was reared on the farm, and has followed agricultural pursuits through life. He was married to Eliza, daughter of William Beatty, of Ohio, and seven children have been born to this union, five of them living: Matilda M. (Mrs. Howard), John A., Mary Belle (Mrs. Shepler), James, William and Sylvester C. Mr. McMillin has retired from farming, and has been an invalid since 1886. He is a member of the Methodist church; politically a Republican.

HARBISON MCMILLIN, farmer, P. O. Darlington, was born in South Beaver township in 1829. James McMillin, his father, a farmer by occupation, was the second son of James, the early pioneer of the family, and married Elizabeth Harbison. Six children were born to to them, of whom Harbison is the eldest. James McMillin died in 1881, aged ninety-one years. His wife, Elizabeth, died in 1829, aged about thirty-five years. Harbison was reared on a farm, and received his education at the log school house. At seventeen years of age he began learning the tanner's trade, serving three years. He followed the trade twenty-five years. Retiring from that business he purchased some five hundred acres of land, situated in several different tracts, and being mostly underlaid with coal. Mr. McMillin is unmarried. In political preference he is a Republican.

RALSTON P. MCMILLIN, farmer, P. O. Achor, Ohio, was born in New Brighton in 1835. His father, William McMillin, who was born and reared in this county, married Martha Marquis, of Washington county, Pa. She bore him six sons and three daughters, of whom Ralston P. is the fourth son. William was a farmer and owned 160 acres of land. He died in 1869, aged sixty-six years. His widow is still living at the age of eighty-five years. Ralston P. purchased his present farm of ninety-three acres in 1875. He was married, in 1864, to Ann Jane, daughter of Robert Wilson, a member of one of the oldest families in South Beaver township, Beaver county. Mr. and Mrs. McMillin have had five children, of whom three are living : William Wilson, born in 1871 ; Robert Edwin, born in 1873 ; and Howard Clarence, born in 1877. Mr. McMillin, in 1862, enlisted in Company I, 134th Regiment. He and his family are members of the Presbyterian church, of which he has for some time been an elder. Politically he is a Republican.

DR. THOS. G. MCPHERSON was born July 16, A. D. 1838, in Economy township, Beaver county, Pa., being the third one of six children born to Reuben and Elizabeth Jane McPherson (*nee* Greer), four sons and two daughters, named respectively : Mary Jane, Robert, Thomas Greer, Reuben Henderson, Mannon, Sarah Ann. His paternal ancestors were Scotch, his maternal ancestors Irish. His grandparents came to America early in life, and were among the pioneers of western Pennsylvania. In 1850 Reuben McPherson, with his family, removed from Beaver county to Sewickley township, Allegheny county, where they resided until 1865, when he came to New Brighton, Beaver county, where he still lives (1888), aged seventy-eight years. The subject of this sketch at an early age manifested a strong desire to secure an education, and at the age of sixteen years was sent to Mount Union College, in Stark county, Ohio. Until twenty-one years of age he continued to attend school in the summer and engage in teaching in the winter. In the spring of 1859 he began the study of medicine under the tuition of Dr. Robert McCready, of Sewickley, where he continued his studies for four years. He then attended lectures at Cleveland Medical College in 1863-64, since which time he has been constantly engaged in the practice of his profession with good success. His literary taste and love of knowledge have made him a persistent reader and an attentive student of the various departments of science and literature. For many years he has written for publication numerous articles on a great variety of subjects, of general or local interest, writing with clearness and a bold independence of popular opinion. In 1859 the Doctor was united in marriage with Miss Jane Riley, of Allegheny county, Pa., and eight children have been born to them : Robert A., L. Luella, Hattie J., Viola, Orvil R., Thomas C., Frank G. and Mabel G. The Doctor inherits the active temperament and sturdy character of his Scotch-Irish ancestry. He is a man of liberal views and progressive ideas, ever true to his convictions of right, and ready to combat that which he believes to be wrong in society, church and state. He courts not popularity nor fears disfavor ; and lives to improve himself and benefit others. Having devoted twenty-five years to the practice of his profession, he is now, at the age of fifty years, in possession of perfect health and vigor of his mental and physical powers, and enjoys the respect and confidence of those who know him, with prospect of spending yet many years of active life. Dr. McPherson became a resident of Beaver Falls in October, 1866. The village was then part of Patterson township, and had about one hundred inhabitants, he being the first physician to locate in the place, now a thriving town, with a population numbering ten thousand souls, and soon to be one of the leading cities of western Pennsylvania.

JAMES McTAGGART, farmer and stock grower, P. O. Vanport, was born in Scotland, May 5, 1834, and is a son of Alexander and Agnes (McCradey) McTaggart, both natives of Scotland, former of whom was a shepherd in that country and came to America in 1858, where he followed farming. James is the fifth of eleven children. He was a shepherd with his father in Scotland, attended the common schools, and since coming to America has worked at farming with marked success. He came to Beaver county in 1870, and settled in Borough township, where he still resides. His farm consists of 225 acres, and he is extensively engaged in gardening and stock raising. Mr. McTaggart was married, in 1866, to May, daughter of Armstrong Jelly, and their children are John, Clara and Thomas E. Mrs. McTaggart is a member of the Presbyterian church. In politics Mr. McTaggart is a Republican.

DANIEL MADDEN, farmer, P. O. Enon Valley, was born in this county in 1818. William Madden came from Columbia county, Pa., to Beaver county about 1815. He was twice married, and by his first wife had two children, Joseph and Savilla (Mountain), both of whom are living. His second wife, Elizabeth Flickinger, bore him eleven children, Daniel being the second son. Our subject received a common school education, and during his lifetime has been principally engaged in farming and coal mining. He was married, in 1852, to Elizabeth, daughter of Samuel Cohn, of Ohio, and they had three sons and three daughters: Samuel, James, Thomas, Mary E., Savilla L. and Ida L. Mrs. Madden died in 1867, and Mr. Madden then married, in 1872, Anna M., daughter of George A. and Eliza Park, of Allegheny county, Pa. Mr. Madden purchased his present farm of fifty-three acres in 1859. He has retired from the active work of the farm, and in the rounding out of a long career he has been financially successful. He had a sister named Mary, older than himself, and has four full brothers, viz.: William, James, Charles and Montgomery, and one sister, Martha. Mr. Madden is a Democrat.

JAMES MADDEN, the fourth son of William and Elizabeth Madden, was born in Little Beaver township, this county, in 1823. He was reared on the farm, and received a good education. For seven years he was engaged in teaching, and afterward was employed as a clerk for twelve years, when, on account of ill-health, he was obliged to give up that occupation in 1859. He purchased 100 acres of land. The discovery of coal rendered this land very valuable. Mr. Madden was married, in 1852, to Nancy, daughter of Esquire Thomas Cunningham, of this county, and they have four sons and four daughters, as follows: Thomas, now in the west; Nora, a graduate of Mt. Union College, Ohio, now teaching in a seminary in Washington, Kan.; William, now gone to California; John, just returned from California; Ellie, married to John McGeorge; Charles, at home; Alice, at home, and Jennie. Mr. Madden has, by his own untiring industry, secured for himself in his declining years a comfortable home. Politically, he is a Democrat.

JOSEPH MALONE (deceased), late farmer, was born in 1817. The family came originally from Maryland. Emery, father of our subject, came here with his parents when a boy. He married Deborah Boen, who bore him ten children, five of whom are now living. Emery died Aug. 2, 1835, and his wife Deborah, Oct. 3, 1835. Joseph, in 1856, with Samuel Jackson, purchased 100 acres of land, which they owned in partnership for less than one year, Jackson's share being purchased by Mr. Malone. Joseph was married, in 1876, to Caroline, daughter of Michael Fry, and they have had five children: Michael (deceased), Josephine, Frances Caroline, Mary Elizabeth and Joseph Elmer. Mr. Malone died in 1887, aged seventy years. The widow with her children now reside on the homestead. Mr. Malone was a member of the Presbyterian church; Mrs. Malone is a Methodist.

IRA F. MANSFIELD, cannel coal dealer, P. O. Cannelton, was born in Poland, Ohio, June 27, 1842, and is a son of Kirtland and Lois Mansfield. His grandfather was Captain Jack Mansfield, of Wallingford, Conn., who for "coolness, firmness and punctuality" in storming Redoubt No. 10, at Yorktown, Va., was commended and promoted to captain by General Washington. Ira F. attended Poland College until he was fifteen years old, when he was placed to learn the machine and moulder's trade at Pittsburgh, Pa. He was married, Dec. 11, 1872, to Lucy E., daughter of Dr. E. Mygatt, and their children are Kirtland Mygatt, born Jan. 29, 1874; Mary Lois, born June 28, 1877; Henry Beauchamp, born April 3, 1880. In August, 1862, Mr. Mansfield enlisted in Company H, 105th O. V. I., and was promoted to orderly sergeant, second and first lieutenant, and for "conspicuous bravery" at the battles of Lookout Mountain and Missionary Ridge, was breveted captain, and assigned as A. Q. M. 14th A. C. He marched with "Sherman down to the sea," up through the Carolinas, and took part in the grand review at Washington in May, 1865. He bought out the cannel coal mines in October, 1865, and has operated them successfully every year since. He was justice of the peace and treasurer of Darlington township eighteen years, and representative of Beaver county in the state legislature in 1880 and 1881. In politics he is a Republican. He is ruling elder and Sunday-school superintendent in Mt. Pleasant Presbyterian church.

R. HOWARD MARKS, farmer and fruit grower, P. O. Beaver, was born in Hancock county, W. Va., June 12, 1854, and is a son of A. J. and Sarah (Hall) Marks. His father was born in Allegheny county April 5, 1825, and was a son of Samuel and Mary (Free) Marks, also natives of Pennsylvania and of French and Dutch origin. A. J. followed farming, but was also engaged in the manufacture of plows for a year. He came to Beaver county in 1869 from West Virginia, and spent the remaining portion of his life on the farm in Brighton township, where he died in 1884. He married in 1851 Sarah Hall, a native of Washington county, Pa., who is of English descent and resides on the farm in Brighton township. Their children now living are Jennie, wife of Charles Summer, and R. Howard. The latter was reared on the farm, received his education in Pittsburgh and the old academy at Beaver, and has made farming and fruit growing the business of his life. He married in Beaver county, in 1876, Viola, daughter of J. L. McKenzie. She was born in Beaver county, and was of English descent. This union was blessed with one child, Edna. Mrs. Marks died in 1883, a member of the Methodist Episcopal church, of which Mr. Marks is also a member. Politically he is a Republican.

ALFRED P. MARSHALL, attorney, a member of the firm of Marshall & McCoy, of Beaver and Rochester, Pa., was born in Lawrence county, Pa., May 17, 1850, and is a son of Joseph and Delilah (Houk) Marshall, natives of Pennsylvania, and of German and Irish descent, former by occupation a farmer. Alfred P. is the fourteenth in a family of twenty children, fifteen of whom grew to maturity, and twelve of whom are still living. He was reared on the farm and attended common schools, and Westminister College, Pa., and Mount Union College, Ohio. Commencing at the age of seventeen he taught school in winters, and attended school in the summers, for seven years. He then began the study of law at Ridgeway, Elk county, Pa., in the office of Hon. John G. Hall, and subsequently came to Beaver, where he completed his studies with S. B. Wilson. He was admitted to the bar in 1876, and has been in active practice ever since. Mr. Marshall was married, Oct. 18, 1886, to Cora F., daughter of Charles H. and Amanda (Clark) Bentel, natives of Pennsylvania and of Irish descent. Mrs. Marshall is a member of the Presbyterian church, Mr. Marshall, of the U. P. church; in politics he he is a Republican.

JOHN MARSHALL, farmer, P. O. New Galilee, was born on his present farm in 1818. His grandfather, Hugh Marshall, who was the early pioneer of the family in this country, came from Ireland about 1790, and located in Westmoreland county, Pa. In 1796 he settled in Big Beaver township, where he purchased a tract of land containing 400 acres. He married Margaret Jack, who bore him four sons, one dying when young. He remained on this property until his death in 1839, previous to which he divided his land among his three sons, John, Hugh and William, each receiving 100 acres, the father reserving the remaining 100 acres until his death. John, the eldest son, was born in 1788. He was all his life a farmer, and at his death owned 500 acres. He married Elizabeth, daughter of David Clark, and had four sons and one daughter. He died in 1863, and his wife in 1865. His son John (our subject) received a common-school education, and has always been a farmer. He owns 250 acres of land, 150 of which is a part of the 400-acre tract purchased by his grandfather. In 1868 he married Mary, daughter of Samuel and Elizabeth (Stevenson) Shurlock, and they have four children: Samuel John, Sarah Elizabeth, Margaret and Mary. Mr. Marshall has been an industrious farmer, and enjoys the comforts of a pleasant home. His wife and children are members of the Methodist church. In political preference he is a Republican.

MARVIN MARSHALL, farmer, P. O. New Galilee, is the third son and fourth child of John and Elizabeth (Clark) Marshall. In early childhood he began work on his father's farm, and now owns 250 acres of the 400 purchased by his grandfather, Hugh. He received a common-school education. April 2, 1863, he was married to Margaret, daughter of John Dowling, and she dying March 14, 1864, Mr. Marshall married, Nov. 17, 1870, Sarah, daughter of John and Sophia (Barnes) Garvin. By her he had six children: James Calvin, Marvin Clark, Elizabeth Bell, Edna Clarissa, John Garvin and Sarah Cornelia. In 1871 Mr. Marshall came into possession of his present farm, and since that time has resided on it. He owns another farm of 120 acres, besides other lands, and has carried on stock raising extensively and profitably. He and his family are members of the New School Covenanters church; politically he is a Republican.

HUGH J. MARSHALL, farmer, P. O. New Galilee, was born in 1831, the youngest son of John and Elizabeth (Clark) Marshall. He was born and reared on the farm and received a liberal education. In 1853 he married Amanda, daughter of Richard Hudson, and by her had five children: John, Mary E. (Mrs. Patterson), Amos, Matilda (Mrs. Crawford) and Robert James, a practicing physician. Mrs. Marshall died in 1870, and in 1871 he married Mary E., daughter of William McCaughtry. By her he had eight children, five of whom are living: Anna Belle, Maggie J., Elmer E., Idella and Edsie. Mr. Marshall purchased his present farm of 194 acres in 1857. It is underlaid with limestone and a superior quality of fire-brick clay, and was formerly the property of Shipman Newkirk. Mr. Marshall has been a justice of the peace for fifteen years. He was also elected county commissioner by the Republican party. He is an industrious and prosperous farmer, highly respected by his neighbors.

J. P. MARTIN, farmer, P. O. Darlington, was born in Beaver county, in 1828, and has resided there ever since. His grandfather, captain, afterward major, Hugh Martin, came from Ireland to America about the year 1770, and afterward served with distinction in the revolution as an Indian scout and commander of reconnoitering parties, in which capacity he met with many unusual and dangerous experiences. After the war Maj. Martin purchased 1,500 acres of land in Western Pennsylvania. At his death this was divided between his three sons, one of whom, James, the father of our subject, came to Beaver county in 1798. He settled upon a portion of the estate, which he cultivated until his death. He married Mary, daughter of Capt. Daniel Leisure, a distinguished resident of Westmoreland county, and a soldier of revolutionary renown. To them were born twelve children. James P., the youngest, received his education at Greersburg Academy, which he left at the age of sixteen, and engaged in farming. He settled upon his portion of the estate purchased by his grandfather, which now amounts to 160 acres. In 1850 Mr. Martin married Mary, daughter of John Imbrie, of Big Beaver township, and became the father of nine children, one of whom is deceased. They are James Rankin, now district attorney; Nancy Rosalie, now Mrs. Duff; John Imbrie, now deputy sheriff: Hugh Wilmer; Mary India, now Mrs. Hall; De Lorme, Lila J. and Jerry C. Mr. Martin has been quite prominent in the political councils of the Republican party in Beaver county, having filled all of the township offices, and also having been elected sheriff of the county, in which position he served from Jan. 1, 1876, until 1879, a period of three years.

J. RANKIN MARTIN, district attorney, Beaver Falls, was born in Darlington township, this county, Jan. 14, 1852, son of James P. and Mary C. (Imbrie) Martin, natives of Pennsylvania and of Scotch-Irish descent. His father, who is a farmer in Darlington township, this county, served one term as sheriff of Beaver county. His family consisted of nine children, five sons and three daughters living, J. Rankin being the eldest child. Our subject received his education in the district schools, Darlington Academy and Westminster College. He remained on the farm until 1876, when he was appointed deputy sheriff under his father, and served in that capacity three years. In 1879 he began to read law with Agnew & Buchanan, and was admitted to the bar Feb. 6, 1882. In 1883 he was elected district attorney, and was re-elected in 1886. He was married in 1880 to Anna, daughter of John R. Eakin, and has two children: Helen and Margaret. Mr. and Mrs. Martin are members of the United Presbyterian church; in politics he is a Republican.

J. H. MARTSOLF, druggist, Beaver, was born in New Brighton, Beaver county, Feb, 21, 1854, and is a son of Philip and Sarah (Schramm) Martsolf. His mother was a native of this county and of German descent. His father was born in Alsace, Germany, came to this country with his parents in 1832, and located first in Maryland, but in 1838 removed to Pennsylvania. He learned the trade of a shoe manufacturer. In 1853 he settled in New Brighton, where he carried on the manufacture of boots and shoes. He had seven children, of whom J. H. is the third. Our subject was reared in New Brighton, and in 1870 became a druggist's clerk, in which capacity he continued till 1877. In that year he established a drug store in the Diamond, Rochester. In the autumn of 1879 he removed his store to Beaver, where he is still in business. In 1876 he was married to Catherine, daughter of the late Daniel Miller, of Bridgewater, and their children are Stanley Miller, Margaretta, Sarah Emma and Clara Blanche. Mr. and Mrs. Martsolf are members of the Presbyterian church. He is a Republican in politics.

GOTTLIEB MAULICK, machinist, Beaver Falls, was born in Würtemberg, Germany, April 15, 1832, and is a son of Jacob and Rosina (Rukert) Maulick. He was reared in Lauffen, on Necker, until fourteen years of age, when he went to Heilbronn, and served an apprenticeship of three years at the locksmith trade. He then traveled through different cities of Europe as a journeyman for four years, and in 1853 landed in New York. He went to Philadelphia, where he worked as a machinist and gunsmith for nine years, after which he engaged in business for himself there. In 1861 he located in Trenton, N. J., where he was engaged nine years in the sword and axe works of Emerson & Silver, after which he went to New York and worked on envelope machinery eight months. He then returned to Trenton and was there employed in the saw works of Mr. Emerson four and a half years. In February, 1872, he came to Beaver Falls. Here he was employed in the saw works of Emerson & Co. six months, and nine years in the Western File Works as a hammerer and machinist. Since 1883 he has conducted a machine shop on his own account. He is a F. & A. M. and member of the A. O. U. W.; in politics a Democrat.

CHARLES W. MAY, Beaver Falls, was born near Wilkinsburgh, Allegheny county, April 8, 1827. He married Miss Mary Anderson, of Pittsburgh, July 27, 1848, and resided in Allegheny and Pittsburgh until 1859, when they moved to Beaver. At the breaking out of the war of the rebellion he raised a company of soldiers and was commissioned captain of the same Nov. 13, 1861. The company was assigned to the 101st Regiment, P. V. and known as Company F. They took part in the siege of Yorktown, the engagements at Williamsburgh, Va., Fair Oaks or Seven Pines, the seven days' battle before Richmond, the engagements at Kinston, N. C., Whitehall, N. C. and Goldsboro, N. C., also in the skirmishes at Blackwater, Va., and South West Creek. He had command of the regiment after the battle of Fair Oaks, but resigned Jan. 17, 1863. He then removed to Pittsburgh, being employed as a master and pilot of steamboats on the Ohio and Mississippi rivers, and lived there until 1875, when he moved to Beaver Falls. He was elected to council for the 6th ward Feb. 18, 1879. He established the hardware store of May & Co. June 19, 1879, and continued in business until

September, 1886, when he sold out to Merriman & Dawson. He had only one child, James M., now superintendent of Beaver Falls Steel Works, who was born in Pittsburgh, Dec. 25, 1849. James M. received his education at the old Beaver Academy, and finished at the Pittsburgh Central High School in 1867. He then read medicine under Dr. C. Emmerling, of Pittsburgh, and attended Jefferson Medical College of Philadelphia, and Bellevue Hospital Medical College of New York, where he was graduated in 1870. He practiced in Pittsburgh and St. Louis, Mo., and came to Beaver Falls in 1875. Oct. 2, 1877, he married Hannah, daughter of John and Cynthia (Murphy) Reeves, and they have four children: Charles Reeves, born April 3, 1879; John Walton, born Oct. 9, 1880; James Moore, born Oct. 14, 1883. and Arthur Largue, born April 10, 1887. Oct. 1, 1875, James M. May accepted a position in the office of the Beaver Falls Steel Works, then known by the firm name of Abel, Pedder & Co., and has been superintendent and general manager for the past eight years. He was elected a school director Feb. 18, 1879, was made secretary of the board June 2, 1879, and held the office during his three years' term. He helped to organize and is a director of the First National Bank, Beaver Falls Street Railway, Beaver Falls Glass Company (Limited), Beaver Falls Marginal Railroad, Beaver Falls Art Tile Company, and Beaver Falls Board of Trade, of which he is also secretary. He is a F. & A. M., Worshipful Master of Beaver Valley Lodge No. 478 A. Y. M., Most Excellent H. P. of Harmony Chapter 306 R. A. M., R. A. (Past Regent); politically he is a Republican.

WILLIAM C. MEGOWN, contractor and builder, Beaver Falls, was born in Butler county, Pa. Dec. 22, 1823, and is a son of James and Jane (Campbell) Megown, the former a native of County Down, Ireland, and the latter of Westmoreland county, Pa. They located in New Brighton, this county, in 1836, and in what is now Beaver Falls in 1837, returning in 1839 to New Brighton, where they lived and died, the father in 1864. James Megown was a bricklayer by trade, also a brick manufacturer, and did some business as a contractor and builder. His children were Jane, Samuel R., Rachel, Sabina, James, William C., Martha, Robert, John, Elizabeth, Thomas J. and Sarah A. William C. was reared in Beaver county from thirteen years of age, and learned the bricklayer's trade with his father and eldest brother, which business he followed until 1855. In 1868 he located in Beaver Falls, where he has since been engaged in business as a contractor and builder. He was one of the contractors who built the Central hotel, the Eleventh Street public school, engine house and old Fire Works of Beaver Falls, and the courthouse at New Lisbon, Ohio. He built the first culvert on the Pittsburg & Erie railroad. He is a F. & A. M.; has served as a member of the council of Beaver Falls; in politics he is a Democrat.

WILLIAM MELLON, miller, Beaver Falls, was born in Westmoreland county Pa., Oct. 28, 1821, and is a son of John and Sarah (Larimer) Mellon. His paternal grandfather was Archie Mellon, a linen weaver, who came from Ireland in 1816 and settled near Greensburg, Pa. He married Lizzie Armour, by whom he had seven sons and two daughters: Armour, Thomas, Andrew, John, William, Samuel, Archie, Nancy (Mrs. Richard Graham) and Margaret. Mr. Mellon's maternal grandfather was David Larimer, of Scotch descent, whose ancestors were pioneers of Westmoreland county. John Mellon was a native of Ireland. In 1831 he located in Allegheny county and erected a grist mill in Wilkins township, which he conducted until 1845. He then removed to New Sewickley, engaged in farming, and died there Feb. 19, 1868. He reared a family of nine children: William, Thomas, Elizabeth (Mrs. William Gill), Archie, Caroline (Mrs. Christian Hershey), John A., Samuel, Andrew J. and George W. William was reared in Westmoreland and Allegheny counties. In 1849, with his brother-in-law, William Gill, he purchased a gristmill in North Sewickley, and in 1874 he bought the Beaver Falls Grist Mill. In 1882 he sold out and opened a feed store, which he carried on until 1885. In 1853 Mr. Mellon married Mary J., daughter of Alexander and Ann (Wiley) Johnson, of North Sewickley township, by whom he had nine children: Alice (Mrs. MacShauer), Caroline, John, William, Anna, Ellen (Mrs. Samuel Miller), Maggie, Thomas and George.

AUGUSTUS MEYER, general superintendent and manager of the Beaver Valley Manufacturing Co.'s works at Bridgewater, was born in Allegheny City, Pa., April 28, 1850, and is a son of Daniel and Lottie (Fisher) Meyer, natives of Germany. His father, who was a professional gardner, came to Allegheny City from Germany in 1835, and carried on gardening. His family consisted of nine children, three of whom are now living. Augustus, the seventh child, war reared in Allegheny county, Pa., and attended the common schools. Early in life he learned the shearman's trade, and after working at same for a time he accepted a position as assistant superintendent of the Hosey House Company, Pittsburgh, manufacturers of steel, which he filled for fourteen years. In 1886 he accepted his present position, and the same year moved to Bridgewater. Mr. Meyer was married, in 1872, to Mary, daughter of John C. Will, and of German descent. Their children are: Callie, Dora M., John H. and Lottie. Mr. and Mrs. Meyer are members of the Lutheran church. He is a Republican, and a member of the council of Bridgewater.

WILLIAM MEYER, glass presser, Beaver Falls, was born in Pittsburgh April 14, 1853. His parents, George and Clarissa (Miller) Meyer, natives of Germany, came to America about 1842 and settled in Pittsburgh, Pa. William was reared and educated in that city, and there learned his trade, which same he has followed since 1862. He located in Beaver Falls in 1879, and has since been in the employ of the Coöperative Flint Glass Works Company. In 1887 he invented and secured a patent for a needle-curtain rack, used exclusively for lace curtains, that has already reached an extensive sale. Mr. Meyer married, in 1881, Mary, daughter of John Maus, of Beaver Falls, and has three children: Ida, William and Harry. In politics he is a Republican.

GEORGE B. MICHEL, merchant tailor, Beaver Falls, was born in Saxonburg, Butler county, Pa., March 14, 1856, and is a son of George and Eliza (Seibert) Michel. His father was a native of Germany, and is now a prominent farmer of Butler county. His mother was a native of Lancaster, Pa., and a daughter of Frederick Seibert, a pioneer of Butler county. Mr. Michel was reared in Saxonburg, and served a three years' apprenticeship at the tailor's trade in Allegheny City, after which he worked as a journeyman seven years in Pittsburgh and three years in Beaver Falls. In 1883 he embarked in business for himself in Beaver Falls. He carries a large and complete stock of goods, and has established an extensive and growing trade.

WILLIAM MILLER is one of the oldest citizens in this section of Beaver county. He was born in 1802, in Northampton county, Pa., the son of Robert and Catherine (Williams) Miller, who were parents of ten children, of whom William was the fourth child. Robert was a farmer, left his native county in 1808 and settled in Washington county; there he remained one year on a rented farm, and in 1809 came to Beaver county and purchased a farm of 200 acres between Big Beaver creek and Little Beaver creek, where he passed the remainder of his life. He was accidentally killed, in 1815, at the age of forty-four years, by a falling piece of timber. His widow died in 1846, aged sixty-eight years. William is now the only remaining member of his family living. Alexander, his grandfather, came from Ireland and settled in Northampton county, Pa., where he remained and died. He was a farmer, and father of ten children. William, the subject of this sketch, was reared on a farm, and has always followed agricultural pursuits. In 1827 he married Margaret Crawford, daughter of Robert Crawford, and six children was the result of this marriage, one now living: Rufina. Mr. Miller has retired from farming, but still owns the property, 120 acres, which he purchased in 1833. His wife died in 1867, aged sixty-four years. Mr. Miller has lived near his present home for seventy-eight years.

W. I. MILLER, secretary and treasurer of the Phoenix Glass Works, Phillipsburgh, P. O. Beaver, was born in Wellsburg, Brooke county, Va., Nov. 27, 1843. His parents, William and Jane (Blair) Miller, natives of Virginia and of Scotch and German descent, came to Carlisle, Pa., about 1836. His father was a prominent man, and served one term as sheriff of Brooke county. Our subject attended school in his native county and the academy in Washington county two years. He worked at farm work until

1861, when he enlisted at Wheeling, Va., in the First Regiment, V. V. I., Company B, and served two years. On his return he carried on the hardware business for two years at Mount Pleasant, Iowa. He then went to Pittsburgh, where he was employed as clerk. Then he was assistant auditor of the fast freight line on the Pennsylvania Railroad for four years. He has been engaged in the manufacturing business since 1877, and was one of the principal movers in the organization of the Phoenix Glass Company, which was organized in 1880. Since then he has been secretary and treasurer of the company, and the success of the business is largely due to his personal efforts and energy. Mr. Miller was married in 1870 to Clara, daughter of Captain William Dean, of Pittsburgh, and of Scotch descent. This union has been blessed with four children : Jane B., Clara D., William D. and Stanley B. Mr. and Mrs. Miller are members of the Presbyterian church. He is a chairman of the Beaver County Republican Committee, and burgess of Beaver borough. He is a member of the G. A. R.

THOMAS LAUGHLIN MINESINGER, merchant, P. O. Smith's Ferry, son of Godfrey and Sarah (Laughlin) Minesinger, natives of this county, was born on the Minesinger farm, near Smith's Ferry, April 12, 1844. His grandfather came from Prussia about 1800, and located near Frankfort Springs. Godfrey Minesinger was a stonemason, and spent a number of years in the building business in Alabama. He took the contracts on the B. & O. Railroad, and built one pier of the Wheeling Suspension Bridge. With his sons, Thomas and John, he bought out the interest of other heirs in the James Minesinger farm near Smith's Ferry, and the farm was divided between the sons. Thomas bought out John's share and subsequently sold it all. Godfrey was a Whig and afterward a Republican. His wife was a member of the Presbyterian church. The subject of this sketch received a common-school education, and when sixteen years old served a three years' apprenticeship at blacksmithing. He followed the river for four years as government engineer. During the war he was on the lower Mississippi river on transport and dispatch boats, and witnessed the engagement at Memphis and the second one at Fort Donelson. After the war he drilled oil wells with good success, and was also with his brother five years on a garden farm, and supplied the oil field. For ten years he was assistant ticket agent at Smith's Ferry. He then spent one year on the farm, and subsequently bought out H. J. Boyd's store in 1880, which he has since carried on, and has become a prosperous merchant. He was also assistant postmaster at Smith's Ferry for five years. His residence is at Glasgow. Mr. Minesinger was married, in 1866, to Narcissa B., daughter of Jesse Smith, of Ohio township. Three children have blessed this union : Jesse, a blacksmith at Pittsburgh ; John L., clerk in his father's store, and Eddie, at school. All are members of the Presbyterian church. Mrs. Minesinger died Feb. 4, 1878, and Mr. Minesinger married for his second wife Mary Ecoff, of German descent, who has borne him one child, Thomas, Jr. Our subject is secretary of Glasgow Lodge, No. 485, F. & A. M. Politically he is a Republican.

DAVID MINIS (deceased) was born in Ireland in 1794, and was a son of John and Mary Minis, who came to America in 1801 and settled on a farm in Butler county, Pa. They had six sons and one daughter, who grew to maturity, of whom David was the youngest. His earliest schooling was received in Butler county; he also attended school in Economy township, where he lived with an elder brother on a farm. Before arriving at his majority he went to Pittsburgh and worked in the woolen mills for several years; then engaged as collector for a book firm, and afterward embarked in mercantile business in Pittsburgh. In 1825 he came to Beaver and established a general country store, which he carried on until past middle life. He then bought a farm and made agriculture the business of his remaining life. He died Feb. 16, 1875. His wife, whose maiden name was Rachel H. Berry, was born in Maryland. She had two children — Anna and David — and died in 1866. Anna is the only living member of the family. Her brother died in the service of his country, in 1862. He was born in Beaver, attended the common schools, was graduated from Jefferson College, studied medicine and was graduated from the University of Pennsylvania. He practiced his profession in Beaver until 1861, when he enlisted in the 48th Regiment of Cavalry, and was appointed surgeon of the regiment. He was on detached service, and was at the battle of Roanoke Island. He died Feb. 14, 1862, from the effects of exposure while in the service. He was married in Beaver, to Sarah H., daughter of Hon. Daniel Agnew. Our subject and his wife were members of the Methodist Episcopal Church, of which he served as steward and class leader. He was a Whig, and afterward a Republican.

JAMES MITCHELL, farmer and gardener, Vanport, was born in Beaver county, Sept. 23, 1833, and is a son of Joseph and Ann (McCreery) Mitchell, the former born in Ireland and the latter in Pennsylvania, of Irish descent. His father, who was a farmer and merchant, was successful in business, and at the time of his death was the owner of 300 acres of land in Borough township. He died in 1877, having been a resident of Borough township since 1838. James, who is the third in a family of six children, attended the common schools, and has made farming his business. He is an industrious and liberal man. He was married, in 1858, to the eldest daughter of Captain Thomas Greenlee, of Vanport, and they have three children, Sue Annie, Floretta and Stella. The family are members of the Presbyterian church. He is a Democrat in politics, and has served fifteen years as school director in Borough township.

J. W. MITCHELL, undertaker, P. O. New Galilee, was born in Beaver county in 1852. His parents, Samuel T. and Nancy, had six children, J. W. being the third son. Samuel T. was a farmer in South Beaver township. J. W. received a liberal education, and at the age of nineteen years learned the blacksmith's trade, serving an apprenticeship of three years. He was married, in 1877, to Miss Mary B., daughter of John W. Funkhouser. of this county, and they have two children, Mary Florence and Pearl B. Mr. Mitchell has for twelve years carried on blacksmithing at his present place. He is also engaged in undertaking, embalming, etc., and has a livery attached. He is a member of the Reformed Presbyterian church; politically, a Prohibitionist.

SAMUEL MITCHELL, retired, P. O. New Brighton, was born in South Beaver township Jan. 24, 1812. His grandfather, Hugh, came from Ireland about 1789 and settled in Westmoreland county, Pa. James, a son of this pioneer, was twelve years of age when his father came to Beaver county. He married Isabella Newell, who bore him three children, of whom Samuel is the eldest. James died in 1842, aged sixty-three years. He was a farmer and owned 400 acres of land. Samuel received a good education and taught school ten years. In 1842 he married Eliza, daughter of James Kennedy, of this county, and by her had three children: James S. (deceased), Scott and Joseph. Mrs. Mitchell died in 1871, aged sixty-two years. Mr. Mitchell has retired from active business life, and resides with his son Scott, on the homestead. He is one of the oldest and most respected citizens of the township. His second son, Scott, was born in 1845, and married, in 1869, M. J. Wilson. Their children are Eliza M., Samuel W., Edwin Scott, Ann L., Frank Stanley, Albert Ross and Eliza Bell. The family are members of the United Presbyterian church; Mr. Mitchell is a Republican.

JOHN G. MOFFET, stonemason, Beaver Falls, was born in Raccoon township, this county, April 18, 1833, and is a son of Robert and Rebecca (Scott) Moffet, the former a native of Ireland and the latter of Scotland. His maternal grandfather was James Scott, a native of Scotland and a pioneer farmer of Ohio township, this county. Robert Moffet was an early settler in Raccoon township. In early life he followed the river, steamboating between Pittsburgh and Cincinnati, and later operated a grist and flouring mill in Raccoon township, near Shippingport, until his death. He had eleven children, of whom seven survive: James, John G., Rebecca (Mrs. William Rambo), Catherine (Mrs. John Weigel), Mary F., Isaac and Emily (Mrs. Charles Moore). Our subject was reared in Raccoon township and learned the trades of bricklayer, stonemason and stonecutter in New Brighton, and with the exception of three years that he was in the army he has followed that occupation since 1850. He enlisted Aug. 25, 1862, in Company A, 17th Pennsylvania Cavalry, participated in the battles of Chancellorsville, Spottsylvania, Cold Harbor, Kilpatrick's raid to Richmond, Winchester, and other engagements, and was mustered out of the service June 16, 1865. In 1867 Mr. Moffet settled in Beaver Falls, where he has since resided. In 1855 he married Matilda, daugh-

BIOGRAPHIES—WEST SIDE.   697

ter of William Knowles, of Raccoon township, and has five children living: Belle (Mrs. Thomas Moore), Sarah (Mrs. Felix O'Neal), Robert M., Tilla and John. Mr. Moffet is a member of the Methodist Protestant church, the G. A. R. and K. of L. He is a F. & A. M.; in politics a Republican.

JOSEPH MOODY, farmer, was born in Hookstown, Greene township, this county, Jan. 4, 1835, and is a son of John and Margaret (McClure) Moody. His father was born in Northampton county, Pa., and his mother in Beaver county. His paternal and maternal ancestors were of Scotch origin, and have been residents of Pennsylvania for many years. His father came to Beaver county and settled at Hookstown, in 1819, on land which is now a part of that village. He died in 1864. Joseph is the second of a family of seven children, four of whom are now living. He attended the school at Hookstown, and remained on the farm until 1862, when he enlisted in Company H, 140th Regiment, P. V. I., serving as second duty sergeant. He was in the battle of Chancellorsville and at Gettysburg; was in Hancock's division in front of Pickett's great charge. About three weeks after the battle of Gettysburg he was detailed by the war department, and served until the close of the war; then returned to Beaver county, and farmed for a time at Hookstown. In 1875 he went to Westmoreland county, where he continued farming and stock raising. In 1884 he sold his farm and retired. He came to Beaver borough and bought seventeen and three-fourths acres of land with a good brick house and other improvements, where he now resides, the land being worth at least $1,000 per acre. In 1866 he was married to Martha, daughter of Thomas (a farmer) and Susan (Allen) Withrow, natives of Chester county, Pa., and of Scotch descent. Mr. and Mrs. Moody have one child living, Mina. The parents are both members of the Presbyterian church. Mr. Moody was an elder in the church while he lived in Westmoreland county. In politics he is a Republican.

COL. SAMUEL MOODY, district passenger agent for the Pennsylvania Company, P. O. Beaver, was born in Brooklyn, N. Y., Aug. 24, 1850, and is a son of Henry and Mary (Foster) Moody. His mother's parents were of English birth, and she left England with an uncle when a few months old, her parents having died. His father was born in England in 1804, and came to New York when fourteen years old; he spent the remaining portion of his life in that state, dying in 1866, at the age of sixty-two. He was a manufacturer and dealer in leather and boots and shoes. Samuel was the sixth in a family of eleven children. He attended private school in Brooklyn, and when he reached his majority came to Beaver county and settled in Darlington township, where he established a general country store on a small scale. In 1877 he sold out, came to Beaver and embarked in the wholesale tobacco business at Rochester, which he followed until 1885, when he obtained a position with the Pennsylvania Company as traveling passenger agent, and Jan. 1, 1887, he was promoted to his present position. Col. Moody was married, May 24, 1871, to Mary K., daughter of Kirtland Mansfield. Her mother's maiden name was Lois Morse. Her parents were natives of Connecticut, and of English origin. This union has been blessed with two children, Lucy Bordman and Oliver Beauchamp. In political preferment Col. Moody is a Republican. He served two years as secretary of the Beaver County Agricultural Society; has been a member of the town council and is at present a member of the school board. In 1887 he was appointed lieutenant-colonel on Governor Beaver's staff.

R. A. MOON, physician, Beaver Falls, was born in Rensselaer county, N. Y., Sept. 17, 1821, and is a son of John B. and Polly (Briggs) Moon (both natives of the above county), and is of Scotch descent. He was reared and educated in Jamestown, N. Y., from twelve years of age. He began the study of medicine in 1840, and was graduated from the Cleveland Medical College, Cleveland, Ohio, in 1844. He located in Hookstown, this county, in 1845, where he was in the active practice of his profession for thirty years. In 1875 he came to Beaver Falls, where he has had a large and lucrative practice since. In 1884 his son, Addison S., became associated with him in business. He studied medicine in the office of his father for several years, and was graduated from Western Reserve Medical College in February, 1884: and also took a special course at the College of Physicians and Surgeons, New York, in 1887 and 1888. Our subject was married, in 1846, to Sarah, daughter of William and Mary (Stewart) Sterling, a pioneer family of Greene township, this county, and they have two children: Mary H. (Mrs. Rev. J. Stewart Brandon) and Addison S. Dr. Moon is one of the oldest practitioners in Beaver county. He and his family are active members of the Presbyterian church. Politically he is a Republican.

ALFRED R. MOORE, justice of the peace, was born in Beaver March 2, 1819, and is a son of Hon. Robert and Mary (Stibbs) Moore, natives of Pennsylvania and of English and Irish descent. His grandfather, Henry Moore, was a physician and practiced in Washington county, Pa.; Robert, his second son, was educated at Jefferson College, when it was an academy. In 1802 he (Robert) came to Beaver county to practice law, and soon gained for himself a prominent place in the county, and was elected a member of the legislature. He represented this district in congress when it embraced a considerable portion of the state, and served two terms. When the project of building the Erie canal was agitated in 1829, the people of Beaver county again turned to him and sent him to the legislature to advocate the construction of the canal, which he did to the satisfaction of his constituents. Alfred R. is one of a family of eight children, of whom four are still living, two in Beaver. His sister, Elizabeth, is the wife of Hon. Daniel Agnew. Squire Moore was brought up in Beaver, attended the old academy and spent two years (1831-32) in Washington College. One of his first business exploits was assisting in the survey of the Erie canal. He afterward went on the river as clerk of a steamboat, and it being a busy time on the river he found it a very congenial place for an ambitious young man. He remained on the water for eighteen years. In 1847 he was elected treasurer of Beaver county; he then clerked for the county commissioners for four years. In 1860 he was elected register and recorder, and was re-elected in 1863. He served nine years as United States storekeeper. In 1887 he was elected justice of the peace, and still holds the office. He was married in November, 1843, to Jane, daughter of Col. Henry Small, of the war of 1812. Her parents were of German and Scotch-Irish descent. Squire Moore has reared his family in Beaver borough. His eldest sons are graduates of Washington and Jefferson College. Robert, the eldest, now deceased, studied law, and at the time of his death was a partner with H. Hice. Alfred S. and Winfield S. are attorneys. Isaac H. is a physician in Jasper county, Iowa, and has served two years as president of the County Medical Society. The last two sons were graduates of the Millersville State Normal School. Isaac H. completed his medical education at the University of Pennsylvania. The Squire and his wife are members of the Methodist Episcopal church. In politics he has been a Whig and a Republican.

ALFRED S. MOORE, the senior member of the firm of A. S. & W. S. Moore, attorneys at law, Beaver, was born in Beaver, Pa., Sept. 13, 1846, and is a son of Alfred R. and Jane (Small) Moore, natives of this county. His mother was of German and Scotch-Irish origin. His father is of English descent, and has been a well-known citizen of Beaver county for many years. He holds the office of justice of the peace in Beaver. In early life he was a clerk on a steamboat, and also served a number of years as a captain. In 1846 he was elected county treasurer. From 1861 till 1867 he was register and recorder. His family consists of seven children, of whom Alfred S. is the second. He was reared in Beaver, attended the common schools and the Beaver Academy. When his father was elected register and recorder, he became clerk in his office, and continued till 1864, when he entered Jefferson College, at Cannonsburg. He was graduated from Washington and Jefferson College with the class of 1867. Immediately upon his graduation he went west, and engaged in railroading, and soon worked up to the position of conductor. He resigned in 1869, returned to his native town, studied law under S. B. Wilson, and was admitted to the bar in 1871. He then went to Warren county, where he practiced for a few months. In March, 1873, he removed to Butler county, where he practiced his profession till the close of 1875. He then returned to Beaver county. In 1880 he was elected district attorney for this county, and served three years. Since then he has been successfully engaged in the practice of his profession in connection with his brother. He was married in Washington county, Pa., Oct. 18, 1882, to Cecelia, daughter of Harrison Richardson. She is of Scotch-Irish origin. Mr. and Mrs. Moore are members of the Methodist Episcopal church, and he is a trustee and a teacher in the Sabbath-school. In politics he is a Republican.

WINFIELD S. MOORE, attorney, Beaver, is the junior member of the firm of A. S. & W. S. Moore, of Beaver and Beaver Falls. He was born in Brighton township June 14, 1852, the fourth in a family of eight children of Alfred R. and Jane (Small) Moore. He attended the public schools here and the Beaver Academy, and was graduated from the Millersville State Normal School in 1873. He then accepted a position as principal of the schools at New Galilee, where he remained two years. He studied law with the law firm of Wilson & Moore, of Beaver, and was admitted to the bar March 15, 1876, since which time he has practiced in this county. June 12, 1879, he was married to Mary, daughter of I. N. Atkins, a merchant of Beaver. Her parents are of English descent. Mrs. Moore was born and raised in Beaver, and is a graduate of Beaver College and Musical Institute. Three children have been born to Mr. and Mrs. Moore: Daniel Agnew (named for our subject's uncle, Hon. Daniel Agnew); Mary Olive, and Maud Atkins. Mr. and Mrs. Moore are members of the Methodist Episcopal church. He takes an active interest in the Sabbath school, and is now superintendent of the Beaver M. E. Sunday school. In politics he is a Republican.

SAMUEL A. MOORE, farmer, P. O. Black Hawk, was born in this county in 1820. His grandfather, Robert Moore, came from County Down, Ireland, in 1788, and located in Westmoreland county, Pa. He subsequently came to Beaver county and bought 100 acres of land near where is now the village of Enon Valley. He married Isabella Chambers, by whom were born five children, all sons. The father died at the age of eighty-eight years. Robert, the second son, was born cn the ocean in 1788, and was twelve years old when his family came to Beaver county. He purchased 160 acres of land. He married Jane, daughter of Samuel Andrews, also of County Down, Ireland, and they had eight children, six of whom are living, Samuel A. being the eldest. Robert Moore purchased the farm now owned by Samuel A. in 1834, and remained there until his death; he died in 1864, at the age of seventy-five years. His wife died in 1877, aged seventy-two years. Samuel A. was educated at the log school house, and remained at home until forty years old; then engaged in mercantile business for six years. He purchased the old homestead at his father's death, and has since resided there. He was married in 1852 to Margaret, daughter of Andrew and Sarah (Hunter) McKinzie, of this county, and they have five children: Robert M., a carpenter; Charles F., a farmer; Sherman Andrews, now a school teacher and student at college; Mattie Jane, now Mrs. McClure; and Meribah Isabella, now Mrs. McMillin. Mr. Moore is a highly respected farmer and has been successful in his business pursuits. He is a member of the Presbyterian church; politically a Republican.

ROBERT H. MORRIS, glass presser, Beaver Falls, was born in Pittsburgh Oct. 9, 1851, and is a son of Henry R. and Catherine (Williams) Morris, of Wales. His paternal grandfather, Robert Morris, and his maternal grandfather, Thomas Williams, were natives of Wales and pioneers of Pittsburgh. Robert H. learned his trade with T. McKee & Bros.; and worked at it in Pittsburgh from 1860 until 1879. He then located in Beaver Falls and became one of the organizers of the Coöperative Flint Glass Works Company, where he has since been employed and is interested as a stockholder. In 1880 he married Agnes, daughter of John and Jane (Nicholson) Bream, of Pittsburgh, and has two children: Robert and John. Mr. Morris is serving his second term as member of the board of directors of the Flint Glass Works Company. He is a member of the I. O. O. F.; in politics a Republican.

GEORGE W. MORRISON, assistant cashier Economy Savings Bank, Beaver Falls, was born in Frankfort Springs, Feb. 24, 1838, and is a son of James and Mary (Dungan) Morrison. His paternal grandfather, James Morrison, was born in Ireland in 1771, came to America in 1788, and settled in Pittsburgh. He was its pioneer merchant, and was one of the founders and directors of the Bank of Pittsburgh. He was also engaged in farming in Hanover township, this county, and afterward removed to Mt. Vernon, Ohio,. where he died. His children were Nancy (Mrs. Benjamin Kendrick), Mary (Mrs. William Robb), James and John. Mr. Morrison's maternal grandfather, James Dungan, Philadelphia, was a bookbinder, and had the contract for binding the first edition of quarto Bibles printed in America, which was published by Mathew Carey in 1802. In 1801 he married Johanna Holland. Her grandfather, Thomas Holland, who was captain of a merchant vessel, left England and settled in Philadelphia. Her father, Nathaniel Holland, served his apprenticeship with Benjamin Franklin, and afterward carried on the printing business established by the latter for over two years. In 1805 James Dungan and wife settled at Frankfort Springs, and engaged in farming, also keeping hotel there. He gave Frankfort Springs its name, and lived there until his death. His wife died when aged eighty-four years, leaving five children, thirty-five grandchildren and twenty great-grandchildren. James Morrison, father of George W., was born in 1801, settled at Frankfort Springs in 1828, and engaged in mercantile business there. He served as postmaster and county auditor, and died in 1871. His children were Jane (Mrs. Robert Shannon), Nancy (Mrs. Robert Mercer), Johanna H. (Mrs. William Mercer), James D., George W., Mary R., Alexander and Lavinia. George W. served as clerk in his father's store until 1869, when he went to Beaver Falls and entered the employ of the Economy Savings Institution, and has been assistant cashier since 1885. He is also secretary and treasurer of the Western File Co., secretary of H. M. Myers & Co. (Limited) Shovel Works, and treasurer of the Beaver Falls School Board. In 1865 he married Mary E., daughter of Hon. William and Jane (Riddell) Sturgeon, of Washington county, Pa., and by her has two children: William S. and Mary R. Mr. Morrison and family are members of the Presbyterian church.

ALEXANDER MORRISON, salesman, Beaver Falls, was born in Frankfort Springs,. Nov. 4, 1841, and is a son of James and Mary A. (Dungan) Morrison. His paternal grandfather, James Morrison, a native of Ireland, was a pioneer of Pittsburgh. His maternal grandparents were James and Johanna (Holland) Dungan, who settled at Frankfort Springs in 1805. [See sketch of George W. Morrison.] Mr. Morrison clerked in his native town for several years, and also practiced dentistry there and at Steubenville, Ohio, ten years. In 1862 he enlisted in the 84th O. V. I. and was honorably discharged after five months' service, and also served as sergeant in Company C. 193d P. V. I. for four months in 1864. In 1865 he married Mary J., daughter of Joseph and Phebe (Floyd) Withrow, of Frankfort Springs, by whom he had four children: Mary D., Charles W., James M. and Helen. Mr. Morrison located in Beaver Falls in 1884, and has since been in the employ of the Western File Company as traveling salesman. He is a member of the I. O. O. F. and G. A. R., served four years as justice of the peace of Frankfort Springs, and in November, 1887, was elected treasurer of Beaver county. Politically he is a Republican.

A. MULHEIM, merchant, Bridgewater, of the firm of B. Mulheim & Son, was born in Bridgewater, Nov. 18, 1855, and is a son of Benjamin and Margaret (Snyder) Mulheim, both natives of Switzerland. The father learned shoemaking in his native country, and coming to America, settled in Pittsburgh, where he worked at his trade, and in 1854 married, the lady of his choice having come to America the same year that he came. March 4, 1855, he removed to Bridgewater, where he continued his trade. When the war broke out he had about twenty men employed, nearly all of whom enlisted in the army. In 1860 he bought a store in company with Mrs. Miller, and three years later he bought his partner's interest. In 1864 he disposed of his interest in the shoe shop to a young man, whom he had reared and taught the trade. Of his five children, four are now living. Our subject received his education in Beaver Seminary and at Duff College, Pittsburgh, where he graduated. He entered his father's store as clerk, and since 1880 has been a partner. In 1870 he learned the machinist's trade, which he followed for ten years. He has three sisters—Mary, Emma, and Bertha. Mr. Mulheim was married Jan. 8, 1880, to Maud Webster. She is of English descent. Their children are Gertrude, Charles and Albert. Mrs. Mulheim is a member of the Episcopal church. In politics Mr. Mulheim is a Republican.

JOHN MURRAY, dentist, P. O. West Bridgewater, was born in Ireland Nov. 22, 1813, and came to the United States in August, 1822, with his parents, James and Mary Murray, who settled in Pittsburgh, Pa. His paternal grandfather, M. J. Murray, was a native of County Down, Ireland, and was descended from the Scotch who settled in the northern part of that country. Our subject passed his early youth in Pittsburgh, attended the common schools, also two terms at Allegheny College, and later pursued his studies at a select school in Pittsburgh. He traveled as a minister of the Methodist Episcopal church for twenty years. In 1855 he asked for a location, and was granted one at the Salem, Ohio, Conference, but still continued to preach where most needed until laid aside by age and infirmity. After retiring from the active ministry he studied dentistry, graduated from the Philadelphia Dental College, and is a successful practitioner. He was commissioned a justice of the peace by Gov. R. E. Pattison, but after a short trial, finding its duties uncongenial to his tastes and life, he resigned the office. July 31, 1838, Mr. Murray married L. A. Gorgas. In politics he has always been a Republican; in religion a Methodist.

HENRY M. MYERS. The Myers family are descended from German ancestry. Henry Myers, the grandfather of the subject of this biographical sketch, removed from Juniata county, Pa., to Columbiana county, Ohio, in 1786, and remained there until his death. His son, Samuel Myers, born in the latter county in 1806, and for many years a popular and successful physician, married Matilda Montz, of Maryland. Their children are Henry M., Noah, John, Mary, Sarah, Elmira and Matilda, of whom all but one are still living. Dr. Myers first pursued his profession in Ohio, and subsequently removed to Elkhart, Ind., where he died in 1861, in his fifty-fifth year. His wife's death occurred in April, 1880, in her sixty-ninth year. Henry M. Myers was born in Georgetown, Ohio, June 17, 1831, and at the age of three years removed to Jamestown, Mercer county, Pa. In 1845 Cohoes Falls, N. Y., became his home, his father having for a brief time engaged in practice at this point. Here he received instruction at the common schools of the place, and became an apprentice to the trade of axe-making and that of a blacksmith. In November, 1849, on the completion of his apprenticeship, he came to Pittsburgh, and for eight years was employed as a journeyman, meanwhile increasing his scanty stock of learning by such means as the night schools of that city afforded. Mr. Myers then accepted an advantageous offer from Newmyer & Graff, of Allegheny City, and became manager of the axe and shovel works owned by them. After a business connection of twelve years a change of firm rendered his retirement necessary, and in 1869 Beaver Falls became his home, and the present works were organized for the manufacture of shovels, spades, etc., under the firm name of Myers & Armor. In July, 1875, the interest of Mr. Armor was purchased and the firm became H. M. Myers & Co., Limited. Mr. Myers, besides giving much time and thought to his business, has acquired some reputation as an inventor, and taken out many patents for inventions and improved methods in manufacture. Since 1868 he has recorded thirty patents in America, ten in Canada, and fifteen in various European countries. These inventions are eminently practical, and materially decrease the cost of manufacture of shovels, to which they are specially directed. In connection with these patents he has already realized from $25,000 to $50,000, and negotiations are now in progress with reference to the organization of a company with a capital stock of $1,000,000 to further develop these inventions. The great saving as a result of their introduction is estimated to exceed $2,000,000 during the lifetime of the patents, which certainly gives Mr. Myers an enviable place on the roll of inventors. He is also with one exception the pioneer in the manufacturing interest at Beaver Falls. Mr. Myers was, Oct. 18, 1855, married to Mary J., daughter of Thomas Bougher, of Pittsburgh. Their children are Charles Henry, George Bennett, Caroline (Mrs. William M. Hamilton), and Amanda (Mrs. Frank M. Wheaton),. Mrs. Myers died Feb. 27, 1864, and on Sept. 14, 1874, he was again married, this time to Ella D., daughter of Nicholas Miller, of Geneseo, Ill. Their children are a daughter, Julia L., and a son, Frank Simpson. Mr. Myers gives little attention to political questions, and has confined his interest in public measures to such aid as he may render in the promotion of a just and economical municipal government. He is a member of the Second Protestant Methodist church of Beaver Falls, and one of its trustees.

A. O. MYERS, traveling salesman, P. O. Beaver Falls, was born in Allegheny county, Pa., Aug. 17, 1860, and is a son of S. H. and S. J. (Dunn) Myers, who located in Beaver Falls in 1868, where A. O. was reared and educated. In 1874 our subject engaged as clerk in the store of E. Autenreith, of New Brighton, where he remained four years. In 1879 he commenced business for himself in Beaver Falls (groceries and provisions), which he continued until October, 1885. In October, 1887, he again embarked in the same business, having purchased the well-known store of H. C. and S. R. Patterson, but later sold this business, and is now traveling for a Philadelphia house. Mr. Myers is a member of the National Aid Union; politically he is a Republican.

CAPTAIN JOHN J. NEVILL, retired farmer, P. O. Beaver, was born in Wayne county, Ohio, March 10, 1810, and is a son of John Nevill, a native of Maryland. His mother was Elizabeth Grant, a distant relative of President Grant. Her father was a spy under General Washington. They were of English and Scotch-Irish origin. His father, who followed farming all his life, came to Beaver county in 1790, and in 1809 removed to Wayne county, Ohio, where he farmed about ten years; then he retired to Beaver county and settled in Ohio township, where he spent the remaining portion of his life. John J. was reared in this county, and made farming the business of his life, operating also a saw-mill. He was married, in 1833, to Sarah, daughter of Edward Nevill, and has been blessed with following named children: Edward, a farmer; Ruth, wife of Andrew G. Johnson; and Milton. The latter was born and reared in the home where he now resides, and attended the schools of Brighton township. He was married, in 1877, to Maria L., daughter of Samuel and Catherine (Meherge) Gibson, and of English and Scotch Irish descent. This union has been blessed with one child, Samuel G. Captain John J. Nevill was a militiaman for many years, and was a good officer. He is still living, at the advanced age of seventy-seven years. In politics he is a Republican.

ROBERT S. NEWTON, grocer, Beaver Falls, was born in Wayne township (formerly Beaver county), Sept. 8, 1840, and is a son of Jacob and Sarah (Wilson) Newton, both of this county. His paternal grandfather, John Newton, formerly of New Jersey, was a pioneer of Wayne township and a soldier of the war of 1812. He reared a family of twelve children: Philip, John, Euphemia, Polly, James, William, Isaac, David, Margaret, Joseph, Betsey and Jacob. The latter was a farmer of Wayne township, and was born, reared and died there. His children were six in number: Mary, Robert S., Sylvester, Charles, Christiana and William. The maternal grandfather was William Wilson, captain of a company in the war of 1812 and a pioneer of Wayne township, where he died at the age of ninety-seven years Our subject was reared and educated in Wayne township., He enlisted August 28, 1861, in Company A, 76th Keystone Zouaves, and participated in nineteen battles. He lost his right arm at the battle of Deep Bottom, Va., Aug. 16, 1864; was then taken prisoner, but made his escape within seven hours. He was honorably discharged from the service March 15, 1865. In 1867 he settled in Beaver Falls and embarked in the grocery business, in which he has since been successfully engaged. In 1865 he married Emma, daughter of Adam and Delilah (Daniels) Shoemaker, of Wayne township, and has three children: Sarah, Minnie and Robert, Mr. Newton is a member of the Presbyterian church; of the G. A. R. and Union Veteran Legion, the I. O. O. F., and Daughters of Rebecca. In politics he is a Democrat.

JOHN H. OHNSMAN, manager Beaver Falls Glass Co., Limited, Beaver Falls, was born in Pittsburgh, May 17, 1854, and is a son of John and Rosina (Speith) Ohnsman, of Germany, who settled in Pittsburgh about 1847. John H. learned the trade of glass presser with Doyle & Co., of Pittsburgh, and worked in the different glass works of that city from 1866 until 1879. He then located in Beaver Falls, and became one of the organizers of the Coöperative Glass Works. of which he has since been a stockholder, and was one of the employes until May 1, 1887. Nov. 8, 1886, with George E. Smith, he organized the Beaver Falls Glass Co., Limited, of which he is the general manager. Plans were made and ground blown for the new works March 14, 1887, and the manufacture of general pressed and blown glass was begun June 22, 1887. The works are said to have the largest furnace in the United States. In 1881 Mr. Ohnsman married Mary R., daughter of William and Emeline (Knowles) Shuster, of Lawrence county, Pa., by whom he has two children living: Nelson J. and Mary G. In 1876 Mr. Ohnsman was one of the organizers of the Greenback party in Pittsburgh (South Side), and took an active part in its interest. He is a member of the Methodist Protestant church, and has been superintendent of the Sabbath-school two years. He is independent in politics, but tends toward the Greenback doctrine.

AUGUST OSCHMAN, glass presser, Beaver Falls, was born in Hesse Cassel, Germany, Nov. 4, 1849, and is a son of William and Christina (Hanner) Oschman, who immigrated to this country in 1854 and settled in Pittsburgh. In 1873 his father removed to West Virginia, and is now engaged in farming there. Mr. Oschman was reared in Pittsburgh, and served a three-years' apprenticeship at his trade in the glass works of Brice, Walker & Co., after which he worked as a journeyman in that city sixteen years. In 1879 he came to Beaver Falls and entered the employ of the Coöperative Glass Company, where he is still engaged. In 1871 he married Caroline, daughter of Jacob Kerlie, of Pittsburgh, and by her has three children: Elizabeth, Alfred and Arthur. He has served as a member of the board of directors of the Coöperative Glass Company for three years. Politically he is a Republican.

JOHN A. PAFF, tailor, Beaver Falls, was born in Bavaria, Germany, March 10, 1826, and is a son of John and Susan (Hein) Paff. He was reared in Bavaria, where he learned the tailor's trade, and in 1848 came to America. He located in Pittsburgh, where he worked at his trade and was in business until 1869. He then located in Beaver Falls. In 1850 he married Caroline, daughter of George and Mary (Raynor) Fischer, of Pittsburgh, formerly of Bavaria, Germany, and by her has five children living: John J., Adam, William, Lena (Mrs. Albert Strub) and Lawrence. Mr. Paff is one of the founders of St. Mary's Catholic church of Beaver Falls, and gave liberally toward the erection of the present church edifice.

JOHN J. PAFF, dry goods merchant, Beaver Falls, was born in Allegheny City, Dec. 8, 1852, and is a son of John A. and Caroline (Fischer) Paff, whose sketch appears above. His paternal grandparents were John and Susan (Hein) Paff, of Bavaria, Germany; his maternal grandparents were George and Mary (Rayner) Fischer, of Pittsburgh, formerly of Bavaria, Germany. Mr. Paff came to Beaver Falls with his parents in 1869, and in 1880 embarked in the dry goods business. In 1885 he began the erection of the store he now occupies, which was completed in 1886. It is a handsome, two-story brick building, with glass front, 95 by 30 feet, and is one of the most attractive dry goods stores in western Pennsylvania. Mr. Paff was married Sept. 14, 1882, to Theresa Wickenhauser, of Allegheny City, by whom he has two children: Clara, born July 4, 1883, and Agnes, born Dec. 25, 1885. Mr. Paff is one of the leading merchants of Beaver Falls; is a member of the Catholic church, and was one of the organizers of the Catholic Mutual Benefit Association, and its first president. Politically he is a Democrat.

WILLIAM H. PAISLEY, manager Coöperative Foundry Association, Beaver Falls, was born in Philadelphia, Pa., May 4, 1844, son of Robert and Anna J. Paisley, who settled in Beaver Falls in 1872. William H. was reared in Philadelphia, where he learned the stove molder's trade. He enlisted in the late war of the rebellion in February, 1864, in Company G., 29th P. V. V., and was honorably discharged July 17, 1865. In 1872 he located in Beaver Falls, and became a stockholder in the Coöperative Foundry Association, where he has since been employed, and has held the position of manager for five years. In December, 1869, he married Maggie M. Morganstern, of Marietta, Ohio, by whom he has seven children living: Laura, Fred, William, Bertha, Charles, McCloud, an infant son. Mr Paisley is a member of the Reformed Presbyterian church, and an honorary member of the Iron Moulders' Union.

NOAH H. PANGBURN, insurance agent, Beaver Falls, was born in Allegheny county, Pa., Feb. 12, 1840, and is a son of Isaac and Susan (Hill) Pangburn. His paternal grandfather was Stephen Pangburn, a pioneer of Allegheny county; his maternal grandfather was Samuel Hill, of Lycoming county. His father, who was born in Allegheny county in 1794, was a millwright, and built many of the pioneer mills of western Pennsylvania. He was in the milling business himself for many years, and died near Elizabeth, Allegheny county, in November, 1869. Noah H. Pangburn was reared and educated in his native county. Aug. 22, 1862, he enlisted in Company E, 155th P. V. I., and participated in twenty-two engagements, among which were Chancellorsville, Gettysburg, Wilderness, Spottsylvania, Bethesda Church, North Anna River, Cold Harbor, Petersburg, Five Forks and Appomattox. He was honorably discharged June 2, 1865, and returning home, engaged in the milling business. In 1868 he located in Beaver Falls, and commenced the insurance business. He represents the leading companies of the world, and his agency extends throughout Beaver county and adjoining territory. Mr. Pangburn served as justice of the peace of Beaver Falls for five years, and was also elected burgess for three consecutive terms, 1881-82-83. He is a member of the G. A. R., Union Veterans' Legion, A. O. U. W., and he is a F. & A. M. Politically he is a Republican.

REV. MICHAEL A. PARKINSON, of Industry, Pa., son of Thomas and Mary Parkinson, was born in Washington county, Pa. His ancestors settled in an early day on the Monongahela river, near Monongahela City, where many of the family yet reside. In 1837 his father removed to Beaver county, and located on a farm in Raccoon township. Soon after their removal to that county, he began a course of study at Bethel Academy, near Pittsburgh, under Rev. George Marshall, D. D. Afterward he attended Frankfort Academy, under the supervision of Rev. James Sloan, D. D., and Hon. Thomas Nicholson, and graduated at Jefferson College, Cannonsburgh, Pa., under the presidency of Rev. Robert J. Breckenridge, D. D.; studied theology at the Western Theological Seminary at Allegheny City, and was licensed by the Presbytery of Ohio, now the Presbytery of Pittsburgh. The greater part of his ministry has been spent in Ohio, in the bounds of the Presbytery of Steubenville. He married Miss Kate C., daughter of William McClelland, Esq., of Cannonsburgh, Pa.

WILLIAM HUNTER PARTINGTON, county commissioner, Beaver Falls, was born in Steubenville, Ohio, March 22, 1840, and is a son of Richard and Ellen (Horner) Partington. His father was a native of England, and a woolen maufacturer, who settled in Chippewa township, Beaver county, in 1846, and died of cholera in 1849. He was a son of Robert Partington, a cotton spinner, who settled in what is now Beaver Falls, in 1830, and kept hotel there. He afterward farmed in Chippewa township, and kept hotel on the stage road between New Brighton and New Castle. His children were James, Nancy (Mrs. James Richards), Mary (Mrs. Wm. Large), Richard and William. Of these, Richard had three children, of whom William H. is the only one living. He was reared in Beaver county, and is a farmer by occupation. In August, 1862, he married Margaret, daughter of Milo and Ellen (Sweezy) McDonnell, by whom he has four children living: Eleanor, Hattie. Frank and Cora B. Mr. Partington was elected commissioner of Beaver county in 1884, and re-elected in 1887. He is a member of the I. O. O. F., and politically is a Democrat.

JOHN PATTEN, farmer and stock grower, P. O. Beaver, was born in Beaver county, Pa., June 3, 1814, and is a son of James and Betsy (Green) Patten, former a native of Maryland, latter of Pennsylvania, and both of Scotch-Irish descent. His father was a farmer, and in early life worked at the carpenter's trade. John is the third in a family of seven children. He was reared on the farm and attended the district school. At the age of eighteen he went to Allegheny county, where he lived until 1863, when he returned to Beaver county and continued farming. He is the owner of 124 acres of land, and has dealt in sheep. He spent two years in California Mr. Patten was married in Allegheny county, Pa., in 1854, to Agnes Hartford, who was born in Beaver county, a daughter of Thomas Hartford. The marriage of Mr. and Mrs. Patten has been blessed with one child, Almira J. The family are members of the U. P. church. Mr. Patten has been supervisor and assessor of Brighton township.

DANIEL O. C. PATTERSON, coal merchant, Beaver Falls, was born in Beaver Falls Sept. 9, 1832, and is a son of James and Eliza (Large) Patterson. His father came when but six years of age from Ireland with his parents, who settled in Albany, N. Y. In early manhood James Patterson located in Philadelphia, where he manufactured tanks for several years. He then erected a cotton mill at Doe Run, Chester county, and in 1829 settled in what is now Beaver Falls, where at one time he owned 1,200 acres of land, also a tract of 160 acres of cannel coal land in Darlington. He erected a grist mill which turned out 200 barrels of flour per day, and built a cotton mill which gave employment to 150 hands. He erected the Mansion House in 1836. In 1854 he sold 400 acres of land to New York parties. Mr. Patterson had large coal interests, and kept the largest general store in the county in the pioneer days, his various interests giving employment to from 200 to 300 people. He was the first postmaster of Brighton, and for several years carried a daily mail at his own expense between his own office and Beaver. He was an active politician and a member of the Whig party. He voted for James Buchanan, but at the breaking out of the rebellion united with the Republican party. He refused the nomination to both houses of Congress, also for Governor of Ohio, when for judicial purposes he had gained a residence there in 1854. He was a public-spirited man, and gave liberally toward all public enterprises. His wife was a daughter of Daniel Large, of Chester county, Pa. He had six children who grew to maturity: Mary (Mrs. Daniel Stone), Daniel O. C., Charles W., Harry C., Samuel R. and Sarah. Mr. Patterson died in September, 1876. Our subject was reared in Beaver county, was actively engaged in farming until 1882, and was the pioneer dairyman of Beaver Falls. He has also been extensively engaged in the coal interests of the county. In 1857 he married Elvira, daughter of Col. John and Elvira (Adams) Dickey. Her father was a native of Greensburg, and a pioneer furnaceman of Beaver Falls. He was a son of Robert Dickey, a prominent citizen of Westmoreland county. Elvira, wife of Col. John Dickey, was a daughter of Dr. and Rev. Samuel Adams, of Essex county. Mass., a pioneer of Beaver Falls. Mr. and Mrs. Patterson have four children living: John D., Grace, James O. C. and Elvira.

JAMES PATTERSON, farmer, P. O. New Galilee, was born in Mercer county in 1830. In 1822 his grandfather, James Patterson, a farmer by occupation, with his wife and nine children emigrated to America from County Armagh, Ireland, and soon after his arrival settled in Beaver (now Lawrence) county, where he purchased 200 acres of land. He was twice married and had four children by his first wife, and five children by his second wife. He died at the age of eighty-five years. William, the eldest son by the first wife, purchased a farm in Mercer county soon after the arrival of the family in America, and here remained until 1833, when he bought 160 acres of land in Big Beaver township. Here he resided until his death, which occurred in 1874, at the age of seventy-three years. His wife was Mary, daughter of Thomas Mathers, of Mercer county, and they had three children: James, Margaret (Mrs. Patterson) and Thomas. William was successfully engaged in canal contracting for many years. James came to Beaver county with his parents when a child, and has since lived here. He was educated in the common schools and Greersburg Academy. In 1858 he married Julia Ann, daughter of James McGeorge, an early settler in Western Pennsylvania, and they have one son, William J., a student in Genna College, at Beaver Falls. Mr. Patterson owns 120 acres of land, ninety of which his father purchased. Many improvements in the way of buildings, etc., have been made. He is a member of the Reformed Presbyterian church; in politics a Republican.

THOMAS PATTERSON, farmer, P. O. New Galilee, is the youngest son of William and Mary (Mathers) Patterson, and was born in Big Beaver township in 1834, on the farm he now owns. He was reared on the farm, attended the "old log school-house" and the Greersburg Academy, and has followed farming as a business. In 1862 he was married to Miss V. C. Irvin, daughter of Mathew and Mattie Irvin, of Lawrence county, and seven children have been born to them, of whom five are living: Eva A., Ira B., James E., Walter S. and Alexander Savidge. Mr. Patterson owns 160 acres of land, nearly all of which is under cultivation. He has held various township offices, including school director. He is a member of the Reformed Presbyterian church; in politics he is a Republican.

REV. SAMUEL PATTERSON was born June 18, 1820, in County Derry, Ireland, and most of his common education was obtained in his native land. In 1836 he emigrated to this country and settled in the city of Allegheny where he remained about thirteen years. In 1843 he entered the Western University, then under the control of Dr. Bruce and Mr. Greerson. When they withdrew from that institution and established Duquesne College, he left the University and graduated at Duquesne College in the fall of 1845. He then entered the theological seminary of the Associate Reformed church in Allegheny, and having gone through the prescribed course was licensed to preach March 29, 1848. By appointment of General Synod, he was sent that summer to preach for three months to a congregation at Indianapolis, also six weeks to Bellefontaine and two weeks to Urbana, Ohio. He then returned to the seminary, and having completed the entire course, he accepted a call from the united charge of Rocky Spring and East Palestine, and entered upon his pastoral work on the first Sabbath of May, 1849. He was ordained and installed Sept. 25, 1849. He remained the pastor of these two congregations till the union of the Associate and Associate Reformed denominations into one body, constituting what is now denominated the United Presbyterian Church of North America. This union took place in 1858. Soon after this he gave up the Palestine branch of his charge, and in a short time afterward all his time was given to Rocky Spring. He is still the pastor of this congregation. Mr. Patterson was married in 1855 to Miss Eliza Jane, eldest daughter of David and Jane Gilliland (deceased). Mrs. Eliza Patterson died in February, 1885, leaving a husband and seven children — four sons and three daughters to mourn her loss. Mr. Patterson owns a large farm near Darlington, managed chiefly by his sons. Politically, he is a Republican.

GEORGE W. PENN, editor of the Beaver Falls *Herald and Globe*, is a journalist of sixteen years' experience. He is a native of Cadiz, Ohio, is on the shady side of forty, and has assisted in clipping three coupons from the bonds of the matrimony. He was reared a farmer's son and began in business life as a clerk in a general store, after which he was successively a mail carrier, an engineer of a stationary engine, and a school teacher, spending eight years in latter capacity in Indiana, Ohio and Pennsylvania. During the past sixteen years he has been employed as a newspaper writer in Ohio, Minnesota and Pennsylvania.

JAMES D. PERROTT, dry goods merchant, Beaver Falls, was born in South Beaver township March 3, 1845, and is a son of Thomas and Mary (Edgar) Perrott, former a native of Ireland, who settled in South Beaver township in 1828. He was a woolen manufacturer, and engaged in that business in South Beaver and Fallston. He had ten children: John R., Nancy (Mrs. Jacob B. Parkinson), Sarah (Mrs. Jacob Ecki), James D., Thomas (deceased), Samuel (deceased), Richard, Mary, Jennie and Clara A. (Mrs. Edward L. Hutchinson). Mr. Perrott's maternal grandfather was Samuel Edgar, of Westmoreland county, Pa., a son of John Edgar, a major in the revolution, the latter being of Scotch descent. Samuel Edgar came to this county with his father in 1811, and settled in Fallston in 1830, where he engaged in milling until his death in 1872. James D. Perrott was reared and educated in Fallston. From 1860 until 1873 he was employed as clerk in the store of Duncan & Edgar. April 1, 1874, he embarked in the dry goods business in Beaver Falls with A. Tomlinson, Esq., and in 1877 purchased his partners interest. In 1884 he erected his present store, which is 125 by 30 feet. In 1884 Mr. Perrott, with Gawn Ward and Jacob Ecki, purchased the plant of the Howard Stove Company, which is among the leading industries of Beaver Falls. In 1875 he married Maggie J., daughter of James and Margaret Jackson, of New Sewickley township, by whom he has five children: Clyde R., Howard D., Frank C., Helen M. and Edward H. Mr. Perrott is a wide-awake business man, and his extensive trade is evidence of his

BIOGRAPHIES—WEST SIDE. 707

popularity. He is a F. & A. M., a member of the Royal Arcanum and N. W. Masonic Society of Chicago; politically he is a Republican.

H. C. PHEIL, butcher, Beaver Falls, was born in Pittsburgh May 13, 1848, and is a son of Philip and Barbara (Snyder) Pheil, of Germany, who settled in Pittsburgh as early as 1830. Mr. Pheil was reared and educated in his native city, where he thoroughly learned his trade. He located in Beaver Falls in 1880, and opened a meat market, which is now one of the neatest, best appointed and most reliable in Beaver county, and is liberally patronized. Mr. Pheil is a member of the M. E. church; politically he is a Republican.

WILLIAM PICKLES, coal dealer, P. O. Enon Valley, was born in Yorkshire, England, in 1829, and came to America in 1853, with his parents, Robert (a farmer) and Elizabeth (Midgley) Pickles, who had ten children, of whom William is the eldest son. He was a coal miner for many years. He came to Beaver county in 1868, and now owns coal land rich with a superior quality of bituminous coal. He was married, in 1849, to Mary Ann, daughter of Thomas and Mary Oldfield, of England, and has had three children: Harrison, a miner with his father; William Henry (deceased); and Emma Jane, at home. The mother died in 1887, aged sixty three years. Mr. Pickles has retired from mining, and devotes his time to selling coal for home consumption. He was in the army from 1864 to 1865. He is a member of the Presbyterian church; in politics he is a Republican.

WILLIAM SWAN PLUMER, D.D., LL.D., one of Beaver county's distinguished sons, was born at Darlington (then called Greersburg) July 26, 1802. His education was received at Washington College, after his graduation from which he entered Princeton Theological Seminary, matriculating in 1824-25. He was licensed to preach by the New Brunswick Presbytery June 14, 1826, and on 19th of May of the following year was ordained an evangelist by the Presbytery of Orange. During the three years following he engaged in evangelistic work in Southern Virginia and North Carolina, organizing churches at Danville and at Warrenton, N. C. In June, 1829, he was appointed regular supply of the Briery, Va., church, and immediately began the duties of pastor. His pastoral charges thereafter were Tabb Street church, Petersburg, Va., from July, 1831, to Sept. 19, 1834; First church, of Richmond, Va., from Oct. 19, 1834, to Nov. 3, 1846; Franklin Street church, Baltimore, Md., from April 28, 1847, to Sept. 10, 1854; Central church, of Allegheny, Pa., from Jan. 17, 1855, to Sept. 19, 1862; Second church, of Pottsville, Pa., from Nov. 19, 1865, to Jan. 2, 1867; and various churches in the vicinity of Columbia, S. C., to which place he removed in the early part of 1867. Besides his duties in the pulpit Dr. Plumer founded in 1837, and was for eight years, sole editor, of *The Watchman of the South*. In 1838 he assisted in the establishing of the Institution for the Blind, Deaf and Dumb. at Staunton, Va. In 1854 he was chosen a professor in the Western Theological Seminary, of Allegheny, Pa., where he continued until 1862, occupying the chair of Didactic and Pastoral Theology. He then received the appointment to a similar position in the Columbia, S. C., Theological seminary. He remained with this institution until its close in 1880, being transferred to the chair of Historic, Casuistic and Pastoral Theology in 1875, at his own request. In addition to his labors as pastor and professor, Dr. Plumer won enviable distinction as an author. In all his efforts he manifested an earnestness of spirit, and a zealous love for the right that left their impress on his many labors. Personally he was tall and erect, with snow-white hair, beaming eye, open countenance and a dignity of manner which, together with his rich, full voice, gave a wonderful effectiveness to his preaching In pulpit, in the school room, and in the editorial chair, he labored for the upbuilding of the Presbyterian church. At the good age of seventy-nine he died in Baltimore, Md., Oct. 22, 1880, firm in the faith which he had so long upheld.

JOHN POPP, farmer, P. O. Industry, was born in Baden, Germany, June 22, 1824, son of Sylvester and Margarette Popp, also natives of Germany. The father was a farmer by occupation, and died in Germany. John came to America in 1849, and worked as a farm laborer in Allegheny county, Pa., for six years; he then rented a farm in the same county, and followed agricultural pursuits until 1869. In the following year he purchased and removed to his present farm in Industry township. He was married, in 1847, to Susan, daughter of Wolfcombe Schuster, a native of Germany, and five children have blessed their union: Maggie, wife of Michael Hardner, of Allegheny county; Caroline, wife of John Paser, of Droversburg, Pa.; John, a farmer in Industry township, and married to Mary Methouse; Mary, wife of Peter Smith, of Droversburg; and George. at home. Mr. Popp is allied to no political party, but always supports the best man; his first vote was cast for Stephen A. Douglas. He and his wife are members of the Lutheran church.

JAMES L. PORTER, blacksmith, is a son of Robert and Eliza (Loyd) Porter, and was born at Unionville, Beaver county, in February, 1854. His parents were natives of Allegheny county, his mother having been born in McKeesport; and his grandfathers on both sides were natives of Ireland. James attended the home school at Unionville, and also one in Stewart county, Tenn. At the age of sixteen years he began learning the blacksmith's trade, and in 1876 opened a shop at Black Hawk postoffice, where he remained for twelve years. He then opened a shop at East Liverpool Ohio, and after sixteen months moved to Fairview, his present location. He married, Dec. 16, 1877, Katharine McFarland, daughter of Benjamin and Mary (Donovan) McFarland, who was born March 26, 1858, in South Beaver township. Two children have blessed this union, Edwin B. and Clyde A., both of whom are at home. Mr. and Mrs. Porter are members of the Presbyterian church.

REV. HENRY N. POTTER, Darlington, was born in Raccoon township, this county, April 6, 1837, the son of John and Eliza Potter. His father was a farmer, but most of his life was employed in active church work; he spent the latter portion of it in missionary work in Philadelphia. Our subject had three brothers in the ministry: James H., now of Eustis, Fla.; John W., who died in 1866; and Gilbert M., of Sharpsburg, Pa. Henry N was reared on a farm, receiving his education at Jefferson College and the Western Theological Seminary. He entered the ministry in 1865, spent the first years of his ministry in the west, and since December, 1870, has been pastor of Mt. Pleasant Presbyterian church, Darlington. He was married, Aug. 29, 1867, to Miss Mary Coe McKown, of Berkeley county, W. Va., and they have had four children, of whom but two, John Elton and Mary Eloisa Walton, are living.

JOHN PURDY, farmer, P. O. Beaver, was born in Allegheny county, Nov. 8, 1833, a son of Farmer and Esther (Richmond) Purdy, natives of Pennsylvania and of English descent. His father is a farmer and makes the raising of sheep a specialty, owning 250 head, and, although eighty-five years old, attends to all his own business. Mrs. Esther Purdy died in 1851. John is the second in a family of three children; was reared on the farm, the pursuits of which he has always followed, and was educated at the common schools. He owns seventy-six acres of land, where he now resides, in Brighton township. He was married, in 1868, to Hannah, daughter of Abraham Christy, and their children are William, now attending the University at Pittsburgh, and Almner. Mr. and Mrs. Purdy are members of the United Presbyterian church, of which he is an elder. He is a Republican, and has served two terms as supervisor of Brighton town ship. He enlisted in 1862, in Company H, 140th Regiment, and was a non commissioned officer; was present at the surrender of General Lee, and was wounded at Spottsylvania in the arm and side; was slightly wounded at Gettysburg, but he remained at his post until the battle was over.

B. F. PYLE, farmer, P. O. New Galilee, is a son of Dr. A. J. and Eliza (Sheppard) Pyle, of New Galilee. Dr. Pyle practiced medicine in New Galilee for twenty years, and died in 1886. B. F. was educated at Allegheny College, Meadville, Pa., and combines carpenter work with farming. He married Jeannetta J. Glass, granddaughter of Robert Harbison, and they reside on the homestead of the latter in Big Beaver township. They have a fine farm of 200 acres, with first-class buildings, and are in a position to enjoy life. They have one child, Mary Elva. Mr. and Mrs. Pyle are members of the United Presbyterian church. Mr. Pyle votes with the Democratic party.

HON. MATTHEW STANLEY QUAY, United States senator, P. O. Beaver, was born at Dillsburg, York county, Pa., Sept. 30, 1833. He is the son of Rev. Anderson Beaton Quay, by his wife Catherine McCain. His father was a prominent Presbyterian clergyman, who was settled for years over flourishing congregations, first at Dillsburg, York county, then at Beaver, Beaver county, and finally at Indiana, Indiana county. The Rev. Anderson B. Quay was a son of Joseph Quay and Ascenath Anderson, who lived in what is now Schuylkill township, in the northern part of Chester county, near Phœnixville. His (Senator Quay's) grandmother's father was Patrick Anderson, the first white child born in the township. Anderson was a captain in the French and Indian war, and, on the breaking out of the Revolution was, along with Anthony Wayne, a member of the Chester county committee. He went into the service in 1776 as captain of the first company in the Pennsylvania Musketry Battalion, and after the battle of Long Island, in which Colonel Atlee was captured and Lieutenant-Colonel Parry killed, he commanded the battalion. In 1778 and 1779 he sat in the Pennsylvania Assembly, and his son, Isaac Anderson, represented that district in Congress from 1808 to 1807. Senator Quay's great-grandmother, Ann Beaton, was the daughter of Daniel Beaton, and the sister of Colonel John Beaton, who, during the Revolution, was most active in military affairs in Chester county. Patrick Anderson's father, James Anderson, came from Scotland in 1713, and afterward married Elizabeth Jerman, daughter of Thomas Jerman, a noted Quaker preacher, who came from Wales with his wife Elizabeth, and settled about 1700 in the Chester valley, where he erected one of the earliest mills in the province.

Senator Quay graduated from Jefferson College, Pennsylvania, in 1850, studied law with Penny & Sterrett, in Pittsburgh, and was admitted to the bar of Beaver county in 1854. The following year he was appointed prothonotary of this county, and was elected in 1856, and again in 1859. In 1861 he resigned his office to accept a lieutenancy in the Tenth Pennsylvania Reserves, and was subsequently made assistant commissary-general of the state, with the rank of lieutenant-colonel. Afterward he was appointed private secretary to Gov. Andrew G. Curtin, and, in August, 1862, was commissioned colonel of the 134th Regiment, Pennsylvania Volunteers. He was mustered out, owing to ill-health, Dec. 7, 1862, but participated in the assault on Marye's Heights, Dec. 13, 1862, as a volunteer. He was subsequently appointed state agent at Washington, but shortly afterward was recalled by the legislature to fill the office of military secretary, created by that body. He was elected to the legislature in 1864, and again in 1865 and 1866. In the latter year he was secretary of the Republican state committee, of which he was chairman in 1878. In 1869 he established and edited the Beaver *Radical.* In 1873–78 he was secretary of the commonwealth, resigning to accept the appointment of recorder of Philadelphia. This office he resigned in January, 1879, when he was again appointed secretary of the commonwealth, filling that post until October, 1882, when he resigned. In November, 1885, he was elected state treasurer by the largest vote ever given to a candidate for that office. He resigned in September, 1887. On Jan. 18, 1887, he was elected United States senator for the term ending March 3, 1893. He is a member of the following senate committees—Manufactures, Pensions, Public Buildings and Grounds, Post Offices and Post Roads, and Claims; and chairman of the committee to examine the several branches of the civil service.

Senator Quay was married, in 1855, to Agnes Barclay, daughter of John Barclay, by his wife Elizabeth Shannon. Her parents were natives of Pennsylvania, and were of Scotch-Irish descent. The children of this marriage, all of whom were born at Beaver, are Richard Roberts, Andrew Gregg Curtin, Mary Agnew, Coral, and Susan Willard. The eldest son is a student at law, while the second is a 2nd lieutenant, U. S. army, having graduated from West Point June 11, 1888.

JAMES H. RAMSEY was born near Frankfort Springs, Beaver county, Pa., son of John and May Hay Harper Ramsey; parents both formerly married; only child by last marriage; of Scotch Irish descent; father a farmer. He received his collegiate education at Jefferson College, Cannonsburg, Washington county, Pa.; graduated at Western Reserve Medical College, Cleveland, Ohio; commenced practice of medicine in

Virginia. He married Agnes S., daughter of William and Nancy Stewart, Hookstown, Beaver county, Pa., in 1856. He was regimental surgeon of the 17th West Virginia Infantry, and part of the time on detached service with the 8th Ohio Cavalry. After the war he practiced his profession sixteen years in Frankfort Springs, Pa.; located in Bridgewater in 1881, and engaged in the drug business and his profession; has had charge of the medical department of the Beaver County Alms House for some years. He has seven children: William S., M. D., a physician and surgeon; Lizzie M., Nina A., Mrs. Laura O. Wineman, Myra B., J. Edgar and Hallie Ethel.

- JOHN W. RAMSEY, superintendent water works, Beaver Falls, was born in North Sewickley township, Oct. 6, 1848, and is a son of Thomas and Sarah (White) Ramsey. His paternal grandfather, Samuel Ramsey, a native of Eastern Pennsylvania, and a pioneer of North Sewickley township, had ten children: Milton, Samuel, James, Thomas, Silas, Matthew, Robert, John, Elizabeth and Mary A. Of these Thomas was a prominent farmer of North Sewickley township, and held several township offices, and served one term as director of the County Poor House. He was accidentally killed on the P. & L. E. R. R. at Brady's Run, in 1880. His children were Clorinda, Eliza, Lycurgus, Edith, John W., Harrison, Mary, Jennie and Anna. John W., in early life, learned the carpenter, machinist and blacksmith trades. In 1861 he embarked in the oil business in Pennsylvania and West Virginia, and operated and drilled a large number of wells. He drilled the largest gas well in the United States at that time (1876) (12-inch bore—2,430 feet deep), for the Economy Society of this county. Since 1876 he has been superintendent of the Beaver Falls Water Works. He has seven valuable patents of his own invention, viz.:—the Ramsey and Corbus fire plug, and automatic natural gas regulating valve, fruit jar cover, furnace for melting pig iron by natural gas, wire nail machine, compression coupling for cold rolled shafting, used by the Hartman Steel Co., of this city, exclusively. In 1870 Mr. Ramsey married Mary, daughter of William and Margaret (Corson) Stafford, of Beaver Falls, and by her has six children: William, Ida, Maud, Effie, Mabel and Beatrice. Mr. Ramsey is a member of the A. O. U. W. Politically he is independent. In 1888 he was elected one of the school directors for White township, for three years, by the entire vote of the township.

B. S. RANGER, merchant, was born in Franklin county, Mass., Nov. 18, 1812. His parents, Moses and Jane (Smith) Ranger, were natives of Massachusetts, and of Scotch-Irish and English descent, former a farmer. B. S. is the eldest in a family of six children. He taught school in early life, and in 1847 he came to Pennsylvania, locating in Johnstown, where he worked in a furnace as assistant manager. In 1852 he accepted a position as railroad overseer, and was sent to Beaver, remaining in the employ of the railroad company for five years. His early life as a school teacher had given him a better insight into human nature than many men who were older had. In 1861 he came to Bridgewater and embarked in the mercantile trade. For many years he has done a large and successful business, and by judicious investments and careful management has succeeded in accumulating a handsome fortune. He is largely interested in real estate, and is the owner of one entire block in Bridgewater. In politics Mr. Ranger is a Republican.

IRA RANSOM, SR., was born in Trenton, Oneida county, N. Y., July 19, 1813, and is a son of Daniel and Mary (Peirce) Ransom. In 1834 he located in Beaver Falls, where he was the contractor for the Erie extension of the Pennsylvania Canal. In 1840 he entered the employ of James Patterson, of Beaver Falls, as a grain buyer. In 1849 he engaged in building railroads, and constructed eight miles of the Pittsburgh, Fort Wayne & Chicago Railway, by contract. In 1852 he removed to Youngstown, Ohio, where he resided until 1869, and during his residence there assisted in building several railroads by contract, among them the Baltimore & Ohio, the Central Ohio (now the Panhandle), and the Steubenville & Indiana. In 1869 he returned to Beaver Falls, and engaged in the flour and feed business for seven years, conducting also the Beaver Falls Flouring Mills two years. In 1877 he built a section of the Pittsburgh & Lake Erie Railroad, Moravia. Mr. Ransom erected the first brick residence in Beaver Falls. In

BIOGRAPHIES—WEST SIDE.   711

February, 1885, he married Margaret, daughter of John and Catharine (McIntire) Braden, pioneers of Chippewa township. They had eight children: Oscar, John, Darwin, Ira, Willard, Thaddeus, Alfred and Mary, all deceased except Ira and Alfred.

JOHN REBESKE, grocer, Beaver Falls, was born in Russian Poland, Nov. 28, 1828, and is a son of Thomas H. and Ellen (Bielohowske) Rebeske. He was reared and educated in his native land, was a refugee of the revolution of 1848, came to America in 1850 and settled in Pittsburgh, where he worked in the machine shops about sixteen years. He then engaged in the grocery business in Pittsburgh (South Side) for six years. In 1870 he removed to Beaver Falls, where he has since been actively engaged in the grocery business. Mis wife was Mary E. Cornelius, a native of Prussia, by whom he has six children: Adolph, Frances (Mrs. John Volk), Edward C., John L., Lena (Mrs. Joseph Schell) and William. Mr. Rebeske is a member of the Catholic church. He belongs to the Druids, and the I. O. O. F. Politically he is a Republican.

IRWIN B. REED, farmer, P. O. Darlington, was born in Fallston, Feb. 22, 1852. In the spring of that year his parents moved on the farm where he now resides, and which was formerly owned by his grandfather. He was educated at the Greersburg Academy and commenced teaching school in Darlington township in 1870, in what is known as the Nebo school. In 1871 he took a trip to Kansas, where, in Ottawa, Franklin county, he attended school one term. The winter of 1871 he taught school in Anderson county, Kan., and when his term closed took a trip South, thence to Emporia, Kan., where, in 1872, he attended the State Normal School one term. Subsequently, he took a trip to the Indian Territory, returned to Anderson county, Kan., Sept. 1, 1872, and taught for six months in the Tipton District. In the spring of 1873 he returned to Pennsylvania, stopped on the way at Atlantic, Iowa, and arrived home April 10. After his return he taught school for six winter terms and then engaged in farming, which he still follows. Dec. 28, 1882, he married Mary E. McGeorge.

J. F. REED, attorney, Beaver, was born in Hopewell township, this county, and is a son of William M. and Nancy E. (Jordan) Reed. His ancestors were early settlers in Pennsylvania, and were a robust class of people, the male members being mostly farmers. Our subject's grandfather, Thomas, was a soldier under General Washington, and being captured by the British together with seventeen others, it was decided that thirteen of them should be shot. They drew lots and Mr. Reed was one of the number to be shot, but the guard was overpowered and they all escaped. Thomas Reed came to this county after the close of the war, and lived to a good old age. Our subject's father was a farmer, and is a well-known and wealthy resident of Hopewell township. He has six children, of whom J. F. is the eldest. Our subject's early education was received in the common and select schools of Hopewell township, and he afterward attended Frankfort Academy and the college at Mt. Union, Ohio. He chose the law as his profession, and studied in the office of the late Frank Wilson, of Beaver, Pa. He was admitted to the bar Sept. 14, 1877, and has since been in active practice. He was married, May 15, 1878, to Anna M., daughter of Robert C. and Jane (Hay) Scott, of Scotch descent. Mr. and Mrs. Reed have four children: Robert, Bessie, Ethel and William. In politics Mr. Reed is a Republican. He is one of the directors of the First National Bank of Beaver, Pa. His wife is a member of the United Presbyterian church.

JAMES M. REED, county superintendent of public schools, Beaver, was born in Hanover township, this county, Nov. 23, 1854, son of John and Jane (Creswell) Reed, natives of this county and of Scotch-Irish descent. John Reed was a miller in early life and afterward a farmer. He twice married and raised seven children; James M. being the second child by the second wife. Our subject remained with his parents on the farm, attending school at the Miller school-house in Hanover township until the death of his father, which occurred in 1861. He then worked on the farm in summer and attended school in winter, employing his leisure time in reading and improving his education. From 1869 until he commenced teaching he worked as a hired hand on a farm during the summer, and attended school during the winter months. He began teaching at the age of eighteen, teaching during the winters and attending to the farm duties and going to Frankfort Academy in the summers. In 1876 he received a state certificate, but feeling the necessity of a more thorough course he entered the Edinboro State Normal School, remained there two terms, and then engaged in teaching again. He has taught in Beaver county in the following places: first at home in the Robert's school-house in Hanover township, one year; next in Industry township, two years. He was principal of Fallston schools, two years, and Vanport school, one year, and, next, principal of the schools in Bridgewater, four years; he was then engaged as principal of the Beaver public schools and teacher in the high school, and served in that capacity, two years. He was then appointed to fill a vacancy as county superintendent, serving two years and nine months. He made it a rule to visit every school in the county at least once a year. The first year he held fourteen educational meetings with the teachers, the second year twenty-two, and the third year thirty-one. He was elected superintendent May 3, 1887, without any opposition, and the directors' convention increased his salary from $1,000 to $1,500 per year. He is devotedly attached to his profession and has done much to improve the schools of his native county. In 1885 he invented the Teacher's Term Report Blank, for which he received a copyright. In 1887 he introduced the graduating system in the common schools of the county. Mr. Reed was married, Jan. 7, 1886, to Amelia Moorehead, daughter of Samuel Moorehead, and they have a son, John M., born Feb. 10, 1887. Mr. and Mrs. Reed are members of the Beaver Presbyterian church, and he has been superintendent of the Sabbath-school three years.

JOSEPH M. REED, assessor and constable, Bridgewater, was born in Beaver, Sept. 29, 1830, and is a son of Eli and Margaret (Daniels) Reed, the former born in Allegheny county, Pa., and the latter at Cape May, N. J. The father was born Sept. 26, 1781; learned the hatter's trade, and moved to Beaver, where he followed his trade for many years. He served several terms as coroner for Beaver county. He was a soldier in the war of 1812. He died in Bridgewater in 1881, having attained the remarkable age of one hundred years and seven months. His family consisted of six daughters and one son, of whom three daughters and one son are now living. Joseph M. has spent most of his life in Beaver county, where he attended the district schools. Early in life he learned the baker's trade. In the late war he served three months in the Tenth Pennsylvania Reserves, and then enlisted in the United States service for three years. He served six months as first lieutenant, was then promoted to captain, and was discharged for disability in 1863. At the battle of Fredericksburg his leg was broken, but he remained on the field until the battle closed. At the battle of Antietam he was shot in the shoulder with a ball which he still has in his possession, and which weighs over one-fourth of a pound. He served three years as coroner, and for several terms has been assessor, constable and collector at Bridgewater. He is a member of the K. of P. Mr. Reed married, in 1855, Eliza, daughter of Henry and Elizabeth Gull, natives of Germany, and they have one child, J. H. D. Reed, who is a resident of Bridgewater. Mrs. Reed is a member of the Methodist Episcopal church.

WILLIAM C. REED, farmer and stock breeder, P. O. Ohioville, was born Dec. 20, 1851, on a farm in Liverpool township, Ohio, where he was reared and received a common-school education. On reaching manhood he engaged for a time in shipping stock, and also in butchering. At the time of the historical cloudburst at Pittsburgh, about 1874 (when many persons lost their lives by the overflow of Sawmill Run), Mr. Reed was engaged successfully in business there, and his entire property was swept away, compelling him to start life anew. Since then he has been engaged in farming, and now gives especial attention to the breeding of shorthorn cattle and Chester-White swine. He also keep a meat market at Ohio City. Politically he is a Republican, and is a member of Line Island Lodge, No. 742, I. O. O. F., at Glasgow. Both himself and wife are communicants in the Methodist Episcopal church at Ohioville. Their marriage occurred Sept. 19, 1872. Mrs. Reed, born in Liverpool March 15, 1856, is Annie, a daughter of Thomas and Eliza Smith, of Pennsylvania. Mr. and Mrs. Reed have three children living, viz.: Thomas Anthony, Ethel Maud and Earl Smith. The second child, Hattie, died at the age of nine years. Mr. Reed's parents were Anthony and Sophie (Caywood) Reed, natives of Ohio, as was probably his grandfather, Anthony.

JOHN and HENRY TAYLOR REEVES. The Reeves family are of Welsh extraction. Joseph Reeves, the great-grandfather of the subjects of this biographical sketch, resided at Mount Holly, and is buried in the cemetery of the Episcopal church of that village. Among his children was a son Joseph, also a resident of Mount Holly, who who married Elizabeth Toy, born July 5, 1758. Their children were sons Daniel and Joseph, and daughters Elizabeth, Mary, Sarah, Jane, Martha and Hannah. Daniel, the eldest of these, was born in 1785, and died Dec. 1, 1837. Removing to Beaver Falls in 1805, he followed the trades of cabinet-maker and carpenter until his death. By his marriage with Margaret, daughter of Matthew Steen, of Washington county, Pa., were born children: Eliza (Mrs. Samuel Corbus), Mary Jane (Mrs. David Whitla), Balleria (Mrs. William Carter), Esther (Mrs. Henry Hipple), Joseph, Matthew, John and Henry T, of whom but three survive. John Reeves was born Feb. 9, 1825, in Beaver Falls, and received a limited common English education at the subscription schools of the day, traveling a distance of two miles on foot to enjoy but meagre advantages. At the age of nine years these opportunities ceased, and Mr. Reeves, by habits of close observation, and reflection, made amends in a great degree for the want of thorough training in youth. His father having died when the lad was but twelve years of age, he at once sought employment with a farmer in the neighborhood, and for three years thus aided in the support of the family. Subsequently becoming a driver on the Pittsburgh & Erie Canal, he soon found himself the owner of boats, and continued this life of comparative adventure until 1852. He then accepted the position of conductor on the Pennsylvania & Ohio Railroad, and at the expiration of the fourth year embarked in mercantile pursuits at New Brighton under the firm name of H. T. & J. Reeves. Disposing of their business in 1865, the brothers engaged in real estate operations, the purchase and sale of which as agents has occupied much of their time until the present. In addition to this, Mr. Reeves became in 1868 one of the projectors and the cashier of the Economy Saving Institution. He is also director of the Beaver Valley Street Railway; of the Pittsburgh, Chartiers & Youghiogheny Railroad; director of the Beaver Falls Bridge Company; of the Art Tile Company; of the Pittsburgh & Chartiers Block Coal Company; director of the First National Bank of Beaver Falls; president of the First National Bank of New Brighton and of the Brighton Bridge Company. To these varied enterprises he gives his personal attention, and has by his trained habits of business and mature judgment contributed largely to their success. Mr. Reeves was, on the 25th of March, 1847, married to Cynthia, daughter of John Murphy, of Beaver Falls. Their children were Daniel F. (deceased); Mary Ann (wife of James F. Merriman; Ada (married to W. H. Nair), Hannah (wife of James M. May), William (deceased), J. Charles F. (deceased), Jessie Benton, Grace (wife of George W. Coats), and Jacob Henrici (deceased). Mr. Reeves is in his political preferences a Republican, but is no sense a politician. Being liberally endowed with public spirit and ambitious for the advancement of his native town, he has at various times accepted local offices, but no others. His religious sympathies are with the Presbyterian church, of which he is both a trustee and member.

Henry Taylor Reeves, the brother and business partner of John Reeves, was born Oct. 14, 1827, in Beaver Falls, then known as Brighton, in which locality the years of his active life have been passed. The old school house of Beaver Falls afforded him the only opportunities for education he enjoyed, after which he sought employment in a cotton factory, and at the age of twenty became a clerk in a general country store. Here his business aptness and fidelity to his employer's interests soon won him a partnership with Samuel McCleary, which continued for a period of four years. He then formed a copartnership with his brother John, which business association has continued uninterruptedly and harmoniously until the present. Mr. Reeves has done much to develop the resources of his native county, and aided many successful enterprises by his influence and capital. He is president of the Beaver Falls and New Brighton Illuminating Gas Company; president of the Beaver Falls Water Works; president of the Beaver Falls Cutlery Company; one of the managers of the Economy Savings Institution, and has been director and a leading spirit in various other projects, Beaver Falls and New Brighton being especially indebted to his energy for their rapid growth. Mr. Reeves was, on the 29th of October, 1857, married to Sarah Jane, daughter of William and Jane Haines, of Mount Holly, N. J. Their children were Harry W., Martha Jane, Walter F. (deceased), Romelius L. B., Albert (deceased), Arthur (deceased), and Orville (deceased). Mr. Reeves has been, since early manhood, an earnest member of the Methodist Protestant church at Beaver Falls and largely instrumental in building churches, both at Beaver Falls and New Brighton.. The prosperity of this denomination has ever been dear to his heart, and enlisted his earnest prayers and most substantial aid. The various church offices, both spiritual and temporal, he has been called upon from time to time to fill. Mr. Reeves has been, since the organization of the party, a Republican, and was formerly a pronounced Abolitionist. He is now one of the most earnest advocates of the Prohibition movement in the county, and a fearless exponent of the cause of temperance, as of every project having for its purpose the welfare of humanity. Other than that of school director and councilman, he has refused all proffers of office. Having in a measure relinquished the cares of business, much of his time for some years has been devoted to recreation and travel.

JOHN B. REEVES, foreman Beaver Falls Steel Works, was born in New Brighton June 5, 1851, a son of Joseph and Sarah (McGachey) Reeves. His paternal grandfather, Daniel Reeves, settled in what is now Beaver Falls in 1804, and was a son of Joseph Reeves, of Wales, who settled at Mt. Holly, N. J., in 1754. His maternal grandfather was Robert McGachey, a farmer and pioneer of Beaver Falls. Joseph Reeves was born and reared in Beaver Falls, was a cabinet maker by trade, and had charge of the wood work department on bridge work for the Pittsburgh, Fort Wayne & Chicago Railway for several years. He ran the first train on the road, and was conductor of the same nearly twenty-five years. He died June 2, 1876, the father of five children: John B., James J., Mary (Mrs. Thomas Marshall), Eliza (Mrs. C. L. Parker) and Margaret (Mrs. A. Siemon). John B. was reared in New Brighton, where he learned the carpenter's trade, which he followed fourteen years, but since 1879 has held his present position. April 18, 1877, he married Mary, daughter of Andrew and Alice Wharmby, of Allegheny county, and has two children: Joseph L. and Grace. Both he and his wife are members of the Presbyterian church. He is a member of the I. O. O. F., and Equitable Aid Union; politically he is a Democrat.

WILLIAM REICH, JR., merchant tailor, Bridgewater, was born Sept. 18, 1844, and is a son of Louis and Amelia (Shaup) Reich. His father, who was a professional gardener in Germany, had seven children, of whom William is the eldest. Our subject was reared in Germany, and received his education in that country. Early in life he began to learn tailoring, and served as an apprentice seven years. When he reached his majority he immigrated to the United States, and settled in Bridgewater, where he worked at his trade three years. His parents came from Germany in 1869 and settled in Rochester, where his father has been engaged as a gardener ever since. William embarked in the merchant tailor business on his own account in 1869, and has met with marked success. He sends considerable work to Pittsburgh and other towns, and carries an extensive stock of fine goods. Mr. Reich was first married in 1869 to Elizabeth Rupp, and by her had three children: Christian, Elizabeth and Harry. Mrs. Reich dying in 1877, Mr. Reich married for his second wife, in 1877, Matilda Winters, and by her has two children: William, Jr., and Lenora. Mr. and Mrs. Reich are members of the German Lutheran church. He is a member of the I. O. O. F. lodge and the encampment.

JOSEPH W. RHODES, farmer, P. O. Achor, Columbiana county, Ohio, was born in this county in 1854. His grandfather, William, who came from Ireland, had seven children, among whom was William, who was a farmer by occupation and owned 140 acres of land in Chippewa township, this county, which was formerly the property of his father, William. William J. married, for his second wife, Eliza, daughter of John McMillin (a major in the war of 1812), and Joseph is the only son born to this couple.

William died in 1883, and his wife in 1855. Joseph was reared on the farm and now owns 100 acres, which was the property of his mother. He was married, in 1875, to Maggie, daughter of Joseph and Jane (Warrick) Moore. They have had six children, five of whom are living: Vincent Orrin, William Fisher, Hido Moore, Mary Jane and Ida Potter. Mr. Rhodes is a member of the Presbyterian church; in politics a Republican.

LYCURGUS RICHARDSON, superintendent Beaver Falls Street Railway, Beaver Falls, was born in Columbiana county, Ohio, March 23, 1843, and is a son of Enoch and Mary (Burt) Richardson. His paternal grandfather was Samuel Richardson, and paternal grandfather, William Burt, pioneers of Columbiana county. Mr. Richardson's parents settled in this county in 1851, where his father engaged in farming until his death in February, 1885. His children are Jason, Delilah (deceased), Lycurgus, Margaret E. (Mrs. J. C. Plummer, now deceased), Hiram B., David (deceased) and Samuel (deceased). Our subject was educated in the common schools of Ohio township. From 1858 until 1859 he was engaged as a ferryman at Smith's Ferry, this county; then served an apprenticeship at the blacksmith's trade at Fairview. In August, 1862, he enlisted in Company A, 17th Pa. Cav., and participated in the battles of Chancellorsville, Fredericksburg, the Wilderness and Gettysburg. He was with Sheridan in the raid through the Shenandoah Valley, and at the surrender at Appomattox in 1865, and was honorably discharged in June, 1865. He returned to Beaver county and was married to Eliza J. Hamilton, daughter of David and Serephina Hamilton; then located at Smith's Ferry, Pa., and worked at his trade until his wife died; then, in 1873, located in Pittsburgh, Allegheny county, Pa.; worked there until June, 1874, when he returned to Beaver county, locating at Industry, where he worked until 1876, when he married Anna F. Appleton, daughter of Joseph and Sarah Appleton. He then located at Fairview, Beaver county, Pa., and worked there until March, 1883; then removed to East Liverpool, Ohio, and worked there until June, 1884, when he removed to Industry and conducted a shop there until June, 1885, when he removed to Beaver Falls and accepted the position of superintendent of Beaver Falls Street Railway, operating the road until Nov. 1, 1887. Resigning at that time, he accepted a position as superintendent of McKeesport Street Railway, in Allegheny county, Pa., where he is at present located. Mr. Richardson has one son by his first wife—Harry H. Richardson (who is a machinist at the Hartman machine shop, Beaver Falls, Pa.); also two children by his present wife—Oakley A. and Anna F. Richardson. Politically Mr. Richardson is a Republican.

J. L. RISINGER, blacksmith, Beaver, was born May 13, 1852, in Beaver. His parents, Daniel and Mary Jane (Eakin) Risinger, were natives of this county and of German and Irish descent. His father and grandfather were blacksmiths. It is related of his grandfather that when he carried on business here his patrons thought he was almost a perfect workman. When asked if he could do anything his answer usually was: "Yes," or "All right, just leave it." When one of his regular patrons brought him a darning needle, which his wife had broken the eye of, and asked him if he could mend it, he told him to "have it." J. L. is the elder of the two children. His sister, Minnie M., resides at home. He learned his trade with his father. He is the owner of valuable real estate in Beaver, and in connection with his father is doing a good business. Aug. 24, 1876, he was married to Nannie, daughter of A. P. Morrow, and born in Beaver county, and of Irish descent. They have had five children: Atha May, Ora V., James (deceased), Daniel M. and Nina Clair. Mrs. Risinger is a member of the United Presbyterian Church. In politics, Mr. Risinger is a Republican.

FRED G. ROHRKASTE, P. O. Beaver Falls, was born near Hanover, Germany, Oct. 31, 1831, and is a son of Frederick and Mary (Wiggraffer) Rohrkaste, who came to America in 1830, located in Pittsburgh and resided there until their deaths. Our subject came to America in 1852, located in Pittsburgh, and in 1855 embarked in the grocery trade in that city, in which he was engaged until 1869. He then removed to Beaver Falls, and engaged in the same business there until 1879, when he purchased the Central hotel, one of the principal hostelries of the place, which he successfully conducted until New Year's, 1888, when he retired and now resides in New Brighton. In 1860 he built the Beaver distillery, which he operated three years. A company, of which Mr. Rohrkaste is a stockholder, is now starting the champion saw works in the distillery. He married, in 1856, Ernstine Stolte, born near Hanover, Germany, and has seven children living: Charles, Emma, Anna, Albert, Otto, Fred and Dora. Mr. Rohrkaste is a member of the German Lutheran church; in politics he is a Republican.

CHARLES RUHE, glass engraver, Beaver Falls, was born in Pittsburgh, Pa., Feb. 13, 1858. He is a son of Charles and Caroline (Rinne) Ruhe, natives of Brunwick, Germany, who came to America in 1848 and settled in Pittsburgh. His father, who was a glass-cutter, engraver and general glass worker, settled in Beaver Falls in 1879, and was one of the organizers and stockholders of the Coöperative Flint Glass Works, of which he was secretary and treasurer two and one half years, and was connected with the business until his death Sept. 6, 1887. He was a prominent citizen, and was esteemed by all who knew him. He was a member of the I. O, O. F. and K. of P., and was a F. & A. M.; he held the office of councilman of Beaver Falls, one term. Our subject was reared in Pittsburgh where he learned his trade, which he has followed since 1876. He came to Beaver Falls in 1879, where he has since been in the employ of the Coöperative Glass Works. He is a member of the I. O. O F., K. of L. and the Flint Glass Worker's Trade Union. He is a member of the council for Beaver Falls, and in politics is a Democrat.

WILLIAM A. SAWYER, physician, Darlington, was born in Washington county, Pa., in 1844. Rev. B. F. Sawyer (of the Seceder's church) was born in Petersburg, Pa., in 1817; was educated at the Cannonsburg College, and ordained when twenty-five years of age; commenced preaching at New Brighton, and in 1845 located in South Beaver township, where he has since resided. He holds services at the Darlington school-house and at the Four Mile church. He married Nancy, daughter of William Anderson, and to them were born three sons and three daughters, all living. Mrs. Sawyer died in 1881, aged sixty-eight years. William A. was educated at Greersburg Academy, and left that institution when eighteen years old. In 1875 he married Ella, daughter of J. C. Thompson, and their children are Benjamin Clark, Georgiana and Nancy C. The doctor commenced the study of medicine when twenty-one years old, D. S. M. Ross, of Altoona, Pa., being his preceptor. He graduated from the Western Reserve Medical College in February, 1869, and commenced practice in Ohioville, remaining there three years. In 1872 he located at Darlington, where he has since practiced. In politics he is a Republican.

PHILIP SCHARFF, foreman of the Coöperative Glass Works, Beaver Falls, was born in Pittsburgh, July 16, 1847, and is a son of Conrad and Wilhelmina (Rupple) Scharff, natives of Hesse Cassel, Germany. They came to America in 1839, located in Pittsburgh, and in 1884 moved to Beaver Falls. They have four children: Mary, Henrietta, Philip and William. Philip was reared in Pittsburgh and learned the trade of glass-blower with McKee Bros., of that city. He worked as a journeyman from 1858 until 1879, when he located in Beaver Falls, working a year and a half in the Coöperative Glass Works, since which time he has held his present position. In 1871 he married Catherine, daughter of Henry and Agnes (Schultz) Gernert, of Pittsburgh, by whom he has six children: Harry, William Agnes, Minnie, Edward and Bessie. Mr. Scharff is a member of the I. O. O. F. and A. O. U. W.; in politics he is a Democrat.

WILLIAM SCHARFF, glass-blower, Beaver Falls, was born in Pittsburgh, April 15, 1850, and is a son of Conrad C. and Mena (Rupple) Scharff, of Germany, who settled in Pittsburgh in 1839. He was reared in that city, and learned his trade with McKee Bros. and Bakewall & Co., and worked in Pittsburgh from 1859 until 1873. He then embarked in the hotel business in Pittsburgh (South Side). In 1879 he located in Beaver Falls, and was one of the organizers of the Coöperative Flint Glass Works, where he has since been employed, and is interested as a stockholder. In 1872 he married Mary, daughter of Henry and Margaret Zell, of Pittsburgh, and has six children: Lillie Catherine, Emma, David, William and Philip. In 1875 Mr. Scharff was the champion oarsman of America. He is an active member of the A. O. U. W. and Red Men (Pittsburgh Lodge). Politically he is a Democrat.

BIOGRAPHIES—WEST SIDE. 717

WILLIAM SCHEFFLER, glass presser, Beaver Falls, was born in Prussia, Jan. 22, 1836, and is a son of Henry and Eva C. Scheffler, who emigrated to America in 1844 and settled in Pittsburgh. Their children were George, Conrad, William and Dorothea. William learned his trade with F. & J. McKee & Co., of Pittsburgh, and was in their employ from 1854 until 1867, when he located in Columbiana county, Ohio, where he was engaged in farming six years, working at his trade occasionally in Pittsburgh. In 1873 he located in that city permanently, and worked for Doyle & Co. until 1878. In 1879 he came to Beaver Falls, and became one of the founders of the Coöperative Flint Glass Works, where he has since been employed. June 5, 1859, he married Catherine, daughter of John Weyand, of Pittsburgh, by whom he has seven children living: William H., Katie M., Lizzie E., Anna D., Cora C., Charles E. and Albert T. Mr. Scheffler has been a member of the board of directors of the glass works for six years, and since May 1, 1886, has been its chairman. He is a member of the German Lutheran church, the A. O. U. W., and in politics is a Republican.

AUGUST SCHWALLER, glass blower, Beaver Falls, was born in Alsace-Lorraine, June 6, 1853, and is a son of Joseph and Anna (Veitlech) Schwaller. He came to America in 1873, and located in Wayne county, Pa., remaining there seventeen months. He then located in Pittsburgh, where he was in the employ of McKee Bros. until the glass strike of 1878. In 1879 he came to Beaver Falls, and became one of the organizers of the Coöperative Flint Glass Works, where he has since been employed, and is also a stockholder. In 1876 he married Mary A., daughter of John Evans, by whom he has five children living: Kate, Annie, Andrew, Maggie and Magdalena. He is a member of the German Catholic church; in politics a Democrat.

JOHN M. SCOTT, clerk of courts, Beaver, was born in Brighton township, this county, April 11, 1842, and is a son of William and Nancy (McKee) Scott, the former a native of Beaver county and the latter of Franklin. His father was engaged in the tanning business in early life, and in farming in later life, until his death, which occurred in Brighton. His family consisted of three sons and five daughters (two deceased), of whom John M. is the youngest living. He was reared on the farm, and attended the common school and the Beaver Academy. He taught school for nineteen winters, and farmed during the rest of each year. He began teaching at the age of eighteen. In 1885 he was elected clerk of the courts of Beaver county, which position he has since occupied. He is well adapted to the position he holds, and has a practical knowledge of the details of the office. He is a member of the United Presbyterian church; in politics he is a Republican.

G. A. SCROGGS, physician and surgeon, P. O. Beaver, was born in New Castle, Lawrence county, Pa., March 23, 1855, and is a son of John A. and Mary J. (Thompson) Scroggs, former a native of Darlington, this county, latter of Columbiana county, Ohio, of Scotch-Irish descent. The Scroggs family were among the early settlers of Beaver county. The grandfather of our subject was Gen. John Alexander Scroggs, who was a general in the war of 1812; he was prothonotary of Beaver county two terms, beginning in 1832. The Scroggs family are descendants of the Lord Chief-Justice of the King's High Bench, Sir William Scroggs. The father of G. A. was a dentist, and practiced in Galena, Ill., for many years. He had four children, of whom G. A. is the second. Our subject was reared in Galena, Ill., where he received his earliest education, and he subsequently attended the Hopedale Normal School, in Ohio. He chose medicine as his profession, and studied at East Liverpool, Ohio, first with Dr. Benjamin Ogden, and afterward with Dr. Daniel Leasure, of Allegheny City, Pa. He then entered Jefferson Medical College, at Philadelphia, in 1876, where he was graduated in 1879. He began practice at East Liverpool, Ohio, and remained there three years, then went to Hazlewood, and in 1884 came to Beaver. He was married, in 1879, to Alexina C., daughter of Alexander C. Gatzmer, of Philadelphia, Pa., of Prussian descent. The doctor is a Republican in politics.

JAMES SCROGGS, JR. physician and surgeon, P. O. Beaver, was born in Allegheny county, Pa., July 19, 1850, a son of James and Emily (Seaton) Scroggs, the former of

40

Scotch and the latter of English descent, and both natives of Pennsylvania. His father was for many years a practicing physician in Beaver borough. He is still a resident of Beaver, but is not in active practice, and is perhaps the oldest physician in the county. He spent the most of his professional life in Pittsburgh, where his family grew up. His two sons are physicians. Our subject, who is the eldest of five children, attended the schools of Pittsburgh, then went to Ann Arbor, Mich., and first attended the literary department of Michigan University, subsequently entering the medical department of the same institution, where he remained one year. He then returned to Fairview, the home of his father, and continued his studies at home until the opening of the Cincinnati College of Medicine and Surgery, which he then entered and from which he was graduated in 1872. He came to Beaver county and commenced the practice of his chosen profession at Fairview. The doctor always speaks of his father in terms of the highest praise. His father first attended to the education of his children and gave them the advantages of the best schools, and then expected them to make their own way. When our subject returned from college his father said to him: "James, I will not buy you anything more than horse and saddle; then you must hoe your own row." He then for the first time in his life felt that he was a man, and must battle with the world single handed. He practiced one year in Fairview, and then came to Beaver where he soon obtained a good practice. He is earnestly devoted to his profession, seldom allowing his time to be taken up with anything else, and takes much interest in the Beaver County Medical Society. In politics he is a Republican, and has served as a member of the school board for ten years in Beaver borough. He is physician to the Beaver County Home, physician to Beaver county jail, also county physician. The Doctor was married, in 1873, to Anna, daughter of John Aber, who was a merchant, and they have had four children: Anna Emily, Joseph J., Hall E. and Fred J. Mrs. Scroggs is a member of the United Presbyterian church, of Beaver. The doctor is a member of the I. O. O. F.

HENRY SECHRIST, farmer, P. O. New Galilee, was born in Cambria county, Pa., in 1840. His great-grandfather came from Germany and was a soldier in the Revolutionary War. William, a son of this pioneer, and a native of York county, Pa., married Esther Saddler, and had six sons and five daughters. He was a farmer, and died at the age of sixty years. Henry, his fourth child, born in 1806 in York county, married in 1834, Nancy, daughter of Frederick and Mary Flinchbaugh, and eight children (six now living) were born to them, our subject being the fourth. The father came to Beaver county in 1860 and purchased the property now owned by his son and namesake. He died in 1872 aged sixty-six years. Henry, our subject, was reared a farmer, and has always followed that occupation. At the death of his father he purchased his farm. He was married, in 1887, to Lizzie, daughter of James Dillon. He is quite extensively engaged in dairying, owns twenty cows, and ships his produce to Pittsburgh daily.

JOHN C. SENNETT, moulder, Beaver Falls, was born in Lake county, Ohio, June 12, 1835, and is a son of Albert and Olive (Cokly) Sennett. He was reared in Erie county, Pa., and Cincinnati, Ohio, and at the latter place served an apprenticeship of four years at the stove-molder's trade, which he followed until 1885. He was in the late War of the Rebellion, enlisting Aug. 11, 1862, in Company I, 145th P. V. I. He participated in the battles of Fredericksburg. Chancellorsville, Gettysburg, the Wilderness campaign, Petersburg and other engagements, and was honorably discharged May 31, 1865. In January, 1871, he located in Beaver Falls, where he has since resided. He is a member of the G. A. R., Union Veteran Legion, I. O. O. F. and Iron Molder's Union; in politics, he is independent.

JOSEPH SHANNON, farmer, P. O. Homewood, is a descendant of an early settler in Pennsylvania, a farmer by occupation, who was born on the River Shannon, Ireland, and was the parent of sixteen children. Robert, his son, settled in Westmoreland county about 1820, where he remained until 1830, when he moved to Beaver county and purchased 100 acres of land. He married Nellie, daughter of Robert Miller, and by her had ten children, seven of whom are living. Robert was a farmer during his whole life. He died in 1868, aged sixty-eight years. His wife died in 1875, aged seventy-seven

BIOGRAPHIES—WEST SIDE.   719

years. Joseph was born in 1826, and is now the oldest living son. He was liberally educated, and was a student at Greersburg academy. He was reared on a farm and is by occupation a farmer. In 1849 he married Eliza Jane, daughter of John Beatty, and they have four children: Ann Mary (Mrs. McCaughtry), John B., Nellie Jane (Mrs. Wallace), and R. Emma (Mrs. Beard). In 1849 Mr. Shannon moved on the present farm of 150 acres, which was the homestead of his wife's father. He is an adherent of the United Presbyterian church; in politics a Republican.

WILLIAM SHANNON, farmer, P. O. New Galilee, the youngest son of Robert and Nellie (Miller) Shannon, was born in Big Beaver township on the farm where he now lives, in 1840. He was married in 1867 to Mary Alloway, of Blair county, Pa. Eight children have blessed this union: Robert A., Aaron M., James B., Elmer E , Nellie J., Royal G., William S. and Annie M. Mr. Shannon received a good common-school education. He enlisted in 1861 in Company K, 10th Pennsylvania Reserves, and served three years, being engaged in the battles of Mechanicsville, Gaines' Mill, Malvern Hill, Second Bull Run, South Mountain, Antietam, Fredericksburg, Gettysburgh, The Wilderness and Spottsylvania. He was taken prisoner at Fredericksburg, was taken to Richmond and to Libby prison, and was in prison for twenty-eight days. He owns 290 acres of land, nearly all of which is under cultivation. He has always been a hard worker and is a successful farmer. He is a Democrat.

EVERETT W. SHEETS, physician, Beaver Falls,was born in East Palestine, Columbiana county, Ohio, Dec. 25, 1860, and is a son of Abraham and Mary A. (Dustin) Sheets. His father was a graduate of Jefferson Medical College, Philadelphia, and was for many years a practicing physician in Columbiana county, Ohio, Beaver county and New Castle, Pa., where he died in 1871. Mr. Sheets' paternal grandfather was Frederick Sheets, a pioneer of East Palestine, and his maternal grandfather, Dr. Barnard Dustin, of Massachusetts, a pioneer physician of Darlington township. He had two sons. Barnard and Nathaniel, both of them physicians of distinction Everett W. Sheets was reared in New Castle. He studied medicine in his father's office, and with his sister, Eugenia C., now Mrs. Dr. Mercer, and later with Dr. Montgomery Linville. He entered Jefferson Medical College in 1883, and was graduated in April, 1885. He was then appointed assistant-surgeon of Lancaster County Hospital. In February, 1886, he located in Beaver Falls, where he has a large and successful practice.

JOHN S. SHEPLER, proprietor of Hotel Summit, in Bridgewater, was born in Allegheny county, Pa., Nov. 3, 1818, and is a son of Philip and Mary (Hill) Shepler. His mother is still living at the age of eighty. His father was a farmer, and later in life a hotel keeper in Pittsburgh. He was a soldier in the War of 1812, and lived to the age of seventy-six. His grandfather was a soldier in the Revolutionary War, and served under George Washington. He, with some others, made a trip in an open flat boat from the headwaters of the Monongahela river to Louisville, then called the Falls of the Ohio. They ran only by night, hiding from the Indians among the willows by day. He died here at the age of ninety, and his wife at ninety-four. Philip had thirteen children, of whom seven are now living. Of these John S. is the eldest. He was reared near Pittsburgh, and attended the common schools. He remained on the farm with his parents till he reached his majority, when he worked in Pittsburgh as a pattern maker and mill-wright. He afterward purchased a flouring mill in Washington county, which he conducted a few years, when it was washed away by a flood. He then purchased property in Monongahela City, and in company with Henry Shearer built a mill there. He sold his interest in this mill, and became part owner of the steamboat Bell, and on that and other boats he was, during a number of years, an engineer. His health failing, he leased, in New Brighton, a hotel which he conducted about four years, after which he removed to Beaver and kept the National Hotel there a few years. He then engaged in the manufacture of agricultural implements, sold out, and built the hotel which he now occupies. On the 4th of March, 1840, he was married to Mary J., daughter of John Megown. She was born in Pittsburgh, and is of Scotch descent. They have had eleven children, of whom seven are now living: Philip L., an engineer and merchant; Albert G., Samuel H. and Charley C., steamboat engineers on the Ohio and Mississippi rivers; Anna Eliza, wife of Oliver K. McKeage, an engineer on the Ohio river; Josephine, at home; and Abbie, wife of J. B. Shumaker, a druggist in Bridgewater. In politics Mr. Shepler is a Republican.

'JOHN A. SHILLITO, merchant, P. O. Beaver, of the firm of Shillito & Brother, was born in Independence township, this county, Nov. 5, 1832, son of George and Elizabeth (Anderson) Shillito, former of whom died in 1869; latter is still living at the age of eighty-five. They were both natives of Pennsylvania, of Scotch-Irish lineage. Our subject's grandfather (George) and father came to Beaver county in 1800, and were tillers of the soil. Samuel Shillito, an uncle of John A., was in the War of 1812, and emigrated west from Beaver county. Our subject is one of a family of six children, three of whom are living: John A. and his partner, R. C., and George M., a prominent physician in Allegheny City. John A. was reared on the farm, attended school in Independence township, and at the age of sixteen went to Clinton, in Allegheny county, where he clerked for one year. Then he moved to Florence, Washington county, and clerked there three years. In April, 1855, he went to California, where he remained thirteen years, and during this time he was employed as salesman in a store, except three years he was mining in Nevada. Jan. 8, 1868, he returned home and embarked in his present business. Both members of the firm have been for many years residents of Beaver county, and John A. has had thirty-seven years' experience in business. Oct. 4, 1871, he was married to Mary G., daughter of John Swearigen, born and reared in Allegheny county, where she was married. They have one child, N. G. L. Mr. and Mrs. Shillito are members of the Presbyterian church, of which he is trustee and treasurer.

THEODORE P. SIMPSON, physician, Beaver Falls, was born in New Brighton, this county, March 19, 1856, and is a son of W. W. and Lavina (Rogers) Simpson. He was reared in New Brighton, began the study of medicine in the office of his father in 1874, and was graduated from Bellevue Hospital Medical College, New York, in 1877. In June of the same year he located in Beaver Falls, where he has built up a lucrative and extensive practice.

DARIUS SINGLETON, lumber dealer and justice of the peace, was born in this county Jan. 9, 1829, and is a son of Henry H. and Rebecca (Maginnis) Singleton, natives of Pennsylvania, and of Irish and English descent. His father came to this county with his parents when a child, spent most of his life here as a farmer, and died in 1867. He had five sons and three daughters, Darius being the youngest son. Our subject was reared on a farm in Greene township, this county, and his early education was received in the common schools in his native county, and at the Twinsburg Institute, Ohio. His business education was obtained at Duff's Commercial College, in Pittsburgh, where he was graduated in 1866. Before the War of the Rebellion he was engaged in the manufacture of lumber, and also in the oil business In 1862 he enlisted in Company F, 140th Volunteer Infantry, and was in eleven engagements. He was promoted from private to sergeant and lieutenant, successively. At the battle of Spottsylvania he received three wounds, one in the left shoulder and arm, which caused him to lose six inches of the bone. At the close of the war he returned to Beaver, and in 1868 embarked in the lumber business. He was appointed justice of the peace in 1876, being elected the next year, and has held the position ever since. In politics he is a Republican. He is a member of the G. A. R., and chaplain of Post No. 473. Mr. Singleton was married, in 1853, to Sarah T., daughter of Sathelius M. and Sarah (Guthrie) Crail, natives of Mercer county, Pa., and of English descent. The living children of this marriage are E. H., Lorena I., Lawrence G., Estella and Dickson Lee. Those deceased are Luenza S., Lenda and Knox. Mrs. Singleton is a member of the Methodist Episcopal church. Mr. Singleton is a Presbyterian, an elder in the church and a teacher in the Bible class.

JAMES SMART, SR., (deceased). The original member bearing this name in Western Pennsylvania was John Smart, who came to Westmoreland county from Philadelphia in the early history of Western Pennsylvania. A son, James, was born to this pioneer in Westmoreland, where he was reared, and in 1796 came to Beaver county and settled on

400 acres of land on the Ohio line in Pennsylvania. After remaining on this tract for some years James was forced to relinquish his claim by depopulation agents, who claimed the right of property. He married Lucy Hartshorn, to whom were born seven children. James, the fourth son, was born in 1802, and was a brother to John Smart, a wealthy bachelor in Darlington township, and one of its most prominent citizens. He was an engineer, having followed steamboat engineering for a number of years. He accumulated considerable wealth and purchased some 400 acres of land, which was part of the original tract settled by his father, James. James Smart, our subject, was born and reared on a farm, and through life followed agricultural pursuits. He was married, in 1831, to Sarah, daughter of Thomas and Jane (Duff) Hartshorn, of this county. They had no children. Lawrence Smart, an adopted son, was born in 1853, and was, in 1873, married to Anna M., daughter of John Roberts, ex-sheriff. Four children were born to them, three of whom are living: Lulu, Ettie and Nannie. James Smart, Sr., the subject of this memoir, died Dec. 4, 1887. He was an industrious farmer, respected by all who knew him; a member of the Presbyterian church, of which his widow is also a member. Politically he was a Republican.

JAMES SMART, JR., farmer, P. O. East Palestine, Ohio, was born in Pittsburgh, Pa., in 1829. His parents, Thomas and Jane (Dillworth) Smart, had seven children, five of whom are now living. Thomas was born in 1798, and died in 1879. He was an engineer twenty-five years, and in early life followed his trade with his brother John. He then came to his native county and purchased 150 acres of land, which was part of the tract of land purchased by his ancestors, and which Thomas owned from 1851 to 1879, and which he left, free of incumbrance, to his family. James Smart, Jr., the remaining male member of the family, with his two maiden sisters, Rebecca and Sarah Jane, now reside on and own the homestead. Thomas was a cabinetmaker by trade, an occupation he followed for a number of years. James, our subject, received a common-school education, and was in early life employed on the river with his uncle. He is now superintending the work on the farm.

ANDREW SMILEY, farmer, P. O. Homewood, was born in Beaver county in 1820. His father, Hugh Smiley, came from County Antrim, Ireland, at an early day and settled in North Sewickley township, where he purchased 150 acres of land. He died there in 1858, aged ninety-six years. He married Martha Richey, of Allegheny county, and had eleven children, five of whom are living, Andrew being the tenth child. Our subject was educated in the common schools, and since early childhood has followed farming. He was married, in 1845, to Elizabeth, daughter of William Beatty, of this county, and she has borne him seven children, five of whom are living: Mary C. (Mrs. Sefton), Abigail, Milton, Annie L. and James. Mr. Smiley owns about 125 acres of valuable land, and is one of the most prosperous farmers in Big Beaver township. He is a man highly respected by his neighbors, and all who know him. He is a member of the United Presbyterian church; politically a Republican.

GEORGE T. SMITH, foreman polishing department, Hubbard & Co.'s Axe Works, Beaver Falls, was born in Pittsburgh, Oct. 21, 1853. He was reared and educated in his native city, where he learned his trade, which he has followed since 1872. He located in Beaver Falls in 1880, where he worked as a journeyman until 1885, when he was promoted to the position he now occupies. He is a respected citizen, a member of the Mystic circle; in politics a Republican.

JACOB SMITH, postmaster and farmer, P. O, Rowe, was born in Allegheny county in 1818. Jacob, his father, came to Beaver county in 1832. He married, near Mahoning town, Catherine, daughter of Powell Smith, of Allegheny county, and they had fourteen children, of whom Jacob is the fifth child. The father died at the age of forty-nine years, and the mother at the age of eighty. Jacob has resided on his present farm since 1854, the property consisting of 120 acres. He was married, in 1843, to Sophia, daughter of William Alexander, of this county, and has had three children, of whom two are living: William A. and Calvin A. Mr. Smith is a member of the United Presbyterian church of Darlington; in politics he is a Republican. His grandfather, Philip, came from Germany, and was in the Revolutionary War.

SAMUEL M. SMITH, farmer and stock grower, P. O. Beaver, was born in Lawrence county, Pa., in August, 1841, a son of David and Catherine (McKee) Smith, who were born in Ireland and came to America when children, former of whom was a carriage maker and followed that business for years in Lawrence county. They raised a family of six daughters and five sons. Samuel M., the second, was reared in Enon Valley, and attended the common schools. Early in life he learned the plastering trade, and later worked at the carpenter's trade until the fall of 1877, when he came to Brighton township, bought a farm, and has since turned his attention to tilling the soil. He was married, in 1877, to Margaret A. McGaffie, whose parents were early Irish settlers of Beaver county. Their children now living are Anna, David and Laura. Mr. and Mrs. Smith are members of the Presbyterian church.

COLEMAN STEINFELD, butcher, Beaver Falls, was born in Prussia Sept. 25, 1849, being a son of Raphael and Rosa Steinfeld, who emigrated in 1854, and settled in Rochester, Beaver county, at which place and New Brighton Raphael carried on the butchering business until 1873. In 1867 he embarked in the clothing business, in which he was engaged until his death in 1882. He had ten children, eight still living: Herman, Lena (Mrs. M. Schiff), Coleman, Hannah (Mrs. Asher Hanauer), Alexander, Rebecca (Mrs. Joseph Ellsoffer), Mary (Mrs. Isaac Spanier), and Amelia (Mrs. Jonas Blumenthal). Our subject engaged in the butchering business with his father in New Brighton in 1868, which partnership existed until Sept. 1, 1873. He then opened a market in Beaver Falls, where he has a large and lucrative business. Mr. Steinfeld married, Sept. 3, 1873, Julia, daughter of Joseph and Mena Lazarus, of Rochester, Pa., and by her he has ten children: Lena, Sadie, Marcus, Cora, Bernard, Harry, Raphael, Charles, Louis and Hannah.

ARCHIE STEWART, agent of the Gas Company and dealer in real estate, Bridgewater, was born in Moon township, Beaver county, Jan. 29, 1844, and is a son of John and Barbaria (Knox) Stewart, natives of Washington county, Pa., and of Scotch and German descent. His father was a farmer and coal dealer, and an early settler of Beaver county. Our subject is one of a family of six children, was reared in Moon township on the farm, and attended the common school and the college at Beaver, Pa. At the age of seventeen he went on the Ohio, and followed the river for several years. He started in, first doing boys' work, was promoted and finally became managing owner of a steamboat, and in 1882 was interested in several other boats. He sold out all his river interests in 1887, and has since been agent for the gas company. He was actively engaged in the manufacture of fire-brick, in Moon township, for a time. He has dealt in real estate in Bridgewater, where he now resides, and is the owner of seven houses and lots. He was married in Beaver county, in 1880, to Gertrude E., daughter of John Miller. This union has been blessed with two children: Anna R. and John A. Mr. Stewart is a member of the Presbyterian, Mrs. Stewart of the English Lutheran church. In politics he is a Republican. He is a member of the I. O. O F. lodge and encampment.

CHARLES E. STEWART, manufacturer, Beaver, was born in Butler county, Pa., in 1847, and is a son of Charles M. and Priscilla (Appleton) Stewart, who were of Engl sh descent, former a manufacturer of lumber, who came to Beaver county in 1827, and spent the greater part of the remaining portion of his life here. He died at New Brighton in 1864. His family consisted of eight children. Charles E., the only son, was reared in New Brighton, and attended the common schools there. Early in life he commenced dealing in wall-paper, and met with success as a dealer. He then engaged in business as a manufacturer of wall-paper, and since 1875 has been manufacturing in New York City. He still owns a neat and substantial residence on Third street, Beaver. He was married in 1871 to Anna M., daughter of George Christian. Her parents were natives of Allegheny City. Mr. and Mrs. Stewart have following named children: Charles E., Jr., Florence M., George T. and Nellie P. Mrs. Stewart is a member of the Methodist Episcopal church. Mr. Stewart is a F. & A. M.; in politics a Republican. The family spend the summer months in Beaver borough.

DAN H. STONE, prothonotary, Beaver, is a native of Beaver county and a son of Dan H. and Mary (Patterson) Stone. His father was born in Connecticut in 1802, and came with his parents to Beaver county in 1812. Our subject's mother was a member of the Patterson family, who were among the early settlers. His father and grandfather were owners of steam vessels. The grandfather was captain on an ocean ship, the father, of Mississippi, Missouri and Ohio river steamers, and was at one time owner of an extensive steamboat line. He met with success in that business, but when in later life he left the water and embarked in other business enterprises, he did not succeed. He died in 1879. His family consisted of seven children. Dan H., the third child, was reared in Beaver county, attended the public school and worked on the farm. When his brother was elected prothonotary in 1879, Dan H. acted as his deputy, and in 1885 he was elected to the office himself. He is eminently qualified to fill the position, having had the experience before he assumed the responsibility. He is thoroughly familiar with all the details of the office. In politics he is a Republican.

STEPHEN P. STONE, bank cashier, P. O. Beaver, was born in this county Sept. 17, 1854, and is a son of Dan H. and Mary (Patterson) Stone. His father was born in Connecticut, but spent most of his life in this county, where he met his wife. She was born in Beaver Falls, and is a descendant of one of the earliest families of the county. Dan H. Stone was on the river in several capacities, and met with success in business. At one time he was principal owner of an extensive line of steamboats on the Mississippi and Ohio rivers. In the latter part of his life he sold out his interest in the steamboat line, bought land and embarked extensively in the sawmill business. He had seven children—three daughters and four sons—Stephen P. being the eldest. Dan H. is now prothonotary of Beaver county. Stephen P. attended the public schools of Beaver, and the Beaver Academy. When sixteen years old he went to work on a farm and steam sawmill owned by his father in Marion township, this county, where he was employed until the panic of 1873 swept away everything that his father owned, and left the family without means of support. His father (who died in 1879) being disabled by advanced age and sickness, Stephen worked as a laborer to support the family. When the new courthouse was built, he worked at the excavation as a day laborer. In the summer and fall of 1876 he was employed on the engineer corps that surveyed and laid out the Pittsburg & Lake Erie Railroad from Pittsburgh to Youngstown, Ohio. In 1877 he was appointed deputy prothonotary, and in 1879 he was elected to the office of prothonotary, being re-elected in 1882. After the close of his second term he accepted the position of assistant cashier of the Beaver Deposit Bank. He was married May 12, 1887, to Louise M., daughter of George W. Knox, a retired attorney of Philadelphia. Mrs. Stone is a member of the Presbyterian church. Mr. Stone is a F. & A. M. and a member of the I. O. O. F. Politically he is a Republican.

JUDGE EDWIN H. STOWE was born Jan. 2, 1826, in the town of Beaver, the eldest son of Hiram Stowe and Martha Darragh, a daughter of Major Robert Darragh, who, at one time represented Beaver county in the state senate. The wife of Major Darragh was Deborah Hart, a granddaughter of John Hart, of New Jersey, one of the signers of the Declaration of Independence. The grandfather of Hiram Stowe was a soldier of the revolution from Connecticut, and his father having purchased a farm near Warren, Ohio, in the western reserve, removed there with his family in 1808. Hiram being a man of enterprise and having a taste for mercantile pursuits, when quite young left his father's home and removed to Beaver county, where, in 1823, he embarked in business in the town of Beaver. In 1827 he removed to a village on the west side of the Beaver river, now known as Bridgewater, and entered into partnership with Mr. Darragh, then engaged in merchandising at that place, the firm becoming H. Stowe & Co. The business, which prospered, was continued until 1836, when Mr. Stowe, having been elected cashier of the Branch Bank of Pittsburgh, located in Beaver, retained that position until 1839, when the branch was withdrawn. He was after that date not actively engaged in any business of his own, but interested in a number of enterprises, and at his death, in 1877, was a director of the Western Insurance Company, and the People's Savings Bank, of Pittsburgh, as also of the Little Sawmill Run Railroad Company. He was at one time director of the Cleveland & Pittsburg Railroad Company. His widow still resides at New Brighton, at the ripe age of eighty-three years. Edwin H. Stowe was carefully nurtured, and enjoyed every advantage of education at command. For a time he was a pupil of the academy at Beaver, but becoming dissatisfied, withdrew from it and recited to Samuel B. Coulter, a graduate of Jefferson College, and an accomplished scholar. In 1843 he entered Washington College, from which he was graduated in 1845. Removing to Pittsburgh in the fall of 1846 he entered the office of the late Judge Hampton, then a member of Congress from Allegheny county, as a student of law. He was admitted to the bar in 1849, and soon after opened an office as an attorney at law. Of a retiring disposition he formed few acquaintances outside the profession, but upon the students and members of the bar he made a favorable impression. His progress was at first slow and discouraging; indeed, so much so, that, at times, he bitterly regretted his choice of a profession. But there was no retreat without disgrace, and he resolved by patience and assiduous study to prepare for better days. In 1855 he entered into partnership with John H. Hampton, Esq., a former schoolmate and the son of his preceptor. Soon business came with unstinted measure to the new firm, and the success of Stowe & Hampton was assured. In 1859 Judge Stowe's name was first mentioned for a judicial position among the members of the bar, and in 1862 he was nominated by the Republican party and elected judge of the Common Pleas Court of Allegheny county. It required but a brief time to gain the confidence of the public as a judge both " competent and honest." In 1864 Judge Stowe married Miss Emma Vick, youngest daughter of Charles Vick, Esq., an English gentleman of culture and means, who came to this country and settled in Allegheny City. Their three sons were Charles H., who died in 1881 in his fifteenth year; Edwin Walford and Percy Van Deusen, born in 1870 and 1874, respectively. In 1872 Judge Stowe was unanimously reëlected a judge of the Common Pleas Ccurt, and in 1882 the same flattering distinction was shown him. His experience on the bench for twenty-five years has extended through all branches of criminal and civil law, and his judicial career has met with public approval. One of the leading Pittsburgh journals thus speaks of him:

A number of the most important cases recently tried in our courts have been tried before him. In the majority of these, of course, the most delicate questions were of a character to be appreciated only by those learned in the law. A few of these are inerestirg even to a lay mind, however. In the famous Clarke-McCully " Bond of Friendship" case, his ruling that Clarke was a competent witness, afterward upon re-argument affirmed by the supreme court, by a divided court, won the case for him. That is known as the " Rising Main Case" is a leading case on the power of the city councils to discriminate between bidders for public work, and award a contract to a bidder other than the lowest. In the Ortwein murder case, which was tried before Judge Stowe, the doctrine was laid down for the first time in this state, that where the defense of insanity was set up against the charge of murder, the insanity must be proved to the satisfaction of the jury. It was not sufficient to merely raise a reasonable doubt in their minds. In this he was sustained by the supreme court, and it is as now settled law. He also presided at the trial of Lane, the poisoner, and Lenkner, who murdered his partner. More recently he has held the scales in the contest of the river men with the Hostetter Smithfield Bridge Company, the protracted Oak Alley church wrangle, and the Lawrenceville graveyard case.

To these may be added the case against James Nutt for the murder of ——— Dukes, who had killed Nutt's father shortly before, and been acquitted by a jury, and in retaliation for which Nutt killed him, sent from Fayette county, and in which " impulsive insanity " was relied upon as a defense; and the Commonwealth vs. Riddle et al, president and director of the Penn Bank, of Pittsburgh, for embezzlement.

ELIJAH STRATTON, farmer, P. O. Beaver Falls, was born in Chippewa township in 1835, a son of John and Hester (Cochran) Stratton. His father, who was formerly of New Jersey, settled in Chippewa township, this county, about 1825, where he cleared and improved a farm, on which he lived and died. His children were Samuel (deceased), John W., Elijah, Margaret and Sarah A. Elijah was reared in Chippewa township,

BIOGRAPHIES—WEST SIDE. 725

and spent fifteen years of his early manhood in Illinois. In 1862 he enlisted in Company C, 84th Illinois Volunteers, and participated in the battles of Stone River and Perrysville, Chickamauga, Lookout Mountain, the siege of Atlanta, Franklin, Nashville and other engagements, and was honorably discharged in 1865. He returned to Chippewa township, this county, in 1874, where he has since resided and been engaged in farming. He has been married twice, His first wife was Jane Craethbaum, by whom he had one son, Charles. His second wife was Emeline B., daughter of Charles and Esther (Hite) McMillan, early settlers of Chippewa township. Mr. Stratton is a member of the Methodist Episcopal church, and a stanch advocate of prohibition.

ULYSSES S. STROUSS, physician, was born in Hanover township, this county, June 5, 1848, and is a son of David and Emily (Woodrough) Strouss, who were of English and German origin. The father was a farmer and tanner, and had eleven children. Our subject was reared on the farm, and attended the district school and the academy at Mansfield, Pa. He studied medicine with Dr. Walker, of Mansfield, Pa., and afterward with Dr. Moon, at Hookstown. He then entered the medical department of the Western Reserve College at Cleveland, Ohio, where he was graduated in 1872. He began practice at Hookstown, where he remained until 1874, when he went to Ohioville, and ten years later came to Beaver, where he has since been in active practice. He is very attentive to his professional duties, and courteous to rich and poor alike. He is a member of the Beaver County Medical Society. The Doctor was married, in 1871, to Esther, daughter of James M. Hatford, and of Irish descent. Their children are Jennie and Martha. Mrs. Strouss is a member of the Presbyterian church. The Doctor is a Democrat; he is a Master Mason.

ALBERT STRUB, glass mould maker, Beaver Falls, was born in Allegheny City, March 31, 1853, a son of Morau and Magdalena (Altenbaugh) Strub, natives of Alsace, Germany. His father settled in Allegheny City about 1847, and has resided in Beaver Falls since 1886. He has eight children living: Joseph, Albert, Louisa, Victoria, Leonard, Caroline, William and Titus. Albert learned the trade of glass mould making in Pittsburgh, and followed it in Allegheny county five years. He came to Beaver Falls in 1874, and for seven years worked as a machinist in the Beaver Falls Cutlery Works and Hartman Nail Mill. Since 1884 he has worked as a glass mould maker in Beaver county. April 11, 1877, he married Mary M., daughter of John A. and Caroline (Fischer) Paff, by whom he has two children: John M. and Agnes. Mr. Strub is a member of the Catholic church and the Catholic Mutual Benefit Association. Politically he is a Democrat.

LEONARD STRUB, furniture dealer, Beaver Falls, was born in Allegheny City, Pa., Nov. 23, 1847, and is a son of Leonard and Catherine (Krepps) Strub, both natives of Alsace. His father came to America in 1832, and was employed in New York City for several years, after which he located in Allegheny City, Pa., where he became a successful and prominent starch manufacturer, and was engaged in that business for upwards of forty years. His wife was a daughter of Joseph Krepps, Sr., of Lorraine, and a pioneer of Allegheny City. Leonard Strub was reared and educated in his native city. In 1868 he embarked in business as a photographer in Allegheny City, having by hard study and indomitable perseverance mastered the art without any instruction from others. He continued in business in Allegheny City and Pittsburgh, until 1885. He has been a resident of Beaver Falls since 1882, and from the spring of 1885 until February, 1886, conducted a photograph gallery in that borough. In May, 1886, he embarked in the furniture business, in which he has since been successfully engaged. He carries the largest stock in Beaver county; his stores, Nos. 805, 805½ and 807, Seventh Ave., now occupy about 6,000 square feet of storeroom, and if his business still increases as it has done he will have to add as much more room. He married, in 1871, Lena, daughter of Peter and Mary Lena Saladin, of Allegheny county, formerly of Switzerland. By this union there are six children: Francis L., Emma R., Tressa M., Carrie A., Stella M., and Walter R. Mr. Strub's residence is on corner of Eighth street and Church avenue.

HENRY STUBER, farmer and milkman, P. O., Beaver Falls, is a native of this county, and was born June 22, 1861. He is a son of Jacob and Kate (Miller) Stuber. Jacob is a native of Germany, but has been a resident of Beaver county upward of thirty years. He is a shoemaker by trade, but of late has been engaged in farming, and is now a resident of Pulaski township. He has three children living: Henry, Catherine and John. Henry was reared in Beaver county, married Mary, daughter of Jacob and Lizzie Klein, of Pulaski township, and has one daughter, Lizzie. He is a prominent dairyman and farmer of Chippewa township. He is a member of the Presbyterian church; politically a Democrat.

R. E. TALLON, contractor, Beaver, of the firm of Harton & Tallon, contractors and builders, was born June 13, 1849, and is a son of Robert and Eliza (Daniels) Tallon, former a native of Ireland and latter of Beaver county. Her father was Stacy Daniels, one of the early settlers of this county. Our subject's grandfather came from Ireland and settled in Pittsburgh in 1824. He soon moved to Westmoreland county, Pa., where he died. Robert, the father of R. E., grew to manhood on the farm, and engaged in the manufacture of boots and shoes. In 1847 he came to Beaver county, and is still in business in New Brighton. He had twelve children, nine sons and three daughters, of whom nine are living, all in Beaver county, R. E., being the fourth son. He was reared in Beaver borough, attended public school and the academy, and early in life learned the carpenter's trade, at which he worked as a journeyman for a time. The firm of Harton & Tallon was formed in 1872, and since then they have done a large part of thd building and contracting of Beaver county. At present they have under way ten contracts, one of them for a church in Ohio, which is to cost $35,000. They employ about sixty men. In 1868 Mr. Tallon was married to Emma Jones, which union has been blessed with five children: Effie, Josie, Fred, Maud and Sadie. Mr. and Mrs. Tallon are members of the Methodist church; in politics he is a Republican. Mr. Tallon served through the Indian war in the Indian Territory, in 1868, with Gen. Custer.

R. T. TAYLOR, college president, Beaver, was born in Otsego county, N. Y., June 29, 1826, and is a son of Epaphro and Caroline (Morse) Taylor, who were of English descent, the father a native of Connecticut and a farmer, the mother of Massa chusetts. Their family consisted of nine children, of whom R. T. is the second Our subject was reared on the farm, attended select school in his native county, and at the age or seventeen commenced teaching school. He taught in winter and worked on the farm in summer until he reached his twentieth year, when he entered the Cazenovia Seminary, in Madison county, N. Y., to prepare for college. He remained there three years, then again engaged in teaching. He was principal of the Brookville Academy for two years; then entered the sophomore class at the Wesleyan University, at Middletown, Conn., in the regular classical course. He was graduated in 1854, and was elected a member of the "Phi Beta Kappa Society." He accepted a professorship in the Rittenhouse Academy, Washington, D. C., where he remained two years. He subsequently taught in a college at Pittsburgh ; also taught in a high school in Ohio, his success as a teacher placing him in the front rank of his profession. He came to Beaver in 1859 as principal of the Beaver Female Seminary, and has been at the head of the institution through its various changes ever since. In 1872 it was chartered as the Beaver College and Musical Institute, and Mr. Taylor was elected president. The growth of the college is largely due to his exertions. The degree of A. M. was conferred on him by his *Alma Mater*, and that of D. D. by Allegheny College, in 1871. He was married July 29, 1856, to Amelia, daughter of Julius and Julia (Berry) Spencer. This union has been blessed with three children: Edmonia, wife of S. A. Hill, who is a professor in Muir College, in India; Caroline A. and Julia E., at home. All are members of the Methodist Church. President Taylor has been a member of the church ever since he was fourteen years old. He was licensed to preach in 1853, joined the Pittsburgh Conference in 1858, and is still a member. He served twenty-five years as superintendent of the Beaver Sabbath school.

J. H. TELFORD, publisher *Daily Tribune*, Beaver Falls, was born in Allegheny City, Aug. 8, 1847, and is a son of James and Sarah (Hamil) Telford, and of Scotch-Irish descent. He graduated from the public schools of his native city, and served an apprenticeship of four years in Pittsburgh, at the printing trade, after which he held several positions of responsibility in that line of business. He was in the employ of the *Christian Advocate* of Pittsburgh, for eight years, the *Methodist Recorder*, eighteen months, and was foreman in the job office of Moore & Nesbit, of Pittsburgh, for four years. He has always been an ardent Republican and strong party man. In December, 1887, he located in Beaver Falls, and purchased of Jacob Weyand a half interest in the *Weekly Tribune*. A year later he bought his partner's interest, and has since conducted the business, which has more than trebled itself under his management. In August, 1884, Mr. Telford started the *Daily Tribune*, which takes front rank among the country dailies of the state, and is quite a factor in county politics. While holding to his own views, Mr. Telford bars none who oppose them from the use of the columns of his paper.

WILLIAM THOMAS, farmer, P. O. Beaver Falls, was born in Chippewa township, Sept. 14, 1821, a son of Ethan and Elizabeth (Eads) Thomas, the former a native of Maryland and the latter of Virginia. They were pioneers of Beaver county, who first located in Patterson township, and later in Chippewa. They had eight children: Isaiah, John, James, David, William, Daniel, Mary A. (Mrs. Jeremiah Britton) and Lena (Mrs. Daniel Daniels). William was reared in Chippewa township, and succeeded to the homestead where he has always resided, with the exception of six years, three of which he was engaged in mercantile business in Beaver, and three spent in New Brighton in private life. In 1850 he married Mary A., daughter of Jacob and Susan Young, of Columbiana county, Ohio. Mr. Thomas is a prominent citizen of Chippewa township, and has served as county auditor for one term, and justice of the peace several terms. He is a member of the Baptist church; politically he is a Republican.

W. H. S. THOMSON, attorney, Beaver, a member of the firm of Thomson & Martin, was born in Independence township, this county, Nov. 16, 1856. He is of Scotch descent, a son of Alexander R. and Hannah (Charles) Thomson, the former of whom was born in Beaver county, and the latter in Allegheny county. His father was a physician, and also studied law, but his health failed and he moved to a farm in Independence township, where he became one of the influential farmers of the county. In 1883 he was elected a member of the legislature. He was twice married, and had four children by his first wife, and one by his second, W. H. S. being the youngest child by the first wife. Our subject was reared here and in the South (where his father used to spend his winters), attended Washington and Jefferson College, and studied civil engineering, thinking to make that his profession; but his father prevailed on him to study law. He was admitted to the bar in 1880, in Cabell county, W. Va.; was admitted here in 1881, and has been in active practice ever since. In politics he is a Democrat, and served two years as chairman of the Democratic committee. Mr. Thomson was married, May 12, 1887, to Mary E., daughter of Hon. D. L. Imbrie, who has been a member of the legislature from Beaver county, and also state senator. Mrs. Thomson is a member of the United Presbyterian church, of Beaver.

NICHOLAS TODD, farmer, P. O. Beaver, was born in Ohio township, this county, April 20, 1823. His parents, Alexander and Sarah (Stephens) Todd, were natives of Fayette county, and of English and Irish descent. His grandfather, John Stephens, was a soldier in the revolutionary war. The Todd family have usually been farmers. Nicholas is the youngest of sixteen children, and after attending the old-fashioned log school-house in Ohio township, he early in life embarked in farming, has met with success, and owns the old home farm of 170 acres. He has served as vice-president and president of the agricultural society, and has also served as school director. He married, in 1844, Jemima, daughter of George and Anna (Daniels) Ingles. Her parents were German and English. The children of Mr. and Mrs. Todd now living are P. P., Thomas J., A. J. and H. S. Mr. Todd is a F. & A. M. Politically he is a Democrat.

WILLIAM TODD, A.M., professor of mathematics and natural science in Beaver College and Musical Institute, was born June 3, 1839. His parents, George and Hannah (Hodgson) Todd, natives of England, came to this country with their parents when they were children. Both were reared in this state, and their fathers were farmers. They were married in Allegheny county and moved to Armstrong county when William was about two years old, settling on a farm where our subject grew almost to manhood. His early education was received in South Buffalo township, near Freeport, Armstrong county. He applied himself so diligently to his studies that at an early age he was able to teach a country school. He was engaged in that occupation when he enlisted, in 1862, in Company L, 14th Regiment, P. V. C., being afterward promoted to regimental steward. He served three years and was honorably discharged at the close of the war, at Fort Leavenworth, Kan., in August, 1865. He returned to Armstrong county and soon afterward entered Allegheny College, at Meadville, Pa., from which institution he was graduated in 1868. The same year he accepted a position as principal of the Toms River (N. J.,) school. He was then professor of mathematics for two years at Wyoming Seminary, Kingston, Pa., and subsequently principal of the public school at Smithfield, Ohio, for two years, after which he accepted a position as principal of the Carrier Seminary, at Clarion, Pa., where he remained three years. In 1877 he was elected by the board of trustees of Beaver College to his present position. He has been a student all his life. He has lectured on educational subjects, but since coming to Beaver has devoted his time to his profession. When he assumed the responsibility of an instructor he did it with a firm determination to succeed, and being blessed with good health he has been able to continue his studies while teaching. Mr. Todd was married, in Butler county, in 1870, to Belle A., daughter of James and Mary (McCafferty) Hunter, who were of Irish origin. Mr. and Mrs. Todd have had three children: Clyde, Pearl and Clarence. Professor Todd and his wife are members of the Methodist church, and he is assistant superintendent of the Sabbath-school. In politics he is a Republican.

J. A. TOMLINSON, oil and gas operator, Beaver, was born in Canada, March 3, 1845, son of Robert and Mary (Harrison) Tomlinson, who were of English origin. The father, who was a farmer, came to New York State in 1831, and settled on a farm there. He spent part of his life in Canada, where he also owned property. He had seven sons and three daughters. J. A., the second son, was reared in Canada on the farm, and attended the common school. Early in life he embarked in the oil business. He came to Beaver county in 1883, being interested in the first gas well here, and has sunk several gas and oil wells. He was married, in 1870, to Amelia, daughter of Nicholas and Diana (Sprague) Bennett, natives of Canada, and of English descent. The children of Mr. and Mrs. Tomlinson are Leora, Jessie, Gilbert, Lee and Everett. Mr. Tomlinson is a Republican. Mrs. Tomlinson is a member of the Methodist church.

SEBASTIAN TRESS, glass mixer, Beaver Falls, was born in Würtemberg, Germany, Jan. 20, 1827, and is a son of Anton and Faronika (Mantz) Tress. He came to America in 1854, stopping in Allegheny county two months; then went to Clarion county, Pa., where he remained until 1858, in which year he located in Natrona, Allegheny county, where he worked in a black ash furnace six years. In 1864 he removed to Pittsburgh and entered the employ of a glass firm, where he learned the trade of glass-mixer, which he has since followed. He settled in Beaver Falls in 1879, and became one of the organizers of the Coöperative Flint Glass Works, of which he is a stockholder. He was twice married; his first wife being Crasin Eck, by whom he has six children living: Frances, Isaac, Anton, Frank, John and Joseph. His second wife was Eva Smith. Mr. Tress is a member of the German Catholic church. In politics he is a Democrat.

B. A. VANCE, physician, Darlington, was born in Columbiana county, Ohio, in 1844, and is the fourth son born to Samuel R. and Marie (Gilfillian) Vance, the latter a daughter of Dr. Alex. Gilfillian, of Lawrence county, Pa. Dr. Vance received in youth an academic education and afterward attended New Wellington College. At the age of twenty-eight years he began the study of medicine, Dr. Robinson being his preceptor, and graduated at Miami Medical College, Cincinnati, in 1874. He was married, in 1878, to Ella, daughter of Rev. Evatron Johnson, of New York. They have no children. In 1877 the Doctor located in Darlington, and since that date has been engaged in a large and lucrative practice. He has a very extensive and valuable medical library. politics he is a Democrat.

BIOGRAPHIES—WEST SIDE. 729

HENRY VEON (deceased) was born June 13, 1794. His father was a German soldier who had, during the revolution, been forced into the service of the English cause by his native ruler, and who, after being captured in the battle of Trenton, espoused the cause of the Americans, which he knew to be the cause of liberty and justice. After the war he removed to Beaver county, where his son was born. Henry, being poor, learned the trade af blacksmithing, and continued at it until 1820, when he married, purchased a farm, and moved thereon, where he lived until Dec. 27, 1882. His eldest son, John, a farmer, of Darlington, was born in 1821 in Beaver county, being one of thirteen children born to his mother, Barbara Douthitt. He was married to Eliza Jane Christy, by whom he had thirteen children, seven of whom are living. They are Walter Scott, Mary Jane, Alice Matilda, James Henry, John Franklin, Jesse Fremont and Albert Logan. Mr. Veon has held several township offices, and is a Republican in politics. The youngest son, George S. Veon, was born in 1838, on the farm which he now resides on and owns. He was married in 1864 to Ella, daughter of Jacob and Ellenora Courtney, by whom he had five children, four living, named: M. H., William S., George C. and Charles Edward. In 1861 Mr. Veon enlisted in Company D, 100th Regiment P. V., known as the "Roundhead" regiment, and was in active service two years, from which he received an honorable discharge. He has been school director; is a member of the G. A. R., and of the Presbyterian church. He is a Republican.

GEORGE W. VERNER, glass blower, Beaver Falls, was born in Pittsburgh, and is a son of William and Priscilla Verner. He was reared in Pittsburgh, and learned his trade in Chicago with John and George Wheeler, assisted by Philip Scharff and John W. Carr. He was in the employ of Hogan & Chandler, of Pittsburgh, for five years. In 1879 he located in Beaver Falls, and became one of the organizers of the Coöperative Flint Glass Works, of which he is a stockholder, and has since been employed there. He came to Beaver Falls with few pecuniary advantages, but by industry and economy has accumulated a fine property. He has served one term as member of council for the borough of Beaver Falls. In politics he is a Democrat.

CHARLES C. VOGELEY, secretary and treasurer of the Coöperative Glass Works, Beaver Falls, was born in Pittsburgh, Oct. 18, 1842, and is a son of Conrad and Catherine (Snyder) Vogeley. His father was a native of Germany, shoemaker by trade, and an early settler of Pittsburgh, where he died Sept. 22, 1884. Our subject was reared and educated in Pittsburgh, and acted as traveling salesman for the Atlantic Glass Company and other firms of that city, from 1875 until 1879. He then located in Beaver Falls and served as shipping clerk for the Coöperative Glass Company for two years. He was then elected chairman, serving three years, since which time he has held his present position. He was married, May 4, 1883, to Laura E., daughter of Philip and Helena (Duer) Metschen, of Phillipsburg, and by her he has two children : Helen and Albert. Mr. Vogeley is a member of the Lutheran church ; in politics a Republican.

JOHN VOLK (deceased) was born April 21, 1852, in Wittenberg, Germany, where he was reared and educated, and learned the brewer and cooper trades. He came to America in 1875, and settled in Beaver Falls. In 1876 he purchased the Volk Brewery, established in 1869 by August Volk and W. Leibold, and successfully conducted it until his death, in October, 1883. It has since been successfully carried on by his widow, Frances Volk. She is a daughter of John Rebeske, of Beaver Falls. She has two children : Alma A. and Alfred H. Mr. Volk was an energetic business man ; a member of the German Catholic church.

LEWIS J. WAGNER, brewer, Beaver Falls, was born in Germany in 1845, a son of Henry and Wilhelmina Wagner, who came to the United States in 1849, and in 1858 settled in Chippewa township and engaged in farming. In 1880 Henry built the brewery in Beaver Falls now managed by Lewis J., which he conducted until his death, May 5, 1884. He left seven children : Lewis J., Henry, Caroline, Lena, Charles, Sophia and August. Lewis J. has been the manager of the brewery since its erection. He married Cornelia, daughter of Ephraim and Margaret Herriott, of Rochester, Pa., and by her he has six children living: Gertrude, Robert, Harry, Ephraim, Margaret and

Bertha. Mr. Wagner enlisted Aug. 8, 1862, in Company F, 140th P. V. I., and participated in the battles of Chancellorsville, Gettysburg, Wilderness and in other engagements; was wounded in the hip at the battle of Bristow Station, and honorably discharged at Washington May 31, 1865. He is a member of the G. A. R. and the Druids. Politically he is a Democrat.

CHARLES P. WALLACE, banker, Beaver Falls, was born in Big Beaver township March 1, 1836, and is a son of Robert and Margaret (Hendrickson) Wallace. His grandfather was John Wallace, who in 1770, with three brothers, emigrated from Londonderry, Ireland. William located in Goshen, N. Y., and many of his descendants, a number of whom occupy prominent positions, still reside in that city and New York. James settled in Philadelphia, and from him spring many of the Wallace families in the eastern part of the state. Hugh went to South Carolina, where there is to-day a large connection; and John, above mentioned, settled in Carlisle, Pa., married and had one son, William, who was reared by his grandparents. He married a Philadelphian and reared a large family, from whom came what are known as the Carlisle Wallaces. Ex-Governor Wallace, of Washington territory, is one of that family. Gen. Lew Wallace, who distinguished himself in the War of the Rebellion, and late Minister to Constantinople, is another. Dr. Wallace, of Springfield, Ill., and ex-U. S. Senator William A. Wallace, of Clearfield, Pa., are also of this family. John Wallace, after the death of his wife, returned to Ireland and married a Miss Crawford, a sister of Mrs. John Scott, well known in the pioneer days of Beaver county. He remained near Londonderry until his children, six in number, were born, and in 1797 returned to America and settled in Cecil county, Md. His youngest son, Robert, when quite a boy, served as a soldier in the War of 1812, and drew a pension. Soon after the close of the war he settled at Beaver Falls, and married Margaret, daughter of Daniel Hendrickson, of New Castle, and by her he had ten children: Dr. John W., of New Castle; Daniel H., of New Castle, late Lieutenant-Colonel of the 76th P. V.; Dr. James J. and Dr. Robert D., of New Castle; Crawford C., of Homewood, Pa.; David W., (deceased), late of Leetonia, Ohio; Charles P.; Elizabeth; Ada (deceased) and William, of Homewood, Pa. Robert Wallace was well and favorably known in Beaver county. He was a man of more than ordinary ability, and was regarded by his neighbors as a man of sterling uprightness, whose word was as good as his bond. He was, in connection with Jeremiah Bannon, owner of the Brighton Furnace; was sheriff of the county from 1848 to 1851; supervisor of the ErieCanal 1836–37–38, and again in 1847. He died March 7, 1883, in his eighty-seventh year. His son Charles P., was reared in Beaver county and married Mary T., daughter of John and Sophronia (Jackson) Tarris, of Big Beaver township, and by her he has five children: David S., Dicky M., Glendia H., Cora and Bertha J. Mr. Wallace was treasurer of Beaver county in 1871–72. He is cashier of the Exchange Bank, treasurer of Beaver Falls Building and Loan Association, treasurer of Beaver Falls Borough, and secretary and treasurer of Grand View Cemetery. He is a member of the A. O. U. W. and I. O. O. F.; politically he is a Republican.

COL. RICHARD WALTON, farmer and blacksmith, P. O., Industry, is a native of this county and a son of Richard and Catherine (Small) Walton, the latter a daughter of Jacob Small. The father was a son of Thomas Walton, who came from Germany and married Nancy Bowers, who bore him four children. Richard, Sr., the eldest child and only son, came to Allegheny county, and later settled on 400 acres of land in this county. He had four sons and six daughters, of whom Richard, Jr., is the third son. The latter at the age of fourteen learned blacksmithing, a trade he followed more or less through life. For thirty two years he has resided on his present farm of ninety-one acres, where he has combined agriculture with his trade. He has been a successful bee-keeper, having had as many as 100 hives at a time. He was married in 1843, to Eliza, daughter of William McElhaney, of this county, and seven children have blessed them: Jane (now Mrs. Swager), Lydia (now Mrs. Munn), R. T., William M., Eliza (now Mrs. Abner), Flora B. and Lou E. Walton. Mr. Walton in early life took active part in the politics of the county, and to-day is the only man living in the township who served

BIOGRAPHIES—WEST SIDE.   731

"Bred Notices" under a law in early times for imprisoning for debt. He and his family are members of the United Presbyterian church. In politics he is a Republican. In 1887 he was elected one of the directors of the alms-house of the county, and Jan. 1, 1888, was elected president of the board of directors. Being a great and successful hunter he gained the title of "Colonel of the Fur Company."

THOMPSON WARNOCK, farmer, P. O. Darlington, was born in North Sewickley township in 1827. His parents, David and Jane (Thompson) Warnock, had a family of four sons and four daughters, Thompson being the third son. David was a soldier in the War of 1812, and was always a farmer. Thompson was reared on the farm, the pursuits of which have been his principal occupation, although for twenty years he was engaged in mercantile business. He received a common-school education, and in 1858 was married to Nancy Jane, daughter of James Wilson, of this county. Their children are Frank Morton (a druggist), Ellen Jane, James T and Margaret. Mrs. Warnock died in 1883, aged forty-four years. Mr. Warnock came to South Beaver township in 1873, and purchased his present farm of 160 acres. He is a member of the Presbyterian church; politically a Republican.

J. MOORE WARRICK, farmer, P. O. Rowe, is a grandson of Isaac Warrick, who settled in Beaver county in 1804. He (Isaac) came from England, and settled in New Jersey, where he married Mary Thatcher, whose parents came from England. In 1797 he moved to Gettysburg, and in 1800 settled in Washington county, whence in 1804 he came to this county. He located where the town of Beaver Falls now stands, and remained there until 1807, when he came to South Beaver township, where he purchased 200 acres of land. He had seven sons and three daughters; he died in 1838, aged eighty-four years. Jesse, the second eldest son, was born in 1787. He was reared a farmer, and in 1810 purchased the farm now owned by our subject. He married Nancy, daughter of William Moore, of Delaware, and had nine children. Jesse died in 1875, aged eighty-eight years, and his wife in 1862, aged seventy-five. Our subject, J. Moore, has never married. He is assisted in the work of the farm by his nephew, Silas N. Warrick, who is also a teacher. The house occupied by Mr. Warrick was built by his father in 1815, and is in a good state of preservation. Our subject is a Republican, and has manifested considerable interest in political matters.

JAMES H. WATERS, farmer and gardener, P. O. Beaver, is a native of Ireland and a son of John and Susan (Greer) Waters, former of whom was a farmer. Our subject, who is the second in a family of five children, was reared in Ireland, receiving his education in the common schools, and has worked at farming all his life. He came to America in 1848, locating in Allegheny county; thence came to Beaver county in 1853, and settled in Borough township, where he has since resided. By industry and economy he has achieved success. He was married, in 1849, to Sarah, daughter of Harry and Belle (McLarnen) Kennedy, natives of Ireland, and their children were Elizabeth (wife of Samuel Black); Sarah (deceased); John (an iron boiler or puddler in Pittsburgh, married to Belle Douds); Mary (wife of L. McCullough), and James, a glass packer at Pittsburgh. Mr. and Mrs. Waters are members of the Presbyterian church. In politics he is a Democrat.

WILLIAM B. WATKINS, D. D., pastor of the Methodist Episcopal Church, P. O. Beaver, Pa., was born in Bridgewater, Ohio, May 2, 1834, and is a son of John and Sarah (Hunter) Watkins. His mother was the fourth white child born in Steubenville, Ohio. His father was born in Jefferson county, Ohio, and was for many years a pilot on the Ohio and Mississippi rivers. He had six children, two of whom lost their lives in the service of their country: John B., a quartermaster sergeant, and Daniel Z, a lieutenant. Our subject's parents moved to Wheeling, W. Va., when he was a child, and he received his earliest education there, attending the first public free schools established in that place. He also attended the Lindsley Institute, and afterward became assistant teacher in the high school in Wheeling, devoting much of his leisure time to the study of classics. He afterward served three years as principal of a graded school. In 1854 he began the study of law, but before he finished his course he was elected a member of the

Pittsburgh Conference, accepting his first charge in 1856. The first five years of his ministerial life were spent in Ohio. In 1861, he was in Wellsburg, and in 1862 he came to New Brighton. He has been in Pennsylvania ever since, except four years spent in Ohio as presiding elder of Steubenville District. Nine years of his life as a minister have been spent in Pittsburgh. In 1884, at the close of a three years' service at the Pittsburgh Smithfield Street Church, he was sent to his present charge. He is the author of the McGuffey Spelling Book, and the Alternate. He also assisted in revising Webster's Dictionary. He is a popular speaker, and has lectured in many states. He has at present an extensive work under preparation: The Etymological Dictionary of American Geographical Names. He has visited sixteen different European countries. He was married in Allegheny county, Oct. 6, 1868, to Rebecca, daughter of Rev. James Mills, and has four children: Annie, a teacher in Ohio; Lucy, who took the first prize at the Beaver High School contest in 1887; Ella and Cora. The family are all members of the Methodist church.

JAMES WATT, P. O. Ohioville, was born in Ireland in August, 1823, where his father, James Watt, died. His mother, Isabella Watt, then removed with her family to America, in 1852, and located at Pittsburgh, where she died in 1858. There James was employed for twenty years as a puddler in an iron furnace. His sister, Eliza, widow of Moses Parks, still dwells there; a brother, Samuel, resides in Darlington township, and another brother lives in Ireland. In 1860 Mr. Watt purchased the farm of twenty-eight acres on which he resides near Ohioville, and settled thereon. He also owns 150 acres in Darlington township, and has been quite successful as an agriculturist and oil producer. Believing in the principles of the Republicans, he adheres to that party. In 1856 he was united in marriage with Mary Ann Arbuthnot, who was born in Ireland, and has been her husband's faithful helpmate and companion through the years of patient toil that have made their pleasant home. She is the mother of eight living children, as follows: Isabella (Mrs. John Potts), in Pittsburgh; Jean (wife of George Duncan), in Darlington; Mary and Margaret, with their parents; James, a carpenter at Pittsburgh; Rachel and Josephine, teachers, and William at home.

REUBEN WATT, farmer and now mill owner, P. O. Cannelton, was born in County Derry, Ireland Jan. 1, 1812, and is the fifth child of Robert (a farmer) and Isabella (Donohue) Watt, who came to America with their family in 1828. Shortly afterward they came to South Beaver township, where the father purchased a farm of 125 acres, and died in 1839, aged sixty-three years. Reuben received his education at the old log school-house, and is the only member of the family now living in this county. He was married in 1838 to Sarah Ann, daughter of Capt. Thomas and Sarah (Cameron) Elmer, of Upper Canada. Her father was a captain in the war of 1812, and fought against General Scott. Mr. and Mrs. Watt have had ten children, six of whom are living: Isabella (Mrs. Gilchrist), Thomas, who was a member of the famous "Round Head" regiment, and was wounded at Petersburg, June 17, 1864; James, a miller by trade; Maggie; George, now in Arizona, and Samuel Elmer, now in New Mexico. Mr. Watt carried on milling in connection with farming. He has retired from active labor, and for a number of years has devoted his time to settling estates, etc. He has been a justice of the peace for twenty-five years, having been first elected in 1847; also president, seven years, and secretary of the school board, eighteen years. He has held many other positions of trust in the township, and is highly respected. He is a member and elder of the Associate Presbyterian church; in politics he is a Republican.

ANDREW WATTERSON, farmer, P. O. Beaver, was born in Scotland, Jan. 13, 1810, and is a son of Andrew and Isabella (Black) Watterson. His father was a weaver, and came to America in 1830; his family came in 1832. Andrew is the third in a family of eight children that grew to maturity. He was reared in Scotland, where he learned the carpenter's trade, after attending the common schools for a short time. When he reached his majority he came to Beaver county and worked at his trade. In 1836 he bought a farm in company with his brother, consisting of 800 acres, of which he still owns 200. He was married in Beaver county, in 1839, to Miss Elizabeth Scott, of

BIOGRAPHIES—WEST SIDE.   733

Scotch-Irish descent, and they have had six children: Alexander (deceased) was a soldier in Company M, Sixth U. S. Cavalry; W. S. (deceased); Elizabeth, wife of B. F. McGaffie; Andrew, farmer, on the home farm; Isabella, wife of Thomas Blackwood, M. D.; Rebecca J. (deceased). Mr. and Mrs. Watterson are members of the Associate Presbyterian church. He is a Republican, and has served as justice of the peace since 1853.

WILLIAM WEIL, dealer in dry goods, Beaver Falls, was born in Pesth, Hungary, April 11, 1858, and is a son of Gen. Herman and Hannah (Houpt) Weil. His maternal grandparents, John and Lena Houpt, were imprisoned for political reasons during the revolution of 1848. Gen. Weil came to America with Kossuth in 1848, and was a refugee from the Austria-Hungary rebellion. In 1851, with others, he was granted amnesty, and returned to his native land to recover property that had been confiscated, but failed. He returned to the United States in 1864, located in Cleveland, Ohio, and engaged in the commission business until his death, which occurred Feb. 4, 1881. William Weil was reared in Cleveland, and in 1866 was sent to Pesth, Hungary, where he attended the State University for three years. He returned to Cleveland in 1869, and graduated from the public schools in that city in 1873. He then studied telelegraphy two years, after which he was engaged in newspaper work on the Reno (Nev.) *Gazette*, the leading paper of that state. In 1879 he embarked in mercantile business in Leadville, Col., remaining there one year; then located in Wooster, Ohio, where he was engaged in business five years. In September, 1887, he embarked in the dry goods business in Beaver Falls, and his establishment is one of the retail trade attractions of this community.

L. F. WEINMAN, dealer in boots and shoes, Bridgewater, was born in Germany, May 8, 1831, and is a son of Adam and Sophia (Hahn) Weinman, former of whom was born in 1800, and in his lifetime did a successful business in contracting, and grading streets. The family consisted of thirteen children, of whom L. F. is the sixth. Our subject was reared in Germany, and received a good education. He came to America in 1853, and in 1854 to Beaver county. He had learned the shoemaker's trade in Germany, and obtained employment with Robert Tallon in Beaver, where he worked for three years. He is now the oldest boot and shoe dealer in this county. In 1856 he was married to Margaret, also of German descent, daughter of John Gress. His children are Louis P., George, Charles, Frank, James, Katie and Minnie. The family are members of the Presbyterian church. Mr. Weinman is a member of the Lutheran church, in politics a Democrat. He is a Master Mason. He was the principal founder of the first building association in Beaver county, and is now president of the Bridgewater Building Association.

WILLIAM S. WELLS, assistant engineer and inspector of bridge materials for the Pennsylvania Railroad Company, Beaver Falls, was born in Altoona, Pa., May 21, 1860, and is a son of James B. and Lucinda H. (Van De Vere) Wells. He was reared in Harrisburg, Pa., where he received his early education in Seiler's Academy. He entered Taylor's Polytechnic Institute, Wilmington, Del., in 1874, from which he was graduated in 1875. In 1877 he began an apprenticeship at the machinist trade in Altoona Pa., serving three years. He filled the position of assistant engineer of construction with the American Iron Works of Pittsburgh, Pa., in 1880-81-83; took a post-graduate course of instruction at Harvard College in 1884; was appointed in 1885 superintendent of physical culture, Y. M. C. A., of Pittsburgh, and at the same time was a member of the faculty of Pittsburgh Female College; and since Jan. 1, 1886, has held the position of assistant engineer and inspector of bridge materials for the Pennsylvania Railroad Company. He located in Beaver Falls in 1867. He is a member of the K. of P.; politically he is Democrat.

A. J. WELSH, sheriff, Darlington, was born in this county May, 6, 1839. His grandfather, James, who was born in South Carolina in 1758, and came to Washington county in 1796, married Mary Peck, by whom were born eight children. Andrew, the fifth son, was born Jan. 5, 1794. In 1796 the family first came to Beaver county where they engaged in the farm and hotel businesses, and Andrew, in early life, was employed in boating on the Ohio river. He married Keziah, daughter of Henry Newkirk, of Ohio, originally of Connecticut. Five children were born to this couple, Andrew J. being the youngest. Our subject was born and reared in Chippewa township, receiving a common-school education, and was for many years engaged in farming. He was married in 1858 to Mary, daughter of Robert and Mary (McBride) Dunlop, and their children are Laura E., Harry G., Ida A. and Charles Ross. Mr. Welsh enlisted in 1861 in Company C, 22nd Illinois Regiment, and served three years. He was justice of the peace nine years. He is now agent for the P. M. & C. Railroad Company, at Darlington. He was elected sheriff of Beaver county by the Republican party, in 1887.

MICHAEL WEYAND, editor and publisher, P. O. Beaver, was born in Somerset, Pa., June 11, 1825, and is a son of Henry and Magdalene (Ginder) Weyand, both natives of Somerset county, and of German descent. He removed with his parents when a year old to a farm in North Beaver township, then in Beaver and now in Lawrence county. The father was a school teacher and a farmer, teaching in winter time both the English and German languages, and he resided on the same farm until his death; he died in October, 1843, aged fifty-four years. The mother died in August, 1862, aged seventy-three years. There were five brothers and sisters; the elder brother died in October, 1843, aged twenty-four; the other brother, Col. Jacob, resides in Beaver, and is in the real estate business; the elder sister is married, and resides near Mt. Jackson; the younger sister is married and lives in Beaver. The subject of this sketch was put to the printing business in the New Castle *Intelligencer* office when but twelve years old, and served as "printer's devil" for one year; then in the spring of 1838, came to the *Argus* office in Beaver; served an apprenticeship of four and one-half years; then for a time played journeyman; and in November, 1851, purchased Hon. William Henry's half interest in the *Argus*, and from that time until the close of 1859 was joint, and for several years, sole editor of that journal; being connected therewith as apprentice, journeyman and editor for nearly a quarter of a century. He was married in November, 1851, to Amanda, daughter of David and Mary Somers, of Beaver; Mr. Somers being county commissioner in 1833-34, and high sheriff in 1839-42. He was a native of Washington county and died in August, 1850, aged fifty seven years. His widow, a native of Cape May, N. J., died a year ago, aged nearly ninety-four years. The fruits of the marriage first above alluded to were two sons and two daughters, all living in Beaver. The eldest, Henry S., married, and is foreman of the *Times* office; one daughter married Dr. J. H. Wilson; and a son and daughter, David and Julia, are at home. After a rest of a few years the *Beaver Times* was founded in April, 1874, by Mr. Weyand, and he is still connected therewith as editor and proprietor, having had with him from the start, his sons as assistants. The paper is republican in politics; has always been independent in tone and action, and is at present the only non-patent journal in the county. He has been connected with the public press in some capacity for over fifty years, and is doubtless the oldest republican editor now in harness in Western Pennsylvania; and next to "Uncle" Jake Zeigler of the *Butler Herald*, perhaps the oldest in service in this section of the State. During his long career as journalist he has had many bitter and exciting controveries, but has always sought to avoid offensive personalities as long as such avoidance was possible. He has been a life long Whig and Republican; a protectionist of the Henry Clay school; he was inflexibly opposed to the extension of slavery, resisted the repeal of the Missouri Compromise, and the introduction of slavery into the territories of Kansas and Nebraska, editorially and on the stump, with all the earnestness and ability he was master of. He held the office of prothonotary of Beaver county six and one-half years, including the time of the late war, one-half year by appointment and six years by election. He was a candidate for presidential elector in 1884 and, with his twenty-nine Republican colleagues was elected with an average majority of about 80,-000. When he came to Beaver fifty years ago he was a lad of delicate health, and it was predicted that he would not live the year out; and yet he has outlived many scores of those who gave much greater promise of long life, and at this writing there are but six male citizens in the town of Beaver who were here when he came.

BIOGRAPHIES—WEST SIDE. 735

JACOB WEYAND, the subject of this notice, was born in Lawrence county, near Mount Jackson, March 29, 1828. He worked on a farm until he attained his majority, after which he attended school in Beaver for a short time. In 1854 he became part owner of the *Argus*, and assisted in editing and publishing that paper until the winter of 1857–58, when he disposed of his interest in the *Argus* and bought the *Free Press* at Carrollton, Ohio. Here he was when the war broke out. Catching the martial spirit of the times he sold the *Free Press*, raised a company of volunteers, was elected its captain, and marched it to Camp Mingo, near Steubenville, Ohio, and was at once attached to the 126th O. V. I. and mustered into the United States service. For sturdy courage and coolness in the midst of great danger he had no peers in the army. He was twice wounded in battle, and participated in nearly all of the bloody battles in which the army of the Potomac took a part. In the battle at Monocacy, Md., July 9, 1864, he was put in command of his regiment; and an officer on the staff of the commanding general that day, in writing a history of the battle, made use of the following language:

Captain Weyand, who was commanding the 126th Ohio Vols. was on the extreme right of the line, with the right of his regiment resting near the Monocacy bridge. After the battle had progressed a short time he was directed by General Wallace to set fire to the bridge, then face his regiment to the left, double quick it to the extreme left of the line, throw it across the pike and hold the position as long as he could. The bridge was fired, and the regiment started off on its perilous mission. It had almost reached its destination, when, as it came abreast of the left of the line of the one-hundred-day men, it met a most unexpected obstruction. Immediately in their front was a farm ditch, about six feet wide and the same in depth, through which a sluggish, shallow stream of water was running. A few feet further was a board fence some five or six feet high, and both running at right angles with the line of battle.

Just beyond the ditch and fence was the Washington Pike. The ditch was literally alive with one-hundred-day men, who, all unused to the sort of treatment they were receiving at the hands of the enemy, had taken shelter there from the raking fire which the Confederates had opened upon the Pike with the view of keeping that thoroughfare open. The enemy were in line of battle on an elevation about four hundred yards in our front and every missile known to savage warfare seemed to be coming down that hard and dusty road. Plowing shot, screaming shell, hurling grape and canister, trimmed out with whistling, zipping, rattling volleys of musketry, falling everywhere, and sending up puffs of dust, or tearing great rifts in the almost impenetrable highway, produced a veritable "pandemonium let loose," and no one who could command calmness enough to considerately behold the scene can ever forget it. Language is not lurid enough, nor is vermillion red enough to catch the scene.

But it must be done! The general had ordered the One Hundred and Twenty-sixth to form across that road.

"Theirs not to make reply,
Theirs not to reason why,
Theirs but to do and die."

To go is death to many; to stay is dishonor and defeat to all. Orders are useless amid this awful din! Example is everything! As a woman who hesitates is lost, so a soldier who falters at the breach is undone. Captain Weyand leaped the ditch, climbed to the top of the fence and pointed "Forward!" In an instant every file was moving after him, and led by the gallant Captain McPeck, the indomitable Captain Hoge, and that sturdy patriot, Lieutenant Crooks, the regiment sprang across the ditch, demolished the fence and wheeled across the road, dressed their line as if on parade, and stubbornly maintained their position. Under the galling fire the men were falling like leaves before an autumn storm, and realizing the dreadful havoc that was being made in the ranks, Captain Weyand broke the battle line and hurriedly moved the regiment some seventy-five yards forward, where an abrupt rise in the ground partially sheltered the men from the merciless storm through which they had just passed. In this movement toward the enemy in the face of a withering fire, the brave men marched with touching elbows and with as regular tread as they ever did in battalion drill or going out on dress parade. All this occurred within the brief period of about fifteen minutes, and yet within that time every fourth man in the regiment that day was either killed, wounded or missing. The saying went undenied then and since that "every officer of the regiment came out of the conflict bleeding; and that *every man in the line* that was not hit had his clothes riddled with bullets. In the eleven preceding battles in which the regiment had borne an honorable part, its splendid discipline and fighting qualities had never shown to greater advantage than on this field. Its brilliant conduct was the theme of officers and men wno had no connection with it. and Chptain Weyand, who had already been complimented highly by his superior officers for gallantry at Cold Harbor, was now honored with recommendations to the Secretary of War for brevet promotions as major and lieutenant-colonel.

The story of Monocacy is that of a battle lost, a victory won. Many other battles were greater in point of numbers engaged and the natural casualties of war; few were greater in results as compared with the numbers engaged; none were greater than the heroism displayed by those engaged. Monocacy saved Washington.

After the war was over he returned to Beaver, bought the *Argus* again, and continued to be its editor and proprietor until 1874, when it and the *Radical* were consolidated and published for four years by Weyand & Rutan. He was married in 1857 to Victoria Adams, daughter of the late Dr. Milo Adams, for many years a leading physician in the county. He has four children living, viz.: Emma, married to Harry W. Reeves, of Beaver Falls; Edwin, who is registered as a law student; Blanche and Paul, who are still living with their parents. Mr. Weyand is considered among the best business men of the Beaver Valley. When the McCreery Bank failed, in 1883, he was selected as assignee, and settled the complicated business of that institution to the satisfaction of all parties interested. He resides now on a small farm near Beaver, and spends much of his time in beautifying and improving his possessions.

WILLIAM WHAN (deceased), whose portrait appears elsewhere in this volume, was born Dec. 24, 1814, in Big Beaver, Lawrence county, Pa., and was reared upon a farm there, his educational opportunities being somewhat limited. He was possessed of sound sense, and attended to his own affairs with success and no ostentation. He sought no public distinction, but was called upon by his fellow-citizens in Darlington township, irrespective of party, to serve them for thirty successive years as justice of the peace. This he did with impartial faithfulness. Politically his affiliations were with the Democratic party. In 1839 he married Miss Margaret Marshall, a sister of Marvin, John and H. J. Marshall, whose biographies will be found in this book. Mrs. Whan was born in Big Beaver, this county, Dec. 5, 1821, and now resides with her daughter at East Palestine, Ohio. Immediately after their marriage this couple settled on the farm in Darlington township, which Mr. Whan had purchased, and there remained until his death, which occurred Nov. 30, 1877. Both were life-long members of the United Presbyterian church. Their children, who grew to maturity, are here named, with their residences : Elizabeth, widow of Robert Mitchell, Darlington township; Mary, wife of John Harvey, Darlington borough; William John, same ; Alice (Mrs. Robert Young), East Palestine, Ohio ; Jonah S., on homestead farm in Darlington ; Robert Emmett, East Palestine ; James Finley, Negley, Ohio ; Ida D., wife of John Sturgeon, Bucyrus, Ohio. The grandfather of our subject, William Whan, emigrated from Ireland and was one of the earliest settlers in what was then Beaver county, now the township of Big Beaver, Lawrence county. He was married twice, and reared a large family. His son John (born March 25, 1791,) married Mary Stinson, who was born in New Jersey Oct. 14, 1795. The former died July 13, 1868, and the latter Dec. 11, 1887. They lived on a farm adjoining the original homestead, and reared ten children to maturity. Their names follow: William, whose name heads this sketch ; Thomas, who now occupies his grandfather's homestead ; Robert, who lives at Galt, Mo.; James, who died at home ; Margaret, widow of Thomas Stevenson, in Bulgers, Washington county, Pa.; Hannah, married John Beatty, and died near Wampum, Pa.; Mary Jane, widow of William Rhodes, resides at Enon Valley ; Elizabeth Celicia (Mrs. Peter Overlander), same ; Isabel, unmarried ; Nancy Adaline, married Capt. Alexander Gilkey and dwells near Blue Mound, Kans. Jonah S. Whan, son of Wm. and Margaret Whan, was born in Darlington township, Beaver county, Aug. 29, 1853. He was educated at Mount Nebo, and has followed farming and coal mining, and is at present a coal operator. He married, Dec. 25, 1873, Sarah M. Billingsley, of Columbirana county, Ohio. They have four children, two boys and two girls.

WILLIAM JOHN WHAN, hotel keeper, Darlington borough, was born in Darlington township, Aug. 5, 1844. He remained on the home farm until of age, after which he followed various occupations. For seven years he was engaged in weighing the output of coal mines, and for three years was employed in the manufacture of lamp oil from cannel coal. After farming for five years in Darlington township and in Ohio, he bought, in 1885, the hotel, which he still conducts. He is extensively engaged in breeding Percheron-Norman horses, and is the owner of a farm of 116 acres adjoining the Ohio line. Mr. Whan is past-master of Meridian Lodge, No. 411, F. & A. M., of which he has been twenty years a member; he has served the township three years as justice of the peace. Like his father he is a life-long Democrat. In 1870 he married Alice, daughter of Samuel and Mary Eleanor Stickel, and their two children, Lena Gertrude and Edwin Marshall, exceptionally bright young people, are at home. Mr. Whan is an expert shot, and takes a great interest in all sporting matters. No boisterous or unbecoming behavior is tolerated about his hotel.

ANDREW G. WHITE, paper hanger, Beaver, was born in Economy township, Beaver county, May 18, 1841. He is a son of Joseph and Margaret (Walton) White, former born in Willsburg, W. Va., and the latter in Beaver county; her paternal and maternal ancestors were among the early settlers of Beaver county. Joseph White was a farmer, and was of Irish descent. He had five children, Andrew G. being the fourth. Our subject was reared in Beaver county, and attended the common schools. He learned the trade of plasterer, and made that his business until 1862, when he enlisted in Company F, 140th Regiment P. V., and became a non-commissioned officer. He was in several severe engagements, was taken prisoner at the battle of the Wilderness, and suffered the horrors of Libby and Andersonville prisons for seven months. He served until the close of the war, and returning home he resumed his trade, finally working into paper-hanging, which he has since made his business. Mr. White was married Nov. 29, 1865, to Margaret, daughter of Socrates and Jane (Williams) Johnson, of German and Irish descent, and their children are Harry L. and Charles F. The family are members of the Methodist Episcopal church, of which Mr. White is a trustee. In politics he is a Democrat.

JOHN WHITE, retired, P. O. Cannelton, was born in Allegheny county, Pa., in 1802. His parents, Thomas and Jane (Martin) White, had four sons and three daughters, John being the second son. Jane (Martin) White was the daughter of Esquire Martin, who was major in the Revolutionary War. Thomas White came from Ireland about 1770, and soon afterward purchased 400 acres of land in Allegheny county, where he engaged extensively in farming and stock raising. Early in life he was engaged as a "trader," an occupation extensively carried on in the early history of Pennsylvania. Thomas died in 1816, his wife in 1827. John White was reared in Allegheny county, and at eighteen years of age left school to engage in farming. He remained at home with his mother and brother till twenty-five years of age. In 1826 he married Polly, daughter of John and Jane (Crooks) Burns. Her father came from Scotland. Five children have been born to Mr. and Mrs. White: Thomas M.; John Burns; Mary. Mrs. Whattenburg, of New York City, (deceased); James (deceased); and Alexander Duncan (deceased). Mr. White, in 1850, sold his homestead farm in Allegheny county, and came to Darlington and purchased 300 acres of farming land, having previous to that period purchased 800 acres of coal land in the same township. For twenty years he was actively engaged on his farm and in superintending his coal lands. In 1852 the Darlington Cannel Coal Railroad Company was incorporated with Mr. White as president, a position he held for eight years. The road is now in a prosperous condition, and known as N. Y. P. & C. R. R. Mr. White was for ten years a justice of the peace in Allegheny county, and has held other positions of trust. Four years ago he retired from active business life and is succeeded by his two sons. He is a strong, intelligent, good-hearted Democrat.

CHAMBERLIN WHITE, chief of police, Beaver Falls, was born in Chippewa township, Feb. 13, 1836, and is a son of Thomas and Elizabeth (Bannon) White. His paternal grandfather, John White, of County Antrim, Ireland, came to America in 1791 and settled in Chippewa township, in 1795, on a farm now owned by James Clayton. In 1796 he took up 400 acres of land in the same township, and lived there until his death. He had ten children: Thomas, John, David, Robert, Sarah (Mrs. Thomas Ramsey), James, Mary (Mrs. William Johnson), Elizabeth (Mrs. Daniel McCann), Anna (Mrs. Samuel Lee) and Hugh. The maternal grandfather of Mr. White was Jeremiah Bannon, a pioneer of this county. Thomas White, father of Chamberlin, was born in Chippewa township in 1810, and died in March, 1887. He had ten children, five of whom are now living: Chamberlin, Jerry B., Eleazor, Martha H. (Mrs. George E. Smith), and Thomas. Our subject was reared in Chippewa township. In 1859 he went to California and worked in the mines four years. In 1866 he located in Beaver Falls, where he has been engaged in various business enterprises. In 1872 Mr. White was elected sheriff of Beaver county. He has been chief of police of Beaver Falls eight years; is a member of the A. O. U. W.; politically he is a Republican.

JERRY WHITE, foreman of the Wire Mills, Beaver Falls, was born in Chippewa township, Feb. 10, 1839, a son of Thomas and Elizabeth (Bannon) White. His paternal grandfather was John White, of County Antrim, Ireland, who settled in Chippewa township in 1795. His maternal grandfather was Jeremiah Bannon, a pioneer iron manufacturer of this county. Jerry White was reared in Chippewa township, and when twenty-one years of age engaged in railroading as manager of contract work. Later he was a foreman in a stone quarry and since 1882 has been foreman of the galvanizing department of the Hartman Wire Mills. In 1866 he and his brother Chamberlin embarked in the manufacture of brick in Beaver Falls, continuing two years. Mr. White has been twice married; first to Isabella, daughter of William and Mary (McEwen) Duard, of Pulaski township, by whom he had six children: Elizabeth, Ellen, Rhoda, Lillie, Maggie H. and Chamberlin. Mr. White is a member of the school board of Beaver Falls; politically he is a Republican.

ROBERT WHITE, farmer, P. O. Beaver Falls, was born in Chippewa (now White) township, Dec. 8, 1816, and is a son of John and Elizabeth (Kelso) White. His father, who was a son of Thomas White, and a native of County Antrim, Ireland, settled in Chippewa township in 1794, and cleared the farm now occupied by Robert. His wife was a daughter of John Kelso, of New Jersey, who settled in Big Beaver township about 1800, where he is said to have built the first gristmill in the county. John White reared a family of ten children: Thomas, John, David, Robert, Sarah B., James, Mary J., Elizabeth, Ann and Hugh. Robert has always resided at the old homestead. In 1856 he married Margaret, daughter of John and Isabel Walker, of Allegheny county, and by her has eight children living: John, Elizabeth, Belle, Mary, Margaret, Ann, Robert, Jr., and Sarah. Mr. White is a prominent farmer of Chippewa township; politically he is a Democrat.

HUGH WHITE, carpenter and millwright, Beaver Falls, was born in Chippewa township, April 13, 1832, and is a son of John and Elizabeth (Kelso) White. His father, who was a son of Thomas White, was a native of County Antrim, Ireland, and settled in Chippewa township in 1794. His maternal grandfather was John Kelso, of New Jersey, who settled in Big Beaver township, about 1800. John White reared a family of ten children, of whom Hugh is the youngest. Our subject was reared in his native township, and served an apprenticeship at the carpenter's trade; which, with the exception of five years spent as a boatman on the canal, he followed until 1876. Since then he has been employed as a millwright in the Beaver Falls Steel Works, and has resided in Beaver Falls since 1867. He was married, in 1856, to Sarah J., daughter of David and Rhoda (Hendrickson) Boyle, of Beaver Falls, and a granddaughter of Henry Boyle and Daniel Hendrickson, pioneers of Beaver county. By this union there are seven children: Eleanor, David, McClellan, Thomas, Malvina, Daniel and Bertha. Mr. White is a member of the I. O. O. F., and K. of P.; in politics he is a Democrat.

CAPT. HENRY WHITFIELD, retired steamboat owner and captain, Beaver, was born in England, Aug. 25, 1809. His father, also named Henry, was a merchant and a farmer. Our subject, who is the only living member of the family in this country, was reared and educated in England, and came to America in 1830. He went to Pittsburgh, where he learned the nailer's trade and worked at it for a time. He afterward studied engineering, and ran an engine on the river several years. He invested in steamboat property, and was at different times interested in many steamboats. He built boats for a time, and was also a captain for many years. In 1864 he bought a farm and retired; lived on the farm until 1882, and then removed to Beaver. He was married, July 31, 1835, to Margaret Adams, of Wheeling, W. Va. Her mother's maiden name was Sarah Marshall, and she was of Irish origin. Captain and Mrs. Whitfield have had five children, of whom three are living: James, in Kansas; Ann, wife of David Auchinbaugh, a tinner in Beaver; and Sarah M., wife of Frank Crawford, who is in the employ of the Adams Express Company, at Cincinnati, Ohio. Captain Whitfield and his wife are members of the United Presbyterian church; he has served as elder for more than thirty years. In politics he is a Republican.

JOHN C. WHITLA. Mr. Whitla, whose name is largely identified with the business achievements of Beaver Falls and New Brighton, is of Scotch descent. His grandfather William Whitla, who resided near Edinburgh, emigrated to America in 1820 and settled in Carroll county, Ohio, where he dwelt during the remainder of his life, being there engaged in farming. He married Elizabeth McGowen, also of Scotch extraction, and had seven children, one daughter, Agnes (Mrs. William Young), and six sons: William, John, James, Hugh, David, and David 2d. The last named and youngest of these was born in Scotland in 1811, and emigrated with his parents when nine years of age. On attaining his majority he removed to Brighton, Beaver county, and there married Mary Jane, daughter of David Reeves, of Beaver Falls. Their children are Margaret, William, Joseph, Elizabeth, Amanda, John C., Esther, Daniel and Henry. Mr. Whitla returned again to Ohio, but finally located permanently in New Brighton, where he followed his trade as saddler, and died Aug. 11, 1878. His son, John C. Whitla, who was born April 9, 1848, in Salineville, Ohio, removed with his parents when a child to Stark county and later to Ravenna, in the same state. In 1864 New Brighton, Beaver county, Pa., became his home. The lad received such education as the common schools of Ohio afforded, and on coming to New Brighton entered the store of H. T. & J. Reeves as clerk, continuing this relation with their successors, Messrs. Duff & Thompson, with whom he remained thirteen years. Mr. Whitla, however, was not satisfied to spend his best years as a clerk, and at the expiration cf this time embarked in the sale of dry goods and carpets at New Brighton, where he remained until 1885. Having become a stockholder in the New Brighton and Beaver Valley Street Railway he then superintended its construction, and in forty-one days successfully completed the project. He also aided in the organization and constructed the buildings of the New Brighton Glass Works, and was one of the projectors and a director of the First National Bank of Beaver Falls. In 1886 he established himself in the clothing business in Beaver Falls, and one year later erected the spacious building opposite the Economy Bank, now occupied by him. In January, 1887, the Beaver Falls Art Tile Company was organized, of which he became a director and is now its president. The same year he with others projected the Whitla Glass Works, Limited, of which he is also president. Mr. Whitla was married Oct. 31, 1869, to Miss Sarah A., daughter of Dr. W. W. Simpson, of New Brighton, and they have had four children, Theodore, the only survivor, being now at Pottstown, pursuing his studies. Mr. Whitla is an active member of Union Lodge No. 59, F. & A. M., of New Brighton, and connected with Harmony Chapter of Beaver Falls, and Askalon Commandery, of Allegheny City. He is identified by membership with the Protestant Methodist church of New Brighton.

JOHN JERVIS WICKHAM, president judge of the Thirty-sixth Judicial District, composed of Beaver county, was born May 14, 1844, in County Meath, Ireland. When between five and six years of age he came to the United States with his parents, who settled in Beaver. He was educated in the public schools and Beaver Academy, and about the age of seventeen learned telegraphy. Soon afterward he entered the United

States Military Telegraph Corps. In July, 1862, while serving as cipher expert at headquarters of the 23d Brigade, he was captured with the command by the rebel General Forrest, in the action at Murfreesboro, Tenn. He was a prisoner of war for a number of months, his last place of confinement being Libby prison, Richmond. Afterwards he served in Telegraph Corps, with different commands in the army of General Sherman. He remained as cipher expert on the staff of Gen. Geo. H. Thomas from the close of the war until the fall of 1867, when, having commenced the study of law, he resigned and returned to Beaver, and was prepared for the bar in the office of S. B. Wilson, Esq. He had been recommended previously for commission in regular army on account of gallantry, etc. [See Plum's History of the Military Telegraph, Vol. I, pages 56 and 274, and Vol. II, page 282.] In 1869 he was admitted to the bar and practiced a short time in Des Moines, Iowa, then returned to Beaver, entered into partnership with S. B. Wilson, Esq., which connection lasted until 1875. He was nominated for the office of president judge by the Republican party, in 1884, and elected in the fall of that year. In 1874 he was married to Lida J., daughter of Charles D. and Abigail K. Hurlbutt, of Beaver. The issue of this union is four children, two sons and two daughters.

JOHN C. WIEGEL, glass cutter, Beaver Falls, was born in Prussia, Feb. 23, 1852, and is a son of Carl and Mina Wiegel, who came to America in 1856 and settled in Pittsburgh. Here John C. was reared, learned his trade of glass cutter, and worked as a journeyman seventeen years in the glass works of McKee Bros. In 1879 he located in Beaver Falls, where he has since followed his trade and been foreman of the cutting shop since 1883. In 1880 he married Elizabeth, daughter of Henry and Margaret Vetter, of Pittsburgh, and they have three children: Albert, Charles and Hilda. Mr Wiegel is a member of the Beaver Falls Building and Loan Association and of the Coöperative Flint Glass Company, Limited; is a member of Tent No. 53, K. O. T. M.; in politics he is a Democrat.

WILCOX BROS., brick manufacturers, P. O., Beaver Falls, are natives of England, and located in New Brighton, this county, in 1884, where they were contractors engaged in the manufacture of brick for Fish Brothers until the spring of 1887. They then embarked in business for themselves in Chippewa township, where they manufacture a superior quality of brick, turning out from 400,000 to 500,000 per annum, giving employment to seven hands, and are the only manufacturers in their line in Chippewa township.

D. R. WILKINSON, general manager and superintendent of the Western File Works, Beaver Falls, was born in Lawrence county, Pa., July 31, 1853, and is a son of George and Margaret (Richey) Wilkinson. He came to Beaver Falls in 1870 and entered the employ of the Western File Works as a clerk; was successively promoted to assistant bookkeeper, bookkeeper and general traveling agent, and in February, 1887, was appointed general manager and superintendent, which position he now occupies. He married in 1873, Mary D., daughter of John Shoemaker, of Beaver Falls, and by her has two children: Bertha M. and Florence L. Mr. Wilkinson is a member of the Presbyterian church; he is a F. & A. M., a R. A. M., a member of the A. O. U. W. and American Legion of Honor; in politics he is a Republican.

CHRISTIAN WILL, manager of the Star Glass Works, at Newark, Ohio, was born in Allegheny City, Pa., May 24, 1835, and is a son of Philip Will. His grandfather, also named Philip Will, was a soldier eleven years, and served under Napoleon Bonaparte. Our subject's parents were French, and his father, who was a tailor, carried on business in Allegheny City. Christian was reared and secured his schooling in Allegheny City; was removed from school at the age of ten years, and commenced work in the glass works. He proved himself a diligent helper, and has climbed from the bottom of the ladder to the top. In 1877 he bought a valuable farm in Brighton township where his family now reside. He was married in Allegheny City to Miss Margaretta, daughter of Jacob and Catherine (Swartz) Sommers, who were of German origin. This union was blessed with five children, only one of whom is now living, Harrison T. Will, who has charge of the farm. He was born at Brownston, Pa., March 29, 1867, and attended the graded school at Pittsburgh, and the high school at Beaver, Pa.; entered Duff's Commercial College at Pittsburgh, graduating in 1887. He was married June 10, 1885, to Miss Stella V., daughter of Marcius Harton, of Brighton township, and of English descent. They have one daughter, Queenette. Both Harrison T. Will and his father are Republicans.

J. H. WILSON, M. D., was born in Beaver borough Oct. 16, 1850, and is a son of Marmaduke and Lucinda (Henry) Wilson. His paternal and maternal ancestors were among the early settlers of Pennsylvania, and were of Irish and Welsh origin. The father is a farmer and resides in Beaver borough, where he owns 33 acres of land. His family consisted of ten children, of whom our subject is the sixth. He attended the old academy here and also Dr. McClean's seminary, commenced the study of medicine in Beaver, and completed the course at New Brighton, with Dr. D. McKinney. His first course of lectures was at Jefferson Medical College in 1873-74, and he completed his course at the Bellevue Hospital Medical College, New York, where he was graduated in February, 1876. He has since been in active practice in his native town. Dr. Wilson was married in 1878, to Eva, daughter of Michael Weyand, editor of the *Times*, in Beaver, and their children are Fred Bailey, Elizabeth and Juliet. Doctor and Mrs. Wilson are members of the Presbyterian church, which he joined in 1867. In politics he is a Democrat. He is devotedly attached to his profession. He is surgeon for the Pennsylvania Railroad Company at Beaver, and for the P. & L. E. R. R. He is a member of the Pennsylvania Railroad Medical Association; has been an active member of the Beaver County Medical Association for many years, and has served in all the offices. He is an active member of the American Medical Association, and has been a member since 1877. He served as jail physician in Beaver in 1884-85.

THOMAS WILSON, retired farmer, P. O. Industry, was born in Ireland in 1808, and is a son of George and Elizabeth (Lindsey) Wilson, who came to America in 1819 with five children, and soon thereafter purchased 50 acres of land, which they failed to hold, owing to invalidity of title. Not long afterward, however, Mr. Wilson purchased 300 acres, which he owned until his death. Thomas was reared to farm life, and has resided on his present farm since 1830. This property now comprises 120 acres, part cultivated and part wood land. Mr. Wilson was married, in 1833, to Jane Burnsides, also a native of Ireland, daughter of John Burnsides. To this union five children were born, four now living: George L, Margaret (now Mrs. Bowers), John B. and Eliza. The mother died in 1872. Mr. Wilson is a member of the Presbyterian church; politically a Republican.

SAMUEL B. WILSON. Mr. Wilson, in his ancestry, unites the blood of the sturdy Scotch race and that of the Knickerbockers. In the early part of the eighteenth century his great-grandfather, Samuel Wilson, who was of Scotch descent, married Mary Van Wier, a Hollander by birth. They owned and occupied a farm on Marsh creek, near Gettysburg, Pa. They had two sons, Samuel and Marmaduke, the latter of whom married Susan Beatty in the year 1744. He remained on the homestead until the death of his parents, who are buried in the cemetery at Gettysburg. He then removed to Westmoreland county. One of his sons, Patrick, who was born in York (now Adams) county in 1772, went to Mercer (now Lawrence) county in 1801, and engaged for a time in mercantile pursuits. In 1804 he married Rebecca, one of the eight daughters of William Morehead, and in 1811 he purchased and removed to a farm (still in possession of his descendants) about six miles north of New Castle, Pa., where he continued to reside, until the time of his death, in 1866. On this farm his son, Samuel Beatty Wilson, was born, Feb. 20, 1824. After having received a common-school and academic education, "Sam B.," as he was called by his associates, entered Jefferson College, at Cannonsburgh, Pa., at which institution he was graduated in June, 1848, standing among the first in his class. His mastery of the construction of the English, Latin and Greek languages was never questioned by fellow-student or professor. Moreover, he has not only kept up, but greatly increased his knowledge of the ancient classics by daily reading and timely reviews. Soon after leaving college, Mr. Wilson was chosen principal of the Darlington academy, a position which he held until the fall of 1849, when he went to Somerset and became a student of law in the office of Hon. Jeremiah S. Black, then president judge of the Sixteenth Judicial District of Pennsylvania. On the 12th of November, 1850, Mr. Wilson was admitted to the bar, and immediately thereafter came to Beaver, where, on the 18th day of November, 1850, he was admitted to practice in the several courts of this county. In due time he acquired a lucrative practice. For more than the third of a century he has been engaged in most of the important legal business that has been transacted in Beaver county, and always "with clean hands." His receipts for professional services have perhaps been greater in amount than those of any other resident lawyer that has at any time practiced at the Beaver bar.

On the 12th day of April, 1854, Mr. Wilson married Elizabeth Robinson, daughter of George Robinson, who was then sheriff of Beaver county. Ever since their marriage Mrs. Wilson has been her husband's faithful assistant in his office. The many legal papers prepared by her, under the direction of her husband, have always been regarded as models in neatness and accuracy. But in a much higher sphere of action, as the mother of four children, viz.: Sarah (now deceased), Anna (wife of A. R. Whitehill, professor of physics in the West Virginia University), Mary (wife of George Davidson, cashier of the National Bank of New Brighton), and George (a student in his father's office), Mrs. Wilson has also performed her duties nobly. Mr. Wilson never engaged in politics. He has decided political opinions, which, on proper occasions, he expresses fearlessly; but the end he aimed at was to become a thorough scholar, and an honest and successful lawyer. Of him it may be said in the words of another: "His learning is sufficient to enable him to realize the comparative littleness of all human achievements. He has outlived the ambition of display before courts and juries. He loves justice, law, and peace. He has learned to bear criticism without irritation; censure without anger; and calumny without retaliation. He has learned how surely all schemes of evil bring disaster to those who support them; and that the granite shaft of a noble reputation can not be destroyed by the poisoned breath of slander."

MARK WISENER. Mr. Wisener is of German extraction and the son of John George Wisener, who, on his emigration from Würtemburg at the age of sixteen, located in Butler, Butler county, Pa., where he established himself as the first butcher in the borough. Here he remained until his death in May, 1849, having married Margaret Nickolas, also of German descent, who came to America with her parents at the age of fourteen. The children of Mr. and Mrs. Wisener were Elizabeth (Mrs Seeger, of Youngstown, Ohio), Philip (who occupies the homestead), Mark (the subject of this sketch), George and Louis (who reside in Ohio), Anne (Mrs. Spear, of Warren, Ohio), and Susanna (Mrs. Elliot). Mark Wisener was born Feb. 5, 1840, in the borough of Butler, Butler county, Pa., where his youth until his eighteenth year was spent. He attended the common schools, and on completing his studies decided upon acquiring a trade. Removing to Pittsburgh for the purpose, he chose that of a carriage blacksmith, and continued his apprenticeship until his removal to Cincinnati, Ohio, in 1860, where for a brief time he followed this trade. The call for troops then occurred at the beginning of the civil war, and Mr. Wisener, with patriotic zeal, enrolled his name with the three-months' men. On the 9th of May, 1861, he enlisted for three years. After some time spent in West Virginia his regiment joined others in forming the army of the Cumberland, and participated in most of its important engagements, among which may be cited the battles of Shiloh, Stone River, Chickamauga, Perryville, Missionary Ridge and all the encounters connected with Sherman's march to the sea. He was discharged in July, 1864, at Covington. Ky., and at once resumed his trade in Pittsburgh. Three years later he removed to New Brighton and embarked in carriage manufacturing. Mr. Wisener continued thus employed until 1869, when he entered the arena of politics, and his name having been presented as the Democratic candidate for the office of sheriff of Beaver county, he was elected by a flattering vote in a district strongly Republican. He filled the office for three years, and not being successful in his candidacy for the office of county treasurer, engaged for a year in the boot

BIOGRAPHIES—WEST SIDE. 743

and shoe business. He next became the lessee of the "Merchants Hotel" in Beaver Falls, and in 1887 erected the "Grand Hotel," a commodious and elegant structure, of which, assisted by his sons, he is the popular landlord. Mr. Wisener was, in 1860, married to Miss Mary Kraus, of Pittsburgh. Their children are Frank L., Mark, Jr., G. Edward, Susan, Anna, Lizzie and Maggie. Mr. Wisener was a second time married, in 1878, to Mrs. Tena Foerstege, daughter of John Strack, of Rochester, in the same county, and their only child is a son, named John.

ABRAHAM B. WOLF, farmer, P. O. Beaver, was born on the farm he now owns June 4, 1814. His father and grandfather were both named John. The latter came to what is now Beaver county in 1782, and settled on the south side of the Ohio river, at what was then known as Logstown. He spent the first twelve years here clearing and farming. Our subject still owns the pack saddle his grandfather brought to Beaver county with him. The Indians stole their horses and drove them off. When this family came, only the old blockhouse was here to mark the place where the handsome borough is now situated. Our subject's father, who was born in 1776, took this farm where our subject now lives, from the government. He took 330 acres. He had eleven children, and died in 1857. Abraham B., who is the fourth child, and the only surviving member of the family, was educated in the common schools, and has made farming the business of his life. He was married, in 1860, to Sarah B., daughter of James Eakin, of Irish descent, and they have four children: George Q., James E., Nannie V. and Esther Mary. Mrs. Wolf is a member of the Presbyterian church. In politics Mr. Wolf is a Republican, and has served many years as justice of the peace.

WILLIAM WOLFSHAFER, contractor and builder, Beaver Falls, was born in Allegheny county March 20, 1856, and is a son of Conrad and Dora Wolfshafer, natives of Germany, who settled in Allegheny county about 1840, and came to Beaver Falls in 1884, where they now reside. William was reared in Allegheny county, and served an apprenticeship at the carpenter's trade, which he followed eight years. In 1883 he located in Beaver Falls, where he has since been actively engaged as a contractor and builder. He has erected a large number of buildings in this and adjacent counties, among which are the Mulberry school-house in Beaver Falls, the German Lutheran church, the Darlington academy, at Darlington, the twelfth ward school building in Allegheny City, and many others. Mr. Wolfshafer is a member of the Evangelical Lutheran church, of the I. O. O. F.; in politics he is a Republican.

JOHN C. WOODRUFF, justice of the peace, Bridgewater, was born Nov. 6, 1857, and is a son of David and Mary A. (Mulner) Woodruff. His parents were natives of Ohio and of English descent. His father, who was a marble cutter by occupation, came to Bridgewater in 1847, and carried on the marble work in that place for over thirty years. He died Nov. 6, 1882. He had two sons, the elder, A. V., being a resident of Brooklyn, N. Y. John C. was born and reared in Bridgewater, attended the common schools, and worked in his father's marble works. When quite young he went on the river, and worked in various capacities for about five years. He then located in Canada, where he remained until 1876, when he returned to his native county and accepted a position as shipping clerk in the Rochester Tumbler Works, where he remained six years. Then for a time he was employed at the Phoenix Glass Company's Works, at Phillipsburg. He is a Republican in politics, and was elected justice of the peace in 1887. He also does gas-fitting work. He is a member of the Republican county committee, and is secretary of the school board. He is a prominent member of the I. O. O. F., and occupies the honorable position of deputy grand patriarch of the encampment; has served two terms as state representative of the Grand Lodge. He is one of the directors of the Bridgewater Building Association, and is agent for the Merchants' Protective Association.

SHANNON R. WORKMAN, farmer, P. O. Beaver, was born in Darlington, this county, Aug. 22, 1820. His parents, James W. and Elizabeth (Shannon) Workman, were natives of Washington county, Pa., where they were married and first settled; thence they moved to this county, residing in the borough of Beaver, where the mother died; the father departed this life in New Orleans, while on a traveling expedition. They had three children: Lucinda (died in Washington county, Pa.), Maria (died in Beaver) wife of Martin Lyon), and Shannon R. The last named acquired his education in Beaver Academy, and was married, Jan. 1, 1850, to Caroline Powers, who was born in this county June 10, 1830, a daughter of James and Ruth (Pumphrey) Powers, the former a native of Darlington, this county, and the latter of Virginia. They both died in this county, and had ten children, four now living. Mr. and Mrs. Workman have nine children: John S., Laura (wife of John Sleight, of Minnesota), Mary P., James P., George W., Samuel S., William F., Charles W. and Bessie E. Mr. Workman carried on mercantile business on his own account for about fifteen years, in Beaver; then, with his family, moved to Minnesota, where he followed farming three years, returning in 1860 to his present farm of 132 acres. In politics he is a Democrat.

HENRY WURTZEL, hardware, stove and tinware merchant, Beaver Falls, was born in Pittsburgh, Pa., in 1857. His parents, Nicholas and Elizabeth (Winters) Wurtzel, were natives of Germany and residents of Pittsburgh, many years. Henry was reared and educated in Pittsburgh, where he learned the trade of tinsmith. He came to Beaver Falls in 1880, and worked at his trade as a journeyman three years. In 1883 he embarked in business with L. C. Ross, in which he continued till 1888; then he established a store by himself. He is a prominent business man, a member of the Catholic church; in politics a Democrat.

EDWARD W. YOUNG, grocer, Beaver Falls, was born in Dubuque, Iowa, Sept. 4, 1859, and is a son of John G. and Anna (Brown) Young, the former of Youngstown, Westmoreland county, and the latter of Greenville, Mercer county, Pa. They were for many years residents of Bridgewater, and have lived in Beaver Falls since 1871. Their family consists of five children: Georgia (Mrs. E. D. Powell), Charles R., Edward W., Perry and Russell. Edward W. was reared in Beaver county, and for several years was employed in the planing mill of Wilson & Brierly. He embarked in the flour and feed business in June, 1886, and in his present business in the spring of 1888.

JACOB YOUNG, farmer and milkman, P. O. Beaver Falls, was born in Germany Sept. 14, 1846, and is a son of Jacob amd Katrina (Homan) Young. The former emigrated to America in 1864, settled in Pittsburgh and later removed to Youngstown, Ohio, where he died. Our subject came to America in 1864, and located in Pittsburgh. He settled in Chippewa township in 1870 and engaged in farming, in which business he has since continued. In 1884 he engaged in the dairy business, keeping twenty-one cows, supplying a milk route to Beaver Falls, and doing a large and successful business. He attends the German Lutheran church; in politics he is a Republican.

JOHN YOUNG (deceased) was born in 1812, and died in 1887. James Young came from Donegal, Ireland, at an early day, and soon after landing upon the free shores of America he came to this county and purchased 100 acres of land in Big Beaver township, where he lived until his death. He married Esther Wickinson, by whom were born four sons and six daughters, John being the third child. James died at the age of eighty-five years. John Young was born on the farm which he owned, and where he died. He married Isabella, daughter of John Crawford, of this county, and they had five children : James R., Mary E. (deceased), Esther T., William J. and G. H. Mr. Young was a prosperous farmer, and was the owner of two farms at his death. His widow survives him. James R., who now superintends the work on the farm, was married in 1877 to Isabella, daughter of Francis and Mary (Douthitt) Gilky, and has three children: John C., Mary E. and Joseph H. William J. lives with his mother on the homestead, and is unmarried. The family are members of the United Presbyterian church.

WILLIAM J. YOUNG, farmer, P. O. New Galilee, was born in Big Beaver township in 1842. Peter Young, his paternal grandfather, immigrated from Donegal, Ireland, about 1795, and soon after landing came to Westmoreland county, where he engaged in farming and remained util 1800. He married Margaret Algeo, of County Armagh, Ireland, who bore him eight children. Peter came to Big Beaver township in 1800, and purchased one hundred acres of land, which was a part of the population tract taken up by Robert Wylie, and here he remained until his death. He died in 1833, at the age of seventy-six years. His wife died in 1830. Robert, the youngest child, and a farmer by occupation, married Jane, daughter of James and Susan (Sleath) McCanlis, also natives of Ireland. Eight children were born to this union, six of whom are living: Margaret, Susan, William, John, Robert, Hamilton Algeo and Elizabeth Jane. The father died in 1862, aged sixty years; the mother is living, at the age of seventy-eight. William J., our subject, was married in 1875 to Hattie J., daughter of John Wallace, and they have five children: Wallace Algeo, Knox McCland, Robert McCanlis, Mary Florence and George Everett. Mr. Young now owns fifty-five acres, part of the 100 acres of his grandfather's farm. He has purchased an additional twenty-seven acres, has erected a new house and made other improvements. He is a Prohibitionist and a member of the Old School Covenanters.

GEORGE YOUTS, wagon maker, was born in Centre county, in 1826. His father, Henry, was born in 1800, was by occupation a distiller, and came from Lancaster county to Centre county about February, 1820. His wife, Sallie, daughter of Samuel Brellhord, bore nine sons and four daughters, of whom George is the eldest. George received a common-school education, and remained with his father until fifteen years old, when he learned the trade of wagon making. In 1846 he came to Beaver county, and has been engaged in manufacturing wagons, buggies, etc., and in repairing. He was married in 1848 to Julia, daughter of Samuel Stricby, of this county. By her he had six children, three of whom are now living: Sallie (now Mrs. Clute), George, who is in Kansas, and Mamie (now Mrs. Esteb). His wife died in 1866, and in the following year he married Mrs. Frances E. Keller, of Cleveland, Ohio, who bore him three children, of whom Monte and Fannie are now living. Mr. Youts has for the past twelve years been a school director, and is now a Mason and Odd Fellow. In religion he is a Presbyterian; politically a Republican.

CHAPTER XXVII.

BIOGRAPHIES—EAST SIDE.

JAMES AGEY, farmer, P. O. Rochester, was born in this county Nov. 16, 1830, a son of George and Ellen (Mackey) Agey. They were natives of Pennsylvania, were married in Youngstown, Ohio, settled in Beaver county, Pa., and remained there until their deaths. James was united in marriage Oct. 20, 1853, with Levina Otto, who was born in Beaver county, March 22, 1835, a daughter of David and Christina (Long) Otto, natives of this state. Her father is deceased, but her mother is still living in Butler county. Mr. and Mrs. Agey have one child, Angie, wife of David Hendrickson. She was born Feb. 7, 1855. Mr. Agey was reared on the farm, the pursuits of which he has always followed. He and his wife are members of the United Brethren church. In politics he is a Democrat.

GEORGE AGNER, proprietor of the Agner Brick Works, Rochester, was born in Butler county, Pa., July 1, 1837. His parents, George and Sophia (Mueler) Agner, natives of Darmstadt, Germany, settled in Lehigh county, Pa., in 1833, and in 1834 moved to Butler county. George, Sr., was a farmer, and the father of six children. Of these, George, the fourth child, was educated in the Butler county common schools, and early in life learned the blacksmith's trade, which he followed for twelve years in Ohio and Allegheny county. In 1867 he embarked in his present business; bought an acre of land near the present site of the Rochester Tumbler Works, and manufactured 400,000 brick the first year. In 1880 he secured an additional four acres of land, put in a new engine and more extensive machinery, and for several years has made on an average two million brick per year. He manufactures three grades; the number 1 is pressed brick for dressing fronts, and all the grades are good; his business is increasing every year and he is said to turn out as good brick as can be made in America. The works are kept running the greater part of the year, giving employment on an average to twenty hands. The venture has been a financial success, though when Mr. Agner came to Rochester he had no knowledge whatever of the business, but being a mechanic with a determination to succeed, he has made his way. He was married, in 1866, to Fannie, daughter of Nicholas King. She is a native of Pittsburgh, Pa., and of German descent. Their children now living are: Ella Lorena, William Henry, Nettie and Beula May. Mr. and Mrs Agner are members of the Lutheran church. He is a trustee of the church; in politics he is a Republican.

GEORGE H. ALTSTADT, farmer, P. O. Knob, was born in Germany Sept. 3, 1831, and is a son of John and Elizabeth Altstadt, who died in that country. He immigrated to America in 1857, resided several years in Pittsburgh, then came to Beaver county, where he has since remained. He married in Pittsburgh, in 1859, Elizabeth, daughter of Henry and Elizabeth Peter, who died in Germany where Mrs. Alstadt was born, March 22, 1828. Five children were born to Mr. and Mrs. Altstadt, four of them living: Mary E., Sophia C., George H. and Minnie E. One daughter, Margaret, is deceased. Mr. Altstadt is by trade a blacksmith, but has been engaged in farming for a number of years, and owns forty-three acres. He served his country in the Civil War in Company G, 5th heavy artillery and was in several engagements. He and his wife are members of the Lutheran church. In politics he is a Republican.

ROBERT BAKER, farmer, P. O. Knob, was born in Beaver county, Dec. 17, 1822, and is a son of Charles and Elsie Baker, both of whom died in this county. Robert was united in marriage Sept. 25, 1849, with Susanna Romigh. She was born July 5, 1828, in Washington county, and is a daughter of Elijah and Mary Romigh, both of whom died in this county. The children of this marriage are Ann, Mary, Charlie, John, Alice, Robert and Elijah. One son, Oliver, is deceased. Mr. Baker has been a farmer all his life and owns about 110 acres of land. He and his wife are members of the Presbyterian church. He is a Democrat and has held the office of school director.

R. G. BANKS, grocer, New Brighton, is. a native of Butler county, born in 1858, the youngest of the nine children of Mathew and Elizabeth (Rogers) Banks, the former of whom was a farmer, engaged also in oil business. R. G. was reared on the farm where he was born, and educated at Washington and Jefferson College, also at Iron City Business College, Pittsburgh, Pa. In 1879 he married Lucretia, daughter of Israel Stephens, of Greene county, Pa., and one child, Luther Ernst, has been born to them. Mr. Banks came to Beaver county in 1882, and has since been almost continuously engaged in the grocery business in New Brighton. In politics he is a Democrat.

WILLIAM BARTON, farmer, P. O. New Brighton, was born in Plum township, Allegheny county, Pa., July 12, 1822. His parents, George and Isabel (Wilson) Barton, natives of Ireland, came to America about 1818. George was a farmer, and first located in Allegheny county, where he remained about four years; thence moved to Allegheny township, Westmoreland county, where he died in 1832; his widow died in June, 1882, aged ninety years. They had eight children: Thomas (deceased), George, Richard, William, Sarah Ann, James (deceased), Eliza Jane (deceased) and Lydia, who keeps house for her brothers, William and Richard, who have never married, but own together and carry on a farm of 95 acres, where they settled in 1853. Richard was judge of election, and William assessor for one year, also supervisor and school director, and for three years served as treasurer of the board. In politics both are Democrats.

WILLIAM W. BEACOM, grocer, New Brighton, was born in Brighton township, this county, in 1841. His father, Robert Beacom, was a farmer, and married Elizabeth, daughter of William Wilson, of Lawrence county. They had four children, of whom

William was the youngest. His grandfather, also named William, came from Ireland, and was a farmer by occupation. He purchased 106 acres of land in this county, where his son Robert was born and died. The farm is now the property of our subject, William W. He was born and reared on the farm, where he always lived until 1883. In that year he came to New Brighton and engaged in the grocery business. He was married in 1869 to Ella, daughter of William Pennell, of Hubbard, Ohio. They have six children: Robert, Edward, William, Ada, Howard and Ernest, all at home. Mr. Beacom is a member of the Presbyterian church; in politics a Democrat.

BENJAMIN BEDISON, retired, New Brighton, was born in this county in 1810. His parents were Shedrick and Jane (James) Bedison, to whom were born two children, Benjamin being the youngest. Shedrick Bedison was a cooper by trade, came from Massachusetts to Beaver county about 1800, and died young. Benjamin was educated at the schools of New Brighton, and at fourteen years of age learned the trade of machinist in Pittsburgh, where he served seven years, then returned to New Brighton and followed his trade for four years. He next engaged in contracting on the canal, which he followed two years; subsequently he built the Star flouring mill, and for twenty years was engaged in the milling business. For the next thirteen years he was engaged in various business pursuits, spending six years in transferring freight on railroad and canal, brick manufacturing and oil prospecting, and retired from active business a few years ago. Mr. Bedison had his ups and downs in life, and were it not for over confidence in man he would to-day be wealthy. He was married in 1832 to Clarissa, daughter of Benjamin Townsend. Six children have blessed this union, one of whom is deceased. Those living are Jane, Charles, William, Adelaide, and Thomas H. Mr. Bedison is a Republican, and has served as member of town council, tax collector and assessor.

THOMAS H. BEDISON, the son of Benjamin Bedison, was born in New Brighton, Oct. 2, 1845. He was eduated in the common schools of his native town, and at the age of sixteen became a grocery clerk. He next worked during three years at the watchmaker's trade, and afteward engaged in different kinds of mechanical business till 1887, when he established himself as a grocer, which occupation he now follows.

CHARLES H. BENTEL, banker, Freedom, was born Jan. 8, 1837, a son of Philip and Margaretta (Smith) Bentel, the former born in Butler county, Pa., and the latter in Germany. They were married in Pennsylvania and lived in Freedom until their deaths. She died in 1881 and he in 1883. They were the parents of four children, two living; Charles H. is the second. He was married June 9, 1859, to Amanda Clark, who was born in Allegheny county, June 21, 1840. Her parents, Captain Samuel and Minerva (Reno) Clark, were natives of Pennsylvania. The former died in Wheeling, W. Va., and the latter resides with our subject. Mr. Bentel and wife have five children: Cora F., wife of Alfred P. Marshall, of Beaver; Mattie, wife of James G. Mitchell; Anna, Thalia and Philip. Mr. Bentel followed mercantile business for seventeen years, and has since been engaged in banking. He and Mrs. Bentel are members of the Presbyterian church. He is a F. & A. M.

JAMES BEVINGTON, pilot, P. O. Freedom, was born in Columbiana county, Ohio, March 22, 1823, a son of Henry and Fannie (Hunter) Bevington, natives of Pennsylvania. They were married and settled in Ohio, and remained until 1867. Henry was married twice in Ohio, and after his last marriage moved to Pennsylvania, and there died. His widow is still living. He was the father of twelve children, nine living. James, the third, was married first in Alliance, Ohio, May 27, 1847, to Catherine Teaters, a native of Stark county, Ohio. After marriage they moved to Birmingham, Pa., and resided until the death of Mrs. Bevington, which occurred Nov. 18, 1860. There were born to this marriage three children, two living. July 3, 1861, Mr. Bevington married Rodiah Teaters, who was born in Harrison county, Ohio, Sept. 1, 1823, and is a daughter of Perry and Levina Chane. Mr. Bevington has been a boatman since 1843, and has been captain and pilot for a number of years. He and his family have resided in Freedom about twenty-five years. He is a F. & A. M. His wife is a member of the Methodist Episcopal church.

748   HISTORY OF BEAVER COUNTY.

WILLIAM F. L. BIDDELL, dentist, New Brighton, was born in Beaver county in 1865, the youngest of the seven children (six yet living) of Henry M. and Selina (Wilson) Biddell. Henry M. was a native of London, England, was a contractor and builder, and came to the United States at an early age. William F. L. was educated at the high school in New Brighton, and soon afterward commenced the study of dentistry. In 1884 he entered Pennsylvania College of Dental Surgery, at Philadelphia, graduated in 1886, and at once commenced the practice of his profession in New Brighton. Politically Dr. Biddell is a Republican.

CAPT. A. J. BINGHAM, grocer, New Brighton, was born in Allegheny county in 1840, the eldest of the eight children born to William and Rebecca (Ray) Bingham. He received a public-school training, and at the age of sixteen commenced learning carriage making, a trade he followed until 1860. In 1861 he enlisted in Company C, 61st Regiment P. V., was present at the principal battles of the war, being thrice wounded ; was promoted to a captaincy in 1864, and was honorably discharged in 1865. Captain Bingham was married in 1867 to Annie, daughter of James and Eliza Dudgeon, of Allegheny county, and five children were born to them: William J., May, Anna, Martha, Kate and Abraham Lincoln. Captain Bingham came to New Brighton in 1871, and has since been engaged in the retail grocery business. He is a F. & A. M.: a member of the A. O. U. W., the K. of P. and the G. A. R. He is an adherent of the Methodist church; politically a Republican.

CHRISTIAN BLACK, retired farmer, Rochester, born in Greene township, Franklin county, Pa., Aug. 12, 1807, is a son of Daniel and Catherine (Etter) Black, natives of Cumberland county, Pa., and of German and English descent. His father was a farmer and had seven children, of whom Christian is the eldest. He was reared in Franklin qounty, received his education in the common schools, and has followed farming all his life. He was married in 1828 to Elizabeth Black, who was of English descent and died Aug. 31, 1869, the mother of two children, George and Daniel. Mr. Black came to Beaver county in 1829 and engaged in farming, he retired in 1872, and has since resided in Rochester. Mr. and Mrs. Black were members of the United Brethren church. He is a Republican, and has served as school director, supervisor, township auditor and overseer of the poor. In 1871 he married Miss Lucinda Hesson, who died March 4, 1886. Mr. Black is a quiet, unassuming man, and has met with marked success in business.

DANIEL BLACK, farmer, P. O. Rochester, was born on the farm where he now resides, April 16, 1837, a son of Christian and Elizabeth Black, who were natives of Pennsylvania, and settled after marriage on the farm where Daniel now resides. The mother died in 1869, and the father was afterwards married to a widow Dunlap, who died in Rochester. Christian Black is still living and resides in Rochester. Our subject was married, Oct. 28, 1870, to Sarah V. Hillman, who was born in Allegheny county, Pa.,in March, 1840, and is a daughter of John Hillman (deceased). She is the mother of two children: William H. K. and John C. Mr. Black owns a farm of 200 acres. In politics he is a Republican.

WILLIAM H. BLACK, postmaster at Rochester, was born in Vanport, this county, April 23, 1854, and is a son of John and Mary Jane Black. John Black has spent a great part of his life in Rochester, where he still resides, and has three sons, of whom William H. is the youngest. Our subject was reared in Rochester, attended the public schools here, also the seminary and Beaver College, Beaver, Pa. He was clerk in the postoffice at Rochester two years (1874–75), then clerked in a dry goods store two years. In 1877 he embarked in mercantile trade in this place. He was senior member of the firm of Black & Breckenridge, dealers in general merchandise, from 1879 to 1887. He was appointed postmaster April 19, 1887. He served five years as secretary of Building and Loan Associations of Rochester. Mr. Black was married, Nov. 13, 1879, to Emma, daughter of Dr. T. J. Chandler, of Rochester. Mr. and Mrs. Black are members of the Methodist Episcopal church, where he has been teacher in the Sabbath school for a number of years. He is an Odd Fellow and a Good Templar, and has twice represented the latter order, as a delegate from Pennsylvania, to the Right Worthy Grand Lodge of the world, in 1882, at Charleston, S. C., and in 1884, at Washington, D. C. At the age of twenty-two years he was elected assessor of the borough of Rochester, and in 1885 he was mercantile appraiser of Beaver county. In politics he is a Democrat. As postmaster Mr. Black is giving universal satisfaction.

A. BLATT, shoemaker, Freedom, was born in France July 9, 1845. His parents, August F. and Margaret Blatt, immigrated to America in 1848, and settled in Pittsburg, where they remained several years; then moved to Phillipsburg, this county, where August F. died in 1884; his widow resides on the homestead. They were the parents of ten children, seven living. Our subject, the eldest, was united in marriage, July 4, 1865, with Nancy J. Bickerstaff, who was born in Beaver county, in February, 1843, and is a daughter of William and Elizabeth Bickerstaff, both living in Phillipsburg, Pa. Mr. and Mrs. Blatt have had seven children, five living. Mr. Blatt learned the trade of shoemaking in 1862, and in 1880 he engaged as a shoe dealer in connection with his trade. He and his wife are members of the Presbyterian church, and have lived in Freedom twenty years

HENRY BLINN, farmer, P. O. New Brighton, was born in New Sewickley township, this county, in 1833, the second son of Philip and Margaret (Gilbaugh) Blinn. He was born and reared on the farm, and was married, in 1852, to Elizabeth, daughter of John Flimmer. They have the following named children: Mary Ann (Mrs. Ferguson), William H., Caroline (Mrs. Bist), Philip, Emma, Charles, Frank and Eva. Mr. Blinn has been engaged in farming for thirty-five years, and purchased his present farm of 100 acres in 1869. He is a member of the United Presbyterian church; he is a Democrat.

CASPER BLUM, farmer, P. O. Brush Creek, was born in Butler county, Pa., Feb. 27, 1854. His parents, John and Laura Blum, natives of Germany, immigrated to America in 1848, settled in Beaver county, and one year later they removed to Butler county, where they remained seven years. They then came to their present farm of sixty-eight acres in New Sewickley township, where they have since resided. They have had eight children, six of whom are living: Adam, John, Lewis, Barbara, Casper and Lizzie. The deceased are Lewis and Katie. Mr. Blum was married June 6, 1878, to Christina Getteman. She was born in Butler county, Pa., April 27, 1857, and is a daughter of Peter and Elizabeth Getteman, both living. Mr. and Mrs. Blum have had four children, three of whom are living: Clara, Alfred and Alma; the one deceased was Anna. Mrs. Blum died March 17, 1885. Mr. Blum is a member of the United Presbyterian church, as was also his wife. In politics he is a Democrat.

G. Y. BOAL, physician, Baden, is a native of Venango county, Pa., and was born in 1840. John Boal, his father, by trade a carpenter, was born in 1804, and married Isabella Huey. David, the grandfather of G. Y., came from Ireland in 1800, settled near the present town of Boalsburg, Centre county, Pa., and in his honor the town was named. John settled in Venango county in 1888, where he purchased two hundred acres of land, and where he remained until his death, at the age of eighty-one years. Seven children were born to John and his wife, Isabella. G. Y., the third son, was educated at the common schools, being a student later on in the high school, Cooperstown, and at Edinboro State Normal School, Erie county, Pa. He commenced the study of medicine in 1863 with Dr. Robert Crawford, of Cooperstown, Pa., took a regular course at the University of Pennsylvania, Philadelphia, in 1865, and in 1866 commenced practicing medicine at Baden, graduating in 1870 at Cincinnati College of Medicine and Surgery. Dr. Boal was married, in 1869, to Mary Emma, daughter of John and Sarah A. (Anderson) Doyle. Four daughters and two sons are the result of this union: George Fay, Elizabeth Isabella, Sarah Effie, Clifford Doyle, Mary and Margaret. Dr. Boal has by his own perseverance secured the position he now holds. He was a teacher in the public schools for seven winters, and since 1866 has been engaged in practice at Baden. He has for the past seven years been practicing physician for the Harmony Society. He is a deacon in the Lutheran church; politically he is a Democrat.

CHARLES BONZO, retired farmer, P. O. Brush Creek, was born in Butler county, Pa., in 1807. His parents, Lewis and Margaret Bonzo, natives of France, were married in their native country; immigrated to America, located first in Butler county, Pa., and afterward removed to Beaver county, where Lewis died, and where his widow is still living. Charles Bonzo was married, June 14, 1837, to Catherine, daughter of Charles and Elizabeth Goehring (both deceased). She was born in Butler county Dec. 25, 1820, and is the mother of nine children, six of whom are living: Henry, Sophia, Elizabeth, Charles, John and Harrison. The deceased are George, Peter L. and Lottie C. Mr. Bonzo, who has always lived on a farm, owned at one time 900 acres, most of which he has divided among his children, but still owns 350 acres. In politics he is a Republican. Mrs Bonzo has been a member of the Lutheran church for many years.

GEORGE BONZO (deceased) was a farmer of New Sewickley township, where he was born Jan. 15, 1815. He was a son of Lewis and Margaret Bonzo, who were natives of France, and came to America after their marriage and settled in Butler county, Pa., whence they removed to Beaver county, where Lewis died. His widow is still living. George Bonzo was married, Jan. 14, 1840, to Margaret Rauscher, who was born in Germany July 15, 1822, and came to America in 1835 with her parents, George and Margaret Rauscher, who settled in Beaver county and from there moved to Tennessee, where they died. Mr. and Mrs. Bonzo had six children, two of whom, Andrew and Caroline, are deceased. Those living are John, George, Mary and Wesley E. Mr. Bonzo was a farmer all his life, and at one time owned 300 acres. He was a member of the Lutheran church, of which his widow is also a member. In politics Mr. Bonzo was a Republican. He died May 6, 1886. Mrs. Bonzo and her son, Wesley E., reside on and manage the homestead.

JOHN BONZO, farmer, P. O. Freedom, was born in New Sewickley township July 14, 1843, and is a son of George and Margaret Bonzo the former deceased. Our subject was married, Nov. 19, 1868, to Martha J. Oliver, who was born in Gallia county, Ohio, May 22, 1850, a daughter of Milton Oliver, who resides in New Brighton. Mrs. Bonzo, is the mother of four children: George M., Andrew W., John A. and Clyde W. Mr. Bonzo has been a farmer all his life, and owns eighty-five acres of improved land. He and his wife are members of the Methodist Episcopal church. He is a Republican.

GEORGE R. BONZO, farmer, P. O. Brush Creek, was born in New Sewickley township July 8, 1845, and is a son of George and Margaret Bonzo. He was reared on a farm, the pursuits of which he was always followed. Nov. 1, 1870, he married Mary J., daughter of James and Sarah Feazel, and born in Beaver county Jan. 16, 1850; she is the mother of six children: Alvira, born Aug. 16, 1871; Cora B., born Oct. 30, 1873; Elton A., born Aug. 27, 1875; Raymond, born July 18, 1877; Eva J., born Aug. 11, 1880, and Wildia M., born March 23, 1883. Mr. Bonzo owns eighty-one acres of land. He and his wife are members of the Methodist church. Politically he is a Prohibitionist.

GEORGE B. BONZON, blacksmith, P. C. Brush Creek, was born in this county Oct. 9, 1850, a son of Peter L. and Rebecca (Brooks) Bonzon, the former a native of France, and latter of America. They were married in Allegheny county, Pa., and settled in Beaver county, where they still reside. George B. was united in marriage, May 1, 1877, with Susan A., daughter of Thomas and Eliza J. Fisher, the former deceased. Mrs. Bonzon was born in Beaver county. Sept. 28, 1852, and is the mother of one child, Bertha I., born March 17, 1878. Mr. Bonzon has been engaged in blacksmithing since his youth. He is a member of the I. O. O. F.; in politics he is a Democrat.

EDMUND BOOTS, wagon maker, P. O. North Sewickley, was born in Sussex, England, Oct. 13, 1811, son of Ambrose and Elizabeth (Bull) Boots, the former of whom, a carpenter by trade, came to America in 1830, and Oct. 13th of the same year settled on Brush creek, North Sewickley township, this county, here remaining until his death. He had four sons, all born in the mother country, three yet living; John is deceased. Edmund was married in 1831 to Eliza, daughter of William Coleman. She died in 1832, and in 1834 Mr. Boots married Eliza, daughter of Samuel Caldwell. By this union there are four children: Samuel C., James D., Ambrose and Edmund R. Mr. Boots owns the property, consisting of seventy acres, where he has resided since 1830. He has been secretary of the school board of his township for eight years, and has held the office of supervisor two terms. He and Mrs. Boots are member of the Methodist Episcopal church; in politics he is a Republican.

EDMUND R. BOOTS, merchant, New Brighton, was born in North Sewickley township, Beaver county, Pa., in 1843, and is the youngest in the family of four children of Edmund and Eliza (Caldwell) Boots, the latter a native of Huntingdon county, Pa. The father, the second son of Ambrose and Elizabeth (Bull) Boots, parents of four children, came from Sussex, England, when eighteen years of age, and in 1833 to Beaver county, where he purchased 160 acres of land, and has since resided. At the age of seventeen years Edmund R. enlisted in Company H, 101st Regiment, P. V., serving four years. He participated in the Siege of Yorktown, battles of Williamsburg and Fair Oaks, the Seven Days' fight, and other engagements. He was a commissioned officer in Company B, Fifth Artillery, during the last nine months of the war; returned to Beaver county in 1865, and the next year engaged in general merchandise business in New Brighton. He married, Sept. 20, 1866, Alice J., daughter of William Barton, of North Sewickley township, and six children have been born to them (five yet living): John S. (assisting his father in the store), E. W., Mary Bell (deceased), Alice E., Frank and Hattie C. The mother died Feb. 12, 1886. Mr. Boots is a member of the town council and treasurer of the borough, and is a Republican in politics. He is an adherent of the Methodist Episcopal church.

SAMUEL BOOTS, carpenter and farmer, P. O. North Sewickley, was born in Sussex, England, May 25, 1816. His parents, Ambrose and Elizabeth (Bull) Boots, came to America in 1830, and settled in North Sewickley township. The father was a carpenter until coming to Beaver county, when he carried on farming, with his eldest son, up to his death in 1844; his widow died in 1852. They had four children: Mary, John, Edmund and Samuel. Samuel received a limited education, and served an apprenticeship at the milling business in his native land, but on arriving in this country learned carpentering and cabinet making, which he followed, together with farming, up to his retirement from active life. He made the coffin for the first interment (remains of James Magaw) in Grove cemetery. He married, in 1837, Harriet Wild, an English lady, who came to America in 1830. They were both on the ocean at the same time but, were not acquainted with each other until they came to America. They have had eight children, four now living: Elizabeth, Mary Ann, Amos C. and Nancy Jane. Since coming to this country Mr. Boots has resided in this township, where he acted as poor director seven years without missing a single meeting of the board; was school director four years, and held the office of overseer of the poor in 1847, before the county home was built. He is now living a retired life with his son, Amos C., on his farm of 150 acres; is a member of the Methodist Episcopal church, of which he has been trustee for many years; in politics he is a Republican. Mrs. Boots died March 16, 1875.

FRANK A. BOSWELL, grocer, New Brighton, was in Beaver county, Pa., in 1859, and is a son of William and Julia (McMichael) Boswell, the parents of twelve children. He received a good public school training, and when nineteen years of age commenced a three years' apprenticeship to the moulding trade, which he followed five years. In 1883 he commenced in the grocery business with his brother in New Brighton, and in 1885 formed the present partnership in the same line with Albert G. Harvey, under the firm name of Boswell & Harvey. In 1875, Mr. Boswell married Ada Wagner, daughter of Mrs. Melissa Wagner, of this county, and by her has two children, Julia and Bernice. In politics Mr. Boswell is a Republican.

JOHN BOSWELL, cigar dealer, New Brighton, is a native of England, born in 1827, second son in the family of nine children of George Boswell, a farmer. He attended the public schools and remained on the farm until fifteen years of age, when he learned blacksmithing, which he followed eight years. In 1849 he came to New Brighton, where he has been engaged in various occupations for the past ten years in the same establishment at his present trade. He married, in 1853, Mary Ann Livsey, also a native of England, who bore him four children, all deceased except one, F. W., at home. Mr. Boswell is a member of the I. O. O. F. and K. of P.; a Republican, politically.

JOHN S. BOYD, physician, New Brighton, was born in Moon township, Beaver county, in 1845. His parents, Samuel and Sarah (Wade) Boyd, had four children. John S., the third child, was reared in the towns of Allegheny and New Sheffield, attending the common schools and an academy. He taught school for six years during the winter and attended school in summer. In 1871 he commenced the study of medicine under Dr. Langford and Dr. Wendt, entered Cleveland Homœopathic College, from which he graduated in 1874, and soon thereafter commenced the practice of his profession at his home, removing in 1883 to New Brighton. He was married, in 1877, to Lizzie J., daughter of James W. and Mary Shannon, of Pittsburgh, Pa., and three children were born to them; two of them are living: Lelia and Faye. Dr. Boyd is a member of the United Presbyterian church; in politics he is a Republican.

WILLIAM M. BOYLE, proprietor Clyde House, New Brighton, was born in Beaver county in 1850. He was reared on a farm in Chippewa township, this county, and received a common-school education. At eleven years of age he left the farm and went to Youngstown, Ohio, where he attended school a short time. He has been engaged in various pursuits, a helper in the oil fields, an oil producer, a manufacturer of cigars, and for eight years was in the upholstery business in New Brighton. He was married, in 1870, to Josephine, daughter of James and Margaret Rager, of this county. They have three children: Annie, Edward and James. In 1877 Mr. Boyle bought and assumed the proprietorship of the Clyde Hotel in New Brighton. He is a member of the A. O. U. W.: politically he is a Democrat.

CHARLES C. BRACKEN, dealer in stoves and house furnishings, New Brighton, was born in 1860, in Butler county, Pa., the eldest of the three children of R. G. and A. J. (Gold) Bracken. He was reared on a farm, received a common-school education, and learned the trade of tinsmith. He came to Beaver county in 1879, and followed his trade until 1887, in which year he purchased his present business in New Brighton. He was married in 1881 to Jennie, daughter of William H. Martin, of Butler county, and one child, Charles H., has been born to them. Mr. Bracken is a member of the Methodist Episcopal church; politically he is a Republican.

WALTER S. BRADEN, postmaster, New Brighton, was born in Beaver Falls, March 15, 1853, and is the eldest son of A. B. and C. R. (Boyle) Braden, who had nine children. His grandfather, John Braden, came from Ireland about 1790 and soon afterward settled in Beaver county, where he was a farmer. He married Catherine McIntyre, who bore him twelve children; A. B., the youngest, was a farmer in early life, later engaged in mercantile business and is now living a retired life in Beaver Falls. Walter S. attended the common schools, and the Iron City College at Pittsburgh, from which institution he was graduated in 1872. He has been engaged in the mercantile and real estate businesses. He was married in 1879 to Miss E. E. Goddard, daughter of John Goddard, of this town, and they have four children: Laura, Edith, Karl and Naomi. Mr. Braden was appointed postmaster at New Brighton in 1886. He is a member of the Royal Arcanum; in politics a Democrat.

BENJAMIN RUSH BRADFORD. The paternal ancestors of Benjamin Rush Bradford were for five generations among the most prominent citizens of Philadelphia, and some of them were distinguished as patriots and statesmen in the history of our country. William Bradford, his great great-grandfather, born in 1660 in Leicester, England, who died May 22, 1752, came with William Penn to America in 1682, and was the first printer for the Middle Provinces as also the first to start a paper mill in Pennsylvania. His son Andrew was the friend and patron of Benjamin Franklin. He was a man of large wealth, a member of common councils and postmaster of Philadelphia. Thomas Bradford, the printer, was born May 4, 1745, and died May 7, 1838. He married, Nov. 23, 1768, Mary, daughter of Samuel Fisher. His son, Thomas Bradford, LL.D., was born April 10, 1780, and died Oct. 25, 1851. Leaving the university of Pennsylvania in his junior year he first learned the art of printing; then engaged in legal studies and became a leading member of the Philadelphia bar. In May, 1805, he married Elizabeth, eldest daughter of Vincent Loockerman, Esq., of Dover, Del., to whom were born four sons and one daughter. The birth of their second son, Benjamin Rush Bradford, occurred Sept. 15, 1813, in Philadelphia. His academical studies were conducted in Pittsfield, Mass., ill health having interfered with a regular collegiate course. He resided for three years in Dover, Del., in 1837 removed to Mercer county, Pa., and in 1839 settled on a farm near New Brighton. He was nominated as a candidate for Governor on the American ticket, and at another and later date received the nomination for Lieutenant-Governor on the Prohibition ticket. During his early manhood when business duties required, Mr. Bradford traveled eighteen thousand or more miles on horseback through Pennsylvania and Virginia, looking after large landed estates entrusted to his care. While thus engaged he had numerous land ejectment cases and other suits in law, not one of which he lost, and for his mode of preparing which he received the encomiums of Chief-Justice Agnew and others. The degree of A. M. was conferred upon Mr. Bradford by Jefferson College. A staunch Presbyterian in his religious faith, he was an elder of the First Presbyterian church, of New Brighton, and in 1849 was elected a director of the Western Theological Seminary; was also one of the founders of the Union Benevolent Society of Philadelphia. He was one of the corporate members of the Board of Colportage, and member of the General Assembly of the Presbyterian church for the years 1849, 1855 and 1860. Mr. Bradford took great interest in the Sabbath-school cause, and was for fifty years scholar, teacher and superintendent. He was also an active worker in the cause of temperance, his life having been one of Christian activity and usefulness until his death, which occurred June 9, 1884. Mr. Bradford was married, Nov. 26, 1840, to Margaret, youngest daughter of William and Jane Campbell, of Butler, Pa., who yet survives him and resides in New Brighton with her son, Hon. Thomas Bradford. Their children were Juliet S. (Mrs. Charles C. Townsend), Thomas, Eleanor (Mrs. Walter Buhl) and William C. (deceased). Thomas was born in Beaver county in 1846, educated at the Polytechnic Institute, Troy, N. Y.; by profession is a civil engineer and was a member of the legislature of Pennsylvania for the years 1879-80. During his father's life he ably assisted him in the real estate business, to which he has succeeded. He is a member of the Presbyterian church.

JACOB P. BRANDT, merchant, P. O. Freedom, was born in New Sewickley township, Beaver county, Pa., on the present site of St. Clair borough, May 21, 1842. His father, Conrad Brandt, a native of Hesse Cassel, Germany, emigrated to America in 1837, and settled in Beaver county. His mother, Christina Walter, a native of Baden, Germany, emigrated with her parents to America in 1832, and also settled in Beaver county. Conrad and Christina (Walter) Brandt were married, July 4, 1841, and have resided in what is now St. Clair, ever since. They had six children, of whom three are living, viz: Jacob P., John C. and Charles F. Jacob P., the eldest, was married, April 10, 1871, to Christina Bishoffberger, who was born in Baden, Germany, Aug. 31, 1847. Her parents, George and Rosanna Bishoffberger, were natives of Baden, Germany. George Bishoffberger died in 1847, and his widow came to America in 1868, and settled in Erie, Pa. Our subject, after receiving a common-school education, such as could be had in a country district at that time, learned the blacksmith trade with his father, and followed it for four years. When the War of the Rebellion broke out in 1861 he enlisted in Company H, 139th Regiment, P. V., and served with his regiment in the army of the Potomac, six months. He was honorably discharged on account of disability. He then learned the cooper trade, which he followed for about twelve years. In the spring of 1875 he engaged in the mercantile business in St. Clair, which he still follows. He and his wife are members of the Lutheran church. He is a charter member of Post 407, G. A. R., department of Pennsylvania; he was twice elected burgess of St. Clair borough, and in March, 1887, he was again appointed burgess of St. Clair by Judge Wickham, of Beaver county, which position he still holds at this writing.

W. H. BRECKENRIDGE, merchant, Rochester, was born in North Washington, Butler county, Pa., Feb. 28, 1852, and is a son of J. B. and Sophia (Ehrenfeld) Breckenridge, natives of Pennsylvania, and of Scotch-Irish and German descent. J. B. is a Lutheran minister, and with his wife came to Beaver county in 1859, settling in Roches-

754   HISTORY OF BEAVER COUNTY.

ter. W. H. is the ninth in a family of eleven children, was educated at the public schools, and early in life learned the carpenter's trade, which he followed for eight years. In 1878 he embarked in mercantile trade, under the firm name of Black & Breckenridge, but in 1887 Mr. Black was appointed postmaster at Rochester, since which time Mr. Breckenridge has continued the business alone. He was married, Aug. 20, 1874, to Miss Jennie A. Thorton, a lady of English descent, and they have two children: Helen T. and Ernest S. Mr. and Mrs. Breckenridge are members of the Lutheran church. He is a trustee and deacon in the church, and a teacher in the Sabbath-school. In politics he is a Republican.

JAMES A. BREWER, farmer, P. O. New Brighton, was born in Allegheny county, in 1820, and came with his parents. Elias and Hannah (Shay) Brewer, to Beaver county in 1830. Elias was a farmer by occupation, and came originally from Eastern Pennsylvania. He had four sons and seven daughters. James A., the second son, started in life without a dollar, and, as a result of his industry and perseverance, now owns 128 acres of land, second in quality to none in Pulaski township, with large and commodious buildings. He was married, in 1842, to Jennie, daughter of Robert Moore. Mrs. Brewer died in 1866, the mother of ten children. Mr. Brewer is a member of the United Presbyterian church; politically he is a Democrat.

F. K. BRIERLY, contractor and proprietor of planing mill, etc., Beaver Falls, residence New Brighton, is a native of Massachusetts, born in 1846, to Samuel and Orilla (Kendrick) Briely, parents of five children, three now living, our subject being the second son. The family is of English origin. Samuel Brierly, who was a wool carder, located in Lawrence county, Pa., in 1848, and in Beaver county in 1858. F. K. received a public-school education, and since youth has been an active business man. When twenty-one years of age he became a member of the firm of Waddle, Wilson & Co., contractors and builders, the present style being Wilson & Brierly. Mr. Brierly is also partner in a flour mill and foundry at Beaver Falls. In 1868 he married Jennie Thompson, who died in 1878, leaving three children: Walter, Ella and Addie. He afterward married Anna Leslie, who has borne him one child, Mabel. Mr. Brierly is a member of the A. O. U. W., and is a Good Templar. He attends the services of the Methodist Protestant church.

HON. HARTFORD P. BROWN, member of the state legislature, of Rochester, was born in Raccoon township, this county, Aug. 7, 1851. His parents, Perry and Mary (McCombs) Brown, were natives of Beaver county and of Scotch-Irish descent. Perry has retired from active business life, and is still living in Rochester. He has two children: Amanda, wife of Samuel R. Campbell, of Beaver Falls, and Hartford P. The family have long been residents of this county. Amasa Brown, grandfather of Hartford P., was the master builder for the fleet built here by Aaron Burr in 1806. Hartford P. was reared in Freedom, Pa., attending school at Freedom, Rochester and the Beaver Academy. His first business was as bookkeeper and teller in the Second National Bank at Pittsburgh, where he remained until appointed cadet at West Point Military Academy, but resigned the cadetship during the first year. He then returned to Rochester and formed a partnership with Hon. Samuel J. Cross in mercantile trade. They kept a general store until 1879, when Mr. Brown sold out. He then built a steamboat called the "Carrier," which he managed until 1884, when he bought the wholesale and retail tobacco and cigar business of Samuel Moody, which he conducted until 1887. In 1886 he was elected to the legislature. He has served as a member of the school board in Rochester and is president of the M. S. Quay Republican Club of Beaver county. Mr. Brown was married, June 26, 1873, to Sue T., daughter of Hon. Samuel J. Cross, and they have five children: Hartford P., Jr., Frances, Emma, Sue and Julia. Mrs. Brown is a member of the Baptist church at Rochester.

CHARLES N. L. BRUDEWOLD, general manager of the New Brighton Glass Company, is a native of Norway, born in 1843, the eldest of the seven children of Canute and Lena (Thomson) Brudewold. The family came to this country in 1859, and soon after settled in Iowa, where Canute was a prominent merchant, but is now retired. Charles

BIOGRAPHIES—EAST SIDE. 755

N. L. is a graduate of the Citizens' Latin School, of his native country, and as will be seen was seventeen years old when he arrived in the land of his adoption. From 1863 to 1879 he was engaged in the manufacture of glass at Pittsburgh, Pa., after which he resided in St. Louis, Mo., until 1885, when he came to New Brighton and founded the glass works, of which he has the entire general management. He married, in 1864, Martha Munson, of Missouri, who has borne him two children, Canute and Lena. Mr. Brudewold is a member of the Methodist church.

CAPTAIN HENRY A. BRYAN, steamboat pilot, P. O. Baden, was born in Beaver county, March 11, 1834. John Bryan, the original pioneer of his family, came to America from Wales at an early period; was a soldier and a captain in the revolution, and settled in Chester county, Pa. He married Barbara Boon, in July, 1763, and by her he had one son, William. John died in 1807, his wife in 1805. William was born in 1767 in West Chester, and reared in Easton, Pa., where he engaged in the hotel business. He married Sarah Price in 1792, the result of the union being five sons and one daughter. William, who was a miller by trade, came to Beaver county in 1811, and engaged in the hotel business, his inn being the general headquarters for the officers and soldiers during the war of 1812. He erected a two-story stone building, which is still standing in a good state of preservation, and is owned by his grandson, our subject. He died in 1840. Aaron M. was among the oldest sons; was born in 1805 and died in 1848. He was a farmer, and like his father, was a hotel man. Aaron married Ann, daughter of Rev. Andrew McDonald, a Presbyterian minister, who organized the first church at Sewickley, and for many years was minister at that place. Born to Aaron and his wife, Ann, were seven children, five of whom are now living: Henry A., Catherine, Sarah, A. Boon and Ann Amanda. Mrs. Bryan now resides on the farm, and occupies the farm-house purchased by Mr. Bryan. Henry was educated at the common schools, and early engaged in steamboating, which he has followed nearly all his life, having recently retired. He was married, in 1865, to Bell, daughter of Thomas Neill. Since 1879 Mr. Bryan has been engaged in mercantile business. He was one of the original projectors of the Baden Gas Company, and the first well for that company was bored on his farm. He is a member of the Presbyterian church, a F. & A. M.; in politics a Democrat.

JACOB F. BUQUO, farmer, P. O. Barrisville, was born in Lancaster township, Butler county, Pa., June 11, 1842, a son of Jacob and Margaret (Hohnadle) Buquo, natives of Germany. The father immigrated to America in 1831, and located in Pittsburgh, where he followed blacksmithing for several years, after which he engaged in merchandising until 1841. He then removed to Butler county and purchased a 160-acre farm, which he carried on until 1867; then sold out and moved to Houston county, Tenn., where he bought a tract of land, to which he added from time to time until he now owns 700 acres, besides several pieces of town property. He had seven children, five now living: Sarah, Jacob F., Henry, Amelia and George. During the rebellion Jacob F. entered the service as teamster, and on his discharge at the close of the war removed to Venango county, Pa., and engaged in the oil business for about two years, at the same time following contracting. He then formed a partnership with Jacob Ifft in leasing land and sinking wells, for some two years more, and in 1868 embarked in the lumbering business in Tennessee. In this he continued three years, after which he moved to North Sewickley and purchased of Daniel Haynes his present farm of 108 acres. Mr. Buquo was married in this township, in 1866, to Gertrude, daughter of Peter Ifft, and they had eight children, seven now living: Anna Margaret, Clara, William Henry, Ferdinand, Gertrude Amelia, Sadie Eleanora and John Jacob Frederick Dillsworth. Mr. Buquo was elected supervisor one term; in politics he is a Republican. He and his wife are members of the United Presbyterian church.

SAMUEL BURNS, farmer, P. O. Bush Creek, was born in this county, Feb. 24, 1816, a son of Samuel and Ellen (Tucker) Burns, natives respectively of Ireland and Maryland. They were married in Pennsylvania, and settled in Beaver county where they died, the parents of twelve children, seven of whom are living. Samuel our subject married,

March 25, 1840, Ruth Shaner, who was born in New Sewickley township in 1822, and is a daughter of David and Ruth Shaner, both deceased. Mr. and Mrs. Burns are the parents of seven children, of whom four are living: Chosten, David, James and Mary. The deceased are Emma and John. Mr. Burns was reared on a farm and has been a life-long farmer. He owns about 320 acres of fine land. He and his wife are members of the Methodist Episcopal church. In politics he is a Democrat.

RICHARD BUTLER, carpenter. P. O. New Brighton, was born in Allegheny county in 1834. His parents Abiah, a farmer, and Jane (Beel) Butler, had fifteen children. Richard being one of the youngest. Richard was born and reared on the farm, received a common-school education, and followed agricultural pursuits for some years. He married, in 1859, Mary E., daughter of Jonathan Houk, and three children have blessed their union: Jonathan Abiah, Harriet B. and Richard. Mr. Butler learned the carpenter's trade at twenty years of age, and with the exception of about three years he has made it his life-long occupation. He enlisted in Company E, 25th Wisconsin Regiment, was with Sherman on his celebrated march, and was engaged in many battles, as he was in active service every day for three years. He is now engaged, besides working at his trade, in the stone quarrying and clay business. He is a member of the Methodist Episcopal church, and of the A. O. U. W. He is a Republican politically.

J. H. CABLE, merchant, Rochester, was born in Beaver March 17, 1831, a son of John and Phœbe (Goehring) Cable, the latter born in Germany and the former in Pennsylvania, of German descent. John was a farmer, and died in Rochester in 1849. J. H. is the fourth in a family of twelve children, ten of whom grew to maturity. He was reared in Beaver county, received his education in the common schools, and later learned the carpenter's trade, which he followed until 1862. He then began work with his brothers, who were masons, and with them carried on that trade until 1885, when he established a general grocery store, which he has since managed with success. He was married, in 1852, to Amanda Kelly, of Irish descent. Their children are Amelia, wife of John Spradley; Henry R., a brick-mason; Phœbe, wife of John A. Miller, a prominent manufacturer, of Rochester; Bessie, wife of David Aldrich; Callie, Joseph and Grace, at home. Mrs. Cable is a member of the Methodist Episcopal church. Mr. Cable is a Republican.

ROBERT M. CABLE, merchant, Rochester, was born in Rochester borough, Dec. 17, 1857. His parents, Charles and Elizabeth (Javens) Cable, were natives of this county, and of Irish and German origin. Robert M. is the third of twelve children, and was reared in Rochester and attended the schools here. His first work was with his father at stone contracting, which business the latter followed successfully many years, dying in Rochester in 1885. When Robert was nineteen years of age he established himself in mercantile trade, and at the age of twenty-one erected his present store building. He keeps a general grocery store, is polite and courteous, and is a man well calculated for the mercantile business. He married, in 1887, Mary J. McKee, of Irish descent, a member of the Methodist Episcopal church. Mr. Cable is a Democrat, and a member of the Junior Order of the United American Mechanics.

JOHN W. CALDER, merchant, Rochester, was born in Huntingdon county, Pa., Nov. 24, 1858, and is a son of Thomas N. and Pheba (Worrell) Calder, natives of Pennsylvania and of English and Scotch origin. Thomas N. is a farmer, an extensive stock dealer and one of the prominent men of Huntingdon county. John W. was the fourth in a family of seven children, of whom four sons and one daughter are living, and at the age of seven years came to live with Lewis Taylor, an attorney at Rochester. He was a great favorite with Mr. Taylor and became greatly attached to him. Mr. Taylor was his teacher, and did not permit him to attend school. He learned the mason's trade, and two years after completing his apprenticeship took a contract amounting to over $75,000, and successfully completed it. The skill and energy displayed in this work attracted the attention of Withrow & Gorden, extensive iron manufacturers at Pittsburgh. He was their general superintendent of construction seven years, and at times had seven or eight hundred men under his charge. In the employ of this company he traveled all

BIOGRAPHIES —EAST SIDE. 757

over the United States. He was then engaged with Reider & Conley, of Pittsburgh, for two years, at the expiration of which time his old friend, Lewis Taylor, was taken ill and Mr. Calder resigned his position, came to Rochester and nursed him until he died. He then bought Mr Taylor's old homestead and has since resided in Rochester. In 1883 he embarked in the dry goods and notion business, which he yet continues. He married Dec. 29, 1886, Jessie A., daughter of Robert B. Clark, of Beaver Falls. They are members of the Presbyterian church. Mr. Calder is a Republican and has been a member of the school board in Rochester, Pa. He is financial secretary of Council No. 140 of the American Mechanics, and is a Sir Knight Templar.

JAMES CARLIN, farmer, P. O. Rochester, was born in Ireland in 1829. Dec. 10, 1849, he left his native land and after a voyage of five weeks and two days, during which time the vessel was wrecked, landed in New York, Jan. 17, 1850. There he lay for six weeks in the hospital from the effects of exposure during the voyage. After his recovery he went to Kittanning; thence to Allegheny county to his brother. There he worked on a plank road for some months and subsequently hired with a farmer in Butler county for eight dollars per month, and the following summer worked at the carpenter's trade for ten dollars per month. He and his brother, who had just come out from Ireland, leased thirty acres of ground for six years, in Hanover township. Leaving his brother to manage the farm, Mr. Carlin, in 1854, went to California, where he worked at mining, sending all his spare money to his brother to buy a farm. In 1858 he returned home, took a trip to Ireland, where he remained six weeks and then returned to this country, bringing his two sisters with him. Leaving them on the farm with his brother he again went to California, and for five years worked as a gardener for from fifty to sixty dollars per month; also worked eight years in a store in Eldorado county. While in California Mr. Carlin married Lizzie Kelly, daughter of William and Nancy (Cowey) Kelly. He met her when in the old country, wrote for her to meet him in San Francisco, where they were married, and there two of their children were born. Mr. Carlin made three trips to California, leaving there the last time July 9, 1867, with his family, and after a voyage of thirty-one days, during which time he again suffered from shipwreck, the vessel arrived in New York. After remaining in Pittsburgh for a short time, he went to Ohio, to the home of his father-in-law, where his family remained until the following year, and Mr. Carlin meantime worked at the machine business until he could get a farm to suit him. Later he purchased his present farm of seventy-three acres, two and one-half miles from Rochester. The third year on this farm, Mr. Carlin was struck by a locomotive and severely injured, from the effects of which he still suffers. Seven children have been born to Mr. and Mrs. Carlin: Aggie (Mrs. White), William, John, Thomas, Ella, Clara and Jennie. Mr. Carlin has been a hard working man, and by perseverance and the aid of an industrious and saving wife has secured a good home. They are members of the Methodist Episcopal church. Politically he is a Republican.

WILLIAM CARR, glass finisher, Rochester, was born at Steubenville, Ohio, Oct. 5, 1848, a son of Robert and Mary (Hall) Carr, natives of Maryland and of Irish descent. Robert Carr was a glass finisher and in early life a glass blower. He had five sons and three daughters and six of the family are now living, of whom William is the youngest. He was only fourteen months old when his father died; was reared in Steubenville and attended the district and public schools. He commenced to learn his trade in Steubenville at the age of nine years, and afterward went to Pittsburgh and worked for a number of years. He then came to Rochester with the firm which established the Rochester Tumbler Works, in 1872, and has been an active member of the firm ever since. He was married at Steubenville, Ohio, Dec. 30, 1860, to Mary E., daughter of R. H. Aldridge, who was a native of Maryland and of English lineage. They have three children: Carrie, Eddie and Nellie. Mr. and Mrs. Carr are members of the Episcopal church. Mr. Carr is a prominent F. & A. M., and has taken thirty-two degrees in that order. He is also a member of the I. O. O. F.

DEWITT C. CHAMPLIN, bank teller, P. O. New Brighton, was born in Onondaga county, N. Y., and came with his parents to Beaver county when eight years of age. He received a good common-school education, and for two years was a student at Jefferson College, Pa. He has been engaged in various pursuits, for a number of years at steamboating, and was a farmer in Maryland for some time. During the war he was at Memphis, Tenn., and for two years was clerk of the military court. Since 1856 he has made New Brighton his home principally. From 1870 to 1883 he lived a retired life, and during the past three years has been teller of the National Bank of New Brighton. He is a member of the Presbyterian church; politically he is a Democrat.

T. J. CHANDLER, retired dentist, Rochester. was born in Bedford county, Pa., Aug. 17, 1807, a son of Jeremiah N. and Sarah (Johnston) Chandler. His mother was born in Pennsylvania, and his father in Norfolk, Va., and they were of English and Scotch descent. Our subject's grandfather, Jeremiah Chandler, was married in 1781. Jeremiah N. studied medicine, but never practiced, and was a hotel keeper in Huntingdon and Bedford counties. T. J. spent his youth in Huntingdon county, received his education in the old-fashioned log school-house, and early in life learned the trade of a silversmith, then that of a tailor, at which he worked until he found it injured his health. He then commenced the study of dentistry, and found his knowledge of work in silver of great advantage to him, as in those days almost all plates were made of silver and gold. He commenced the practice of dentistry at Alexandria, Pa., removed thence to Beaver county in 1834, and in 1883 retired from practice. During the war he went South, and was with the Union army for over two years, receiving from Secretary Stanton a pass which enabled him to go through the lines at all times. He returned home in 1863, and was so overrun with work that he could hardly get out of the house day or night. He was married, Aug. 28, 1829, to Eliza J., daughter of Thomas and Hattie (Stearns) Sherman, natives of Pennsylvania, and of German and Irish descent. The children of Mr. and Mrs. Chandler are as follows: William, a dentist; Henry B. (deceased), also a dentist; Harrison, a dentist; Harriet, Matilda, Josephine, Clara, Emma Q. and Mary (an adopted daughter), all married. Mr. and Mrs. Chandler are members of the Methodist Episcopal church, in which he has been steward and class leader. He became a member of this church in 1827. He is a prominent member of the Good Templars; in politics a Prohibitionist. He has been ticket agent for the Pittsburgh & Fort Wayne Railroad for thirty-five years.

H. J. CHANDLER, dentist, Rochester, was born in Bridgewater, Pa., Sept. 4, 1840, a son of T. J. Chandler, a retired dentist of Rochester. He is the seventh in a family of twelve children, seven now living; he was reared in Rochester, attended the public schools, and learned dentistry with his father. In the winter of 1860 and 1861 he went to New Orleans and opened an office, but owing to the excitement of the war he returned to Rochester. When he reached home he enlisted in the Curtin Riflemen, which became Company F, of the 10th Pennsylvania Infantry. He was a non-commissioned officer, and was three times slightly wounded, at Gaines' Mill, Charles City Crossroads and second Bull Run; after which was sent to the hospital, and was discharged from the army Feb. 27, 1863. He regained his health, and Jan. 4, 1864, reënlisted in Company K, the 76th P. V. I., as a recruit, and was wounded at Chester Station, Va., May 7, 1864, and also at Fair Oaks Oct. 27, 1864 (the two last times severely), and was promoted for bravery, after having command of his company as a non-commissioned officer in five different engagements, to second lieutenant, and was the officer in command when he was wounded the last time. He was then sent to Pittsburgh on detached service, was appointed a member of the military court there, and served until the close of the war. He then returned to Rochester and entered again upon the practice of his profession. He was married, in 1869, to Adda C. Critchlow, who is of English descent. This union has been blessed with four children: Benjamin L., Thomas P., Harrison C. and Eunice E. Mr. and Mrs. Chandler are members of the Presbyterian church. He is a member of the G. A. R. Post, of Rochester; in politics a Republican.

C. H. CLARK, proprietor of the St. James hotel, Rochester, was born April 4, 1841, a son of Samuel and Martha (Shirk) Clark, natives of Lancaster county, Pa., and of

Scotch and German descent. Samuel was a farmer all his life, and died in 1874, the father of four children. C. H., the eldest child, was reared on the farm and educated in the common schools. Later he became a teacher, which occupation he followed until 1870, when he embarked in the hotel business in Rochester. He kept the "Johnson House" three years, then the "Pavilion Hotel" for ten years, and in 1886 bought the "St. James' Hotel" property; he is a popular landlord. He enlisted, in 1864, in Company A, One Hundred and Ninety-sixth O. V. I., and served as orderly sergeant. He is a member of the United Workmen, the Royal Arcanum, and the Garfield Council of American Mechanics. In politics he is a Republican. He has been school director. He was married in Butler county, Pa., in 1866, to Mary, daughter of Phillip Stefler, and of German origin. They have four sons now living: Howard, at college; Harry, Maurice and Walter.

IRA CLEVELAND, retired, Freedom, was born in Ohio July 9, 1831, a son of Jonas and Sarah (Voorhees) Cleveland. His parents were married in New York, and removed to Ohio, where they remained about ten years. In 1833 they moved to Southern Michigan, and remained on the same farm until their deaths. They had ten children, of whom six are living. Ira, the fifth child, was married in Michigan, Dec. 4, 1854, to Ruth A., born in New York Aug. 30, 1828, daughter of Joshua and Deborah (Dwelley) Baker, who died in Michigan. Mr. Cleveland learned the carpenter's trade, which he followed for many years. When the war broke out he enlisted in Company G, 13th Wisconsin Volunteers, and remained in the service four years. He then engaged in farming until Sept. 1, 1879, when he moved to Freedom, Pa., and has since resided there. In 1887 he was elected justice of the peace, and still holds the office. He has had three children, two of who are living, one married and the other single. Mr. Cleveland owns five houses and lots in Freedom, renting all except the residence which he and family occupy.

GEORGE H. COLEMAN, farmer, P. O. Brush Creek, was born in Beaver county, Nov. 29, 1843. His father, Edward Coleman, a native of England, immigrated to America with his parents when fourteen years of age, settled in Beaver county and married Elizabeth Hinds. Both died in this county. George H. was married, Nov 4, 1869, to Elizabeth, daughter of Charles and Catherine Bonzo. She was born in this county July 14, 1846, and to them have been born nine children, one of whom, Colleda T., is deceased. Those living are Warren W., Charles E., Laura E., Eva C., Lottie S., Ross C., Delbert L. and George W. Mr. Coleman followed teaching thirteen winters, and his father was also a teacher. He has been engaged in farming nineteen years. In 1861 he enlisted in Company H, 101st Regiment P. V., and was at the siege of Yorktown, at the battles of Williamsburg and Fair Oaks, and the Seven Days' fight. He was honorably discharged in 1862, and reënlisted in 1863, in Company I, 52d Regiment, and was discharged the same year. He is a member of the G. A. R., at Rochester, and has filled the offices of justice of the peace and school director. He owns 250 acres of improved land.

JOHN CONWAY, banker, Rochester, president of the John Conway Company Bank, was born in this county March 27, 1830, and is a son of Michael and Mary (O'Brien) Conway. His parents came from Ireland in 1825 and settled in Economy township, this county, on a farm where they spent the remaining portion of their lives. John is the fourth in their family of six children. He grew to manhood in the rural district of Beaver county, obtaining his education at the public schools and the college at Vincennes, Ind., where he attended two years. His first business was as a steamboat clerk on the Ohio, at which he remained from 1847 to 1854. He then embarked in the dry goods trade and established a store at Newcastle, Pa., remaining there until 1856. In 1858 he came to Rochester and was engaged in mercantile trade until 1871, when the present firm was established. The business of this firm was safely conducted by Mr. Conway through the panic of 1873, and the dismal business times of 1874 and 1875, and he has won the confidence of the community. He has spent most of his life in this county, and for years has been prominently identified with its commercial interests and progress. He married, in 1857, Miss Thalia, daughter of Philip Bentel. She was a native of Freedom and of German origin. They have two children: Lillian, wife of N. F. Hurst of Rochester, and Charles B. Mr. and Mrs. Conway are members of the Presbyterian church, of which he has been a trustee for sixteen years. He is president of the Olive Stove Works and of the Union Street Railway Company of Rochester; is also a director of the Rochester Heat & Light Company, is a prominent member of the Masonic fraternity and has taken thirty-two degrees in that order. In politics he is a Democrat.

O. H. COUCH, undertaker and furniture dealer, P O. New Brighton, was born in Allegheny county in 1829, a son of Nathan and Emily (Light) Couch. His father, who was a shoemaker, had six children. O. H., the eldest, was reared in his native county, and received a common-school education. In youth he was employed in a woolen establishment; during the war was engaged at railroad engineering, and afterward was for ten years in the mercantile business. In 1884 he located at his present place of business, where he carries a full line of furniture and follows the undertaking business. He was married, in 1851, to Charlotte, daughter of William Dunbar, of Philadelphia, and they have eight children: Esther, John, Nathan, Eliza, Charlotta, David, Mary Ann and Orlando. Mr. Couch is a Democrat.

CHARLES COVERT, dealer in groceries, provisions, notions and tinware, P. O. New Brighton, is a native of Butler county, Pa., born in 1853, second son in the family of nine children (seven of whom grew to maturity), of Rufus P. and Susan (Radenbough) Covert. The father was a school teacher and manufacturer of tubs. Charles Covert came to this county when three years of age with his parents, and here received a common-school education. When eleven he commenced learning tub making; worked at that until the business was discontinued, then was employed in the manufacture of cutlery, and other business, and afterward, for several years, followed the trade of a carpenter. In 1883, with no previous experience, he embarked in his present successful business in New Brighton. He was married, in 1877, to Margaret, daughter of Madison Phillis, of this county, and by her has four children: Margaret, Rufus P., Allen and Elsie. Mr. Covert is a member of the K. of P. and R. A. In politics he is a Democrat.

P. H. COYLE, farmer, P. O. New Brighton, was born in Allegheny county in 1830, and came to Beaver county in 1853. Edward, his father, by trade a plumber, came from Ireland about 1829, settled in Pittsburgh, married Ann McSwiggin, of County Tyrone, Ireland, who bore him three children, P. H. being the eldest. · Edward Coyle returned to his native land, where he died. His widow survived him and came to this country with her children in 1853. P. H. was educated in the common schools, and at the age of eighteen years began to learn the glass-blowing trade, which he followed until 1869. He married in 1859, Mary Ann, daughter of Daniel and sister of E. B. Dougherty, of this county. They have two sons and two daughters: Elizabeth, at home; Daniel, a druggist; Harry, a practicing physician; and Alice, at home. Mr. Coyle purchased his present farm in 1869, and, with the exception of three years, has since devoted his time to agricultural pursuits. He is a Democrat, and has been justice of the peace for twelve years, besides holding other township offices. He is a member of the Catholic church.

B. F. CRAIG, ship carpenter, Freedom, was born in Beaver county, Pa., Nov. 22, 1829, a son of Joseph and Elizabeth (Manor) Craig, natives of Pennsylvania, and who died in Beaver county. Joseph, after the death of his wife Elizabeth, married Eliza Stoops, who is still living. He was the father of seventeen children, of whom ten are living. B. F. is the eldest child, and was united in marriage, May 9, 1850, with Catherine Lambert, who was born in Beaver county, a daughter of Moses Lambert (deceased). Two children have been born to them, Harriet (deceased) and Anna L., wife of William Kronk. Mrs. Craig died July 31, 1852, and Mr. Craig married Oct. 14, 1856, Jessie Stewart, who was born in Scotland in 1827, and is a daughter of James and Anna (Craig) Blyth. The former died in Scotland, and the widow and children came to America and settled first in Pittsburgh, and later in Freedom, where the mother died in 1878. Mr. Craig has followed ship and house building all his life, and settled in Freedom in 1834, where he owns four houses and lots.

BIOGRAPHIES—EAST SIDE. 761

STEPHEN A. CRAIG, physician, Freedom, was born in Freedom borough, March 4, 1848, a son of William and Angeline (Rogers) Craig. His parents, natives of Pennsylvania, have resided in Freedom since their marriage, and have had ten children, eight now living. Stephen A., the eldest child, was married, Jan. 19, 1872, to Fredricka Miller, who was born in Freedom Dec. 31, 1854. Her parents, George and Elizabeth Miller, were natives of Pennsylvania, where they were married, settled and remained. Her mother died in June, 1884. Dr. and Mrs. Craig have two children: Gertrude M. and Elizabeth A. He began the study of medicine in 1866, graduated in 1877, and has continued in practice in Freedom, Pa., ever since. His brother, W. H., is associated with him in practice. When the war broke out he enlisted in Battery D, 1st P. L. A., and served one year. He and Mrs. Craig are members of church. He is a F. & A. M , and member of the I. O. O. F.

NICHOLAS CRESS, justice of the peace, P. O. Brown's, is a native of Butler county, and was born in 1838. Henry Cress, his father, married Lizzie Reifer, and by her had ten children, nine of whom are now living. Henry came from Germany to America about 1830, was by trade a shoemaker, and died at the age of sixty-three years. His widow is still living at the age of seventy four years. Nicholas the second son, received in youth a common-school education, and at the age of seventeen learned the trade of blacksmith, which he has followed for twenty-five years. He married, in 1865, Susie S., daughter of Adam Younker, and by her had two children: Lewis L. and George A. Mrs. Cress died Oct. 28, 1878, and Mr. Cress next married Maggie, daughter of Nicholas and Caroline Rieb. Four children are the result of this marriage: Cora Bell, Edward, Daniel and Jennie May. He purchased his present farm, containing seventy-three acres, in 1876, and also conducted a blacksmithing shop until 1887, when he discontinued the latter on account of ill health. He was elected justice of the peace in 1880 and reëlected in 1885. He enlisted in 1862 in Company B, 12th P. C., and served his country three years and two months. Among the battles in which he took an active part were Bull Run, Antietam and Cedar Creek; and was in numerous raids through Virginia, Maryland and Pennsylvania.

CHARLES CUNNING, farmer, P. O. Brush Creek, was born in Allegheny county, Pa., Oct. 3, 1842. His parents, Patrick and Elizabeth Cunning, natives of Ireland, were married in Pennsylvania, and settled in Allegheny county. They afterward moved to Beaver county, where they died. Charles was reared on a farm, and when starting out in life for himself engaged in merchandising in New Brighton, after which he engaged in farming, and now owns 140 acres of fine land. He was married in September, 1867, to Sarah, daughter of John and Jane Schrista, the latter deceased. Mrs. Cunning was born in Washington county, Pa., in 1846, and is the mother of seven children: John, Samuel, Jane, Elizabeth, Mary, Anna and George. Mr. Cunning and his wife are members of the Catholic church. In politics he is a Democrat.

A. J. DANIELS, farmer, was born in New Sewickley township, April 21, 1853, a son of William and Jane Daniels. William was a native of Wales, and died in Beaver county; his wife was born in Pennsylvania, and is still living. A. J. Daniels was reared a farmer, and has followed that business through life on the old homestead. Aug. 9, 1882, our subject was married to Mary, daughter of Benjamin and Emeline Piersol. The former died in this county Aug. 30, 1885; his widow is still living on the old homestead. Mrs. Daniels was born Feb. 20, 1862. Mr. Daniels is a Republican; a member of the Baptist church.

MAJOR JOHN S. DARRAGH, retired merchant, P. O. Rochester, is a descendant of one of the early settlers of this county, where he was born, July 16, 1804, a son of Robert and Deborah (Hart) Darragh. Mrs. Deborah Darragh was a native of New Jersey, a daughter of Jesse Hart and a granddaughter of John Hart, one of the signers of the Declaration of Independence. Robert Darragh was born in Ireland, came to America in 1798, and to Beaver county in 1808. He taught school at Sharon (now called Bridgewater), and subsequently kept a hotel and general store. Sharon was then the best business point in Beaver county. He was successful in business and succeeded in accumulating a handsome fortune. The Major is the eldest of a family of eight children, was reared in Beaver county, where he obtained his schooling, and early in life worked in his father's store and also carried on business for himself for about twenty years, as a merchant. From 1836 to 1837 he was collector for the canal company. He then embarked in business in company with his brothers and conducted a general store at Sharon; also erected a foundry and machine shop. In 1844 he sold out his entire interest to his brothers, and built a steamboat called the "Gondolier." The boat was run with a good profit to the owner until 1848, when she sunk. He was then appointed mail agent on the Fort Wayne & Chicago Railroad, having been the first mail agent appointed on that railroad, and was afterward assistant treasurer for all express transfer at Pittsburgh. He next went on a steamboat as clerk, for eighteen months. In 1860 he was elected county treasurer and served one term. He served two years in the pension department at Washington. He has been for many years president of the Big Beaver Bridge Company; is a prominent member of the I. O. O. F. and a Republican. He served seven years as major of militia. He was married, in 1827, to Mary, daughter of James Lyon. Her mother's maiden name was Electa Smith; she was of English descent. Her grandfather was killed by the Indians in Allegheny county, Pa. Her father and his brother were taken, when children, by the Indians, and carried to Ohio, where they were afterward exchanged. Major Darragh and wife have had eight children: James and Robert, mechanical engineers, the latter a first lieutenant in the late war; Thomas, a clerk; Jesse, who was one of the body guard of General Anderson: George; (the two last named died within a few days of each other, in 1887, of typhoid pneumonia;) Anna, wife of Captain Charles B. Hurst, of Rochester; Louisa and Martha. Mr. Darragh has been a member of the Methodist Episcopal church for more than half a century.

SAMUEL DEAN, farmer, P. O. Freedom, was born in Ireland Jan. 9, 1823. His parents, Samuel and Mary Dean, came to America in 1833 and settled in Beaver county, where they died. Samuel was married, June 24, 1847, to Ann Hunter, also a native of Ireland, who died in 1866, the mother of five children, of whom four are living. Mr. Dean next married, Dec. 10, 1868, Catharine J. Miller, who was born in Allegheny county, Pa., March, 16, 1839. Her parents, Philip and Jane Miller, were natives of Pennsylvania and died in Butler county. To Mr. and Mrs. Dean two children have been born, Samuel C. and Jennie A. Mr. Dean has been a farmer most of his life, and owns about 150 acres of land. He and his wife are members of the United Presbyterian church.

FRITZ DEGNER, draftsman, P. O. New Brighton, was born in North Germany in 1854, and came to America in 1883. His parents, Carl and Bertha (Eichler) Degner, had a family of eleven children. Fritz, the tenth child, was educated in the gymnasium schools of Germany, and at twenty years of age served one year as a soldier. For four and a half years he was a student of civil engineering, taking a thorough course in that branch of study and graduating at Berlin in 1881. He married, in 1883, Anna, daughter of Fritz Frundt, also of Germany, and to them has been born one son, Carl. Mr. Degner came to New Brighton in 1884, and since that date has been head draftsman for the Penn Bridge Company of Beaver Falls.

F. A. DEITRICK, locomotive engineer, New Brighton, was born in 1842 in Marion township, this county, the youngest of the five children of Frederick and Dorothy (Flugh) Deitrick. Frederick came from Alsace, France (now Germany), to this country in 1828, located on a farm in Butler county, Pa., in 1829, but afterward moved to this county. F. A. remained on the home farm until his fifteenth year, then learned blacksmithing, which he followed for some time; and later carried on a boot and shoe business in Pittsburgh for three years. In 1862 he enlisted in Company A, 123d Regiment, P. V., and during a nine month's service participated in the battles of Antietam, Fredericksburg and Chancellorsville. Returning from the army in 1862 he commenced railroading in Allegheny City and has been an engineer for twenty-two years. He married in 1867, Louisa, daughter of John McKnight, and seven children have blessed their union: Florence, Robert, Mary, Frederick, Edith, Lula and Ethel. Mr. Deitrick is a member of the G. A. R. and of the United Brotherhood of Locomotive Engineers. In politics he is a Democrat.

JOSEPH DEWHIRST, brick manufacturer, New Brighton, was born in England in 1843; came to America in 1865 and soon afterward located in New Brighton. His parents were Richard and Mary Dewhirst, to whom were born seven children, Joseph being the eldest son. He received a good education and left school at the age of seventeen. He was married, in 1866, to Hannah, daughter of Thomas Dewhirst, who was also from England. Five children have been born to this marriage: Mary Ann, Amy, Joe Demain, Faith and Fred. Mr. Dewhirst began to learn the carpenter's trade at the age of seventeen, and served an apprenticeship of three years. He followed his trade six years, but in 1866 began the manufacture of red brick, which he still continues, and turns out one million of brick per year, giving employment to from nine to fifteen men.

JOHN H. DIPPOLD, JR., steamboat captain, P. O. Baden, was born in Allegheny county, Pa., in 1847. His grandfather, Clements Dippold, was a soldier under Bonaparte for six years, and was in the cavalry at the great battle of Waterloo. His wife was Margaret Cemmets, by whom he had nine children. He died in 1817, and his widow in 1829. Captain John Dippold, Sr., their youngest child, was born in Bavaria in 1816. He left school at the age of fifteen years and learned the trade of a stonecutter and mason. In 1841 he came to this country, landing in Baltimore in November of that year. In 1842 he came to Pittsburgh, and soon afterward to Baden, this county, where he has since resided. From 1842 to 1859 he was extensively engaged in contracting, and built the largest bridges for the Pittsburg & Ft. Wayne, and the Cleveland & Pittsburg railroads, and over thirty bridges for the Pan Handle road. In 1859 he gave up bridge contracting and engaged in steamboating and the coal business; has owned several boats, but retired from business in 1878. He married, in 1840, Anna, daughter of John and Catharine Hoffman, and to them were born eight children, seven of whom are living: Frederick, Barbara, John H., Martin, Catherine, Jacob and George. Mr. and Mrs. Dippold are now living retired on a small farm. They are members of the Lutheran church, and politically he is a Democrat. John H. received a common-school education, and at the age of twelve years went on a steamboat with his father, and has followed the river ever since, having filled the position of pilot and captain on a steamboat. He was married, in 1866, to Isabella J., daughter of Price Bryan, of this county. They have one daughter, Annie B. The captain resides in Baden, where he has a comfortable home. He is a F. & A. M., a member of the I. O. O. F. and K. of P. He is a member of the Lutheran church. Politically he is a Democrat.

REV. S. T. DODD, M. D., P. O. Rochester, was born in Marshall county, Va., Sept. 26, 1836, a son of Dr. George and Mary (Henon) Dodd, the former a native of Virginia and the latter of Pennsylvania. They were of English and Scotch-Irish descent. His grandfather, Rev. F. S. Dodd, was educated for a Catholic priest in Dublin. Dr. George Dodd was a physician and practiced in Washington county, Pa., and in Virginia for many years; was also a farmer and woolgrower. Our subject attended common school in Virginia and the normal school and academy in Washington county, Pa., and studied medicine with his father. In 1866 he graduated at Mount Auburn college, Cincinnati, Ohio, having previously taught school and practiced medicine. He then went to the Cleveland, Ohio, Medical College, where he graduated in 1867, and practiced for fifteen years. In 1862 he enlisted in the 22d Pa. Cavalry, was appointed hospital steward, and was discharged at the close of the war. During the last year and a half of service he was acting assistant-surgeon of the regiment. At the close of the war he continued his practice at West Middletown, Pa., until 1871. He then removed to Wellsburg, W. Va., and commenced preaching, and was ordained in 1878 as minister in the Disciple church of which he has been a member since he was fifteen years old, and was employed in missionary work in Kansas for five years. He is the author of several works, among which are "The History of the Christian Church," "Sunday-School Manual," "The Pastor" and numerous tracts. He was married, in 1866, to Virginia C., daughter of William Marlatt. Mrs. Dodd was of French descent, and was the mother of four children: William M., Charles S., James C. and George L. She died in Wellsburg in 1874. Mr. Dodd afterward married Hettie A., a daughter of Squire John Engle, of Industry, this county. She lived but three years after their marriage. He married his present wife at Deersville, Harrison county, Ohio. By her he had one child now living, Francis Merit. Mr. Todd is a Master Mason, a member of the I. O. O. F. and K. of P., of the Good Templars and of the G. A. R. He came to Rochester in 1886 and bought what is called the Deer Lane property, formerly owned by John Javens. He organized a society at Beaver Falls in 1886 known as the First Christian church. He now preaches at several points on Lord's days, and spends his week days at home in recuperation, on account of broken health from overtax in former years.

RICHARD DONCASTER (deceased) was born in England, Feb. 2, 1801. His father, Daniel Doncaster, died when Richard was only three years old, and the latter was reared by an Episcopal minister, receiving a good education. In 1826 he came from England to Pennsylvania and engaged at the miller's trade, which he had learned in England. He owned and operated a mill in Westmoreland county for more than twenty years, but in later life made hotel-keeping his business. He kept hotel for twelve years in Butler county, Pa., but in 1865 he came to Rochester and carried on the same business until his death, in 1882. In politics he was a Democrat. He married, in 1826, Ann, daughter of Richard North. Mrs. Doncaster was of English descent. and the mother of eleven children, of whom four daughters and one son are living. The daughters have managed the hotel since the death of their father. The mother died in 1871. The living members of the family are Daniel, a millwright in Jefferson county, Pa.; Sarah, Anna, Elizabeth and Jemima, at their old home, the Doncaster hotel.

JAMES DOUGLAS is superintendent of the American Fire Brick Clay and Blast Furnace Linings Works of S. Barnes & Co., Limited. This business was established in 1840 by S. Barnes, and to him may be attributed a large amount of the success of the company. When he first started here he did all the work himself; was a natural mechanic and could turn his hand to almost anything. He died in 1885, and since then the business has been superintended by James Douglas, who has been in the employ of Mr. Barnes and this company for over a quarter of a century. Mr. Douglas was born in Antrim, Ireland, Aug. 7, 1839, a son of Robert and Mary (Black) Douglas, who came to America in 1855, and settled in Beaver county. He is the third in a family of four children, two sons and two daughters; was reared on a farm in Ireland and attended the common school there. Since 1861 he has been at work at fire brick manufacturing. He was married, in 1860, to Louise Wigley, who was born in Beaver county, of English descent. Of their twelve children eight are now living: Anna, Maggie, Emma, Laura, Nettie, Arthur, Gertrude and Fred. Mr. and Mrs. Douglas are members of the Presbyterian church, of which he is a trustee. He is a Democrat, and has served as school director for seventeen years.

A. J. DOUGLASS, carpenter, New Brighton, was born in this county in 1851. William Douglass, his father, was by trade a millwright, and married Sarah Moser, by whom he had three children, A. J. being the eldest son. He received a common-school education and at the age of sixteen began to learn the millwright's trade, which he followed from 1867 to 1876. Afterward he took up the trade of a carpenter, and since 1879 has followed that occupation. He was married, in 1876, to Ella, daughter of I. J. Shearer, of Westmoreland county, Pa. By her he has one child, Jesse. Mr. Douglass was elected a member of the town council in 1887 by the Republican party. He is a member of the I. O. O. F. encampment. In religion he is a Presbyterian.

ROBERT J. DOUTHITT. farmer. P. O. North Sewickley, was born in this county in 1840, a son of Robert and Phœbe (Newkirk) Douthitt, the former born in Beaver county in 1802, and the latter in Washington county, Pa., in 1809. Our subject's grandfather, Joseph Douthitt, a farmer, was born in Carlisle, Pa., in 1764; was a teamster in the Revolutionary War, and in 1796 settled in Chippewa township, this county. The maternal grandfather of Robert J. was of Irish descent. Robert Douthitt had five children:

Anthony W., Mary E. (deceased), Shipman N., Robert J., and Ada. The father was a blacksmith twenty years; then carried on a hotel in Chippewa township twenty years, on the State road, between Rochester and Ohio. He then retired and lived for twelve years in Beaver Falls, after which he moved to Mercer county, where he still lives. Robert J. enlisted in 1861, in Company D., 100th Regiment, P. V., serving four years less one month. This regiment belonged properly to the Army of the Potomac, but in 1863 it was detached and sent to the siege of Vicksburgh, remaining until the surrender, when it was transferred to the Army of the Cumberland, and finally returned to the Army of the Potomac, with which it remained until the close of the war. Mr. Douthitt participated in many hard-fought battles through Tennessee, Virginia and Maryland. He received a gun-shot wound in the head at Campbell's Station, near Knoxville, Tenn., was held a prisoner for three months at Columbia, S. C., and was discharged with rank of second lieutenant at Harrisburg, July 24, 1865. On his return home he farmed in Chippewa township until 1871, when he bought his present place, of 130 acres, in this township. He married Matilda Crowl, by whom he has two children: Alice May and Theodore A. Mrs. Douthitt died in 1873, and in 1879 Mr. Douthitt married her sister, Sarah. He is township auditor, and has served on the board several terms; is a member of Post 164, G. A. R., Beaver Falls; in politics he is a Democrat. He and his children are members of the Methodist Church, Mrs. Douthitt of the Presbyterian.

REV. M. F. DUMSTREY, pastor of St. John's church, Zelienople, was born in Germany, June 5, 1854, a son of Charles and Henrietta (Winkelman) Dumstrey, who still reside in Germany, the former being a merchant there. M. F. received a theological education in Germany, came to America in 1871, and for about five years traveled in different parts of the United States, stopping for a short time in New York, Philadelphia, Chicago and other cities. In 1876 he went to Lancaster, Pa., where he took a special course to perfect himself in the English language, and remained there three years. In 1879 he went to Pittsburgh, where he took charge of a church until 1887, when he came and assumed charge of St. John's Evangelical Protestant church. In 1879 he married Annie Thoma, who was born Dec. 4, 1858, in Pittsburgh, a daughter of John and Sophia (Shanhoefer) Thoma, who were also natives of Pittsburgh. Two children have blessed the union of Mr. and Mrs. Dumstrey: Edwin and Renate. Mr. Dumstrey is an active young church worker and is destined to do well in his new field, as St. John's church is one of the oldest church organizations of Beaver county.

JOHN W. DUNLAP, farmer, P. O. Brown, was born in Allegheny county, in 1837. His father, William, married Mary Adams, who bore him four sons and two daughters, and after her death he married Margaret, daughter of Dr. John Waldron, of Butler county. Seven sons were born to this union, of whom John W. is the eldest. The mother of these children died in 1852, and William next married Catherine Lockard, who died without issue. His fourth wife was Lucinda Hesson who had no children. William came from Germany in 1825, and settled in Allegheny county, where he remained until 1839. He then came to Beaver county and purchased 200 acres of land where he remained until his death at the age of seventy-eight years. John W. was educated at the common schools, and has always been a farmer. He was married in 1860 to Mary Ann, daughter of William and Ann (Hammer) Kapper. Nine children were born to this union, seven of whom are living: James F., John E., Orlando, William Joseph P., Sylvester H., Ida Mary and Emma Bell. Mr. Dunlap purchased, in 1877, his present farm of 100 acres, a part of the tract purchased by his father. Mr. Dunlap is a school director and supervisor. He is a member of the Lutheran church; in politics a Democrat.

JOHN W. EBAUGH, baggage-master, P., Ft. W. & C. Ry., New Brighton, was born in Maryland in 1854, and is the fifth son of Joseph and Caroline Ebaugh. Until he was sixteen years of age he attended the public schools. Since the age of nineteen he has been engaged in railroading, for the past fifteen years on the Pittsburg, Fort Wayne & Chicago Railway. He came to New Brighton in 1874, and was married, in 1882, to Oroe, daughter of Henry Fetter, an old and respected citizen of Beaver county, and by her has one child, Millard. Mr. Ebaugh is a F. & A. M., and a member of the K. of P. In politics he is a Republican.

DANIEL EISENBRAUN, farmer, P. O. Knob, was born in Germany, July 7, 1818, and is a son of Michael and Fredericka Eisenbraun, who died in Germany. Daniel was married, Aug. 12, 1842, to Barbara Binn, who was born in Germany, April 1, 1817, a daughter of Jacob F. Binn (deceased), and the mother of ten children, nine of whom are living: Margaret, Mary, Jacob, Laura, George, Catherine, John, Henry and Willie. One daughter, Caroline, is deceased. Our subject is a weaver, and follows that trade in connection with farming. He owns seventy-six acres of land. He and his wife are members of the Lutheran church.

B. F. ELLIS, merchant, Rochester, was born in Bordentown, N. J., Feb. 25, 1847, and is a son of A. P. and Elizabeth (Strock) Ellis. His mother was born in Philadelphia, his father in New Jersey, and they are of German and English descent. His father, who is a cabinetmaker, came to Rochester in 1856, and has worked at his trade here most of the time since. He had a family of nine children, seven of whom grew to maturity. B. F., the eldest, was educated in the public schools at Philadelphia and Rochester, and when fourteen years old he became clerk in a store in Rochester for the late Hon. Samuel J. Cross, with whom he stayed fourteen and one-half years. In 1876 he established a small grocery store, and has succeeded in building up a good trade. Since 1881 he has carried an extensive stock of general merchandise, and has done a fine business. He was married in Fairfax county, Va., in 1871, to Ada V., daughter of Thomas Javens. Her mother's maiden name was Emily Scarce, and her parents were of Welsh origin. This union has been blessed with five children: Olive M. (who is a valuable assistant to her father in the store), Ada V., Florence F., Grace B. and Eva B. Mrs. Ellis is a member of the Episcopal church; Mr. Ellis and Olive M. of the Baptist church. In politics he is a Republican. He has served as school director and assessor, and member of the town council at Rochester. He is an active member of the R. A. and the J. O. A. M.; is a past officer in the K. of P., and a Master Mason.

HENRY EMRICK, Rochester, was born in Butler county, Pa., Aug. 10, 1832, a son of Jacob and Catharine Emrick, who were natives of Pennsylvania, and died in Beaver county. He was married, Dec. 13, 1860, to Amelia Romigh, who was born in Beaver county, March 14, 1833, a daughter of John and Juliet Romigh. By this marriage were born five children, four of whom are living: Belle Z., Johnson, James A. and Nannie. The one deceased was Eldora. Mrs. Emrick died Jan. 5, 1876. April 15, 1885, Mr. Emrick was again married, to Ellen Ashworth, who was born in Brownstown, Allegheny county, Pa., Aug. 28, 1853, a daughter of Samuel and Lizzie Ashworth, the latter deceased. Mr. Emrick has been a farmer all his life, and owns forty-eight acres of improved land, which he rented Feb. 29, 1888. and now resides in Rochester. When the war broke out he enlisted in Company G, 168th Regiment. In politics he is a Republican. The family are members of the Presbyterian church.

ZACH. EMRICK, farmer, P. O. Lovi, was born in this county March 15, 1852, a son of Jacob and Catherine Emrick, who settled in Beaver county and remained here until their death. Zach. Emrick was married, Feb. 4, 1875, to Elizabeth Huffman, who was born in Butler county, Pa., Sept. 23, 1850. Her mother, Margaret Huffman, was a native of Germany. She settled in Beaver county, afterward moved to Butler county, and is still living. Mr. and Mrs. Emrick have seven children: William O., David E., Samuel C., Tillie R., Joseph W., Maud G. and Jacob C. Mr. Emrick owns fifty acres of improved land. In politics he is a Republican.

DANIEL ENDRES, dealer in cattle, etc., was born in this county in 1847, the eldest of the eleven children (five yet living) of Adam and Elizabeth Endres, the former a farmer. Daniel was reared on the farm, and remained at home until twenty-three years of age, and since his fifteenth year has dealt in live stock. He came to New Brighton in 1872, and has since carried on butchering here. He married, in 1870, Sarah, daughter of Christian Daumbach. He is a F. & A. M.; a member of the Presbyterian church. In politics he is a Republican.

BIOGRAPHIES—EAST SIDE.   767

CAPT. SAMUEL ERWIN, pilot, P. O. Baden, was born in Moon township, in 1844. His grandfather, William Erwin, was by occupation a school-teacher, and came from Crawford county, Pa., to Beaver county at an early day. He had seven sons and four daughters. John was the youngest son, and in early life followed the river as a keel-boat man, and was also a captain and pilot. He purchased a farm in Hopewell township, where he spent the latter part of his life. He married Margaret, daughter of John Baker, and by her had seven sons and one daughter. John died, aged sixty-nine years, and his wife in 1878. Samuel is the fifth son born to his parents. His early life was spent on the farm and in the common schools. At the age of sixteen he engaged in steamboating, and has been for twenty years captain and pilot. He was married in 1872, to Havanna, daughter of Mathew Wilson, of Hopewell township. Five children are the result of this union: Frederick E., Edith, Mathew W., Clarence E., and Myrtle G. Mr. Erwin has been for a number of years in the employ of William H. Brown's Sons, of Pittsburgh. He is a F. & A. M., a member of the I. O. O. F., and the Methodist church. Politically he is a Democrat.

THOMAS G. EVANS, steamboat pilot, P. O. Rochester, was born in Bridgewater, Pa., March 24, 1836. His parents, George and Letitia (Scott) Evans, were natives of Pennsylvania, of Welsh and Irish descent, and members of the Society of Friends. George Evans was a captain and a pilot on the Ohio river, was the owner of fleet boats, and was the first to pilot a stern wheel boat down the Ohio. He had two sons and three daughters. Thomas G., the youngest son, was reared in this county. His education was obtained at the common schools, and early in life he went on the river with his father. He served three years and was then appointed pilot. In 1861 he enlisted in the 10th Pennsylvania Reserves. Col. M. S. Quay, now United States senator, was the first lieutenant. Mr. Evans was wounded at the battle of Gaines' Mill, July 2, 1862, and still carries the ball in his arm. He was a non-commisssoned officer and was discharged in 1863. He participated in several battles, including what is known in history as the Seven Days' Fight. He is a member of Rochester Post, No. 183, G. A. R. Since the war he has been engaged at piloting, and also owns a one-half interest in the extensive livery stable of Evans & Reno. They keep eleven head of horses and a good supply of carriages. Mr. Evans is a member of the I. O. O. F. of Rochester.

RAWDON EVANS, New Brighton, was born in New Brighton Oct. 14, 1845. His father, Ross B. Evans, a native of Utica, N. Y., was by occupation a harness manufacturer and shoemaker. He married Mary, daughter of Hiram Gillmore, of Queen Anne's county, Md., to whom were born three sons and two daughters, Rawdon being the youngest son. This family originally came from Wales and located in Connecticut, coming to Beaver county in 1831. Rawdon was a student at the Normal School until he was fourteen years of age, and was employed for two years as messenger boy by the Ohio & Pennsylvania Railway Company. After that he learned the machinist's trade, serving a full apprenticeship, and was employed as locomotive fireman and engineer for several railroads. In 1868 he was chief engineer for the Beaver Falls Cutlery Works, a position he continued to hold for two years. From 1870 to 1876 he was general supply and Division passenger agent for the Baltimore & Ohio Railroad Company. with headquarters at Pittsburgh. Leaving the service of that road in 1876, Mr. Evans continued in the railroad business for different roads until 1880, when he entered the service of the Pittsburg & Lake Erie Railway Company, and from that time up to the present has held various prominent positions, being now engaged as assistant to the general superintendent and purchasing agent. Mr. Evans was married, in 1868, to Lois, daughter of John Tintsman, of Westmoreland county, Pa. He is a member of the Episcopal church of New Brighton; a F. & A. M.; in politics a Republican.

JAMES FEZELL, farmer, P. O. Brush Creek, was born in Beaver county, Feb. 13, 1812. His parents, John and Jane (Stewart) Fezell, were natives of Washington county, Pa., and after marriage settled in Beaver county, where they died. They had nine children, six of whom are living, James being the eldest. He was married, in January,

1843, to Sarah Goehring, who was born in Butler county, Pa., Sept. 4, 1817, a daughter of Adam and Mary Goehring, who died in Butler county. After his first marriage Mr. Fezell settled on the farm where he now resides. He has had ten children, of whom seven are living: William H., John C., James T., Mary J., Matilda, Sarah H. and Charles F. Those deceased are George W., Emma A. and Elmer. Mr. Fezell has been a farmer all his life, and owns about 250 acres of land. He and his wife are members of the Baptist church.

JOHN FERGUSON (deceased) was born April 1, 1814, on the farm where he died. He was a son of John and Elizabeth (Brandeth) Ferguson, the former born near Coleraine, Ireland, and the latter in New Jersey. They had four sons and one daughter. The father, who was a farmer, came to North Sewickley township in 1809, and bought the farm on which his son John always lived, now comprising 150 acres. John was married, in 1848, to Janiza Elliott, born in Allegheny county, Pa., and who, at the age of twelve years, came with her parents to Beaver county. To Mr. and Mrs. Ferguson were born five children: Agnes, wife of Henry Sloan, in New Brighton; Sarah Jane, in Beaver Falls; Mary E., wife of Abram Berry; John F. and Thomas B. Mr. Ferguson served as school director three years and supervisor one year. He was a member of the Methodist church, to which his widow also belongs; politically a Republican.

THOMAS FERGUSON, farmer, P. O. New Brighton, was born in Pulaski township in 1822. His father, James, came from County Antrim, Ireland, about 1797, locating in Beaver county, where he purchased 500 acres of land and died at the age of eighty-six years. His wife was Catherine Beer, who bore him nine children. Thomas, the second son, received a common-school education. His father left him 150 acres of land, which was part of the original 500 acres. Thomas has purchased 100 acres more, and now owns 250 acres of as good land as there is in Pulaski township. He married, in 1848, Eliza Ann, daughter of Robert Jackson, of this county, and ten children have been born to them: Emmet, Mary Jane (Mrs. Longenecker), James M., Thomas B., Ann (Mrs. Thomas), Norman, Courtney, Charley, Kate and Bertha Grant. Three of these sons are now engaged in farming in Washington Territory. Mr. Ferguson has retired from active work, but still superintends the farming. He has spent some part of his life traveling through the states of Ohio, Indiana, Missouri, Illinois, Colorado and Iowa. He is a member of the Methodist church; in politics a Republican.

WILLIAM FISH, stone-mason and contractor, P. O. New Brighton, was born in England in 1836, and came with his parents, James and Ann Fish, to New Jersey in 1839. He was educated in the common schools and academy, and at the age of seventeen was employed as a clerk in a country store, an occupation which he followed two years. After that he engaged with his father in stone-mason and contracting work. He married, in 1875, Mina, daughter of Lewis Friday, of Lawrence county, Pa. They have four children: Jennie, at home, Edward, Henry and William. Mr. Fish and his brother own extensive and valuable stone quarries, and are now engaged in contracting. He is also engaged in farming. He passed three months in the Civil War in Company C, 6th Regiment. He is a Republican.

LEVI FISH, stone contractor, New Brighton, is a native of England, born in 1837, fourth son in the family of eight children of James and Ann (Brindle) Fish, who came to these shores with their family in 1839. James Fish was a stone contractor, and located in New Jersey, where he remained until 1848, then moved to this county. Levi received a good public-school training, and since the age of eighteen he has been engaged, more or less extensively, in his present business, owning large quarries of valuable building stone, also in manufacturing brick and farming, giving employment to from twenty-five to fifty hands. He was united in marriage, in 1860, with E. E., daughter of John Hays, of this county, and by her had five children, four yet living: James C., Nellie I., John M. and Thomas M. Mr. Fish served one term (from 1878) as county commissioner, and has been school director. He is a F. & A. M., and a member of the A. O. U. W.; holds membership in the Methodist Protestant church, of the Sunday school of which he is superintendent. In politics he is a Republican.

BIOGRAPHIES—EAST SIDE. 769

ROBERT FISHER, farmer, P. O. Brush Creek, was born in Beaver county, Sept. 16, 1844. His parents, Thomas and Eliza (Bradley) Fisher, were natives of Pennsylvania, and settled in Beaver county. Thomas died in 1876 ; his widow is still living, and makes her home with her children. Robert was married, Sept. 24, 1868, to Eliza, daughter of James and Isabella Gray, both deceased. She was born in Allegheny county in 1846, and is the mother of two children: Dollie E. (born July 20, 1869) and Lillie B. (born July 30, 1876). Mr. Fisher was reared on the farm where he and his family reside, and has been engaged in farming all his life. In politics he is a Democrat; he holds the office of school director.

ADAM FLINNER, farmer, P. O. New Brighton, was born in Jackson township, Butler county, Pa., in 1851. His parents, John and Eve (Miller) Flinner, natives of Germany, now reside in Butler county. Mr. Flinner was born and reared on the farm, and received a good common-school education. He was married, in 1873, to Mary, daughter of Casper Schaffer, of Beaver county. They have seven children: Henry J., Frank E., Clara Emma, John, Harry George, Ira Arthur and Ada Pearl. Mr. Flinner purchased his present farm of fifty-seven acres in 1874. He has since that time made great improvements in the way of buildings. He is a member of St. John's church of New Sewickley township; in politics he is a Democrat.

CAPT. SAMUEL FOWLER, pilot, Baden, was born in Pittsburgh, Pa.. (South Side), in 1849. Capt. Thomas W., his father, was born in Mahoning county, Pa., in 1813, and died in 1882. He married Sarah Ann Vanhook, and by her had three sons and four daughters, of whom Samuel is the second son. Thomas was a ship carpenter, which trade he followed for a number of years, after which he was a captain on the Ohio river for thirty-five years, and lived nearly all his life in Birmingham, now known as South Side, Pittsburgh, Pa. Samuel left Allegheny county with his people when he was ten years of age, and has lived nearly ever since that age in Beaver county. He was educated at the common schools, and was a student at Duff's college for eight months. He has followed steamboat piloting for eighteen years. He was married, in 1871, to Mattie J., daughter of Capt. John McDonald, of Hopewell township. Three children have been born to this union: Pearl E., Edwin Vanhook and Thomas Quay. Mr. Fowler now lives in the town of Baden, Pa., and is captain and pilot of steamboats plying between Pittsburgh and Louisville, Ky. He and his wife are members of the Methodist church. Politically he is a Republican.

JOHN FRESHCORN, farmer, P. O. Knob, was born in Germany Dec. 27, 1831. His parents, Daniel and Catherine Freshcorn, immigrated to America about 1837, and settled in New Sewickley township, where they died. John was married March 31, 1855, to Caroline Mink, who was born in Pittsburgh July 18, 1837. Her parents, John and Catherine Mink, natives of Germany, were married in their native country, came to America about 1834, and settled in Pittsburgh, where they remained about ten years; then moved to New Sewickley township, where they died. Mr. and Mrs. Freshcorn are the parents of twelve children: Mary, Caroline, William, Lewis J., Henry N., Katie A., Lizzie A., Jacob J., Tillie E., George A., Harvey W. and B. Frank. Mr. Freshcorn has been engaged in farming all his life, and owns about 130 acres. He and his wife are members of the German Reformed church. He has filled the offices of supervisor and school director.

MICHAEL FRESHCORN, farmer, P. O. Knob, was born in Beaver county May 10, 1837. His parents, Daniel and Catherine Freshcorn, came from Germany and settled in Beaver county, where they remained until their deaths. Michael was married, Aug. 9, 1858, to Amelia, daughter of William and Elizabeth Graham, who died in Butler county. Mrs. Freshcorn was born Nov. 17, 1841, and is the mother of thirteen children, ten of whom are living: John, Sarah J., William F., Hulda J., Henry N., Charlie F., Joseph M., Mary E., James L. and Lillie M. Mr. Freshcorn has been a farmer all his life and owns 110 acres of improved land. He and his wife are members of the German Reformed church. In politics he is a Democrat.

WILLIAM FRESHCORN, farmer, P. O. Knob, was born in Germany Sept. 20, 1835, son of Daniel and Eva C. Freshcorn, who came to America in 1837 and settled in Beaver county, where they died. William was married, Dec. 26, 1860, to Sarah, daughter of John and Fannie Deemer, who died in Butler county. Mrs. Freshcorn was born in Beaver county July 1, 1832, and is the mother of six children, five of whom are living: Edwin R., Andrew C., Anna J., Addie L. and Harry L. A daughter, Lizzie A., is deceased. They have also an adopted child, Nellie M. Mr. Freshcorn owns about 156 acres of land. He and his wife are members of the Lutheran church.

J. G. FRIEDERICK, saddler, New Brighton, was born in Butler county, Pa., in 1853, to Fredrick and Elizabeth Barber (Diehl) Friederick. He is the third son of ten children, was reared on the farm and received a common-school education. He was married, in 1878, to Mary, daughter of William Thomson, of this county, and three children have been born to them: Lewis Wilber, Edith Amelia and Blanche Elizabeth. Mr. Friederick came to New Brighton in 1869, and was engaged in various employments, until 1877, when he took up his present occupation. He has now one of the finest stores in the town. In politics he is a Republican.

HENRY C. FRY. Two brothers, John and William Fry, emigrated from Dublin, Ireland, after the close of the Revolutionary War, and landed in New York, of whom William was the paternal grandfather of the subject of this biography. They were educated young men and descended from a well-to-do and highly respectable family of tradesmen. Both were married, and while tarrying in New York a son was born to William and christened Thomas C., who became the father of Henry C. Fry. The other children of William Fry were William and Eliza. The brothers above mentioned settled in Wilkesbarre, Pa., and became prosperous in business. The children of William were left orphans at an early age, the eldest two removed to Cadiz, Ohio, where they died at an advanced age, highly esteemed by all who knew them. Thomas C., the younger settled in Washington county, Pa., married there, became deputy sheriff of the county, and later removed to Pittsburgh, were he was actively engaged in the glass business, in the still remembered firm of Curling Robinson & Co. John Fry, the elder, lost his wife about the year 1800, and was afterward married to Elizabeth Miller, a Scotch lady, in 1803. Their only child, Charlotte, born in 1806, became a woman of much personal beauty and charm of character, and was the mother of the subject of this sketch. John Fry soon after that event moved to Lexington, Ky., and, possessing ample means, purchased an extensive tract and erected an attractive home near that city. His estate included a part of the present city of Lexington and the cemetery, where repose the remains of the distinguished statesman, Henry Clay, of whom Mr. Fry was a warm friend and political supporter. Both Mr. and Mrs. Fry lived honored and beloved in their Kentucky home until their deaths, and are buried side by side in the Lexington Cemetery in sight of the beautiful home, which still remains in possession of the family. Mr. Fry, whose death occurred in 1835, was interred with Masonic honors. In 1837, Thomas C. Fry married his cousin, Charlotte, then a widow with one child. Their eldest son, Henry C. Fry, was born Sept. 1, 1840, near Lexington, Ky., and received in his native town a common-school education. In April, 1857, being desirous for a more extended field of activity than was opened to him at home, he repaired to Pittsburgh, being well fortified with introductory letters from his father to former Pittsburgh friends. Here he entered the glass manufacturing works of William Phillips & Co., as assistant shipping and time clerk, and remained until 1862, having filled the various positions in the works, preliminary to those of manager and head salesman. In August, 1862, leaving his business, he enlisted as a private in the 15th Regiment, Pennsylvania Cavalry, and served until mustered out in 1864, having participated in all the engagements of the army of the Cumberland. Returning to Pittsburgh he embarked in the manufacture of glass under the firm name of Lippencott, Fry & Co., who were succeeded by Fry & Scott, and they by Fry, Semple & Reynolds. Retiring from the last named firm in 1869, he accepted a lucrative position as general manager of the business of James B. Lyon & Co., of Pittsburgh, and conducted this establishment with great success. In 1872 Mr. Fry removed to Rochester, and organized the Rochester

Tumbler Co., meantime superintending personally the entire construction of the works, of which he has since been the president, undoubtedly the largest of their kind in the world. Tumblers are made a specialty; five hundred men are employed, and a product valued at $500,000 is disposed of annually, a market for which is found in all parts of the world. Mr. Fry was, in the spring of 1883, the principal factor in the organization of the First National Bank of Rochester, and has been since that time its president. He was also one of the projectors, and is a prominent director of the Bridgewater Gas Company. Mr. Fry was married, in 1862, to Miss Emma Matthews, of Pittsburgh, and their children are Harry C., Gertrude E., Clara B., Jesse Howard and Mabel M. The death of Mrs. Fry, a lady possessing many attractive qualities of mind and heart which rendered her greatly beloved, occurred in 1884. Mr. Fry is an active member of of the First Baptist church of Rochester, and has been since its organization superintendent of the Sunday-school.

C. T. GALE, physician, New Brighton, is a native of Washington county, Ohio, born in 1850, eighth in the family of twelve children of Dr. G. W. and Catherine A. (Wells) Gale, of Newport, Ohio. He was educated at the public schools and St. Thomas Seminary, after which he commenced the study of medicine under his father in 1870; entered Jefferson Medical College, Philadelphia, in 1876, and was graduated in 1878. He commenced the practice of his profession in 1878 at Parkersburg, W. Va., and in 1880 moved to New Brighton. He married, in 1879, Lucy L., daughter of Hon. James M. Stephenson of Parkersburg, W. Va. Dr. Gale is a member of the Roman Catholic church; politically he is a Democrat.

T. F. GALEY, superintendent of the Bridgewater Gas Company, P. O. Rochester, was born in Clarion county, Pa., of German and Irish parentage. His father was a farmer and oil producer, and his family consisted of eight sons and two daughters. T. F., the second child, attended the public schools and the high school in Clarion county. His first business was dealing in sheep, but later he embarked in oil producing in Venango county, where he met with marked success. In 1885 he was induced to accept the very important trust of superintendent of the Bridgewater Gas Company, of which Judge Henry Hice is president. Mr. Galey takes an active interest in schools, and served three years as school director in Clarion county. He was married in Warren, Ohio, in 1871, to Olive, a daughter of David Yingling, and a native of Clarion county, Pa., of German origin. They have two children: Jessie A. and Clara. Mr. and Mrs. Galey are members of the Methodist church. He is a F. & A. M.; politically a Democrat.

A. D. GILLILAND, dealer in dry goods, New Brighton, was born in 1838, in Darlington township, this county, the third of ten children born to Samuel and Lois (Dunlap) Gilliland, the former of whom followed farming all his life. The paternal grandfather, William Gilliland, also a farmer, emigrated from Londonderry, Ireland, in 1829. A. D. was reared on the farm where he was born, and between the ages of twelve and fifteen attended the high school. In 1852 he commenced the dry goods business, in which he has ever since been actively engaged. He was married, in 1861, to Emma, daughter of Charles M. Stewart, of New Brighton, and by her he has five children: Charles A., Carrie A., Louis A., Laura B. and May Ella. Mr. Gilliland is a member of the United Presbyterian church; politically a Republican.

JOHN GODARD, retired, New Brighton, was born in Beaver county, Pa., in 1822, the eldest son in the family of fourteen children of James and Mary (Godard) Godard, the latter a daughter of John Godard, of Kentucky. James Godard was a son of James and Elizabeth (Dawson) Godard, the former a revolutionary soldier. John attended the common schools and was reared on a farm, where he remained until twenty-two years of age. For fifteen years he was engaged in the coal business, and later for six years carried on merchandising, but since coming to New Brighton has lived retired. In 1847 he married Elizabeth, daughter of Samuel and Margaret Elliott, of Lancaster county, Pa., and four children have blessed them: Rebecca (Mrs. Stratton), Mary Virginia (Mrs. Ryan), Laura (Mrs. Dr. Jordan) and Edith (Mrs. Braden). Mr. Godard has been a member of the town council, tax collector and assessor twelve years, besides holding other offices of trust. He has been affiliated with the I. O. O. F. for thirty years; is a member of the Presbyterian church; in politics a Republican.

CHRISTIAN H. GOEHRING, farmer, P. O. Freedom, was born in Butler county, March 20, 1834. His parents, Christian and Elizabeth Goehring, came from Germany and settled in Butler county, Pa., where the father died. The mother is still living, and is the wife of William Fahl. Christian H. married, April 10, 1857, Margaret Metz, who was born in New Sewickley township, Beaver county, Pa., in January, 1836. Her parents, George and Christina Metz, immigrated to America and settled in Beaver county, where they died. Mr. and Mrs. Goehring have had eight children, of whom five are living: Adam, Elizabeth, Charles, William and Henry. The deceased are Tillie, Emma and an infant. Mr. Goehring has been engaged in farming all his life and owns fifty acres of improved land. When the war broke out he enlisted in Company D, 2d Pa. Heavy Artillery, and was wounded in front of Petersburg, June 17, 1864. He and Mrs. Goehring are members of the English-Lutheran church. He has filled the offices of supervisor and assessor, and has been collector three times.

JOHN GOEHRING, farmer, was born Dec. 20, 1846, in New Sewickley township, a son of William and Magdalena (Dambacker) Goehring, natives of Germany. His grandfather, John Goehring, settled in New Sewickley township about seventy years ago. Our subject received his schooling in Marion township, and at twenty-three years of age began farming with his father, who died Dec. 16, 1872. He was married, May 3, 1870, to Caroline Pflug, who was born Feb. 20, 1849. Six children have blessed this union, viz.: William Henry, now at school at Edinburgh, Pa.; Emma M , Henry Daniel, Charles John, Gilbert Jacob and Harvey L. Mr. and Mrs. Goehring are members of St. John's church in New Sewickley.

ZENO GOEHRING, farmer, P. O. Zelienople, Butler county, Pa., was born in New Sewickley township, July 9, 1861, a son of Henry and Sophia Goehring, the former a native of Pennsylvania and the latter of Germany. Henry Goehring died in this county, Aug. 18, 1884, and his widow resides in Butler county. Zeno was married, Sept. 21, 1882, to Amelia Ruby, who was born in Butler county, Jan. 8, 1863, and is a daughter of Andrew and Catherine Ruby, the former a native of Pennsylvania and the latter born in Germany. Andrew Ruby died in 1879 ; his widow is still living. Mr. and Mrs. Goehring have two children: Alma H., born Jan. 9, 1884, and Harvey J., born Dec. 21, 1885. Mr. Goehring owns 100 acres of improved land, and is a successful farmer. He and his wife are members of the English Lutheran church. In politics he is a Republican. He is a member of the Junior Order United American Mechanics.

MARCUS T. C. GOULD. This distinguished gentleman was born at Rome, N. Y., in 1792. He was educated in an academy in his native state, graduating at the age of eighteen, and delivering the leading oration on the occasion. For a time he engaged in business in New York, but, failing, he went to Philadelphia and began the publication of certain works for the Friends or Quakers. He published for them a paper called '' The Friend or Advocate of Truth,' which had an extensive circulation. Some difficulties arising in the denomination, he came westward in 1831, and stopped for a time at Steubenville, Ohio, to report the sermons of Elias Hicks, the founder of the branch of the Quakers usually called the Hicksites. On his return to Philadelphia, he was charmed with the beauty and grandeur of Beaver Valley and its superior advantages for manufacturing purposes. This was in 1832. He at once closed his business in Philadelphia, and gave the energies of his ardent soul to the building up of the valley. Being a cousin of Zachary Taylor, he was induced to go to Kentucky to aid in the sale of some real estate. For a time he was very successful, but the prevalence of cholera in that region broke up his resort, and he returned to Beaver Valley. He established a Boys' School in New Brighton, and was successful in arousing an educational interest. Not in the educational field did he achieve most fame. The best energies of his life were given to the development of the material resources of the valley. Unselfishly he labored for the interests of others, content to see his efforts successful though he did

BIOGRAPHIES—EAST SIDE. 773

not share the fruits thereof. Like General Lacock, Mr. Gould predicted the building of railroads along the valley. Though regarded visionary at the time, his predictions were fully realized, and his children are permitted to see the steam horse speeding by on either side of Big Beaver. His greatest project, perhaps, was the effort to consolidate and build up a large city at the mouth of Big Beaver, to be known as Beaver City, and to embrace all the towns within a radius of five or six miles. His hopes may yet be realized. Mr. Gould was a keen writer and a vigorous, fascinating talker, who readily enlisted his audience in his enterprises. He was a superior short-hand reporter, and frequently was called upon to take down the speeches of Webster, Clay and other distinguished orators. He had two children, both daughters, one of whom, Mrs. Harvey Mendenhall, is still a resident of New Brighton, where Mr. Gould resided the greater part of his Pennsylvania life. He died in Rochester in 'October, 1860, just after the state election; his wife in 1872.

DAVID A. GRAHAM, farmer, P. O. New Brighton, was born in North Sewickley township Feb. 9, 1857, and is a son of David and Sarah (Moffit) Graham, natives of Pennsylvania, the latter of Irish origin. David was born in 1807, was reared on the farm where David A. now lives, and had a family of eight children, seven now living: Mary, wife of Henry Fink, of Rochester; Thomas W., a merchant in Braddock, Pa.; William Nelson; Sarah, wife of Neil Love, in Pittsburgh; Agnes, wife of Charles C. Wilson, in Lawrence county, Pa.; David A., and Emmett, a merchant in New Brighton. David A. was educated in the common schools and began life as a carriage painter, a business he followed two years; he then took up farming and now owns 110 acres. He married, in 1879, Mrs. Caroline (Snyder) Bunzo, a widow, whose first husband, Andrew Bunzo, of French descent, died in 1875, leaving one child, Anda Ella. Mrs. Graham is a daughter of John Snyder, of German origin, who came to this county when young; his wife was Anna Eliza Bolland, also of German birth, who came to this country when eighteen years of age. Mr. and Mrs. Graham have one child, Edna Idelletta. They are members of the United Presbyterian church. In politics he is a Republican.

WILLIAMSON GRAHAM, ex-postmaster of Rochester, Pa., was born in Phillipsburg, Pa., Nov. 25, 1839, and is a son of Capt. Avery W. and Margaret (Moore) Graham, natives of Beaver county, and of English and Irish descent. His father was a captain and pilot on the river, which business he followed during many years. He was a staunch Republican and a good citizen. Williamson is the eldest of six children. He was reared in Beaver county, was educated in the English branches in the common and select schools, and was two years under the instruction of the late Rev. Dr. Winter. Early in life he learned from his father the river business, and studied mechanical engineering. At the age of nineteen he became chief engineer of the steamboat "Princeton" and afterward of the "Porter." In April, 1861, he enlisted in the "Curtin Rifles," and served his country valiantly during the War of the Rebellion, passing through the battles of Drainsville, the seven days' fight on the Peninsula, second Bull Run, South Mountain, Antietam and Fredericksburg. After two years of faithful service he was honorably discharged for disability. He recovered his health, in a measure, and during several years was engaged on the river. In April, 1864, he married Philie M., youngest daughter of William and Sophia (Evans) Reno, of French and English descent They were among the pioneers of this region. Her grandfather, Rev. Francis Reno, was the first ordained Episcopal clergyman west of the Allegheny Mountains. Her mother was the daughter of Eli Evans, an early settler here. Her father built and commanded the first steamboat on the Western rivers. Mr. Graham became a member of the Methodist Episcopal church in Bridgewater, in 1865. His wife had been a member of the same church from the age of twelve. In 1867, when the Rochester M.E. church was organized, both were constituent members. They have been active members, and Mr. Graham has, from time to time, filled positions of trust and responsibility in the society. Both he and his wife have been active workers in the Sunday-school. He has filled all the chairs in the lodge and encampment of the I. O. O. F., he is a member of the A. O. U. W., and an ex-post commander in the G. A. R. He has been a life-long Republican, and a strict temperance man. In 1874 he invented, and patented, an excellent strainer for starch, fruits, etc. He was made postmaster of Rochester in 1877, and held the office by successive reäppointments till 1887. During his administration he did much to promote the efficiency of the postal service in Rochester, though at a sacrifice, to some extent, of his pecuniary interest. From the first his wife was his able assistant. He has always been genial, courteous and kind, and has never incurred the suspicion of compromising principle for expediency. He is now engaged in the insurance business.

FRANCIS M. GRIM, postmaster at Freedom. was born in Glasgow, this county, Aug. 5, 1846, and is the third son of Charles and Catherine S. (Wiseman) Grim, both natives of Pennsylvania, and of German descent. After they were married in Freedom, Pa., they settled and remained in Beaver county until 1855, then moved to Augusta, Ga., and resided for five years. They returned to Beaver county, where Charles remained until 1879; then removed to Pittsburgh, where he died in 1879. His widow resides in Freedom. They had thirteen children, eight living. Francis M. was married, Nov. 4, 1868, to Maggie J. Davis, who was born in Allegheny county Feb. 7, 1850, a daughter of Basil W. and Margaret J. Davis. To Mr. and Mrs. Grim have been born six children, four living: Lillie B., M. Pearl, Alberta F. and Francis M. Those deceased are Maggie L. and Lizzie M. Mr. Grim is a steamboat builder by trade. In 1864 he enlisted and entered the ranks for his country in Company F, 140th regiment, under Capt. Thomas Henry. On the 18th of June he was wounded by a Minie ball in front of Petersburg, causing the loss of his left leg near the hip joint. He was then sent to the hospital in Philadelphia, from there transferred to the Pittsburgh hospital, and discharged March 16, 1865. July 12, 1865, before the wound was healed, he had to have a second operation performed. After coming out of the army he taught school for a short time, then began making cigars, which he followed until his appointment as postmaster of Freedom borough March 1, 1886. He and Mrs. Grim are members of the Methodist Episcopal church; he is a member of the G. A. R.; in politics a Democrat.

WILLIAM H. GROSSMAN, farmer, P. O. Rochester, was born in Beaver county in 1838. His father, John Grossman, came from Germany about 1833 and purchased thirty-five acres of land in this county. He married Ziporah Stiles, by whom were born two children. William H., the youngest, was born and reared on a farm, where he has always remained, and now owns 125 acres of land, most of which is under cultivation. He was married in 1859 to Christena, daughter of Thomas Elliott, from Washington county, Pa. Six children have been born to them, four of whom are living: Emily A., John S., Nettie W. and W. H. Mr. Grossman has been engaged in steamboating. He has been school director for several terms. He is a Democrat, and has been auditor of the township eighteen years.

MICHAEL GUTERMUTH, farmer, P. O. Brush Creek, was born in Germany, Feb. 24, 1831. His parents, Nicholas and Anna A. Gutermuth, emigrated to America in 1833, and settled in New Sewickley township, where the mother died many years ago, and the father was afterward married to Caroline Deitrich. Michael was united in marriage, Oct. 12, 1856, with Sarah Deitrich. She was born in Beaver county, Pa., March 24, 1836, and is a daughter of Frederick and Dollie Deitrich, both deceased. Mr. and Mrs. Gutermuth are the parents of eight children, seven living: Nicholas. Frederick, Anna, Mary, John, Joseph and George; William is deceased. Mr. Gutermuth has been engaged in farming all his life. He and his wife are members of St. John's church. In politics he is a Democrat.

P. D. HALL, retired, New Brighton, was born in Pittsburgh in 1832, the only child of Alexander and Mary A. (Devenny) Hall (both deceased), who came to Beaver county in 1831. The father came from Ireland, and carried on silk manufacturing east of the Alleghanies. When nineteen years of age, P. D. commenced railroading, which he followed for thirty-three years in the employ of the same company, part of the time in charge of their freight department at Pittsburgh. In 1885 he retired from active life, and purchased his present home in New Brighton. Mr. Hall was united in marriage, in 1866, with Mrs. E. C. Bonbright. He is a F. & A. M.; politically a Republican.

O. J. HAMILTON, ship builder, Freedom, was born in Beaver county, April 4, 1825, a son of James and Elizabeth Hamilton, natives of Beaver county, where they resided all their lives. Mrs. Elizabeth Hamilton died May 7, 1866, and her husband Oct. 12, 1870. They were the parents of ten children, five living. O. J. was united in marriage March 1, 1849, with Lovina Manor, who was born in Beaver county, Sept. 29, 1820, a daughter of James Manor (deceased). Mr. and Mrs. Hamilton had four children, only one of whom is living, James O. The deceased are Deloss, Adam L. and Nancy J. Mrs. Hamilton died Aug. 15, 1855. Jan. 5, 1857, Mr. Hamilton married Mary J. Calvert, who was born in Allegheny county, July 13, 1827, a daughter of James Calvert (deceased). To this union seven children have been born, of whom six are living: John C., William D., Milo J., Frank S., Alexander O. and Thomas A. Lizzie L. is deceased. Mr. Hamilton learned the trade of ship carpenter, and has followed that and house building since 1849. He and his wife are members of the Methodist Episcopal church, and have lived in Freedom since 1852.

A. HANAUER, millinery, New Brighton, was born in Würtemberg, Germany, in 1841. His parents, Sampson and Fannie Hanauer, had a family of four sons and two daughters, of whom our subject is the eldest. Sampson Hanauer was a merchant and farmer. A. Hanauer was educated at the public schools, and at the age of fourteen came to America. Soon after his arrival he located in Rochester, N. Y., where he carried on the millinery business for nine years. He came to New Brighton in 1867, where he has since remained. In 1884 he started a branch establishment at Beaver Falls, which has grown to great proportions. He was married in 1865, to Hannah, daughter of Raphael Steinfield, of this county, and two sons have been born to them, Sampson and Raphael, both living. Mr. Hanauer is a member of the I. O. O. F. and K. of P. He is of the Jewish faith; politically a Democrat.

WILLIAM G. HARKER, manufacturer, P. O. New Brighton, was born in this county in 1851. His parents, William and Mary A. (Peatling) Harker, had seven children, William G. being the eldest son. He was born and reared on the farm, received a common-school education, and at the age of eighteen years learned the trade of a moulder, which he has since followed. He married in 1875, Irene, daughter of Joseph and Isabella (Sillaman) Wilson, and to them have been born three children, only one of whom is living, Herbert Clyde. For eight years previous to engaging in his present business, Mr. Harker was employed by the Beaver Falls Car Works Company in the capacity of foreman. In 1883 the present firm, Novelty Works, Knott, Harker & Co., Limited, was established. The business is yearly increasing and to-day ranks first of its kind in the county. The concern is known as the "Beaver Falls Novelty Works". Mr. Harker is a member of the K. of P.; politically he is a Republican.

JOHN C. HART, furniture dealer and undertaker, P. O. New Brighton, was born in Butler county, Pa., in 1840, the elder of the two children of John and Nancy (Nixon) Hart. He was reared on the farm where he was born, until his eighth year, when he came with his mother to Beaver county, and here remained, receiving a common-school education, till 1861, in which year, August 28, he enlisted in Company D, 100th Regiment, P. V. He served three years and eleven months, and participated in the following named battles: Secessionville, Second Bull Run, Chantilly, South Mountain, Antietam, Fredericksburg, siege of Vicksburg, Blue Springs, Campbell's Station, siege of Knoxville, Wilderness, Spottsylvania Court House, North Anna River, Cold Harbor, at Petersburg, June 17th, July 30th (mine explosion), Aug. 19th, Aug. 21st, and Oct. 27th, the general siege of Petersburg and the battle of Fort Steadman, 1865. Mr. Hart was married, May 24, 1870, to Sarah, daughter of William Johnson, of Mahoning county, Ohio, and to this union were born four children, only one of whom, Frank Donald, is living. Our subject was elected clerk of the court of Beaver county in 1869, serving until 1879, having been elected for three successive terms. He is a member of the A. O. U. W., I. O. O. F., K. of P., G. A. R. and U. V. L. In politics he is a Republican.

JOHN HARTZELL, farmer, was born in Marion township, in 1818, a son of George and Catherine (Krohn) Hartzell, of Eastern Pennsylvania. He bought a part of his present farm in 1841, and his father also gave him a part. He married, in 1839, Dorathea Knauff, who was born in Germany in 1821, a daughter of Michael and Margaret Knauff. Mrs. Hartzell died in 1869, the mother of nine children, as follows: George, in Butler county; Michael, in Lawrence county; John, in Marion towrship; Henry and William Andrew, in the furniture business in Rochester; Herman, in Marion township; Jacob, who conducts his father's farm; Catherine, married to Frederick Wolf (now deceased), and Margaret, wife of Henry Keterrer, of Marion township. Mr. Hartzell is a member of the German United Presbyterian church, and has held several township offices. His son, Jacob, was born in 1858, and Sept. 29, 1881, married Catherine, daughter of John and Catherine Beuller, natives of Germany. She was born 1856, and died Oct. 21, 1887, the mother of three children: Alma, Edna and Effie.

HERMAN HARTZELL, farmer, was born March 25, 1851, on the farm of his father, John Hartzell, in Marion township. He married, in 1876, Elizabeth Kaufman, who was born in 1857, in New Sewickley township, a daughter of Austin and Mary Freshcorn, natives of Germany. Four children have been born to them, as follows: Agnes Matilda, Birdie M., Amanda, and Mollie (who died in August, 1883). Mr. and Mrs. Hartzell are members of St. John's church.

ALBERT G. HARVEY, grocer, New Brighton, was born in Butler county, Pa., in 1846, eldest son of Andrew (a carpenter) and Margaret (Glass) Harvey, parents of eleven children. The Harveys came originally from Ireland. Albert G. received a commonschool education, and at the age of fourteen commenced the battle of life. After trying various occupations he finally served a three years' apprenticeship to the machinist's trade, which he followed nineteen years. In 1864 he enlisted in Company B, 5th Heavy Artillery, and served until the close of the war. Mr. Harvey married, in 1869, Caroline, daughter of William Boswell, of New Brighton, and seven children were born to them, six yet living: Wilbur, Edward, Fred Lewis, Hattie, Howard and Walter. In 1885 Mr. Harvey formed a partnership with Frank A. Boswell, under the firm name of Boswell & Harvey, in their present grocery business at New Brighton. Mr. Harvey is a member of the G. A. R.; in politics a Republican.

JAMES HASTINGS, merchant, P. O. Freedom, was born in Allegheny county, Pa., Sept. 8, 1845, and is a son of Nasbet and Mary (Meredith) Hastings, who were natives of Pennsylvania and were married in Allegheny county. After marriage they lived in that county for a time, then moved to West Virginia and from there to Ohio, and finally returned to Allegheny City, where they now reside. James Hastings was united in marriage July 10, 1869, with Sarah J., daughter of Richard and Nancy A. Holsinger, natives of Pennsylvania (both deceased). She was born in Allegheny county, June 2, 1852, and is the mother of seven children: Amanda, Frank, Nannie, Walter, Perlie, Myrtle and Fred J. After marriage Mr. Hastings settled in St. Clair borough, where he has remained ever since. He was engaged in quarrying stone for about twenty years. In 1884 he established his present business in St. Clair. He owns five houses and lots in the borough, and has filled several borough offices.

ISAAC HAZEN, farmer, P. O. North Sewickley, is a son of James and Jerusha (Runyan) Hazen, natives of New Jersey, who came to Beaver county at an early day and settled in North Sewickley township; but since the division of the township they have been in Franklin. They had thirteen children, eight yet living: James, Ann (widow of Hugh Thompson), Isaac, Jeremiah, Maria (widow of Hugh Bennett), Amariah, Loring and Absalom. The father was a gunsmith, a trade he followed through life, at the same time superintending his farm. Isaac was married, in 1843, to Mary Jane, daughter of Mathew Kelly, and five children have blessed them: Mathew (deceased), Rachel, wife of John Rosenberg, in West Virginia; Jerusha Ann (deceased), James and Adoniron. The mother died in 1854, and Mr. Hazen afterward married Mary, daughter of Isaac Eolinger, a native of Armstrong county, Pa. By this union there were eight children: John P. (deceased), Amariah, William R., Laura (wife of Samuel Thompson), Jennetta,

Violetta, Elizabeth and Howard. Mathew, the eldest son by the first wife, was a soldier in the Civil War, serving in Company H, 101st Regiment P. V.; he was taken prisoner at Plymouth, N. C., and died in Andersonville prison. Mr. Hazen was reared, educated and has continually resided in North Sewickley township. He has been judge of election one term. In politics he is a Democrat. He and his wife are members of the Baptist church.

NATHANIEL W. HAZEN, farmer, P. O. North Sewickley, was born Dec. 5, 1816, in Franklin township, the eldest son of Samuel and Eliza (McDannel) Hazen, who were born Aug. 27, 1791, and 1798, respectively, on Peters Creek, Washington (now Allegheny) county. His father was the youngest of eleven children born to Nathaniel and Mary (Bell) Hazen, who came to Washington county from New Jersey, and shortly after to Franklin township. The patent issued from the government to the eldest son of Nathaniel Hazen, Sr., bears date 1790 for the old homestead where Smith Hazen now resides. Samuel Hazen died Sept. 7, 1855, and his wife in 1847. At the age of twenty-three years Nathaniel W. began farming his father's farm on shares; later on he bought 100 acres known as the "Severance farm," and with his faithful wife labored to clear the place from debt; and just as their earnest work was about to bring its reward, Mrs. Hazen died, after a few days' illness, in 1851. She was Rebecca, daughter of Joseph and Mary (Runyan) Morton; her grandfather was one of the early settlers of this place. To her and her husband two children were born, Ezra (whose sketch appears below) and Elzena, married to Andrew Jackson, who died two years later, and she now resides with her father. Mr. Hazen after about eight years on the Severance farm exchanged it for his present place, where he as built up a beautiful home and has lived a useful life. He married his second wife, Nancy M. Dobbs, in 1854. She was born Feb. 22, 1835, a daughter of James and Isabella Dobbs, and has borne her husband four children: Maggie D., wife of John W. Irwin, of Franklin township; Elmer E. and Clara Bell, at home, and Eliza Jane who died at the age of fifteen years. All the family, except the youngest son, are members of the North Sewickley Baptist church. Mr. Hazen is a Republican; he has been school director about thirteen years, and has also held other township offices.

EZRA HAZEN, farmer, P. O. North Sewickley, the eldest son of Nathaniel W. Hazen, was born on the Severance farm, in Franklin township, Sept. 7, 1842. He attended the schools of this township and North Sewickley Academy, and after reaching his twenty-first year worked his father's farm on shares for six years, and taught school four winters. After that he bought a part of his father's farm, erected a fine dwelling, and has a pleasant home. He married, March 31, 1868, Rebecca S. Knox, who was born Nov. 21, 1844, in Butler county, a daughter of Obed and Sarah (Dunn) Knox, natives of Butler county, and both now deceased. Her mother was born March 14, 1814, and died July 27, 1886. Two children have been born to Mr. and Mrs. Hazen: Gilbert Nathaniel and Charles L., both at home. Mr. Hazen is a Republican, and with his wife and eldest son is a member of the North Sewickley Baptist church.

NATHAN HAZEN, farmer, P. O. North Sewickley, was born in Franklin township, this county, Dec. 15, 1829, a son of Samuel and Eliza (McDannel) Hazen, also natives of this county, and parents of eight children, all of whom lived to maturity: Nathaniel; Margaret, widow of John Thompson, residing in New Brighton, this county; Mary Ann, deceased wife of H. R. Alter (Mr. Alter had been three times married, and his third wife, together with the youngest three daughters, was killed at the railway accident which occurred at or near Chatsworth, Ill., Aug. 11, 1887); Rebecca, who was twice married, first to William Mortain, and at his decease to Alexander Cavin, died in 1883; Hannah, deceased wife of James C. Thompson, also deceased; Nathan; Samuel, who died at the age of twenty-two; and Smith, in Franklin township, this county. The father of this family died Sept. 7, 1855, at the age of sixty-four years. Nathaniel Hazen, grandfather of our subject, a native of New Jersey, and a farmer, came to this county at a very early day; the maternal grandfather, Jethro McDannel, was also a farmer. Nathan Hazen was educated in the common schools of his native county, and has followed farming pursuits all his life, in connection with which he carried on mercantile pursuits for eight years in North Sewickley. He was married, March 4, 1851, to Judith, daughter of Abraham Zeigler, a native of this county, whose father, Christopher, a farmer and cabinet maker, was among the earliest settlers of Franklin township, and died in Mahoning county, Ohio, about 1853, at the age of ninety-seven years. Mr. and Mrs. Hazen have six children: Christopher; O. T.; Elizabeth, wife of Stewart Thompson, a merchant in New Castle, Pa.; Mary, wife of Dr. W. H. Morrison, in Struther, Ohio; Ida and Lillie, at home. Mr. Hazen has held the office of supervisor, and served on the board of electors several terms; in politics he is a Republican. The family are members of the Baptist church, excepting the married daughters, who have joined the churches of their respective husbands.

SMITH M. HAZEN, farmer, P. O. Frisco, was born on his present farm in 1835, youngest son of Samuel and Eliza (McDannel) Hazen. Samuel was the youngest of eleven children born to Nathaniel and Mary (Bell) Hazen, who settled here in 1790. He was a soldier in the war of 1812. Smith M. received his education in the old log schoolhouse, and after his father's death took the farm. He married, March 5, 1857, Mary Ann Nye, who was born in 1835, in North Sewickley township, a daughter of Andrew and Sarah (Seth) Nye, whose grandfather, also named Andrew, settled here about 1790. Seven children have resulted from this union, as follows: Edwin P., a dentist, at Fort Madison, Iowa; Elwin S., a farmer, in Missouri; Ira R., at home; Austin Pierce, a farmer, in Franklin township, this county; Ora E., who died in 1869; Samuel Grant and Bertha, at home. Mr. Hazen is a Republican, and all but one of his family are members of the North Sewickley Baptist church.

PHILIP H. HERRMANN, farmer, was born May 4, 1839, in Alsace, France (now Germany), a son of Philip and Kate Zehner, who were born May 1, 1809, and March 12, 1812, in Germany. They located in 1852 in Marion township, Beaver county, where the father died March 25, 1888. The paternal grandfather of Philip H. was Philip Herrmann; his maternal grandfather was Henry Zehner, and both died in Germany. Philip H. received some schooling in the old country, attended school one month here, and learned the English letters, but by his own individual study he is now able to read English well. When he was twenty-six years old he married Margaret, a daughter of Frederick and Margaret (Smett) Danbacher, and born July 1, 1846. Following named children were born to this union: Maggie C.; John Adam; Kattie, who died in 1874; Clara; Sophia, who died in 1883; Albert and Emma. Mr. Herrmann bought his present farm four years after he was married. He has served in several township offices, and is now filling his third term as town assessor. He is a member of the United Presbyterian church.

JOHN HERZOG, farmer, P. O. Knob, was born in Germany, Feb. 7, 1829. His parents, John and Mary Herzog, immigrated to America in 1849, and in 1850 returned to Germany, where the father died. The mother afterward came to this country, and again returned to Germany, where she died. Our subject came to America in 1848, and was married in Pittsburgh, Aug. 16, 1848, to Margaret Heid, who was born in Germany March 20, 1826. Her parents, John and Catherine Heid, started for America in 1852. The mother died at sea, and the father in Baltimore soon after landing. Mr. and Mrs. Herzog have had nine children, eight now living: William, Anna M., Mary E., Sevilla, Mary B., John, Emma M. and Eva B. Mary A. is deceased. The family have lived in Beaver county since 1865. Mr. Herzog owns ninety-five acres of improved land. He has held the offices of supervisor and assistant assessor in New Sewickley township.

TOBIAS HETCHIE (deceased), whose portrait appears elsewhere in this work, was a native of Freedom borough, where he passed all his life. He was born Oct. 4, 1846, and passed away on the day he was thirty-nine and one-half years old. His parents, John and Anna Mary (Schmidt) Hetchie, were natives of Germany, and were among the early residents of Freedom. Mrs. Hetchie survived her husband several years, dying at the age of seventy-four. Tobias Hetchie was a notary public and conveyancer, and transacted a great deal of business for other people. He never sought political preferment, and the only society with which he was ever connected was the local Loan Association, of which he was president at the time of his demise. In 1867 he was wedded to Miss Anna M. V., daughter of Thomas Freeman and Hannah (Vickery) Robinson, natives of Beaver and Allegheny counties, respectively. Mr. Robinson received a medical degree, but gave his attention to his farm at Freedom, where Mrs. Hetchie was born. He died in 1876, aged sixty-three years, and Mrs. Robinson passed away four years later, at the age of fifty-six. Captain William Vickery, father of the latter, was a son of John Vickery, an English seaman, and came from Philadelphia to Allegheny county about the beginning of the present century. In 1826, he began the erection of the fine stone mansion in Freedom, now occupied by Mrs. Hetchie, and moved in with his family two years later. He lived to the age of seventy years, and was highly respected. Mr. Hetchie is succeeded by a son, christened Willliam Vickery, now seven years old.

J. G. HILLMAN, teacher, P. O. Freedom, was born in Lebanon, Pa., a son of Robert T. and Mary (Shalk) Hillman, the former a native of New Jersey, born in 1811, and the latter a native of Lebanon, Pa., born in 1812. They were married in Columbiana county, Ohio, where they remained until the death of Robert T., which occurred in 1872. His widow resides on the old homestead near New Lisbon, Ohio. They were the parents of ten children, six living. J. G., the eldest, was united in marriage March 18, 1874, with Sarah A. Nickum, who was born in Freedom, a daughter of John and Lydia (Cooper) Nickum, both natives of Beaver county, Pa. Mrs. Nickum died in October, 1875; Mr. Nickum is still living. They were the parents of six children, of whom Mrs. Hillman is the only one living. To Mr. and Mrs. Hillman have been born three children, two living : Nellie L. and John A. The one deceased is Robert C. Prof. Hillman acquired his education in New Lisbon, Ohio, and has engaged in teaching all his life. When the war broke out he enlisted in Company K, 104th O. V. I., and served his country three years. He has resided in Freedom for seventeen years.

GEORGE HINKEL, house plasterer, P. O. Rochester, was born in Germany May 19, 1820, a son of John and Barbara (Miller) Hinkel. His father, who was a farmer all his life, had nine children. George was reared in Germany and came to America when twenty-three years old. He learned his trade in Pittsburgh, serving seven years, and has worked at it since, first as a hand, then as boss, for one year. Since 1846 he has been in business for himself as a contractor. He has met with success; is the owner of the farm where he resides in Rochester township, and has made his own way in the world. He married in Allegheny county, Pa., Miss Margaret Kress, who was born in Germany. Of their ten children, only four are living: Nicholas, Mary, Anna and John. The family are members of the Catholic church. Mr. Hinkel is a Democrat in politics.

WILLIAM H. HOOPER, merchant and engineer, Freedom, is a member of the firm of Dambach & Hooper, merchants, of Freedom, Pa. He was born in Pittsburgh, Jan. 17, 1831, a son of Philip and Margaret Hooper. Philip was born in Allegheny county, Pa., June 10, 1805, and his wife in Beaver county Feb. 23, 1807. They were married in Pittsburgh, where they settled and remained about five years, when the father died. They were the parents of two children: Jane, the wife of Thomas Dripps, of Freedom, and William H. After Philip's death the family moved to Freedom, where the mother died Aug. 17, 1854. William H. was united in marriage Nov. 21, 1850, with Merie Benner, who was born in Butler county, Pa., April 19, 1831, daughter of John and Sarah Benner, the former deceased, the latter yet living. After William H. was married he settled in Freedom, Pa., has been a resident of the town for fifty years, and has been a steamboat man all his life. He has one child living, Olive E., born April 8, 1864, and married June 29, 1882, to Charles Dambach, a member of the firm of Dambach & Hooper. Charles Dambach was born in Butler county, Pa., Oct. 12, 1860. His parents, Nicholas and Catherine Dambach, natives of Germany, emigrated to this country and have resided in Butler county. They are the parents of three children, two living, Charles, and Tillie (wife of W. A. Goehring).

EDWARD HOOPS. Joshua Hoops, the progenitor of the Hoops family in America came with William Penn in 1682, and located in Bucks county, Pa. His son

Daniel married Jane Worrellow, of Bucks county, in 1696, and soon after removed to Chester county. They were blessed with seventeen children, most of whom attained a great age. Among them was Thomas, whose two sons were Thomas and David. The latter was by trade a tanner. He married, in 1766, Esther, daughter of Joseph and Lydia Townsend, of East Bradford, Chester county, in the same state, and in 1802 removed to New Brighton. Their children were Thomas, Joseph, Susanna, Jesse and Lydia. Joseph, of this number, born Oct. 28, 1770, married, April 5, 1798, Ellen, daughter of J. and Rachel V. Hamilton, of Wilmington, Del. His death occurred Dec. 10, 1840, and that of his wife Oct. 4, 1850. Their children are Francis, Edward, Francis 2d, Charles, William, Mary, Charles 2d and Hamilton, of whom four died in infancy. Edward Hoops, the subject of this biography, was born Dec. 18, 1800, in Wilmington, Del., and removed with his parents when but two years of age to Beaver county, where he has since, with the exception of a brief interval, resided. He was for a few months, only, a pupil in a Quaker school, and at the age of twelve entered a store as clerk, acting in that capacity until 1818. Returning home, he embarked with his brother in the coach making business in Brighton, and continued this relation until 1830. He then became a merchant at the same point, and gave his exclusive attention to this department of industry until 1840. Mr. Hoops has since that date been variously employed, confining himself to no special branch of business. He was for a period secretary of an insurance company, and agent for the collection of claims for the trustees of the branch of the United States Bank, located at New Brighton. In 1857 he was made cashier of the Bank of Beaver County at the latter point, and continued agent for the lands belonging to the Chew estate, in Beaver and Lawrence counties. He also engaged in private real estate operations, but has recently devoted his attention exclusively to the management of his own property. Mr. Hoops was, in 1826, married to Cynthia, daughter of Benjamin and Pamelia Townsend, and their children were William P. (deceased), Henry (deceased), Henry 2d, Ellen, Pamelia and Edward, who lost his life in the battle of Fredericksburg. The death of Mrs. Hoops occurred in 1878. Mr. Hoops was reared in the faith of the Society of Friends, to which he still adheres.

H. N. W. HOYT, insurance agent and dealer in real estate, New Brighton, is a native of the state of Maine, and was born in 1842. His father, Benjamin G. Hoyt, a native of England, was for ten years a professor in and president of Beech Grove Seminary, Tennessee, where he died. H. N. W. Hoyt graduated from Baden College, Brunswick, Maine, and soon thereafter removed to Ohio, where for eight years, he was superintendent of schools. Coming to Beaver county, in 1875, he was appointed by the board of school directors superintendent of the county schools, and later on was for some years principal of the public schools of New Brighton. Mr. Hoyt is now engaged in insurance and real estate business. He is a member of the Presbyterian church; in politics a Democrat.

ELIAS HUNTER, baggage master, P , Ft. W. & C. Ry., New Brighton, was born in that town in 1838, the fourth son and youngest child in the family of seven children of John C. and Jane (Moore) Hunter. The paternal grandfather, William H., came from Ireland at an early date, and purchased a farm in this county. Elias was educated at the public schools of his native town, and early in life commenced railroading, having now served some twenty-five years, twenty as baggage master. He was for a time conductor for the same company. He married in 1868, Josephine, daughter of John and Sarah (Foutz) Sheets, and to this union have been born two children, Edward C. and Lewis S. Mr. Hunter is a member of the K. of P. and A. O. U. W., and of the Methodist Episcopal church. In politics he is a Republican.

N. F. HURST, proprietor of real estate and loan agency office, Mansfield block, Rochester avenue, Rochester, was born in Bridgewater, this county, Dec. 19, 1850, a son of William and Amanda (Parsons) Hurst. His parents were natives of England, and settled in Bridgewater in 1832. His father learned mercantile business in England, for which privilege his parents paid five hundred pounds. In Bridgewater he carried on a dry goods store and grocery until his death in 1879. He had five children, of whom N. F. is the fourth. He attended the public school in his native town, and the school which

BIOGRAPHIES — EAST SIDE. 781

afterward became Beaver College, in Beaver, Pa. He went into his father's store as a clerk, and was a diligent and successful salesman. After his father's death he continued mercantile trade as clerk for his brother, A. C. Hurst, in Bridgewater, until 1884, when he embarked in his present business in company with Samuel Moody. Mr. Moody retired from the firm in 1885, since which time Mr. Hurst has continued the business alone. He was married in 1881, to Lillian, daughter of John Conway. Mr. Hurst is a brother to Capt. Charles B. Hurst, of Rochester, and A. C. Hurst, a merchant at Bridgewater. He is a Democrat in politics, and is a member of the council of Rochester. He has two children: John Conway and Edwin Moody. Mr. and Mrs. Hurst are members of the Presbyterian church, of which he is a trustee. He is a Sir Knight Templar.

JOHN C. IRVIN, farmer, Rochester, was born in Rochester township, this county, Oct. 8, 1821. His parents were Joseph and Ellen (Carlen) Irvin, the former a native of Ireland, the latter born in Pennsylvania, and of Irish descent. Joseph Irvin, a prominent farmer, served for several years ae associate judge of Beaver county, where he located in 1803 with his parents. He died in Rochester township in 1884, in his eighty-seventh year. He reared a family of seventeen children, thirteen of whom grew to maturity, and ten are now living. Thirteen of the children were sons; eight of them still survive. John C. is the smallest of the sons, and his weight is about 224 pounds. Our subject's great-grandfather, Joseph Irvin, was a prominent man, and was compelled to leave Ireland in 1796, during the rebellion. He came to the United States, settled in Pennsylvania, and carried on farming. His son, John Irvin, grandfather of John C., was also a farmer, and spent a part of his life on the farm in Rochester township. John C. received a common-school education, and has been a farmer, contractor and successful trader all his life. He is interested in almost every enterprise of importance in Rochester, and is the owner of more real estate than any five men in Rochester. He is popularly known as "Uncle Jack," except by some of the colored people, who call him "Grandpap." In politics he is a Democrat. He is a prominent F. & A. M., and has taken thirty-two degrees in that order. He was married Dec. 25, 1844, in Darlington, Beaver county, Pa., to Miss Martha Mann, of English descent. Their living children are Edward, James C. and Joseph B., and those deceased are William L., Martha, Milton, Jesse and Mary L. Mrs. Irvin died Aug. 14, 1871.

JAMES IRVIN, farmer, P. O. Rochester, was born in this county in 1835, a son of Joseph and Ellen (Carlin) Irvin, who were also the parents of twelve other children, James being the tenth. Joseph was a farmer by occupation. He came from Scotland to America about 1802, and purchased 300 or 400 acres of land in Beaver county. James was educated at the common schools in Rochester, and has always lived on a farm. He married, in 1858, Isabella, daughter of Jessie Nannah, of this county. They have had nine children, of whom eight are now living: Hugh, Blanche (Mrs. Brewer), Jessie, Joseph, Edith, Clyde, Martha and Clarence. Mr. Irvin purchased his present farm of ninety-two acres in 1865. It is beautifully located and on it are erected good buildings, etc. He is a Democrat, politically.

JOSEPH IRVIN, farmer, P. O. Rochester, was born on the farm where he now lives April 9, 1842. His parents, Joseph and Nellie Irvin, are both deceased. Joseph, Sr., served as associate judge, was a farmer and among the early settlers of Beaver county. Our subject attended school here, and chose farming as a business. Jan. 9, 1866, he married Maria Sample, of Butler county. She was born July 26, 1840, and is a daughter of James and Susannah Sample. They have had three children, of whom two are living : Richard and Walter. A daughter, Nellie, is deceased. Mr. Irvin owns eighty acres of land. Mr. and Mrs. Irvin are members of the Presbyterian church. He is a Democrat.

THOMAS J. IRWIN, farmer, P. O. North Sewickley, was born in Plum township, Allegheny county, Pa., July 17, 1822. His parents, Joseph and Lydia Ann (Wilson) Irwin, natives of Ireland, came to this country in 1818, first locating in Allegheny county. They had nine children: Sarah (deceased), Alexander (deceased), Wilson, Thomas J., Eliza Jane, Samuel, Isabella and two (unnamed) who died in infancy.

44

Joseph was a farmer, and died in 1852. Thomas J. was educated partly in the subscription schools of Allegheny county and partly in the common schools. He engaged in farming in early life in Allegheny county, then moved to this township, where he bought his present farm of 130 acres. He was married, March 13, 1851, to Elizabeth J., daughter of Frederick Hillman, and by her had eleven children: Joseph F., in Deadwood, Dak.; Ann Jennie, wife of Dr. Judson Hazen, of North Sewickley; Alexander (deceased), John W., Rachel (deceased), William A., Carrie I., Mary Loretta, Sarah E., Harry and Walter M. Mr. Irwin is a Democrat, and has held the offices of school director three years, supervisor one year, assessor one year, and was judge of election for several years. He and his wife are members of the Presbyterian church, of which he has been elder for thirty years.

CHARLES E. JACKSON, physician, New Brighton, was born in Beaver county in 1863. James Jackson, the first member of this family in America, came from Ireland when eighteen years of age, and soon after his arrival here located in Allegheny county, where he remained only a few years, settling finally in Beaver county, where he purchased a farm containing seventy-five acres. He married Jane Jackson, who was also from Ireland, and to whom were born eight children Dr. James E. (deceased) being the youngest. He was born in 1818, and died in 1875. He received in youth an academic education, and at the age of nineteen learned the blacksmithing trade, which he followed for a number of years, during which time he took up the study of medicine. He graduated from Cleveland Medical College, and for twenty-nine years practiced his profession at Fallston, where he died. He married, in 1861, Pamelia, daughter of John and Margaret (Hazen) Thomas, also of this county. They had two children, Charles Elmer and John Thomas. Charles E. was educated at the high school in New Brighton, and at Geneva College, and in 1882 commenced the study of medicine with Dr. W. C. Simpson. He entered Bellevue Hospital Medical College, New York, in 1882, and graduated in 1885. After graduating he practiced at Fallston for one year, and is now located at New Brighton, where he has a lucrative practice. He is a member of the Beaver County Medical Society; politically he is a Democrat.

JAMES JACKSON, farmer, P. O. North Sewickley, was born Feb. 14, 1812, in North Sewickley township. His parents, Andrew and Agnes (Robison) Jackson, had nine children: Martha, Mary, Robinson, Jane, Robert, Ann, James, Agnes and Andrew. Four of these are yet living: Mary and Jane residents of Indianapolis, Ind., aged respectively, eighty and eighty-four years; Ann, now seventy-eight years, living in Allegheny City, and James aged seventy-six. Andrew Jackson was born in Ireland, and came to America in 1798, first settling in Sewickley Bottom, this county, where he lived for several years. In 1808 he bought the farm where James Smith now resides, in the extreme southeast corner of North Sewickley township, and there died in 1846. In his native country he learned to be a farmer, which he followed in this country. He was a cousin of President Andrew Jackson, and was one of the first elders elected in the Presbyterian church in Beavertown, Rev. William McLean, pastor. His wife was born in Newark, N. J., her parents coming from England in the latter part of the last century and settling in Newark, where they remained until 1790, then removed to North Sewickley township, where they died. James received a common-school education and learned the trade of stone cutter, which he followed for five years, then purchased the farm adjoining the one on which he now resides, and, in 1849, bought his present property consisting of over 200 acres, to which he subsequently removed, and where he has since resided. He was married, in 1838, to Esther Akin, and they had eight children, (six living): Kate Agnes, Jane (deceased), James A., Andrew (deceased), Sarah Ann (wife of Harry Potter, of Franklin township, this county), Henderson, John and Robert. Mr. and Mrs Jackson are members of the Methodist Episcopal church. In state or national elections he votes for the nominee of the Democratic party, but in county elections, for the man who, in his judgment, is best suited for the particular office. He is an honored citizen, highly respected by all who know him.

SAMUEL F. JACKSON, superintendent of Penn Bridge Works, New Brighton, was born in this county in 1851. His father, Hugh Jackson, a boat-builder, married Ann Ferguson, who bore him eight children, of whom Samuel F. is the fifth. He was educated in the common schools, and at the age of eighteen commenced to learn the cutlery trade, serving an apprenticeship of three years. He followed that business until 1881. He was married, in 1875, to Jennie, daughter of Samuel Dunbar of this town, and two children, Adnie and Eva, have been born to this couple. Since 1881 Mr. Jackson has been in the employ of the Penn Bridge Works, and since July, 1886, has held the position of superintendent. In 1887 he was elected to the town council by the Republican party, and in 1886 was a delegate to the Republican state convention. He is a F. & A. M., and a member of the K. of P.

THOMAS H. JAVENS, druggist, Rochester, was born in Bridgewater, Pa., April 21, 1856, a son of John and Mary (Crossgrave) Javens. John Javens was born in Beaver county, a son of Henry Javens and grandson of John Javens, who came to Beaver in 1800. He went from this county to the war of 1812. He reared a family of thirteen children, but most of his descendants have gone into the Western states. Mrs. Mary Javens was a native of Maryland, and the family have been residents of Maryland for several generations. Our subject's father was of French descent, and a stone mason and contractor. His family consisted of five children, three now living: Thomas H. and two daughters. Thomas H. was reared in Rochester, attended the schools of his native town and spent one year at the University of Michigan. He was in the medical department of the University, which eminently qualified him for the business he was destined to follow. He had selected the drug business and has worked at it most of the time since he was fourteen years old. He was in business in Mercer county for a time, but in 1881 came to Rochester and embarked in the drug business in company with C. A. Danals. This partnership continued until 1886, when Mr. Danals retired from the firm. Mr. Javens was married, in 1877, to Olive Hunter, and to them have been born four children: Fred, Cyrus, John and an infant. Mr. Javens is a Democrat.

A. M. JOHNSON, real estate agent, Rochester, was born in this county June 11, 1858. His parents, Samuel and Mary (Guiceler) Johnson, were natives of Allegheny county and of German origin. His father was a coal miner by occupation. Of his twelve children, ten grew to maturity, of whom A. M. is the fifth. He was reared in Beaver county, where his parents had resided for nearly one-half a century. His father was baggage agent for the Pennsylvania Railroad Company, and subsequently kept a hotel. When he retired our subject took up that business and kept the "Point Hotel" for four years. The present real estate agency was established in 1884. When first started Mr. Johnson was in company with others, but since 1885 he has been alone. He lately issued the *Beaver County Real Estate Journal*, a handsome volume containing nearly forty pages, which he circulates to all parties sending their names and address. He is also ticket agent in Rochester for the Pittsburg & Lake Erie Railroad, and is an agent for fire insurance. He was married, in 1880, to Anna, daughter of Peter Shupbert, a weaver by trade. Her parents were of German descent. The children of Mr. and Mrs. Johnson are Howard and Nellie. The parents are members of the Lutheran church. In politics Mr. Johnson is a Democrat. He is a member of the Royal Arcanum.

WILLIAM DAVIS JOHNSON (deceased) was a merchant in Rochester at the time of his death in 1881. He was born in Connecticut in April, 1803, a son of John Johnson, and of English descent. He was reared in Connecticut, attended the common schools, and early in life learned the mason's trade. In 1826 he settled at Rochester, and worked at his trade for a few years. He then embarked in mercantile trade and met with success in business. He was a highly respected citizen, and had many warm friends. He was married in Rochester, in 1829, to Jemima, daughter of John and Jane (Wier) Irvin, natives of Ireland. Mrs. Jemima Johnson was born in Rochester township, Sept. 10, 1807, a sister of Joseph Irvin who was associate judge of Beaver county. She has resided in Rochester for over fifty years. The marriage of Mr. and Mrs. Johnson was blessed with one son George J. who was reared in Rochester married and died there, leaving one child, George, who is now in California. Mr. Johnson was a professor of religion, but did not unite with any church. He was a Republican in politics. Mrs. Johnson is a member of the Reformed Presbyterian church.

CHARLES W. KATZ, retired, New Brighton, was born in Germany in 1811. His parents were Christian and Caroline Katz, the former a manufacturer of paper in Germany. They had six children, of whom Charles W., the youngest, came to America with his parents about 1836, and for several years worked at his trade, that of a papermaker. In 1870 he came to Beaver county, and during five years worked in a paper-mill at Fallston. He also passed five years at the same business in West Newton, Westmoreland county, Pa. In 1854 he purchased a farm in Patterson township, Beaver county, on which he remained seventeen years. He then removed to New Brighton, where he has since resided. He was married, in 1843, to Louisa Gilboch, who bore him three children: Louis H. (deceased), Amanda and Caroline. Mr. Katz is a member of the German Reformed church; in politics a Republican.

JOHN KETTLEWOOD (deceased), late of Rochester, was born in England in 1820, and died in 1880. At the age of nine years he came with his father to America and located in Wellington, removing thence to Bridgewater, Pa. He was married, in 1847, to Amy Gardner, who bore him seven children, four of whom are living, viz.: John, George, Frank and Mary (Mrs. Murray). Mr. Kettlewood followed his trade, that of blacksmithing, for twenty-five years. The farm he owned at his death was purchased and settled by his father-in-law in 1802. Mrs. Kettlewood and her son Frank reside on the farm, which is beautifully located and under good cultivation. The family are members of the Methodist church.

JOHN KIRCHNER, farmer, P. O. Knob, was born in Germany Dec. 27, 1822. His parents, Michael and Elizabeth Kirchner, came to America in 1833, and settled in Beaver county, where they died. John was married, Sept. 2, 1855, to Catherine Stichling, who was born in Baden, Germany, April 22, 1832, a daughter of Everhart and Catherine Stichling, natives of Germany, and who immigrated to America in 1841, settling in Beaver county on the farm where our subject now resides. Mr. and Mrs. Kirchner have five children: Jacob, Margaret, Henry, Sophia and Mary. Mr. Kirchner has been a farmer most of his life, and owns sixty acres of land. He and his wife are members of the German Evangelical church; politically he is a Democrat.

JACOB KLEIN, farmer and dairyman, P. O. Beaver Falls, was born in Bavaria, Germany, in 1832, and came to America in 1852. His parents were Philip, a farmer, and Caroline (Keiser) Klein, who had five children, of whom Jacob is the third. Soon after his arrival in this country Mr. Klein located in Beaver county (in 1853), purchased 250 acres of land, and also engaged in the butchering business. He came to Pulaski township in 1875 and purchased his present farm, containing 166 acres, including 25 acres of woodland. He was married, in 1858, to Elizabeth, daughter of Philip and Margaret (Gilbaugh) Blinn. They have three children: Jacob, Charles and Mary. Mr. Klein has made great improvements on his farm in this township. He is engaged in dairying, keeping sixteen cows. He is a Democrat, and has held the offices of supervisor and school director. He is a member of the Presbyterian church.

JOHN H. KNOTT, superintendent of flouring mill, Beaver Falls, residence in New Brighton, was born in this county March 16, 1854, third son of Moses and Ann (Whiteworth) Knott, the latter a daughter of Henry and Sallie Whiteworth, natives of England. They had six children. Moses Knott came from England in 1849, and first located in Mercer county, Pa., for three years; then in 1853 settled at New Brighton; he is by trade a woolen manufacturer. John H. was educated at the public schools, and when eighteen was apprenticed to the carpenter's trade, which he followed eight years; then entered Iron City College, at Pittsburgh, after leaving which he was engaged for two years as shipping clerk, and in 1882 accepted his present position. He was married, in 1883, to Mary E., daughter of John Edgar, of Fallston, this county, and one child, John Edgar, was born to them. Mr. Knott is a member of the Mystic Circle, R. A., at Beaver Falls, and of the Methodist Protestant church. In politics he is a Republican.

BIOGRAPHIES—EAST SIDE. 785

FREDERICK KORNMANN, farmer, P. O. Freedom, was born in Germany, Nov. 22, 1833. His parents, Frederick and Anna G. (Brandt) Kornmann, were natives of Germany, and died there. Frederick came to America in 1853, and settled in Freedom, Pa., where he learned the blacksmith's trade. He was married in Pittsburgh, in 1856, to Barbara Schnessler, who was born in Germany, May 1, 1831, a daughter of George Schnessler (deceased). The fruits of this marriage are nine children: Mary A., Jeannette, Frederick, Adam, Catherine, George, Charles, Maggie and John. Mr. Kornmann followed blacksmithing twelve years, then engaged in farming. He and his wife are members of the German Lutheran Church. In politics he is a Democrat.

JOSEPH KREBS (deceased) was born in Butler county, Pa., in 1819, and was a son of John H. and Barbara Krebs, who died in Butler county. Joseph was married, in 1857, to Matilda, daughter of William and Elizabeth French, the former deceased. This union was blessed with ten children, eight of whom are living: Anna, Arrema, Joseph A., Elizabeth, George, Matilda, Grace and William. Those deceased are Abigail and Emeline. Mr. Krebs departed this life April 12, 1888, aged sixty-eight years. He had been a farmer all his life, and owned eighty acres of improved land. He was a member of the United Brethren church, of which his widow is also a member. In politics he was a Republican.

J. H. KUHL, merchant tailor, Freedom, was born in Germany Oct. 24, 1843, a son of Henry and Hetchie Kuhl, who died in Germany, and who were the parents of six children, five living. J. H. was married, in 1873, to Hattie Geisler, who was born in Economy township, this county, in 1854, a daughter of Jacob and Barbara Geisler. Mrs. Kuhl died March 12, 1884, the mother of three children, two living: Anna B. and Lottie M. Mr. Kuhl learned the tailor's trade when he was fourteen years old, and has followed it ever since. He owns a nice home in Freedom, Pa., where he has lived for eighteen years. In politics he is a Republican.

ABNER P. LACOCK was the youngest son of Gen. Abner Lacock, and was born April 12, 1812, in the house in which he lived all his life. He early chose his father's profession, that of a civil engineer, in which he became thoroughly proficient. He and his father surveyed the route of the Crosscut canal, running from Mahoningtown, Ohio, to Zanesville, connecting the Erie with the Ohio Canal. Unlike his father Abner P. Lacock never took an active part in politics, though he was a staunch Whig, and afterwards a Republican. He was always a prominent citizen of this county, and ranked among her foremost men. He never joined any secret order, and was never married. He lived an honest, honorable, upright life; was a sincere friend, generous and unselfish to a degree seldom found among men. He died on the 20th of April, 1888, loved and respected by all who knew him, and was buried beside his father in the cemetery belonging to his family.

CHARLES M. LINE, train baggage master, for the Pennsylvania Railroad Company, Rochester, was born in Holmes county, Ohio, Sept. 16, 1840, a son of William G. and Mary (Hoover) Line, natives of Carlisle, Pa., and of German origin, former of whom was a farmer. Charles M., the youngest of nine children, was reared on the farm in Holmes county, Ohio, attended the district school and also school at Hayesville. He enlisted in 1861 in Company E, 4th Regiment O. V. I. His regiment was in sixty-nine skirmishes and battles, among them the battles of Gettysburg, Antietam and Chancellorsville. He was under Generals Hancock and Carroll. He had many narrow escapes, and at the expiration of his service came home, and in less than three months obtained a position with the Pennsylvania Railroad Company, with which he has since remained. He was a brakeman two years, and has since been baggage master. Mr. Line was married, March 24, 1868, to Margaret, daughter of John Boley, and of German and Scotch origin. Mr. and Mrs. Line are members of the Presbyterian church of Rochester. He takes an active interest in the affairs of the church, and has served as secretary of the board of directors for eleven years. He is a member of the G. A. R., and is a Master Mason.

WILLIAM LLOYD, machinist, P. O. New Brighton, was born in Beaver county in

1844, and is of Welsh descent. His parents, John and Elizabeth (Words) Lloyd, had sixteen children. William being the youngest. John Lloyd was a wire drawer by trade, and came to Beaver county as early as 1829. William was educated in the common schools of Fallston, this county, and at the age of eighteen began to learn the machinist's trade, serving an apprenticeship of three years. He was married, in 1871, to Caroline, daughter of Robinson and Ann Jackson, of this county, and they have one child, Ada Jackson. In 1864 Mr. Lloyd enlisted in Battery B, 1st P. A., and served until the close of the war. He is a Republican and has been twice elected to the town council, in 1883 and 1886. He is a member of the G. A. R. and of the A. O. U. W.

J. R. LOCKHART, physician, Freedom, was born in this county Aug. 22, 1842. His parents were Jeptha and Edith (Applegate) Lockhart, the former born in New Jersey and the latter in West Virginia. They were married in West Virginia, settled in this county and remained here until their deaths. They had five children, four living, our subject being the third. He was married Dec. 1, 1875, to Frances M. McCaskey, who was born in Freedom, Pa., a daughter of Robert and Frances McCaskey, natives of Pennsylvania, who settled in Freedom, and there remained until his death; his widow is still living. Our subject began the study of medicine in 1865, graduated in Cincinnati, Ohio, in 1870, and has been engaged in the practice of his profession in Freedom ever since. The doctor and his wife are members of the Methodist church; he is a F. & A. M. When the Civil War broke out he enlisted in Company F, 140th Regiment, P. V. I., and remained in the service eighteen months.

D. E. LOWRY, retired merchant, P. O. Freedom, was born in Bridgeport, Ohio, May 15, 1837. His parents, John and Sarah (Waggoner) Lowry, natives of Pennsylvania, were married in Beaver county, and from there moved to Bridgeport, Ohio, and thence to Allegheny county, Pa., where they lived until 1856, when they removed to Beaver, and here remained until their deaths. Our subject is the eldest of the family. He was first married, in 1868, to Mary A., daughter of Jacob Coas, and born in Beaver county. She died in 1875, and Feb. 20, 1878, Mr. Lowry married M. Jennie Dillworth, who was born in Beaver county Sept. 24, 1855, a daughter of Rev. Robert and Eliza J. (Slom) Dillworth, the former of whom died in 1858 and the latter in 1868. Two children have been born to Mr. and Mrs. Lowry: Mabel, born Nov. 25, 1878, died Jan. 8, 1881; and Annie, born May 18, 1884. Mr. Lowry was a merchant in Freedom from 1854 to 1875, retiring in the latter year. He and his wife are members of the Presbyterian church, of which he is a trustee. He is a F. & A. M.

GEORGE F. LUKENS, forwarding and commission merchant, Rochester, was born in Sharon, Pa., Nov. 23, 1827, and is a son of John M. and Mary (Jones) Lukens, the father a native of Beaver county, and the mother of England. His father was a merchant in early life, and later a forwarding commission merchant. When the canal was built through Beaver county he contracted to build bridges for it. In his later years he resided in Rochester, where he died in 1863. The grandfather of George F. (Thomas H. Lukens) was among the earliest permanent settlers in Beaver county. He was born in Chambersburg, Franklin county, Pa., and was a merchant. George F. is the eldest of seven children, and attended school at New Brighton. The first business he did for himself was keeping a store boat on the Ohio river, which he followed for one year. He has been on the Ohio since 1846, and owned and operated the wharf boat at Rochester until 1863. He is a Republican in politics. In 1861 he enlisted in Company E, 134th P. V., was a non-commissioned officer, and was discharged in 1862. He is a member of the Royal Arcanum, the I. O. O. F. and encampment, and has been a Mason for years, having taken thirty-two degrees. He is also member of Post 188, G. A. R.

WILLIAM MCCAGUE, treasurer of the Point Bottle Works, Rochester, was born in Franklin township, Westmoreland county, Pa., and was brought to Allegheny county when five years old. His parents were natives of Westmoreland county, Pa., and of Scotch-Irish descent. His father, who was a farmer, was killed by an Indian in the war of 1812; his mother's maiden name was Jane Crookshanks. William and his sister, the only children of their parents, were left orphans when he was only six years old. He

BIOGRAPHIES—EAST SIDE. 787

learned the wagon-maker's trade in Pittsburgh, and also the art of making plows, serving nearly three years as an apprentice. In 1833 he became foreman in a manufactory of wagons and plows at Manchester. In 1836 he established such a manufactory in Pittsburgh, and followed that business for twenty years. He bought a farm in 1865, in Brighton township, Beaver county; retired from active business, and resided on the farm for six years, but being used to active life he sold the place and moved to Rochester in 1874. He became interested in the Point Bottle Works at Rochester in 1882, and was elected treasurer of the company. He has been twice married, first in 1884, the fruits of which union were two children, one of which is now living, Rebecca G., wife of John Hines, of Allegheny City. In 1872 Mr. McCague married Elizabeth Worrick. They are members of the Methodist church, in which he takes an active interest, and has officiated as steward. class leader and treasurer, and teacher in the Sabbath-school. He is the oldest Odd Fellow in Pennsylvania, having joined the order in Pittsburgh in 1830. He served for several years as district deputy grand-master of four counties. His lodge is the Western Star, No. 24, of Pittsburgh. In politics he is a Democrat, and during his eventful, life he has served thirty-two years as school director. He was burgess of Lawrenceville, five terms, in the early part of his life. Since he came to Rochester he has made many warm friends.

GEORGE MCCASKEY, ship carpenter, P. O. Freedom, was born in Freedom, Aug. 31, 1839, and is a son of Robert and Frances McCaskey, the former of whom died in March, 1880; the latter resides with her son-in-law, C. T. Fowler. They had ten children, of whom eight are living, George being the fourth. Our subject was united in marriage, Jan. 20, 1870, with Mary Kerr, who was born in Freedom, Pa., Dec. 23, 1838, and is a daughter of Thomas G. and Grizzy H. (McCurdy) Kerr, who died in Freedom, the former April 19, 1886, and the latter Oct. 8, 1885. They were the parents of twelve children, three only remaining, of whom Mrs. McCaskey is the youngest. She is the mother of five children. three now living: Harlan, Stanley A. and Ella H. Those deceased are Francis L. and Robert L. Mr. McCaskey has followed his trade, that of steamboat building, for many years. When the war broke out he enlisted in Company F, 39th Regiment P. V., and served three years. He and his wife are members of the Methodist Episcopal church.

LEANDER MCCAULEY, farmer, P. O. Rochester, was born on the farm where he and his family reside, Dec. 6, 1834, and is a son of Robert and Mary (Mitchell) McCauley, the former of whom, a native of Ireland, emigrated to America with his mother in 1819, his father having died in the old country; the mother of Leander was a native of Pennsylvania, and died at the home of her daughter, in Rochester, June 9, 1887. They were married in Pennsylvania, and located for a short time in Allegheny county. In 1825 they bought the farm where our subject resides, and on which his father died, Jan. 9, 1867. Leander was married, Oct. 13, 1859, to M. Margaretta, daughter of John and Elizabeth (Harnit) Andrews, natives of Pennsylvania, now deceased. She was born in Lawrence county, Pa , Jan. 28, 1840, and is the mother of four children: John C. and Evelyn S., living, and Willie J. and Mary M., deceased. In 1857 Mr. McCauley went to Williams county, Ohio, and engaged in lumbering and teaching school. In 1862 he moved to Rochester, Pa., where he also taught school. In 1868 he moved to his present residence, and has since been engaged in farming. He and his wife are members of the Presbyterian church. In politics he is a Prohibitionist.

WILLIAM MCCLELLAND, farmer, New Brighton, was born and reared on the farm he now owns. consisting of 115 acres, in Beaver county, in 1828, second son and fourth of the five children of William and Jane (Hays) McClelland, former of whom, a farmer by occupation, was in the war of 1812, and drew a pension; he came to America in 1776 from Ireland, purchased the farm his son William now owns, and died at the age of ninety-two years. Our subject was married, in 1852, to Rebecca, daughter of Valentine and Susanna Long, of Allegheny county, and ten children have been born to them: Frank. George, Susanna, Jacob, William, Elmer, Jennie, Rebecca (deceased), James and Lula. Mr. McClelland moved, in 1887, from the old homestead to New

Brighton, where he now lives, retired, though still looking after the management of work on his farm. He is a Republican.

H. S. McCONNEL, physician, New Brighton, was born in Freedom, Beaver county, Dec. 17, 1848, and was educated at Beaver Academy and Beaver College. His grandfather came from Ireland at an early date. James McConnel, father of our subject, was a steamboat draftsman and builder. He married Elvira, daughter of Stephen Phillips, in whose honor Phillipsburg was named. They had ten children, the doctor being next to the youngest. James McConnel died in 1862, aged sixty years. The doctor was graduated from Bellevue Hospital Medical College in 1875, and immediately began practice in New Brighton, where he has continued, enjoying a lucrative practice in the town and surrounding country. He was married in 1879 to Georgiana, daughter of G. L. Eberhart, of New Brighton, and they have two children: Florence May and Donald Vinton. Dr. McConnel is a Republican, and a member of the school board. He is a member of the K. of P.

FRANK McCRACKEN, farmer, P. O. Freedom, was born in Beaver county in September, 1851, and is a son of John and Sarah McCracken, the former deceased. He (Frank) was married, Jan. 1, 1874, to Sarah A. Piersol, who was born in Beaver county Nov. 6, 1851. Her parents, Jacob and Eliza Piersol, were natives of Pennsylvania, and after marriage settled in Beaver county, where they remained until the father's death; the mother is still living. Mr. and Mrs. McCracken have four children: William, Elmer E., Lillian and John C. Mr. McCracken has been engaged in farming all his life, and owns eighty-seven acres of improved land. He and his wife are members of the Methodist Episcopal church. In politics he is a Democrat.

BENJAMIN A. McCREARY, farmer, P. O. Beaver Falls, was born in North Sewickley township, Beaver county, Pa., Oct. 20, 1850, and is a son of William and Mary (Ferguson) McCreary, both of Irish descent. The father was born in Franklin county, Pa., in 1813, and came to Beaver county in 1841, settling in North Sewickley township, where he has since carried on farming and the practice of law. He had nine children: Robert A., who was a soldier in the War of the Rebellion, was taken prisoner, confined in Andersonville prison, and died of starvation and rough treatment, while on his way home; Jemima A., William A., Thomas H., James F., Benjamin A., Charles H., Joseph P., (in Wisconsin), and Franklin E. The mother died in March, 1882. Benjamin A. received a common-school education, and has followed farming all his life. now owning fifty-seven acres. He was married, Oct. 20, 1875, to Mary, daughter of Isaac and Maria (Boots) McDaniel, natives of Pennsylvania, both now deceased, latter a daughter of Samuel Boots, of North Sewickley township, this county. Mr. and Mrs. McCreary have three children: Laura E., Grace V. and Mary E. The parents are members of the Methodist church; politically Mr. McCreary is a Republican. He has in his possession the first dog-power churning machine invented by his brother, James F., made after patent was taken out in June, 1879.

CHARLES H. McCREARY, farmer, P. O. New Brighton, was born in this county in 1853, seventh in the family of nine children of William and Mary (Ferguson) McCreary. He was born and reared on a farm, and received a common-school education. He was married, in 1879, to Jennie S., daughter of Elizabeth Bennett, and has one child, Robert Victor. Besides the home farm of thirty-five acres, Mr. McCreary owns seventy-two acres in North Sewickley township, which he purchased in 1885. In politics he is a Republican.

ABRAM McDONALD, pilot, Freedom, was born in this county, June 2, 1834. His parents were Andrew and Katy (Riddle) McDonald, natives of Washington county, Pa., where they were married. They moved to Hopewell township, this county, in 1810, and here remained until their death. Andrew McDonald came to Beaver county as a missionary, before he was married. He was a minister of the Presbyterian church, and preached a great many years. He and his wife were the parents of eight children, four living, Abram being the youngest. Abram was united in marriage the first time, May 6, 1856, with Phœbe McDonald, who was born in Hopewell township, and was a daughter of John W. McDonald. She died in 1857, and Nov. 3, 1859, Mr. McDonald married Sarah J. Noss. She was born in Moon township, this county, Oct. 5, 1835, and is a daughter of Jacob J. and Ann (Irwin) Noss, the former born in Mifflin county, Pa., March 8, 1810, the latter in Moon township, Feb. 16, 1817. They were married and settled in Beaver county, and remained until her death, which occurred May 27, 1866; Mr. Noss now resides with his son-in-law, Mr. McDonald, and is in his seventy-eighth year. Our subject and wife are the parents of five children, three living: two sons and one daughter. Mr. McDonald has been engaged on the river since he was fourteen years of age, and has been a captain and pilot for over thirty years. He and his wife are members of the Presbyterian church. He is an honorary member of the Masonic order; has resided in Freedom twenty-eight years.

THOMAS J. McDONALD, pilot, Freedom, was born in Columbiana county, Ohio, April 12, 1829, and is a son of James and Rachel (Cook) McDonald, former of whom was born in Ireland and came to America with his parents when three years of age, they settling in Columbiana county, Ohio. Rachel (Cook) McDonald was born in Ashtabula, N. Y., where she and her husband were married. After marriage they settled in Columbiana county, and remained there until their deaths. The family consisted of three children, all living: Thomas J., Eleanor and Matilda. Thomas J. was united in marriage in Allegheny county, July 16, 1849, with Sarah A. Oliver, who was born in Beaver county Feb. 15, 1832, daughter of Joseph Oliver. Mr. and Mrs. McDonald have had three children, two living: Elizabeth, wife of Charles W. Coffer, and Ella, wife of Captain George Whitefield. A son, James, came to his death by drowning, in 1857. Mr. McDonald has been steamboating all his life, and has been a pilot for thirty years. He owns a nice property, where he and family reside. He has lived in Freedom since 1861, and has filled various borough offices.

W. H. McDONALD (deceased) was born in Warren county, Pa., in 1839, and was a son of William R. and Rebecca (Magee) McDonald, the former of whom carried on lumbering in this county. They were the parents of eleven children, W. H. being the third son. When two years of age our subject was brought by his parents to Beaver county, where he received his education at the common schools, and remained nearly all his life, dying in 1886. In 1862 he enlisted in the 139th Regiment, P. V., and served three years. He received a sunstroke, from the effects of which he suffered to the day of his death. Mr. McDonald returned home in 1865, and soon afterward embarked in the grocery business in New Brighton, which he carried on up to his decease. He married, in 1868, Hannah, daughter of John and Cornelia Ervin, and by her had three children: John W., Lizzie and William H. Mr. McDonald was a member of the Methodist Episcopal church; a member of the K. of P. and the G. A. R.; he was a F. & A. M.; in politics a Republican.

R. L. McGOWEN, retired, P. O. New Brighton, was born in Pittsburgh, Pa., in 1823, and is a son of Samuel and Jane (Strain) McGowen, natives of Belfast, Ireland. He received a common-school education, and in youth learned blacksmithing; then for six years manufactured brick. In 1854 he became foreman of a railroad machine shop, a position he held until 1885, when he retired from active labor and located at his present home. Mr. McGowen married, in 1848, Rebecca Jane, daughter of Edward Oldham, and by her has three children: Marion C. (now Mrs. Magaw), Mary J. (now Mrs. Kinsley) and R. F. (in Pittsburgh). Mr. McGowen is a F. & A. M.; and politically he is a Republican.

JAMES McGUIRE, farmer, P. O. New Brighton, was born in this county in 1816, son of Hugh and Mary (Dougherty) McGuire, latter a daughter of Edward Dougherty. They had sixteen children, of whom James is the fourth child, and the eldest now living. James McGuire, grandfather of our subject, came from Ireland in 1789, and located in Chester county, Pa., where he remained ten years. Coming to Beaver county in 1799, he purchased 400 acres of land in New Sewickley township, where he resided until his death. James, our subject, was born and reared on the farm, receiving his education in the common school and academy, and at the age of eighteen he left school to engage in business. After three years spent in clerking he turned his attention to agriculture and purchased his present farm, which is a part of the tract originally bought by his grandfather. He owns 120 acres, including some mineral lands. Mr. McGuire married, in 1840, Abby, daughter of Michael and Mary (O'Brien) Conway, and they had six children, five of whom are living: Hugh C., Michael, Joanna, Eliza Ann and Abby Alice. The mother died in 1882. Mr. McGuire has always been a prominent Democrat; he is a member of the Catholic church.

W. J. McKee, dealer in staple and fancy groceries, New Brighton, was born in Allegheny county, Pa., in 1843, being the eldest of the three children of William and Jane (Rea) McKee. He received a common-school education, and during boyhood learned the grocery business. From 1857 to 1874 he was engaged in railroading (in 1868 and the following six years in Beaver county), and then embarked in his present business in New Brighton. He was married, in 1868, to Myra, daughter of J. E. Sharrer, of New Brighton, and four children have blessed them: Nettie, William, Nellie and Hazel, all at home. Mr. McKee is a F. & A. M. and a member of the K. of P.; he is an adherent of the United Presbyterian church; in politics a Republican.

Frank W. McKim, farmer, P. O. North Sewickley, was born in Big Beaver township, this county, Feb 28, 1824, a son of William and Margaret Gilkey, natives of Burgettstown, Pa., and of Beaver county, and born in May, 1797, and Sept. 6, 1806, respectively. His grandfather, James McKim, a native of Ireland, came to America before the revolution, and with his brother John, served seven years and three months in that struggle, being members of Washington's body guard. Our subject received his education in Big Beaver township, and remained at home until his father's death, July 5, 1858. He married, Sept. 23, 1859, Martha Miller, who was born in Big Beaver township, Jan. 25, 1834, a daughter of William and Margaret (Crawford) Miller. Mrs. McKim died March 5, 1860, and Nov. 17, 1864, our subject was united in marriage with Margaret Campbell, a native of Big Beaver township, born Jan. 29, 1843, a daughter of James and Rebecca (Morrow) Campbell, also natives of Lawrence county, Pa. After his father's death, his mother made her home with him until her death, Sept. 15, 1878. By his second marriage, Mr. McKim is the father of eleven children: Ella Rebecca, William J., Mattie Jane, Charles M., Robert L., John G., Frank C., Mary A., Samuel P., Wilbert Calvin and Margaret Madessa (twins), all at home, also Maggie S. McKim, whom they have reared since she was two years old. In January, 1865, Mr. McKim bought his present farm and moved thereon in March following, but Aug. 2, 1871, his house was burned with half its contents. He is a Republican, and has served as school director and assessor. He has been general appraiser for the Brush Creek Protective Association since January, 1881, and has secured $400,000 worth of property for the Association. He and Mrs. McKim are members of the United Presbyterian church.

Joseph McKnight, of the firm of J. McKnight & Son, Rochester Foundry, manufacturers of the improved Howard, Servant, Prize, Star and Veto cook stoves, hollow-ware and castings, was born in Washington county, Pa., Feb. 5, 1826. His parents, Robert McKnight, who was all his life a farmer, and Sarah (Willison) McKnight, were natives of Pennsylvania and of English and Irish descent. Joseph was reared on the farm, attended the common schools, and learned the miller's trade, which he followed for over thirty years. He conducted a mill at New Galilee, Beaver county, for eleven years; in 1876 he sold out and farmed until 1880, when he sold his farm. In 1883 he embarked in his present business. He was married, in 1855, to Mary, daughter of James Clark, of Irish descent, and their children are Kate, wife of James Freed; W. J., in business with his father: Anna, wife of John Sparks; Maggie, wife of James Gaston; Nettie and Myrtle. Mr. McKnight is a Democrat in politics. He enlisted in 1862, in Company C, 104th O. V. I., and was under General Sherman.

Rev. D. H. A. McLean, D.D., Rochester, was born in Crawford county, Pa., April 5, 1816, and is a son of Rev. Daniel and Mary (Glover) McLean. His father was an Associate Presbyterian minister, and preached for over half a century in Crawford county, Pa. He died June 5, 1855, in the same county where he had labored so long and so well. His widow died five years later, in Erie county. Of their family of nine children four are now living. Our subject entered the ministry early in life. May 12, 1842, he was married to Elizabeth, daughter of Andrew and Eliza (Brown) Patterson, and born Dec. 9, 1821, in Mercer, Mercer county, Pa. Their children are Dr. E. P., a practicing physician in Virginia; Mary E., wife of Dr. J. E. Libbey, of Pittsburgh; Daniel B.; Ella I.; and Margaretta G., wife of A. S. Lewis, of near Xenia, Ohio. Our subject graduated from Jefferson College in 1836. He also took a regular theological course, and received his first license to preach in 1840, and took charge of the Mercer and Greenville congregations in 1841, which he served jointly four years, remaining in charge of the Greenville congregation for eleven years. In 1852 he accepted a professorship in Westminster College, Lawrence county, Pa. In 1856 he was elected principal of Pittsburgh High School, and resigned in the fall of 1859. In 1858 he became joint proprietor and editor of the *United Presbyterian*, of Pittsburgh, and four years after sold his interest in that paper. In 1861 he was pastor of Beaver and Four Mile congregations, and continued as pastor of Beaver congregation until 1868. In 1867 he took charge of Beaver Ladies' Seminary, continuing the charge over six years. Since then he has resided for several years in Allegheny county, teaching and preaching. In 1882 he came to Rochester township, Beaver county, Pa. He still continues to preach in vacant congregations, under appointment of his Presbytery.

R. H. McPherson, contractor and builder, New Brighton, is of Scotch-Irish extraction, born in this county in 1839, third son of Reuben (a farmer) and Elizabeth (Greer) McPherson, parents of six children. He was reared on the farm until his eighteenth year, and then taught school and studied at Mount Union College. In 1862 he enlisted in Battery G (Young's), Pittsburgh Artillery, stationed at Ft. Delaware, and served until the close of 1865. On his return home he took up carpentering, which he had partially learned before enlisting, and for ten years was engaged in the planing mill business under the firm name of McPherson & McLean, but has since been a contractor and builder. Mr. McPherson married, in 1865, Margaretta J., daughter of Mathew H. and Harriet Hamilton, and by her has six children: Lizzie Greer, Anna May, Hattie Gertrude, Elmer Elsworth, Ira Hamilton and Winnie Leona. Mr. McPherson is a member of the A. O. U. W., K. of P. and E. A. U. He is a member of the Methodist Episcopal church; in politics a Republican.

J. C. McWilliams, butcher, Rochester, was born in Washington county, Ohio, May 23, 1838, a son of James and Deborah (Caldwell) McWilliams, natives of Fayette county, Pa., and of Scotch-Irish descent. James McWilliams, a dealer in leaf tobacco for many years, was twice married, and became the father of eight children. J. C., the eldest child by the second marriage, was reared in Washington county, Ohio, attended the schools of his native district, and early in life learned the butchering trade, to which he has since given his attention. For a short time after completing his trade he worked for other parties, but in 1872 established himself in business in Washington county, Ohio. In 1874 he came to Rochester, and established his present business. He was married, Aug. 7, 1860, in Washington county, Ohio, to Miss S. A. Vansant, a native of that county, and of German descent. They have six children: Eva L., Lillie, Sarah, Edith, Mary and Ross Vansant. Mr. and Mrs. McWilliams are members of the Presbyterian church, and he is chairman of the board of trustees. In politics he is a Democrat.

David Magaw, owner and proprietor of the "Park Hotel," New Brighton, was born in North Sewickley township, this county, in 1820. and is the youngest surviving child of James and Eunice (Dye) Magaw, parents of twelve children (seven sons and five daughters), two now living. James was a shoemaker, and later in life followed farming. David was reared on the home farm until he was twenty-one; he received a good school training, and for fourteen years was engaged in teaching, chiefly during winters. In 1850 he embarked in a general merchandise business in New Brighton, which he carried on three years; then for six years was in the lumber business, and the following two years, was railroad division superintendent. In 1862 he took charge of the hotel then known as the "Keystone Hotel" but later as "Park Hotel." He married, in 1856, Elvira D., daughter of John Braden, of this county, and three children were born to them: James A., John M. and David. The mother and two sons, James A. and David, died in 1860. Mr. Magaw has been a member of the town council several years. In politics he is a Republican.

STUART MAGEE, merchant, New Brighton, was born in Ireland in 1827, and came to America in 1872. His parents were George and Jane Magee, to whom ten children were born, Stuart being the fourth child. His grandparents were Stuart and Nancy (Jackson) Magee, who had nine children, George being the second son. Our subject received a common-school education, and at fourteen years of age joined his father in the bleaching of linen. He was married, in 1876, to Lizzie, daughter of William Hardy, also a native of Ireland. For five years previous to Mr. Magee's emigration to America he served in the Royal Irish Constabulary. Soon after coming to this country he located in this town and during four years was employed in manufactories here and in Pittsburgh. In 1886 he started his present business. He is a member of the United Presbyterian church; politically a Prohibitionist.

ABNER MAJORS, truckman and farmer, P. O. New Brighton, was born in this county, in 1837, to George and Martha (Mercer) Majors, who had six children, Abner being the eldest. His grandfather, Samuel, married Abigail West, and became the father of seven children, of whom George, the eldest, was a farmer. Abner was born and reared on a farm, and for sixteen years has been engaged in farming and trucking. He married in 1857 Mary Ann, daughter of David Pane, and ten children were born to them, of whom eight are living: John, Henry, Emma (Mrs. Brewer), Alfred, Harley, Hugh, Cedar and Benjamin. Mr. Majors has 150 acres of land, and on this farm are four large fish ponds stocked with German carp. He finds a ready market for his produce at Beaver Falls and New Brighton. In politics he is a Democrat.

GEORGE W. MAJORS (deceased) was born in New Sewickley township, Beaver county, Pa., Nov. 29, 1855. His parents, Samuel and Ella Majors, were natives of Pennsylvania, and lived in Pulaski township, Beaver county, sixteen years; then moved to New Sewickley township, where Samuel died Dec. 30, 1883. His widow is still living. George W. was reared on a farm, was always engaged in agricultural pursuits, and owned forty acres of improved land. He acquired a common-school education in his native township, and was a member of the Methodist Episcopal church and of the I. O. O. F. In politics he was a Democrat.

JAMES H. MANN, dealer in boots and shoes, New Brighton, was born in Mercer county, Pa., in 1840, and is the youngest survivor of the five children of James (a farmer) and Rebecca (Lindsay) Mann. James H. was brought up on a farm, on which he remained until eighteen years of age. He attended public school, and studied at Mt. Union College, Ohio, for several years. From 1864 to 1865 he served in the 6th Regiment, Pa., Heavy Artillery, and coming to New Brighton in the latter year found employment for one year as bookkeeper, then served as principal of North Sewickley Soldiers' Orphan School six months ; after which he established a boot and shoe business under a partnership, which was dissolved in the fall of 1873. Mr. Mann was then elected county treasurer, and at the expiration of his term embarked in the hardware business, continuing four years. During the next four years he was employed as bookkeeper for Sherwood Bros., manufacturers of pottery, after which he began his present business. He married, in 1873, Sallie A., daughter of William H. Bebout, and six children were born to them, five now living: William Horace, Robert Stanley Quay, James Howard, Earl Clifford, and an infant daughter. Mr. Mann is a member of the I. O. O. F., the K. of P. and the A. O. U. W., and of the Methodist Episcopal church. In politics he is a Republican.

JAMES MANOR, carpenter, P. O. Freedom, was born in Virginia, Sept. 22, 1826, a son of James and Elizabeth Manor, natives of Pennsylvania, and who departed this life in Beaver county, Mr. Manor in 1848, and his widow in 1862. They were the parents of eight children, four living. James Manor, our subject, was married twice: first in

BIOGRAPHIES—EAST SIDE. 793

1856 to Rhoda R. Phillips, daughter of William Phillips. She became the mother of three children, and died Sept. 21, 1862, two of her children dying the same year. After her death he married Annie J. Sloan, who was born in Beaver county in 1826, a daughter of Jackson Sloan. Alice A., only daughter of Mr. Manor, is the wife of Albin H. Baldwin. Mr. Manor learned the ship carpenter's trade, and followed that and house building thirty-five years. He and his wife are members of the Presbyterian church, of which he has been an elder twenty years.

DAVID S. MARQUIS, M. D. David Marquis, the grandfather of Dr. Marquis, was at an early day one of the representative farmers of Washington county, Pa. He was the father of nine children, as follows: Joseph, William, Robert, Samuel, John, David, Ellen, Martha and Eliza. David, of this number, was born in Washington county, and on becoming a master of the saddler's trade, removed to Beaver, and resided in that borough until 1842, when the vicinity of Brighton became his home. There he spent the remainder of his life. He married Mary, daughter of James Moore, a lieutenant in the War of the Revolution. Their children were James (who died in the service during the Mexican war), Lydia (deceased wife of Dr. Chapman), David S., Milton M., Edwin (who fell a victim to the horrors of Andersonville prison during the Civil War), Albert, Addison, and Mary E. (deceased). David S. Marquis was born April 14, 1821, in Beaver, Beaver county, and received an academic education; after which he began the study of medicine with Drs. Oliver and Smith Cunningham, of Beaver, meanwhile attending two courses of lectures at the Ohio Medical College in Cincinnati, from which institution he was graduated in the class of 1845-46. He made Hookstown, Beaver county, the scene of his first professional labors, and three and a half years later removed to Freedom, in the same county, where he continued for ten years in practice. In 1859 Dr. Marquis came to Rochester, where he soon established himself as one of the successful physicians of the borough, with a correspondingly extended field of operations. He is a member of the Pennsylvania State Medical Society; of the American Medical Association; and of the Beaver County Medical Society, of which he is the president and the only surviving charter member. Apart from his membership in the Presbyterian church of Rochester, the Doctor is connected with no other organizations. Dr. Marquis was in May, 1847, married to Miss Emeline S., daughter of Jacob Jones, of Sharon, Pa. Their children were Benjamin Franklin (deceased), Addison (deceased), Mary Eliza (Mrs. A. M. Whistler, of New Brighton), Elizabeth A. (Mrs. William Bentley, of Parkersburg, W. Va.), and Lorena M. (Mrs. H. L. Umstead, of Indianapolis, Ind.).

WILLIAM H. MARSHALL was born in Brownsville, Pa., Oct. 4, 1836. His parents, Henry and Mary (Rathmill) Marshall, came from Yorkshire, England, and settled in Brownsville, Pa., about 1830. W. H. Marshall is the third of a family of six sons, and spent his early life in Brownsville until he was about seventeen years of age, when he removed to Pittsburgh, Pa., and worked at the marble trade until he located in the marble business in Rochester, at which he is still engaged. He was married, March 8, 1858, to Asenath J., daughter of Robert and Jane Wallace, of Pulaski township, Beaver county, and they have five sons and one daughter.

JOHN F. MARTIN, foreman of the Enterprise Pottery, New Brighton, was born in that town in 1860, to Ephraim and Mary (Collins) Martin, also of New Brighton and of American parentage. He received a common-school education, and from his seventeenth year has been engaged in the pottery business, four years with the firm of which he is now foreman. He married in 1885, Violet, daughter of Joseph Knott, of this county. In politics Mr. Martin is a Democrat.

J. D. MARTSOLF, contractor and builder, New Brighton, was born in Butler county, Pa., in 1856, the fourth of nine children born to Frederick and Margaret (Miller) Martsolf. He received a common-school education, and at the age of eighteen learned the trade of a carpenter in the town of Butler, serving a three years' apprenticeship, and working at the trade two years afterward. He came to Beaver county in 1878, and in 1882 formed a partnership with John Hatter, under the firm name of Martsolf & Hatter. In January, 1887, this partnership was dissolved, and the firm of

Martsolf & Bro., consisting of J. D. and John Martsolf, was formed. He was married in 1879 to Annie, daughter of David Miller, of Beaver county, and by her had four children, one, David, now living. Mr. Martsolf purchased his present residence in New Brighton in 1886. He is a member of the K. of P., and of the Presbyterian church; politically he is a Republican.

W. G. MASTEN, station agent, Rochester, was born in this county, Feb. 8, 1854, a son of Cornelius and Hattie (Adams) Masten. His mother was born in Beaver county, and his father in Kingston, N. Y., and are of Scotch and English descent. Cornelius was a telegraph operator in Rochester, and for many years clerk on a steamboat, but at present is a clerk in the Pennsylvania Railroad freight office at Rochester. W. G. is the eldest of eight children, and was reared in Bridgewater. Early in life he entered the employ of the Pennsylvania Railroad Company as a clerk, and has been with that company ever since. Since 1883 he has served as ticket and freight agent, and by care and prudence has eminently qualified himself for the railroad business. He married, in 1879, Miss Anna E. Neely, a lady of German descent, and they have three children: Rial, John and Hattie. Mr. and Mrs. Masten are members of the Lutheran church at Rochester. In politics he is a Democrat; he is a F. & A. M., a member of the I. O. O. F., and for five years has been collector for the Royal Arcanum.

MATHIAS S. MECKLEM, contractor and builder, Rochester, was born in Marion township, this county, May 8, 1840, a son of William and Nancy (Strock) Mecklem, natives of Beaver county, the former born in 1808. His paternal and maternal grandfathers, Samuel Mecklem and Mathias Strock, who came to Beaver county about 1806, were both farmers, and were among the early German and Scotch settlers of Beaver county. Mathias S., the eldest of a family of seven children, attended the district school, and was with his parents on the farm until he reached his nineteenth year. He then learned the carpenter's trade, serving an apprenticeship of three years with Henry Alleman, and worked by the day for two years, but in 1864 commenced contracting and building. He married, March 7, 1862, Mary E., daughter of John and Ella (Wine) Hunter, who were early settlers here, of German and English descent. Mr. and Mrs. Mecklem have seven children: Nancy, wife of Charles Musser; Eliza, wife of Joseph Ecoff; William, Joseph and Sarah, twins; Rachel and Lester. Mr. Mecklem is a Democrat in politics; a member of the I. O. O. F. and of the K. of P.

MILLARD F. MECKLEM, attorney, Rochester, was born in Pittsburgh, Pa., Oct. 15, 1851, a son of Archibald and Margaret (Thompson) Mecklem, natives of Pennsylvania and of Scotch-Irish origin. His father was a merchant, and carried on business in Pittsburgh until 1856, when he came to Darlington, this county, and remained until 1869, whence he moved to North Sewickley township, where he died in 1874. He had two daughters and three sons. Millard F., the second child and eldest son, was reared in Darlington, attending the common schools and the North Sewickley Academy, while the latter was yet under the principalship of Rev. Henry Webber. He taught school several terms, and then studied law in New Brighton, in the office of ex-president Judge Chamberlin and Mr. Pearsol. He was admitted to the Beaver county bar March 10, 1882, and has been engaged in the active practice of his profession since 1883, in Rochester. In politics he is a Republican, and in 1886 served as chairman of the Beaver county Republican committee. He was elected burgess of Rochester in 1883, and has been five times re elected to that office. He is a member and a trustee of the Rochester Baptist church. He was married, in 1881, to Ella, daughter of Robert and Eliza (Thompson) Jackson. She too is of Scotch-Irish origin. Her grandfather Jackson was a cousin to President Andrew Jackson. He settled upon a farm near Beaver Falls, whence her father went, in about 1841, to North Sewickley township where she was born. Her grandfather and father were Democrats. She is a member of the Presbyterian church. Their children are Erle Homer, Norman Jackson, Ella and Marguerite.

E. D. MELLON, oil refiner, P. O. Freedom, was born in Pittsburgh, Pa., July 6, 1856, a son of Patrick and Sarah J. (Knox) Mellon, natives of Ireland, who came to America and were married in Pittsburgh, where they located until 1868, when they

BIOGRAPHIES—EAST SIDE. 795

moved to Beaver county and here have since resided. They were the parents of seven children, five living. E. D. married, Sept. 17, 1881, Nettie W. Cumming, who was born in Beaver county, March 2, 1862. Her parents, David and Sarah A. Cumming, were natives of Pennsylvania, and settled in Beaver county after they were married. David is deceased ; his widow is still living in Freedom. Mr. and Mrs. Mellon have had three children: Eugenia and Grace, living, and Helen, deceased. Mr. Mellon has been engaged in the oil business most of his life, and has filled several borough offices.

JOHN MENGEL, farmer, P. O. Freedom, was born in Germany, Aug. 5, 1830, a son of Peter and Elizabeth (Wagner) Mengel, who died in Germany. They were the parents of six children, all living. John, the third child, immigrated to America in 1848; remained three months in New York, and then came to Freedom and has resided there and in New Sewickley township ever since. He was united in marriage, May 8, 1856, with Catherine E., daughter of John Hartmann (deceased). She was born in Pittsburgh July 8, 1838, and is the mother of ten children, nine living: Maggie A. W., John A., Edward H., Lillie L., George F., Cora A., Elmer J., Laura M. and Euretta C. Mr. Mengel learned the trade of shoemaking, which he followed twenty years in Freedom. He afterward bought seventy acres of land in New Sewickley township, where he now resides. The family are members of the German Lutheran church.

HENRY J. METZ, retired, New Brighton, was born in Würtemberg, Germany, in 1811, to George M. and Margaret (Olnhausen) Metz, the former of whom was a farmer and for many years a justice of the peace. Henry J. was reared on the farm, and received a common-school education. He came to this country when twenty-one years of age, and shortly afterward located in Pittsburgh, where he followed butchering until 1856, in which year he came to Beaver county, and purchased 142 acres of land, which he farmed for fifteen years. In 1872 he moved to New Brighton, where he has since lived retired. He married, in 1839, Amelia, daughter of John Stann, of this county, and by her had thirteen children, seven yet living: Herman, George, Richard, Frank, Christ, Edward and Augustus. Our subject is a member of the town council; an adherent of the Presbyterian church; in politics a Republican.

WILLIAM MILLER, of the firm of Miller & Sons, proprietors of the Keystone planing mill and box factory, and manufacturers and dealers in rough and dressed lumber, packing boxes, sash, doors, mouldings, etc., scroll sawing and turning, Rochester, was born in Beaver county, Feb. 19, 1835. His parents, John and Elizabeth Gripp) Miller, were natives of Germany, and came to America in 1834, settling in Beaver county. His father was a cooper by trade, but became a farmer after he came to Beaver county. William is the third in a family of six children. He was reared on a farm, attended the common schools in winter, and in his eighteenth year went to New Brighton and learned the carpenter's trade. After working as a journeyman for two years he engaged in contracting and building; came to Rochester in 1855, and in 1870 established his present business, employing about twenty men. He married, May 26, 1857, Catherine Hollermann, who was born in Butler county, Pa., of German descent. They have seven children: John A., George W., Charles M., W. L., H. J., Maggie E. and Emma J. The eldest two sons are partners in the firm of Miller & Sons. John, the eldest son, is taking an active interest in the new Pottery Works at Rochester. All the boys work in the Keystone factory. The family are members of the German Lutheran church, of which Mr. Miller has been a trustee. In politics he is a Republican. He is a charter member of the A. O. U. W. at Rochester.

JOHN A. MILLER, secretary of the Rochester Pottery Company, was born in Rochester, March 26, 1858, the eldest son of William and Catherine Miller. He was reared in Rochester, receiving his schooling there and at Duff's Commercial College at Pittsburgh, where he graduated in 1876. He worked in his father's planing mill, where an extensive business in contracting and manufacturing woodwork, and dealing in lumber, is done, from 1883 until August, 1887, and has been a partner with his father. When the pottery company was organized he was elected secretary. He is a Republican in politics. He is a prominent member of the Masonic fraternity, having taken thirty-two degrees in that order. He married, in 1880, Phœbe Cable, born in Rochester, of German descent, daughter of J. H. Cable, a merchant. They have one child, Olive.

GEORGE H. MILLER, farmer, P. O. Knob, was born in New Sewickley township, this county, Oct. 24, 1839, a son of John and Elizabeth Miller, natives of Germany. They came with their parents to America, settled in Beaver county and died on the farm where George H. now resides. The latter was married Aug. 18, 1863, to Matilda Phillips, who was born in Butler county, Pa., July 11, 1839, a daughter of George and Mary Phillips, natives of Germany, where they were married. They immigrated to America and settled in Butler county, Pa., but afterward moved to Beaver county, where they died. Mr. and Mrs. Miller have seven children living: Mary C., Wesley C., William H., Edward L., Emma E., George A. and Albert J. One daughter, Lizzie, is deceased. Mr. Miller has been engaged in farming all his life, and owns about 100 acres of land. He and Mrs. Miller are members of the Evangelical church.

JOHN MINER was born in Onondaga county, N. Y., Aug. 27, 1806, the son of Amos and Phœbe Miner, both New Englanders, of English descent. His ancestor, Thomas Miner, came to New England in 1630. Mr. Miner received his education in the common schools of his native state. In 1826 he came to New Brighton, of which place he has ever since been a resident, and engaged in the manufacture of what were then called "patent buckets." He continued in that business nearly forty years, or till the close of the Civil War, when he retired from active business. During about twenty years he was the president of the Beaver County National Bank at New Brighton, and has been president of various other corporations. In 1832 he was married to Caroline, daughter of John Pugh, a prominent member of the Society of Friends. They had one daughter, Caroline, now the widow of Major David Critchlow. In 1835 he was married to Mary Ann Pugh, and they had three children: J. F., Henry (deceased) and Henrietta, now the widow of Dr. George W. Read. Her children are Harry M., Bessie F., Marion P., Emily H., and George W. Read. Mrs. Critchlow's children are John Miner, Mary Emily, Edward Coe, Caroline Townsend (Whysall), Louis Warren, Helen, Charles Dilworth, and George Read Critchlow.

J. F. MINER, county treasurer, New Brighton, was born in this county Dec. 21, 1837. His parents were John and Mary Ann (Pugh) Miner, natives of New York and Pennsylvania. He was reared in New Brighton, attended the schools of his native town, and embarked in the business of his father. He was afterward bookkeeper and teller in the National Bank at New Brighton, four years. From 1865 to 1884 he was engaged in the lumber business at New Brighton. In 1884 he was elected county treasurer, and has served one term of three years. In politics he is a Republican. He was married in New Brighton, May 20, 1862, to Emma, daughter of Thomas and Elizabeth (Pugh) Read, former of whom was a miller, and of English descent. Their union has been blessed with three children: Elizabeth, John R. and Mary Ethel. The family are members of the Presbyterian church.

JOHN MINKE, cooper, P. O. Freedom, was born in Rosenthal, Germany, Dec. 31, 1822, a son of Jacob Minke, who departed this life in Germany. John came to America in 1847, and was married in New York to Margretha Schleiter, who was born in Rosenthal, Germany, Nov. 10, 1828, and is the daughter of John Schleiter. After marriage they removed to New London, Conn., and resided there four years, during which time Mr. Minke went to California, and returned in 1852. He then moved to Pittsburgh, Pa., and remained two years, when he came to New Sewickley township, now St. Clair, where he has resided ever since. He has four children: Mattie, wife of Charles Bischoffberger; Mary, wife of Charles Mohr; Katie, wife of John Brandt; and August J. Mr. Minke has been a cooper all his life. He owns a nice property, where he and his family reside. His son, August J., owns the Freedom Oil Works Mr. and Mrs. Minke and their entire family are consistent members of the Lutheran Trinity church.

C. O. MITCHELL, farmer, P. O. New Brighton, was born in Rochester township, this county, a son of David and Jane (Davidson) Mitchell, natives of Pennsylvania.

David was born in this county in 1801, and was the son of Robert Mitchell, a farmer. Our subject's maternal grandfather, James Davidson, was a soldier in the war of 1812. They were of Irish descent, and were among the early settlers and farmers of Beaver Creek, near New Brighton. C. O. is the fifth of a family of eight children, four of whom are now living. He was reared on the farm, attended the common schools and Duff's Commercial College at Pittsburgh, where he was graduated in 1876. He has made farming his business. He is a prominent member of the I. O. O. F., and is past officer in both lodge and encampment.

JAMES S. MITCHELL, carpenter and lumber dealer, New Brighton, was born in this county in 1847, a son of James W. and Mary J. (Neill) Mitchell; the former, a stone cutter, came from Allegheny county to this county in 1832. They had four sons and five daughters. The paternal grandfather, J. W. Mitchell, came from Scotland at an early day. James S. was reared in New Brighton, attended the public schools until seventeen years of age, and at nineteen learned the trade of carpenter, which he has since followed. He is now also engaged in the lumber business, as successor to Miner & Co., New Brighton. In 1864 he joined the 204th Pennsylvania Fifth Artillery, and served eleven months. He married, in 1868, L. E , daughter of David Johnson, of Fallston, this county, and four children have been born to them: Jennie M., Frederick S., David J. and Juliet. Mr. Mitchell was for seven years a member of the town council of New Brighton, but now resides at Beaver Falls, where he has been three years a member of the council. He is a member of the A. O. U. W., K. of P., I. O. O. F. and G. A. R., and an adherent of the Methodist church. Politically he is a Republican.

JOHN R. MOHLER, lumberman, P. O. Freedom, was born in Allegheny county, Pa., in 1824, a son of Samuel and Mary Mohler. Samuel, a native of Switzerland, emigrated to America in 1806, and first located in Pittsburgh, Pa. His wife was a native of Pennsylvania, and after marriage they located in East Liberty, but in 1844 moved to Beaver county. They afterward went to Missouri, and finally to Oregon, where Samuel died in 1880, and where his widow still resides. They were the parents of four children, three of whom are living. John R., the eldest, was united in marriage, April 27, 1847, with Sarah A. Irwin, who was born in Beaver county, Pa., Aug. 14, 1827, a daughter of Thomas Irwin. Mr. and Mrs. Mohler are the parents of ten children, five living, one son and four daughters. They are members of the Methodist Episcopal church. Mr. Mohler is a member of the I. O. O. F.

WILLIAM T. MOHLER, lumberman, Freedom, is one of the enterprising business men of that place, a member of the firm of William T. Mohler & Co. He was born in Beaver county, Dec. 11, 1849, a son of John R. and Sarah A. Mohler, natives of Pennsylvania, where they were married, and have remained all their lives. They are the parents of ten children, five living. William T. was united in marriage, March 27, 1878, with Maggie E. Epple, who was born in Freedom, Pa., Dec. 28, 1844, a daughter of Lewis Epple (deceased). Mr. Mohler is a ship carpenter by trade, and engaged in lumbering in 1883. He and his wife are the parents of five children, two living: Elvernia M. and Ross C. He is a member of the I. O. O. F.

OLIVER MOLTER, proprietor of livery, New Brighton, was born in Beaver county, Pa., in 1841, the fourth son in the family of thirteen children born to J. C. and Fanny (Camp) Molter, the former a miner and brick maker. Oliver received a liberal education at public school and academy, finishing in his fifteenth year. In August, 1864, he enlisted in Company B, 204th regiment P. V. He has been twice married; on first occasion, in 1859, to Margaret Brown, who bore him four children—William, Frank, Nora and Ida—and died in 1871. The following year Mr. Molter married Ada Laney, by whom he has five children: James, Grace, Bird, Herbert and Ralph. From early age Mr. Molter was engaged in the coal business, and since 1865 has owned and operated coal mines. In 1878 he commenced his present livery business. He has been town councillor, school director and assessor, and president of the Beaver County Agricultural Society; he is a member of the A. O. U. W., K. of P. and G. A. R.; he is a Republican

A. G. MOORE, farmer, P. O. Rochester, was born in Pulaski township in 1859. There is probably not a more widely known family in Beaver county than that of the Moores. Samuel Moore came from Westmoreland county to Beaver county at an early day; was a boat builder by trade, and married Nancy Reno, who bore him four children. His first wife dying, he married Hannah McCleary, to whom were born seven children. Alfred, a son of the first wife, was educated in the public schools, and, following the ambitions of his father, from early life engaged in boating, and for many years was captain of several steamboat lines. He was thus engaged until 1855, when he purchased 150 acres of land in Pulaski township, where he lived until his death in 1875. He married Elizabeth R., daughter of James and Elizabeth Porter, of this county, and became the father of eight children, six of whom are now living. Alfred G., the third son and sixth child, was reared on the old farm, receiving a liberal education. In 1875 he went to California, where he remained until the following year. In 1881 he was married to Deborah, daughter of Oliver and Patience Houlette, of New Brighton, this county, and three children have been born to them: Linnie Z., Oliver H. and Mabel. The mother of our subject resides at Rochester, and is in her sixty-sixth year. The family are members of the M. E. and Episcopal churches. In politics Mr. Moore is a Republican.

DUNLOP MOORE, D.D., pastor of the First Presbyterian church, New Brighton, was born in Lurgan, County Armagh, Ireland, July 25, 1830, and is a son of Dunlop and Margaret Moore. He studied at Edinburgh and Belfast, and graduated in 1854. He was missionary of the Irish Presbyterian church to Gujurat, India, in 1855-67, and to the Jews in Vienna, Austria, in 1869-74. Since 1875 he has occupied his present pastoral position. He assisted in translating the Scriptures into the Gujurati language, composed treatises on Mohammedanism and Jainism, and edited a monthly periodical, *The Gnyandipaka*, in the same tongue. He also translated, with Dr. S. T. Lowrie, Nägelsbach's commentary on Isaiah in the American Lange series, and has contributed articles to various reviews. The degree of Doctor of Divinity was conferred on him by Washington and Jefferson College in 1877. He was married to Rosetta Anne Luis, in Hamburg, Germany, Aug. 20, 1870. Their children are Dunlop, John, Luis, William Hermann, Rosetta Anne and Alfred Kerr.

JAMES MOORE, retired, P. O. Baden, was born March 18, 1812, at Enniskillen, County Fermanagh, Ireland. His father, James, came to this country from County Derry, Ireland, in 1815, and landed in Baltimore, Md., where he remained three years in the furniture business, having learned the trade of a cabinet maker in London. After the war of 1812, business became so dull that he, imbued with the spirit that still rules, was prompted to "Go West," in the hope of greater success. He sold out his business and came to Pittsburgh in 1818, only to find trade as stagnant as he had experienced it in the East. No money being in circulation he was compelled to trade his wares for country produce and orders on stores for the necessities of life. The first actual silver money he received was for making the coffin for Commodore Barney, about one year after he removed from Baltimore. Tiring of this unsatisfactory and profitless way, he purchased in 1822, from Mrs. McKean Buchanan, through Hon. Trevanion B. Dallas, a tract of 407 acres of land on the Ohio river, and now included within the boundaries of Baden borough, with the intention of engaging in agricultural pursuits, paying therefor $950.00, $500.00 of which sum was in furniture for Judge Dallas' wedding outfit. He finally, in 1828, closed out his business and removed to his farm. In 1787 he married Margaret, daughter of James Porteus, also of County Fermanagh, Ireland, and by her had ten children. He died at the age of ninety years and his wife at eighty-seven.

James Moore, our subject, is the only child now living of this union, and is numbered among the oldest and most respected citizens of Baden, or neighboring portion of the county. He was educated in the common pay schools of the period in Pittsburgh, and at the age of sixteen years began to work at the pattern making trade, which he followed for thirty years as an exceptionally skilled and careful workman. With large ideality and constructiveness, he manifested from early childhood considerable mechanical and inventive genius, as his models of various creations of his brain, in the patent office, testify. When ten years old he made a paper row boat large enough to carry him, by pasting and varnishing successive layers of strips of paper over wooden ribs and keel, an idea only recently patented and advantageously used by prominent scullers. When twelve years old, he made the patterns for the various parts, and completely fitted and set up a small brass steam engine and boiler, with only the limited inspection allowed a boy of the half dozen very crude steam engines then in Pittsburgh, as his guide or instructor in its construction. In 1834-35 he designed and made the patterns and shapes for the first locomotive built west of the Allegheny mountains, "The Mountaineer," for use on the levels between the inclines in connection with the Pennsylvania canal; and with the aid of Joseph Bridges and James Boustead, both now dead, fully and successfully constructed it. He married, in 1837, Harriett, daughter of Samuel Pierce, of England, who established the first steam marble cutting works west of the mountains. Four children were born to them: Margaret A. (now Mrs. R. C. Machesney), William H. (married to Adelia A. Duncan), Alciphron (now Mrs. W. S. Pier) and Charles P., who in infancy died with his mother in February, 1848. Mr. Moore for the past thirty years has lived with his son and daughters at Linmore, in Baden borough, upon the land purchased by his father two-thirds of a century ago, and where he in his boyhood days chased the deer, foxes, wild turkeys, etc. That disputed his title to what is now a portion of an almost continuous city from Pittsburgh to Beaver. Politically he has always been a Republican, and the esteem of his fellow citizens has manifested itself in his selection, by their votes, for the various offices of honor and trust in the borough.

WILLIAM MOORE, farmer and stockgrower, P. O. New Brighton, Pa., was born on Beaver Creek, in Rochester township, this county, Aug. 5, 1805, and is a son of James Moore, who was of Scotch-Irish descent and a soldier in the Revolutionary War; he was a lieutenant under General Washington; was wounded, and carried a ball for many years in his right shoulder; he was a farmer by occupation and settled in Rochester township in 1794, on Beaver Creek; his log house, being the first erected in this part of the county, was regarded by the Indians as an encroachment on their rights, and it was necessary for him to have a man to stand on guard while he was at work. William is the only survivor of a family of ten children. He has been twice married, and by his first wife, who died in 1828, had two children. He was again married, March 26, 1838, to Elizabeth, daughter of Solomon and Susannah (Vinks) Lightfoot. Solomon Lightfoot was born March 2, 1783, in Maryland, and died April 1, 1861; his wife, also a native of Maryland, was born Feb. 5, 1792, and died Nov. 2, 1858. The marriage of Mr. and Mrs. Moore was blessed with seven children, six now living: David J., in California; Isabella, wife of J. Donaghy, of Brooklyn, N. Y., a landscape and portrait painter, with office in New York City; Susannah, wife of Jackson Bebout, a railroad conductor; Celesta, wife of Addison Sloan; Isphene H., wife of J. W. Nippert; Clara, wife of Joseph J. Snellenburg; and William C. Mrs. Moore is a member of the Methodist church. In politics Mr. Moore is a Democrat.

٠J. P. MOORE, druggist, Rochester, was born Feb. 10, 1857, a son of Alfred and Eliza (Porter) Moore, natives of Pennsylvania, and of English and Irish descent. Alfred, a steamboat pilot for many years on the Ohio river, was the father of six children, and died in 1885. The paternal and maternal ancestors of J. P. were among the early settlers of Beaver county. James Moore, his great-grandfather, went from Beaver county to the war of 1812, and his name is prominently mentioned in the United States History for gallant conduct in that war. Samuel Moore, grandfather of J. P., was a farmer, and settled here before the town of Rochester was thought of, and shot wild deer where is now the center of the borough. He died in Rochester, in 1883, nearly one hundred years old. J. P., the fourth child, was reared in Beaver county, attended the seminary at New Brighton for two years, and subsequently Beaver College. At the age of fifteen he commenced the study of pharmacy, entered a store in Pittsburgh, Pa., and clerked there until 1885, when he established his present business. He is a member of the I. O. O. F. and the A. M., of Rochester. He traveled in the West for two years, and visited nearly all the states and territories.

W. J. MORGAN, farmer, P. O. Knob, was born in Beaver county, on the farm where he now resides June 28, 1849. His parents, Lyghtle and Susanna Morgan, were natives of Pennsylvania, and after marriage settled on the farm where W. J. was born. There Lyghtle died; his widow is living in Freedom. W. J. was married, in September, 1871, to Kate Eisenbrann, who was born in Beaver county, June 20, 1849, a daughter of Daniel and Barbara Eisenbrann of this county. She is the mother of nine children, eight of whom are living: Ira, Crawford, Maud, Charlie, James, Herby, Callie, Stephen. Savilla is deceased. Mr. Morgan has been engaged in farming all his life, and owns seventy-six acres of improved land. He and his wife are members of the Presbyterian church. He holds the office of school director.

WILLIAM S. MORLAN, attorney at law, P. O. New Brighton, was born in Fallston, this county, in 1828, the fourth son of Richard and Mary (Erwin) Morlan, who had seven sons, six of whom grew to maturity. Stephen Morlan, grandfather of William, had six sons and two daughters, Richard being among the juniors; he came from Virginia to this county in 1825, and was here engaged in the manufacturing of linseed oils; also erected a gristmill in Fallston; and died at the age of seventy-six years. William S. received a public-school education, and learned the trades of blacksmithing and coachsmithing, which he followed for about ten years; then commenced the study of law, was admitted to the bar in 1857, and has since continued in practice. He enlisted, in 1861, in Company F, 101st Regiment, P. V., and served three and one-half years, finally becoming sergeant. He was a prisoner for about eight months at Plymouth, N. C., and at Andersonville. In 1852, he married Elizabeth Wilson, by whom he had four children, three of whom are living: Carrie (Mrs. Milligan), Marion (a teacher in Ohio) and Alice (an artist in New York City). The mother of this family died and Mr. Morlan afterward married Emma Young. In politics he is Independent.

ANDREW MORROW, conductor, New Brighton, was born in this county in 1829. His parents, John and Elizabeth (Moore) Morrow, had five children, of whom Andrew is the eldest. Charles and Rebecca (Moore) Morrow, grandparents of Andrew, came from Ireland and settled early in this country. Charles was a tailor by trade, and received a common-school education. Andrew was born and reared on his grandfather's farm, where he remained until eighteen years of age. He was engaged at different pursuits until 1852, when he commenced railroading. He now holds the position of conductor on the P., Ft. W. & C. Ry., in which capacity he has served for twenty-seven years. He was married, in 1853, to Mary, daughter of R. B. and Mary (Gillmore) Evans, and they have had four children, two of whom are living: Louie F., now dispatcher in the superintendent's office of the P., Ft. W. & C. Ry., at Pittsburgh, and Vesta at home. Mr. Morrow is a F. & A. M., politically a Republican.

THOMAS MUSE, steamboat captain and pilot, Rochester, is a native of England, born July 12, 1823. He is a son of Thomas and Hannah (Brown) Muse, the former a miller. His parents were born in England, came to Pennsylvania and settled at Pottsville. They had eight children, Thomas, the third child was reared in Allegheny county, where he attended the common schools. Early in life he went on the Ohio and has served in almost every capacity since the time that the boats were floated down the river and pushed or pulled up by hand. He has witnessed all the changes and progress made in boating, and has himself done much for the advancement in methods. He has owned and managed boats, and has successfully made his own way in the world. He has resided in Rochester since 1870. Mr. Muse was married in 1845 to Sarah, daughter of John Danks, and a native of Pennsylvania, of English descent. Mr. and Mrs. Muse have been blessed with three children: Homer, a pilot; Jennie and Charles, the latter a student at Ada, Ohio. The captain and wife are members of the Methodist church at Rochester.

THOMAS NANNAH, farmer, P. O. Rochester, was born in Rochester, Pa., June 8, 1831, and is a son of Reese and Sarah (Bell) Nannah, natives respectively of New Jersey and Beaver county. They were married in Beaver county and lived here until the death of Reese. His widow resides in Rochester. Thomas was married, Aug. 28, 1855,

BIOGRAPHIES—EAST SIDE. 801

to Elizabeth Musser, who was born in New Sewickley township Nov. 8, 1835, a daughter of Abraham and Matilda Musser, natives of Pennsylvania. Abraham is deceased; his widow resides with her son-in-law. Mr. and Mrs. Nannah are the parents of four children: Electia M., Ada A. and Joe M., living, and Frank S., deceased. Mr. Nannah was a pilot on the Ohio river about thirty-five years, but left the river in 1877, and since that time has been farming. Mrs. Nannah is a member of the Methodist Episcopal church. In politics Mr. Nannah is a Democrat.

W. J. NANNAH, undertaker, P. O. New Brighton, was born in this county in 1837, the second child and eldest son of Jesse and Catherine (Javens) Nannah. Reese Nannah, father of Jesse, and a native of Scotland, came to the United States with a brother in early times, and soon after arriving located in Beaver county. W. J. Nannah attended the common schools, and at the age of sixteen joined his father who was a pilot on the Ohio river and followed that vocation until 1864. He also learned the painter's trade, which he carried on twelve years, and in 1881 embarked in his present business. He married, in 1863, Alice, daughter of Robert Jackson, of Beaver county, and to them have been born two children: Fred J. and Lula C. Mr. Nannah is a member of the I. O. O. F., K. of P. and A. O. U. W. He attends the service of the Presbyterian church; in politics he is a Democrat.

H. J. NEELY, physician, P. O. Brush Creek, was born in Allegheny county, Pa., Oct. 24, 1851, a son of William and Margaret M. R. (Brewerman) Neely, natives of Pennsylvania. Mrs. Margaret Neely died in 1866, and Mr. Neely afterward married Mary A. Philips. H. J. Neely was married, May 11, 1882, to Frances M. Philips, born in Butler county, Pa., Nov. 11, 1860, a daughter of John and Sarah (Miller) Philips, natives of Pennsylvania, the former deceased. Mrs. Neely is the mother of one child, Sebertius O., born April 9, 1883. Mr. Neely began the study of medicine in 1878, and was graduated from the Jefferson Medical College of Philadelphia, in 1881. He located in Unionville, Beaver county, Pa., where he has been engaged in practice ever since. He and his wife are members of the Baptist church. He is a member of the I. O. O. F.; in politics he is a Democrat.

JOSEPH A. NELSON, tax collector, Rochester, was born in West Greenville, Mercer county, Pa., Feb. 22, 1839, a son of John and Nancy (Carman) Nelson, natives of Pennsylvania and Delaware, respectively, the father of Scotch descent. John Nelson, who was a silversmith, came to Rochester in 1852, and carried on business there until his death. Joseph A. learned the silversmith's trade in Rochester, where he was reared and attended the common schools and the Academy at Beaver. He then went to the Ohio river as steward on a steamboat, where he remained for twelve years, and subsequently engaged for a time in packing medicine for Dr. Shallenberger, of Rochester. He enlisted Aug. 21, 1861, in Company C, 63d P. V. I., and served three years. He is a Republican, and served three terms as assessor; also several terms as tax collector. He was married, in 1879, to Catherine Marsh, a native of New York state. She is a member of the Methodist Episcopal church. He is a Baptist, and is secretary and treasurer of the Sabbath-school. He is a member of the G. A. R.

JOHN R. NIBLO, bookkeeper and general manager for L. H. Oatman, lumber merchant and manufacturer of woodwork, Rochester, was born in Beaver county, Pa., Sept. 8, 1840, a son of John R. and Mary (Small) Niblo. His maternal grandfather, John Small, who came to Beaver county about 1800, was a farmer, and served in the war of 1812. His paternal grandfather, John R. Niblo, came from Ireland to Beaver county, and was a farmer in Brighton township. His two sons, our subject's father and his brother, Alexander R. Niblo, were printers by trade, and among the first to publish a paper in Beaver county, Pa., called the *Aurora*. Their circulation was very limited, for the county was sparsely settled. Our subject's father died in 1842. He had three children. John R., the second child, was reared in Vanport, Pa., attended the district school and the old academy at Beaver. His first business was teaching school, which he followed for twelve years. He has held his present position since 1883. He married, in 1861, Millcent J., daughter of James Worrick, a prominent farmer in Beaver county. She is of English descent. They have one child, Lizzie. Mr. and Mrs. Niblo are members of the Methodist Episcopal church, in which he has served as trustee, steward and class leader, and assistant Sabbath school superintendent. He has served eight years as secretary of the K. of P., and a member of the A. M. and the T. of H.

JOHN NOONEN, farmer, P. O. Rochester, was born on the farm where he now resides, in New Sewickley township, March 6, 1838. His parents, Martin and Mary (Kline) Noonen, were natives of New York, where they were married and first located. They afterward moved to Erie, Pa., thence to Rochester, and finally located on the farm where their son John now resides. The latter was married, April 16, 1874, to Margaret Musgrave, who was born in Beaver county, Pa., Oct. 19, 1843, and is a daughter of James and Margaret (Hendrickson) Musgrave, the former born in England, and the latter in America. They were married in Pennsylvania, and settled in Beaver county. The mother is deceased. Mr. and Mrs. Noonen have one child, Charles E., born Feb. 9, 1875. Mr. Noonen learned the blacksmith's trade, which he has followed twenty-eight years, being also engaged in farming. He and his wife are members of the Methodist Episcopal church. In politics he is a Democrat.

MICHAEL PIERSOL NYE, civil engineer, P. O., Fombell, was born in January, 1836, at Unionville, Pa., a son of Samson S. and Ruth (Piersol) Nye, natives of Ohio and of Marion township, this county. He began teaching in 1853, and has taught every winter but two since, having received his education at North Sewickley Academy and at a branch of Pennsylvania University at Zelienople, and was a classmate of the president of Thiel College at Greenville, Pa. From 1857 to 1860 he was principal of Webster High School at Portsmouth, Ohio. In 1862 he married Hattie Hartzel, daughter of George and Charlotte (Stamm) Hartzel, who were natives of Bucks county, Pa. Nine children have been the fruits of this union, as follows: Ruth (now Mrs. Frederick Twentier), Charlotte, King, George, Benjamin, Fred, Joseph, Richard and Peire.

L. H. OATMAN, dealer in and manufacturer of lumber and all kinds of woodwork, also contractor and builder, P. O. Rochester, was born June 26, 1826. His parents, Arnold and Abigail (Hays) Oatman, were natives of Vermont and Connecticut, respectively, and of English and German descent. His father, a carpenter, contractor and millwright, had a family of six children, of whom L. H. is the fifth, and the only son living. He was reared in Connecticut, worked in a sawmill in early life, and at the age of twenty set out for himself. He took up the painter's trade, and worked at house and sign painting for ten years. He then built a sawmill in Beaver county, which he conducted for three years. In 1861 he embarked in his present business at Rochester, and has met with uniform success. He married, in 1844, Eliza, daughter of Martin Noonen, and born in the State of New York, of German origin. They have three children: Lewis, Arnold and, Minnie. They attend the Episcopal church. In politics Mr. Oatman is a Democrat, and has served as a member of the council of Rochester. He has traveled extensively in the United States. In 1885 he built the Ellis Hotel at Conneaut Lake, Crawford county, Pa., of which he is still the owner.

CHARLES W. PALMER, real estate agent, P. O. New Brighton, was born in Fayette county in 1847, a son of Rev. Henry Palmer, now a minister in Beaver Falls. Mr. Palmer received a liberal education in youth, and has since early life led an active business career. He married, in 1837, Maggie, daughter of William and Elizabet1 Geddes, of Scotland. They have had five children, only two of whom are now living: William and Charles. Mr. Palmer was for many years employed as baggage master of the Pittsburgh & Fort Wayne Railroad. He served in the Civil War in Company B, 58th Regiment, P. V. I., and enlisted in the 112th or 2d Cavalry. He was actively engaged in the battles of the Wilderness and Cold Harbor. He is a member of the Methodist church; in politics he is a Republican.

JACOB PANNER, farmer, P. O. Knob, was born in Germany, Dec. 12, 1825. His parents, Henry J. and Elizabeth Panner, immigrated to America in 1837, and settled in Pittsburgh, where they lived many years. The father died in that city and the mother in this county. Jacob Panner was married, June 27, 1847, to Mary, daughter of John

BIOGRAPHIES—EAST SIDE. 803

and Catherine Mink, who came from Germany in 1834. They first settled in Baltimore, Md., afterward moving to Pittsburgh, and thence to Beaver county, where they died. Mrs. Panner was born in Germany June 25, 1825. She has an adopted child, Jacob H. who married and has two children. Mr. Panner owns 121 acres of land. He and his wife belong to the English-Lutheran church.

JAMES I. PARKS, lumber dealer, P. O. Freedom, was born in Allegheny county, Pa., June 8, 1830, a son of David and Anna (Hamilton) Parks, natives of Allegheny county, where they were married, settled and remained there until 1845, when they moved to Beaver county, and remained there until their deaths. They were the parents of eight children, six living. James I., the eldest, was married first to Emeline McDonald, who bore him four children: W. A , John H., Anna V. and George J. After her death he was united in marriage with Mary, daughter, of Samuel Dean, and born in Beaver county; she is the mother of two children: Mabel Dean and Nellie Duff. Mr. Parks is a carpenter by trade, and has been engaged in the lumber business for thirty years. He owns a valuable farm in this county.

SIMON C. PHILLIPS, farmer, P. O. Knob, was born in Germany, June 24, 1836, a son of George and Mary C. Phillips, who came to America in 1837, and settled on the farm where Simon C. now resides. Both died here. Simon C. was married, Jan. 27, 1859, to Elizabeth Miller, who was born in Beaver county Aug. 8, 1841, a daughter of John and Elizabeth Miller, natives of Germany, both of whom died in this county. Mrs Phillips is the mother of four children: Henrietta, William H., George L. and Catherine E. Mr. Phillips has been a farmer most of his life, and owns eighty-one acres of improved land. He and Mrs. Phillips are consistent members of the Methodist Episcopal church.

HENRY PHILLIS, retired farmer, Beaver Falls, was born in Independent township, this county. Aug. 27, 1814, a son of Joseph and Elizabeth (Cowen) Phillis. Joseph was a wheelwright early in life, but later became a farmer, and had a family of six sons and six daughters. Henry, the eldest son, was born and reared on the farm, and learned a trade which he followed one year. He then bought a farm in Moon township, where he lived eight years, at the expiration of which time he came to Pulaski township, purchased eighty acres of land, and resided on a farm belonging to his wife until 1886, when he purchased property and moved to Beaver Falls. He was married, in 1843, to Malinda. daughter of Francis Alcorn. Five daughters and one son have been born to them: Elizabeth, Rebecca (Mrs. Stewart), Euphemia (Mrs. Allen, deceased), Alice, Malinda (deceased) and William H. Mr. Phillis has been a prominent citizen, and has held numerous positions of trust, and has, as executor and administrator, settled several estates. For thirty years he has been an elder in the Presbyterian church at New Brighton. In his political preferences he is a Republican. His grandfather, Joseph Phillis, came from Kentucky opposite Cincinnati, about 1777, and settled in Washington county, where he purchased 300 acres of land, and followed farming and stock raising, being one of the first settlers in that part of Pennsylvania. He had seven sons and four daughters, Joseph, father of Henry, being his fourth child.

JOSEPH POLLOCK, dealer in hosiery, notions and household goods, New Brighton, was born in Mercer county, Pa., eldest son of David and Isabella (McColl) Pollock. He was educated at the common schools, and when nineteen years of age learned carriage building, which trade he followed for several years, seven in Beaver county, whither he had come in 1876. He enlisted, April 25, 1861, in Company H, 7th Ohio Infantry, served three years and three months, and participated in some of the most memorable battles of the war. In 1864 he married Mrs. Esther Bogardus, who bore him two children: Emma, and Nellie. After her death he married, in 1878, Lizzie Tobin, who blessed him with three children: Edwin, Willis and Laura Bell. Mr. Pollock commenced in his present business in 1884. He is a member of the Baptist church; in politics a Republican.

JOHN B. PORTER, farmer, P. O. Rochester, was born in New Sewickley township, this county, Jan. 1, 1831. His parents, John and Nancy (Sharp) Porter, natives of Ireland, came to Beaver county in 1797. His grandfather, Edward Porter, a farmer, settled in this county. John Porter, a farmer, lived to be seventy years old, and had ten children, all of whom lived to maturity. John B., the sixth child, was educated in the old log school-house He has been a farmer all his life, and now owns a well-improved farm and dairy in connection, known as the Rochester dairy. He was married, first in 1858, to Martha Ellen, daughter of James Prentice, a prominent farmer of Beaver county. She was of Scotch descent, and died in 1872. Of their eight children only four are now living. Mr. Porter next married, in 1884, N. M., daughter of James Young. They have one child, Mabel Nell. Mr. and Mrs. Porter are members of the United Presbyterian church; in politics he is a Republican.

JOSEPH POWELL, farmer, P. O. Knob, was born in Beaver county May 14, 1830. His parents, Henry and Sarah Powell, were natives of Pennsylvania and settled after their marriage in Beaver county, where they died. Joseph was married, first May 10, 1853, to Margaret, daughter of Joseph and Jeannette Zahler, both deceased. She was born in Beaver county, and died in 1866. They had six children, three of whom are living: Sarah J., Amelia and Charles S. In 1869, Mr. Powell was married to Anna Deemer, who was born in Butler county, Pa., a daughter of John and Fannie Deemer, both deceased. By this marriage were three children, two living: Ida E. and Edmund H. Mr. Powell has been a farmer most of his life, and owns fifty-nine acres of improved land. He and his wife are members of the Lutheran church.

GENERAL THOMAS J. POWER, of Rochester, was born in Beaver county July 7, 1808, a son of Samuel and Elizabeth (Penny) Power, natives, respectively, of Loudoun county, Va., and New Jersey, and of Scotch-Irish descent. Samuel Power came to what is now Beaver county in 1796, and settled where is now the county seat. He was a farmer, and took care to have his children taught the English language. He was elected sheriff of Beaver county in 1809; served as a member of the legislature, also as adjutant-general of the state. In later life he was a merchant at Freedom, where he died. Thomas J., the fifth of ten children, was reared in Beaver county, is a civil engineer by profession, and has spent twenty-seven years of his life on public works. He also served one term as adjutant-general of the state. He was married, in 1832, to Mary Ann, daughter of Samuel Johnson. Her father built the first house in Beaver, Pa. They were of Scotch-Irish descent. General Power and wife have six children living. In politics he is a Republican.

EVAN PUGH and JOHN PUGH, sons of Jonathan and Naomi Pugh, of Pughtown, Chester county, Pa., and their wives, Lydia and Sarah, who were daughters of brothers by the name of Townsend, came to Beaver county in May, 1804, and settled at the lower falls of Beaver, now known as Fallston. Soon after their arrival they erected a flouring mill (both being practical millers), which they continued to operate for many years, when Evan withdrew from the business, and John continued until the year 1858, when he rented to another party, and on the morning of the 5th of July of that year, the mill was totally destroyed by fire together with all its contents. It is proper, however, to state that a large and very substantial four-story brick and stone building, with four run of stones had taken the place of the original frame building. During the existence of the mills very many thousand barrels of flour were made therein, which found a market in Philadelphia, Pittsburgh and southern cities, but chiefly in the two first named places. A very large amount of custom or "grist" work was also done, it being almost the only mill for many miles in either direction that could be relied upon during the dry season. It was no uncommon thing for grist work to come the distance of fifteen to thirty miles, and often customers had to wait two and sometimes three days for their grinding. In addition to the street being filled with wagons, etc., might also be seen from three to five canoes in the creek, from the Ohio river nearly as far up as Pittsburgh. This only occurred during the dry period in the summer and fall. The brothers Evan and John were also engaged in wool carding and cloth dressing for several years, also in the manufacturing of cotton yarn, the style of the latter firm being Pugh, Wilson & Co. In connection with the mills was a store of general merchandise. They were also at one time connected with Talbot Townsend in the manufacture of salt on Yellow Creek, in Jefferson county, Ohio; and in boring two or

BIOGRAPHIES—EAST SIDE. 805

more wells for salt on "Hollow Rock Run," near to the aforesaid place. After many attempts and ultimate failure to obtain salt water in sufficient quantity at the latter wells, the company erected a building in which they made linseed oil and did wool carding for a few years. In February, 1832, there was an unprecedented flood in the Ohio river, and the village of Fallston suffered to such an extent as to cause Evan to seek higher ground for a home. He therefore built a residence on the east side of the Beaver creek, in New Brighton, to which he removed the same year. In May, 1837, his wife (Lydia) died, being in the sixty-seventh year of her age, and he (Evan) died in July, 1841, in his seventy-sixth year. They died without issue. Sarah, wife of John, died in 1826, in her fiftieth year, and he afterward married Ann Peck (widow), of Baltimore. About 1836 he built a residence in New Brighton, to which he removed and occupied to the time of his death, which occurred in May, 1860, being nearly eighty-one years of age. He was president of the Branch bank of the United States, at one time located in New Brighton, and continued as such until the institution wound up its affairs by appointing trustees. Soon after the death of John Pugh, his widow, Ann P. Pugh, returned to Baltimore, where a few years later she died. There were no children by the second marriage. John and Sarah Pugh had four children, two sons and two daughters. Jonathan, the eldest, died at an early age; Caroline died in 1831; Mary Ann died in 1881 or 1882; Joseph T., the third in age, now seventy-nine, has living: sons, John, Evan and Henry; and daughters, Sarah Ann, Caroline Cecelia, Irene Ida—Mary Elizabeth is deceased.

FRANK S. READER, editor and proprietor of the *Beaver Valley News*, New Brighton, was born Nov. 17, 1842, in Greenfield (now Coal Centre), Washington county, Pa., a son of Francis and Ellen Reader, the former a son of William Reader, a native of Warwickshire, England. Frank S. passed most of his early life on the farm and in working at the carpenter's trade; he attended the public schools and Mount Union College, Mount Union, Ohio. He married, Dec. 24, 1867, Merran F. Darling who bore him two children: Frank E. and Willard S. Mr. Reader entered the Union army April 27, 1861, serving in the 5th W. Va. Cavalry, and while scouting June 20, 1864, was captured, but succeeded in escaping from the train while on his way to Andersonville July 19 following, arriving in the Union lines at Petersburg July 30. In July of the following year he entered the civil service and became chief deputy collector for the Twenty-fourth Collection District of Pennsylvania. He established the weekly *Beaver Valley News* at New Brighton May 22, 1874, and the daily edition Feb. 5, 1883. He has been a member of council and secretary of county committee; is a member of the Methodist Episcopal church; a Republican in politics.

JAMES REED, ship builder, P. O. Freedom, was born in Butler county, Pa., Dec. 24, 1814. His parents, James and Mary (Winghart) Reed, settled in Butler county and remained there until their deaths. They had nine children, three of whom are living. James was married, March 10, 1842, to Eunice Dull, who was born in Pennsylvania Dec. 10, 1816, a daughter of John and Catherine Dull, both of whom died in Butler county. Mr. and Mrs. Reed have five children, three of whom are living: Anna J., wife of H. P. Wilson; Eli M. and Charles W. Those deceased are Martha and William J. Mrs. Reed died Jan. 10. 1884. Our subject is a ship and house carpenter, and has followed this trade all his life; he owns the property where he resides. He was elected justice of the peace in 1867, and has filled that office ever since. In politics he is a Republican. He is a member of the Methodist Episcopal church, and has lived in Freedom and St. Clair since 1849.

NICHOLAS REEFER, farmer, P. O. Knob, was born in Germany Sept. 26, 1828, a son of Ommert and Catherine Reefer, who came to America in 1857, and settled in Beaver county. Ommert died here, but his widow still lives in Pittsburgh. Nicholas married, May 2, 1852, Catherine Freshcorn, who was born in Germany March 26, 1833, to Daniel and Catherine Freshcorn, who came to America in 1837 and settled in Beaver county, where they died. Mr. and Mrs. Reefer have had ten children, nine of whom are living: Catherine, John, Elizabeth, Henry, Nicholas, Caroline, William, Charlie and Margaret. One daughter, Mary, is deceased. Mr. Reefer is a shoemaker by trade, but is engaged in farming at the present time. He owns 150 acres of land. He and his wife are members of the German Reformed church.

JAMES J. REEVES, merchant, Beaver Falls, is a son of Joseph and Sarah (Maghey) Reeves, the latter a daughter of Robert and Rachel (Parks) Maghey, of Butler county, Pa. Our subject's parents were married in 1845, and had two sons and three daughters: Mary Jane (now Mrs. Marshall), Eliza (deceased), Margaret (now Mrs. Sieon, of Beaver Falls), James J. and John (art tile manufacturers). The paternal grandfather, Daniel Reeves, a cabinet maker, came from Mount Holly, N. J., to this county at an early day, and purchased three pieces of land, on part of which Beaver Falls now stands. He married Margaret Steen, who bore him four sons and three daughters. Joseph, the eldest son, was born in this county in 1818, received a common-school education, and learned carpentering which he followed for a few years. He then engaged in boat-building with his brother John on the Erie Canal, continuing in same until the building of the Pittsburgh & Fort Wayne railroad from Pittsburgh to Alliance, when he was appointed master mechanic for that road and its several branches, a position he held up to his death in 1875. The family are members of the Methodist church; politically they are Democrats.

OZIAS RENO, farmer, P. O. Freedom, was born in New Sewickley township, July 24, 1834, a son of Isaac and Nancy Reno, natives of Pennsylvania, and who died in Freedom. They were the parents of two children. Ozias, the only one living, was united in marriage, Oct. 12, 1854, with Lydia, daughter of William Carey (deceased). She was born in Maryland, May 8, 1835, and was the mother of eleven children, five living. She died Feb. 8, 1879. July 26, 1880, Mr. Reno married Talitha A. Pritchard, who was born in Allegheny City Feb. 6, 1839, and is a daughter of Daniel and Esther Pritchard, both living. Mr. Reno was reared on a farm. When the war broke out he enlisted in Company H, 139th Regiment, P. V., and served his country nearly three years. Mrs. Reno is a member of the Methodist Episcopal church. They moved to St. Clair borough from New Sewickley township in 1883, and bought the place where they now reside.

WILLIAM D. RENO, steamboat captain and pilot, also a member of the firm of Evans & Reno, liverymen, at Rochester, Pa., where he was born and reared, is the son of William and Sophia (Evans) Reno, the latter born in 1796. They were natives of Pennsylvania, and of French and Welsh descent. William was born in 1794, and died in March, 1860; he was a pilot and captain on the Ohio river in early life; in later life he retired to the quiet of the farm; his farm included forty acres of what is now the town of Rochester. He had eleven children, nine of whom grew to maturity, and four are now living. William D. attended school in Rochester and at the Beaver College, and early in life went on the Ohio river. He enlisted in April, 1861, in the 10th Pennsylvania Reserves; was a non-commissioned officer; was taken prisoner at the battle of Charles City Crossroads, and held on Belle Isle for five weeks, and then exchanged. He rejoined his regiment, and was engaged in the battles of Antietam, Fredericksburg and Gettysburg. In the last named battle the 10th Reserves took a very conspicuous part. He was discharged in 1864, and since the war has been a pilot and captain on the river most of the time. He embarked in the livery business in company with Captain Thomas G. Evans, in 1884. He was married, in 1877, to Bella, daughter of George and Ann S. (Mitchell) Graham, and their children are Lewis Evans, Blanche Ethel and Anna Sidney. Mr. and Mrs. Reno are members of the Methodist Episcopal church; in politics he is a Republican. He is a member of the I. O. O. F., the R. A. and the G. A. R.

AMOS ROMIGH, farmer, P. O. Freedom, was born in Allegheny county, Pa., April 12, 1812, a son of Jacob and Susanna Romigh, who died in this county. Amos was married, June 24, 1851, to Lottie, daughter of Calvin and Jemima Leonard (both deceased). She was born in Warren county, Pa., Nov. 10, 1829, and is the mother of eight children, only two of whom. Laura F. and Calvin L., are living. Those deceased are Anna J., Nancy A., Susan A., Jackson M., Lotta C. and Jacob A. Mr. Romigh has been engaged in farming nearly all his life, and owns 104 acres. Mrs. Romigh is a member of the Lutheran church.

JACOB ROMIGH, farmer, P. O. Freedom, was born in Washington county, Pa., Feb. 3, 1824, a son of Jacob and Susanna Romigh, natives of Washington county, who moved from there to Beaver county, where they died. Our subject was married, Nov. 27, 1849, to Elsie, daughter of Charles and Elsie Baker, who died in this county. Mrs. Romigh was born March 11, 1825, and is the mother of nine children, eight of whom are living: Louisa, James B., Caroline, William O., Lizzie M., David F., Alice and Jacob C. One daughter, Nettie A., is deceased. Mr. Romigh has followed farming all his life and owns about eighty-one acres. He and Mrs Romigh are members of the Presbyterian church.

JAMES RONEY, grocer, and agent for Adams Express Company, New Brighton, was born in Rochester, this county, in 1837, being the eldest of the three children of Arthur and Jane Roney. He received a public school training in his native town, and from ten years of age followed boating on the Erie Canal extension, until it was closed up. For the past sixteen years he has been engaged in his present grocery business. He was married in 1858 to Matilda McDonald, who bore him one child, Charles W. Mr. Roney is a member of the I. O. O. F.; politically a Democrat.

WALTER A. ROSE, M. D. Walter Rose, the grandfather of Dr. Rose, who emigrated from Scotland to the province of Canada, settled in Elgin county, Ontario, where his death occurred at the age of one hundred and three years. His children were five sons and one daughter, of whom Alexander, the father of Dr. Walter A. Rose, also a native of Scotland, resided in Elgin county, where he was a manufacturer of various implements of wood. He was married to Catherine Monroe, whose children were Isabella, wife of John Warburton; Jennetta (deceased wife of Elihu Moore): Catherine (wife of Colin McDougall); Margaret, (wife of Edward Capsey); Rachel (deceased) and Walter A. The last named child was born in the county of Elgin, Ontario, April 17, 1842, and received his education at the common schools of his native town and the graded schools at St. Thomas, near his home. In the year 1862 he began the study of medicine with Dr. Robert Lyon Sanderson, of Sparta, Ontario, and in 1863 and 1864 attended two courses of lectures at the University of Michigan, Ann Arbor, together with two additional courses at the Medical University of Buffalo, N. Y., where he was graduated in 1867. Dr. Rose at once chose Rochester as a favorable point in which to begin his professional career, and has since that time found no occasion for seeking a change of locality. During the years 1875 and 1876 he also maintained an office in Allegheny City. His practice, which is of a general character, has been large and successful, and has given him an enviable rank among the leading physicians of the county. Dr. Rose has, since Rochester became his residence, identified himself with the growth and advancement of the borough, and done much to promote its prosperity. He is one of the incorporators of the Rochester & Beaver Street Railway, and director in the Second and Third National Building Associations of Rochester. He is a member and examining surgeon of the A. O. U. W., and prominently identified with the Masonic order as a member of Rochester Lodge No. 229, F. & A. M.; member of Oskalon Commandery, Knights Templar, of Allegheny City, and of Pennsylvania Sovereign Grand Consistory, of Pittsburgh. He is also connected with Syria Temple, Nobles of the Mystic Shrine.

LEWES ROSENMUND, farmer, P. O. New Brighton, was born in the city of Basel, Switzerland, in 1832, and came to America in 1845. His parents, John and Catherine (Gysin) Rosenmund, had fifteen children, and the nine surviving ones came with their parents to America, locating in Pittsburgh, Allegheny county. Mr. Rosenmund came to Beaver county in 1874 and purchased fifty acres of land, where he now resides He was married, in 1862, to Wilhelmina, daughter of John Flinner, of Zelienople, Butler county, Pa. They have had six children, three of whom are living: Mary Louise, Emma Catharine and Charles Henry. The family are members of the United Presbyterian church.

NICHALIES ROSENBERGER, farmer, P. O. Brush Creek, was born in Germany, April 3, 1826, a son of John and Margaret Rosenberger, natives of Germany. After the death of his wife, John emigrated to America and settled in Beaver county, where he died. He was the father of three children, two living. Our subject was united in marriage, Jan. 9, 1848, with Catherine Strutt, who was born in Germany, May 18, 1824, a daughter of Henry and Catherine Strutt, both of whom died in Germany. Mr. and Mrs. Rosenberger are the parents of nine children, six living, viz.: Catherine, Casper, George, William, Lizzie and Mary. Those deceased are Lizzie, John and Henry. Mr. Resenberger came to America in 1846. He was employed several years in digging coal, and then engaged in farming. He owns 218 acres of improved land. He and his wife are members of the Presbyterian church.

JOHN RUCKERT, farmer, P. O. Freedom, was born in Germany, Feb. 28, 1831, a son of John and Christine E. Ruckert, who died in Germany. John came to America in 1850, and remained in Pittsburgh three years, then moved to Freedom. He married, in October, 1854, Lucinda, daughter of Casper and Magdelena Coffman. She was born in Butler county, Pa., in 1836, and is the mother of fourteen children, ten of whom are living: John, Mary, Henry, Elizabeth, Emma, Margaret, Ida, Amelia, George and Charlie. The deceased are Matilda, William, Jacob and Anna. Mr. Ruckert learned the shoemaker's trade, which he followed about twenty-five years, and since that time has been farming. He owns 160 acres of land. He and his wife are members of the Lutheran church. In politics he is a Democrat.

JOSEPH SANTS, designer, New Brighton, was born in Bath, England, in 1834, the eldest child of Joseph and Sarah (Griffith) Sants, who were parents of fourteen children. He was educated at college in his native country, left school at the age of sixteen years and served eight years in the English navy. From early childhood Mr. Sants has made designing and modeling his special study, and to-day ranks among the most skillful in the profession. He came to this country in 1859, from South America, landing in Baltimore. He has been through Australia and India, and was engaged in the Crimean War. For the past twenty years he has been employed by different firms in New Brighton, having but recently permanently located here. He is now employed in the large pottery establishment of Elverson, Sherwood & Barker, and is the designer and modeler for all goods manufactured by that firm. He was married in 1865 to Maggie, daughter of Martin Kappler, of Pittsburgh, Pa., and they had one child that died. Mr. Sants enlisted in 1862 in Company B, 122d Regiment, P. V. I., for nine months, and at the expiration of that time enlisted in the 50th Regiment, in which he remained until it was disbanded. He then enlisted in the Construction Corps, in Tennessee, Company B, 1st Regiment, 2d Battalion. He is a Republican, a member of the G. A. R., and a F. & A. M.

CONRAD SCHLEITER, marble dealer, Freedom, was born in Germany, Dec. 11, 1839, a son of John and Catherine Schleiter, who died in Germany. Conrad was married, Oct. 30, 1865, to Fredricka Fliehman, who was born in Germany, May 21, 1844, a daughter of Conrad and Charlotte Fliehman, who died in Germany. Mr. and Mrs. Schleiter are the parents of twelve children, of whom nine are living. Mr. Schleiter learned the trade of marble cutting in New London, Conn., and has followed the same ever since. He came to America in 1854, and to his present home in 1868. He served in the Civil War in the 13th Connecticut Regiment. He and his wife are members of the German Lutheran church; in politics he is a Democrat.

WARWICK SCOTT, New Brighton, is a native of St. Louis, Mo., born in 1851, a son of Thomas and Agnes (McCready) Scott, who had three children. Warwick being the eldest. Thomas Scott was a manufacturer, and died in 1869, aged forty-eight years; his widow now resides with a daughter in Philadelphia. Warwick was educated in the public schools, which he left at the age of eighteen years to engage in farming and manufacturing. He came to New Brighton in 1874, and engaged in carriage manufacturing until 1880. He was then elected secretary of the Building and Loan Association of New Brighton, which position he held for six years. He is superintendent and proprietor of the Beaver Valley Art Tile Works, which were established in 1887. He was married, in 1878, to Anna, daughter of Jacob Price (deceased), late of Philadelphia, Pa. They have two children: Thomas and Edward. Mr. Scott has been collector of New Brighton borough. He is a member of the A. O. U. W. and R. A.; he is a Republican.

WILLIAM S. SHALLENBERGER. "Schallenberg," the name given to a mountain in Canton Uri, Switzerland, from very early times, because of its remarkable echo, is at the same time the origin of the family name Schallenbergers, a hardy race of people dwelling on this mountain, which was covered with pasture to the top, and was a favorite gathering place for the people. A few traces of the family appear in history. Three of the name were killed at Lempach in 1385. One Ulric Schallenberger led a company of the men of Uri against Charles the Bold at Grandsen, in 1476. In the same year he served as aid to Hans of Holwyl, at the battle of Murton, and was present, with all of the family name who could bear arms, at the battle of Nancy, Jan. 5, 1477, where Charles was killed. The paternal ancestry of William S. Shallenberger is traced with certainty to Ulric Schallenberger, born in Canton Uri, in 1694. John, son and only child of Ulric above mentioned, was born at Altdorf, Switzerland, in 1720, and the same year Ulric emigrated from Switzerland and settled in Lancaster county, Pa. Abraham, the son of John, and youngest of three children, was born in Lancaster county; Pa., Oct. 15, 1764. Abraham, son of the last mentioned, was born in Fayette county, Pa., Aug. 22, 1797.

William S., the son of Abraham, and subject of this biography, was born Nov. 24, 1839, at Mount Pleasant, Westmoreland county, Pa., his mother being Rachel Newmyer, daughter of Peter and Susannah Newmyer. His early years were spent at the public school, and in learning the trade of his father, who was a saddle and harness-maker. In October, 1855, when not quite sixteen years of age, he was elected teacher of one of the district schools of Washington county, Pa., and taught during the following winter. He removed with his father's family to Beaver county, Pa., in the spring of 1856, and has since resided in Rochester. He attended the University at Lewisburg, Union county, Pa., during a portion of two years, but was compelled to leave before graduating on account of failing health. He has since received the honorary degree of A. M. from this university. In 1862 he enlisted in the army. We quote from material before us, a few leading estimates of the public services and personal characteristics of Mr. Shallenberger. His army record we find well summarized in the following paper prepared by the surgeon of his regiment, afterward division surgeon, Dr. I. Wilson Wishart, and signed by all the officers of the regiment.

HOSPITAL 1ST DIV. 2D. CORP A. OF P. Sept. 17, 1864.

Adjutant Shallenberger, in response to the call for volunteers in 1862, enlisted as a private, and contributed largely by his influence and personal efforts to the formation of the 140th Regiment, P. V. Upon the organization of the regiment he was appointed adjutant, and has served in that capacity until the present time. At the battle of Chancellorsville, the first in which the regiment was engaged, he received a slight wound, which, however, did not require him to leave the field. At the battle of Gettysburg he was severely wounded in the leg, but rejoined the regiment at Morrisville, Va., before his wound was healed, and participated with his comrades in all the marches and fighting of the fall campaign.

Just recovering from a severe attack of illness he started upon the campaign of 1864, when scarcely able to keep the saddle; was in the battle of the Wilderness and at the fight of Corbin's Bridge, near Todd's tavern, May 8th; received a very severe wound in the thigh, from which he is now suffering.

Adjutant Shallenberger has remarkable business capacity. Having full confidence in his ability to discharge the duties of paymaster to the satisfaction of the department, I very cordially recommend his appointment.

(SGD.) I. WILSON WISHART,
Surg. 140th Pa. Vol.

In forwarding this paper Gen. Nelson A. Miles says:

"Adjutant Shallenberger has served under my command, and I know him to be a most reliable, efficient and worthy officer."

Gen. Hancock adds: "This young officer made, I think, more recruits for us in Western Pennsylvania in the winter of 1863-64 than probably any other officer; but aside from this he is a gallant young officer, richly deserving promotion."

The last wound compelled the retirement of Adjutant Shallenberger from active service. After the lapse of two years the ball was extracted from the thigh, and the wound healed. From that time until 1876, when he was elected to his first political office, that of Representative in Congress, Mr. Shallenberger was engaged in mercantile pursuits. He represented in Congress the 24th District of Pennsylvania, composed of Washington, Beaver and Lawrence counties; was reëlected in 1878, and again in 1880. In a Washington City paper published in June, 1880, the following estimate of his official character appears:

"Mr. Shallenberger is scrupulously attentive to his public duties; rarely out of his seat in the House; faithful in committee work; extremely courteous and genial in his relations with his colleagues; always practical, and never obtrusive or out of place in his conduct of legislation. He has had remarkable success in securing the favorable action of Congress upon bills which he has had in charge. He has reason to feel proud of the endorsement recently given him by his constituents. For the first time in nearly forty years a renomination for a third term has been made by his district, and by the most flattering popular vote of all the counties at their primaries."

During his third term he served as chairman of the Committee on Public Buildings and Grounds, but devoted much time to the study of the tariff, a subject of controlling interest to his constituents. His speech of April 15, 1882, has been widely circulated and highly praised. General J. K. Moorhead, of Pittsburgh, himself an able defender of the tariff for ten years in Congress, acknowledged the receipt of a copy of the speech under date of May 1, 1882, as follows:

"DEAR SIR:—I thank you a thousand times for your very able tariff speech, which I have just read. It should be spread over the United States by thousands; and it places you at the very head of protectionists. I have just finished reading it, and as my time for leaving my office has arrived, I can say no more, but could not leave until I had said this."

Hon. Wm. Lawrence, of Ohio, then first comptroller of the treasury, wrote under date of Dec. 18, 1882, in regard to this speech, as follows:

"Prior to the last political campaign, I had occasion to prepare some matter to enable me to make speeches in Ohio, and I procured a copy of your speech, which I read and studied with great care. I congratulate you and your constituents on the excellence of your speech. It has a vast fund of information compressed in comparatively small space, and is one of the most able and exhaustive speeches upon the subject which I have read."

Since his retirement from Congress, Mr. Shallenberger has been engaged in the banking business in Rochester, and as treasurer of various corporations. He was on the 1st of December, 1864, married to Josephine, daughter of Gen. Thomas J. Power of Rochester, and their children were Thomas P., Laura, Francis W., Elizabeth, Mary, William and Josephine, of whom Thomas P. and Francis W. are deceased. Mr. Shallenberger is a member of the Baptist church, of Rochester, and has been a deacon since its organization.

A. T. SHALLENBERGER, physician, Rochester, was born in Westmoreland county, Pa., Feb. 20, 1825, a son of Abraham and Rachel (Newmyer) Shallenberger, natives of Pennsylvania and of German and English descent. His father, a saddler in early life, was afterward, for many years, engaged in mercantile trade. From 1856 to 1868 he resided in Rochester. He had five sons and three daughters. Dr. A. T., the second child, was reared in Westmoreland county, attended the academy at Greersburg, and early in life commenced the study of medicine in the office of Dr. W. C. Reiter, where he remained three years. He then entered Jefferson Medical College, graduating in 1846. He began practice with his preceptor, came to Rochester in 1847, and continued in active practice for eight years. Since then he has devoted his time to the manufacture and sale of the well known medicine, "Shallenberger's Fever and Ague Antidote." He was married in Westmoreland county, Sept. 1, 1846, to Mary, daughter of Daniel Bonbright, and born in Westmoreland county, of German descent. Their children are H. M., a physician now in active practice in Rochester; Oliver B., of Pittsburgh; Herbert B. and Alethe, wife of A. A. Atterholt, of Pittsburgh. The family are members of the Baptist church. The doctor is a trustee of the church. He is a Republican, and has frequently served as a member of the school board of Rochester, also as trustee of Beaver Academy for eleven years.

H. M. SHALLENBERGER, physician and surgeon, Rochester, was born in Rochester, Pa., Oct. 4, 1853, and is a son of Dr. A. T. Shallenberger. He was reared in Rochester, attended school here, also attended the Bucknell University, Pa., a Baptist Institution, where he graduated in the regular literary course in 1873, and the same year commenced the study of medicine in the office of Dr. Clark, at Mount Pleasant, Pa. In 1874 he entered the Jefferson Medical College at Philadelphia. remaining in that college and the hospitals of that city until 1876, obtaining a thorough preparation for practice. Since 1876 he has been successfully engaged in practice in Rochester. In politics he is a Republican. He is a member of the Medical Society of Beaver county, and has served as borough physician one term. He is a member of the Baptist church.

D. B. SHANER, retired farmer, P. O. Brush Creek was born near Unionville, Beaver county, Nov. 22, 1820. His parents, David and Ruth (Peirsol) Shaner, were natives of Pennsylvania, and settled in Beaver county where they remained until their deaths. D. B. was united in marriage April 22, 1842, with Elizabeth Peirsol, who was born in New Sewickley township Feb. 25, 1826, and is a daughter of John and Neoma (Mace) Peirsol, who were natives of Pennsylvania, and both of whom died in this county. Mr. and Mrs. Shaner are the parents of six children, of whom three are living: Malissa, wife of William Feezel, Mac and John. Neoma and two infants are deceased. Mr. Shaner has been a farmer all his life. He and his wife are members of the Methodist Episcopal church. In politics he is a Prohibitionist, and has filled the office of school director a number of terms.

JOHN SHARP. merchant, Rochester, was born May 3, 1825, near New Castle, in that part of Beaver county which is now a part of Lawrence county. His parents, Moses and Margaret (Armstrong) Sharp, were of Scotch and Irish origin and natives of Pennsylvania. His father and grandfather were farmers, and the latter was among the earliest settlers at Darlington. Moses Sharp was born and reared in the county where he spent his life and died in 1830. He had three children. John. when five years old, went to live with his uncle, John Armstrong, with whom he remained, working on the farm and in the mill, until he reached his majority. He learned the shoemaker's trade in Bridgewater; then went on a steamboat as a deck hand for two years, and was engaged on the Ohio in various capacities for a number of years; he was watchman on a steamboat for two years, and was a clerk on the wharf boat at Rochester for two years, and for a like period was captain and part owner of a steamboat. He then bought a boat and ran it between Rochester and Warren, Ohio, for fifteen years. In 1868 he embarked in his present business, under the firm name of Sharp & Hoffman. He was married, in 1853, to Rebecca Keister, a native of Pennsylvania. Mrs. Sharp is of German descent. She is a member of the Methodist Episcopal church. Captain Sharp is a Republican in politics; he is a F. & A. M.; a member of the I. O. O. F. and encampment.

GEORGE W. SHERWOOD, superintendent and proprietor of pottery, P. O. New Brighton, was born in Hancock county, W. Va., in 1852, the son of John and Hannah (Bryant) Sherwood, who had four children, George W. being the youngest. John was a lumber dealer, and died at the age of forty-five years; his widow is living at New Brighton. They had three children, who are living. George W. is a practical pottery man, having followed the business since he was ten years old, and was for nine years employed by Thomas Elverson. In 1876 Mr. Sherwood, in partnership with his brother, commenced business in a building 30 by 50 feet, with one kiln and propelled by horse power. By their personal supervision and close application to business they built up one of the largest establishments of the kind in Western Pennsylvania. Mr. Sherwood married, in 1873, Annie E., daughter of Nathan Wood, of New Brighton, and they have three children: Gay Oakley, George P. and Louie E. Mr. Sherwood is a member of the I. O. O. F.; in politics a Republican.

THOMAS Y. SHILTON, oil refiner, P. O. Freedom, was born in England, Aug. 25, 1849, a son of Joseph and Jane (Young) Shilton, the former a native of England, the latter of Scotland. They were married in England, where Joseph died, after which the widow and Thomas, who is the only child, came to America, and settled in Beaver county, where she died in 1886. Thomas was united in marriage, March 20, 1881, with Frances White, who was born in Beaver county in 1862, a daughter of E. N. White. To Mr. and Mrs. Shilton have been born three children (two living): Thomas L., Edwin B. and Edwina J. (deceased). Mr. Shilton was formerly engaged in the drug business, but since marriage has been in the oil business. He owns a fine farm of over 200 acres in Economy township. He is a F. & A. M., a member of the I. O. O. F. In politics he is a Democrat.

JAMES SHOUSE, captain and pilot, P. O. Baden, was born in Steubenville, Ohio, in 1831. His father, Jacob; was born in Easton, and died at the age of seventy-five years. He married Jane Harper, of Jefferson county, Ohio, and by her had twelve children, three of whom are now living. Jacob was a ship carpenter and boat builder, being among the oldest of his trade in Western Pennsylvania. In company with one hundred and thirty-two he went to Allegheny county and settled in a place, which has since become a town and is called Shousetown. James was born and reared in Steubenville, Ohio, where he remained until 1876. He was educated at the academies and at Washington college. He left school at the age of fifteen years to engage in steamboating, and has since spent his life at that business, being familiar with all the work connected with steamboating. He was married in 1871 to Rosa Bell, daughter of Henry and Sarah Welch. Seven children, five of whom are living, were the result of this union: Alice Margaret, Sarah Amelia, Emma Carlton (deceased), Laura M. (deceased), Anna Mary, Richard E. and George Boal. During the war Mr. Shouse was engaged in the transporting service, having enlisted in Company B, 6th Ohio Regiment. He is a member of the Lutheran church; of the I. O. O. F.; politically he is a Democrat.

LAWRENCE SHUSTER, passenger conductor, New Brighton, was born in this county Nov. 19, 1846, the seventh child of M. and Sarah (Davis) Shuster, who were the parents of eleven children. His father was by trade a blacksmith. Lawrence received a common-school education, and at the age of fourteen years learned the blacksmith's trade. He has been employed on the railroad twenty-three years, ten years of that time as passenger conductor for the P., Ft. W. & C. Railway Company. He was married in 1867 to Mollie, daughter of James and Mary (McClosky) Walsh, natives of Ireland. Four children have been born to Mr. and Mrs. Shuster: Charles M., Lewis Davis, Lillie Amanda and Lawrence Lane. For several years past Mr. Shuster has made his home in New Brighton, where he owns some property. He is a member of the K. of P., and of the A. O. U. W.; politically he is a Republican.

ALEXANDER F. SMITH, brick manufacturer, New Brighton. was born in Butler county, Pa., in 1839, and is the third of the five children of Ephraim and Ann (Lee) Smith. Ephraim Smith, a woolen manufacturer, moved with his family from Fallston to Mt. Ephraim, Pulaski township, this county, in 1852. Jonas Smith, great-grandfather of Alexander F., lived in Yorkshire, England, and had a son Alexander, who married a daughter of Ephraim Ellsworth, of Kirkstall, near Leeds, in Yorkshire, to which union was born a son, Ephraim, father of our subject. Ephraim Smith was but four years of age when his father died, and he was reared by his grandfather Ellsworth. Alexander F. was educated in Beaver county, attending the public schools. and until twenty-four years of age worked in a woolen mill. Soon afterward he commenced the manufacture of brick for building purposes, as well as fire brick. He is also engaged in farming, owning nearly 200 acres of land. He resided in Pulaski township until 1886, when he removed to New Brighton. He was married, in 1866, to Hannah Rebecca, daughter of John Backus, of Erie county, Pa., and by her had seven children: Perry Alexander, Ellen Lydia, Myra Ann, Edward, Mary Celia, Lee Backus and Bessie Edith. Mr. Smith was a justice of the peace in Pulaski township, a school director, and director of the New Brighton Bridge Company. He and his family are members of the Methodist church. In politics he is a Republican.

CHARLES W. SMITH, dealer in real estate, Cucamonga, California, was born in Rochester Oct. 13, 1857, son of Jacob and Christiana (Walter) Smith. His parents, natives of Germany, came to this country when children, their parents settling in New Jersey, where they grew up and were married, coming to this county in 1851. Their family consisted of seven children. The eldest son, John F. Smith, is a prominent merchant in Rochester, and keeps a general store. It was here that our subject did his first work as a clerk, which occupation he commenced as soon as he left the public school. On reaching his majority he became a partner in the business, and continued with success until 1884, when Charles W. retired. In 1885 he went to Cucamonga, Cal., and bought a ranch, which he afterward sold, and bought another of 1,600 acres, which he sold in 1887. He has since made other investments, and intends making California his permanent home. He was married, Sept. 23, 1880, to Louise, sister of Emmett Cotton, a prominent attorney at Pittsburgh, Pa. Her parents are of Irish and French descent. Mr. and Mrs. Smith have four children: Charles D., Emma C., Bertha and an infant. Mrs. Smith is a member of the Episcopal church; in politics he is a Republican.

JAMES SMITH, farmer, P. O. Beaver Falls, was born in Lancashire, England, in 1834, a son of James and Grace Smith, natives of England, and the parents of thirteen children. James, the seventh child, came to this country in 1842, locating first at Lowell, Mass., where he resided until the spring of 1868; then came to New Brighton, this county, where he was engaged as foreman of the carding department of Wild & Co.'s Keystone Woolen Mills until 1872, in which year he bought and moved to his present farm of fifty-seven acres in North Sewickley township. He has two coal banks on his place, which he operates with profit. He was married, in 1857, to Sarah Turner, of New Brighton, by whom he had six children, three now living: Joseph, Anna and Ires. The mother dying in 1867, Mr. Smith married, the same year, Ann Taylor, and by her has three children: Sarah, Frank and Grace, all at home. Mr. Smith was school director for three years in North Sewickley township; in politics he is a Republican. Mrs. Smith is a member of the Episcopal church.

W. A. SMITH, merchant, Rochester, was born in Monroe county, Ill., March 16, 1844, and is a son of J. B. and Eliza (Ramey) Smith. His mother was born in Illinois, and his father in Ohio. J. B. Smith was a merchant and a photographer; of his four children by his first wife, W. A. is the only son. After seven years of age, our subject was reared in Greenville, Mercer county, Pa., and attended the public schools and academy. He chose law as a profession, went to Liverpool, Ohio, and contemplated taking a regular law course, but financial matters prevented. He learned the business of photographing with his father, and in 1867 moved to Beaver, and embarked in mercantile trade. Since 1868 he has carried on business in the same line in Rochester. Mr. Smith was married, Dec. 20, 1870, in Zanesville, Ohio, to Miss Katie Hibbard, of St. Clair, Mo. Mr. and Mrs. Smith are members of the Methodist Episcopal church, and he served for fourteen years as a Sabbath-school superintendent. He is president of the Equitable Aid Union Life Insurance Company of Rochester, a beneficiary society for both sexes, also president of the Grand Union, E. A. U., of the state of Pennsylvania, an annual meeting of delegates from 240 Subordinate Unions in that state.

WILLIAM H. SMITH, stone mason and contractor, P. O. New Brighton, was born in Perry county, in 1840, the eldest son of seven children of S. C. and Matilda (Page) Smith. His father is a stone mason by trade, and came to Beaver county in 1858. William H. received a common-school education and learned the trade of his father, which

814   HISTORY OF BEAVER COUNTY.

he has followed all his life. He was married in 1866 to Marie, daughter of John and Mary (Beets) Tinsman, of Butler county, Pa. They have seven children: Mary A. (Mrs. Fisher), Miles C., Maud, Lois C., Kate, Mark S. and Elizabeth Grace. Mr. Smith has resided at his present home for twenty-five years. In 1864 he enlisted in the 50th Regiment, Heavy Artillery, and served until the close of the war. He is a member of the G. A. R., politically he is a Republican.

JOHN SNYDER, merchant and farmer. P. O. Brush Creek, was born in New Sewickley township, Beaver county, Dec. 3, 1846, a son of John and Anna E. (Bolland) Snyder, natives of Germany. They were married in this country and settled in Beaver county, where they remained until their deaths. Our subject was married, July 15, 1869, to Mary, daughter of George and Margaret Bonzo, the former a native of America, the latter of Germany. George Bonzo died in 1886; his widow resides in New Sewickley township. Mr. and Mrs. Snyder are the parents of seven children, five living: Wesley H., Jacob W., Mollie N., Carrie D. and John E. The deceased are George H. and Bertha A. Mr. Snyder was reared on a farm, engaged in merchandising in 1873, and handles everything from a spool of thread to a steam saw-mill. He owns 273 acres of fine land. He and his wife are members of the Methodist Episcopal church. He is a member of the I. O. O. F.

GEORGE C. SPEYERER. Mr. Speyerer is of German ancestry and the grandson of a manufacturer living in Frankenthal-on-the-Rhine, from whence he removed on the invasion of Napoleon's army to Heidelberg. His son, Frederick C., was born in Frankenthal, and was a soldier in the army that fought against the French invader, after which he retired to civil life and became a successful farmer. He was twice married, his wife by the second union being Christine Maria Stezel, of Schweinfurt, in Bavaria. Their children are two daughters: Justinia Maria (Mrs. Ebel) and Christine W. (Mrs. Buhl), and one son, George C., the subject of this biographical sketch. He was born Dec. 6, 1818, near Heidelberg, in Baden, and on his immigration to America in 1828, settled in Butler county, Pa. He became a pupil of the common schools during the winter months and devoted the remainder of his time to labor on the farm. His health failing, a trip to Europe proved advantageous, after which, on his return, he made Rochester his home and embarked in mercantile ventures. With the exception of a brief interval in the service of the German Manufacturing Company, he has for forty years been engaged in business at the same point. Since his advent in the town, Rochester has grown materially and become one of the most prosperous boroughs of the county. In all movements tending to its prosperity Mr. Speyerer has been a leading spirit and has unhesitatingly contributed both influence and capital to many worthy projects. He founded and is the president of the Beaver County Banking and Safe Deposit Association of Rochester. Mr. Speyerer was, in 1842, married to Anna Eliza, daughter of Henry Krebs, of Butler county, Pa., and their children were Henry Frederick (deceased); Herman J. (cashier of the Beaver County Banking and Safe Deposit Association); and William J. (who died, leaving the following named children: Frederick G., Maud, Anna Eliza and Mace, orphans, and residing with their paternal grandparents). Mr. Speyerer is a leading member of the Lutheran church at Rochester, of which he is a trustee.

HERMAN J. SPEYERER, cashier of the Beaver County Banking and Safe Deposit Association, Rochester, was born Sept. 4, 1845, the only son of George C. Speyerer. He was reared in Rochester, where his parents have resided since he was one year old. He received his education in Rochester and at the Beaver College. Early in life he embarked in mercantile trade, and was in his father's store until he reached his majority, when he became a partner. He remained with his father until 1874, then carried on a banking business till 1881, then mercantile business alone for two years. In the spring of 1885 he was elected to his present position. He was married in Butler county, Pa., May 25, 1876, to Sadie E., daughter of Dr. Adam Endres, and born in Beaver county, of German descent. The fruits of this union are three children: Elizabeth, Harrah and William. Mr. and Mrs. Speyerer are members of the Lutheran church. He is a

Republican in politics, and has served as a member of the council of Rochester borough for three terms. He is a F. & A. M., and a member of the I. O. O. F. and A. O. U. W.

PHILIP STEINBACH, farmer, P. O. Zelienople, Butler county, Pa., was born in New Sewickley township, Sept. 8, 1843. His parents, John A. and Dora Steinbach, natives of Germany, were married in Allegheny county, and settled in Beaver county, where they died. They had four children, of whom only Philip is living. He was married, March 23, 1866, to Mary A., daughter of Daniel and Charlotte Brenner, both living in New Sewickley township. She was born Feb. 7, 1842, and is the mother of five children: Emma D., Sophia E., John D., Charlotte A. and Henry P. Mr. Steinbach owns 180 acres of improved land. He and his wife are members of St. John's church.

E. P. STEWART, railroad clerk, P. O. Freedom, was born in Allegheny county, Aug. 13, 1836. His father, James H. Stewart, was a prominent attorney and died in 1838 at an early age. His mother was Anna Pentland, daughter of Ephraim Pentland, ex-judge of Allegheny county and editor of the first paper in that county. She died in 1844, leaving two children, of whom E. P. is the elder. With his brother he was placed in the care of his granduncle, Abner P. Lacock, an old and prominent citizen of Beaver county. E. P. received a common-school education, and commenced business life at the age of eighteen years. In 1861 he enlisted in Company F, 10th Pennsylvania Regiment, and served until 1862. He returned to this county, and remained here until 1868, when he located in Ohio and engaged in the railroad business. In 1881 he moved from Sewickley, this county, to New Brighton, where he remained until Feb. 22, 1888, when he removed to Rochester. In 1866 he was married to Susan E., daughter of M. S. and Charlotte (Eckert) Johns, and they have four children living: Susan E., Charlotta, Anna and Charles. Mr. Stewart is a member of the Knights of Honor of Sewickley, and Post No. 208, G. A. R., of New Brighton; politically he is a Republican.

TURNER STROBRIDGE. William Strobridge, who was of Scotch lineage and born in 1687, married Margaret Henry. His son James was the father of William Strobridge, a native of Saratoga county, N. Y., who married Hannah Tuttle on the 10th of October, 1784. Their children were E. Hinds, Phedoras, Tulley, Meroe, Parnel, Turner, James, Susanna, William, Oliver and Hannah. Mr. Strobridge ultimately removed to Barnet, Vt., where he engaged in farming. His son, Turner, who also resided in the latter place, first as a farmer and latterly as a successful merchant, married Eliza, daughter of Capt. Edward Clark, a soldier of the Revolution, wounded at the battle of Yorktown, whose home was in Peacham, Caledonia county, Vt. Their children were Lydia (who died in childhood), LaFayette and Turner. The last named and youngest of this number and the subject of this biography, was born July 9, 1826, and left fatherless at the early age of ten months. He was, during his infancy, adopted by R. R. Livingston, of Pittsburgh, Pa., the latter city then becoming his residence. His education was received at the common schools in Vermont, and the public schools of Pittsburgh, with a supplementary career at the Western University in the latter city. He then entered the Pittsburgh Novelty Works, of which his benefactor was owner, and mastered the intricacies of the business with such readiness as to warrant his management of the foundry department of the works at the age of eighteen. He was afterward admitted to a partnership and remained thus engaged until the establishment was destroyed by fire when, discerning a more favorable field in New Brighton, he removed thither and built the New Brighton Novelty Works, of which he is the present head. He is here engaged in the manufacture of novelty goods and domestic hardware, a market for which is readily found in the United States and South America. Mr. Strobridge also devotes some attention to farming, and resides upon his farm adjacent to the borough. He was, in August, 1847, married to Elizabeth, daughter of George Irvine, of Pittsburgh, and their children were Emma, Livingston R., Frank (deceased), and Turner, Jr. Mrs. Strobridge died in May, 1884, and our subject was a second time married, in the fall of 1884, to Mrs. Jane Robinson, daughter of Gen. Charles Carter, of Beaver.

C. W. TAYLOR, traveling salesman, New Brighton, was born in that place in 1853.

His father, C. W. Taylor, who was justice of the peace for many years in this county, married Mary, daughter of W. W. Willis, of New Brighton, and they had eight children, C. W. being the eldest. Joseph Taylor, grandfather of our subject, came to America from England. C. W. attended public school in New Brighton until he was fifteen years of age; was then employed on the railroad and some time afterward engaged in pottery business. For a number of years he was employed as a salesman, and held other positions in connection with potteries. He was married, in 1880, to Jennie, daughter of John Rupert and grand-daughter of Casper Weitzell. They have two children: Annie and Lila.

THOMAS M. TAYLOR, merchant, justice of the peace and notary public, Rochester, was born in this county March 31, 1818, a son of William and Ann (Wilson) Taylor, the latter born in Pennsylvania, of German descent, and the former born in Ireland. William came to America in 1798, and to Pennsylvania when a mere lad, soon afterward locating in Darlington, this county. He served in the War of 1812, and was a farmer all his life; his family consisted of eleven children, all of whom grew to maturity, and were all married before a death occurred in the family. Our subject's eldest brother, John Taylor, who was born in Northumberland county, in 1802, now resides on a farm in Iowa. Thomas M., who is the youngest of five brothers, was reared in Beaver county, attending the public schools and the Greersburg Academy, at Darlington. He clerked in a store and on a steamboat in early life, and subsequently embarked in mercantile trade at Rochester, at which place he was appointed postmaster in 1862, serving fifteen years. Since then he has been justice of the peace and notary public. He also carries on the boot and shoe trade in Rochester. He was married, in 1845, to Margaret, daughter of Daniel Skillenger, and a native of Beaver county; her parents were born in the New England States. Mr. and Mrs. Taylor's only son, Eugene W., now deceased, was a physician in practice in Venango county, Pa., at the time of his death. He was married and left two children: William and Thomas. Mr. Taylor is a Republican. He has been a member of the I. O. O. F. for thirty-six years.

CHARLES TEA, contractor and builder, also dealer in sand used for building purposes, New Brighton, was born in Beaver county, Pa., in 1847, and is the elder of the two children of Richard and Margaret (Hunter) Tea, the former of whom was the second son in the family of six children of Josiah and Hannah (Luther) Tea. The family are descended on the mother's side from Daniel Boone. Charles received a public-school training, and at the age of sixteen enlisted in Company B, 205th Regiment, P. V., serving one year as orderly sergeant. In his eighteenth year he commenced to learn carpentering of his father, and is now a successful contractor and builder, employing from ten to fifteen men. Mr. Tea married, in 1866, Mary M., daughter of Eugene Fleeson, of Irish parentage, and by her had five children, three now living: Amelia N., Eugene F. and Sarah Floretta. Politically our subject is a Republican. He is a member of the K. of P. and G. A. R.

GEORGE L. TEETS, farmer, P. O. Zelienople, Pa., was born in New Sewickley township, Aug. 22, 1852, a son of Lewis and Caroline Teets, the former a native of Pennsylvania and the latter of France. After their marriage they settled in Beaver county, where they have since resided. They have four children: Adam, George L., Lottie C. and Mollie. Lottie C. was married, Oct. 27, 1881, to W. H. Ifft, a merchant at Zelienople; Mollie was married May 5, 1881, to W. H. Stockey, a hotel keeper at Evans City, Butler county. George L. married Jan. 26, 1881, Emma, daughter of Henry and Magdelena Zehner, and born in Butler county, Pa., Aug. 4, 1862. She is the mother of three children: Clara P., Mary and Carrie. Mr. Teets owns 118 acres of improved land. In politics he is a Democrat. He and his wife are members of the United Presbyterian church. They live in the old home where Mr. Teets' father and mother have resided for thirty-seven years.

JOHN TEETS, farmer, P. O. Zelienople, Pa., was born on the farm which he now owns and where he resided, in New Sewickley township, Aug. 8, 1848. His parents, George and Margaret Teets, were natives of this county and died here. John was married March 14, 1883, to Ann C. Gudekunst, who was born in Butler county, Pa., June 11, 1860, a daughter of Jacob F. and Charlotte Gudekunst, both living in Butler county. Three children are the result of this marriage: Clifford A., Vesta A. and May E. Mr. and Mrs. Teets are members of the English Lutheran church. In politics he is a Republican. He owns seventy-five acres of land where he resides.

ETHAN H. THOMAS, retired, P. O. New Brighton, was born in Beaver county, Pa., in 1856, to John and Margaret (Hazen) Thomas, the former a farmer, and the latter a daughter of Samuel Hazen, of this county. They were the parents of ten children, three yet living. Ethan H., when fourteen years old, was brought by his mother to New Brighton, and here attended the high school. After finishing his education he was employed in the drug business for five years, then carried on a feed store three years. In 1878 he married Ella, daughter of Daniel and Margaret (Riley) Kirkpatrick, and by her has had three children: Edith and Edna (twins, the former deceased), and Clara. Mr. Thomas was a member of the town council and of the Baptist church. In politics he is a Republican.

J. W. THOMAS, baggage master, P., Ft. W. & C. Ry., New Brighton, was born in Butler county, Pa., in 1845, to Austin (a carpenter), and Sarah (West) Thomas, parents of five children. J. W., the second child, and first son, attended the common schools and remained on the home farm until he was sixteen years of age, after which he was employed in a store and factory for a few years. In 1869 he commenced railroading, and for the past ten years has held his present position. He married, in 1866, Mary, daughter of James Rowland, and by her had five children: Agnes (deceased), Andrew M., George W., Lewis W. and Bertha B. Mr. Thomas is a member of the I. O. O. F.; in politics a Democrat.

R. H. THOMAS, superintendent New Brighton Glass Company, was born in Allegheny county in 1851, only child of James (an iron-worker) and Ella (Winton) Thomas. He was educated at the public schools, and has been connected with glass manufacturing ever since he was eleven years of age. For several years he was with Bryer & Bros., Pittsburgh; was a stockholder in the Coöperative Glass Works, at Beaver Falls: two years foreman for A. B. Mills, at Chartiers, on Lake Erie; and after that was appointed to his present position. He is the patentee of a new glass tank, which, though yet in its infancy, has proved one of the most complete of the kind ever introduced for use in the manufacture of cheap glass. He resides with his mother at New Brighton. In politics he is a Republican.

JAMES K. THOMPSON, farmer, P. O. New Brighton, was born in this county, May 31, 1814, the eldest child of James and Margaret (Kennedy) Thompson. His grandparents were Moses and Margaret (Whittaker) Thompson. James, father of our subject, was a wheelwright, and later in life a farmer. James K. was reared on the farm and received a common-school education. In 1867 he bought his present farm of 100 acres. He was married in 1846, to Margaret, daughter of James and Sarah (Welch) McCleary, and they have had nine children, five of whom are living: Sarah (Mrs. Wallace), Margaret (Mrs. Davidson), Dwight, Grant and Eva (Mrs. Phillis). Mr. Thompson is a Republican, and has been school director. He is a member of the United Presbyterian church.

JAMES W. THORNILEY, retired machinist, New Brighton, was born May 20, 1819, the second son of Thomas and Margaret (Wiley) Thorniley, parents of eight children. The father came from England when four years of age (about 1790), and in 1813 settled in Beaver county, where he carried on cotton manufacturing. Caleb Thorniley, the paternal grandfather, was a farmer in Ohio. Our subject was reared in his native town, where, with the exception of a few years, he has always remained. He left school when nineteen, learned his father's trade, that of machinist, and for twenty-two years carried on a foundry and machine shop. He is now retired from active business, residing near the spot where once stood Braden block-house, a noted resort during the early period of this county. Mr. Thorniley married, in 1849, Sarah, daughter of Jacob and Eliza Wiands, of Ohio. He is a F. & A. M., and has been a member of the I. O. O. F. In politics he is a Republican. He is a member of the Presbyterian church.

818   HISTORY OF BEAVER COUNTY.

ROBERT TOWNSEND was born in Washington county, Pa., April 9, 1790, his father having removed a short time previous to that date from Chester county, Pa. When sixteen years of age he repaired to Baltimore, Md., and there learned the trade of wire working, establishing himself, in 1816, in Pittsburgh, in that business. In 1828 he removed to Fallston, Beaver county, and erected a factory for the manufacture of iron wire, continuing this enterprise, as well as that in Pittsburgh, until 1861, when, owing to failing health, he retired from active business. His eldest son, William Penn Townsend, became associated with him in 1840, and he, with his two sons, Charles C. and Edward P. Townsend, now continue the business, to which has been added the manufacture of iron rivets, and recently of steel wire nails. Robert Townsend is a descendant of Richard Townsend, who came with William Penn to America in the ship "Welcome," in 1682.

JACOB TRAX, merchant, Rochester, born in Allegheny county, Pa., Sept. 7, 1824, is a son of Lewis Trax. His parents came from Alsace, France, in 1817, and settled at Pittsburgh, where his father worked for a while at the weaver's business, having learned the trade in the old country. Lewis was a farmer, and had thirteen children. Jacob, the youngest, was reared in Allegheny county and educated in the public schools. He learned the cabinet maker's trade, which he followed for several years. In 1850 he came to Beaver county, and in 1877 he moved to the eastern shore and bought a farm of 200 acres, near Baltimore. He returned in 1886 and engaged in different kinds of business until he built his present store. He is an extensive owner of real estate in Rochester. Mr. Trax was married in Allegheny City, in 1847, to Catherine, daughter of Henry Knomeshu, and of German descent. Their children are Catherine, wife of D. A. Steiner; George H.; Emma, wife of Harry Hawkins, of Beaver Falls; John T.; Henry C.; Lydia Ann, wife of E. B. Furnace, and Lewis. Mr. and Mrs. Trax are members of the Methodist Episcopal church, and he has been steward, class leader, trustee and Sabbath-school teacher. In politics he is a Democrat.

- J. JACOB WAGONER, farmer, P. O. Knob, was born in Germany, Feb. 21, 1809, a son of George P. and Christina E. Wagoner. He was married in Germany in June, 1825, to Eva, daughter of Henry Massenhold; came to America in 1839, and in 1840 settled on the farm where he still resides. They had nine children, eight of whom are living: Elizabeth, Conrad, Eva C., Jacob, Elnora, Margaretta, Caroline and George. Mr. Wagoner is a painter by trade, but has been engaged in farming all his life, and owns fifty acres of improved land. He and his wife were members of the German Reformed church. In politics he is a Democrat. Mrs. Wagoner died Jan. 8, 1870, and since that time Mr. Wagoner and his son George have been living together. The latter married a daughter of Christian Wahl.

GEORGE WAHL, farmer, P. O. Knob, was born in Germany, Jan. 15, 1810, and is a son of John and Soloma Wahl, who died in Germany. George was married in Germany, in January, 1838, to Christina, daughter of Henry and Elizabeth Burg, and born Sept. 1, 1819. Mr. Wahl and his wife came to America in 1846, and settled in Beaver county, where they have since lived. They have had ten children, seven of whom are living: Jacob, Elizabeth, Caroline, George, Sophia, Margaret and Emma. Those deceased are Henry, John and Maltilda. Mr. Wahl is a tailor by trade, but has been engaged in farming since coming to America. He owns sixty acres of improved land. He and his wife and children are consistent members of the Lutheran church.

CHRIST WAHL, farmer, P. O. Knob, was born in Germany, May 18, 1812, a son of John and Sallie Wahl, who died in Germany. He immigrated, in 1838, to America, settled in Beaver county, and was married Jan. 28, 1842, to Charlotte Geier, who was born in Germany, Dec. 13, 1819, a daughter of Nicholas and Charlotte Geier, who came to America in 1840, and settled in Beaver county, where they died. Mr. and Mrs. Wahl have had nine children, two of whom, George and Charlotte, are deceased. Those living are Sophia, Elizabeth, Catherine, Christina, Caroline, Mary and Christ. Mr. Wahl is a shoemaker by trade, but has been engaged in farming all his life. He owns about ninety-four acres of land. He and his wife belonged to the Lutheran church. Mrs. Wahl died March 30, 1883.

BIOGRAPHIES—EAST SIDE. 819

MICHAEL WAHL, retired farmer, P. O. Brush Creek, was born in Germany, March 14, 1825, a son of John and Sarah Wahl, both of whom died in Germany. Michael married, March 10, 1855, Sarah, daughter of Jacob and Magdelena Martzolf, both deceased. Mrs. Wahl was born in Pennsylvania, Oct. 6, 1830, and has six children living: Mary, Charles, Jacob, Henry, Caroline and Emma. One daughter, Amelia, is deceased. Mr. Wahl was engaged in blacksmithing about twenty-five years. He owns 246 acres of fine land. He came to America in 1853, and has resided in Beaver county about thirty years. He and his wife are members of the German United Presbyterian church.

FRANK WALLACE, farmer, P. O. New Brighton, was born in Pulaski township, this county, in 1837. William Wallace, with his wife, Mary, came from Ireland in 1790, and located at Sheffield, Pa., where he engaged in farming and the timber business. He had four sons and four daughters. James, his eldest child and father of our subject, was nine weeks old when he landed in America with his parents. William Wallace came to Beaver county and purchased 200 acres of land in Pulaski township. James was a wagon-maker, and purchased part of the 200-acre tract at the death of his father. He married Eleanor McClelland, who bore him nine children. Two daughters and three sons are now living, of whom Frank is the youngest. James Wallace served in the War of 1812. He died in his seventy-eighth year, and his wife in her eighty-sixth year. Frank was born and reared on the farm which he now owns, and which is part of the original tract purchased by his grandfather. He was educated at the public schools. In 1865 he married Euphemia, daughter of Henry Alcorn, of Pulaski township, this county; they have no children. Mr. Wallace has held various township offices, and is a Democrat. He is a member of the Associate church.

JAMES D. WALLIS, dealer in groceries and provisions, New Brighton, was born in Allegheny county in 1857, and is the eldest son in the family of seven children of David B. and Nancy A. (Carroll) Wallis, the former a carpenter. James spent his boyhood in his native county until eleven years of age, and then came with his parents to New Brighton, where for nearly sixteen years he was engaged in grocery and dry goods business, and in 1886 located at his present place. He married, in 1879, Sarah F., daughter of James D. and Ellen Harris, of this county, and to this union were born four children, three now living: Lewis J., William H. and Robert M. Mr. Wallis is a member of the I. O. O. F.; in politics he is a Democrat.

DAVID WARNOCK, farmer and justice of the peace, P. O. North Sewickley, was born on the farm where he now resides Feb. 11, 1825, a son of David and Jane (Thompson) Warnock, natives of Pennsylvania, the former a farmer by occupation. They had eight children, five now living: Margaret, widow of Warren B. Parkinson; David; Thompson; Martha E., widow of John McClure; Maria A., married to T. J. Marshall; ann Robert Q. David was married, in 1851, to Eliza Jane, daughter of Jonathan Evans, a native of Pennsylvania, and a miller by occupation. To this union were born nine children: Horace G. and David E., attorneys in Dakota; Maggie Bell, Lewis D. and John J., commercial travelers; Robert, a merchant in Westmoreland, Pa.; Henry W., clerk; James C., bookkeeper, and Ralston K., with Lyons & Co., Pittsburgh. Shortly after his marriage Mr. Warnock moved to Lawrence county, Pa., and there carried on farming until 1867. In 1864 he was elected auditor of that county, serving until 1867; then returned to his old homestead in Beaver county, where he has since resided. He was elected to his present position of justice of the peace in 1868; also held the office of school director two years. He and his wife are members of the United Presbyterian church, of which for many years he has been an elder. Politically Mr. Warnock is a Republican.

ABRAHAM WEST, farmer, was born in Knob, New Sewickley township, in 1825, a son of Peter and Agnes (Boyd) West, who were natives of Virginia and Allegheny county, Pa., respectively. His father moved to the farm where Abraham now resides, in 1830, and died there April 30, 1865, and his wife in November, 1869. His paternal grandfather was Joseph West, who died in 1827, aged eighty years, and his maternal grandfather was William Boyd. Abraham received his education in Franklin township and always lived at home, and continued on the same farm at his father's death. He married, in 1860, Mary Jane Sowers, who was born in this county Sept. 6, 1837, and seven children have blessed this union, as follows: Virginia, wife of Omer Wilson; William Boyd, in Zelienople; Clinton P.; Joseph, who died April 27, 1888; Abraham Garret; Charles F. and Francis F. Mr. and Mrs. West are members of the Zelienople Presbyterian church.

ABELARD WHISLER, secretary of the American Fire Brick Works of S. Barnes & Co., Limited, was born in Pulaski township, Beaver county, May 13, 1841, a son of Benjamin and Mary (Robinson) Whisler, natives of Pennsylvania, the former of German, and the latter of Scotch descent. His father was a carpenter, contractor and merchant. He had seven children, of whom Abelard is the third. He was reared in Beaver county and attended the public schools, the Kenwood Institute and an academy in North Sewickley township. He taught school for five years and then embarked in mercantile trade in company with his father at New Brighton and at Beaver Falls, and carried on a successful business for seven years. His health failed, so he sold out, and for a time engaged in business which gave him outdoor exercise. In 1878 he accepted his present position and since 1884 has been a stock holder and secretary of the company. He has been twice married: first, in 1865, to Mary A. Coulson, who died in 1883. They had three children: Liola (deceased), Sewell and Ernest. He was again married, in 1886, to Jennie E., daughter of Adam Winlow, of English descent. Mr. and Mrs. Whisler are members of the Methodist Episcopal church. He has held the offices of steward, class leader and trustee; is leader of the choir and Sabbath-school superintendent. In politics he is a Democrat.

JAMES K. WHITE, physician, New Brighton, was born in Allegheny county, Pa., in 1845, is the second son of Samuel M. and Alice (Phillis) White. He was reared on the farm where he was born, and attended the public schools during winters until twenty years of age. In 1873 he commenced the study of medicine under the preceptorship of Dr. J. H. Ramsey; in 1878 he entered Cleveland Medical College, and graduated at the University of Louisville, Ky. After three years' practice in Washington county, Pa., he came to New Brighton, where he has since been engaged in his profession. In 1878 he married Nettie, daughter of John Graham, of Pittsburgh, Pa., and to this union have been born two children: Frederick Graham and Blanche Amelia. Doctor White was school director two years and re-elected; he is an adherent of the United Presbyterian church; in politics he is a Republican.

JOHN WHITE, farmer, P. O. Rochester, was born in this county Oct. 15, 1833, and is a son of Jacob and Catherine White. They were natives of Pennsylvania, and after marriage they settled in Beaver county, where they remained until his death. His widow is still living. John White was married, Feb. 11, 1856, to Mary A., daughter of James and Eliza A. Prentice, who died in this county. Mrs. White was born July 24. 1838, and is the mother of eleven children: Frank, Jacob, Samuel A., Elmer, Oscar, John P., Charles R., Walter, Minnie V., Nora E. and Martha A. Mr. White has been engaged in farming since his marriage, and is the owner of 119 acres of land.

T. S. WHITE, manufacturer, New Brighton, is a native of that town, and was born in 1852. His parents, Timothy B. and Olive B. (Howland) White, had six children, five of whom grew to maturity, T. S. being the third son and youngest child. His grandfather, Samuel White, a native of Burlington, N. J., married Sarah Balderston, and Timothy B. was their second son. The family came to Beaver county in 1838, locating in Sharon, and in 1840 moved to Fallston, where Timothy B., for several years, was engaged as a contractor and builder. In 1860 he commenced the building of bridges, and in 1868 established the manufacturing business now carried on by his sons, T. S. and Samuel P., at Beaver Falls. T. S. was reared in his native town and graduated in civil engineering at Cornell University in 1873, since which he has followed his present business. He married, in 1876, Annie, daughter of George and Caroline (Appleton) Appleton, residents of Philadelphia and of English origin. Mr. and Mrs. White have

BIOGRAPHIES—EAST SIDE. 821

had three children, two of whom are living: Samuel and Theresa. Mr. White is a member of the school board, junior warden of the Episcopal church; politically he is a Republican.

JOHN J. WICKHAM, physician, Rochester, was born in Rochester, Pa., June 15, 1862, a son of Jervis and Anna (Hurst) Wickham, natives of Ireland. His father is a mechanical engineer, and has devoted most of his time to that occupation since he came to Rochester. He has been twice married. By his second wife he has two sons, of whom the Doctor is the younger. Our subject attended the public schools in Rochester, and commenced the study of medicine in that place while engaged in teaching school. In 1882 he attended the Medical College at Cincinnati, where he graduated in 1884. He practiced for a time in the hospital in Cincinnati, but not being satisfied with his knowledge he went to New York City, where he took a post-graduate course. He then began practice in his native town, and has met with success. The Doctor is a congenial and social gentleman, and has many friends. He is a F. & A. M. and a member of the I. O. O. F.

JOHN WILHELM, farmer, P. O. Knob, was born in Germany, Nov. 13, 1847, and is a son of Jacob and Christina Wilhelm. The father died in Germany, but the mother came to America and resided with her son John, until her death; she died Jan. 22, 1888, aged seventy-seven years and three months. Mr. Wilhelm was married April 17, 1873, to Elizabeth Drebert, who was born in Butler county, Pa., Jan. 19, 1854, a daughter of Conrad and Anna Drebert, the former of whom was born in Germany, and died in Butler county; the latter was born in Pennsylvania, and is still living in Butler county. Mr. and Mrs. Wilhelm are the parents of five children, three of whom are living: Amos, Frederick A. and Flora C. Martha M. and an infant are deceased. Mr. Wilhelm learned the shoemaker's trade in Germany. He owns eighty-five acres of land. He and his wife are members of the Lutheran church.

AARON WILSON, merchant, Rochester, was born in North Sewickley township, this county, March 9, 1842. His parents James and Barbara (Showalter) Wilson, were natives of Pennsylvania, and of German origin; the father was a farmer, and his family consisted of twelve children, of whom seven are living. Aaron, the seventh son, was reared on a farm, attending the district school and the Beaver Academy and Mount Union College, where he took a scientific course. He also took a theological course in Allegheny City, where he was graduated in 1870. He then accepted the charge of the Baptist church at Sharon, Pa., and for nearly ten years he was engaged in pastoral work. In 1877 he embarked in the mercantile trade at Rochester. He was married, in 1870, to Mary B., a daughter of Rev. A. K. Bell, D. D., a Baptist minister. Mrs. Wilson is of Scotch origin. They have five children: Adie K. B., Mary Bell, Nellie, Clara B. and James Earl. In politics Mr. Wilson is a Republican. He and three of his brothers were soldiers in the Union army. He was a member of Company B, 56th O. V. I., for four months. In early life he took an active interest in secret societies, and was a member of the Masonic fraternity and others. He now expresses himself as opposed to all secret societies. He takes an active interest in the Sabbath-school, and often preaches. He is a fluent speaker, and a candid and honest man.

JOSEPH WILSON, manufacturer, Beaver Falls and New Brighton, was born in North Beaver, (now Lawrence county) Pa., in 1822. His parents were Jeremiah and Lydia (Davidson) Wilson. The latter, a daughter of William Davidson, of Scotch-Irish extraction. They had six children, five of whom grew to maturity, Joseph being the eldest. Joseph Wilson, grandfather of our subject, was a commissioned officer in the War of 1812, and at an early period settled in this county, where he followed farming. Our subject was educated in the public schools, and when twenty-one began farm life. He also learned the trade of a carpenter, which he followed for some time. In 1852 he located in Fallston, this county, and in 1854 settled in New Brighton, where he operated a planing mill. In 1860 he formed a partnership with T. C. & C. Waddle. In 1864 the firm became T. C. Waddle and Joseph Wilson, and continued till 1867, when it became Waddle, Wilson & Co. (F. K. Brierly becoming one of the firm), and the business was removed to Beaver Falls, where it has since been conducted. The firm is now Wilson & Brierly. At the time of the removal to Beaver Falls many business men had no faith in the success of the enterprise. The firm persevered, however, and the results have demonstrated their superior judgment. When success was assured those who had been skeptical invested in the undertaking, and by so doing achieved fortunes. Mr. Wilson has also been identified. since 1866, with various other business enterprises. He is president of the Knott, Harker & Co. Novelty Works, of the John H. Knott & Co. Flouring Mill, member of the Tile Works Co. and of the Beaver Falls Glass Works Co.; vice-president of the First National Bank at Beaver Falls, besides holding other positions of trust. He was married, in 1844, to Isabella, daughter of Thomas Gilliman, of Lawrence county, Pa., and seven children were born to them, four now living: T. S., Martha Irena (Mrs. Harker), Ada A. (Mrs. Peatling), and Ella C. Mr. Wilson has been ten years a member of the town council, is an adherent of the Methodist Protestant church, and in politics he is a Republican.

T. S. WILSON, brick manufacturer, New Brighton, was born Nov. 25, 1849, the oldest son of Joseph Wilson. He was educated at the common schools, and at the age of fifteen years began to learn the carpenter's trade. He was married, in 1871, to Emma, daughter of Philip Martsolf. They have five children: Harry, Ella, Sadie, Ada and Flora. In 1882, Mr. Wilson commenced his present business. The site of his yard has been used for brick making since 1830, and is the oldest brick yard in the county. The partnership of Wilson & Peatling has existed since 1887. They manufacture the line of fire brick known as "Oak Hill." Mr. Wilson is a member of the I. O. O. F.; in politics a Republican.

CHARLES F. WINTER, insurance agent, New Brighton, is a native of this county, the eldest son of Rev. Ferdinand E. and Hannah (Swartz) Winter, who were the parents of twelve children. Rev. Ferdinand Winter, a minister of the Reformed German church, was born in Germany, and soon after his immigration to this country settled in Beaver county, where he has preached to one congregation for forty-three years. Charles F. received a good common-school education, and at the age of twenty-one years learned the watchmaking trade, which he followed eighteen years. He was married, in 1861, to Adelaide, daughter of Benjamin Bedison. They have had eight children, six of whom are living: William E., Benjamin B., Charles Lewis, Amy S., Alfred T. and H. May. Mr. Winter is at present engaged in the insurance business, representing the Germania Life Insurance Company, of New York. He is also engaged in the manufacturing and introducing the valuable Keefer R. R. splice bar. For fifteen years he was leader and instructor of the New Brighton Cornet Band, and was a musician and drum major in the army. He is a F. & A. M. and a member of the K. of P.

STANTON WOODS, foreman, Rochester, was born in Rochester July 25, 1855. His parents, Elisha and Harriet (Garver) Woods, were natives of Pennsylvania and of English origin. His father was a carpenter and contractor, and also learned tanning. His family consisted of eleven children, of whom Stanton is the youngest now living. The latter was reared in this county, educated in the common schools, and early in life learned the stone-moulding business. He worked for ten years with the Olive Stone Company at Rochester, and is now superintendent of the moulds. In politics he is a Republican.

JACOB WOOSTER, farmer, P. O. Beaver Falls, was born in New Sewickley township Oct. 24, 1828. His parents were Jacob and Magdalene (Gohering) Wooster, the former a native of Bavaria, Germany, a farmer, and the latter of Alsace, France (now Germany), daughter of William Gohering, a native of France; her mother's maiden name was Catherine Bear. Mr. and Mrs. Wooster were the parents of six children: Catherine, Charlotta, Charles, Sophia, Elizabeth and Jacob. The parents were both born in 1786, and emigrated to America, the mother in 1802, and the father some ten years later. They settled on Brush Creek, this county, where they died, the former in 1872 and the latter in 1876. Jacob was married to Adda, daughter of Joseph Girard, of French descent, and to this union have been born nine children, following living: Josephine, Stephen, Susan, Olive, Georgiana, Charles and Maud Augusta, all at home. Mr. Wooster held the offices of school director, supervisor and township auditor one term each. In politics he is a Prohibitionist. He and his wife are members of the Methodist Episcopal church. Mr. Wooster is the owner of a beautiful home and farm of 211 acres highly cultivated.

JACOB YOUNG, JR., farmer, P. O. New Brighton, is a son of Jacob and Catherine Young, both of whom reside in this county. He was born in Deichweiler, in the county of Rhinefalz Baerer, Germany, Feb. 20, 1838; came to America in 1847 and settled in this county. He was married, Sept. 13, 1863, to Sophia Goehring, who was born in New Sewickley township July 10, 1842. Her parents, John and Margaret Goehring, were born in Germany, and came to this country when quite young. They were married and settled in Lawrence county, Pa., but afterward moved to Beaver county, where they resided for a number of years. They are at present living in Lawrence county. Mr. and Mrs. Young have ten children living: Katie M., Lizzie M., Emma V., Anna S., Bertha, Charles, Albert D., Mollie G., Amanda R. and John W. One son, Walter, is deceased. Mr. Young owns 150 acres of improved land. He and his wife are members of the United Presbyterian church.

JOHN H. YOUNG, oil refiner, P. O. Freedom, was born in Beaver county, Pa., Jan. 30, 1852, and is a son of William and Jeanette Young, natives of Scotland. Soon after their marriage they came to America and settled in Beaver county, where they remained until the father's death, which took place in 1865. His widow survives him. They were the parents of six children, two living. John H. was married, Dec. 28, 1876, to Agnes M., daughter of Capt. T. W. and Sarah A. Fowler (now deceased). They have two children ; Edith Fern and Myrtle A. Mr. Young was elected to the office of justice of the peace, and has held three commissions He was engaged in the drug business eight years, and has been in the oil business four years.

JOHN Y. ZERGLER, farmer, was born Dec. 3, 1830, at Harmony, Butler county, Pa., a son of Andrew H. and Mary (Yotter) Zergler, natives of Northampton county, Pa., and of Ohio, respectively. His father was a tanner, carrying on that business at Harmony about thirty-seven years, and then traded for a farm in Butler county. About 1846 he bought the farm where our subject now resides, and the latter moved on to this place in 1851, having been married, Jan. 12, of that year, to Hannah Wise. She was born in the next house west of Mr. Zergler's farm, March 10, 1828, a daughter of John and Mollie (Funk) Wise. Seven children have been born to Mr. and Mrs. Zergler: Andrew, (a druggist in Pittsburgh), Sarah (now Mrs. John Liebendorfe), John W., (a carpenter in Kansas), Caroline, (now Mrs. John Curry, of Lawrence county), Emmet, Elmer, Harvey H. and Ferdinand at home.

GEORGE ZINKHAN, farmer, P. O. Knob, was born in Germany Feb. 16, 1826. His parents, John and Mary Zinkhan, came to America in 1845 and settled in New Sewickley township, this county, where they died. George was married, Nov. 12, 1850, to Mary, daughter of Martin and Margaret Zinkhan. She was born in Germany, July 15, 1830, and the same year her parents came to America and settled in Beaver county, where they died. Mrs. Zinkhan is the mother of eleven children, nine of whom are living: William, Caroline, George, Charles, Henry, Nicholas, Albert, Edwin and Anna. Those deceased are John and Lizzie. Mr. Zinkhan has been a farmer all his life, and owns forty-five acres of improved land. He and his wife are members of the Presbyterian church; in politics he is a Democrat.

W. H. ZORTMAN, farmer, P. O. Freedom, was born in Butler county, Pa., Jan. 17, 1819, and is a son of Henry and Margaret Zortman, natives of Pennsylvania. They lived some years in Butler county, then moved to Adams county, Ohio, where they died. Our subject was married, Nov. 25, 1841, to Hannah Wallice. She was born in Allegheny county, April 4, 1821, and is a daughter of George and Jane Wallice, who died in Allegheny county. Mr. and Mrs. Zortman have had ten children, of whom eight are living: George, James, William, David, Margaret J., Lida, Albert and Nannie. Those deceased are John and Lewis. Mr. Zortman has been a farmer all his life, and owns sixty acres of improved land. He and his wife are members of the United Presbyterian church; in politics he is a Republican.

CHAPTER XXVIII.

BIOGRAPHIES—SOUTH SIDE.

ARCHIBALD AGNEW, farmer, P. O. Sheffield, was born July 4, 1823, on a part of the old McCoy place, where his father then resided. His grandfather, Robert Agnew, was a native of Ireland, came to America, joined the continental army, and became one of the heroes of the revolution. He was captured, and taken to Quebec and confined on an English prison ship three months. After the war he went to Cannonsburg, Pa., and from there to the wilderness of Beaver county. He settled on Raredon's Run, lived here about fifty years, and died at the home of his son, William, aged eighty-five years. He was a member of the Old Seceder's church. His wife was Margaret Cornagy, who died young. They had three sons and three daughters. Of the sons William married Jane, daughter of David and Nancy (Shearer) McCoy. They had eight children, four of whom are deceased: John, Agnes, Esther and William. The last mentioned died in Libby Prison. Those living are Archibald, David, Jane and Samuel. William Agnew died at the age of seventy-eight years. He was a member of the United Presbyterian church; in politics a Democrat. Archibald Agnew, subject of this sketch, married Mary J., daughter of John Purdy. Three children have blessed this union: James P. (died young), John C. and Margaret, the latter wife of John Greene. Mr. and Mrs. Agnew are active members of the United Presbyterian church. He is a Democrat and has held various township offices.

JOSEPH ALEXANDER, farmer, P. O. Seventy-Six, is a grandson of Robert Alexander, of Scotch descent, who came to Beaver county at an early day and settled near Seventy-Six, then in Hopewell township, and died there. His wife was Nancy Phillis, and they had nine children: David, Joseph, James, Alice, Nancy, Rebecca and Margaret reached maturity; Alice (Mrs. Gilbreth) and Rebecca (Mrs. Glaspey) are yet living. David married Mary, daughter of Jacob Phillis. David Alexander was a man well known throughout the country, was born Feb. 14, 1806, and died on the old homestead, July 20, 1869. His widow was born in 1804, and is yet living. He was a Democrat and held the office of constable for twelve years or more. He was the father of six children, Margaret A. (Mrs. Johnston), Jacob P., Joseph, Eliza A., James M. and David S. Of these Joseph married Louisa, daughter of James S. Alexander. They have two children: James Ray and David A. Of these James Ray is married to Anna Newingham, and has two children: Joseph S. and William. Mr. Alexander is a Democrat, and has served sixteen years as constable and assessor of Independence township. He owns a farm of eighty-two acres.

JOSEPH ALLEN, farmer, P. O. Industry, is a native of Washington county, Pa., born in 1817, of Scotch-Irish descent. Eli Allen, a farmer and a native of the same county, married Sarah Griffith, by whom he had three sons and two daughters, the eldest of whom, Joseph, father of our subject, also born in Washington county, was a farmer and boat builder. He married Annie Thompson, of Fayette county, Pa., and she bore him five children. Joseph, the third child, remained in his native county until 1866, when he came to Beaver county. He received a common-school education, and in early youth learned carpentering, which he afterward followed in connection with ship-building. For thirty-five years he was engaged on the river in various kinds of work on steamboats, as mate, engineer and captain. Retiring in 1878 he purchased the property where he now resides, and devotes his attention to farming. He was married, in 1837, to Rebecca Jane, daughter of Robert and Elenor Lyons, of Irish extraction, and they have five children: Ruth Ann (now Mrs. Reed), Florilla, (now Gallagher), Margaret Marie (now Mrs. Gormley). Joseph, at home, and Sarah Jane (now Mrs. Surles). Mr. Allen and family are members of the Presbyterian church; he is a Democrat.

. BENJAMIN ANDERSON, farmer, P. O. Murdocksville, Washington county, is a grandson of Benjamin Anderson, of Scotch descent, but a native of Ireland. He first settled in Washington county, and later moved to Hanover township, Beaver county, where he died, aged about fifty-eight years. His wife was a Miss Campbell of an old Scotch family. They had eleven children, all born in Hanover township, of whom two are now living: Mrs. Betsey Shillito, of Beaver, and Mathew Anderson, of Hookstown. The others were John, Ella, Nellie, Mary, James, Edward, Benjamin, Robert and Benoni. Of these John moved to what is now Bockstown, then known as "Anderson Still House," and carried on distilling and milling until about 1848, when he removed to Independence and continued milling for a few years, and then went to California, where he died in 1857, aged fifty-eight years. His wife was Elizabeth, daughter of David Miller, and died young, leaving six children: Elizabeth, Benjamin, David M., Mary E., John and Samuel. Of these Benjamin and David M. accompanied their father to California. David lived awhile in Chili, South America, returned to Beaver county, studied medicine, and settled in Washington county. He was a surgeon in the late war. Benjamin left California and went to Honda, United States of Columbia, where he was superintendent of mining for an English syndicate. He remained for five years, superintending from 100 to 150 natives, none of whom could speak English. He returned to Beaver county in 1877, crossing the Gulf of Mexico in a small boat. He owns 284 acres of land in Beaver county. In 1882 he went to Colorado in the interest of the Comstock Mining Company of Beaver, for whom he has made several trips. His wife is Orrie Burretta, daughter of David P. and Elizabeth (McDonald) Scott.

JAMES R. ANDERSON, farmer, P. O. Murdocksville, was born Aug. 30, 1830, on the old Anderson homestead settled by his grandfather, William Anderson, a native of Ireland. The latter married a widow Logan, who had one child, James Logan. William Anderson was shot through the shoulders by the Indians early one morning, but managed to escape to Fort Dillow, which place his wife and youngest child reached in the night, James Logan, aged six years, and William Anderson, aged two years. James Logan remained with the Indians until he was twelve years old, and then made his way to Fort McIntosh, but William Anderson never returned. Years afterward his children wrote to their uncle, Thomas Anderson, making inquiries about their white relatives and stating that their father had become a chief. Their descendants had been educated at Carlisle, Pa. William Anderson, the pioneer, had six children: William, Alexander, Thomas, David, Mrs. Robert Calvin and John. Thomas was twice married. His first wife, a Miss Patton, had ten children: Juliet, David, William, Esther, Angeline, Mary, Sarah, Armor, Clarissa and Matilda. His second wife was Jane, daughter of James Patton, a native of Maryland. She died April 9, 1881, aged ninety-one years, the mother of three children: Catherine J., James R. and Alexander H. The parents were members of the Hopewell Presbyterian church, which Mr. Anderson helped to build, and of which he was for many years a trustee. James R. has been a successful farmer and owns 200 acres of land, a part of the old homestead. He has been twice married. His first wife was Elizabeth, daughter of Joseph Culley. She had one child, Ada M., who is the wife of Edward Inglefield. His present wife is Sarah, daughter of Peter Lance. She has four children: William T., Charlie B., Bertie J. and Ida May. Mr. and Mrs. Anderson are members of the Presbyterian church; he is a Republican.

JOHN ANDERSON, miller, P. O. New Sheffield, was born Nov. 5, 1531, in Washington county, Pa. His grandfather, John Anderson, came from Ireland and settled in West Virginia in an early day. His son, Andrew, was born in West Virginia and settled in Washington county, Pa., where he farmed until 1837; then removed to Raccoon township, Beaver county, where he died at the age of seventy-three years. He was a member of the old Seceder's church, in which he was for some time an elder. In politics he was a Democrat. He was an excellent fifer, and was always on hand muster day. His wife, Hannah Wykoff, died at the age of eighty-two years. Their children were Mary J., Nancy Ann, Margaret, Sarah, John, Catherine, James W., Andrew J. and William M. John was a farmer in Raccoon township until 1869, when he came to Hopewell township and engaged in milling. He first owned and operated a water and steam mill half a mile from New Sheffield, and in 1878, built the steam mill, which he has since operated in New Sheffield. He also has a farm of fifty acres. He was married, June 21, 1855, to Mary E., daughter of James and Margaret (McCuone) Buchanan. Mr. and Mrs. Anderson are members of the United Presbyterian church, of which he has been an elder many years. In politics he is a Democrat; has held many township offices, and is now justice of the peace.

SILAS ATEN, farmer, P. O. Frankfort Springs, is a son of Jacob and Eliza (Brown) Aten. His paternal grandfather was a native of Germany, settled in Hancock county, W. Va., and raised a large family. Jacob and Eliza Aten had nine children. The parents moved to Jefferson county, Ohio, where they died. Silas was married in West Virginia to Mary, daughter of Peter and Elizabeth (Carson) Peterson, the former of German and the latter of Irish descent. Mr. and Mrs. Aten have four children living: Eliza E., Emma E., Luda C. and Ira O. Mr. Aten and wife are members of the Presbyterian church, of which he is an elder. He came to Beaver county in the autumn of 1864 and bought 166 acres of land, which he has well improved. He owes his success in life to his own perseverance and industry.

GEORGE BAKER, farmer, P. O. New Sheffield, was born on Raccoon creek, April 28, 1837, and is a grandson of George Baker. The latter, with his parents and brothers, was captured by the Indians, but escaped while the savages were drunk. The father, who was a Bavarian, came to this country in the pay of the British during the Revolution, but deserted and fought for the colonists. George Baker, Sr., was a farmer, and died at the age of ninety years. His children were George, Charles, Michael, John, Nellie, Isabella, Jane and Betsey. Michael married Mary Jane, daughter of George and Mattie (Young) Nickum, and by her had nine children: John, George, Joseph (killed at the battle of Chancellorsville), Martha, Eliza J., Malinda (deceased), Isabella, Adaline and Mary. Our subject was reared in this township, and chose the business of farming. Starting in life with nothing, he now owns two farms, containing 102 and seventy-six acres, respectively. His wife is Emeline, daughter of James and Agnes (Christy) Warnock. They have nine children: James O., Calvin Q., Daniel W., Joseph H., Michael, Lillie M., Vistie A., Vinnie J. and Eddie C. The parents are members of the Presbyterian church at New Sheffield, of which Mr. Baker has been an elder. He takes great interest in church and school matters. Two of his sons, Daniel W. and Michael, have been teachers.

GEORGE BECHTEL, merchant, P. O. Water Cure, was born May 30, 1843, in Schemmern, near Cassel, Germany. His father, Rev. George Bechtel, a minister of the Reformed church, lived and died in Germany. He was educated in the universities of of Leipsic and Heidelberg, and could speak seven languages. He was an earnest worker, and had charge of seven congregations. His wife, Margaretha Tourte, was the mother of eight children: Wilhelm, Matilda and Charlotte who are deceased, and Ernst, Mary, Henry, George and Fred, living. Wilhelm was a captain in the civil war. Fred is a music teacher in Allegheny, and Henry is also a resident of Allegheny. George was educated in Germany, and learned mercantile business there. At the age of twenty he came to this country and located in Pittsburgh, where he clerked for four years. He then came to Phillipsburg, where he has since been engaged in mercantile business, keeping a general store. His first wife was Emelia, daughter of Antony Knapper. She died here. His present wife is Mary Miksch, a native of Bohemia. She has two children: Emelia and William. The parents are members of the Reformed church. Mr. Bechtel is a Democrat, and has filled several town offices.

ROBERT BIDDLE, gardener, P. O. Water Cure, is a grandson of Spencer Biddle, who came from England with his brother. The family is of French descent. Spencer Biddle married Sarah S. Pierce, and settled on the eastern shore of Maryland, where he kept a merchant mill. He lost a vessel loaded with goods, and this loss caused him to move west. He settled on Fish Creek Island, in the Ohio river, in Marshall county, Va., where he bought a large tract of land; brought negroes and fine blooded stock with him and became a leading man in his section. He kept a hotel there, and was nearly ninety years old when he died. His wife died in Wheeling, W. Va. They had seven children. Of these Lloyd was a farmer, and died in Pleasant county, W. Va., aged ninety years. His wife, Francis Wikart, of German descent, died at the age of eighty-seven years. They had eleven children. Of these Robert followed the river from an early age until he was forty-five years old. He was a deck hand two years and then was mate twenty-four years on the upper and lower Mississippi and Missouri, the upper and lower Ohio and the Red and Ouchata rivers. In 1865 he came to Phillipsburg. After this he was for a while engaged in steamboating, then began gardening, which he has continued to the present time. He has a garden of about twenty acres, and supplies New Brighton and Beaver Falls with his produce. He is married to Mary E. Hayward. They are members of the Presbyterian church. Mr. Biddle is a Republican.

SAMUEL BIGGER, farmer, P. O. Frankfort Springs, was born Oct. 19, 1819, in Hanover township. The progenitor of the family in America was Thomas Bigger, a son of Matthew Bigger, a native of Scotland, who, on account of religious persecutions, fled to Ireland. Matthew was the father of six children: John, James, Samuel, Thomas, Jane and Elizabeth, wife of John Anderson. They lived in County Antrim. The three eldest sons remained in Ireland; the rest, accompanied by the mother, came to America, landing in Baltimore Oct. 16, 1773. Thomas was thirty-five years old when he came to America. He settled near Raccoon creek, Washington county, Pa.; was a weaver by occupation, and was a leading man in those early days. He married in Ireland, in 1773, Elizabeth Moore, of an old and wealthy family, who objected to her marriage with Mr. Bigger, which fact prompted them to emigrate. They were the progenitors of a numerous family, and died on the old homestead. Of their ten children James married Mary Biggart, and in 1816 settled in Hanover township, where they died. James Bigger was a man of good sense and ability, and became the father of nine children: Samuel, Jane, Mary, Thomas, Eliza A., Ellen, James M., John and Robert. Of these Samuel, our subject, is a thoroughly self-educated and well-informed man. He married Jane, daughter of James Fulton, of Washington county, and four children have blessed this union: James, a lawyer, in Chicago; John, Laura, and Mrs. Nettie Stephenson. Mr. and Mrs. Bigger are members of the United Presbyterian church; politically he is a Democrat.

THOMAS BIGGER, farmer, P. O. Frankfort Springs, was born Jan. 9, 1826, on the old Bigger homestead in Hanover township, where his father, James, settled in 1816. The farm consisted of 400 acres of wild land originally entered by Magnus Tate, an eastern man. Thomas Bigger was reared and educated in his native county, and has always been a farmer. He still has a farm of sixty-one acres near the famous Frankfort Springs. He was married, Nov. 2, 1854, to Mary Nicholson, a native of Frankfort, where she was born May 6, 1834. She is a daughter of Hon. Thomas and Rebecca (Stewart) Nicholson. The former settled in Frankfort in 1833. Mr. and Mrs. Bigger are the parents of three children: Ellis N., an attorney at Beaver; Inez J., and James Carl. Mr. Bigger, wife and daughter are members of the United Presbyterian church. He has been a Republican since 1860, having been a Democrat previous to that time.

J. M. BIGGER, hotel-keeper, P. O. Frankfort Springs, was born March 31, 1834, on the old Bigger homestead in Hanover township. His father, James Bigger, served in the War of 1812, and was stationed at Fort Malden, on the lakes. J. M. was reared and educated in this county, and previous to engaging in the hotel business, was a farmer. He owned 200 acres of the old farm, which he sold in 1884, and bought the Frankfort Mineral Springs property, on which he has made great improvements. The summer resort opens July 1st.

HENRY BIMBER, lumber merchant, P. O. Water Cure, is a native of Germany, and a son of George Bimber, of Hesse-Cassel, who was a large hotel-keeper, a prominent man in his town and a major of militia. George married Marie Tourté, a descendant of an old Huguenot family that was driven out of Paris at the time of the French revolution. Mrs. Bimber died in 1876, aged sixty-four years, the mother of four boys, of whom only Henry is living. The latter was well educated in his native country, in the gymnasium and polytechnic institute in his native town. In 1854 he came to America and settled in Phillipsburg. He has spent much time in traveling. In 1870 he returned to Germany on the occasion of the death of his father, and sailed on the last German ship that crossed during the Franco-Prussian war. The vessel was bombarded by a French man-of-war, and landed in England. He remained in Germany until 1884, when he returned to Phillipsburg. He was married here to Josephine, daughter of Dr. Acker, the founder of the Water Cure at Phillipsburg. They have four children: George A., who was educated in Germany and is now a druggist in Allegheny City; Mary, born in America; Edward and Carl, born in Germany. The parents are members of the Lutheran church. Mr. Bimber has been a teacher in the German school of Phillipsburg. He is an active worker in and superintendent of the Sunday-school. He is a Republican.

THOMAS BLACKMORE, blacksmith, P. O. Hookstown, was born Sept. 9, 1832. His great-grandfather was a native of Maryland, and lived for some years in Beaver county. His grandfather, Nathaniel Blackmore, married Mary Patterson and resided several years in Greene and Hanover townships, this county, but died in Meigs county, Ohio. Their son John was born in Hookstown in 1804, and died at the age of seventy-six years. John married Mary, daughter of Robert Laughlin, and they had eight children: Matilda, Thomas and William (twins), Mary, Elizabeth, Sarah, Lucinda and John. Thomas, the subject of this sketch, married Sophia Wright, and to them have been born three children: John W., Mary A. and Bertha. Mr. Blackmore is a thorough mechanic. His father and grandfather were both blacksmiths, as is his son, John W. Mr. Blackmore has also been successful as a stockman, and in his stables may be seen the "Duke of Dunblane," "Prince of Normandy," "Messenger Billy," and the colt, "Pride of Scotland."

JACOB BORN, farmer and dairyman, P. O. New Sheffield, was born June 16, 1849, in Canton Berne, Switzerland. His parents, John and Magdelena (Sherich) Born, came to America with their children in 1853, and settled in Pittsburgh, where the father followed his trade, that of carpenter, until his death. He left four children, John, Jacob, Barbara and Magdalena; the last two died about four years ago. John is janitor of the City Hall, Pittsburgh. The mother afterward married John Kaiser, and moved to Monroe county, Ohio, with the family, and engaged in farming there. He married Mary Kanzig, by whom he has six children: John W., Charles A., George J., Benjamin H., Lena and Louis F. Mr. Born is a Republican. He resides on his brother's farm, which he cultivates for him, and which contains a gas well. He ships about 200 quarts of milk to Pittsburgh daily.

JOHN M. BOYCE, farmer, P. O. Seventy-Six, is a son of Robert Boyce (deceased), a man of sterling worth and a prosperous farmer, who was born near Cannonsburg, Pa., Sept. 15, 1800, and moved to Beaver county in 1851. He started in life poor, and accumulated a valuable property of 140 acres, where John M. now resides. He was a member of the Hopewell Presbyterian church, and in politics a Republican. His wife, Flora, was born Jan. 10, 1804, and was a daughter of Samuel and Jane (Patterson) Stewart. She had two children, who are now living, Jennie P., born July 26, 1836, and John M., born July 27, 1839. The latter is a successful farmer and a respected man, following in the footsteps of his father. He was married to Louisa E., daughter of Samuel Eachel. They are members of the United Presbyterian church; Mr. Boyce is a Republican.

AARON BOYD, farmer, P. O. Harshaville, was born July 1, 1823, on the farm where he was reared and educated and where he now resides, containing 340 acres. His grandfather, John Boyd, who was of Irish descent, settled near Frankfort, in Hanover township, Beaver county, and died at the home of his daughter, Mrs. Sallie Moore. He was a farmer, and had a large family. His son, John Boyd, was born July 20, 1782, and died April 2, 1870, at the home of his son, Aaron. He was married, in October, 1807, to Agnes, daughter of Thomas Moore, who came here when the Indians were still in the county, and a blockhouse stood near where Mrs. Eliza Moore now resides. Mrs. Boyd was born Dec. 15, 1789, and died Aug. 13, 1869. She was the mother of twelve children: Margaret, Martha, Mary, Thomas, Sarah, Eliza, Samuel, Aaron, Eleanor, Agnes, John and Esther. Aaron married, Feb. 2, 1871, Martha, daughter of James Plotts, a bugler, who was killed in the Civil War. Seven children have been born to Mr. and Mrs. Boyd: Harvey, Ava, James, Robert A. (died at the age of seven years), Hally, Mitchell and Maud. Mr. Boyd is a thorough-going business man; in politics a Democrat.

JAMES BRADEN (deceased) was a native of Raccoon township, Beaver county, Pa., born in 1812. His ancestors were among the pioneers of this county, whose experiences in the wilderness and among the Indians are recorded in history. He was a son of John and Mary (Phillips) Braden; who were the parents of five children, he being the second son, born and reared on the home farm. At the death of his father he inherited the property, consisting of 422 acres, subsequently reduced to 300 acres. Mr. Braden married, in 1835, Ellen, daughter of William and Margaret (Patterson) Elliott, of Jefferson county, Pa., and to this union were born eleven children, six yet living: John, Thomas (married), Isabella and Beckie J., at home, Margaret and Rachel, married. Mr. Braden died in 1866, a life-long farmer; in politics a Republican. His widow is a member of the United Presbyterian church, as are her children, with the exception of John and Isabella, who are Methodists.

WILLIAM BRUCE, farmer, P. O. Shafer's, was born on the old Bruce homestead in Hopewell township, Jan. 21, 1829. His great-grandfather, Charles Bruce, was born in Scotland, came to this country in youth, and is buried on the old homestead in Moon township, and his son, George, lived and died on the above place, where he had a large tract of land, which was divided among his sons. He (George) married Hannah Gun, whose second husband, Joseph Rambo, lived on Raccoon creek. George Bruce had seven children: Charles, Abraham, Jacob, John, William, Peggie and Jane. Of these Charles married Margaret, daughter of Daniel Christy, a native of Ireland, and a well-known man who held the office of county commissioner and auditor. Charles Bruce and wife died near the old homestead. Their children were George, Daniel C., David, William, Joseph R., J. Rodgers, Robert, Rebecca and Hannah. J. Rodgers died in Andersonville prison. William Bruce owns a farm of 135 acres. He has been married twice. His first wife was Malinda Baker, whose grandfather was captured by the Indians. She died, leaving three children: Margaret J., Elmer and Ida. Mr. Bruce's present wife is Elizabeth, daughter of Michael Mateer, Sr. She has five children: Caroline, Louisa, Elizabeth, William J. and Charles R.

HOMER BRYAN, farmer, P. O. Shafer's, was born in Mechanicsburg, this county, Nov. 14, 1857. His great-grandfather, John Bryan, a native of Ireland, came to America when a young man, and died in Beaver county. He had nineteen children. His son Thomas, was a doctor, and practiced under the old school twenty-five years; then adopted the Homeopathic system, which he followed twenty-five years. He died in Sheffield, in September, 1877, aged about seventy-eight years. His wife was Jane P., daughter of Samuel Nichols, and died in July, 1877, aged seventy-eight years. Her children were, Mary S., Samuel N., Jane P., John and Margaret, who are living; and George, who was killed at the battle of Gaines' Mill, and Henry, who was drowned in Raccoon creek. John Bryan read medicine with his father and Dr. J. F. Cooper, and in 1866 was graduated from the Cleveland Homeopathic College. He resides in Moon township, where he owns a farm of 140 acres. He married Elizabeth, daughter of James Reed. Their son, Homer, was married, in Beaver Falls, March 28, 1883, to Ida Bryan, adopted daughter of Anderson and Rebecca (Alcorn) Braden. She was born Feb. 14, 1857. They have one son, John Bryan, Jr., born May 13, 1884. Mr. and Mrs. Bryan are members of the North Branch Presbyterian church.

830   HISTORY OF BEAVER COUNTY.

ROBERT BRYARLY, farmer, P. O. Frankfort Springs, was born Feb. 14, 1805, on the old Bryarly homestead in Hanover township, where his grandfather, Patrick Scott, entered 420 acres of land in February, 1785, besides several other large farms in the neighborhood. This was about the time old Thomas Armour and James Hartford first settled in this county. Robert Bryarly was named after his father, who was born in Maryland, of Scotch-Irish descent. He married Sarah, daughter of Patrick Scott, near Little York, Pa. The young couple came west about 1796, and settled on one-half of the original 420 acres mentioned above. They had six children: Susannah, John, James, Patrick S., Robert and Mrs. Nancy Smith, of Iowa. Robert Bryarly, Sr., was born Oct. 16, 1772, was married Oct. 14, 1792, and died March 29, 1842. His wife was born May 11, 1774, and died April 18, 1827. Our subject is a farmer, and holds 118 acres, a part of the old homestead. He married, April 22, 1828, Elizabeth Smith, who was born June 18, 1800, at Saw Mill Run, seven miles west of Pittsburgh, and died Aug. 19, 1884. Her children were Jane, Sarah, William C., Elizabeth, Margaret and Robert S. The family are all members of the United Presbyterian church. Mr. Bryarly is a Republican. His son, William C., works the home farm.

JOSEPH KERR BUCHANAN, farmer, P. O. Kendall, was born in Hancock county, W. Va., near Chapman's Landing, and is a son of John and Margaret (Chambers) Buchanan. His father died when Joseph was three months old, and, at the age of three years he was left an orphan by the death of his mother. He had three brothers, James, Thomas and John. James went to Nebraska, and from there enlisted in the army where he suffered severe hardships, which eventually caused his death. Thomas started for California in the spring of 1852, and died on the Platte river. John, a mute, is a carpenter at Hannibal, Mo. Joseph at the age of four years, was bound out to Aaron Moore, whose parents, Thomas and Margaret (Hutchinson) Moore, came from Lancaster county, Pa. They were classed among the wealthy people of Beaver county and owned over 1,000 acres of land. Aaron Moore married Polly, daughter of David and Nancy (Kennedy) Stevens. The latter's mother was captured by the Indians. Aaron Moore was a miller on the west branch of Little Traverse, and also owned 100 acres of land. He died childless, Feb. 17, 1879, and his wife died Feb. 27, 1874. They were members of the Mill Creek Presbyterian church. In the article of indenture it was stipulated that Joseph K. Buchanan should be bound to Mr. Moore until age of seventeen; should receive board and clothing, and be sent to school till he could learn to read and write and cipher " till the single rule of three." He was treated as a son by Mr. and Mrs. Moore. At the age of fourteen he went into the mill, asthma having prevented Mr. Moore's active life there, and he continued to operate the mill until after he was seventeen years old, and helped to pay off a debt incurred by Mr. Moore in building a house. Feb. 16, 1855, he was married to Martha T., daughter of James Bigger. She was born April 19, 1830. They have two sons: Rev. Aaron M., of Morgantown, W. Va., and James B. Mr. and Mrs. Buchanan are members of the Mill Creek Presbyterian church; in politics he is a Democrat. He is the largest land holder in the township, owning 700 acres.

JAMES BURNESON, farmer, P. O. Water Cure, was born May 29, 1824, a son of Samuel and Mary Ann (Cochran) Burneson, natives, respectively, of County Armagh, Ireland, and Scotland. They came to America about 1815, and located in Pittsburgh. About 1821 they moved into Moon township. Samuel Burneson was a farmer, and died March 3, 1863, aged eighty-two years. His wife died May 27, 1837, aged forty-three years. They had eleven children: William, Agnes, Jane, Samuel, Thomas, James, Mary A., Isabella, John, Margaret and Andrew. The parents were members of the Associate church; the father was a Democrat, and he filled several township offices. James was educated here, and owns a farm of 100 acres, a part of the old homestead. He is married to Rebecca J. Thompson, and had nine children: Martha J., Mary J., Rebecca J., Robert S., Maggie E., Sarah M., James T., Thomas A. and Fannie J. Mary J. and Maggie E. are deceased. The parents are members of the United Presbyterian church; Mr. Burneson is a Republican.

THOMAS BUTLER, farmer, P. O. Seventy-Six, is a grandson of Simon Butler, who settled in Beaver county about the beginning of this century. He was of Welsh descent and came here from the eastern part of the state. He had six children: Eliza, Benjamin, Simon, Sarah, Peter and John. Benjamin was born here and married Jane, daughter of Thomas and Catherine McElhaney, and now resides in Alabama. His wife died in Beaver county. Their son, Thomas, subject of this sketch, has lived all his life in Beaver county with the exception of a short time spent in California. He owns 230 acres. He is married to Sarah A., daughter of Samuel Morgan. They have had seven children: Emma J., Benjamin, Samuel M., John T., Charles H. and Clara K., living, and Mary E., who died at the age of fourteen. Mr. and Mrs. Butler are members of Mount Olivet Presbyterian church, of which he is a trustee. Politically he is a Democrat.

J. W. BUTZ, wagon maker, P. O. Frankfort Springs, is of German descent. His grandfather, Nicholas Butz, was born in Germany, and was married there to Maria Magdalena Younker. They located in Northampton county, Pa., but later came to Mercer county, where the father died; the mother died in Wayne county; both were over eighty-five years of age. They had five children; of these David, born Jan. 29, 1801, came to Ginger Hill, Washington county, and from there went to Beallsville, where he learned the shoemaker's trade. He married, July 21, 1824, Amy, daughter of Job Pyle. She was a native of Washington county, and died July 13, 1871, aged sixty-four years. David Butz resided at Beallsville from date of settling there until 1884, when he made his home with his son Joe W., where he died Sept. 22, 1887. They had eight children: Eli, Emily, David, John, Joe W., Job, Mary A. and Sarah C. Our subject was born March 11, 1831, in Beallsville, Washington county, Pa. He learned the cabinet maker's trade in Washington, Pa., and followed it for some time. He went west five times, visiting twelve states. Later he began work as a wagon maker, and although he never learned that trade, he has been very successful. He was married, in Frankfort Springs, Pa., to Kate, daughter of J. S. Campbell, and they have had two children, only one of whom is living—Mrs. Ella M. McKenzie. In July, 1863, Mr. Butz enlisted in Company E, 61st P. V., Capt. William Glenn, and participated in the battles of the Wilderness, Spottsylvania, Cold Harbor, and in the battles in front of Petersburg. Politically he is a Republican. Mrs. Kate Butz' mother was Rosannah Teel. The latter was a daughter of John Teel who fought in the Revolution, and afterward settled in Hanover township; he was captured by the Indians, but escaped from them at night, and while being pursued, he ran around a tree followed by a big Indian; then suddenly wheeling, Mr. Teel sank the Indian's own tomahawk into his pursuer's head; then scalped him and escaped.

MILTON CALHOON, farmer, P. O. Hookstown, was born in Greene township, Feb. 12, 1818. His grandfather, William Calhoon, a native of Ireland, came to Beaver county at an early day, and finally settled near Shippingport, in Greene township, where he died. He was a prosperous man and a large landholder. He had nine children, of whom William, a farmer by occupation, was born in Greene township, and died there at the age of sixty-two years. His brothers, John and James, were tanners in Hookstown; Richard died in Raccoon township, aged four score years; Samuel lived near Smith's Ferry, and died in Ohio, aged eighty-seven years. William Calhoon married Elizabeth, daughter of James Hutchison, an old pioneer on the Raccoon creek. Mr. Hutchison was a grand old man, honest and upright. Besides his own family of four children, he brought from Scotland four poor children, who lived and died with him. Elizabeth Calhoon died at the age of eighty-five years; she had ten children: John, James, Richard, Robert, Milton, George, Thomas, Joseph, Elizabeth and Mary. Milton Calhoon has been a successful farmer. Beginning life poor, by industry and good management he has succeeded in accummulating a competence. He owns three farms containing altogether about 360 acres. He married Phœbe, daughter of James and Polly (Foster) Mackall. Mrs. Mackall's father was Thomas Foster, a leading man in Georgetown in his day. Mr. and Mrs. Calhoon are members of the Presbyterian church. They have seven children: Mary, James, Thomas, Walter, Ida, Samuel and

Hamilton. Mr. Calhoon is a Republican. Five of his brothers were captains and four were owners of vessels. His son Walter is general agent for the State of Missouri for the German Insurance Company.

,THOMAS S. CALHOON, steamboat captain, Georgetown, was born Aug. 15, 1834. His grandfather, William Calhoon, was a farmer in Greene township, and died young; his wife, Elizabeth (Hutchison) survived him many years, and was the mother of nine children: John, Richard, James, Thomas, Joseph, Elizabeth, Mary, Milton and George. Of these, John was born on the home farm near Georgetown; he was a river captain, and was drowned in the Ohio river. Elizabeth died young. Mary is the wife of Captain Stockdale, of Allegheny City. All the boys were captains. John married Nancy, daughter of Thomas Stephenson; she died a few years after her husband, the mother of seven children, and those living are Thomas S., Mrs. Hattie Nelson, Mrs. Elmira Smith, and William. Thomas S. began life on the river at an early age, and when twelve years old he made a trip to Nashville on the "Caledonia." He has been a captain since 1862, and is now in command of the "Katie Stockdale," plying between Cincinnati and Pittsburgh. He was married, Jan. 8, 1867, to Amanda, daughter of Charles Calhoun, and they have two children: Harriet, at Beaver College, and Mary E. Captain Calhoun is a Democrat.

JOHNSTON CALHOUN, of Hookstown, Greene township, was born Sept. 19, 1812. The progenitor of this family was Gloud or Thaddeus Calhoun, of Ireland, who married a sister of Lord Blaney, at Blaney's Castle (now called Blarney). His son William married a Miss Sprowl, a daughter of Jane Johnston, who escaped the siege of Derry by hiding in a potato furrow. Since her time Johnston has been a family name among her descendants. William had a son Johnston and a daughter Jane. Jane married a distant relation in Ireland, named Samuel Calhoun. They came to America and settled in South Carolina. The great statesman, John C. Calhoun, was their son. Johnston also came to America in 1790, in the brig "Cunningham," and landed in Philadelphia. He lived three years in Kennigojig, Pa., then went to Washington county and rented a farm where the Washington County Home now stands. He sold provisions to the government troops commanded by George Washington, when he was sent to quell the whisky insurrection. In 1800 he bought over 300 acres of land at Mill Creek, where he died Dec. 10, 1835, aged eighty-two years. His wife, Jane Donnehay, died in 1883, aged eighty-two years. Their children were William, Joseph, Robert, George and Ann (Mrs. Littell). Joseph married Jane, daughter of William Littell, Esq. He and his wife both died at Mill Creek, the former June 30, 1845, aged fifty-eight years, the latter Nov. 21, 1863, aged seventy-one years. They had six daughters and two sons: Johnston, Mary, Ann, Eliza, Alice, Lovina, Joseph and Agnes. Johnston, the subject of this sketch, carried on farming and sheep raising successfully till 1872, since which time he has lived a life of retirement, for some years in Beaver, this county, and for the last few years in Hookstown. His first wife died leaving eleven children: Jane (now Mrs. Isaac D. Sibley, of Colorado), Mary (now Mrs. John Gallaspie, of Colorado), Isabella A. (now Mrs. Fleck, of Wyoming), Joseph (now pastor of the United Presbyterian church of Indianola, Iowa), John and Henry D. (both now of Colorado), Eliza (now wife of Rev. M. M. Carleton, both missionaries in India), Johnston C. (now a minister in Viola, Ill., United Presbyterian church), George N. (now of Washington Territory), Emma (now Mrs. Andrew Hunter, of Colorado), and Samuel (who died in Huntsville, Ala., about 1866). His second wife, Sarah Shirts, died leaving one child, Alice, now Mrs. Frank Pittenger, of Ohio. His present wife is Maggie A. Calhoun, daughter of Samuel Calhoun, of Bellaire, Ohio. He has been from time to time called to fill positions of trust and responsibility, and has never failed to give full satisfaction. He was elected a school director, and served as such for a number of years; also as justice of the peace of Beaver county. Was a delegate of the Christian Commission twice during the war; first, to the Potomac army at Washington City, and sent from there to Virginia; second, to Cumberland army in Tennessee and Alabama. He organized and taught a Bible class in each army, over and above the duties devolving upon him as a delegate, and was presented by them with a written testimonial of their esteem and regard of him as a Bible teacher.

BIOGRAPHIES—SOUTH SIDE. 833

JAMES S. CALVERT, farmer. P. O. New Sheffield, was born in Allegheny City, May 1, 1832. The history of the Calvert family may be traced back to three brothers of the name, who fled from Scotland on account of political troubles, and settled in three different counties in the North of Ireland. The descendants of these brothers are scattered throughout the United States. The progenitor of the Beaver county Calverts was Alexander, a native of County Down, Ireland. His son, James, was married in Ireland, to Ann Small, and coming to this country settled in Pittsburgh, where James worked at ropemaking. In 1835 he came to Moon township and bought 116 acres of land, on which he died in 1859, aged sixty-six years. His widow died in 1880, aged eighty-two years. They had seven children. all of whom are living. James and Ann Calvert were active members of the United Presbyterian church. He was a Democrat. His son, James S., was reared on the homestead, on which he now resides. During the gold excitement he went to California by the Vanderbilt route, via Nicaragua and Costa Rica. He engaged in mining and prospecting there with varied success, and was for a time foreman of the Rodgers quartz mill, near Virginia City, Nev. He had many thrilling adventures with the Indians. At one time his party of twelve was surrounded by 300 Indians, but escaped by making a bold rush. He is unmarried and his sister Kate keeps house for him. He is a member of the United Presbyterian church at Raccoon; in politics a Republican, and has been justice of the peace fifteen years, and jury commissioner, one term.

WILLIAM M. CALVERT, merchant, New Sheffield, was born April 2, 1839, in Moon township. His grandfather, Richard Calvert, was born in the highlands of Scotland, where his two uncles fought under Sir William Wallace. After his defeat the family were banished and went to County Down, Ireland, where James, father of William M., was born. James Calvert was married in Ireland to Ann, daughter of James Small. The latter participated in the great Irish rebellion, was taken prisoner and died soon after his release. James Calvert came to America and settled in Baltimore, Md., in 1815: thence he came by wagon across the mountains to Pittsburgh, and followed his trade of rope making in Allegheny county until 1832; then came to Moon township, Beaver county, and bought a farm of Robert Potts. He died at the age of sixty-six years, his wife at the age of eighty-three years. They had seven children, all of whom are now living: Bella, Mary, Alice, James, Catharine, Rev. A. H. Calvert, of the United Presbyterian church, and William M. The last named was educated in Beaver county, and began his mercantile career in November, 1863, in New Sheffield, where he bought out David Patton. He started with little capital, and has been successful. He was burned out Jan. 31, 1887, and in six weeks from that time he had erected a handsome two-story store and resumed business. He buys and sells large quantities of wool, and owns a farm of sixty-five acres, on which is the largest gas wells in the county. His wife is Elizabeth, daughter of Joseph Wallace, and they have ten children: Joseph, James, Bella, Charles, Anna, Vallie, Bessie, Willie, Guy and Alice. Mr. and Mrs. Calvert are members of the United Presbyterian church; in politics he is a Republican.

WILLIAM CAMPBELL was born of Scotch parentage,and while young was indentured to a Mr. Henry Craig to learn the weaving trade in the State of Maryland. Soon afterward this Henry Craig moved to Pennsylvania, and located at the head waters of Service Creek, now Greene township, Beaver county (but what Mr. Craig supposed was Virginia). In 1778 Mr. Craig purchased 200 acres of land, agreeing to give William Campbell 100 acres of this land in lieu of his trade, if he would stay with and work for him until his indentures were out; which he did, and received his deed for the 100 acres of land William Campbell was married in 1786 to Miss Nancy Vance, and by this union were born four sons and two daughters: Henry, William, Margaret, Nancy, Arthur and James. Said Henry Campbell, after coming to years of maturity, purchased the old Craig farm, and with his sister Margaret lived on said farm until their deaths. They lived until a good old age, and neither of them was married; Nancy died in about her twentieth year. James, the youngest son, bought out the heirs of the Campbell farm and lived on same until his death at a good old age. This James had but one son, William, who now owns both the old Craig and Campbell farms. Arthur Campbell was born in 1798; was married to Miss Sarah Mercer in 1822, and by her had four sons and four daughters: Nancy, Joseph, William, Comfort, Mary, Marshall, Louisa and James. Arthur Campbell and his brother William bought a farm near the old Campbell farm in 1822, and lived on said farm until 1831; they then sold it and bought 400 acres of land on Service Creek, four miles below the old home farm, and moved on to the same in 1832, dividing it equally between them. They both lived and died on these farms. William Campbell was born in 1790, and died in 1863. He had three children, who still survive him, and live on the old farm. Arthur was a prominent man in his day; he was commissioner of said county at the time of his death, which occurred in 1844. Four of Arthur's children died, leaving no heirs, viz.: Comfort, Louisa, William and James. Nancy married W. W. McCoy; Mary married T. Shane; Marshall married Isabell Smith, by whom he has nine children (he has a part of the home farm); Joseph was born in 1824, was married, in 1849, to Isabell Bryan, daughter of John and Mary Bryan, and to this union have been born three sons and four daughters: Sarah (deceased), John B., William A., Mary A. (married to J. H. Smith), James O. (in Kansas), Jennie (deceased) and Ella Bell (deceased). Joseph and his family are members of the United Presbyterian church; in politics he is a Republican. He still resides on a part of the farm bought by his father in 1832, with other land added to it.

WILLIAM CAMPBELL, farmer, P. O. Hookstown, was born on the old family homestead, Jan. 29, 1833. The Campbell family were early members of Dr. Anderson's church at Service. William Campbell, Sr., was but two years old when he left Scotland, and soon after reaching this country was bound out to a weaver named Henry Craig, with whom he remained until the latter's death, when, having served faithfully and well, inherited the Craig farm of 100 acres, which is yet in possession of his heirs. He married Nancy Vance, who became the mother of the following-named children: Henry, William, Margaret, Nancy, Arthur and James. Of these James was born June 15, 1801, and joined the United Presbyterian church in 1826. He was a thrifty farmer, and died March 8, 1883. His wife was Margaret, daughter of John and Isabelle (Duncan) Craig, the former a soldier of the revolutionary war. Mrs. Margaret Campbell was born Aug. 29, 1809, in Hanover township, joined the church in 1828, and has been a faithful and devoted member ever since. Her life has been marked by kind deeds, and she is greatly respected for her qualities of head and heart. William Campbell married Jane, daughter of David and Jane (Crooks) Kennedy. Their union has been blessed with five children: Mrs. Margaret J. Reynolds, James, Mrs. Elizabeth M. Leeper, Thomas K. and John Newton C. Mr. Campbell and his wife are members of the United Presbyterian church. He has a farm of 180 acres, on which he resides, near the old homestead. In politics he is a Republican.

MARTIN W. CAREY, merchant, P. O. Water Cure, is a grandson of John Carey, who came from England and settled in Beaver county, where he died at the age of fifty-seven years. They had five children who reached maturity: Daniel, George W., Emeline, Harrison and Mary Ann (Mrs. Lutton, deceased). Daniel Carey, father of Martin W., was born, Oct. 8, 1827, in Moon township. He married Mrs. Adaline Minor, nee Wilson, who is the mother of three children: Martin W., John W. (deceased), and Mrs. Maria J. Gunther, of Ohio. Mr. and Mrs. Daniel Carey are members of the Methodist Episcopal church. Martin W., was married, to Mary A. McCullough, and they have six children: Harry W., Mary L., Mertilla and Modina (twins), Martin W. and Helena. Mr. and Mrs. Carey are members of the Methodist church of Philipsburg, of which he has been financial steward and trustee. He is a Democrat and has held the office of assessor. He was with his parents five years in Ohio, and for the past five years has been a merchant in Philipsburg.

JOHN J. CAROTHERS, farmer, P. O. Frankfort Springs, was born June 10, 1822, on Brady's Hill, Patterson township, this county, His grandfather, James Carothers, was born in Carlisle, Pa. His parents were Scotch-Irish. James Carothers was reared and educated in Carlisle, and at the age of twenty-two years he came to Hanover township, taking up 212 acres of government land in 1787. He was a civil engineer, held the position of county surveyor, and was known far and wide as Colonel Carothers. He came here a single man, and in 1789 returned to Carlisle and married Alice Carothers, not a relative. She died in 1848, aged eighty-three years. He died about 1817, aged fifty-two years. Both were members of the Presbyterian church. Their children were Mary (or Polly), John, William, James, Jesse, Matilda and Thomas. Thomas was a Presbyterian minister, and died young. Jesse was cashier of the Merchants and Manufacturers Bank, of Pittsburgh. Mary married John Glasgow, and Matilda married Alexander Duncan. John Carothers was born on the old homestead, and married Agnes (McGlester) White. After his marriage he removed to Patterson township where he died. He was a Democrat and served as judge of Beaver county eighteen years, besides filling nearly all the township offices, and was deservedly popular. He died in December, 1860, aged sixty-seven years. His children were James, John J., Andrew, Mary (wife of Wm. Anderson), Jesse, Jane (wife of Wilson Cunningham), William and Nettie (wife of Robert Ferguson). John J. returned to the home farm in Hanover township at the age of fourteen. Sept. 2, 1847, he married Ellen, daughter of John and Sarah (Ferguson) Ewing. They have had five children: Emeline, Agnes S. and Jeanette, all of whom died, within ten days, of diphtheria, aged respectively nineteen, sixteen and ten .years; James W. and Ella, wife of A. D. Matchett, a carpenter, of Frankfort. James W. married Maggie Forner. Mr. and Mrs. Carothers are church members. The former is a Democrat, and has been justice of the peace in Frankfort nearly ever since it became a borough.

.WILLIAM M. CAROTHERS, retired, P. O. Frankfort Springs, was born March 5, 1833, in Hanover township, where his grandfather, William Carothers, settled at an early date. He left seven children: Ann, Jane, Mary, William, James, Thomas and John. Of these John married Eleanor, daughter of William and Catherine (Gordon) Murray; they died aged sixty-eight and seventy-six years, respectively. William Murray, our subject, was their only child, and was raised and educated in his native county. He married Mary A., daughter of William and Rebecca (McDole) Hoge. William Hoge was a native of Harrisburg, Pa., and came here with his parents when a child. Rebecca McDole was a daughter of Matthew and Elizabeth (Adams) McDole, natives of Ireland. They all died on the same farm. Mr. and Mrs. Carothers are members of the United Presbyterian church of Frankfort Springs.

B. H. CHAMBERS, farmer, P. O. Frankfort Springs, was born Aug. 7, 1823. His grandfather, James Chambers, the progenitor of the family in this country, was born in Fifeshire, Scotland, and the old family name was Chalmers. James came to this country as a British soldier with Cornwallis, and served in the British army three years. Having become imbued with the spirit of freedom he deserted and enlisted in the colonial militia. After the war he went to Florence, Pa., and there, with Miles Wilson, and finally married Jane, daughter of Samuel and Nancy Miller, of Montour's Run, in Allegheny county. In 1797 they came to Hanover township, in Beaver county, where he purchased of Samuel Swearingen, Sr., 150 acres of land for £76, 17s. He died here at the age of seventy-eight years and his wife died January 1, 1830, aged sixty-seven years. They had eight children: Thomas, Samuel, James, Nancy, John, Jane, Margaret and William. Of these Thomas, and Samuel Chambers, father of our subject, were born in Allegheny county. Samuel was a farmer there, but removed to the old Chambers homestead, where he died Jan. 3, 1871, aged seventy-eight years. He was a member of the Presbyterian church; in politics a Republican. His wife was Isabella, daughter of Benjamin and Margaret (Miller) Hall, and died Dec. 11, 1865, aged sixty-eight years. She had four children: Jane, Margaret, James and Benjamin H. The latter now owns the Mansion farm of 247 acres. He married Jane, daughter of John and Margaret (Barclay) McDonald, the former of Scotch and the latter of Irish origin. Mr. and Mrs. Chambers are members of the United Presbyterian church, of which he has been a trustee. He is a Republican. Their children are Mrs. Margaret Cotter; Lizzie C., wife of J. Cooley; Martha B., S. Elmer and Viola S. S. Elmer married Sept. 22, 1885, Laura Lee, daughter of John and Sarah (Cavitt) Erwin, and they have one son Howard C., born Aug. 15, 1886. He represents the fifth generation living on the same Chambers Homestead.

MICHAEL CHRISTLER, late of Greene township, a native of Switzerland, emigrated to this country at a very early age. He was a great hunter, and one of the pioneers and Indian scouts in the early days of the country's settlement. He was one of the first residents of Greene township, Beaver county, living near Shippingport. During the Revolutionary War he was active in the patriot cause, and lived through many exciting adventures. He was the father of four children: Samuel, Mrs. Rosannah Kerr, John and George. He died at an advanced age.

JOHN C. CHRISTY, farmer and justice of the peace, P. O. Holt, is a native of Philadelphia, Pa., born in 1823, a son of James and Mary (Clark) Christy, natives of Ireland, former of whom was a farmer the greater part of his life, and came from his native land about 1821. He and his wife were the parents of six children, four now living. John C., the second son, received a common school education, and studied also at a business college in Philadelphia. Coming to Beaver in 1844, he, in 1863, purchased 111 acres of land, now nearly all under cultivation. He married, in 1844, Agnes, daughter of John Covit, and two children were born to them, James Harvey and John Lawrence, both of whom met with untimely deaths in 1883. Mr Christy was elected to his present office of justice of the peace in 1885, was jury commissioner, and held other positions of trust. He is a member of the Presbyterian church; in politics he is a Republican.

JOHN CHRISTY, farmer, P. O. Holt, is a native of Allegheny county, Pa , born in 1824, a son of Abraham and Hannah (Bricker) Christy. Abraham was the eldest of five sons and four daughters of John Christy, who came with his family from Switzerland to America about 1806, his first settlement being at Wilmington, Del., after which he moved to Pittsburgh, Pa., and finally to Kentucky, where he died. Abraham was a miner for many years, and was engaged in ferrying at Pittsburgh, but in later life purchased a farm, were he lived the remainder of his days. He had a family of three sons and six daughters, of whom John is the second son. The latter received a common-school training, and worked on his father's farm until thirty-two years of age, part of the time in this county, his father having purchased 143 acres here in 1839. John bought his present property in 1856, and the same year married Mary A., daughter of J. J. Anderson, of Rochester, this county. Five sons and one daughter have blessed this union: Abraham A., married to a Miss Ewing; John J., in California; Francis M., married to Emma I. Minor, of this county, and assisting his father on the farm; Daniel G. and Mary J., at home; William L. is deceased. The mother dying in 1868, Mr. Christy married, in 1870, Annie, daughter of Samuel W. and Elizabeth (Leggett) Moore. Mr. Christy and wife are members of the United Presbyterian church; in politics he is a Republican.

JAMES CHRISTY, farmer, P. O. Shippingport, is a native of Allegheny county, Pa., third son of Abraham and Hannah (Bricker) Christy. He was married, in 1871, to Annie, daughter of Rev. J. M. Smith, of Butler county, Pa., and seven children were born to them, five now living: Daniel. Smith, Clarence, Margaretta and Florence, all at home. Mr. Christy has been a successful farmer, and now owns 140 acres of the old homestead, which originally contained 150 acres. He is a member of the Presbyterian church; politically he is a Republican.

T. A. CLIFTON, farmer, P. O. McCleary, was born in 1850 in Raccoon township, the eldest son of John and Rachel (McHenry) Clifton; the latter, a daughter of Charles McHenry, of this county, died in 1872. John and Rachel were married, in 1846, and had six children, three living: T. A., S. G. and D. L. Thomas Clifton, the grandfather of our subject, came from Washington county, Pa., to this county, and married a Mrs. Hunter, who bore him five sons and three daughters, John being the youngest. He (John) and his brother, Thomas, bought in this county 100 acres of land, and soon after a third brother joined them, purchasing seventy-five acres. This piece of land was deeded to an unmarried sister, who held it until 1875, when it was bought by John Clifton's sons. John bought his brother's fifty acres, which he owned up to the time of his death; he left 100 acres of land to his three sons. Our subject purchased from his brothers their interest in the 175 acres, and is now sole proprietor of the farm. He received a good common-school education, working on the farm during vacations. He married, in 1879, Jennie, daughter of James and Margaret Sterling, natives of Ireland, and by her has two sons: Cory and Carlton. Mr. Clifton is a member of the United Presbyterian church; in politics he is a Republican.

HENRY CONKLE, farmer, P. O. Hookstown, was born on the homestead which he now owns, Nov. 23, 1821. His father, Henry Conkle, Sr., was born in Germany, and was brought to America when but six months old by his parents. They settled in Washington county. Henry and his father came to Greene township when the former was twenty-one years old, and bought a farm of 212 acres, where Henry, Sr., lived and died. He was twice married; his first wife, Margaret, was the mother of eight children. His second wife, Christine Shafer, had four children: Henry and Martha (twins), William and Margaret. Henry Conkle, Sr., was eighty years old when he died, and his father was ninety-eight years. Henry, our subject, married Catharine, daughter of Adam Metts. She bore him eight children: Robert F., a physician at Coraopolis, Pa.; Anna M., Samuel M, Allihue A., Sarah M., John S., George E. and Harriet A. Mr. and Mrs. Conkle and children are members of the Mill Creek church. Politically Mr. Conkle is a Democrat.

SCOTT A. CONNELL, farmer, P. O. Clinton, was born in Independence township, Nov. 6, 1862. His grandfather, John Connell, was a native of Ireland and of Scotch descent. He came to America about 1818, and settled on the farm where Scott A. now resides. He was a carpenter by trade. His children were Nancy, Betsey, Martha, Joseph and Jane. Joseph was born in Ireland, and was married here to Lucinda Gilliland, who is still living. Their children are John, James, Jane, Frank, Mattie, Mary E. and Scott A. Scott A. received a common-school education, and has been a farmer all his life. He was married, Dec. 7, 1886, to Mattie L. Ferguson. Mr. and Mrs. Connell are members of the Hebron Presbyterian church. He was formerly a Democrat, but is now a firm advocate of the principles of the Prohibition party. He owns a farm of 185 acres.

WILLIAM COOK, ferryman, P. O. Shippingport, was born Aug. 20, 1842, in Westmoreland county, Pa. His grandfather, George Cook, lived and died in Trenton, N. J., where his son, George W., was born. The latter was married in Kingessing, Philadelphia, Pa., to Margaret A., daughter of George Fuhr, a basket maker, and landlord of the "Blue Bell Tavern." She died May 30, 1874, aged fifty-two years, the mother of eight children: Caroline V., William, Deborah A., Amanda, Sarah J, Ernest A., Bertha and Clara C. George W., in youth, was bound out to a basket maker, but, disliking his master, left him and finished the trade with George Fuhr. He resided in Westmoreland county, Pa., for fifteen years, and in 1853 came to Phillipsburg, this county, where he farmed and worked at his trade. In 1858 he came to Shippingport and bought the ferry, also became ticket agent for the C. & P. R. R. Co., which position he still holds. He and his son William are both Democrats. The latter has been connected with the ferry over thirty years, and never has had an accident. He was married July 3, 1866, to Harriet, daughter of Andrew Swaney, an old settler. She is the mother of seven children: Harry F., Ernest G., Ella V., Claude R., Albert M., Thomas M. and Sarah I. Mr. and Mrs. Cook are members of the Presbyterian church, of which he is an elder.

JOSEPH COOLEY, farmer, P. O. Frankfort Springs, was born May 19, 1848. His grandfather, Robert Cooley, came to Hanover township, this county, from Pittsburgh, where he had followed the blacksmithing trade. He was married there to Jennie Smith, and then came here shortly afterward, and they had a farm of 160 acres. Both were members of the Presbyterian church of which Mr. Cooley was an elder. In politics he was a Republican. He had a family of nine children. His son, Joseph, married Matilda Anderson, and both died on the farm, aged sixty-two and thirty-two years, respectively. He was also an elder in the Presbyterian church. They had six children who grew to maturity: Anna, Elizabeth, Robert, Latitia, Joseph and Matilda. Joseph, our subject, was reared by his grandparents from the time he was three weeks old. He has a farm of 230 acres, which includes his grandfather's farm. He was married, Nov. 12, 1873, to Lizzie, daughter of Benjamin Chambers, and five children have been born to them: Laura, Chambers R., Lizzie E., Joseph D. and Leola M. Mr. and Mrs. Cooley are members of the Presbyterian church; politically he is a Republican.

J. F. COOPER, physician, P. O. New Sheffield, was born in East Liverpool, Columbiana county, Ohio, Sept. 25, 1822. His great-grandfather, Philip Cooper, a native of Germany, came to this country at the age of four years, lived in Monmouth county, N. J., nine miles from the old battle ground, and died in 1798, aged ninety-four years. His son, Gasper, was educated in Europe and became a teacher in New Jersey. At the breaking out of the Revolution he accepted a commission in the army. He died in New Jersey. Another son, Jacob, was decoyed from home at the age of fifteen years, and served three years in the British army. He was wounded and taken prisoner at the battle of Trenton, and after several months' confinement was sent home, where he remained until after the war. He became an iron manufacturer, and while superintendent of Turnbull's work in Pennsylvania was thrown from a horse and killed. A daughter of Philip Cooper married a Tory, and moved to Canada. David Cooper, son of Philip, removed to Williamsport, in 1796, and two years later went to Chippewa township, Beaver county, and engaged in farming. His wife died there, the mother of six children. From Chippewa David Cooper removed to Ohio, and died in 1809 near Ashtabula. His son, Philip Cooper, was born in New Jersey in 1792. He learned the trade of a carpenter, and followed it for many years. He returned to Beaver county in 1841, and became a farmer. He died in Moon township, July 7, 1879. His wife was Elizabeth, daughter of Joseph Hamilton, and died in May, 1884. She had nine children, five of whom are living. Dr. J. F. Cooper, subject of this sketch, attended the common schools in Ohio and Pennsylvania. In 1843 he engaged in teaching at the same time pursuing his studies. Two years later he was compelled to give up his studies on account of poor health. After three years he resumed his studies and graduated from the Homeopathic Medical College of Pennsylvania in 1853, in the class with Prof. Helmouth, and other distinguished men. He remained with his preceptor, Dr. C. Bayer, of Allegheny City, two years after graduating, then opened an office in Allegheny City, where he has practiced ever since. He bought a farm of 425 acres in Hopewell township, in 1866, which he has greatly improved, and on which are two gas wells. The Doctor is a member of the American Institute of Homeopathy, the Homeopathic Medical Society of Pennsylvania, the Allegheny County Homeopathic Medical Society, and the Allegheny County Anatomical Society. He was married, April 4, 1844, to Sarah, daughter of John and Margaret (Davis) Johnson. They have had six sons: Philip L., an attorney, a graduate of Columbia Law School; Henry; John, a physician, a graduate of the Hahnemann Medical College, Philadelphia, office in Allegheny City; George; William, a chemist in Denver, Colo., and Sidney. The doctor and his wife are members of the Methodist Protestant church of Allegheny City.

HENRY COOPER, oil producer, P. O. New Sheffield, is a son of Dr. J. F. Cooper, and was born Dec. 12, 1848, in Allegheny City. At the age of seventeen years he began to learn the machinist trade; was with Andrew Hartupee one year, and two years with Armstrong & Andrew, in Allegheny City. He then came to Hopewell township, and followed farming and building until August, 1883, when the production of oil first engaged his attention. He helped to take out the first lease, and lent his energy to the new enterprise. He is a member of the Raccoon Oil Company. Nov. 23, 1870, he was married to Sarah J., daughter of George and Eliza A. (Harper) Nevin. George Nevin came to Beaver county in 1838, his parents, John and Margaret (Murray) Nevin, having settled here in 1834. Mr. Cooper has four children: Laura H., Roy C., Jean N. and John F. The parents are members of Mount Carmel Presbyterian church. Mr. Cooper is a Republican, and has held township offices. He served as county auditor three years.

L. M. COTTER, miller, P. O. Service, is a native of Allegheny county, Pa., born

BIOGRAPHIES—SOUTH SIDE. 839

in 1848. He is a son of James and Christiana (Miller) Cotter, parents of six children, L. M. being the second youngest. The father, some years ago, purchased the mill property originally owned by Mr. Shillito. At the age of twenty-three years L. M. learned the milling trade, which he has since followed, having purchased the mill of his father. The power used in operating the mill is steam, and a large business is done. Mr. Cotter was married, in 1870, to Mary, born in Washington county, a daughter of David Wilson, of Washington county, Pa., and the result of this union is three children: John P., James W. and Lizzie. The mother dying in 1876, Mr. Cotter married, June 19, 1878, Maggie, daughter of Benjamin Chambers, of this county. Politically Mr. Cotter is a Democrat.

HENRY COWAN, farmer, P. O. Frankfort Springs, was born in Hanover township, Washington county, Pa., Sept. 29, 1830. His grandfather, Henry Cowan, a native of Ireland, of Scotch descent, came to America when young, and raised a family in Allegheny county, where he died at Half Crown Run. He had five sons and three daughters. Of the sons, Henry married Sarah A., daughter of James and Margaret Stewart, who came to Fort Pitt, where he was offered land at ten shillings per acre, but refused the offer and bought land near Clinton, Pa. Henry and Sarah A. Cowan died in Greene township. They were members of the Presbyterian church. They had six children: Margaret, Eliza J., James S., Henry, William G. and Sarah A. Our subject was educated in this county, and has been a farmer all his life. For sixteen years he was also engaged in buying and selling wool. His farm contains 322 acres. He married Harriet A., daughter of Robert Smith, of Washington county. They have four children: Ella M., William S., Eliza J. and Harry M., the two last being twins. Mr. and Mrs. Cowan are members of the Presbyterian church, of which he is an elder. He is a Republican, and has held several township offices.

JOHN R. COWLING (deceased) was a native of London, England. He came to this country with his father, Edward Cowling, who resided in Allegheny City, and died at his son's residence. Sophia, wife of Edward Cowling, died when John R. was nine years old. Of her children, only two are living; George, of Metropolis, Ill., and Mrs. Gunnell. John R. was educated in Allegheny City and followed the river many years. He enlisted in the 62d Regiment, P. V., and at the second day's fight at Gettysburg received a wound, in consequence of which his leg was afterward amputated. He was subsequently employed in the Arsenal at Lawrenceville, Pa., and later was in business in Beaver Falls. He removed to Hookstown, where he was a merchant, and bought a farm of 100 acres near the village. He died Nov. 28, 1886, aged forty-four years, a member of the Baptist church. He was married, May 26, 1870, to Martie W., daughter of William Sterling. She was born in Beaver county, and died May 27, 1878, aged thirty-four years, a member of the United Presbyterian church. Their only surviving child, Ralph Erskin Sterling, was born Sept. 19, 1872.

J. C. CRAIG, farmer, P. O. McCleary, was born in 1837, on the farm he now owns, in Raccoon township, and is a son of James and Margaret (Crooks) Craig, parents of three sons and three daughters. John, the original pioneer of the Craig family, came from east of the mountains to this county in an early day, and purchased 106 acres of land; he married Isabella Duncan, by whom he had six children, James, the father of our subject being the eldest son. He (James) when comparatively a young man, purchased 190 acres of land, and followed farming all his life. Our subject commenced life a poor boy, and is now one of the most substantial farmers in the county. He married Mary, daughter of James Louthan, of South Beaver township, this county, and by her had seven children, four now living: Charles R., Simon H., William S. and Lizzie B. The entire family are members of the United Presbyterian church; In politics Mr. Craig is a Republican. He enlisted, in 1861, in Company F, 46th Regiment, P. V., and after eighteen months' active service was compelled, through ill health, to return home. He was present at the battle of Cedar Mountain, where he was wounded, and participated in other engagements.

JOHN CRAIG, farmer, P. O. Hookstown, is a member of an old and respected family on the south side, whose ancestors were of sturuy Scotch stock. James Craig came from Scotland with his parents. He was a Revolutionary soldier, and after the war lived several years in Washington county, Pa., but died in Beaver county. He married Elizabeth Carson, and they were among the first and prominent members of Dr. Anderson's church, and boarded twelve of his theological students. Of their children, James was born Nov. 26, 1786, in Washington county, and died in Beaver county in 1861. His wife was Mary, daughter of David McCoy, a Revolutionary soldier. She was born June 1, 1786, in Hopewell township, where she died April 12, 1855. Both were members of the Seceder's church, and they were the parents of David, Eliza, John, Mary J. and Sarah. John was born Jan. 10, 1815, near Murdocksville, in this county. He has been a farmer, and still owns eighty-two acres. With filial devotion he cared for his parents until his forty-fifth year. He married Sarah Nevin, whose father was a prominent character in his day. Three children have been born to them: Wilda M, Emma L. and Rosa J. The family belong to the United Presbyterian church.

L. L. H. CRAIL, farmer, P. O. Holt, was born in Raccoon township, Beaver county, Pa., in 1831, son of Sethelius Middleton and Sarah B. (Guthrie) Crail, the former the second youngest of the ten children of John and Alethia (Irvin) Crail, the latter a daughter of Robert Guthrie. The father of Sethelius M. Crail came to this county from Maryland at an early day, and served three years in the Revolutionary War. L. L. H. is the second son in a family of five children (two now deceased), and was born and reared on the farm he now owns and lives on, consisting of 160 acres of the original tract of 245 acres. He received a good public-school education, and studied at Pittsburgh Business College, graduating from the same in 1854. For several winters he was engaged in teaching school, saw-milling and farming in the summer, which latter pursuits he still follows successfully. Our subject was married, in 1857, to Elizabeth, daughter of John Cristler, of this county, and by her has five children: Alfaratta, Ida May (now Mrs. Ewing), Atlas Omar, Clara Emma and Ernst Jansen. Mr. Crail has been school director for six years, also township auditor. He is a member of the Methodist Episcopal church. In politics he is a Republican. His grandfather, John Crail, was one of the first M. E. church adherents in Raccoon township, and his house the first place where Methodist preaching was held.

REV. P. J. CUMMINGS, P. O. New Sheffield, was born in Coshocton, Ohio, Nov. 23, 1834. His grandfather, George Cummings. was a native of Scotland, and is supposed to have come to this country previcus to the Revolution. He settled in Fauquier county, Va., and moved thence to Coshocton, Ohio, where he died at the age of eighty-three years. He was an Episcopalian in religion, and politically a Democrat. He married a Miss Tullus, and they had five children who reached maturity: Eli, Maria, K. Bruce, Susan and Ludwell. Of these K. Bruce Cummings was born in Virginia, Dec. 5, 1803, and still resides in Ohio. He married Harriet Humphrey, of Rhode Island. Her father was a sea captain, and afterward a farmer. She was born in June, 1815, and had five children: Abraham J., Philander J., George M., William W. and Francis M. Philander J. attended the common schools and the Millwood Academy, after which he taught school several years. He entered Washington College in 1859, and was graduated in 1863. He then attended the Western Theological Seminary at Allegheny City, finishing his course there in 1866. In October of the same year he was installed pastor of Mount Carmel church at New Sheffield, and there remained until the spring of 1882. He then took charge of the church at Industry until April 1, 1887, when he returned to his first charge at New Sheffield. He was married in Allegheny county, to Hattie C., daughter of John and Elizabeth (Ferguson) Miller. They have two children: William H. and S. Florence. Mr. Cummings was the first principal of Woodlawn Academy, a position he filled for several years. He was afterward principal of the academy at Industry for two years.

JAMES DAVIS, farmer and justice of the peace, P. O. Seventy-Six, was born Aug. 30, 1846, on the old Davis homestead in Independence township. At a very early age he moved with his father, John Davis, to Moon township, where the latter bought the old Campbell farm, but afterward the Edwards farm, where his widow Margaret Davis, now resides. He was a member of the Presbyterian church. He was in the boatyard in Elizabethtown in early life. His ancestors are supposed to have been of Welsh origin. His widow, Margaret, is a daughter of Francis Flannegan, who was an attorney of Pittsburgh. She is the mother of twelve children, eleven of whom are living: F. F. Davis, M. D., of Oil City, Pa.; William, a preacher in Iowa; John, Henry, James, Sarah (Mrs. Wilson), Margaret (Mrs. Usleton), Hugh, Elizabeth (Mrs. Tucker), Emma (Mrs. Hicks), and M. S. Davis, a physician of Shippingport. Of the sons, James was educated in his native county and at Edinboro, Pa. He taught school two winters, and then engaged in farming. He owns 145 acres, a part of the old Davis homestead. His wife is Susan C., daughter of Stacy and Mary (Robinson) Engle, and they have five children: John, Francis F., Henry, Maggie and Anna; Mr. and Mrs. Davis are members of Mount Carmel Presbyterian church, of which he is a trustee. He is a Republican; has been school director five years, and is auditor and justice of the peace.

HUGH H. DAVISON, physician, P. O. New Sheffield, was born Jan. 21, 1851, in this county, and is a son of Robert Davison. The latter was married to Margaret J., daughter of Hugh and Sarah (Veazey) Hamilton. Sarah Veazey was a daughter of Elihu Veazey. He located here after the close of the Revolutionary War, on or between 1780 and 1790, on 400 acres of land, and his descendants have filled many positions of trust and honor. Hugh H. Davison was educated in this county and at Clinton, Pa. In 1871 he began the study of medicine under Dr. R. S. Kennedy, who was then located at New Scottsville. Three years later he entered the Medical School at Cleveland, Ohio, and was graduated in 1876. He is engaged in practice in Hopewell township, and resides on a part of the old Veazey homestead. In political preference he is a Republican.

REV. JAMES L. DEENS, P. O. Bellowsville, was born in County Armagh, Ireland, Jan. 3, 1820. His parents, James and Margaret (Graham) Deens, were natives of Ireland and of Scotch descent. The father died in Ireland, and the mother came to America and settled in Pittsburgh when James L. was an infant. She married John Lompre, and both died in Pittsburgh; only one daughter, Mrs. Eliza Irwin, a widow, survives. James L. was educated in Pittsburgh, and there joined the Methodist Episcopal church while clerking for E. Day, and entered the Western University. That institution burning down, he continued his studies with Rev. Wesley Kenney. He entered the Pittsburgh Conference in 1847, and in 1885 he became a supernumerary minister. He now resides in Moon township, Beaver county, on a farm of seventy acres. He married Mary, daughter of Samuel McKinley, well known in Western Pennsylvania, one of the most prominent members of the Masonic fraternity. Mr. and Mrs. Deens have six children: Margaret, Minnie, Anna, Charles, James and John. Anna is a member of the high school of faculty of Pittsburgh, in the Normal department.

JACOB H. DIEHL, farmer, P. O. Georgetown, was born in Lancaster county, Pa., Jan. 29, 1820. His grandfather, Henry Diehl, was a native of Germany, who came to this country at an early age, and whose father died the day before the family landed in Philadelphia. They settled in Reading, Pa., where Henry was a blue dyer for many years. In old age he walked twenty-five miles beyond Lexington, Ky., where he died at the home of his son, William. Of his children, Jacob was a chairmaker, and worked at his trade in various places. His wife was Mary Peterman, and they raised a family of seven children: Charles, Henry, George, Jacob H., Rosannah, Mary A. and Sophia. Of these Jacob H., the subject of this sketch, was also a chairmaker. In November, 1837, he came to Georgetown, where he worked at chairmaking with his father. The latter died on the Ohio river, of heart disease, aged sixty-four years. Jacob H. then engaged in mercantile business with James Todd, continued for thirty-six years, and gained the esteem of all by his just business transactions. He finally gave up mercantile life, and engaged in farming, and now owns 230 acres. He married Anna, daughter of Samuel Smith, a Quaker, and a prosperous farmer, who came here from Maryland. Mrs. Diehl is the mother of three children: Rachel L., wife of Rev. J. E. Wright; Mrs. Anna Jones and Rosa L. Mr. and Mrs. Diehl are members of the Methodist church; in politics he is a Republican. He started in life with $100 capital, and by his own efforts has accumulated a comfortable competency. He received only twelve weeks' schooling, and learned the English lauguage after he was eighteen years old.

WILLIAM P. DIEHL. gardener and fruit grower, P. O. Georgetown, was born, raised and educated in Georgetown. His grandfather, Jacob Diehl, came here from Lebanon county, Pa., but lived for a time in Cincinnati, Covington and Pittsburgh. He was a painter and chairmaker, and died in Georgetown. He was a liberal, openhanded man, a member of the Lutheran church, and of German descent. His son, Charles, who was also a painter, died here, aged seventy-four years. William P., our subject. was in early life a farmer, and at the age of twenty-one, in the fall of 1861, enlisted in Company F, 101st Regiment, P. V., serving three and one-half years. He participated in many engagements, including the siege and battles of Yorktown, Williamsburg, Fair Oaks, Suffolk, Va., the three skirmishes at Blackwater, Va., Kingston, Goldsboro and Washington, N. C. At the battle of Plymouth, N. C.. he was taken prisoner, and held eight months at Andersonville, Ga., Charleston and Florence, S. C., (of thirty prisoners from Company F, only sixteen came home alive). Since the war he has lived in Georgetown and vicinity, making specialties of gardening and fruit growing. Mr. Diehl married Lucy, daughter of John and Mary A. Winch, and they have three children: Elsie M., Jacob J. and Mary E.

GEORGE DOCKTER, farmer, P. O. Water Cure, was born in Alsace, Germany, Jan. 28, 1835. His parents, Christian and Caroline (Sturm) Dockter came to America in 1875, with the following named children: Martin, Christian, George, Catharine, Caroline and Salome. They settled in Butler county, Pa., where the parents died. George was educated in Germany, and there learned the carpenter's trade. After coming to this country he worked in a brickyard in Beaver county, then farmed in Butler county nine years. At the expiration of that time he sold out and went to Michigan, where he farmed one year, and then returned to Beaver county and bought a farm of 100 acres, where he now resides He has added to his possessions by purchase till he now owns 520 acres adjoining Phillipsburg. on which he has built a fine residence, all of which he has accumulated by his own industry and perseverance. Mr. Dockter married Elizabeth, daughter of Conrad Ebert, and she has borne him six children: Frederick, George, Christian, Charles, Caroline and Henry. The parents are members of the Lutheran church. In politics Mr. Dockter is a Republican.

JOHN DOUDS was born about six miles from Carlisle, Pa., on what is called Yellow Breeches Creek. Oct. 29, 1778, the only son of an Englishman, Robert Douds, who had immigrated to America previous to the outbreak of the Revolution, and who was killed in the colonial service in 1777. His mother (before marriage Miss Elizabeth Dawson) was a resident of Carlisle, her parents being of German origin. For the first three and a half years of his life young John remained in the locality of his birth. At the expiration of this period, in company with James Braden, with whom he lived until attaining his majority, he removed to Pittsburgh, remained there during the following winter and in the succeeding spring, John and his foster parent removed to the region of Raccoon Creek, Beaver county. The first abode they entered consisted of a small log hut, about twelve feet square, so low that one could not stand erect within it. In this house the family lived for over three years, Mr. Braden, meanwhile, clearing away the adjoining timber, and preparing for future improvements. At length a larger house became necessary, and a log one, 18 by 24 feet in dimensions, was "raised," with the assistance of neighbors, and occupied shortly afterwards. In this structure, surrounded on every hand by forest and wilderness, young John was reared. The territory in which he lived was the theatre of many an Indian outrage and massacre; and it is related that John was so much thrown into Indian society that he became acquainted with the savage language, and could converse quite readily in it. At the age of twenty-one Mr. Douds decided to embark upon the sea of matrimony, and Oct. 18, 1799, was united in wedlock to Miss Mary Hutchison, daughter of James and Elizabeth Hutchison, the ceremony being performed by Rev. Reno, of Beaver. Immediately afterward the new couple removed to the farm, on which they passed the remainder of their lives. Their housekeeping equipments consisted of two chairs, a few stools made out of puncheons, a table constructed in the same manner, pewter dishes and other utensils of a like primitive nature. The implements with which the husband began cultivating his farm were also novel. His horse-collars were platted corn husks, sewed together by a wooden needle with a flax cord; his trace chains and bridle were made out of home-twined rope; backbands of double tow linen; and hames of wood, with two auger holes through it, and ropes put through them so as to lengthen or shorten, as might be required. The plows were wooden, the shares and coulter were of iron, while the harrow had wooden teeth. Notwithstanding these inconveniences, it is related that the Douds' farm was kept in a condition that would cause envy among many of the farmers of to-day. His wife, Mary Hutchison, was born June 23, 1782, at Kilrea, county Derry, Ireland, emigrated to America in June, 1789, in company with her parents; located first at Brandywine, later at Middletown, in Allegheny county, Pa., and afterwards in Moon township, Beaver county. Shortly after her marriage she joined the White Oak Flats Presbyterian church, and by the influence of her Christian life secured her husband's entrance into the fold of the same congregation, of which, under its later name of Mount Carmel church, he became a leading and honored member. The union of these worthy pioneers was blessed with eleven children: Agnes, born July 25, 1800, and married, Aug. 28, 1817, to Mahlon T. Stokes: Robert, died in infancy; James H., born Jan. 15, 1805, married, Aug. 16, 1827, to Margaret Caldwell, died Sept. 7, 1856; John, born March 17, 1807, married, Dec., 1832, to Mary McDonald; Benoni D., born Aug. 23, 1809, married in March, 1833, to Mary Irons; Eliza, born Jan. 30, 1813, married, Nov. 7, 1833, to James Moore; Mary Ann, born Nov. 6, 1815; William McC., born Feb. 19, 1818, married, May 6, 1841, to Rebecca Wyant; Edward Hill, born July 27, 1820, married, April 29, 1845, to Maria Fronk; Margaret H., born Oct. 11, 1822, married, April 8, 1841, to Joseph Irons; and Mahlon S., born Dec. 9, 1824, married, April 23, 1850, to Rebecca Brotherton.

B. D. DOUDS, farmer, P. O. Green Garden, was born in Moon township, this county, on the old Douds homestead, where his grandfather, James Hutchison, first settled. The latter was a native of Ireland, and of Scotch descent. Robert Douds, grandfather of B. D., was a light horseman, and was shot from his horse during war. The quarter section of land, which his family were entitled to was never obtained, though it lies in the limits of Beaver county. John Douds, son of Robert, was born near Carlisle, Pa., and at the age of two years was bound to James Braden, who lived at the mouth of Raccoon creek, and was engaged in carrying salt from Carlisle to Beaver county. John Douds was married at the age of twenty-one years to Mary, daughter of James Hutchison and both died in Moon township, he, April 4, 1867, aged nearly eighty-eight years, and she, March 24, 1868, aged nearly eighty-six years. They had the following named children who reached maturity: Agnes (Mrs. Stokes), John, Benoni Dawson (our subject), Edward H., Margaret (Mrs. Irons) and Mahlon S., living, and James H., Elizabeth and William M., deceased. B. D. came to Hopewell township in 1852, and bought the John R. and Mary A. McCune farm. He sold a part of it, retaining sixty-one acres. He also owns a farm of eight-seven acres across the Ohio river. He was married March 16, 1833, to Mary, daughter of Solomon Irons. She died April 29, 1887, aged nearly eighty years. She had five children that reached maturity: Mary (Mrs. Orr), James I., John B. (killed at Spottsylvania, May, 12, 1864), Robert C. and Agnes A. The latter is the wife of William Brunton Smith, and has three children: Mary I., William J. and Dawson D. Mr. Douds is an elder in the Presbyterian church. In politics he is a Republican.

MCALLISTER DUNLAP, farmer, P. O. Murdocksville, was born in Westmoreland county, Pa., Feb. 22, 1819. His grandfather, Thomas Dunlap, was of Scotch-Irish descent. John Dunlap, father of McAllister, was born in Westmoreland county, and married Jane, daughter of John McClure. They came to Beaver county, afterward lived a short time in Washington county, but returned to Beaver county, and bought the old John McComb farm. They were members of the Presbyterian church. Their children were John, William, Alexander, Lucetta J., McAllister and Violet (twins) and James, who died at the age of sixteen. McAllister Dunlap married Margaret, daughter of Robert Cooley. They are active members of the Presbyterian church. Mr. Dunlap has a farm of 107 acres, where he resides, and another farm of sixty-five acres. He is a Democrat, and takes an active interest in local and national affairs.

JOHN C. DUNN, farmer, P. O. Water Cure, was born near Glasgow, Scotland, Nov. 14, 1842. His parents, Walter and Ellen (Brownlee) Dunn came to America with nine children: William Nicol (a son of the mother by a former marriage), Jessie, Catharine, Jeanette, David, Walter, John C., Mary and Ellen. They had two children, Robert and James, born in this country. In 1852 the family settled in Beaver county, where the father died at the age of seventy-two years. John C. was a pit boss at the coal mines of McKeesport for about twenty-five years. In 1882 he came to Beaver county, where he has a farm of sixty-seven acres, a part of the homestead of his father-in-law. His wife is Martha B., daughter of William Shroads. They have six children living: Nettie, John, Ellen, Samuel, James and Alice N. The parents are members of the North Branch Presbyterian church, of which Mr. Dunn is a trustee. In politics he is a Republican.

CHARLES EACHEL, oil producer, P. O. Ethel Landing, was born in Allegheny county, Pa., Oct. 23, 1844. His grandfather, Andrew Eachel, was of German descent, and came from Redstone, Pa., east of the mountains. He settled in Hopewell township in 1810, and died there at the age of ninety-three. His wife, Mary Ann, also died in Hopewell township. His son, Samuel, bought the homestead of his father, and died Feb. 9, 1884, at the age of seventy-six years, a member of the United Presbyterian church. He was a weaver by trade, and lived for many years in Allegheny county, having held office there. He was a Democrat. His wife was Isabelle Johnston, who died at the age of sixty-six years. Of their children seven lived to maturity: Mary Ann, Margaret J., Matilda, Verlinda, Louisa E., Elizabeth and Charles. The latter was educated in this county, and here followed farming until the oil business opened a new field of industry. As an oil producer he has been successful. His wife is Sarah J., daughter of Thomas Brunton. Their children are Vinnie L., Charles E., Edna Laura, Edith Lilian and Gertie. The parents are members of the United Presbyterian church. Mr. Eachel has six wells on his farm of 106 acres, all of which is leased, except five acres, which he operates himself.

JOHN H. ECKERT, farmer, P. O. Water Cure, was born in Baden, Germany, Jan. 16, 1828. His parents, John H. and Margaret (Reicherd) Eckert, came to America in 1843, bringing seven children, viz.: Peter, Jacob, John H., Charles, Margaret, Rosa and Adam, William, the eldest son, having come three years before the rest. They settled in Economy township, Beaver county, where the father died at the age of seventy-two. John H. was engaged in butchering in Allegheny City for many years, having learned the trade in Germany. He came to Moon township in 1868, and engaged in farming and dairying, in which he has been successful. He owns nearly 170 acres, which he has greatly improved. His wife, Charlotte Koener, was born March 16, 1834, in Hesse Darmstadt, Germany. They have had eight children: Albert, Emma, Ferdinand, Henry, William, Ernest, Charles and Theodore. The parents are members of the Evangelical Protestant church. Mr. Eckert is a Democrat, and has held several township offices.

WILLIAM P. ELLIOTT, farmer, P. O. Bellowsville, was born in Hubbard township, Trumbull county, Ohio, Sept. 29, 1817. His father, William Elliott, Esq., a native of Ireland, came to this country with his brother James, who settled in Carlisle, Pa., and whose decendants live in Pittsburgh. William settled in Jefferson county, Pa., and subsequently went to Trumbull county, Ohio, with his uncle, Dr. John Mitcheltree. He sold his farm there, and in 1824 came to Moon township and bought the farm where George Sohn now lives. His wife was Margaret Patterson. Their children are Jane, Nancy, Arabella, Ellen, Susan, Rachel, John, William P., James and Thomas. The father died at the age of eighty-three, a member of the Presbyterian church, and the mother at the age of eighty-five years, a member of the Methodist church. William P. was educated in this county, and owns a farm of eighty-two acres. His wife is Adeline, daughter of George Nickum, and their children are Margaret, Narcissa S., Oliver B., James, Washington and Elizabeth. James and Washington are stockmen in Oregon. The family are members of the North Branch Presbyterian church, of which Oliver B. is an elder. The father and sons are Republicans.

CHRISTIAN ERBECK, farmer, P. O. Water Cure, is a son of Balthasar Erbeck, who was a farmer in Körle, Cur Hesse, Germany, where he died when Christian was fifteen years old. His wife, Mary Miller, also died there. She had four children: Wilhelm and Mary (deceased), Anna M. and Christian, living. Christian learned the saddlery and upholstery business in Germany, and at the age of nineteen came to America, and followed his trade in Pittsburgh and Rochester, where he worked in the car shops, and where he afterward had a shop of his own for two years and a half. He was successful, but was compelled to give up the business on account of ill health. He removed to Moon township, where he followed farming and butchering about twenty years; then ceased butchering, and devoted his whole attention to farming; he still owns a farm of 109 acres. He married Phillipine, daughter of Jacob Wagner. They have four children: Ernest, Walter, Frank and Clara. The family are members of the Lutheran church. Mr. Erbeck is a member of the I. O. O. F. He is a Democrat, has been member of the council several times and member of the school board for fifteen years.

DAVID EWING, farmer, P. O. McCleary, was born in Raccoon township, Beaver county, Pa., in 1818, of Scotch-Irish descent. Five brothers by the name of Ewing came to America at a period anterior to Penn's arrival in the country, and Alexander Ewing, a descendant of these, born in Delaware county, Pa., came to this county in 1788. John, a son of his, married Jane, daughter of David McAllister, also a native of Ireland, and they had seven sons and four daughters, of whom David is the eldest son and third child. Our subject worked on the home farm until his thirtieth year. He received a good common-school education, and at the age of twenty-two learned coopering, a trade he followed ten years. He married, in 1857, Elizabeth, daughter of David Kennedy. She dying, Mr. Ewing was united in wedlock with Sarah Ann, daughter of Elisha and Nancy (Brinton) Thornsburg, of this county, and by her there were four sons and two daughters: R. S., at home,; Stanton F., in Kansas; Ellis and Willis (twins, latter deceased); Lizzie and Jennie, at home. Mr. Ewing bought, in 1847, his present farm, consisting of 150 acres. He has held many positions of trust in the county, and was for twenty-one years a justice of the peace; he is a school director, etc. In politics he is a Republican. He and the family are members of the United Presbyterian church.

JAMES M. EWING, farmer, P. O. Holt, was born in 1827, in Raccoon township, the fifth son of John and Jane (McAllister) Ewing, and a descendant of Alexander Ewing referred to in the sketch of David Ewing above. James M. was born and reared on a farm, and for thirty years was a school teacher in his district during the winter months, attending to his farm duties in summer, He is the oldest school teacher in the county south of the river. He was married in 1851 to Nancy Robertson, who bore him five sons and one daughter: Wellington (deceased), William M., Samuel L. (in Illinois), Frank (in Iowa), Lizzie Jane (now Mrs. Rogers) and Alva A. (in Illinois). The mother died in 1865, and Mr. Ewing subsequently married Nancy, daughter of Thomas Purdy, of Allegheny county. Mr. Ewing has been school director, judge and clerk of elections and township auditor. He is a member of Session of Service United Presbyterian church. Politically he is a Republican.

J. H. EWING, merchant, Shippingport, was born in Raccoon township, this county, in 1834, youngest son of John and Jane (McAllister) Ewing. He remained on a farm while a young man, receiving a common-school education, and his first venture in mercantile life began in 1868, when he engaged in the wholesale grain trade in Pittsburgh, continuing three and a half years. Coming to Shippingport in 1871, he embarked in his present general merchandise business. Mr. Ewing was married, in 1864, to Nannie, daughter of James and Jennie (Wallace) Nelson, and by her has three sons: William H.,

J. Wallace and John LeMont. The parents are members of the United Presbyterian church. Mr. Ewing is a Republican.

JAMES P. EWING, farmer, P. O. Holt, was born on the farm he now owns, in Raccoon township, in 1830. Henry Ewing, the eldest child born to Alexander and Margaret (McConnell) Ewing, was brought, when a child, from Lancaster county to Allegheny county, Pa., in 1786, and four years later they moved to Beaver county. The journey was made on horseback, and when crossing the Susquehanna river, the boy slipped from his mother's lap into the water, and but for the timely assistance of the father, who rescued him, would have been drowned. Arriving at maturity, this Henry, with his brother, James, purchased a tract of land known as "Panther Grove," part of the Martin survey, and containing 337 acres, 207 of which are now owned by the subject of this sketch. Henry Ewing married Jane Purdy, of Allegheny county, and three children were born to them; James P., the youngest, secured a common-school education. In 1853 he married Frances, daughter of Samuel Kennedy, and by her had two children: Samuel (deceased) and Caroline, now Mrs. A. A. Christy. The mother dying, Mr. Ewing married Marie, daughter of William Littell, of this county. Nine children blessed this union, five sons and two daughters yet living: Alice Jane, William L., Cyrus Alexander, Mary Frances, Randall Ross, Oliver Sheridan and Horace Warren. The family are members of the United Presbyterian church. Politically Mr. Ewing is a Republican.

WILLIAM EWING, farmer, P. O. McCleary, was born in Raccoon township, in 1825, was reared on the farm, and received a good common-school education. During the early part of his life he traveled through different parts of the West, and in 1862 he enlisted in Company H, 140th Regiment, P.V., serving nearly three years. He participated in the battles of Gettysburg and Spottsylvania, receiving at the latter a wound which incapacitated him from duty for six months, and at the close of the war he returned home. On the death of his father he purchased 100 acres of land—part of the original tract bought by his father. He was elected county commissioner in 1867. He is a member of the United Presbyterian church. In politics he is a Republican and a Prohibitionist.

WILLIAM EWING, farmer, P. O. Frankfort Springs, was born in Frankfort Feb. 5, 1833, and is a son of John Ewing, a native of Allegheny county, His ancestors were natives of Chester county, and of Scotch descent. John was a tanner by trade, and carried on business in Frankfort many years. He was a popular man in the township and filled the office of justice of the peace for many years. He died in 1863 aged sixty-three years. His wife was Sarah, daughter of John Furgeson, and their children were Jane (deceased), Ellen, Sarah A., Eliza, James (deceased), William and John. William was educated at Frankfort Springs, and has been a farmer all his life. He was married, Nov. 13, 1856, to Margaret, daughter of Jacob Keifer, and she is the mother of seven children: John B., William K., Jacob G., Charles S., Margaret, Horace G. and Sarah A., who died at the age of nine years and seven months. Mr. and Mrs. Ewing are members of the Frankfort Springs Presbyterian church, of which he has been a trustee. He is a Republican, and has been elected school director.

DANIEL B. FIGLEY, farmer, P. O. Shafer's, was born on the old Figley homestead in Hopewell township, Dec. 5, 1827. His grandfather was one of the pioneers of Western Pennsylvania. He was of German descent and had five children: Jacob, Hannah, William, Margaret and Elizabeth. William married Nancy, daughter of Daniel Baker, and they had nine children: Margaret, Zachariah, Daniel B., Mary, William, Hannah, Jacob, Sarah and John. The parents were members of Mount Carmel Presbyterian church. They died on the old homestead. Daniel B. married Mary, daughter of James McCallister, and they have four children: William, David, Nancy and Daniel. Mr. and Mrs. Figley are members of Mount Carmel Presbyterian church. He is a Republican, and has held various township offices.

WILLIAM FLOCKER (deceased) was born in Darien, Conn., May 22, 1830, and was a son of Cornelius Flocker, a native of New York. At the age of nineteen years, Cornelius Flocker was on the brig "General Armstrong" in the war of 1812. This vessel was scuttled and sunk at New Orleans. William Flocker went to Allegheny City when a boy, and there learned the trade of rope maker. He married Eliza Snider Miller, who was born Feb. 22, 1831, in Lewistown, Pa. and who is the fifth descendant from the Duchess of Holland, who came with a colony from Amsterdam in the seventeenth century, and settled near the present site of New York, which they called New Amsterdam. She is the mother of six children: Miller, George C., Frank J., Thomas M., William H. and Washington W. Mr. Flocker came to Bellowsville, Beaver county, in 1873, and in 1876 was killed by a railroad train near Glendale. He kept a store, which has been continued by his widow, who is now postmistress. Three of the sons, George C., William H. and Washington, are engaged in butchering. Mrs. Flocker is a member of the Methodist Episcopal church. Mr. Flocker served in the War of the Rebellion in the 40th Regiment O. V. Mrs. Flocker's parents were Peter and Susan (Young) Miller; the former was a soldier in the War of 1812, a son of Adam and Mary (Ensminger) Miller, who lived at Little York during the Revolution. General Washington was a frequent visitor at their house.

MILLER FLOCKER, merchant, Bellowsville P. O., was born in Steubenville, Ohio, April 28, 1852, and is a son of William and Eliza Snider (Miller) Flocker, natives respectively of Connecticut and Pennsylvania, and of English and German origin. His maternal grandfather, Peter Miller, was a soldier in 1812, as was also his paternal grandfather. His father was a rope maker, and came to Beaver county from Allegheny in 1871, and died in 1876. Miller is the eldest of the family. He traveled considerably in early life in Canada, Michigan and Ohio. He worked at his father's trade, commencing when he was ten years old, and followed it until he was twenty. In 1881 he embarked in the mercantile trade, and at present is running a general store at Vanport, and also one at Bellowsville. He has made his own way in the world and has met with success. He was married April 11, 1878, to Julia Ramsey, of Pittsburgh, and daughter of Samuel and Rebecca (Agnew) Ramsey, natives of Allegheny county and of Scotch-Irish origin. Mr. and Mrs. Flocker are members of the Methodist Episcopal church. He has been superintendent of the Sabbath school. In politics he is a Prohibitionist.

JAMES A. FORSYTHE, farmer, P. O. Shafer's, was born in Hopewell township, Jan. 27, 1843. His paternal grandfather came from Ireland and settled in Beaver county at an early day. His son Alexander, father of James A., was a farmer most of his life, but followed the river in youth. He was born in Hopewell township, and died there at the age of seventy-six years. He married Aleyan McGary, who is yet living, and had seven children that lived to maturity: Mary J., James A., Rachel A., Agnes, Benjamin, Margaret E. and William H. The latter was drowned in the Ohio river, below Louisville, at the age of eighteen years. James A. was educated in Hopewell township; followed the river for about eighteen years, beginning at the age of eighteen, and was mate of a number of steamers. He now resides on a farm of 106 acres, which he has greatly improved. He was married, in Beaver county, to Caroline, daughter of Michael Mateer, and they have three children: Margaret A., Clara and Harry E. Mr. and Mrs. Forsythe and daughter are members of the North Branch Presbyterian church; politically he is a Democrat.

JOHN N. FRAZER, farmer, P. O. Frankfort Springs, was born July 27, 1836, in Hanover township, Washington county, Pa. His grandfather, Thomas Frazer, was a native of County Down, Ireland, and of Scotch descent. His wife died in Ireland, and he came to America with his son, William H., when the latter was eleven years of age. They came to Hookstown, this county, where William H. was left with his uncle, William Frazer. His father revisited Ireland, but afterward returned to Beaver county. William H. was a miller in early life, then a carpenter and then a merchant; he was engaged in mercantile business in Frankfort about thirty years, and was a popular man, greatly esteemed. He was a Whig, later a Republican, filled many township offices, and was once a candidate for associate judge of Beaver county. He was for many years an elder in the United Presbyterian church of Frankfort. His wife was Mary, daughter of John Nelson, one of the pioneers of Greene township. She had seven children: John N., James T., Thomas S., William M., Mary E., Margaret J. and Robert L. John M. was educated in this county, and married Elizabeth, daughter of Robert Bryarly. They have three children: Robert B., James T. and Lizzie J. Mr. Frazer, his wife and family are members of the United Presbyterian church. He served in the Civil War, being orderly sergeant of Company G, 168th regiment. His brothers, James T. and Thomas S., served in Company F, 46th regiment. Mr. Frazer owns two farms containing eighty-four and forty acres, respectively. He is a Republican, and has filled nearly all the township offices.

SOLOMON FRONK, farmer, P. O. Hookstown, was born in Allegheny county, Pa., May 24, 1816. His great-grandfather came from Germany. His grandfather, Jacob Fronk, was born in Eastern Pennsylvania, and afterward came to Beaver county, where he died. His son, George, came with him to this county, and was a farmer in Raccoon township. He finally moved to Ohio, where he died at the age of seventy-five years. His wife was Rebecca, daughter of Casper Metts, and died in Ohio, aged over seventy years. They had nine children: Solomon, Lavina, Rebecca, Elizabeth, Maria, Sarah, Elmira, George and John. Solomon moved to this county with his parents, in 1828. He has been a successful farmer, and owns 118 acres of land in Greene township. He married Rosannah, daughter of John Cristler, whose father, Michael was one of the pioneers of Beaver county. She was born in Ohio in 1820, and they have four children: John, Rebecca, Sarah and Elizabeth. The parents are members of the Episcopal church; in politics Mr. Fronk is a Democrat.

FREDERICK FUCHS, farmer and gardener, P. O. Water Cure, was born in Sausenheim, Canton Frankenthal Phaltz, Germany, Sept. 29, 1817, and is a son of Adam and Eve (Neushafer) Fuchs, both of whom died in Germany. They had seven children. One of the two sons, Henry, spent a short time in this country, and returned to Germany. Frederick was educated in Germany and learned his trade there. He came to America in 1848, returned to Germany in 1849, and in 1850 came again to America, bringing with him the Hartenbach family. In the latter year he married Fredericka Hartenbach, who bore him four children: Katie, Daniel, Adam and Emma. Daniel and Katie (Mrs. Niemes) live in Cincinnati. Mr. Fuchs owns a farm of 100 acres, which his son manages. His second wife was Mrs. Anna C. Walter, *nee* Schaffer. He is a member of the Evangelical church.

JOHN S. GIBB, farmer, P. O. Clinton, is a great-grandson of Alexander Gibb, a native of Botriphnie, Scotland, who was born Nov. 11, 1751, and coming to this country settled on the farm where John S. now resides, in the year 1794, and died there. The place was first entered by a Mr. Maxwell, who sold to George McElhaney, and he to Alexander Gibb. His wife, Jane Innes, was born in Botriphnie, Scotland, in May, 1757. They had eight children: Anna, Adam, Margaret, John, Alexander, Martha, Mary and Jean. Alexander Gibb owned four farms at his death which he left by will, one farm to Adam, one to John, one to Alexander and the homestead to Anna and Margaret; the rest of the heirs receiving their shares in money. Adam Gibb, son of Alexander Gibb, was born in Piqua, Scotland, in October, 1785, and died Sept. 27, 1855. His wife, Susannah Duncan, was born Oct. 10, 1781, and died May 10, 1849; both were members of the Seceder's church of Service, of which he was an elder for many years. Their children were Alexander, John A. and Jane. Alexander, grandson of Alexander Gibb, came into possession of the homestead. He married Ruth Tagert, who was born about 1820, and died July 10, 1884. He was born March 11, 1812, in Hanover township, and died March 24, 1882. They had no children. The homestead, called "Prosperity," finally descended to John S., its present owner, who has 207 acres. John A., father of John S., was born in this county July 16, 1814, and died Jan. 30, 1888. He was a machinist, and built many of the old fashioned threshing machines. He married Sarah, daughter of John Shaffer. She was born in 1821, and died July 25, 1874. She had four children who lived to maturity: Susannah (Mrs.

Elder), Sarah E. (married to William Whiston), Emma (died at the age of eighteen) and John S. The latter moved to the old Gibb homestead in 1879. He was married in Cambridge, Ohio, and afterward lived four and a half years in Noble county, Ohio. His wife is Jane, daughter of James and Margaret Geary. They are both members of the United Presbyterian church of Clinton. They have two sons: Wilbert C. and and Willis G. Mr. Gibb is a Republican.

JOHN A. GIBB, ESQ., farmer, P. O. Harshaville, was born July 16, 1814, in Hanover township, a son of Adam Gibb. The latter, a native of Scotland, came to this country with his parents, Alexander and Jane (Innes) Gibb, both natives of Scotland and members of the old Seceder's church. They were weavers by occupation, and came to America in 1787 or 1788, settling on Peter's creek, in Washington county, Pa. They afterward came to Independence township and settled on Prosperity farm, where they remained until their deaths. They had eight children: Anna, Adam, Margaret, John, Alexander, Martha and Mary (twins) and Jean. Adam was born in October, 1785, in Piqua, Scotland, settled in Hanover township in 1811, and died there Sept. 27, 1855. He was married, May 13, 1811, to Susannah, daughter of John Duncan, and born Oct. 10, 1781, died May 10, 1849. She had three children: Alexander, John A. and Jane. John A., who is the only son living, is a well-educated and well-informed man. He has been twice married: first to Sarah, daughter of John and Mary (Geary) Shafer. She left three children, now living: Mrs. Susannah Elder, John S. and Mrs. Sarah E. Whiston. Mr. Gibb's present wife, Ann, is a daughter of Samuel Bigger (deceased). Mr. and Mrs. Gibb are members of the United Presbyterian church, and he is a member of Session. He is a Republican, and has been justice of the peace fifteen years.

WILLIAM GILLILAND, farmer, P. O. Cometttsburgh, was born June 6, 1822, in Hanover township, Washington county. His grandfather, James Gilliland, was of Scotch-Irish descent. He had three children: John, James and Margaret. Of these James married Jennie Anderson, a native of York county, Pa., and they lived in the vicinity of Frankfort after they came to Western Pennsylvania. The father died in 1862 at the age of sixty, in Beaver county, and the mother died in Washington county ten years later, at the same age. They were both church members. Their children were Margaret, Archibald, Elizabeth, David, Eleanor, James, Jane, Lucinda, William and George B. William was put to work at an early age, and for this reason his education was limited. He was the chief support of his mother after his father's death, the other children all marrying. He was married, Nov. 11, 1847, to Elizabeth, daughter of Joshua and Jane (Hooper) Witherspoon, early pioneers of Washington county. She is the mother of eight children: Jane L., James W., Mary E. (died at the age of twenty-one years), Lizzie A., William O., Lucy L., Maggie E. and Mattie B. Mrs. Gilliland died Dec. 26, 1877, aged fifty years. She was a faithful member of the United Presbyterian church, as are all the family. Mr. Gilliland has been an elder in three different churches. He is a Republican. As a farmer and business man he has been successful, for he started poor and now owns two farms, one of 138 acres and the other of seventy acres.

JOSEPH GILMORE, farmer, P. O. Shoustown, is a son of Archibald and Jane (Bigham) Gilmore. Archibald Gilmore is a native of Ireland, and of Scotch descent. He came to this country in 1829, and first settled near Pittsburgh. His wife is a daughter of Joseph Bigham, who settled here about 1812. They are members or the United Presbyterian church. They have had three sons and one daughter: James, Joseph, Alexander, and Sarah, who died young. Joseph and Alexander enlisted Aug. 15, 1862, in Company I, 140th Regiment, P. V., and served until the close of the war, and were in many battles. Joseph was taken prisoner at Gettysburg and suffered the horrors of prison life at Belle Isle and other Southern prisons until exchanged. After the war he returned home. and has followed farming ever since. He is a Republican.

DORSEY K. GLASS, farmer, P. O. Hookstown, was born Oct. 30, 1838. His grandfather, Robert Glass, was born in Washington county, Pa., and was of Irish descent; and his son, John, a farmer by occupation, was also born in Washington county. He was taken to West Virginia by his father when quite young, and died in Hancock county, aged seventy-two years. He married Rachel, daughter of Isaac and Mary (Pentecost) Kinney. She is still living at the age of seventy-one years, and is the mother of seven children: Malinda, Dorsey K., Eliza J., Rachel H., John T., Andrew J., and Lawrence W. Dorsey K. worked for his father until he was twenty-five years old, and received a horse and cow as his reward. He has been a successful farmer, and owns 115 acres. He married Elizabeth A., daughter of Ebenezer Langfitt, and born in 1836, in Hancock county, W. Va. She has one son, Harry G. L., born Sept. 18, 1868. Mr. Glass is a Democrat.

WILLIAM C. GOLL, farmer, P. O. Shafer's, was born in Knittlingen, Würtemberg, Germany, Oct. 25, 1839. His parents, Jacob F. and Anna C. (Burk) Goll, died in Germany. They had four children, all of whom came to this country. Their names were William C., Jacob F., John T. and Christina. William C. came to this country in 1853, and settled in Philadelphia, where he learned the shoemaker's trade. He removed to Economy, Beaver county, in 1855, and followed his trade there. He subsequently went to Pittsburgh, and carried on coopering for one year; then engaged in business in Freedom, where he remained eighteen years, and at the expiration of that time came to Moon township, purchased the Daniel Baker farm of ninety-three and a quarter acres, and has since been engaged in farming. He was married, in Pittsburgh, to Caroline Bayha, a native of Würtemberg, and they have the following-named children: Emma (wife of Otto Kind), Catharine, Maggie, Louis R. and Jacob. The parents are members of the Evangelical church. Mr. Goll is president of the school board; politically he is a Democrat.

ROBERT GORSUCH, farmer, P. O. Service, was born Jan. 19, 1825. His grandfather, John Gorsuch, was a native of Ireland, but of Scotch extraction. The family were Protestants, and strict adherents of the old Covenanters church. John came to America when a young man and settled in Maryland, where Robert Gorsuch, Sr., was born. Robert came across the mountains at the age of six years, in 1798, with his father, when the Indians were numerous in Pennsylvania. He settled in Washington county, and at one time, when pursued by the Indians, swam the Ohio river with his son Robert on his back. John Gorsuch died near Paris, Pa., in 1828. His wife, Nancy McClelland, was a native of Scotland, and became the mother of six children: Robert, David, Thomas, John, Sarah and Rebecca. Robert Gorsuch, Sr., married Elizabeth, daughter of James McCoy, and by her had four children: John, James, Robert and Rachel. By his second wife he had five children. His third wife was Nancy Cooper, who had no issue. Robert Gorsuch, Sr., was a farmer and died in 1871. Robert, Jr., owns the farm of 230 acres where he lives, and two of 160 acres each in Hanover township, where his sons Robert A. and John M. reside. Our subject married Maria, daughter of Richard Cooper. She is the mother of three children: Robert A., John M. and Nancy J. All the family are members of the United Presbyterian church, and Mr. Gorsuch is an elder in the Hanover church. He is a Republican in politics, and a warm advocate of the principles of prohibition.

SAMUEL GORSUCH, farmer, P. O. Service, is a son of Robert and Nancy (Searight) Gorsuch, who had five children: Eliza J., Margaret, Samuel, Martha and Mary Ann. Samuel was reared and educated in this county, and has been a successful farmer and stockman. He owns 156 acres which he and his father have greatly improved, the land lying in a wilderness when the latter first settled on it. Samuel Gorsuch married Martha J., daughter of John and Mary (Anderson) Brunton. By her he has two children: Mary A. and Robert Wilson. The parents are members of Mount Olivet Presbyterian church. Mr. Gorsuch is a Republican; has been justice of the peace for nine years, and has held other township offices.

ROBERT GREENE, farmer, P. O. New Sheffield, was born in Hopewell township, July 6, 1863. His grandfather, William Greene, settled here in 1790, and married Mary Boyd for his second wife. They had four children. Their son, William Greene, married Sarah E., daughter of Robert McCartney. She was born July 27, 1840, and died March 30, 1872. She had four children: Robert, Mary (deceased), Jennie and

BIOGRAPHIES—SOUTH SIDE. 851

Lillie. William Greene owns a farm of 120 acres. Robert Greene owns a farm of sixty-nine acres. He was married Dec. 2, 1886, to Belle B., daughter of James Marks (deceased). All the members of the Greene family belong to the United Presbyterian church.

GEORGE N. HALL, farmer, P. O. New Sheffield, was born in Raccoon township, this county, Dec. 9, 1836, a son of James F. Hall, who came to Raccoon township where his father bought 400 acres of land, of which James F. got 100 acres. The Hall family were early settlers in Beaver county. George N. was educated in his native county, and became a tiller of the soil. In 1861 he came to Hopewell township, where he owns a farm of 112 acres. He married Lizzie, daughter of James McCormick; she is the mother of four children: Mrs. Nettie Mercer, James K., Adda B. and George Mc. Mr. and Mrs. Hall are members of the Raccoon United Presbyterian church. In politics he is a Republican.

J. R. HALL, merchant, P. O. Shippingport, is a grandson of Robert Hall, who was a farmer of Chartiers, Allegheny county, and died in Freedom. His ancestors were English and Scotch. His son James, father of J. R., was a well-known boat-builder on the Ohio, and is still living at the age of eighty-six years. He married Isabella, daughter of George Baker, who was taken prisoner by the Indians. She died in this county, the mother of nine children, who are all living. J. R. was educated in Beaver county, and followed boat building for fourteen years. He then farmed one year, and has since been in mercantile business. He has been in business in Shippingport for sixteen years; he also deals in grain and wool. He married Lizzie A., daughter of David Gilliland, and they have three children: William G., Sarah B. and Lina. Mr. and Mrs. Hall are members of the Presbyterian church; politically he is a Republican. David Gilliland was a foreman in the laboratory at the Pittsburgh arsenal, where, at the age fifty-three years, he was killed in the fatal explosion.

ZACHARIAH HALL, farmer, P. O. New Sheffield, was born Sept. 11, 1833, in Freedom, Beaver county, Pa. His grandfather, Robert Hall, was born in Lancaster county, Pa., of Scotch descent. He owned 400 acres of land in Raccoon township, and afterward removed to Freedom, where died. His wife was Isabella Fowler, who died at the age of ninety-three years. They had twelve children. Two of his sons, Benjamin and James, came first to Raccoon township, where they built a cabin and remained until spring, when the family came on. The sons built a large distillery on their father's farm, and Benjamin conducted the distillery when whisky sold for twenty five cents a gallon in the barrel. He finally removed to Freedom, where he followed the trade of ship carpenter, and later came to Hopewell township, where he resided until his death. He was eighty-three years old June 17, 1887, and died Sept. 3, 1887. His wife, who was Elizabeth, daughter of Zachariah Figley, died aged about seventy-six years. She had four children: Isabella, Margaret and Nancy (twins) and Zachariah, the latter of whom was reared and educated in this county. Mr. Hall has been constable, supervisor, election judge and inspector, and is postmaster at New Sheffield. He owns a farm of 104 acres, and his father owned one of about 118 acres. His wife was Ellen, daughter of Charles Barry. She died of consumption, Jan. 16, 1864, aged twenty-seven years. She left two children: J. P. and Eleanor J. (Mrs. Bruce). J. P. received his education in the schools and academies of Beaver county. He was admitted at the university of Ann Arbor as a law student in the fall of 1885, and got his diploma from the university in July, 1887. He was admitted to the bar at Ann Arbor, Mich., at the Common Pleas Court, and shortly afterward at the Supreme Court in Lansing, Mich.; was admitted to the bar in Pittsburgh, Allegheny county, in September, 1887, and is now practicing law in Pittsburgh: office, 408 Grant street. He taught school in Beaver county four years. The Hall family are members of the United Presbyterian church.

ADAM HARTENBACH, farmer, P. O. Water Cure, was born in Rhein Baiern, Germany, Dec. 19, 1832, a son of Conrad and Fredericka (Hamman) Hartenbach, both natives of Germany. They came to America in 1852, with the following named children: Catharine Schlupp (daughter of Mrs. Hartenbach by a former husband);

Barbara, now the wife of J. Vogt; Fredericka, now the wife of F. Fuchs; Elizabeth (now deceased); Jacob, of Ohio, Christopher and Adam. The last named was educated in Germany, where he learned the blacksmith's trade with his father. The family settled in Moon township, and the father died there Dec. 24, 1871, aged seventy-two years. The mother died Oct. 10, 1884, aged eighty-eight years. They were both members of the German United Evangelical Protestant church of Phillipsburgh. Adam was married here, March 15, 1863, to Rosa Eckert, and they have two children: Henry C. and Rosa F. The parents are members of the above mentioned church, of which Mr. Hartenbach has been a trustee for fourteen years. He owns the homestead of 100 acres. He is a Democrat, and has been school director six years.

WILLIAM HARTFORD, farmer, P. O. Murdocksville, was born in Hanover township, Beaver county, Pa. His great-grandparents, James and Nancy (Armor) Hartford were born in Ireland, of Scotch descent, and were among the very first settlers in Hanover township, locating on what is known as the McClung farm, now owned by Joseph Cooley. Their children were William, James, Thomas, John, Abraham. Peggy, Polly (or Mary), Julia, Nancy, Rachel and Mrs. Valina Smith. Of these William married twice; by his first wife, Margaret Morrison, he had four children: James, John, Jane and Matilda. His second wife, Nancy Caughey, had no children. James, father of our subject, and a farmer by occupation, married Sarah, daughter of David and Mary (McGeehen) Elder. She died Feb. 20, 1886, aged eighty-four years, and James Hartford died March 14, 1878, aged seventy-six years; both were members of the Presbyterian church. Their children were Mary, William and Elder D. The latter served during the Civil War, as one of the Berdan sharpshooters, Company A, Second Regiment, U. S. A. He participated in many engagements including Bull Run, South Mountain, Antietam, Chancellorsville and Gettysburg. He died in Wisconsin from the effects of a wound in the ankle. William and Mary have the farm of 205 acres. He also owns another farm of 146 acres. Politically he is a Democrat.

MILO A. HOLMES, farmer, P. O. Shafer's, was born in Independence township, this county, May 17, 1827. His parents, Joseph and Jennie (McComes) Holmes, natives of Ireland, settled in Independence township and died there. They had ten children: John, Maria, Lazarus, Rachel, Joseph, George, James, Jane, Leander and Milo A., all of whom lived to maturity. Milo A. was raised on a farm, the pursuits of which he followed all his life. He owns a farm of 140 acres in Independence township. He has been twice married. His first wife, Nancy, daughter of William McElhaney, died at the age of twenty-seven years, leaving three children: William, Joseph and George. His second wife, Margaret A., daughter of John Short, died Jan. 25, 1886. She had one child, Elizabeth S. Mr. Holmes is an elder of the North Branch Presbyterian church. He is a Republican, politically.

WILLIAM HUNTER, foreman, P. O. Water Cure, was born Feb. 28, 1850. His great-grandfather, Enoch Hunter, was born in Ireland, and was of Scotch descent. He came to America and settled in New Jersey, where his son, Enoch, was born, and at the age of nineteen years, settled on Brush Creek, in New Sewickley township, Beaver county, Pa., where he was engaged in farming. He died at the age of ninety-three years, his wife, Mary (Musser), at the age of eighty-nine. They had eleven children: Abraham, Caroline, John, Abel, Margaret, Samuel, William, Mary, Thomas, Kate (deceased) and Nancy. Of these, John is a farmer near the old homestead. His wife, Ellen Wines, of Washington county, Pa., died in 1880, of cancer. They had seven children: Sarah, George, Lizzie, Bob (deceased), Albert (deceased), Mary and William. William left home at the age of nine years. He worked at farming three years, then on a canal one summer, and afterward learned the carpenter's trade, which he followed until 1880. In that year he took a contract to build the Phœnix Glass Works, with which he has ever since been connected. After the burning of the original building in 1883, he erected the present structure, and he is foreman of the etching department. He is married to Barbara Bloom, and they have eight children: Clara, John, Lester, Elmer, Willie, Olive, Leo and Clyde. Mr. Hunter is a Democrat.

BIOGRAPHIES—SOUTH SIDE. 853

JAMES A. INGLES, farmer, P. O. McCleary, was born in Raccoon township, Beaver county, Pa., in 1840, son of James and Nancy Ingles, parents of four children, James A. being the third. Mrs. Nancy Ingles had been previously married to a Mr. Purdy. James Ingles, grandfather of our subject, came from Scotland to America, and soon after his arrival located in this county. His children were Andrew, John, Isabella, James, Nathaniel, Eliza. Our subject was reared on the farm where he was born, and received a common-school education. He married, July 1, 1869, Lizzie, daughter of John McClester, of this county, and five children were born to them: John A., Clara B., Nathaniel W., William Leroy and Nannie Ella. Mr. Ingles now owns the farm, part of the original tract purchased by his grandfather. He has been school director; is a member of the United Presbyterian church: in politics a Republican. Mr. Ingles has one sister living, Mrs. N. J. Kerr.

JAMES A. IRONS, justice of the peace, P. O. Water Cure, was born Jan. 12, 1837, in Hopewell township, on the river bank, the site being washed away by the flood. John Irons, father of James A., was born in the old Irons homestead, and married Ann, daughter of Joseph Moore. He died March 11, 1851, aged forty-two years, and his wife died March 18, same year, both being victims of the Hookstown fever. He was a ruling elder in the United Presbyterian church, had accumulated considerable property, and stood high in the community. In politics he was a Whig. He had seven children: Joseph, James A., Elizabeth A., Rachel J., Rosannah, John D. and Margaret A. James A. was a blacksmith before and during the war. He was assistant engineer and blacksmith on the Mississippi flotilla, on the ram, "Lioness," operating on the lower Mississippi. After the destruction of the rebel fleet at Memphis the town was surrendered to Captain John M. Shrodes, of the ram "Lioness." After the war, Mr. Irons returned to Phillipsburg where he followed his trade at times, but has been engaged principally in the real estate business. He has been justice of the peace since 1883, and is filling his second term of office as burgess. He was married in Moon township to Margaretta Quinn. Her grandfather, William Quinn, made the cordage for Commodore Perry's fleet on Lake Erie, and his descendants became noted men in Northern Ohio. Mr. and Mrs. Irons have had four children: John E., Anna E. (deceased at the age of eighteen), James Clyde and Will. Bert. Mr. Irons is a member of the Equitable Aid Union, and of Rochester Post G. A. R. In 1870, while in Virginia, he was a local minister of the Methodist church, a position he filled three years. While in Washington, in 1873, he was a sub-contractor on the James Creek Canal, where he was engaged six months.

WILLIAM W. IRONS, farmer, P. O. Woodlawn, was born Jan. 9, 1814, on the old Irons homestead in Hopewell township. His grandfather, James Irons, lived and died in Ireland. He had six children, of whom Joseph first came to America and settled in Washington county, Pa., where he died. His son John, better known as Major John Irons, kept public-house in Washington county and Pittsburgh. His son Joseph was educated at West Point, and served in the Mexican war under Gen. Scott. He became a colonel, and distinguished himself at the storming of Chapultepec. Samuel and Solomon Irons, sons of John, came to America and settled near Noblestown, Pa. Solomon married Rachel Dixon, removed to Hopewell township in 1807, and with his father-in-law bought 300 acres of land, of which he retained 200 acres. He died in 1845 aged seventy-one years. He and his family were members of the Seceder's church. His wife died in 1829, aged forty-seven years. They had twelve children: James, Rachel, Rosannah, Mary, George, John, William W., Elizabeth (died at the age of fourteen years), Joseph, Andrew (a United Presbyterian minister, who had charge of two congregations, Portersville and Mountville, Lawrence county, Samuel and Agnes (died at the age of six years). William W. and Joseph are the only ones living. William W. received a common-school education, attending fourteen different schools. He has been a successful farmer and owns about 250 acres of land, besides Crow's Island. His first wife was Hannah Dixon. She died here at the age of forty-three years. She was the mother of eight children, three of whom are dead: Rachel, Leander and Agnes. The living are

Sarah, John D. (sheriff of Beaver county), Martha, James and Davison. The latter is a minister of the United Presbyterian church of Barlow, Ohio. Mr. Irons' present wife is Sarah J., daughter of Archibald Harper, and by her he has two sons, Harper and Joseph. He has been an elder in the United Presbyterian church since 1852. He was formerly a Whig, and is now a Republican.

JOSEPH IRONS, farmer, P. O. Woodlawn, was born May 8, 1818, on the old Irons homestead, where his father, Solomon Irons, settled in 1808. The latter, a son of James Irons, and a native of Ireland, came to this country at the age of fifteen years and finally settled in Allegheny county, where he married Rachel, daughter of George Dixon, one of the pioneers of Allegheny county. She died in June, 1828, aged forty-seven years. She had seven sons and five daughters. Solomon Irons came to Hopewell township and bought 100 acres of land, t) which he added by subsequent purchase. He died here in 1847, aged seventy-one years. He was a prominent member of the Seceder's church. His son Joseph followed the river for twelve years, beginning at the age of sixteen years, then returned to the farm, and owns 115 acres. His wife is Margaret H., daughter of John Douds. Their children are Rev. John D., president of Muskingum College, Ohio; Rachel D., Rev. William D., pastor United Presbyterian congregation, of McDonald, Pa.; Joseph M., Mary A., Elizabeth J. and James H., a bookkeeper in Pittsburgh. The parents are members of the United Presbyterian congregation of Ohio, of which Mr. Irons has been ruling elder for fifteen years. He was formerly a Whig, and is now a Republican. His first vote was cast for General Harrison for president. He has been supervisor and county commissioner.

WILLIAM JOHNSON (deceased) was a farmer of Hopewell township. He died of consumption, May 4, 1877. He was twice married: first to Jane Barry, by whom he had two sons Michael B. and J. Preston. His second marriage was with Sarah A. Neely, who survives him. She was born in Moon township, Allegheny county, on the old Neely homestead, settled by her grandfather, who at one time owned 1,000 acres. Her parents were Nathaniel and Elizabeth (Boyd) Neely, the former of whom died at the age of eighty years, and the latter at the age of seventy-two. They had eight children: George, Letitia and Esther (deceased), and Matilda (Mrs. Thompson), Samuel, Sarah A., Nancy and James, living, the last two residing on the old homestead. Sarah A. was married to William Johnson, Dec. 10, 1868. She has no children. She is a member of the United Presbyterian church, and resides on the farm of 250 acres belonging to her late husband's sons.

THE JOLLY FAMILY. The representatives of the Jolly family resident in Beaver county are descended from revolutionary stock, their progenitor having been Colonel Henry Jolly, a brave officer during that eventful struggle, who afterward settled in Marietta, Ohio, became a distinguished citizen, and presided as Judge over the first court held in that state. His wife, formerly a Miss Ghreist, was no less distinguished as the victim of Indian atrocities. She was scalped and tomahawked, and though the wound never healed, she survived this barbarity for forty-three years, and died at an advanced age. The children of Colonel and Mrs. Jolly were William, Kenzie, Albert and Siddy, wife of Vashel Dickerson. Kenzie Jolly was born in 1778 in Washington county, Ohio, where his life was devoted to the pursuits of a farmer. He married Elizabeth, daughter of Thomas Dickerson, born in 1795, and still living in her native county. Their children are Rachel (Mrs. John Ankrim, of New Orleans); Rebecca (Mrs. Abner Martin, of Washington county, Ohio,); Siddy (Mrs. Charles Hutchison, of Phillipsburg); Henry (of Washington county); Dickerson and Andrew Jackson, residing in Phillipsburg; Alpheus B., who removed to Keokuk, Iowa; William M., who died in infancy; Electa M. (wife of James Hutchison, of Washington county); and Owen F., of Dayton, Ky. Andrew Jackson Jolly was born May 23, 1828, in Washington county, Ohio, where he resided until 1844, availing himself during his boyhood of such advantages of education as the primitive schools of the day afforded. At the age of sixteen he came to Pittsburgh and embarked as a boatman on the Ohio and Mississippi rivers, beginning as a deck hand and advancing through various grades until he became captain of a steamer. This was continued until 1866, when he engaged in prospecting and drilling for oil in Beaver county, a venture in which his accumulated savings were speedily absorbed without a corresponding return. He then resumed the life of a boatman, and continued this pursuit until 1872, when the business in which he is at present engaged had its beginning in the furnishing of stone for large buildings, and cobble stones for street paving. Like many great enterprises, the business of A. J. Jolly & Sons, Limited, has developed from small beginnings, and is the outgrowth of hard labor, perseverance and indomitable energy. It is unnecessary to detail here the obstacles overcome, the severe toil necessary to secure cobble stones from the river banks, and finally the opposition met from older firms in the same business. These have been happily overcome, and the subjects of this sketch now rank among the most successful contractors in the state. The first contract was awarded them by the Pittsburgh & Lake Erie Railroad Company, since which time they have been largely engaged in furnishing stone and masonry for this road and other railroads in various portions of this country. The firm supplied the stone for the Pittsburgh courthouse and custom house; built a bridge one and a half miles long and 108 feet high on the Ohio River Railroad at Point Pleasant, W. Va.; erected the bridge at Parkersburg in the same state, furnished the stone for Lock Number Four on the Monongahela river, and for the bridge at Cold Centre, Pa., on the Baltimore & Ohio Railroad. For five years nearly all the masonry and stone work on the Pittsburgh & Lake Erie Railroad has been done by them. Mr. Jolly has for many years devoted his time to business, and given little attention to politics. He supports the nominees of the Democratic party, but is not himself ambitious for office. He was married, Sept. 26, 1850, to Miss Sarah, eldest daughter of Captain John M. Shrodes, of Beaver county, and their children were William A. (deceased), John K., Albert M., Marilla E. (married to J. D. Anderson), Eddie (deceased), and Frank L. Mr. Jolly has relegated the details of the business largely to his sons, who are his partners. The eldest of these,

John K. Jolly, was born March 20, 1854, in Phillipsburg, and spent his early youth with his parents. He received instruction at the common schools, and at the age of fifteen began the life of a pilot on the Ohio river, making Pittsburgh and Louisville his objective points. Continuing thus employed for six years, he then engaged in the retail coal business in his native county. In 1874 he became associated with his father as a general contractor in stone and stone work, to which business he gives his exclusive attention. He is much of the time in Pittsburgh, where the main offices of the firm are located, or superintending the work in the field. His presence is also frequently required at the quarries in Beaver and Lawrence counties. Mr. Jolly was married, July 3, 1873, to Emeline G., daughter of Samuel Cameron, of Pittsburgh, and their children are Birdie G., Sadie, Alice C. and A. Eugene. Mr. Jolly is connected with no orders other than Rochester Lodge, A. O. U. W. Though interested in local politics he has never accepted office.

Albert M. Jolly, the second living son of Andrew J. Jolly, was born Dec. 11, 1855, in Phillipsburg, and received a modest English education in his native town, after which he spent two terms at Duff's Mercantile College, in Pittsburgh, from which he graduated in 1874. Returning to Phillipsburg he at once became interested with his father in the business of contracting, and is now the secretary and treasurer of the firm of A. J. Jolly & Sons, Limited. This was at that date chiefly confined to the quarrying of stone, but has since been largely extended, and made its principals well known throughout the state as contractors. Mr. Jolly gives much attention to the details of the business, and is frequently to be found in various localities where work is progressing, West Virginia having recently been his base of operations. He was, on the 23d of March, 1882, married to Jennie E., daughter of S. J. and Elmira Small, of Beaver Falls. Their only child is a son, Clarence D., born March 30, 1883, in Beaver Falls, his parents' home. Mr. Jolly is a member of Valley Echo Lodge, No. 622. I. O. O. F., of Beaver Falls; of Lone Rock Lodge, No. 222, K. of P., also of Beaver Falls, and of Mechanics Lodge, No. 28, A. O. U. W.

JAMES JORDAN, farmer, P. O. Ethel's Landing, was born Feb. 20, 1813, in Hopewell township, one and a quarter miles from where he now resides. His grandfather, James Jordan, was a native of Ireland, and came to this country with his wife and son John, before the Revolution. He entered the Continental army, and fought the battles of Germantown, Brandywine and others, under General Washington. At the battle of Germantown, having no gun of his own, he seized one of a fallen comrade, and did good service. He made four charges for a battery and finally captured it, receiving several bullets in his hat and clothes. He was taken prisoner and nearly starved to death, and his best team was stolen by the Hessians. He lived in Philadelphia county on the Schuylkill river, came west in 1784 and settled on the farm now owned by Charles Eachel, in Hopewell township. He died at the home of his daughter, Margaret, in Allegheny county, aged eighty-six years, He was an elder in the Presbyterian church. He was twice married, and his children were John, William, Jane and Margaret. William married Elizabeth Ann, daughter of George McClellan. Their children were James, George, John, Margaret, Eleanor, Jane, Nancy E. and Mary A. William Jordan was an elder in the Presbyterian church, and died at the age of sixty-seven years where his son James now lives. His wife died Oct. 17, 1864, aged seventy-four years. James Jordan was a farmer all his life, except eighteen months, when he was a ticket and freight agent for the P. & L. E. railroad company. He owns about eighty-three acres, and a two-thirds interest in the remainder of the old homestead. He is a member of the Presbyterian church; in politics is an independent Democrat.

EDWARD KAYE. Mr. Kaye is of English parentage. His grandfather, Joshua Kaye, resided in Yorkshire, England, until 1817, the year of his removal to Pittsburgh, Pa., where he spent the remainder of his life. He married Hannah Poole, also of English birth, and their children were as follows: William, Joseph, David, Edward, Timothy P., Mary and Lydia, of whom all but the eldest three were born on American soil. The birth of David Kaye occurred at Henry Bridge, Huddersfield, Yorkshire, England, in 1817, from whence he came, when a child, with his parents, to America. Settling in Pittsburgh, he at an early age learned the trade of a glass blower, and until his recent retirement from active labor, was a skillful workman in the latter city. By his marriage with Sarah Jane McCoy were born children as follows: Edward K., Mary K. (Mrs. James B. Simpson), David K., Jr., Sarah J., Hannah P., Belle (wife of Edward Eaststep), Timothy P. and George B. Edward Kaye, the eldest of these children, was born Aug. 6, 1854, in Pittsburgh, and spent much of his early youth with his grandparents in Washington county. His education was limited to the common English branches, and the years usually devoted to study were spent in acquiring the glass blower's trade, his first employers being Messrs. Atterbury & Co., of Pittsburgh. A year later he entered the works of Messrs. Plunkett & Co., of the same city, where his father was assistant foreman, and finally completed his apprenticeship with Messrs. Chandler & Hogan. Mr. Kaye followed his trade at various points, and in 1880 came to Phillipsburg as a glass blower for the Phœnix Glass Company. In February, 1881, he was made foreman of the works, and now fills that responsible position. In politics the subject of this biography is a Republican, and has been active in municipal affairs as member for four years of the common council of the borough of Phillipsburg. Mr. Kaye was married, in December, 1875, to Anna Catherine Koedle, of Butler, Butler county, Pa., and their children are two sons: Melvin Wesley and Clarence Edward. Mr. Kaye is connected with various orders, being a member of Rochester Lodge, No. 229, F. & A. M.; of Eureka Chapter No. 167; of Rochester; of Rochester Lodge, No. 786, I. O O. F.; No. 99, K. of P., of Phillipsburg; of No, 921. R. A., and of the J. O. A. M., No. 24, also of Phillipsburg.

JOHN KEBER, glass worker, P. O. Water Cure, was born in Allegheny City, Oct. 18, 1851. His parents, Michael and Elizabeth (Keefer) Keber, who were both natives of Germany, lived many years in Allegheny City and Pittsburgh. They had two children, who are now living: Henry A. and John. The mother died in Pittsburgh. The father, who is a farmer in Moon township, married for his second wife Elizabeth Sitzman.

John Keber was educated in Pittsburgh, and at an early age began labor in the glass works. He worked at Bellaire, Ohio, from 1872 to 1877, returning to Pittsburgh in the latter year. In 1880 he came to Phillipsburg, and was one of the founders and stockholders of the Phœnix Glass Company. He married Hattie, daughter of Leonard Hahn, one of the pioneers of Phillipsburg, and they have had two children: Nora Lee, born Feb. 1, 1886, died July 1 the same year; and Edward E., born April 21, 1887. Mr. Keber is a Republican; a member of Rochester Lodge, No. 274, K. of P.

WILLIAM KEIFER, farmer, P. O. Frankfort Springs, is a son of Jacob Keifer, and was born Dec. 17, 1837. He was raised and educated in this township, and is a wide-awake farmer, managing a farm of 183 acres. He married Miss Martha Strouss, who died Aug. 22, 1884, a faithful, loving wife and devoted Christian. She had nine children: Jane M., Emily E., Agnes M., David S., Jacob F., Dickey, Martha M. and Anna B., twins, and William H. Three of the children died: Dickey, March 15, 1874; Anna B., Sept. 3, 1875; Jane M., March 18, 1883. Mr Keifer, three daughters and two sons are members of the Frankfort Presbyterian church, of which he has been a trustee. Politically he has been identified with the Republican party.

JACOB KEIFFER, farmer, P. O. Frankfort Springs, is a son of Henry and Anna. (Byers) Keiffer. Henry Keiffer was of German descent, came west when a young man and settled in Allegheny county, but made nineteen trips across the mountains with pack-saddle horses, carrying salt, etc. He was married at the age of forty years, his wife being a native of Allegheny county. He died at the age of eighty-two, and she at the age of fifty-one. They had ten children, of whom only Jacob and Henry came to this county. Jacob was born in Allegheny county June 11, 1803, and in 1826 married Nancy, daughter of Robert and Jane (Moore) Smith. She died Aug. 10, 1881, aged seventy-nine years. They had eight children: Jane M., Henry B., Robert S., Samuel, Margaret, Anna, William and John C. Anna married R. M. Bigger, who died Oct. 9, 1862. She afterwards married John Martin, a native of Virginia, and he died April 27, 1885. John C. was killed during the war. Mr. Keiffer has been a successful farmer. He is a true Christian member of the Presbyterian church, and has been a member of Session. Politically he is a Republican, and has held many responsible offices, including supervisor, assessor, etc.

WILLIAM C. KELLEY, oil producer, P. O. Ethel's Landing, was born May 7, 1857, in Pittsburgh, where he was reared and educated. He is a son of Amer and Elizabeth (Vandergrift) Kelley, of Irish and Scotch descent. Amer Kelley was a merchant in Pittsburgh, and enlisted in Company D, 13th Regiment, and died of fever while in the army. His widow is still living in Allegheny. The children now living are Sophia, Ellen, Harriet, Carrie, William C. and Jacob V. William C. has been in various occupations, having assisted in the support of the family since he was twelve years old. At the age of fifteen he removed with his mother to Cleveland, and four years later he went to Butler county, Pa., where he worked as pumper on an oil well. He soon sent for his brother and they worked there six years; then went to Byrank Center, where they drilled the first well on their own account. A year later, William C. went to McKean county, and operated there three years. He then went to Garfield, in Warren county, and operated there two years, coming from there to Beaver county. In 1884 he bored a gas well on Raccoon Creek, on John Zimmerly's farm. He has extended operations in all directions and at the present time has sixty-five wells in operation. In March, 1886, he formed the Raccoon Oil Company, consisting of the Kelley brothers, Henry Cooper and E. H. Jennings. The company employs about forty-two men, and produces about 2,000 barrels of oil per day. Mr. Kelley was married, Nov. 14, 1883, to Miss Martha A. Kohl, and they have one son, Howard B.

WILLIAM KELLY, glass packer, P. O. Water Cure, was born in County Down, Ireland, Feb. 21, 1841. His father, William Kelly, died in Ireland, at the age of sixty-five years. Our subject followed farming in his native country until 1869, when he came to America and settled in Pittsburgh. He worked in a glass factory until 1875, when he came to Moon township, where he bought a small farm. He sold the farm in

1882, and came to Phillipsburg, where he is employed by the Phœnix Glass Company. He was married, in Ireland, to Jane E., daughter of Arthur Brady, and they have five children: Mary A., William, John B., Rebecca J. and George A. The parents and the eldest daughter are members of the Presbyterian church. Mr. Kelly is a Republican.

ALEXANDER KENNEDY, farmer and merchant, P. O. Shoustown, was born in Independence township, this county, July 14, 1839. His grandfather, Ambrose Kennedy, was a native of Ireland and of Scotch descent. He married Drucilla Inman, and they came to this country and settled in Allegheny county, Pa. Their son, Alexander Kennedy, Sr., was born in Allegheny county, was a farmer, and died there at the age of forty-five years. He was married to Emeline, daughter of John and Agnes (Shipman) McMurtrie. She was born near Philadelphia, and came to Allegheny county when four years old. She is the mother of four sons and three daughters. Of the sons, only our subject is living. He was educated here, and married Mary J., daughter of A. P. Morrow. They have five children: Alexander M., Anna Z., Hugh, Sarah A. and Laura May. The parents are members of the United Presbyterian church. Mr. Kennedy was formerly a Democrat, but is now independent in politics. He has held the office of supervisor, is an extensive farmer, and keeps a general store.

HENRY KENNEDY, farmer, P. O. Holt, is a native of Allegheny county, Pa., born March 6, 1818, second son in the family of eight children, four boys and four girls, of Alexander and Elizabeth (Myers) Kennedy, former of whom, a twin son of Ambrose Kennedy, was a farmer and blacksmith, which trade he followed up to his death. Ambrose Kennedy, who came from Ireland to America in an early day, had three children. Henry learned his father's trade at home, and in 1836 came to this county, where he has followed agriculture. He was married, in 1841, to Isabella, born Oct. 25, 1817, a daughter of Hugh Orr, of this county, and the result of this union has been four children: Martha Jane, born Sept. 2, 1842; Alexander and an infant (deceased), twins, born March 27, 1844, Elizabeth Ann, born July 24, 1846, died June 18, 1861. Mrs. Kennedy died Jan. 6, 1888, a member of the Presbyterian church, of which Mr. Kennedy is also a member. In politics he is a Democrat.

WILLIAM A. KENNEDY, farmer, P. O. Green Garden, was born in Findlay township, Allegheny county, Aug. 19, 1815. He is a grandson of William A. Kennedy, who left Ireland on account of religious intolerance, and settled in Butler county, Pa., dying at the age of ninety years in Steubenville, Ohio. His children were Alexander and William A. (twins), and Mrs. Stephenson. Of these William A. was four years old when the family came from Ireland. He died in Jackson county, Ohio, aged sixty-five years. His wife, Druzilla (Inman), was of Scotch descent, and died in Jackson county, Ohio, aged seventy-one years. Their children were Ezekiel, Alexander and William A. and John (twins). William A., subject of this sketch, was educated in Allegheny county, where he learned the cooper's trade, and followed it for ten years. In April, 1841, he came to Independence township; he owns a farm of 160 acres, that township, and another of 143 acres in Raccoon township. In 1878 he went to New Brighton, where his son, Dr. Robert S., kept a drug store. Two years later he moved to Beaver, where he was in partnership with his son in the office of the *Star*. After seven years he returned to the farm, where he has since remained. He was married to Rosa B., daughter of Robert Shannon. She died in 1881, aged sixty-seven years. Two children are now living: Dr. Robert S. and Mary D. Mr. Kennedy is a member of the United Presbyterian church; in politics a Democrat. In early life he was a lieutenant of a militia company.

FRANKLIN D. KERR, physician, P. O. Hookstown, was born in Hookstown Aug. 16, 1844. His father, grandfather and great-grandfather were each named David. The great-grandfather was a native of County Antrim, Ireland, and his wife was Jane Black. He settled near Frankfort Springs while the Indians were still about. He raised a good crop of corn the first summer, with his family safely housed for weeks at a time in Dungan fort. He died on the homestead which he settled. He had five children: David, Mary, Jane, Sallie and Margaret. Of these David married Rachel, daughter of Thomas

BIOGRAPHIES—SOUTH SIDE.   859

and Nancy (Phillis) Moore, and had five children: Thomas, David, Samuel, Mary A. and Agnes. The father died in Hookstown, aged eighty-seven years. The mother died in Greene township, aged ninety years, having had her thigh broken three weeks previous to her death. Her son David was a carpenter. He was made captain of militia by Governor Porter. He married Mary, daughter of Capt. Thomas Swaney, of Hanover township. She died July 7, 1887, aged seventy-six years. His death occurred Nov. 25, 1887, in his seventy-sixth year. Mr. and Mrs. Kerr were members of the Presbyterian church for about forty-eight years, and he was an elder thirty-two years. Their children were Jane, Rachel, Samuel, Frank D., Sylvester and Estella. Rachel, who married William F. Johnson, D. D., was a graduate of Beatty's Female Seminary, Steubenville, Ohio, and was a missionary in India for twenty-five years. Franklin D., the subject of this sketch, was married Sept. 7, 1871, to Susan M., daughter of James Nelson, Esq., of Hanover township, and they have four daughters living: Helen, Jennie, Edith and Nellie, and had three sons and two daughters deceased, Olive, four years old, being the eldest deceased. The Doctor is a brother-in-law of Rev. William F. Johnson, D. D., president of Biddle University, N. C., a missionary to India for twenty-five years, and of J. C. Langfitt, Esq., of Allegheny City. He was schooled in his native village and for sometime worked at carpentering. When past seventeen he enlisted with his only brother, Samuel, who was breveted major for gallant services as a private in the 140th Regiment P. V. He took part in the battles of Chancellorsville, Gettysburg, Maryland Heights, Bolivar Heights, Halltown aud other engagements. After Gettysburg he was transferred and promoted to first lieutenant, Company G, 1st Maryland Cavalry (Cole's Cavalry), and was for a time in command of Company B. He afterward served as adjutant, assistant adjutant-general, commissary, quartermaster, commander of blockhouse with parts of two companies at Back Creek, Va., and aide-de-camp to Gen. William H. Seward, and his last services were as judge advocate of a military commission, which sat at Harper's Ferry under General Stevenson, for the trial of bushwhackers confined there. He was recommended to President Lincoln for appointment as a cadet at West Point by General Seward, Colonel Cole, Colonel Vernon and others, but the consent of his parents was withheld. He served in the army three years before he reached his majority. After the war he attended Washington and Jefferson College; taught school, traveled in the West, and after three years' study was graduated from Cleveland Medical Colleges of Wooster University, Ohio. He has been practicing in his native village for a number of years. Dr. Kerr was elected an elder in the Presbyterian church in 1888, of which he he has been a member since he was sixteen years of age.

PRESLEY M. KERR, M. D. (deceased), was born in Raccoon township, Beaver county, Pa., in 1835, a son of James W. and Mary (Allen) Kerr, parents of eight children, our subject being the second youngest. He was born and reared on the home farm, attended both public and high schools, graduated from the Allopathic College at Cincinnati in 1860, and at once commenced the practice of his profession in his native township, in which he continued up to his death in 1884. At the outbreak of the Civil War the Doctor was appointed field sergeant, which position he had to resign, owing to ill health, and return home, but was soon called again into service, attending in the practice of his profession Hairwood and other hospitals, for over a year. On his return from the army he was appointed physician to the County Home, which position he filled for fourteen years, at the end of which time he resigned on account of ill health. He was married, in 1862, to Nancy J., daughter of James and Nancy (McAulley) Ingalls, by which union there are six children, all at home: Alvin H. and James Purdy, studying medicine, Nancy A., Emma, John F. and Anderson J. The family are all members of the Presbyterian church, as was also the Doctor. In politics he was a Republican.

CHARLES KUGEL, farmer, P. O. Water Cure, was born in Baden, near Heidelberg, Germany, April 1, 1848, and is a son of George and Catherina (Epert) Kugel, the former a native of Baden, and the latter of Hesse Darmstadt. Both died in Moon township, on the farm where they first settled. They came to America in 1849, reaching Rochester, Pa., July 4 of that year. George followed the trade of carpenter and cabinet-maker one year, then engaged in farming. He had nine children, six of whom lived to maturity: Charles, Catherine, Elizabeth, Caroline, Bertha and George. Charles was educated in Beaver county, and owns eighty-two acres of land, a part of the old homestead. He married Pauline Kaercher, a native of Beaver county, and a daughter of Charles F. Kaercher, who was born in Wurtemberg, Germany. She has three children: Albert J., C. Frederick and William George. The parents are members of the Lutheran church. Mr. Kugel is a Democrat, and was supervisor of the township in 1885.

WILLIAM LANGFITT, farmer, P. O. Kendall, has been a life-long resident of Hanover township, where he was born March 31, 1820. His grandfather, William Langfitt, the hero of the frontier of Beaver county, was born on the eastern shore of Maryland, came West in youth, and "tomahawked" the road from Washington to Georgetown. He married Margaret, daughter of James Campbell, a pioneer of Virginia. They settled in Hanover township, where Ephraim Langfitt now resides, and where they died, he at the age of ninety-eight and she at the age of eighty-eight years. They had five sons and five daughters: James, William, John, Philip and Thomas; Bettie, Sarah, Katie, Rebecca and Hannah. Of these, James married Sarah, daughter of Henry Russell. They had eleven children: Philip, William, John, James, Margaret, Elizabeth, Rebecca, Sarah, Mary, Hannah and Catherine. James Langfitt died Jan. 2, 1884, aged ninety-eight years and one day. He was a soldier in the War of 1812, and a stranger to sickness and pain. On the day of his death, he told his family that he was going to die. He walked to the door, took one look at the outside world, bid it farewell, then walked to his bed, where he lay down and died, without a groan or sign of pain. His wife died in 1841. William Langfitt has been a farmer all his life in Hanover township, where he and his sister own 200 acres of land. He is a Democrat, as was his father before him.

EPHRAIM W. LANGFITT, farmer, P. O. Kendall, was born May 22, 1849. His grandfather, William Langfitt, born in 1737, came west in youth, and was the third man west of the mountains. He was shot by the Indians, but recovered from his wounds and lived to be ninety-four years old. He was a hardy pioneer. His son, Philip, was born Oct. 12, 1799, on the old homestead, where all his children were born. On Dec. 22, 1836, he was married to Mary A , daughter of John and Charity Cristler. She was born Sept. 10, 1815, and died Jan. 29, 1879. Philip Langfitt was a farmer all his life, and died Jan. 28, 1875. Both he and his wife were members of the Presbyterian church. Their children were William, Margaret, John, George, Frank, Ephraim W., Mary E. (wife of William Salman) and Joseph. Ephraim W. married Clara E. Porter. She was born March 11, 1850, and is a daughter of Nathan and Julia A. (Anderson) Porter. Her father was a boat builder for many years, and a well-known and esteemed character along the Ohio river. Mr. and Mrs. Langfitt are members of the Presbyterian church. He owns 150 acres of the old Langfitt homestead, which originally contained 343 acres, and was called "Indiana." An old blockhouse built for protection from the Indians stood on the farm. Politically Mr. Langfitt is a Democrat.

CHARLES B. LAUGHLIN, steward, P. O. Georgetown, was born Nov. 6, 1841, in Greene township. His grandfather, Thomas Laughlin, settled in Beaver county at an early day. His son, Robert, father of Charles B., was a farmer in Greene township, and died there. His wife was Rebecca, daughter of Robert Dawson. They had eight children: Sarah A., George, Thomas, Jane, John, Benjamin, Robert and Charles B. The latter commenced life as a cabin boy at the age of fifteen years, and has followed the river almost ever since, except three years spent in the army. He enlisted July 20, 1861, in Company A, 147th Regiment, P. V.; was in many engagements, including Antietam, Gettysburg, Lookout Mountain, Missionary Ridge and Ringgold, and was mustered out at Louisville, Ky. In 1873 he went to Salineville, Ohio, where he engaged in the bakery and confectionery business for eighteen months. He is now in the employ of Joseph Walton & Co. He married Pauline, daughter of Hiram Cornell, and they have two children: Victor Clyde and Gertrude Lytton. Mr. Laughlin is a Republican.

THOMAS J. LAUGHLIN, farmer, P. O. Hookstown, was born Sept. 30, 1814. His grandfather, Thomas Laughlin, of Irish descent, was one of the early settlers of Beaver

BIOGRAPHIES—SOUTH SIDE. 861

county, and lived and died on a farm between Hookstown and Georgetown. He lived to be over eighty years old; his wife was Sarah Simpson, who died at the age of eighty. Their children were John, Robert, Thomas, James, William, Mary, Betsey, Ann, Sarah and Nancy. All married and raised families. John was born and died here. His death occurred in 1822, in his thirty-fourth year. He was a farmer by occupation, and his wife, Martha Bell, died in 1849, aged sixty-two years. They had two children. Mary and Thomas J. The latter was a carpenter for about thirty years, and has since been a farmer. He owns about 125 acres. He married, Nov. 9, 1843, Clara, daughter of Jacob and Sarah Strieby, who died Aug. 2, 1878, aged fifty-five years. She left three children: Adele (wife of James Calhoon), Walter S. and Ada M. Mr. Laughlin is a member of the Presbyterian church; politically a Republican.

WILLIAM LAUGHLIN, farmer, P. O. Hookstown, was born June 18, 1818, on the farm of 130 acres, where he now resides. His grandfather, William Laughlin, was of Irish descent, and lived and died near Cannonsburg, Washington county, Pa. His son, Samuel Laughlin (father of our subject), was born in the above named place and died on his farm in Greene township in 1819, aged twenty-five years. He settled on the land that his father had taken up in 1797, which then contained 460 acres. William Laughlin came here when the Indians were still in the vicinity, and he had no neighbors within seven miles. Samuel Laughlin married Hannah, daughter of Robert Reed, of Ireland, and had two children: William and Martha, the latter of whom married John Murphy. William is a successful farmer. He married Agnes, daughter of David Kerr, and has had the following named children: Marianna (deceased), Rachel J., Ida M., Lizzie, Anna, Samuel (deceased), John, Sylvester (deceased), Maggie, Lillie, Frank W. and Mabel C. Mr. and Mrs. Laughlin are members of the Mill Creek Presbyterian church, of which he is a trustee. He is a Democrat.

FELIX LAY, assessor, collector and treasurer, P. O. Water Cure, was born in Phillipsburg, in March, 1841. His grandfather and his father, George Lay, were born in Germany. George Lay married Mary Baker, and they had eight children, Felix and George being the only survivors. The others, who all died in the prime of life, were named Edward, William, Alonzo, Kate, Etta and Maggie. Felix learned the shoemaker's trade and followed it for many years. Since 1877 he has engaged in various occupations, including gardening. He has been assessor and collector for several years. He was married here to Wilhelmina, daughter of Simon and Christina (Smith) Wagner, the former of whom died in 1843. Mr. and Mrs. Lay have four children: Richard, Edward, Josephine and Libbie M. In political preferences Mr. Lay is a Democrat. He enlisted in August, 1862, in Company E, 134th Regiment, P. V., Captain J. A. Vera, and served nine months. He was wounded in the battle of Fredericksburg, and draws a pension.

THOMAS LEE, hotel keeper, P. O. Water Cure, was born in Yorkshire, England, Dec. 16, 1841, a son of Thomas Lee, who died in England. He was raised and educated in Lancaster county, England, and was foreman of the saw room in a cutlery factory. At the age of twenty-three he came to America with his mother, Sarah (Travise) Lee, who died in Lawrence, Mass. His brother and sister are living in the East. Thomas Lee was married in Darlington to Ann Woolley, by whom he has two children: Sarah A. and Nora H. Mr. Lee came to Phillipsburg in March, 1883, and purchased the Point Breeze Hotel, which he has since conducted. Politically he is a Democrat.

SAMUEL H. LEEPER, Frankfort Springs, Pa., is a grandson of James Leeper, a native of County Antrim, Ireland, and who was of Scotch descent. James Leeper came to America with his parents when a small boy; his parents settled in York County Pa., and died there. James, his son, married Nancy McCleary. They moved to Washington county, Pa., and thence removed to Hanover township, Beaver county, Pa., in 1794. They had ten children—five boys and five girls. Robert was the eldest, and father of S. H. Leeper. Joseph Washington Leeper lives on the farm his great-grandfather settled on, and, together with his son Robert, erected a cabin in 1794. James

49

Leeper died March 13, 1814, aged sixty-six years. Nancy, his wife, died April 15, 1815. They were members of the Seceder's Church, James also being an elder. He was a man of great intelligence and piety. Robert inherited fifty acres of the old homestead farm, afterward adding 150 acres by purchase, for which he paid $750. He died Aug. 28, 1862, in his eighty-fifth year. He held a commission as captain in the War of 1812, and he carried a sword which his father-in-law, Samuel Harper, brought from Scotland, and which is now in the possession of his son, S. H. Leeper. He was training his company one day when the word came that the British were at Youngstown. He ordered the drum-muffled, and beat around for volunteers. But only three volunteered. He threw down his uniform and marched after the drum and almost all of his company followed him. He was an elder in the old Seceder's church of King's Creek. The congregation afterwards built a new church at Frankfort Springs, Pa. His wife, Nancy A., daughter of Samuel Harper, was born Oct. 10, 1782, in York county, Pa., and died in May, 1868, in her eighty-seventh year. Their family consisted of seven children: Jane, Margaret, Samuel H., Agnes, James K., Emeline and Levina. During his younger years S. H. was in mercantile business, but farming and stock-raising have constituted the principal part of his occupation. He spent the winter of 1836-87 in Rock Island, Ill., having arranged to go into business in that place. His parents wishing him to return home, he did so, feeling it to be his duty to return home to promote their comfort. His wife, Mary J., daughter of Joseph Miller, Esq., died April 17, 1887. Their family consisted of seven children: Robert Newton, Joseph W., Mary A., Estella S., Robert C., James L. and Samuel Harper. Politically S. H. Leeper is a Republican, and an advocator of tariff for protection to American productions. Of his sons, J. L. is pastor of the First Presbyterian Church, Reading, Pa., and S. Harper is a student, senior year, at the Theological Seminary. Both were educated at Princeton College and Seminary.

JOSEPH W. LEEPER, farmer, P. O. Frankfort Springs, was born July 4, 1841, and is a son of S. H. Leeper. He was reared on the farm he now owns, consisting of 150 acres, He was married Oct. 19, 1871, to Nancy E., daughter of James Fulton, of Washington county. She was born Oct. 23, 1845. Their children are Estella S., aged fifteen; Ira F., aged thirteen; Mary Jeannetta, aged eleven, and Harland H., aged nine years. Mr. and Mrs. Leeper are members of the United Presbyterian church of Frankfort Springs, and he is a trustee and a member of Session. In politics he is a Republican.

SAMUEL H. LEEPER, farmer, P. O. Hookstown, was born on the home farm at Frankfort Springs, Aug. 1, 1821. His father, Hugh Leeper, was born near Frankfort Springs in 1793, and died near Hookstown in 1869. He was an elder in the United Presbyterian church, and a member of Session. His wife, Esther, daughter of Samuel Harper, was born in Beaver county, and died in May, 1871, aged seventy-five years. She was the mother of fifteen children, twelve of whom reached maturity, viz.: Jane, James, Samuel, William, Anderson, Robert, Archibald, Mary A., Harriet, Amanda, Joseph and Hugh. Two of the sons were college graduates, and Archibald became a physician in St. Louis. Samuel taught school eight years, beginning at the age of nineteen years, receiving a certificate from Thomas Nicholson, the first county superintendent. Since then he has been a farmer, and owns 116 acres. He has been married twice; first to Margaret Patterson, who bore him four children: Harper, Elizabeth J., Esther J., and William A. His present wife is Jennie, daughter of Walter Denny. They are members of the United Presbyterian church, and he is a member of Session. He is active in church and school work, and has been secretary of the board nine years. He was formerly a Whig, and is now a Republican.

ROBERT LEEPER, farmer, P. O. Hookstown, is a son of Hugh and Easter (Harper) Leeper. His parents were of Scotch-Irish descent, and were members of the old Seceder's church. Their fathers, James Leeper and Samuel Harper, with their wives, emigrated from Ireland to America, and settled in York county, Pa.; thence they moved to Frankfort Springs, Beaver county, where Robert was born Nov. 10, 1827. At the age of six years he came to Greene township, where his father bought land. He taught school for nine years, four years in Greene township, one in Hanover township, two in

Allegheny county, one in Washington county, and one year more near Xenia, Ohio. He owns the old homestead farm of 150 acres, where he resides, and another of eighty-eight acres. His first wife was Mary, daughter of Joseph Collins, of Greene county, Ohio. She died Aug. 10, 1863, leaving two sons: Hugh C. and William R. His present wife is Elizabeth, daughter of John Dallas, of Springfield, Ohio, and she is the mother of three children: Mary H., John B. and Robert J. The parents are members of the United Presbyterian church, Mr. Leeper being an elder. Politically he has been successively a Whig, Republican and Prohibitionist.

THE LEIPER FAMILY. Five brothers of this family, of Scotch-Irish extraction, emigrated to America in the latter part of the eighteenth century. James Leeper (so formerly spelled) did not stop in York county, as did his four brothers, but came farther west, locating for a time in Washington county, and subsequently at Frankfort, Beaver county. Here he became the father of five sons—Robert, James, William, John and Hugh. William was a soldier in the war of 1812, and died of fever contracted while lying in a marshy, malaria-breeding camp near Erie, Pa. Hugh married Esther Harper, in 1818, and located on a farm near Frankfort. He became the father of fifteen children, the last three of whom were born on a farm of 250 acres near Hookstown, which he purchased in 1836, and upon which he located. Three of these died in infancy; four of the eight sons who lived to mature life graduated in letters and theology, and one in medicine, the remaining three becoming farmers. The names of the brothers in order of birth are James, a farmer in Randolph county, Ill.; Samuel, a farmer in Beaver county, Pa.; William, an editor in Malvern, Ark.; John Anderson, a minister, who died in October, 1855; Robert, a farmer in Beaver county; Archibald, a physician. died in December, 1886, at Coulterville, Ill.; Joseph H., a minister and secretary National Reform Society, Philadelphia; and Hugh G., pastor United Presbyterian congregation at Yellow Creek, Ohio. The four daughters, Mrs. Jane Patterson, Mrs. Mary Ann Littell, Mrs. Harriet Andrews and Mrs. Amanda Blythe, are still living.

ANDREW LEITCH, farmer, P. O. Shoustown, was born in 1815. His grandfather, John H. Leitch, came from Ireland and settled in Hopewell township, where Andrew now lives. His son, Daniel, was born in Ireland, and died here in 1862, aged eighty years. He married Eliza, daughter of James McFarland, and they had twelve children. Andrew Leitch has been a hardworking, successful farmer. His wife was Nancy Biggerstaff, by whom he had one child, Joseph. Joseph married Mary J., daughter of Samuel Neely, and they had two children: Albert S. and Rosa A. Mr. Leitch is a Democrat.

GEORGE LITTELL, farmer, P. O. Service, was born Jan. 24, 1825. William, grandfather of the present Littell family was a native of Ireland, and with his brother James came to this country during the Revolutionary struggle; they both entered the army. During James' thirteenth battle, William, who was a staff officer, was taken prisoner and held at Philadelphia, but was finally exchanged. He married Elizabeth Walter, and settled on a farm in Hanover township, Beaver county, Pa., where he died. He was one of the first members of Service Congregation; he was a justice of the peace, and for a time the only one from Pittsburgh to Georgetown. His children, all of whom were born on the old homestead, were Betsy, Jane, Mary, Alice, Agnes, James, William, David and Thomas. David, who remained on the old farm, was born in 1801, he married Jane, daughter of George and Nancy (Miller) Shillito; he died July 8, 1865, and she died Oct. 10, 1885. They had eight children: Belinda, Elizabeth, Agnes, George, James, William, David S. and John R., all of whom united with the Congregation of Service. James and William emigrated to Iowa in 1855; David S. is now pastor of the Second United Presbyterian Church, Pittsburgh. George, the eldest, and J. R., the youngest, divided the old home farm of near 400 acres. George married M. A. Leeper, and their family consists of eight children: Joseph A., Hugh F., James H., David W., William A., John D., Robert R. and Ella J., all of whom are members of the United Presbyterian church. Joseph A. married Clara, daughter of Judge Munger, of Xenia, Ohio, and is pastor of the First United Presbyterian church of Albany, N. Y. They have unanimously voted the Republican ticket.

WILLIAM McCAGUE, farmer, P. O. Service, was born Aug. 24, 1817. His grandfather, James McCague, was a native of County Down, Ireland, and a tiller of the soil. He was of Scotch descent, and married Jeanette Cochrain, a native of Scotland. They came to this country with two children: William and Jane, the latter of whom married first a Mr. Langan, and afterward James Logan. James McCague settled on Peter's creek, Washington county, Pa., and became a successful farmer there. He was a member of the United Presbyterian church. Both he and his wife died at an advanced age. Their children born in this country were Thomas, John, James, Mary, Martha and Ann. William McCague, Sr., came to Beaver county in 1807, and settled on the farm of 150 acres, where his son, William, now lives. He died in 1866, aged eighty-five years. He was a member of the old Seceder's church. His wife was Mary, daughter of John and Hannah Reed, old settlers of Allegheny county, and they had eight children: Hannah, Jane, Mary, Tabitha, William, Elizabeth, Martha and John. Of these William was educated in this county, and has been a successful farmer on the old homestead. He married Lucinda, daughter of Alexander and Jane (McElhaney) Thompson, and by her had three children: Jane M., who died at the age of seven years; William F., of Beaver, Pa., and Anna Cora, at home. The parents are members of Mount Olive Presbyterian church; Mr. McCague is a Republican.

WILLIAM C. MCCOLLOUGH, farmer, P. O. Frankfort Springs, was born in Hanover township, Washington county, Pa., Aug. 25, 1820. His grandfather, George McCollough, was born in Scotland. He came to America, and with his brothers, Alexander and William, and two half brothers, settled at the head of Big Traverse in Hanover township, this county. Alexander and George were farmers. William started the salt works, and became wealthy. His son, John N., is a prominent railroad man. George McCollough died at the old homestead. He had seven children, of whom George, Jr., was born in 1795, and died in Missouri in 1843. He married Jane, daughter of William and Margaret (Clagston) Carothers. She was born in October, 1797, and died Dec. 4, 1871. Her children were Elizabeth, William C., John, Peggie Ann, George, David, Mary and Alseta. William C. was raised in this county, and has lived here all his life, except three years spent in Missouri. He is a farmer and carpenter, started in life poor, and, as the result of his own labor and industry, now owns 196 acres of land. He and his brother John supported their mother and her family. He married Eliza, daughter of Henry and Mary A. (Smith) Keifer. She is the mother of seven children: George H., David K., Jennie N., Anna Mary, Amanda, Sarah E. and Alsetta. Mr. and Mrs. McCollough and their family are members of the Presbyterian church, of which he is a ruling elder. Politically he is a Democrat.

JOHN MCCOLLOUGH, farmer, P. O. Frankfort Springs, is a son of George McCollough. He was born in Frankfort Springs borough Jan. 4, 1823, and at the age of ten years moved with his parents to Halliday Cove, in Brooke county, W. Va. From there they went to Missouri and settled in Adair county, where the father died. The family came to this county in 1845, and John came six months later. He was also a house carpenter and joiner, having learned his trade in Paris, Pa., and Steubenville, Ohio, and followed his trade in this county about five years. He married Sarah A., daughter of John Ewing, and entered into partnership with his father-in-law. They carried on the tannery business for five years, and for about twenty years Mr. McCollough followed the business on his own account, working first in Beaver and then in Washington county. When his father-in-law gave up business, he returned to Frankfort Springs and remained in business until 1873. He then moved to a farm of 100 acres, which he purchased. He now owns 350 acres of land in Beaver and Washington counties. He has three children: John E., Frank and Sarah F. He is a Democrat. He now resides in the house he helped to build while he was working for seventy-five cents a day, in order to help pay for a home for his mother in Frankfort Springs. While in Missouri he gave all his money to help the family at home.

CYRUS MCCONNELL, physician, P. O. Service, is a native of Washington county, Pa., born in 1836, the fourth of the ten children (six sons and four daughters) of John

D. and Sarah (Morrison) McConnell. The father was born in 1802, on the farm of his father, at whose death he came into possession of the property by purchasing his brothers' and sisters' shares; he was a son of Daniel McConnell, who had four sons and six daughters, John D. being the eldest son. Daniel was a native of Maryland, came to Washington county, Pa., when a young man, and followed blacksmithing for a considerable period, afterward purchasing and operating a farm of 200 acres. Cyrus received a good common-school education, studied at Florence Academy, Washington county, for six years, and at the age of twenty-five commenced the study of medicine with Dr. James McCarell, then of Washington county, now of Allegheny City; entered college at Ann Arbor in 1863, from which he graduated, commencing the practice of his profession in 1868 at his present location. He was married, in 1872, to M. H., daughter of Samuel Reed, of Greene township, this county. The doctor and his wife are members of the Presbyterian church.

JOHN B. McCONNELL, farmer, P. O. Seventy-Six, was born March 18, 1831, on the old homestead, where his father, Joseph, settled after his marriage with Elizabeth M., daughter of James Wallace. Joseph and Elizabeth McConnell had seven children: Nancy, Susannah, Rachel, Alice M., James, John B. and Joseph. The mother died young, but the father lived to the age of eighty-two years, and both were devoted members of the United Presbyterian church. John B. McConnell, father of Joseph, came from the vicinity of Philadelphia to Beaver county at an early day. John B., our subject, married Mary, daughter of Joseph McCorkle, and a native of Mahoning county, Ohio. She is the mother of two children: Harry S. and Elizabeth I., wife of A. Allen, of Ohio. Mr. and Mrs. McConnell are members of the United Presbyterian church, of which he has been trustee and treasurer. He has been a farmer all his life, and owns 107 acres of land, on which there is an oil well. Politically he is a Democrat.

ALEXANDER L. McCOY, farmer, P. O. Service, was born Feb. 16, 1814, in Allegheny county, Pa. His grandfather, James McCoy, was a farmer in Allegheny county, and of Scotch-Irish descent, and his son, James, Jr., (father of our subject) was born and married in Allegheny county; was a farmer and came to Raccoon township at an early day. He finally bought land where his grandson, J. E. McCoy, now resides, and died there at the age of fifty-six years. He married Elizabeth Bridewell, who lived to be over eighty years of age, and had six children: William, Alexander L., James, Mary, Martha and John. Alexander L. married Margaret McCoy (not a relative), who was born in 1814. They have nine children: James E., John L., Alexander, Samantha, Martha, Melissa, Roberta, Seymour and Edwin. Mr. McCoy is a self-made man and a successful farmer; he owns 128 acres of land. He is a Republican.

DAVID McCOY was born in Scotland, and came to this country at an early day. He purchased in 1772, the old homestead in Beaver county, where his granddaughter, Agnes S. McCoy, now resides. He was one of the heroes of the Revolution, and was discharged in 1779. In April, 1783, David McCoy, of Chartiers, was married to Nancy Shearer, of Path valley, Cumberland county, Pa. She died in 1826, leaving four children: Mrs. Polly Craig, Mrs. Jane Agnew, Mrs. Nancy Eachel and Archibald. David McCoy and wife were members of the old Seceder's church, and were married by Rev. Samuel Dougal. Mr. McCoy used to spell his name in the old Scotch way "McKeay." He owned a farm of 600 acres. He died in December, 1831, aged eighty-seven years. His son, Archibald, was born July 24, 1803, and died Sept. 15, 1883. He was a farmer on the old homestead, and married Jane, daughter of Daniel Leitch, of an old pioneer family. She was born on the old Leitch homestead, and is the mother of six children: Agnes S., Elizabeth (Mrs. Douds), David, Mary J. (deceased), Hannah (Mrs. Creese), and Rosa Ann, who died at the age of nine years. Archibald McCoy was a quiet man, greatly esteemed and respected. In politics he was a Whig and a Republican. He was a member of a militia company. The family have a letter written July 1, 1788, by Sally Shearer to Nancy McCoy, and an old gun and sword found under a log by Mr. McCoy. These arms undoubtedly belonged to a French officer. Cut in an old tree on the farm is the picture of a hunter with his gun on his shoulder, and a turkey in his hand, and underneath the words "Aurgaurst, 1772," supposed to have been executed by one of the French hunters. An old Indian trail crosses the farm from southwest to northeast.

JAMES E. McCOY, farmer, P. O. Service, was born June 26, 1837, on the old homestead where he now resides, and which was settled by his grandfather, James McCoy. He was raised and educated in this county, and was married, Oct. 25, 1860, to Ann, daughter of Alexander McCoy. She was born Jan. 3, 1837, and has three children: Laura C., Jennie M. and Albine R. Mr. McCoy lived four years with his uncle before he was married, and after marriage went to Richland county, Ohio, where he settled sixteen miles northeast of Mansfield, and engaged in farming three years. He then bought a farm in Hanover township, this county, and remained there until 1881. He now owns the old homestead; has 230 acres and has been financially prosperous in life. His parents had nine children, all of whom are living, and eight are married and have children.

JAMES H. McCOY, farmer and stockman, P. O. Clinton, was born Sept. 19, 1820, in Greene township, Beaver county. His grandfather, James McCoy, a weaver by trade, and a native of Ireland, lived in Allegheny county, Pa., where he died at an old age. He had seven children: William, James, Alexander, Hugh, Isaac, Betsey and Polly. Hugh married Rachel, daughter of William Schooler, and died at the age of seventy-nine. He was an active member of the Baptist church. His wife died in Independence township at the age of sixty-seven years. Her children were Polly, Ann, Elizabeth, James H., Rachel, William, Isaac A., Sarah J. and Lucinda. James H. received a common-school education, and at the age of ten years began farming, which he chose as his occupation. Gradually, with pluck and perseverance, he made his way in the world. He bought his first land while a young man, and went in debt for it, but now owns 176 acres. He married Martha, daughter of William McCague, and they had six children: John, Lucinda, Mary Ann, Martha J., William Frank and Thomas. Lucinda died at the age of fourteen years. John is a merchant in Bocktown, and William F. in Gringo. Mr. McCoy is a Democrat, and has been school director. He has dealt extensively and successfully in stock.

JOHN R. McCOY (deceased) was born Jan. 22, 1828, on the old McCoy homestead, in Greene township, He was in early life a farmer, later a stockman, and purchased the old homestead of 260 acres, to which he added eighty-four acres, and on which his widow now resides. He was a member of the Presbyterian church; politically he was a Republican. He married, June 20, 1850, Martha, daughter of Alexander and Mary (Wood) McCoy, and born Nov. 27, 1830, in Service. Mr. McCoy was a good business man, esteemed for his many excellent qualities of head and heart. His early education was limited, but he was a well-read and intelligent man. He died June 22, 1881, mourned by a large circle of friends.

JOHN B. McCREADY, Hookstown, was born on the old McCready homestead, Aug. 5, 1837. His great-grandfather, Joseph McCready, was a native of Ireland, and settled in Greene township while the Indians were still living in the neighborhood. He took up 400 acres of land, receiving patent dated 1784, and died in 1798. His wife was Katy Laughlin, and they had five daughters, who became Mrs. Bruce, Mrs. Ralston, Mrs. Bay, Mrs. Martin and Mrs. McClure, respectively, and two sons. Joseph and John, the latter of whom was a doctor at New Bedford, where he died. Joseph, born July 9, 1786, married, May 14, 1805, Elizabeth Ewing, and died Oct. 3, 1862. His wife was a daughter of James Ewing, and died March 22, 1846. He was a man of most remarkably strong mind and clear judgment, an earnest Christian and staunch Presbyterian. He had four sons, James, Joseph, John B. and W. E., and four daughters, Catharine, Jane, Eliza A. and Isabel. James was born May 10, 1806, and died Sept. 30, 1872. He married Mary A. Reed, daughter of Thomas and Sarah (King) Reed. She was born Sept. 11, 1801, in Cumberland county, and died in Hookstown, July 3, 1882. They had five children, two sons and three daughters: Joseph J., John B., Sarah E., Elizabeth I. and Mary Jane. Three are deceased and two living, John B. and Mary Jane. John B. came to Hookstown in 1873, built a mill, has carried on a successful business, and still owns 120 acres, a part of the old homestead. He married, April 25, 1861, Sarah A., daughter of Henry and Sarah A. Cowan, and they have two children living: James H. and Frank, the former of whom is married to Mary E. Stewart, and has one child, Edith B. The family have been members of the Presbyterian church for many generations. Mr. McCready is a Republican.

CYRUS MCCREARY, harness-maker, P. O. Frankfort Springs, was born May 11, 1848, in Columbiana county, Ohio, in the village of Fairfield. His grandfather McCreary, who died at Gettysburg, Pa., was of Scotch-Irish descent. His son, Henry B., was born in Adams county, and was a harness-maker by trade. He came to Beaver county at an early day, and married Anna Carothers, who died here. She had eight children, five of whom lived to mature age. Henry B. followed his trade in Frankfort Springs in the shop now occupied by his son, Cyrus, and died at the age of eighty-three. Cyrus McCreary married, Oct. 3, 1882, Laura E., daughter of Alexander and Margaret (Wilcoxon) McConnell. Mr. and Mrs. McCreary are both active members of the Presbyterian church. Mr. McCreary is a Democrat, and has filled the offices of burgess and councilman of Frankfort Springs. He is greatly esteemed and respected by his fellow-citizens.

S. L. MCCULLOUGH, M. D., Frankfort Springs, was born June 27, 1853, near Buffalo, Washington county, Pa., a son of John L. and Julia A. (Logan) McCullough, the former a native of Ireland of Scotch descent, and the latter a native of Lancaster county, Pa., and still living. Her children are Jacob L., John L., Nathaniel G., Joseph E., Matthew W., S. L., Mattie and Julia A. The first four served in the Civil War in Company A, 100th Regiment, and were all wounded. John died at home; Nathaniel is still living, and the other two died on the battle-field. Matthew W. enlisted, but was rejected. S. L. received his education at the California State Normal School, after which he taught school nine years. He studied medicine with Dr. T. C. M. Stockton, and was graduated from the University of the city of New York, in 1883. He first located in McDonald, Washington county, Pa., and then came to Frankfort Springs, where he has built up a good practice. He was married June 7, 1878, to Miss Maggie Proudfit, of Burgettstown, Pa., and they have three children: William, J. L., Charles L. and Gracie G. The Doctor and his wife are members of the Presbyterian church, of the Sunday-school of which he is assistant superintendent. In politics he is a Republican.

ALLEN MCDONALD, farmer, P. O. Hookstown, was born on the farm he now owns, Jan. 27, 1844. His father, John McDonald, was a native of Inverness, Scotland, and came to America at the age of ten years, his parents having preceded him some years. Allen's grandfather, Daniel, settled in Greene township, this county, at an early day and died there. He was a member of the Presbyterian church. His children were Mrs. Nancy Randolph, Mrs. Jennie Cronk and John. The last named married Margaret Barclay, daughter of Andrew Barclay, of Irish descent, who is yet living, aged eighty-five years. She used to make annual visits to her old home, doing the journey of forty miles on horseback, and carrying a child in her arms. Hotels in those days were few and far between. In the shearing of sheep, the women performed that labor, and the flocks then, on ordinary sized farms, consisted usually of twenty in number, which was considered a large flock; they would shear each an average of three pounds, and the carcass would sell at one dollar per head. John died in 1859, aged sixty-two years. He was a successful, energetic farmer; a member of the United Presbyterian church; in politics a Republican. His children were William, Jane, Joseph, Andrew, Elizabeth, James, John, Sarah, Margaret, Allen and Maria. Allen was reared and educated in this county, and was married, Dec. 31, 1874, to Cordilla J., daughter of David and Jane (Henry) Anderson, and born Aug. 24, 1851. Mr. and Mrs. McDonald are members of the Tomlinson Run Presbyterian church, of which he is a trustee. In politics he is a Republican. He has one child, Emma J., born Oct. 21, 1875.

C. I. MCDONALD, contractor, P. O. Woodlawn, was born Nov. 26, 1846, in Logstown Bottom, Hopewell township, on the place where Rev. Andrew McDonald settled in 1810. The latter preached at White Oat Flats, now Mount Carmel. Our subject graduated from Duff's Business College, in Pittsburgh, learned the carpenter's trade, and after working at it some time, severely cut himself. He then became a clerk for Simon Harrold, contractor, of Beaver Falls, and two years later a partner. At that time his work was mainly for the Cleveland & Pittsburgh Railroad, building shops, bridges, etc. During dull times he ran his sawmill at Logstown, and dealt in lumber. He was engaged with B. J. McGrann in the construction of the Pittsburgh & Lake Erie Railroad, about one year. From 1878 to 1880 he managed his sawmill, and in 1880, in connection with Capt. D. A. McDonald, established the Point Bottle Works at Rochester. In 1881 he sold out, and engaged once more in contracting. He built bridges across the Allegheny river, and the Mahanoy river, Ohio; lock and dam No. 7 on the Monongahela river, also second lock at No. 3 for same company, and enlarged the tunnel for the P. C. & Y. Railroad. In 1884 he began dam 6 on the Great Kanawha river for the U. S. government, and completed it in October, 1886. He was married in Mount Pleasant, Ohio, to Mattie V. Sharon, daughter of John Sharon, who was brother of Senator Sharon, of California. John Sharon was born in Carlisle, Pa., of Scotch descent. Mr. and Mrs. McDonald have had six children: Clement B., John S., Chauncy I., Mabel V., Harold H. and Helen. Mabel V. died when two years of age. Mr. McDonald established the postoffice, and was the first postmaster at Woodlawn, which place was on his farm, and named by his wife. He supplies many families with natural gas, which is found on his place. He is now engaged with the C. & O. R. R. in Virginia and West Virginia. In politics he is a Republican.

ALEXANDER T. McELHANEY, farmer, P. O. Service, is a grandson of George McElhaney, the old Indian scout and pioneer. He was educated in his native township, and has followed farming all his life. His wife is Jane, daughter of John McMurtrie, and they have nine children: Elizabeth, Mary A., Joseph Alvin, Thomas A , Richard E., Clara, Lossie B., Elvira Lucretia G. and Harry. Mr. McElhaney has been identified with the Republican party all his life. He owns a farm of seventy-six acres near the old homestead.

JOHN S. McELHANEY, farmer, P. O. Seventy-Six, is a grandson of George McElhaney, who was born in Lancaster county, Pa., and whose father came from Scotland. In 1782 George McElhaney made application for a tract of 400 acres of land where John S. now resides. He died at the residence of Thomas Butler, at the age of sixty-two years. At the time of his settlement the Indians were numerous, and he was one of the most daring Indian scouts on the frontier. He married Martha Stringer, of Lancaster county, and of Welsh descent. The young people failed to obtain the permission of their parents, but, escaping the vigilance of the latter, they were married and settled in their new home in the wilderness. They reared five children, whose descendants are numerous in Beaver county, and have contributed much to its wealth and advancement. The names of the children were William, John, Thomas, Jane and Martha. Of these William married Lydia, daughter of John Strouss. She died at the age of seventy-six, and he died at the age of seventy-six years. They had eight children: Martha, John S., George, William, Eliza, Nancy, Jane and Alexander. John S. has been a farmer all his life, and owns 151½ acres. He married Hannah, daughter of William and Nancy (Baker) Figley. They have four children living: Zachariah F , Strouss D., Richard W. and Frank R. Mr. McElhaney is a Democrat, and has held several township offices, including that of school director.

WILLIAM McELHANEY, farmer, P. O. Seventy-Six, is a grandson of George and a son of William McElhaney. He was educated in this county, chose the occupation of farming, and owns 104 acres. He was married in Hopewell township to Eliza, daughter of John and Margaret (Davis) Johnston, of an old pioneer family. This union has been blessed with seven children living: Margaret M., Francis H.. Charles B., David S., Martha, Ida J. and Elva N. The mother is a member of the United Presbyterian church. Mr. McElhaney has held a number of township offices, including supervisor, for several years.

JOHN H. MCELHANEY, farmer, P. O. Service, is a grandson of William, and a son of George McElhaney. The latter was born July 7, 1821, in this county, has been a life-long farmer, and owns 300 acres. After his marriage he settled near his father's residence, and lived there sixteen years. He then purchased 199 acres, and by subsequent purchase has accumulated his present property. He was married to Elizabeth, daughter of Isaac McCoy, and they have four children living: Lydia (Mrs. Mateer), William J., John H. and Isaac M. The mother and daughter are members of Mount Olive Presbyterian church. John H. was born in Independence township, and is a successful farmer and business man, owning about 200 acres. He married Maria, daughter of Thomas Wilson, and their children are George, Alexander G., Sarah E. and Nora B. Mr. McElhaney is a Republican.

WILLIAM J. MCELHANEY, farmer, P. O. Seventy-Six, was born on the place where he now resides, Jan. 27, 1845. His grandfather, William McElhaney, was born in Beaver county, where his father, George McElhaney, owned a large tract of land. William J., is a son of George and Elizabeth (McCoy) McElhaney, and was reared and educated in Beaver county, where he is a prosperous farmer. He was married, Oct. 24, 1867, to Mary E., daughter of Hugh Miller, and they have five children: Jane A., Margaret E., George W., Hugh Calvin and an infant daughter. Mr. McElhaney is a Republican.

JOHN MCHENRY, retired farmer, P. O. Service, was born in Hopewell township, this county, in 1818, and is the eldest son and second of the six children (four yet living) of Charles and Martha (Devine) McHenry, both of Irish parentage. John McHenry, grandfather of our subject, with his wife and children, came from Ireland to these shores, locating soon after arrival in Washington county, Pa., and afterward removed to Beaver county. He had five children, the eldest of whom, Charles, born in 1785, was a hatter for several years. In 1820 he came to Raccoon township, purchased 130 acres of land, and settled down to farm life. He married Sarah McCracken, who bore him one son, Dr. William McHenry. This wife dying, Mr. McHenry married Martha Devine, as above. He held the office of justice of the peace for fifteen years. John was reared on the farm, receiving a good education. He married, in 1861, Cynthia, youngest daughter of William Littell, and sister to Gen. John S. Littell, the family being one of the oldest in the county. Seven children, three now living, have blessed this union: Agnes (graduate of Edinboro College), Jennie Estelle and John Edgar, at home. Mr. McHenry was a school director for fifteen years, and held many other positions of trust. He and family are members of the United Presbyterian church; in politics he is a Republican.

WILLIAM E. MCKEE, farmer, P. O. Woodlawn, was born in Birmingham, now Pittsburgh (South Side), May 5, 1835. His grandfather, James McKee, a native of Ireland, settled in Cumberland county, Pa., and finally removed to Pittsburgh, where he died. His son, John McKee, father of William E., was born in Cumberland county, Aug. 19, 1798, and was reared in Pittsburgh. He was a prominent man in his day, was well known throughout the country, and was justice of the peace for twenty-five years; also served as borough treasurer and poorhouse director of Allegheny county. He died July 11, 1863. His wife was Charlotte, daughter of Henry Wendt, one of the first glass manufacturers of Pittsburgh. She was born in Pittsburgh (South Side) Sept. 11, 1808, and died Jan. 5, 1870. John McKee was class leader in the Methodist church for many years. Politically he was a Whig and afterward a Republican. His brothers, James, Samuel and Thomas, were prominent glass manufacturers in Pittsburgh. William E. McKee, our subject, had two brothers, John and Henry, and one sister, Sarah, who lived to maturity. John is a member of the Board of Health of Pittsburgh. William E. was educated in Pittsburgh, and learned the trade of glass-cutting; enlisted Aug. 5, 1861, in Company B, 62d Regiment, P. V., and served until November, 1862. He participated in the battles of Hanover Court House, Gaines' Mill, Antietam and South Mountain, and at Gaines' Mill he received a wound, on account of which he was discharged. After the war he came to Moon township, where he has a farm of 100 acres.

He was married in Pittsburgh, to Mary, daughter of George and Catharine (Roth) Haas, and they have five children living: Thomas, Sarah, John, William and Charles.

JOHN R. MCKENZIE, farmer, P. O. Harshaville, was born in Washington county, Pa., Nov. 22, 1827. His grandfather, Kenneth McKenzie, was born near Fort George, Scotland, and came to America between 1780 and 1790, settling in Maryland, where he was married to Jane Clark. They moved to Bevington Mill, Washington county, Pa., and in 1812 came to Hanover township, this county, where Mr. McKenzie died April 25, 1814. His wife died Sept. 22, 1836. They had six children: John, Mary, Jane, William, Collin and Sarah A. William, who was a farmer and tanner, was born in Washington county Jan. 10, 1803, and died Sept. 3, 1835; his wife, Isabella Ralston, was born in 1803 and died in 1886. They were members of the United Presbyterian church. They had three children: John R., James and Jane C. John R. was married to Elizabeth, daughter of David Strouss, and they have five children living: Nettie, David, William J., John and Joseph. Mr. and Mrs. McKenzie are members of the United Presbyterian church; politically he is a Democrat. He owns 200 acres of land. Of his sons, David and William J. are farmers; John teaches school in winter, and farms through the summer. Mrs. Isabella McKenzie was a daughter of John Ralston, whose father was assisted and partly carried to Fort Frankfort in one of the early Indian alarms. He died at Youngstown, Ohio, aged 104 years.

ALEXANDER and J. B. MCKIBBIN, farmers, P. O. Green Garden, are sons of Alexander McKibbin, who came to the United States from Ireland about 1825, and shortly after his arrival located in Pittsburgh, where for seven years he followed his trade, that of stone mason. He then moved to Beaver county, purchased 125 acres of land, commenced farm life, and managed successfully a country store. He married a Miss Gregg, sister of the well-known wholesale dry goods merchant of Pittsburgh. Two children were born to this union: John T., of Kansas, and Ellen (now Mrs. Campbell), of Perrysville, Allegheny county, Pa. The mother of these dying, Mr. McKibbin married Nancy Bryson, who bore him seven children, five of them now living.

Alexander McKibbin, the second son born to the last marriage, was reared on the homestead, and received a good education, graduating from the Commercial College at Pittsburgh, in 1868. He enlisted in 1862, in Company H, 140th Regiment, P. V., served three years, and participated in many decisive battles. In 1871 he bought 100 acres of land, all under cultivation, and the same year married Tillie J., daughter of William Irwin. By her he has four children: Ella May, Mattie Jane, Amie Mary and Alvin Stewart. Mr. McKibbin has been a member of the county and state board of agriculture for six years, serving his second term as member of state board of agriculture; is school director and secretary (third term); was county auditor from 1876 to 1879. He is a member of the United Presbyterian church; in politics a Republican.

J. B. McKibbin, also a son of Alexander and Nancy (Bryson) McKibbin, is a native of Allegheny county, Pa., born in 1840, and was reared on the farm purchased by his father, at whose death he inherited the property. He married, in 1865, Lizzie Ellen, daughter of James White, and to this union were born three children: Aggie, Jane and Bessie. Mr. McKibbin is a member of the United Presbyterian church; politically a Republican.

WILLIAM MCKIRAHAN, minister, Hookstown, was born Feb. 25, 1845, in Belmont county, Ohio. The genealogy of the family dates back to the days of religious persecution in Scotland, when all the family were killed, save two brothers, who fled to Ireland, where one was killed by the Catholics on landing. The other one escaped and settled in the North of Ireland, where many of his descendants still reside. Samuel McKirahan, grandfather of William, came to America in 1790, in the Brig "Cunningham." He settled near Hickory, Washington county, Pa., and died in Belmont county, Ohio. He married a Miss Gamble, who was the mother of nine children, five sons and four daughters. Of these children, Joseph was a minister. John was born in Washington county, Pa., in 1806, and is still living in Logan county, Ohio, and is a farmer by occupation. He married Elizabeth Porterfield, who is the mother of nine sons and three daughters. Five sons were soldiers in the Civil War. William was graduated from Eastman's Business College, Poughskeepsie, N. Y., received his literary diploma from West Geneva College, his theological education in Allegheny Seminary, and has a certificate from Dr. Harper of Yale College, professor of the Semitic languages, where he studied Hebrew. He is now studying the Assyrian and Arabic languages. He received the first appointment in Indiana county, Pa., where he remained six years, and Oct. 14, 1883, came to Hookstown, where he has charge of the United Presbyterian church. He was married in Pittsburgh, Pa., Sept. 4, 1876, to Ida L., daughter of Rev. J. M. Johnston, and they have one son living, Ralph, born May 30, 1878.

JOSEPH McLARN, merchant and postmaster at Murdocksville, was born in Findley township, Allegheny county Pa., in April, 1815. He is a son of Hugh McLarn, a native of Ireland, who came to America when a young man in company with his brother, Robert, and settled in Mercer county, Pa. He afterward moved to Findley township, where he carried on the business of farming, and died in August, 1825, aged fifty-eight years. He was a Whig, and a member of the Seceder's church. He married, Jennie, daughter of John Harper, an old settler of Allegheny county. She bore him eight children. Joseph was educated in his native county, and was in early life a farmer. At the age of twenty-five he started a store in Moon township, Allegheny county; opened his store in Murdocksville in 1840, and has been very successful. He owns 150 acres of land in this county, and twenty acres in Washington county. Dec. 11, 1849, he was married to Mary Ann Donaldson, who is the mother of four children: Joseph H.; Jennie M., wife of Rev. J. L. Leeper, of Reading, Pa.; Anna M., widow of Dr. Henry Burns; and Esther. Mr. and Mrs. McLarn are members of the United Presbyterian church of Robinson. Mr. McLarn has been postmaster since 1841, and is a Republican. He is a thorough-going successful business man.

JOHN McMURTRIE, farmer, P. O. Clinton, Allegheny county, was born Dec. 10, 1809, in Sussex county, N. J. His grandfather, John McMurtrie, was a native of Sussex county, of which he was the oldest justice, and died there. His son, John, father of the subject of this sketch, was also born in Sussex county, but died in Clinton, Pa. He was a farmer, and married Ann, daughter of Joseph Shippen, and granddaughter of Dr. Shippen, of Philadelphia, from whom she received an annuity as long as she lived. She died in Clinton, Pa., leaving six children: William, Nancy, John, Emeline, Angeline and Horace. Of these John, our subject, came west at the age of four years. He farmed until he was twenty years old, then worked on the road to Philadelphia as a broker and dealer in stock. He purchased land in Beaver county in 1840, and now owns 143 acres. He married Elizabeth, daughter of John Connel, and she has borne him five children: Jane, Ann, Elizabeth, Nancy M. and Joseph. Mr. McMurtrie has been a Democrat all his life.

ADAM MANOR, farmer, P. O. Bellowsville, is a native of Allegheny county, Pa., born in 1812. His parents were James and Elizabeth (Graham) Manor, the former of whom came to Western Pennsylvania from east of the Alleghanies at an early day. They had seven children, four now living, Adam being among the eldest. Our subject was reared on a farm, and in 1836 came to Beaver county, where he purchased, in 1862, his present farm of fifty-four acres, in Raccoon township, where he has since resided. He was united in marriage, in 1842, with Elizabeth S., daughter of Peter Lance, of this county, and eight children have blessed them. Mrs. Manor died in 1871, and in 1872 our subject wedded Emeline Lance, sister to his first wife, and she has borne him one daughter, Dora. The mother dying, Mr. Manor married Mrs. Ralston, of Washington county, Pa., the mother of four children by her first husband. Mr. Manor is a member of the Presbyterian church. In politics he is a Democrat.

JAMES MARKS (deceased), son of John Marks, was born in Allegheny county, Pa., Dec. 25, 1812, and died Dec. 19, 1884, of cancer of the stomach. His father, John Marks, was a fuller by trade, and came here from over the mountains. He first settled on Montour's Run, Allegheny county, where his descendants became honored members of the community in which they lived. Our subject became a member of the Associate

Reformed church at the age of sixteen years. In 1838 he moved within the bounds of the Raccoon church, in the same year was installed ruling elder of the congregation, and remained for about forty years in the discharge of his duties as an officer of the church. In 1877 he changed his membership to the New Bethlehem church. The memory of his true, Christian life will ever be cherished by those who were privileged to know him. He was married three times. His third wife, whom he married Dec. 26, 1861, and who survives him, and was faithful and devoted to him, was Margaret, daughter of Samuel Eachel, and she became the mother of two children: Isabella, wife of Robert Green; and Ulysses Grant, a student at the Western University of Pennsylvania. Mr. Marks was a Republican. Of his children, three sons and four daughters are yet living, one son having given up his life in the service of his country. The Marks farm contains ninety-six acres, on which are three oil wells.

MICHAEL MATEER, farmer, P. O. Shafer's, was born July 14, 1839, in Moon township, to which place his father, Michael Mateer, Sr., had moved the previous spring. The latter was born at Alsace, Germany, and was married in Pittsburgh, to Margaret Rook. He died Oct. 12, 1882; his widow died Nov. 23, 1887, aged eighty-two years. She was the mother of seven children: Margaret, Mary A. (deceased), Elizabeth, Michael, Caroline, George and Louise. Michael, our subject, followed the trade of carpenter for twenty years. He owns a farm of 155 acres, part of the old Baker homestead, and which contains probably the oldest orchard in the county. Mr. Mateer married Lydia A., daughter of George McElhaney, and she has borne him five children: Elizabeth A., Anna M., Margaret L., Thomas F. and Albert M. Mr. and Mrs. Mateer are members of the North Branch Presbyterian church, of which he is a trustee. He is a Democrat, and has been school director, treasurer, auditor and collector.

SAMUEL MAXWELL, farmer, P. O. Bellowsville, was born Aug. 17, 1833, in Findley, Washington county, where his father lived from 1815 to 1833. The parents died in Allegheny county, the father at the age of seventy-six, and the mother at the age of eighty-three years. James Maxwell was born in Scotland, and had fourteen children, of whom nine reached maturity: Jane J., Mary, Fanny, Isabella, Ann, Rachel, James A., Joseph B. and Samuel. The last named was educated in Allegheny City, and learned several trades. Firrt he learned the iron moulder's trade, and then the blacksmith's bellows trade, from which occupation the village of Bellowsville received its name. In Allegheny he was in partnership with his brother, Joseph B., who died in Bellowsville. Samuel came here and bought land Aug. 17, 1870, and now owns fifty-six acres. When Mr. Maxwell and his brother came here they erected a substantial ferryboat, which plies between Bellowsville and Vanport, and kept the ferry about ten years. During the war they had a large factory and forge, and filled many government contracts. Samuel Maxwell married Eliza, daughter of William Morrison, Esq., and they have three children: Harriet J., Rachel A. and Ella E. The parents are members of the United Presbyterian church. Mr. Maxwell is a Prohibitionist.

JOSEPH MEHAFFEY, farmer, P. O. Harshaville, was born in Cumberland county, Pa., Sept. 6, 1815. His father, also named Joseph, and a native of County Tyrone, Ireland, came to America at the age of twenty-one years, and settled in Cumberland county, Pa., where he carried on farming. He married Jane Patterson, who was also a native of Ireland, and who came with her parents to this country when she was two years old. After marriage, Mr. and Mrs. Mehaffey settled in Washington county, where they died. They had nine children. Joseph, our subject, was married in Washington county, to Jane, daughter of William Chapman, and six children have been born to them: John L., William Alexander, Joseph H., Elizabeth J. (died at the age of eleven years), Sarah E. and Emma A. Mr. Mehaffey and wife are members of the United Presbyterian church of Hanover, of which he is an elder. He came to Beaver county in 1844, and has since been successfully engaged in farming here, owning 140 acres. He is a Democrat, and has held several township offices.

J. H. MEHAFFEY, merchant, P. O. Service, was born in 1827, in Beaver county, Pa. His grandfather, Joseph Mehaffey, came from Ireland and settled in Washington county, Pa. Of his family of three sons and five daughters, Joseph, the eldest son, came to this county in 1842, and purchased the farm on which he died; he married Jane Chapman, by whom he had six children, five yet living, J. H. being the youngest. Our subject was reared on the farm, where he remained until his twenty-fourth year, then engaged in huckstering, Pittsburgh being his shipping port; and for thirteen years he has been engaged in general mercantile business, the past eight years at his present place. He was married, in 1870, to Sarah, daughter of Allison Robertson, of this county, and two children have been born to them: Lillie Dickson and Fred Arden. Mr. Mehaffey is a member of the United Presbyterian church; he is a Democrat.

JUSTICE MERKEL, blacksmith, P. O. Water Cure, was born May 3, 1824, in Hesse-Darmstadt, Germany, in the village of Swingenberg. His father, Johannes Merkel, was a blacksmith in the German army, was with Napoleon Bonaparte in the war with Russia, and received three medals for bravery. He died in Bessengen, Hesse-Darmstadt, aged ninety-three years. His wife was Elizabeth Merkel, who died in Germany, aged eighty-three years. They had ten children, seven of whom are living. Justice learned his trade with his father, and was with him in the army at the age of fourteen years. He traveled seven years in Germany and came to America Oct. 1, 1847, and worked a while in the carriage shops at Albany, N. Y., and then went to Philadelphia, where he worked two years in the horse-shoe shops. After this he worked two years in Pittsburgh, and then two years in Stewardstown. In October, 1854, he came to Phillipsburg, where he has since carried on his trade. He was married here to Margaretha, daughter of Michael and Margaret Matter, and now supports his aged mother-in-law.

JAMES MILLER, farmer, P. O. Clinton, Allegheny county, was born in County Derry, Ireland, Jan. 18, 1822, is a son of John and Elizabeth (Scott) Miller. James came to this country with his mother, at the age of twenty-two years, and in 1845 he bought from John Hice the place where his brother John S. now lives. There the family settled, and from there the children started out for themselves and became good and useful citizens. James married Sarah, daughter of Hiram Lockhart, and they have eight children living: John, Joseph, Archibald, Robert, William, Elizabeth M., Margaret Ann and Sarah. Mr. Miller and wife are members of the United Presbyterian church, and he is an elder in the New Bethel church. He owns the farm of 134 acres where he lives, and about 200 acres in the neighborhood. He is a Democrat.

JOHN S. MILLER, farmer, P. O. Seventy-Six, was born March 26, 1830, in County Derry, Ireland, and is a son of John and Elizabeth (Scott) Miller. The father died in Ireland, and the mother in this country, in 1869, aged sixty-nine years. She had nine children: Mrs. Mary Sherrard, (who died in the old country), Mrs. Margaret McGarvey, Mrs. Jane Thompson, Mrs. Martha McGarvey, Mrs. Eliza A. McAllister, James, Archie (deceased), Joseph (of Kansas) and John S. The mother showed great courage in leaving her friends in Ireland, and bringing her family to this country. John S. has followed farming all his life, except nine years spent in mining in California. He owns 125 acres. His wife was Jane, daughter of John and Sarah (Carr) Mateer. She died, leaving six children: Sarah, Eliza A., Mary J., Martha, John S. and Andrew. Mr. Miller is a member of the New Bethlehem church, of which he has been a trustee. In politics he is a Democrat.

JOHN MONTGOMERY, farmer, P. O. Hookstown, is a grandson of James Montgomery, of Irish descent, who was a farmer and millwright for many years in Washington county, Pa., and Columbiana county, Ohio, where he died. He raised eleven children, of whom James was a tanner by trade, and worked many years near Frankfort with John Ewing, who taught him the trade. He finally bought a farm of 250 acres in Greene township, where his son John now resides. He died Aug. 14, 1866, aged fifty-six years. He was a Presbyterian, and took a deep interest in church and school affairs. Politically he was a Republican, as is his son. His wife was Sarah, daughter of John Stevenson, who built the Stevenson mill in Allegheny county. She died July 1, 1881, aged seventy-two years. She had two children, John and Nancy J., who farm the home place. They are members of the Mill Creek church.

ALEXANDER MOORE, farmer, P. O. Service, was born in Allegheny county, Pa., April 18, 1826. His paternal grandparents were John and Letitia (Watt) Moore, of Scotch-Irish Presbyterian stock. His father, Samuel W. Moore, was born in County Antrim, Ireland, and was the eldest of six children. He was born in October, 1797, came to America at the age of twenty, and died Feb. 14, 1873. He first landed in Philadelphia, where he worked about a year, and then came to Pittsburgh, and worked for a time on the abutment of the old Allegheny bridge. In 1831 he bought 300 acres of land, and in the fall of that year moved to the farm. His wife was Elizabeth, daughter of Alexander Liggett. She died Sept. 17, 1875, aged seventy-nine years. They were members of the United Presbyterian church of Service. Their children were Isabella, John L., Alexander, Letitia, Ann, Hugh, Eliza J. and Samuel N. Alexander has been a farmer all his life, and owns a farm. He has been a successful farmer, and has accumulated a competence.

JAMES MOORE, farmer, P. O. Hookstown, was born Feb. 16, 1817. His grandfather, Thomas Moore, was born near Easton, Pa., and married Margaret Hutchison, a Scotch lady. They settled in Washington county, but soon afterward came to Hanover township, and purchased 400 acres of land, where our subject now resides. Thomas Moore was one of the wealthy men of Beaver county, and owned about 1,000 acres of land. He had seven children: James, Nancy, Mary, Samuel, Aaron, Andrew and Margaret. Of these, James married Sarah, daughter of John and Martha (Mahan) Boyd. James Moore died at the age of eighty-four years, and his wife at the age of sixty-two. They were members of the United Presbyterian church: in politics he was a Democrat. Their children were John, Thomas, James, Margaret, Martha, Aaron and Sarah. Of these, James, the subject of this sketch, is the only one living. He married Rachel, daughter of Samuel Lindsey. They have three children: Martha A. (Mrs. Ewing), Mary A. and James E. Mr. and Mrs. Moore are connected with the Tomlinson Run United Presbyterian church; politically he is a Democrat.

SAMUEL W. MOORHEAD, farmer, P. O. Hookstown, was born July 30, 1817. The progenitor of the family in this country was Samuel Moorehead, a native of Scotland, and supposed to have been a descendant of the old Moore family of that country. He came to America, and first located in Wilmington, but soon afterward left his tools and an unfinished cellar to investigate lands further west. He settled in Washington county, and died there at an old age. His wife, Elizabeth Sproul, died at the residence of her son John, aged nearly 100 years, having been blind for seven years before her death. She had five children: John, James, David, Robert and Elizabeth (Mrs. McLaughlin). Of these John was a mason by trade, and owned a farm in Washington county, where he died, aged over seventy years. He married Sarah, daughter of John Buchanan. She died young, leaving five children: Samuel W., John, William, George, and Eliza J., who died young. Samuel W. followed farming in Washington and Allegheny counties, and in 1872 came to Greene township, where he has a farm of 101 acres. In 1843 he married Ellen Wilson, granddaughter of old Rev. Dr. Wilson. They had four children, only one of whom, Mrs. Sadie Campbell, is living. Mr. and Mrs. Moorhead are members of the United Presbyterian church. He is a Prohibitionist.

DAVID MORRIS, farmer, P. O. Service, was born "east of the mountains," Jan. 19, 1818. Isaac Morris, his grandfather, was born in Ireland, of Scotch descent; his wife was Mary Lockhart, and they lived in Bucks county, Pa., whence they moved to Allegheny county. They had eighteen children. Of these, Thomas settled in Greene township, Beaver county, and died there; his wife was Mary E. Benwood, and they had nine children, of whom David, the subject of this biography, lived in Greene township until he was twenty-one years old. He then lived two summers in Washington county. He married Elizabeth, daughter of William Schuler, and they have six children, John, George, William, Levi F., James A. and Eliza Ann. The parents are members of the Presbyterian church of Mount Olivet, which Mr. Morris helped to build, and in which he has been an elder. He has been a life-long Republican.

THOMAS J. MORRIS, pilot, P. O. Water Cure, was born in Wood county, W. Va.,

Oct. 9, 1820. His parents were Thomas and Nancy (French) Morris, the former of English and the latter of Scotch descent, and both died in West Virginia. They had three children: William, Thomas J. and Isabella. Thomas J., the only survivor, was educated in his native county, and at the age of sixteen made a trip to New Orleans with produce. On his return he commenced to learn the business of piloting in Pittsburgh, and has followed that occupation since 1846. His usual run is from Pittsburgh to Louisville, Ky. He was married in Rochester to Mary, daughter of Samuel Moore The latter erected the third house in Rochester, which is still standing, and died in 1884, aged ninety-six years. His father, James Moore, cut a road across the mountains, and settled near New Brighton. The children had to be taken to the blockhouse at night to avoid a massacre by the Indians. Mr. and Mrs. Morris have seven children: James H., Charles T., Alfred L., Clinton H., Frank R., George S. and Carrie A. Mr. and Mrs. Morris and daughter are members of the Presbyterian church of Phillipsburg. Mr. Morris is a Democrat. His maternal grandfather, William French, located at the present site of Williamsport, Pa., which was destroyed by fire by the Indians, the family being saved by a friendly Indian. Of Mr. Morris' children, James H. is engaged in the coal and steam business at Allegheny City and Pittsburgh. He is married to Rebecca Shires, and has three children: Shires, Max and Lillie.

ALEXANDER MORROW, farmer, P. O. Seventy-Six, was born Sept. 4, 1846, on the old Morrow homestead, in Hopewell township, Beaver county. His father, Alexander P. Morrow, was also born there. They are descendants of Hugh and Sarah (Herdman) Morrow, natives of Ireland, and probably of Scotch descent. Our subject was educated in the schools of his native county, and has been a successful farmer. He owns about 160 acres of land, besides a gristmill, which was formerly operated by the Anderson and Bock families. Mr. Morrow married Mary J., daughter of Robert McBride, and they have had nine children, eight of whom are living: Ida M., Sadie, Minnie, Lulu W., Lizzie B., John Lee, Charley B. and Myrtle Pearl; Alexander H. died Jan. 17, 1881. Mr. Morrow is a Democrat, and has held township offices.

WILLIAM MORROW, farmer and stockman, P. O. Seventy-Six, is a grandson of Hugh Morrow and a son of Alexander P., one of the large landholders of Beaver county. William was born on the old Morrow homestead, in Hopewell township, Aug. 14, 1849, and was educated in his native county. He worked for his father until six months after he reached his majority, then began for himself. He was married, Dec. 29, 1872, to Miss Melvine Jane, daughter of Henry Twiford, of West Virginia. She was born in Independence township Jan. 12, 1851; was educated in Raccoon township, and resided with her grandparents until her marriage. They have seven children now living: Laura B., Sadie A., Alexander P., William Wilson, Mary J., Seth W. and Phoebe A. The parents are members of the United Presbyterian church of New Bethlehem, and Mr. Morrow has been teaching in the Sabbath-school for seven years. Politically he is a Democrat, has held the office of school director, and has been reëlected for three years more.

JOHN MORROW, farmer, P. O. Ethel Landing, was born in Hopewell township May 21, 1844. His grandfather, Hugh Morrow, was born in the North of Ireland, of Scotch descent, came to this country when a young man and settled on the old Morrow homestead, in Hopewell township. John Morrow was educated in the county and became a farmer. He married Fannie, daughter of James Alexander, and their children are J. Alexander, William J., John, Hugh, Nancy J., Mary and Edith L. Mrs. Morrow died Nov. 17, 1886, aged thirty-nine years. She was a member of the United Presbyterian church. Mr. Morrow is a Democrat, and has held the offices of supervisor and school director.

JAMES MULLEN, glass worker, P. O. Water Cure, was born in Philadelphia May 6, 1832. His parents, George and Catherine (McLaughlin) Mullen, were both natives of County Derry, Ireland. They came to America in 1818, and settled in Philadelphia where they lived many years. In 1835 they removed to Pittsburgh, where the father followed the blacksmith trade, and died at the age of seventy-two years. The mother died young. They had seven children. James began labor in the Fort Pitt Glass Works, and has followed the business in different places for forty-four years, becoming one of the finest glass blowers in Western Pennsylvania. He was in the employ of Bakewell, Pierce & Co., for twenty-nine years, and was one or the originators and stockholders of the Phœnix Glass Company in 1880. Since 1883 he has been employed by George A. McBeth & Co., in the Keystone Glass Works, at Pittsburgh. He married Mary Milligan, who died in 1871. Three children are the result of this union, all living: Ella E., a well-known singer in Pittsburgh, now married to W. J. Mellon, a prominent attorney of Beaver, Pa.; George V. and Agnes B. Mr. Mullen politically is a Democrat.

JAMES NELSON was born May 4, 1804. The first of the family to settle in this country was William Nelson, who was born in Ireland and came to America with five children: John, Matthew, James, Anna and Margaret. The mother died on the voyage. William Nelson settled in Beaver county, four miles northwest of Service. The first Seceder's congregation of Service was formed at his house, and he was a prominent member. His son Matthew married Hannah Hunter, and both died in Greene township. They had ten children: John, William, David, Mary, Esther, James, Alexander, Margaret, Samuel and Nancy. James Nelson married Jane, daughter of Hezekiah and Nancy (McCullough) Wallace. She was born April 20, 1811, and is the mother of nine children: John, Hezekiah W., Mrs. Hannah Ewing, Matthew, Mrs. Nancy Ewing, Mrs. Martha Swearingen, Susan M. (wife of Dr. F. D. Kerr, of Hookstown), David A. and Esther J. Mr. and Mrs. James Nelson were members of the United Presbyterian church, of which he was for forty years an elder. Politically he was formerly a Whig, but is now a Republican. During the anti-slavery excitement he aided and sheltered fugitive slaves. Hezekiah W. Nelson was reared and educated in Beaver county and Pittsburgh. He was lieutenant of Company H, 53d Regiment State Troops, in the Civil War, and served three months. He was sent to relieve General Kelly at New Creek, W. Va., and afterward spent much time in recruiting, and in the Christian commission. Politically he is a Republican. The old family name was spelled Nielson.

JOHN NELSON, farmer, P. O. Hookstown, was born May 23, 1830, on the old homestead, where he remained only one year, when his father removed to Greene township, where he lived until nine years of age, then lived on a farm near Service twelve years. In 1851 he returned to the homestead, then owned by the heirs of his grandfather, Hezekiah Wallace. After living there ten years he was married March 31, 1861, and then settled on a farm of fifty acres, which was a part of the homestead. In the spring of 1867 he bought a farm on Service creek, where he resided until 1880, when he purchased a farm of 160 acres near Hookstown; he also owns another farm of 135 acres. His wife was Mary J., daughter of Thomas and Susan (Allen) Withrow, both natives of Chester county, Pa., and of Scotch-Irish descent. This union has been blessed with two children: Susan E. (wife of George R. Stewart, who has one son, Clyde N.) and Flora J. (now at school in Beaver). Mr. and Mrs. Nelson are members of the United Presbyterian church, of which he is an elder. He is a Republican. Early in life he taught school and conducted a saw-mill. He has also done much work as a surveyor.

MATTHEW NELSON, farmer, P. O. Harshaville, was born Dec. 4, 1839, on Service creek, in Greene township, where his parents, James and Jane Nelson, resided for about twelve years. He was reared and educated in this county, and has been a farmer all his life, with the exception of the time spent in the army. He enlisted Aug. 22, 1861, in Company F, 46th Regiment, and served over three years, being honorably discharged in September, 1864. He was in General Banks' campaign in the Shenandoah Valley; was with General Pope on his retreat from Cedar Mountain; was captured at Chancellorsville, and taken to Libby prison. He was shortly afterward paroled, and when exchanged, joined the regiment in Tennessee. He was in the engagement at Buzzard Roost, Resaca, Kenesaw Mountain, Dallas and Peach Tree Creek, South Mountain and Antietam, and his brigade was the first to enter Atlanta. He had typhoid fever at the time of the battle of Gettysburg. Mr. Nelson was married, Sept. 21, 1865, to Hattie, daughter of John Calhoun, and sister of Captain Thomas Calhoun. This union has been blessed with three children: Rosella J., Frank E., and Ernest J., who died Jan. 16, 1881. Mr. and Mrs. Nelson are members of the United Presbyterian church. He is a Republican.

JAMES NELSON, mechanic, P. O. New Sheffield, was born Aug. 11, 1814, on the banks of the Ohio river, in Beaver county. His grandfather, John Nelson, a native of Ireland and of Scotch descent, a farmer by occupation, died in Pittsburgh. His son, John Nelson, was a farmer and died in Pittsburgh, aged ninety-five years. His wife was Elizabeth, daughter of Nicholas Conly, who was a soldier in the Revolution, serving all through the war. Mrs Elizabeth Nelson died on the farm where James Nelson now resides, in 1884, aged eighty-six years. She had two children: James and Mary (Mrs. Maratta). She was one of a family of twenty children, who lived to maturity. John Nelson was a well-read man, and had the most extensive library in the neighborhood. He fought in the War of 1812, and received injuries from which he suffered concussion of the brain. James Nelson attended the common schools, and at the age of fourteen began learning the trade of steam engine building. He served an apprenticeship of seven years, at the close of which he went into partnership with his employers, Samuel Stackhouse and James Thomson. The firm eventually became James Nelson & Co., and continued until 1862, when Mr. Nelson went to St. Louis, where he built two coasting monitors for the U. S. navy, the "Etlah," and the "Shiloh." After the war he returned to Pittsburgh, and again engaged in engine building till 1876, when he removed to Hopewell township where he owns a farm of 146 acres. In 1850 he was elected to the executive department of the water works in Pittsburgh, and filled the office with ability for twelve years. He was one of the founders of the Mercantile Library Association, formerly the Merchants and Mechanics Institute. His life has been one of great activity and usefulness. He has never married. He was formerly a Whig, and is now a Republican.

SAMUEL NELSON, farmer, P. O. Hookstown, was born in August, 1815, on the homestead where he now resides. His father, Mathew Nelson, was a native of County Armagh, Ireland, and when four years old came to this country with his father, William. Mathew Nelson married Hannah Hunter, who died on the farm now owned by Samuel. They were members of the United Presbyterian church, of which Mr. Nelson was an elder for many years. He was a fluent speaker, and was identified with the old Whig party. Samuel was reared and educated in this county. He was the youngest son, and retained the homestead farm, which he has greatly improved. He is a member of the United Presbyterian church; politically he was formerly a Whig, and is now a Republican. He has been township auditor for several years, and justice of the peace ten years. In 1878 he was elected county commissioner, and served three years.

THOMAS NICHOLSON (deceased), whose portrait appears elsewhere in this work, was the first superintendent of schools for Beaver county. He was emphatically a self-made man, having had no early educational advantages, and was compelled to support himself from a very youthful age. His parents, John and Margaret (Hays) Nicholson, were natives of Ireland, and lived in Lancaster county, Pa., where our subject was born on Aug. 26 of that year. From early childhood until 1833 he lived in Washington county, and removed in the last named year to Hanover township, this county. At first he taught a subscription school, and afterward opened an academy at Frankfort in company with Rev. James Sloan. Nearly all the time of his residence here he filled the office of justice of the peace. In 1844 he was elected to the legislature on the Whig ticket, and served three terms; in 1867 he was again elected to the same position, which he held two terms. For the last three years of his legislative service he was a member of the committee of ways and means. While an ardent champion of the Republican party, he was fair to his opponents, and was influential in debate. A faithful laborer in the cause of free education, temperance and the abolition of slavery, he was respected alike by his allies and opponents. He knew when to say a word in time, and killed a bill to prohibit the free range of cattle with these words: "Great God! What will you do with the poor woman's cow?" Resigning the office of assemblyman at the close of the last session to which he was elected, Mr. Nicholson accepted the position of cashier of the state treasury, which he held under four preceding treasurers, being often left in entire charge, and without giving bond. During the last term of such service, under treasurer Mackey, he was obliged to resign on account of ill health, and returned to Frankfort, where a long life of usefulness was brought to a close Jan. 14, 1872. During his judicial service he labored to prevent litigation among his fellow citizens, and was known in the legislature as the uncompromising foe of extravagance with public funds. For a helpmeet Mr. Nicholson espoused Rebecca, daughter of David and Mary Stewart, of Ireland. She was a native of Washington county, Pa., and died at Frankfort Springs Dec. 12, 1887, in her eighty-first year. Mr. and Mrs. Nicholson were communicants in the Methodist Episcopal church. Their only children now living are Mary T., wife of Thomas Bigger, of Frankfort Springs, and Thomas C., of Altoona, Pa. The latter was for some time editor of the *Argus*, in Beaver, where he subsequently studied law. He practiced for some time in Paola, Kas., and served as lieutenant in the 140th Regiment, P. V. I. John H., the eldest child of Thomas Nicholson, died at Macomb, Ill. David S. died at Fairview, W. Va. Margaret, wife of Dr. J. A. Bingham, died in Frankfort Springs. Eliza Jane died at the age of six years.

ALEXANDER NICKLE, farmer, P. O. Kendall, was born Nov. 18, 1824, in Washington county, near Frankfort Springs, where his parents, David and Mary (Murrey) Nickle resided. The latter's mother, Mary Murrey, died at the home of her daughter, Mrs. Margaret Kevan, aged eighty years. Our subject's parents were of Scotch origin. The father died aged seventy-seven, and the mother aged seventy-one years. They belonged to the Associate church, of which he was an elder. They had eight children: James, George, William, David, Elizabeth, Mathew, Alexander and Margaret. Alexander was reared and educated in this county, became a farmer and owns 124 acres. He was married, in October, 1866, to Mrs. Minerva A. Stevenson, *nee* Evans. They have had three children: John C. C., James E. and Mary V. Mr. and Mrs. Nickle are members of the United Presbyterian church of Hookstown, in which he has been an elder ever since the war. He is a Democrat, and has been supervisor eleven years.

MATTHEW NICKLE, farmer, P. O. Hookstown, was born July 7, 1822, and was raised and educated in this county. His father, David Nickle, was born in 1781, near Edinburgh, Scotland, and was a merchant in his native country. His wife was Mary Morrow. They had five children born in Scotland: James, George, William, David and Elizabeth. They came to this country in 1820, and settled near Frankfort Springs, where the old Dr. McElwee place now is. They were members of the old King's Creek Seceder's church under Dr. John Anderson's charge. They subsequently moved to the northwestern part of the township, where the father died in 1847, aged eighty-six years. The mother died at the home of her son, Alexander. They had three children born in this country: Matthew, Alexander and Margaret. Matthew married, Aug. 7, 1847, Margaret Patterson, of Carroll county, Ohio. She died, leaving seven children: John B., Thomas M., Alexander M., James, Mary (who died at the age of sixteen years), Margaret R. and William P., the adopted son of Alexander and Mary Scott, of Carroll county, Ohio. Mr. Nickle was married, on second occasion, to Mrs. Jane Hall, daughter of James Bigger. Mr. and Mrs. Nickle are members of the Tomlinson Run United Presbyterian church, of which he has been an elder for fifteen years. He has been a hard working, successful business man, and has accumulated a property of 450 acres. He is a Democrat, and has filled several township offices.

DAVID NICKLE, farmer, P. O. Frankfort Springs, was born Nov. 13, 1834, in Hanover township. His grandfather, David Nickle, was a native of Scotland, and was married there to Mary Murray. He came to America with his son James was twelve years old. He had eight children: James, George, William, David, Matthew, Alexander, Eliza and Margaret. The grandfather settled in Hanover township, where he died. He was an elder in the Seceder's church. In politics he was a Democrat. James Nickle married Jane Dobbin, from West Virginia, and both lived and died in this township. They were members of the United Presbyterian church. Their children were Mary, Jane, David, Leonard, James, John, Mathew, Margaret and Ann. David married Eliza A., daughter of James Bigger, and they have one son. Robert J., born Dec. 18, 1861. Mr. and Mrs. Nickle are members of the Presbyterian church, of which he is an elder. Politically he is a Democrat.

JOHN NICKLE, farmer, P. O. Kendall, was born May 7, 1840. His grandfather, David, and his father, James, came from Scotland when the latter was eight years old, and both died in this county. James Nickle married Jane, daughter of James and Jane Dobbin, natives of Ireland, and ten children were born to this couple: Mary, Jane, David, Leonard, James, John, Matthew, Margaret, Charles D. and Anna. John was born on the homestead, and followed farming until the war. He enlisted Aug. 22, 1862, in Company H, 140th Regiment, and participated in many engagements, among which were the Wilderness, Cold Harbor, Spottsylvania and Chancellorsville. He was at Mine Run, near Petersburg, and lost his right leg. He afterward returned home, has since followed farming, and now owns 138 acres. July 9, 1879, he married Belle, daughter of Andrew and Eliza (McCready) Moore. They have one child, Anna Orra Ethel, born Nov. 23, 1886. Mr. and Mrs. Nickle are members of the Mill Creek Presbyterian church; in politics he is a Republican.

CHARLES OBNEY, farmer, P. O. Service, was born at Montour's Run, Allegheny county, Pa. When he was but fourteen years old he came to Beaver county, and lived in Independence township for ten years, on the farm where Robert Gorsuch now resides. At the age of eighteen years he commenced working out for other people. He married Mary, daughter of John Ralston. She was born on King's creek, Washington county, and died Oct. 14, 1885, leaving two children now living: John R. and William A. Of these John R. married Elizabeth Bell, and had seven children: Charles O., Alice Bell, Mary I., Emma I., Cora E., Annette O. and James C. Charles Obney married for his second wife Eliza J. Shillito, who was born at Service, Beaver county. Both are members of the United Presbyterian church of Service, and take a deep interest in church affairs. Politically Mr. Obney is a Republican. He has been supervisor, and is now school director.

JOSEPH PALMER, decorator, P. O. Water Cure, was born in Falkenau-bei-Heide, Bohemia, Feb. 18, 1845. His father, Joseph Palmer, Sr., was an expert decorator on glass, and early in life our subject evinced a love for the profession, in which he has since proven himself so proficient. He learned his trade with his uncle, August Palmer, whose son, William, is now in a factory in New York City. Joseph Palmer was in business in Germany for twenty years, having twenty employes under him. He came to America in 1883, and after remaining in New York City three years, in 1886 came to Phillipsburg, where he is engaged in the Phœnix Glass Works. He has been twice married; his first wife Helene Paul, died in Germany, leaving two sons, Joseph and Richard, who are employed in the glass works. His present wife, Caroline Budelmeyer, is a native of Germany and the mother of one child.

CAPTAIN A. H. PARR. P. O. Georgetown, is a son of Abraham S. Parr, who was a blacksmith, and died in Georgetown, Dec. 30, 1839, in his thirty-ninth year. His wife was Mary A. Hague, who was born near Hagerstown, Pa., and died Oct. 9, 1866, aged seventy-five years. She was the mother of five children by her first husband, Frederick Ebbert, viz.: Capt. George W., Theodore, Harrison, Mary A. and Susan. By her second husband, Mr. Parr, she had eight children: Sarah M., William J., Parthenia, Myrtilla, Andrew H., Lucinda B., Jessie S. and John Q. A. Andrew H. was born Jan. 14, 1831, in Georgetown, and at the age of fourteen became cabin boy on the river, and has worked his way to his present position. He has been with J. C. Risher & Co. for sixteen years, and is now running on the tow boat "Smoky City" between Pittsburgh and Louisville. He married Lizzie H., daughter of James Calhoon. They have nine children living: Mary A., J. Frank, Flora B., Quincy A., Parthenia C., Jackman T. S., Myrtilla M., Lizzie R. and Homer S. K. The family are members of the Methodist church. Captain Parr is a Republican. During the war he was for a time on the government boat, steamer "Melnotte," on the Cumberland and Tennessee rivers, carrying troops and forage.

JAMES PETERS, farmer, P. O. Harshaville, is of Scotch descent, his grandfather, Peters, going from that country and settling in County Antrim, Ireland, where the family became well-to-do, and were members of the Presbyterian church. The father of our subject, John Peters, married Mary, daughter of Peter Madill, and had eight children. James, the youngest, was born in 1814, and was educated in his native country. He came to this country when a young man, and first settled in Pittsburgh, where he was employed in a wholesale grocery about six years. In 1844 he came to Hanover township. He was married to Rebecca, daughter of Samuel Kelley, who settled here in 1809. She was born in 1828, and is the mother of eleven children: Samuel, John, Sarah, Mary, Agnes, William, Cyntha, Alla, Minnie, Nettie and James. The parents are members of the Presbyterian church of Hookstown. Mr. Peters began life without means, and by industry and perseverance has accumulated a good home and property, owning over 400 acres of land. In politics he is a Republican.

JOHN R. PETERS, civil, mechanical and mining engineer, P. O. Georgetown, was born in New York City, June 19, 1818. The first of the family came to England with William the Conqueror. They came to New England at an early day, and settled in New Hampshire. Absalom, grandfather of John R., was aide-de-camp to General Bailey in the Revolutionary War. He was best known as Gen. A. Peters. His father was a nail maker in New Hampshire when slaves were employed to make them. John R., Sr., son of Gen. A. Peters, was a wholesale cotton merchant in New York, and sent the first vessels to Mobile to bring cotton to the North. He was familiarly known as "Alderman Peters," having served as alderman several years. He died in New York City, in 1858, aged seventy-four years. His wife was Abbey Covil, of Providence, R. I., and they had nine children. John R., our subject, was educated in New York City, and was in mercantile business a number of years; then entered the University of the City of New York, where he took a course in mathematics, Spanish and other languages, paying special attention to engineering. He was one of a corps of engineers in Allegheny county, N. Y., under Chief Major Brown, who died in Russia. In 1843 he was attached to the first embassy to China under President Tyler's administration. Fletcher Webster being secretary of legation, and Dr. E. K. Kane, the arctic explorer, the surgeon. In 1845 he returned to America, and brought with him the Chinese collection which was exhibited in Boston and New York, and at the Philadelphia Exposition. In 1865 he went to West Virginia to prospect for oil for a New York firm. He finally came to Beaver county, where he developed several wells in Greene township, near Georgetown. He left here in 1866, and spent twelve years in Morris county, N. J., directing mining operations. He returned to this county in 1878. He was married to Susan M., daughter of Capt. Richard Calhoon, and they have three children: Lizzie, Harrie and Grace.

SAMUEL PLUNKET (deceased) was a son of Isaac and Lydia (Hannah) Plunket. The father died when Samuel was fourteen years old, and the mother died about eleven years later. Samuel was the second eldest child, and the burden of raising the rest of the family fell principally on him. He remained with them until they were grown up. He had two sisters, Mary and Bettie, and four brothers, John, James, William and Robert. The boys all learned trades except William, who died young. John was educated for a United Presbyterian minister; Samuel worked for several years by the month, then learned the carpenter's trade, which he followed for a time in Pittsburgh. He then bought 151 acres where he resided until his death March 13, 1888. By other purchases he increased his property to 341 acres. His widow is Margaret, daughter of John Spence, a native of Ireland, who lived to be nearly 100 years old. Of Mr. Plunket's children, five are living: John S., Isaac, Thomas, Amanda J. and Ida S. The parents were members of the United Presbyterian church, of which Mr. Plunket was an elder. He was a Republican and had been assessor and supervisor of his township.

BIOGRAPHIES—SOUTH SIDE. 881

THE POES. Of the early settlers along the Ohio river, no better examples of strong physical form and development, together with heroic daring, were to be found than those of Adam and Andrew Poe, two brothers who were born near the present city of Frederick, Md., and who migrated to the West in the year 1774, settling in what was then Westmoreland, but subsequently Washington, county. Later, in life, they were residents respectively of the vicinity of Hookstown and Georgetown. The contest which these stalwarts had with Big-foot, the mighty Indian chief, in the autumn of 1781, has been so frequently told that it need not be related here. Suffice it to say, no more thrilling hand-to-hand contest has ever been chronicled than that in which Andrew Poe (not Adam, as the old story has it) measured strength and prowess with the Ajax of the forest, together with the smaller Indian who was with him when the conflict ensued. Both these sons had large families, who became prominent citizens and members of Beaver and other counties. Andrew died near Hookstown, in 1831, more than an octogenarian, while Adam died at Massillon, Ohio, during the presidential campaign of 1840, at some ninety-three years of age. He had been invited to attend a mass meeting at which General Harrison was the chief speaker, and having drunk a large quantity of ice-water, became ill and never recovered. His only surviving child, Sarah, the seventh of ten children, died near Congress, Wayne county, Ohio, in March, 1888, in the ninety-eighth year of her age.

WILLIAM J. PORTER, merchant, P. O. Water Cure, is of Scotch ancestry. His great-great-grandfather fought under Sir William Wallace, and fled to the North of Ireland, where he died. His son returned to Scotland, where he was married and died. His son, James, grandfather of William J., came to America and settled in Findley township, Allegheny county, then a part of Virginia. He died near Clinton, aged seventy years. He married an eastern lady of Scotch descent, who died aged sixty-five years. They had seven boys and two girls, and all went to Ohio except Samuel, who died in Clinton, aged seventy-one years. He married Elizabeth Kindley, also of Scotch descent. The name was formerly spelled Ginley or Kindley. She died in Burgettstown, Pa., aged seventy-eight years. She had seven sons and three daughters. Of these William J. married Mary Anna, daughter of Isaac and Margaret (Greenlee) Onstott. Mr. Porter followed farming in early manhood. In 1863 he removed to Pittsburgh, Pa., where he resided until 1873, when he came to Phillipsburg, and has since been engaged in the mercantile business. Mr. and Mrs. Porter are members of the Presbyterian church of which he is an elder. They have no children, but their home is brightened by the presence of two adopted nieces: Robba and May Porter. The former is organist in the Presbyterian church.

ROBERT POTTER, farmer, P. O. Bellowsville, is a native of Venango county, Pa., born June 10, 1806, son of James and Mary (Quigley) Potter, both of Irish descent; former born and reared on a farm, latter a daughter of James Quigley. They have five sons and three daughters, Robert being the eldest. James Potter's father, Robert, came from Ireland to America about 1774, and soon thereafter settled in Allegheny county, Pa., where he died. Our subject remained at home until the age of thirty, and then moved to his present place. Same year (1835) he married Margaret Irvin Braden, by whom he had five children, three now living: William, Emily (now Mrs. Dunn) and John; the deceased are James and Mary. The mother dying in 1843, Mr. Potter married, in 1855, Rosanna, daughter of James and Agnes (Baker) Reed, of this county. Three children blessed this union: Mary Ida (now deceased), Robert Calvin, at home, and Washington M., at present a student at Mercer College. Mr. Potter was for thirty years a justice of the peace; was a jury commissioner, and held other positions of trust. He is a member of the Presbyterian church. In politics he is a Democrat.

THOMAS POTTS, JR., pilot, P. O. Georgetown, was born Dec. 15, 1827. His grandfather, Noah Potts, was a native of Wales, immigrated to Pennsylvania, and married Barbara Hagethorn, of German descent. They came to Beaver county, and he was on one occasion chased by the Indians, and saved his life by swimming the river at the head of Georgetown Island. He and his wife both died near Georgetown, each aged over eighty years. Their children were Sarah, Thomas, Rachel, James, Polly and Robert. Of these Thomas married Nancy, daughter of Nathan Potts; they lived to be eighty-two years old, and raised twelve children. Thomas, our subject, was a cabin boy when quite young, became a pilot at the age of seventeen years, and has been captain or pilot ever since, at times filling both positions, and has been in the employ of John A. Wood & Son for the last nineteen years. He married Ann, daughter of John Scott, and she has borne him five children: Luella (wife of Harry Hughes), Mrs. Harriet McCormick, Mrs. Isadore Hisley (now residing in Germany), Estella H. and Thomas H. Mr. Potts is a Democrat.

FARMER PURDY, farmer, P. O. Frankfort Springs, is a son of James Purdy, a native of Ireland, whose parents and two sisters died on the ocean while coming to America, when he was but eleven years old. He (James) landed in Philadelphia, and remained with his aunt for some time; then went to Lancaster county, Pa., where he married Mary, daughter of Gregor Farmer. They finally moved to Allegheny county, near Mansfield, and died near Clinton, Pa. They had ten children. Of these, Farmer was born Feb. 11, 1803, was educated in Allegheny county, and was married there to Miss Esther Richmond: She died in this county, leaving nine children, three of whom are living: James, John and Esther. His present wife is Mary, daughter of Thomas Frazer. She has two children: Maria and Sadie, the former being the wife of James Hood. Mr. and Mrs. Purdy are members of the United Presbyterian church, of which he has been an elder since 1854. He owns a farm of 150 acres. He is a self-made man, and his only capital when he started in life was energy and perseverance. He is a Republican. James Purdy was a soldier in the Revolution, and one of the heroes of Valley Forge. His grandsons, William and John, enlisted in Company H, 140th Regiment, and William was lost at the battle of Spotsylvania.

ELI RAMSEY, farmer, P. O. Kendall, was born Dec. 3, 1822, in Hanover township, this county. His grandparents, Robert and Mary (Mitchel) Ramsey, resided in Hanover township, Washington county. They had fourteen children, all of whom lived to maturity. Robert, Jr., was married twice. His first wife, Susannah Leeper, died, leaving four children: Robert, James, William and Mary. His second wife was Mrs. Deborah Whitehall, nee Stephens. She had three children: Eliza, Eli and Jane. Robert Ramsey, Jr., came to Hanover township, Beaver county, April 1, 1812, and died May 9, 1862. His wife died Sept. 10, 1830. Eli was reared and educated in this county, and has been married twice. His first wife was Elizabeth Stephenson, who died June 23, 1850, leaving four children: Thomas S., Robert M., Louis and Elizabeth J. His present wife is Mary E., daughter of Andrew and Eliza A. (McCready) Moore. She has three sons: James P. M., Andrew G. and Joseph W. The parents are members of the United Presbyterian church. Mr. Ramsey is a Republican, and has been school director twelve years. His bachelor half-brother, Robert, resides with him, and owns 100 acres of land. Eli owns 150 acres.

F. R. RAMSEY, farmer, P. O. Hookstown, was born Sept. 2, 1845. His great-grandfather, Robert Ramsey, lived near Florence, on King's Creek. He was one of the pioneers of Western Pennsylvania, was of Scotch descent, and the father of fourteen children. Of these, Robert married twice. By his first wife, Susannah Leeper, he had five children, and by his second, Deborah Whitehill, three. Robert and Susannah Ramsey were members of the Presbyterian church. Of their children, William L., born July 4, 1814, on King's Creek, Beaver county, came to Greene township in 1840, and in 1845 bought fifty acres of land. He married Mary J., daughter of William and Elizabeth (McHarg) Ewing. She died March 13, 1881, aged sixty-two years. She had five children, of whom Frank R., our subject, is the only one living. He went west in 1867, and was married in Davenport, Iowa, Feb. 16, 1869, to Mareta R., daughter of Dr. A. S. Maxwell. She was born March 25, 1850, in Holmes county, Ohio. Mr. Ramsey has spent considerable time in the West, was for some time engaged in the drug business in Davenport, and also followed farming for a while. He now occupies the home farm of 212 acres. Mr. and Mrs. Ramsey are members of the Hookstown Presbyterian church, and he is a fifth degree member of the I. O. O. F. in Iowa, and a Master Workman in the A. O. U. W.. Davenport, Iowa. They have six children: Jennie E., William M., Lottie M., Blanche A., John W. and Nellie M. Mr. Ramsey is extensively engaged in the fruit business. His brother, Watson J., was an able, well-informed man, an elder in the Presbyterian church, and died Oct. 28, 1879, aged thirty-seven years. Mr. Ramsey's grandfathers, Robert Ramsey and William Ewing, were elders in the church at Mill Creek. The first apple trees in this section were planted by his great-grandmother Ewing, who brought apple seed with her from east of the mountains. Some of these trees yet remain on the farm where our subject resides. One-half mile distant from his farm was a blockhouse, where his great-grandparents and their neighbors took refuge from the Indians.

DAVID REED, farmer, P. O. Poe, was born in Hanover township Jan. 17, 1837. His grandfather, Adams Reed, was a native of Ireland, and settled in the eastern part of the United States. He was twice married. His son, Adams Reed, came to Beaver county with his father in 1812, and when he was sixteen years old his father purchased 100 acres of land from James Miller, the patentee. The grandfather died at the age of ninety-four. Adams Reed, father of David, married Susannah, daughter of David and Isabella (Adams) Beal, who were Quakers, and came from Westmoreland county. Adams Reed and his wife died on the old homestead; he at the age of ninety-two. They had seven children: William, Isabella, David, Margaret J., Martha Ann, Agnes and Rachel. William married Jane Ralston; Agnes married Joseph Bell; Rachel married William Strauss. David and Mrs. Rachel Strauss are the only ones now living. David inherited the home farm. He was married, June 28, 1860, to Hattie E. Durbin, who bore him five children: Anna, Joseph B., Agnes Bell, Minnie and Elizabeth. Mrs. Reed is a Methodist. Mr. Reed, politically, is a Republican.

T. JEFFERSON REED, farmer, P. O. Service, is a grandson of Andrew Reed, who came to Western Pennsylvania from the vicinity of Philadelphia at an early day. He had ten children: William, James, Moses, John, Andrew, Isabella, Mary, Dorcas, Samuel and Hannah. Moses was a thrifty farmer, and owned 100 acres of land. He married Mary A., daughter of Robert Toland, and had seven children: Andrew M., Thomas Jefferson, Susannah, Sarah J., Elizabeth, Matilda and Julia A., who died at the age of thirty years. The boys sold the old farm, and bought another of 200 acres, where they now reside. The farm is longer east and west, and the 45th degree line of the gas belt passes through the center of the place. There are now three gas wells on the place, each well of greater capacity than the first one drilled. Moses Reed was a Whig, and his sons are Democrats. Mr. Reed has in his possession an old music book, written one hundred and twenty-seven years ago by his grandfather's uncle. It was all done by his pen, and it is said to be as fine a piece of penmanship as can be produced to-day; some of the verses are written in Latin and translated into English. It is highly prized by music teachers to-day. He was a good scholar. His name was John.

WASHINGTON B. REED, farmer, P. O. Holt, is a native of Beaver county, Pa., born Jan. 14, 1825, a son of James and Agnes (Baker) Reed; former a farmer, latter a daughter of Michael Baker, of this county. They were the parents of eleven children, Washington B. being the eldest son. He remained on the home farm until twenty-one years of age, receiving a common-school education, and in 1851 married Eliza, daughter of Sampson and Agnes Kerr, of this county. To this union have been born seven children, all now living: Lizzie Alice, John Allen, Lewis Washington, Cornelius Weygnantd, Sampson Kerr, Harriet Isabella and Agnes Marie. With the exception of twelve years our subject has always lived on the farm which he now owns, originally consisting of 200 acres, now of 150, of which 100 are under high cultivation. Mr. Reed is a member of the Presbyterian church. All his life he has been one of the leading Democrats of the county, though never aspiring to any political office, but has served his township by filling several township offices to which he had been elected.

DAVID REID, farmer, P. O. Seventy-Six, was born in Hopewell township, Beaver county, March 21, 1820. His paternal grandfather was born on the ocean while his parents were crossing to this country. The family came from the North of Ireland, but were of

Scotch ancestry, and the name was formerly spelled Reed. The grandfather married a Miss Finnley, and settled in Fayette county, Pa., whence he removed to Allegheny county, and died near Clinton. He was a farmer and had eight children: Andrew, Samuel, William, James, Moses, Isabella, Mary and Dorcas. Of these Samuel was a farmer, and married Agnes, daughter of David Scott. They removed to Independence township, thence to Hopewell, and settled near what is now the village of Independence, where they both died. He died April 10, 1840, aged sixty-three years, and she at about the same age. They were members of the Associate church at Scottsville, known as the Ohio congregation, of which Samuel Scott was an elder from the age of nineteen years. They had six children: Jane, William, David, Maria, Samuel and Agnes. David received a common-school education, and adopted the business of farming, in which he has been successful, owning 160 acres. His wife is Mary, daughter of Thomas W. McKee, born in Ireland of Scotch ancestry, and came to America at the age of five years. They have four children: Agnes (Mrs. Purdy), Samuel, Elmer W. and Valeria A. The parents are members of the old Ohio congregation, and Mr. Reid is an elder. In politics he is a Republican.

WILLIAM RENDALL, miller. P. O. Frankfort Springs, was born March 28, 1831, in Seavington, Somersetshire, England, and is a son of Simon Rendall, who was a member of one of the oldest families in his native county. William was educated in his native country, and served a three years' apprenticeship at the milling business. He came to this country in 1853, and for four years worked at the "Black Rock" mill, near Buffalo, N. Y.; then six years in the "Pearl" mill in Allegheny City, and from 1863 to 1866 worked in various places; in September of the latter year he bought the Frankfort steam mill. He has made great improvements in the property, and has established a lucrative business. The capacity of the mill is fifty barrels per day. He was married, Sept. 5, 1861, to Eliza, daughter of Alexander and Elizabeth (Lawhead) Anderson, pioneers of Pine township, Allegheny county. Three children have been born to them: Asenath S., Walter A. and John S.

JAMES C. RITCHIE, farmer, P. O. Woodlawn, was born in Hopewell township March 10, 1824. The Ritchie family came from Center county, Pa., and is probably of Scotch descent. Robert, father of J. C., became an orphan in early childhood, and was raised by his uncle and aunt, Jonas and Jeanette Davis. They settled in Hopewell township in 1796. Robert was eighteen years old, and as they had no children he inherited the homestead, where he died at the age of eighty-four years. He was an industrious farmer, and member of the Presbyterian church of Mount Carmel. He married Elizabeth, daughter of William and granddaughter of Alexander Thomson, who came from Scotland, and settled near Chambersburg, Pa. Elizabeth Ritchie died in 1839, aged fifty-two years. She had eight children: Jane, Frances, Alexander, William, Robert, James C., Elizabeth and Jonas D. James C. was educated in his native county, and became a farmer. He was married, May 15, 1851, to Margaret, daughter of William and Phoebe (Williams) McDonald. Their children are William, Mattie, Robert and Phoebe. Robert was graduated in 1886 from Washington and Jefferson College, and is now a law student. Mr. and Mrs. Ritchie are members of Mount Carmel Presbyterian church. He is a Democrat, and was elected county auditor. In 1849 he was elected county commissioner, in 1853 and again in 1878, being the first man elected to that office a second term. He has been a school director over twenty years.

JAMES RUSSELL, farmer, P. O. Service, is a grandson of William and a son of James Russell. The latter was a farmer in Washington county, Pa., and died there. He married a Miss Scott, and they had eight children: Abraham, Jane, Samuel, Sarah, James, Mary, William and Margaret. Of these James was educated in Washington county, and was married there to Martha, daughter of James Dunlap. They have two children now living: Finley J. and Franklin. The latter is married, has two children, and is farming his father's place of 155 acres in Hanover township. Mr. and Mrs. James Russell are members of Mount Olivet church, of which he is a trustee. In politics he is a Democrat. He owns 235 acres of land, and is a successful farmer.

BIOGRAPHIES —SOUTH SIDE. 885

WILLIAM J. SALISBURY, farmer, P. O. Water Cure, was born in Sligo, near Pittsburgh, Sept. 2, 1835. His grandfather Salisbury died in Wheeling, W. Va., and was descended from an old English family. His son, James Salisbury, is yet living in Pittsburgh, where he was a glass blower and a manufacturer for some years. He was married to Lydia Gallagher, who is also living, and is the mother of six children who lived to maturity: Mary Ann, Elizabeth, William J., John, David and Henrietta. The parents celebrated, some years ago, their golden wedding, on which occasion the minister who united them, the Rev. Mr. Williams, was present. William J. Salisbury was educated in Pittsburgh, where he learned and followed the glass blower's trade. He went to California in 1863, and followed his trade there until 1873, when he returned to Pittsburgh. The next year he bought a farm of 100 acres of land in Moon township, where he now resides. He was married, in California, to Margaret J. Fuller, who was born in Nantucket, Mass., March 3, 1845. Mr. Salisbury is a Republican.

MICHAEL SCHADE, farmer and dairyman, P. O. Water Cure, was born in Gruenberg, Saxony, Germany, March 2, 1822, and is a son of Melchior and Rosina (Schmidt) Schade, both of whom died in Germany. They had twelve children, only six of whom reached maturity. Michael learned the trade of shoemaker in Germany. He came to this country in 1850, and followed his trade two years in Buffalo, N. Y. In 1852 he came to Independence township, and opened a small shop, where he carried on his trade until 1856. He then removed to New Scottsville, where he was postmaster, besides carrying on his trade until 1863, when he purchased a farm of sixty acres, to which he has added forty acres more, and owns two houses in Phillipsburg. He was married in Buffalo, to Miss Justine Klotz, who was born April 6, 1826, in the same town that her husband was born in. She had eight children, five living: Emma, Agnes, Rosa, Frank and Louis. Mrs. Schade died Dec. 19, 1880, a member of the Lutheran church. Mr. Schade has been school director six years, and also held the office of supervisor for one year.

HENRY G. SCHMOUTZ, farmer, P. O. Water Cure, was born in Würtemberg, Germany, Aug. 31, 1837. His parents, Gotlieb and Christine (Kapphahn) Schmoutz, came to America in 1840 and settled in Pittsburgh, where the father was a gardener. They had five children who lived to maturity: Caroline, Rachel, Henry G., Mary and Catharine. Henry G. worked in the glass works of McKee Brothers, in Pittsburgh, for twenty-four years. He came to Moon township in 1886, and bought of John Wilhelm the farm of 112 acres where he now resides. He was married in Pittsburgh to Caroline Shaffer. They have four children: William, Thomas, John and Flora. Mr. Schmoutz is a Republican.

DAVID SCOTT, a native of Aberdeen, Scotland, was educated when a boy for a merchant's profession, and, after attaining manhood, was sent to Philadelphia in the interests of a Liverpool firm, whose employment he entered at the time. He had been prepared for his new position by being made thoroughly conversant in the French language, owing to the fact that the trade of his firm was conducted largely with Frenchmen as well as Americans. Not long after his arrival in Philadelphia he espoused the patriot cause, and entered the army of Gen. Anthony Wayne, serving in the capacity of quartermaster. While his division was stationed at Fort Duquesne, now Pittsburgh, young David was sent with a company of men to Legionville, a short distance below Economy, on the Ohio, to aid in erecting a temporary fort. While engaged in its construction he met with the accident of having his right leg broken, which so disabled him that when he recovered the war was over. In compensation for this misfortune he was subsequently given by the government a 500-acre tract of land lying across the river from Legionville, about one mile from Economy, which he retained in his possession until the time of his death. Outside the learned professions, few men of his day obtained as liberal an education as he possessed, or as much general information. His legal advice was much sought by his neighbors, and, when given, was received with confidence. It passed into a general saying among his friends and associates that "if old Davy Scott said that was *law*, there was positively no use in consulting a lawyer." While Mr. Scott never sought any office, he received (under the old law) a life appointment as justice of the peace, a position which, it is needless to say, he filled with honor and credit. It was his custom, while occupying this official position, to hold court in his private residence every Saturday; and upon that day it was not an uncommon thing to see from twenty to fifty horses tied in front of the justice's door. When quite a young man he married Miss Jane McLellan, a native of Armagh, Ireland, although of Scotch parentage. Miss McLellan crossed the Atlantic in an ordinary sailing vessel, the trip being made in 105 days. The ceremony of marriage was performed in this country. They became the parents of a large family, many of whom arrived at distinction in later years, and nobly upheld the credit of the family name, which, upon the side of David, was rendered illustrious by its having once numbered royalty within its ranks, the ancestor thus noted being Robert Bruce, King of Scotland, to whom the line of descent could be clearly traced.

JOHN SCOTT, farmer, P. O. Holt. John Scott, the grandfather of the subject of this biography, married Margaret Steward, daughter of Elisha Robinson, of Maryland. He emigrated from Ireland to America, and became a resident of Washington county, Pa. His son William Scott, the eldest of seven children, married Frances Robinson. John Scott, the second son in a family of seven children, was born in 1809, in Washington county, Pa. The farm, and its varied labors, occupied his attention until his twentieth year, when he chose to become independent by mastering a trade, and for eighteen years thereafter was a successful cooper. In 1852 he purchased 180 acres of land, and at a later date 220 in addition, giving him the ownership of 400 acres, on which he and three sons reside. Mr. Scott married, in 1832, Nancy Gilmore, whose three children are William, David and Samuel. He married, for his second wife, Ellen, daughter of Elisha Stansbury, of West Virginia, whose children are McKendre M., Joseph L., L. H., E. S. and Charles W. All these sons have chosen the vocation of their father, and are industrious farmers. Mr. Scott and his family are members of the Methodist Episcopal church, he being its only survivor of the congregation of fifty-one years ago. He has been for thirty years one of its officers; for twenty years a steward; in 1850 assisted in building the Green Valley M. E. church, and in 1872 aided in the erection of the Mount Zion church of the same denomination; in politics he is a Republican, and has held positions of trust. His son David manifested his patriotism by joining the 140th P. V. I., and serving for three years during the Civil War. He was wounded in both feet by the same ball at Hackett's Run, and was also in the battle of Gettysburg. He died in December, 1880, in his thirty-seventh year.

M. M. SCOTT, farmer, P. O. Holt, was born in Raccoon township, Beaver county, Pa., in 1854, the eldest son of John and Ellen (Stansbury) Scott. He was reared on the farm where he was born, and received a good common-school education. In 1879 Mr. Scott visited Colorado to improve his health, and while there engaged in mining, but returned after one year. In 1885 he married Lynda M., daughter of John Springer, of Raccoon township, and two children were born to them: Catherine E. and John W. Mr. Scott is a member of the Methodist church. In politics he is a Republican.

J. L. SCOTT, farmer, P. O. Holt, was born in Raccoon township, Beaver county, Pa., in 1856, the second eldest son of John and Ellen (Stansbury) Scott. He received a good common-school education, and was reared to agricultural pursuits on the farm where he was born. He has bought a farm in the same township, and now lives on it. He was married, in 1881, to Lizzie A., daughter of John L. and Jane (Adams) Moore. He is a member of the Methodist church, and his wife of the United Presbyterian. Politically Mr. Scott is a Republican.

L. H. SCOTT, farmer, P. O. Holt, was born, in 1859, on the farm where he has always lived, in Raccoon township, Beaver county, Pa. He is the third son of John and Ellen (Stansbury) Scott, and was brought up to agricultural pursuits. In 1880 he married Jessie, daughter of William and Mary (Wallace) Barnes, by which union have been born two children: Mary Ellen and Alice Iona. Mr. and Mrs. Scott attend the services of the Methodist church. In politics he is a Republican.

WILLIAM SCOTT, farmer, P. O. Murdocksville, was born in Hanover township,

Washington county, Pa., Oct. 26, 1833. His grandfather, Joseph Scott, was born in the eastern part Pennsylvania, and was of Scotch descent. He was one of the early settlers of Washington county, and died there aged ninety-six years. He was a farmer. Both he and his wife, Martha Paden, were members of the Cross Roads Presbyterian church. They had five children: Benjamin S., Jane, Martha, Betsey and Joseph. Of these Joseph was born on the old homestead in 1799, and died there in 1878. He was a farmer, and married Isabelle, daughter of Samuel Nelson, a native of Hookstown, Beaver county, Pa. She bore him five children: Louisa, William, Margaret A., Elizabeth and Joseph. The parents were members of the Presbyterian church. William, our subject, was a farmer in Washington county until 1858, when he came to this county. Jan. 23, 1861, he married Agnes H., daughter of David Moreland She was born June 7, 1836, in Robinson township, Washington county, and is the mother of six children: Mary Bell, David M., James A., Jennie L., Ada Robertine and Leona A. Mrs. Scott is a member of the Hebron Presbyterian church. Mr. Scott is a successful farmer, and owns 163 acres, which he has greatly improved. In politics he is a Democrat.

SAMUEL SHAFER, blacksmith, P. O. Shafer's, is a son of Daniel Shafer, and was born in Moon township Jan. 16, 1829. He was reared and educated in Moon township, and learned his trade in the village of Scottsville with George Denny. He has a farm of ninety acres. His wife is Agnes, daughter of James McCallister, and they have seven children: Mary E., James M., Ann E., Emma R., William M., Daniel P. and Nancy J. The parents are active members of the Raccoon United Presbyterian church. Mr. Shafer has been a chorister about thirty-seven years, and Sunday-school superintendent two and one-half years. He takes a deep interest in all things pertaining to the welfare of the community. He has been a Republican ever since the inception of that party, having previously been a Whig.

JOHN SHAFER, farmer, P. O. Shafer's, was born on the old homestead, in Moon township, June 9, 1831. His father, Daniel, was born in Pennsylvania east of the mountains, and settled on Raccoon creek in Independence township, but subsequently came to Moon township, where he died. His wife was Mary, daughter of Samuel Wade, and they had nine children: Sarah A., William, Eliza J., Samuel, John, Daniel, James, Mary and Joanna. John Shafer is by trade a wagon maker, which business he followed in New Scottsville from 1854 to 1865. He then returned to Moon township, where he owns a farm of 147 acres. He married Esther. daughter of John McClester. They have seven children: Lizzie (Mrs. Bell), Anna M., Frank E. (in Missouri), Mattie J., Ella A., John M. and James A.

. J. B. SHANE, M. D., P. O. Service, is a native of Raccoon township, this county, born in 1832. a son of Cornelius and Mary (Bryan) Shane (parents of nine sons and three daughters), the latter a daughter of John Bryan. Cornelius Shane, also a native of this township, by occupation a farmer, was the second son of Timothy Shane. The latter came from Ireland to America at an early day, took part in the Revolutionary War; he was the father of five sons and two daughters. J. B. was reared on the farm where he was born, and for some time followed school-teaching; then commenced the study of medicine with his brother, Dr. S. C. Shane, and attended college at Cleveland; following which he located in Raccoon township, and has since practiced his profession here. He was married, in 1857, to Lizzie, daughter of James Craig, and eight children were born to them, six now living: Maggie (now Mrs. George), Mary Bell (at home), William P., Joseph W., Ernest Elmor and Thomas N. The entire family are members of the United Presbyterian church. In politics the Doctor is a Republican.

ᐟ ROBERT SHANNON (deceased) was a son of Robert Shannon, Sr., and grandson of Robert Shannon, a native of Ireland who came to America before the Revolution, and settled in Independence township. He took up a tract of several hundred acres, and died here in 1831, aged seventy-four years. His wife Isabella died in 1843, also aged seventy-four years. They had five sons and five daughters. Of the sons, Robert, father of our subject, a farmer by occupation, was born in Independence township, Beaver county. Pa,, where he also died, aged about forty years. His wife was Mary, daughter of William Thomson, and their children were William, Thomson, Robert, Lindsey, and Rosa Bell (deceased in 1881,) who married William A. Kennedy. Robert, our subject, was a farmer, went to California in 1852, and remained five years. He drove a pair of mules over the plains with a company from Pittsburgh, and worked in the gold mines. His health failing he returned to the old homestead, and there died Nov. 4, 1871. He was married, in 1859, to Nancy A., daughter of Alexander Thomson, and she is the mother of two children: Alexander Thomson (deceased) and Jennie M. (wife of Edward Snyder). Mrs. Shannon is a member of Raccoon church. She owns a valuable property of 312 acres, including the old homestead.

GEORGE SHILLITO was born in Ireland, and brought to America at the age of eleven years. His parents settled near Germantown, Pa. George served in the Revolution, and at the termination of that contest married Miss Nancy Miller, of Robinson's Run, Washington county, Pa., and settled in Raccoon township in April, 1812. He became the father of seven children: Samuel, John, Elizabeth, Jane, James, Mary and Ebenezer. He died at the age of eighty-four years, on the old homestead; and his wife, in Hanover township, at the age of ninety-one years.

W. W. SHILLITO, retired farmer, P. O. Service, was born in Raccoon township, Beaver county, Pa., in 1831, eldest son of James and Violet (Smith) Shillito, who were married in 1830, and had eight children, seven of whom are yet living. James, at the age of nineteen, learned the trade of tanner and currier, which he carried on in addition to farming, having received from his father, in 1828, fifty acres of land. George Shillito, grandfather of W. W., came to this county from Allegheny county, about 1812, and here purchased 424 acres of land near where Service church now stands. He married Nancy Miller, who became the mother of eight children, James being the fourth son. Our subject has always lived on the old homestead and followed agricultural pursuits, having also learned the trade of tanner and currier. He married, in 1858, Jane, daughter of Samuel and Elizabeth (Thompson) Reed. Mr. Shillito has been assessor of his township, was on the board of election, and filled other positions of trust. Mr. and Mrs. Shillito are members of the United Presbyterian church; he is a Republican.

DANIEL B. SHORT, farmer, P. O. Water Cure, was born in Moon township, this county, June 16, 1826, and is a son of John Short. The latter was born on the ocean, while his parents Hugh and Ann Short were coming to this country from Ireland. They lived for a short time in Little York, Pa., then came to Irons Ridge, Beaver county. John Short married Elizabeth, daughter of Daniel Baker, whose father, George Baker, was captured by the Indians. Mrs. Elizabeth Short died Dec. 9, 1867, aged nearly sixty-eight years. She had three children: Daniel B., John H. and Margaret. Daniel B. received his education in a log school-house. He married Jane McCallister, of Hopewell township, and she has borne him seven children: Lizzie, Nancy, James M., John B., Reuel R., Jane I. and Margaret E. Mr. Short owns two farms containing 194 and seventy-two acres, respectively. By his own energetic efforts he has achieved success. He worked at brickmaking six years, receiving only eight and ten dollars per month. In politics he is a Republican. He and his wife are members of the Presbyterian church.

GEO. W. SHROADS, farmer, P. O. Bellowsville, was born in Moon township Oct. 3, 1831. His great-grandfather, Jacob Shroads, a native of Germany, located in Pittsburgh when that place was a borough, and removed to Moon township, Allegheny county, where he farmed. He was accidentally killed while crossing a pair of bars. He weighed about 250 pounds. He had five sons. George was a farmer first in Allegheny county, and afterward in Ohio and Virginia. In 1824 he came to Beaver county and ferried at what is now Vanport ferry. He died in Moon township at the age of sixty-seven years. His wife, Mary, was a daughter of James Minor, and died here at the age of sixty-five years. She had six children: Jacob, William, Samuel, Margaret, Eliza and John. William was a farmer and a man of local prominence. He filled the office of county commissioner, and was steward of the county home for thirteen years; also held many township offices, including constable, fifteen years, and justice of the peace, thirty years. He was an auctioneer for fifty years, and was a major of militia. His wife taught him how to write. He died June 9, 1885, aged seventy-eight years. His wife Margaret was a daughter of Anthony Baker, who came from Virginia and settled here about 1800. She died March 22, 1881, aged seventy years. Her children were George W., Mary (deceased wife of Dr. David Müller), Margaret (deceased wife of John B. Potter, of Phillipsburg), Martha (Mrs. Dunn), Viannah, Lossan (Mrs. Badders) and William James E. George W. received a common-school education, and has made farming the business of his life. He was county commissioner in 1876-79, and has also filled township offices. He is a Republican. He was school director many years. His wife is Jane, daughter of Moses Rambo, and granddaughter of William Rambo, one of the early pioneers. Mr. and Mrs. Shroads have eight children living: George W., Jr., John M., James M., David, Porter, Zoa, Stanley Quay and Edwin Forrest. The parents are members of the Presbyterian church.

JAMES B. SIMPSON, glass blower, P. O. Water Cure, is a son of William Simpson a, native of Ireland, and of Scotch descent. When a young man, William Simpson came to this country with his wife. They settled in Lancaster county, Pa., and he became a gardener and florist, having learned the business in his native country. He was a leader among the Orangemen, and a member of the United Presbyterian church. He finally removed to St. Louis, where he died, and was buried with great ceremony by the Masonic fraternity, of which he was a prominent member. His widow, Susannah E. Simpson, now resides in Pittsburgh. She has seven children, all living: John, Harry, George, James B., Emma (Mrs. McDonald), Virginia (Mrs. Allen) and Cora A. James B. was educated and learned his trade in Pittsburgh. In 1881 he removed to Phillipsburg, and became a stockholder in the Phœnix Glass Company. He worked there until the fall of 1887, when he became a stockholder in the New Brighton Glass Company. He is president of the school board, and takes a deep interest in educational matters.

JOHN E. SMITH, retired, Georgetown, was born March 28, 1828. His great-great-grandfather left Scotland during the religious revolution, and his great-grandfather John was born in New Jersey. William Smith, the grandfather of our subject, married a daughter of Joseph Smith, but not a relative. He (William) died on Terre Haute Prairie, Ind., in 1818, being one of the pioneers of that locality; his wife died the same year, [and they left ten children: Sarah, John, Joseph, James, William, Steel, Robert, Washington, Smiley and Rebecca. All except John lived to a good old age, and all returned to Belmont county, Ohio, where the parents had formerly lived. The sons were all millers by occupation, as was the father. John was born in 1801, in Washington county, Pa., and died in Belmont county, Ohio, in 1848. He married Martha, daughter of John and Mary (Stewart) Kirkwood. She died March 10, 1887, in her eighty-second year. She had ten children: William S., John Edie, Mary E., Rebecca J., Joseph W., Sarah A., Martha E., Margaret A., James S. and Campbell K. John E. was a miller and farmer until he was nineteen years old. He then went on the river, followed engineering eighteen years, and was a captain three years. He then carried on mercantile business at Smith's Ferry and Glasgow. While at the latter place, he lost his two sons, William S. and James K., aged eleven and thirteen years respectively. This loss caused him to leave the place and remove to Georgetown, where he bought "Rose Point," which he has greatly improved and beautified. His wife was Emily, daughter of James and Mary Boyles Kelsey. She had five children, all deceased except Callie K., wife of T. Stephen Laughlin. The family are members of the Presbyterian church. In politics Mr. Smith is a Republican.

JULIAN J. SMYTH, farmer, P. O. Service, was born in Wellsville, Ohio, March 2, 1847. His grandfather, John Smyth, who was born of Irish descent, came to Beaver county about the close of the War of 1812, from Adams county, Pa., bought land and settled in Hanover township, where he died at the age of seventy-two years. His wife was Nancy, daughter of John McClure, and they had eight children: James, John, Cynthia, William, Eliza J., Violet, Nancy and Washington R. The last named was born near Cannonsburg, Pa., and was a mere boy when he came to this county. Early in life he was a tanner and harness-maker, but later became a farmer; was also a merchant for several years, and a hotel-keeper. He died July 23, 1866, aged fifty-six years. His wife was Melvina D., daughter of John M. Jenkins, an attorney at law at Wellsville, Ohio. She died Dec. 26, 1881, aged sixty years. Washington R. Smyth was a Democrat, and a prominent man in his day. He was brigadier-general of state militia under Governor Bigler. He had three children: Wellington W., Julian J. and Clarence C. The latter is chief clerk for the master mechanic of the Bee Line Railroad; Wellington W. is an engineer on the I. & St. L. Railroad; Julian J. married Elizabeth, daughter of John McMurtry, and they have seven children: Frank H., Blanche F., Mortimer C., Bessie M., Ralph W., Libbie D., and Lillian. Mr. Julian J. Smyth is a Democrat. He owns a farm of 230 acres.

JOHN L. SNYDER (deceased) was born Nov. 27, 1829, in Allegheny City, Pa. His father, Martin Snyder, was born on the Rhine, in Germany, came to Pittsburgh when a young man and kept a dairy. He died in Wall Rose, Beaver county, where he owned a farm, which is yet in the possession of his widow, Mary (Black) Snyder. Martin Snyder had eleven children, including two pairs of twins. Only six are living. John L. was educated in his native town, where he lived until a young man, when he moved with his father to Economy township, Beaver county. There he was married, Feb. 22, 1855, to Susan, daughter of Thomas and Isabella (Porter) Neill, both of whom died in Beaver county, he at the age of ninety, and she at the age of seventy one years and eleven months. The Neill family came from near Belfast, Ireland. Mr. and Mrs. Snyder had eight children, who are now living: Alfred L., Thomas M., Isabella A., Mary A. (deceased). Edward R., Callie M., Clara E. and Anna L. Mr. Snyder was a ruling elder in the Presbyterian church. He was in the dairy business, which his widow has continued successfully in spite of many discouragements. She has erected new buildings, and made great improvements on the farm generally.

VALENTINE SOHN, farmer, P. O. Woodlawn, was born in Gross Karlbach, Rhein-Baiern, Germany, Dec. 22, 1819. His grandparents were Heinrich and Catharine Sohn. The former died at the age of seventy-seven years, and the latter at the age of nine ty-six. His parents were John G. and Ann Maria Sohn, former of whom died at the age of forty-two years, and the latter at the age of eighty-four. They had eleven children. Valentine came to this country at the age of nineteen, in 1838, reaching Pittsburgh on Aug. 20. He worked as a gardener and florist, six years, and after his marriage followed gardening on his own account, five years. He then purchased a farm of fifty-five acres in Hopewell township, and to this he subsequently added thirty-three acres. He owns two other farms, containing respectively seventy-two and 160 acres. He is a member of the Protestant church at Phillipsburg; in politics a Republican. He married Louise Eirich, who has borne him nine children: Maria L., Sarah, George J., William, Heinrich, Louise, Carl, Emma (deceased at the age of twenty-two years) and Elizabeth Gertrude.

GEORGE J. SOHN, farmer, P. O. Shafer's, was born in East Liberty, Allegheny county, Pa., June 14, 1851, a son of Valentine Sohn. He was educated in Beaver county, and has been a farmer all his life. He married, March 31, 1880, Miss Lizzie Wilhelm who was born July 5, 1854, in Moon township. Her father, John Wilhelm, a native of Hesse-Darmstadt, Germany, came to America in 1852, and settled near Pittsburgh. One year later he went to Huntingdon county, where he worked in the woods; thence came to Quincy, Ill., and one year later returned to Allegheny county, where he was married, in 1844, to Gertrude, daughter of Conrad Hert, and who died April 22, 1883. She had three children: John, in Allegheny City; Heinrich, living in the South on account of ill health, and Lizzie. Mr. and Mrs. Sohn have two children: Elmer, born Dec. 19, 1881, and Gilbert, born Feb. 15, 1886. In 1880 Mr. Sohn came to Moon township, where he has a farm 165 acres, equipped with the finest farm buildings and machinery in the township. He and his wife are members of the Lutheran church at Phillipsburg.

W. H. SOHN, farmer, P. O. Woodlawn, was born March 20, 1853, in Hopewell township. He is a son of Valentine Sohn, who settled in Beaver county, in February, 1853. W. H. received a common-school education, and adopted the business of farming, in which he has been successful. He was married, Sept. 22, 1881, to Alice, daughter of William McDonald, and they have one child, Bessie, born July 4, 1884. Mr. Sohn is a Republican.

HON. EDWARD SPENCE, justice of the peace, Georgetown, is a son of Edward Spence, a native of Ireland, of Scotch descent. The father married Ann Smythe, whose four nephews were Presbyterian ministers, and one of whom was a member of parliament. Mr. and Mrs. Spence came to America with two children, Richard and Samuel, and settled in Rhode Island. They afterward lived in Massachusetts, and later came to Allegheny county, Pa., where the father engaged in farming and gardening. They finally came to Georgetown, where the father and mother died, aged, respectively, eighty-one and eighty two years, both members of the Baptist church. They had four children born in America: Mary, Edward, John and Margaret. Edward was born in Pawtucket, Mass., April 9, 1829, and was educated in Allegheny county. He has been a farmer and merchant, and engaged in producing petroleum oil. He was married Jan. 2, 1879, to Jennie, daughter of R. D. Dawson. Mr. Spence has been a Republican ever since the inception of that party. He was in Kansas during the border troubles, and took an active part in making it a free state. When the war broke out, being in West Virginia during the formation of the state, he received a commission as second lieutenant from Gov. Pierpont. He has filled the office of burgess for a number of years, and has been justice of the peace for five years. In 1880 the people showed their appreciation of his sterling worth by electing him representative, which office he filled with honor and ability.

MICHAEL SPRINGER, retired farmer, merchant and postmaster, Green Garden, is a native of Beaver county, born in 1819. His paternal great-grandfather came from Switzerland. His grandfather, Michael Springer, a farmer, born in Eastern Pennsylvania, married Susan Sunderland, who became the mother of five sons and six daughters. Daniel, the eldest son, was born in Allegheny county, and remained on the home farm until a young man; then came to Moon township, this county, where he purchased a farm on Raccoon Creek. He married Rebecca Meanor, who bore him eight children. Michael, the second son, remained on his father's farm until his twenty-second year; married Elizabeth, daughter of John Cooper, and by her had six children, five now living: Elizabeth Susan (now Mrs. Ewing), John C., Christina Maggie (now Mrs. White), Mary R. and James E. When Mr. Springer arrived at maturity his father gave him sixty-three acres of land, and soon afterward he purchased seventy-five more, and is now the owner of 140 acres. In addition to farming he has followed mercantile business for twenty-two years. He has been postmaster at Green Garden since 1867, and has also been mercantile appraiser and school director. He is a member of the United Presbyterian church. In politics he is a Republican.

HENRY SPRINGER, farmer, P. O. Clinton, Allegheny county, was born in Allegheny county, Oct. 11, 1835. His grandfather, Mathias Springer, was born at the forks of Yah on the Allegheny river, and was a farmer there. He came to Allegheny county in 1785, was a soldier in the Revolution, and participated in the battles around Lake Erie. His son, Joseph, was born in Findley township, Allegheny county, and died on the old Springer homestead there, aged sixty-six years. He was a farmer, in politics a Democrat; a member of the United Presbyterian church at Clinton under Rev. William Wilson, then called the Seceder's church. His wife was Nancy McMurtrie, and they had ten children. Of these Henry came to Beaver county in 1860, and settled on the old Bier farm owned by his father. He still owns the farm which contains 175 acres. His wife is Rebecca, daughter of John and Sarah (Carr) Mateer, and they have seven children now living: Nancy E., Sarah M. (Mrs. Doughty of Beaver Falls), Ulysses A., Joseph H., Lillie M., Martha J. and John M. Mr. and Mrs. Springer are active members of the Hebron church, and he is one of the trustees. He is a Democrat, and has held various township offices, serving six years as school director.

HON. ROBERT L. STERLING, farmer, P. O. Seventy-Six, was born in the village of Independence, Nov. 14, 1835. His grandfather, Robert Sterling, was born in Ireland, of Scotch descent, and came to America in 1887. James Sterling, father of Robert L., came to this country in 1829, being twenty-nine years old at the time. He worked for some time in Pittsburgh in the rolling mills, and as a salesman. He married Margaret Ebbernethy, and came to Bocktown, where he opened a store. He next moved to Seventy-Six, where he was the first postmaster, and was a merchant there seven years; then went to Bloomfield, Hanover township, and eighteen months later removed to the farm in Independence township, where he died at the age of seventy-eight. His widow survived him two years, dying in 1880. They were the parents of five children: Robert L., Margaret, Elizabeth, William (who died in the army) and Martha J. Robert L. was educated in his native county, and at the Iron City Mercantile College. He owns a farm of 112 acres, on which were a saw and grist mill. He rebuilt the sawmill in 1859, and the gristmill in 1863. His wife is Elizabeth M., daughter of James Shillito. They are members of the United Presbyterian church, of which he is an elder. He is a Republican, and has held many township offices, including justice of the peace thirteen years. In 1885 he was elected a member of the legislature.

ANDREW STEVENSON, farmer, Frankfort Springs, was born Dec. 5, 1822, in Moon township, Allegheny county, Pa., a son of John Stevenson, who was born in Pigeon Creek, Allegheny county. He (John), married and settled in Moon township, where he died at the age of seventy-two years. His wife, Nancy, a daughter of Philip Hooper, died, aged sixty-two years. She raised nine children. At the age of twenty-five, Andrew came to Frankfort Springs, Hanover township, and engaged in milling in partnership with his brother John, to whom he sold out two years later. He then returned to Washington county, where he carried on agriculture five years; then came back to Beaver county, where he farmed and kept store at Frankfort Springs two years. He owns two farms in Beaver county, one of 170 acres and the other of 200 acres, and also one of 191 acres in Washington county. His wife, Ann Maria, was a granddaughter of Mrs. Mary Dungan, and daughter of John Roberts, an old pioneer, who was born Aug. 13, 1780, and died at the age of ninety-five years, and whose son, Colonel R. P. Roberts, fell at Gettysburg. Mrs. Stevenson is the mother of four children: John, Richard P., Mrs. Agnes M. Bryte and Samuel M. Mr. and Stevenson are members of the Presbyterian church. He is a Republican.

W. S. STEVENSON, farmer, P. O. Hookstown, was born Dec. 20, 1851, on the farm where he now resides. His great-great-grandfather was born in Scotland, and emigrated to Ireland. His great-grandfather, James Stevenson, was born in Ireland, emigrated to America, was an orderly sergeant in the Revolutionary army, was captured by the British, confined in Philadelphia nine months, and exchanged at New York. He lived after the war in Chester county, Pa., was collector of fines for that county, and was twice married. His first wife was Hannah Bull, sister of Colonel Bull, of the Revolutionary army. She bore him seven daughters and three sons. His second wife was Catharine Moore, who bore him eight sons and one daughter. In 1808 he moved to Poland, Ohio, and lived on a farm which he cleared, dying in the eighty-fifth year of his age. Two sons by his second marriage survive him: Silas, of New Castle, Pa., and McCurdy, of New Bedford, Lawrence county, Pa., the latter now in his eighty-second year. Thomas Stevenson, a son of James Stevenson by his first marriage, was born Aug. 25, 1788, was a farmer and owned the farm now occupied by W. S. Stevenson and on which he died July 17, 1847. He was a Democrat, and an adherent to the O. S. Presbyterian church. He was married, Dec. 19, 1811, to Jane Smith, who was born July 23, 1783, and died Oct. 27, 1853. Their children, all of whom are dead, were Nancy, Esther, James, Jonathan, Thomas and Elizabeth (twins), Martha, Andrew, Sampson and Mary J. Of these, Sampson was born Sept. 8, 1824, and died Aug. 28, 1880. He was a farmer, a member of the United Presbyterian church, and politically a Republican. He was twice married, first to Rachel Stewart, who was born Feb. 27, 1828, and died June 2, 1854, and whose only surviving child is our subject, a younger child, Laura E., dying in infancy. His second wife, Rebecca Manor, survives him. W. S. Stevenson was married, April 23, 1879, to Mary A., daughter of Robert N. Graham. Three children have blessed this union: S. Percy, Willis R. and Samuel N. The parents are members of the United Presbyterian church. Mr. Stevenson, politically, is a Republican.

RICHARD D. STEWART, undertaker, Hookstown, was born June 5, 1838. His grandfather Stewart, one of the first settlers of Findley township, Allegheny county, bought 1,000 acres on Potato Garden Run, a small part of which was cleared, probably by the Indians. He afterward sold 200 acres for what he had paid for the whole tract, and died on the property. His widow died in 1842, aged eighty-four years. They had eleven children: Jane, John, James, Richard, Joseph, Thomas, Ann, Ellen, Polly, Sarah and Peggie. Of these Richard was married, April 12, 1821, to Mary Stuard, who died Feb. 19, 1872, aged seventy-four years. He died Jan. 2, 1860, aged sixty-two years. They were members of the Presbyterian church of Hopewell, of which he was an elder many years. Their children were James, Catherine, John B., Margaret, Mary, Joseph, James R. and Richard D. John B. is a Presbyterian minister at Riverside, Cal, Richard D. was born on the old homestead, which he farmed until 1876, when he sold out and moved to Hanover, this county, where he bought 170 acres of land. He afterward sold out and came to Hookstown, where he has since been engaged in the undertaking business. He married Matilda, daughter of Russel Moore, and they had six children: Mary E., wife of James McCready; Margaret J., Nancy M., John M., Frank and Harry. The parents are members of the Hookstown Presbyterian church, of which the father is trustee and deacon. Politically he is a Republican.

ROBERT W. STEWART, farmer, P. O. Hookstown, was born Sept. 15, 1819, and is of Scotch descent. His grandfather Stewart was a colonel in the army in his native country; he had a large family, his sons in America receiving a dowry from him many years ago. Of his sons, Benjamin lived in Westmoreland county, Pa. He removed to Virginia when a young man, and was married in West Virginia to Rebecca Cochran. They sold their farm in Virginia, and came to Greene township, where Robert W. now lives, and where they died. They had seven children: Charles, Mary, Susan, Rebecca, Robert W., Samuel Elihu and Margaret J. Robert W. has been twice married. His first wife, Isabella Ewing, died, leaving three children: Mary J., Sarah and John, all married. His present wife was Mrs Jane Stevenson, neé Ramsey. His children by her are Oliver, Laura, Anna, Harriet and George. Mr. and Mrs. Stewart are members of the Presbyterian church of Hookstown, of which he is an elder. He was formerly an elder in the Mill Creek church. He has taken much interest in church and school work. Politically he is a Republican.

WILLIAM STEWART, plumber, P. O. Water Cure, was born and educated in this county. His father, Samuel Stewart, was born in Scotland, and came with his parents to this country when a mere youth. He settled in the northeastern part of West Virginia, and became a farmer. He lived for a while in Bridgewater, this county, but finally returned to the old homestead, where he died at the age of sixty-four years. His wife, neé Elizabeth Grim, died at the same age. She was of German descent, and had two children: Josephine and William. William married Louisa Brady, a native of Cassel, Germany, who died Jan. 1, 1881, aged forty-six years. She had four children who are now living: Felix, William, Albert and Clara L. In early life, Mr. Stewart was a shoemaker. For sixteen years he worked for the Gray Iron Line of boats, but for the last five years has been employed by the Phœnix Glass Company, of Phillipsburg.

JAMES STORER, farmer, P. O. Holt, is a native of Washington county, Pa., born in 1858, son of Richard and Mary Jane (Cooper) Storer, latter a daughter of David Cooper. Richard Storer was for many years a boat-builder in Pittsburgh, Pa., but for the past thirty years has carried on farming in Allegheny county. He had thirteen children, nine of them yet living, James being the youngest son. Our subject worked on his father's farm until twenty-two years of age; then commenced on his own account, and in 1884. came to this county, where he settled on his present farm. He married, in 1880, Phebe Ann, daughter of David and Mary (Gibson) McMillin, and by her has three children: Mary Elva, Richard William and Harper Beacom. Mr. Storer and family are members of the United Presbyterian church at Mt. Pleasant; in politics he is a Republican.

DAVID M. STROUSS, farmer, P. O. Harshaville, was born May 9, 1857, on the Strouss homestead, and is a son of David Strouss. He was reared and educated in this county, and has been a successful farmer. He has a portion of the old homestead, consisting of 134 acres. He married Aug. 12, 1879, Della F., daughter of James and Jane (Leeper) Patterson. By her he has three children: Junius M., James C. and Charles A. Mr. Strouss and wife are members of the Olivet Presbyterian church, of which he is trustee and treasurer. Politically he is identified with the Democratic party.

HENRY STROUSS, farmer, P. O. Clinton, Allegheny county, was born Jan. 28, 1807, in Northampton county, Pa. His grandfather, David Strouss, was born in Germany, and died in Pennsylvania; and his father, Henry, was born in New York City, in 1768, married Barbara Rouch, and died in 1861. He bought 100 acres of land in Independence township, His son Henry, the subject of this sketch, yet owns ninety-three acres of this land, which he has greatly improved. He has been twice married. His first wife was Nancy Bolger, and his present wife is Sarah, daughter of Joseph Gunnett, a millwright by trade, who died in this county, aged seventy-four years. Mrs. Strouss is a member of the Hebron church. Mr. Strouss has been a hardworking, industrious man, and all the buildings on his farm have been erected by himself.

WILLIAM J. STROUSS, farmer, P. O. Harshaville, was born March 1, 1837, in Allegheny county, Pa. His grandfather, John Strouss, was born in Germany, came to Lancaster county, Pa., when eight years old, was by trade a millwright, and died near Clinton, Allegheny county, at the age of ninety years. He was the founder of the Hopewell Presbyterian church of Allegheny county, was a plain, straightforward man, a strong Presbyterian and an elder in the church. He built the Potato Garden Mill, still known as the Strouss Mill, and hauled the buhrs from Philadelphia. These French stones are now in the Hookstown mill. He was married three times, and reared a large family. His first wife, Mrs. Mary (Rauch) Strouss, had eight children: John, Jonas, David, Simon, Mary, Betsey, Hannah and Martha. Of these David, born in Allegheny county, was a tanner by trade, came to Beaver county in 1847, and engaged in farming. His death occurred when he was sixty-five years old. He was examining a loaded gun, when the contents were discharged in his head. His wife Emily, daughter of Josiah and Elizabeth (McCleary) Woodrow, was born Sept. 6, 1813, and is still living. Her children were John (deceased), Josiah (deceased), William J., Junius M. (deceased), Ulysses S., David M., Elizabeth, Martha (deceased), Melissa J. and Mary A. Of these William J. came into this country at the age of ten years. He has been a farmer all his life, and owns 161 acres. He married Rachel, who was born near Frankfort Springs, Beaver county, a daughter of Adam Reed, and they have three children: Anna, Emily E. and Mary A. Mr. and Mrs. Strouss are members of the United Presbyterian church of Hanover. He is a Democrat.

JEHIEL B. SWANEY, farmer, P. O. Hookstown, was born March 17, 1850, on the homestead. His great-grandfather, James Swaney, was born in Ireland, of Scotch parentage. He was one of four brothers, who all came to America and settled in different states. Thomas settled in Beaver county, while the Indians were still here. His son, James, was a farmer, and died on the old mansion farm near Hookstown. He was father of seven children: Thomas, Andy, Benjamin, Mary, John, Robert and William. Of the sons, John, the father of Jehiel B. was born on the homestead June 1, 1815, and died May 20, 1876. He was well-known and highly esteemed. He was married, Sept. 19, 1839, to Sarah, daughter of Hezekiah and Nancy (McCollough) Wallace, of Scotch descent. She was born Dec. 18, 1818, and reared eight children: Hezekiah, Cynthia, James, Jehiel B., Anna, Robert, Homer and Emmet. Jehiel B. was married, Sept. 15, 1874, to Eva, daughter of William and Anna (Gibb) Trimble, and they have one child, Jerome J., born in 1875. Mr. Swaney is a Republican.

BASIL SWEARINGEN, farmer, P. O. Poe, was born Feb. 23, 1835, in Hanover township. His father, Zachariah Swearingen, also a native of this county, was born on the old homestead, and died May 31, 1867, aged eighty-one years. He was a successful farmer, and at the time of his death owned about 910 acres of land, which was divided among his children. He was a man of large physical proportions, and industrious habits, was firm and decisive in all his dealings, yet never sued nor was sued. He was twice married; his first wife, Elizabeth, or Ruth Wilcoxon, died June 13, 1880, aged thirty-eight years, the mother of five children: Thomas, Samuel, Garret, Catharine and Zachariah. His second wife was Malinda Swearingen, and her children were Leonard, Basil, Mary (Mrs. Duncan), John, Captain William, Henry and Rezin. Henry died in the army. Basil was raised and educated in his native county. He owns a farm of 320 acres, which he has greatly improved. He married Melissa J., daughter of David Strauss, and they have five children: Mary O., Mattie V., David S., Zachariah and Nina E. Mr. Swearingen is a Republican, and has been school director for many years.

DUNCAN SWEARINGEN, farmer, P. O. Poe, was born Dec. 5, 1820, in Hanover township, this county, and is a son of Bazel and Sarah (Wilcoxen) Swearingen. He was reared in the county, and has been a successful farmer, owning 218 acres. He was married April 28, 1842, to Sarah, daughter of Jonathan and Jane (Reed) Hoge. She was born July 15, 1819. Her grandfather, John Hoge, served in the Revolution, was taken prisoner, and afterward drew a pension. He took up 400 acres of land in Hanover township in an early day. Mrs. Swearingen is the mother of ten children: Mary M., Washington (deceased at twenty years), Amanda J., Sarah A., Basil D., Jonathan D., John C., Samuel D., Martha M. and Arnet Swearingen. Mr. Swearingen and his sons are Republicans.

JOHN A. SWEARINGEN, farmer, P. O. Kendall, was born in Hanover township, Oct. 3, 1851. His grandfather, Basil Swearingen, married Sarah Wilcoxen, who bore him ten children. She died at the age of seventy-four. and he at the age of seventy-one years. Their children were Samuel, Leathy, Catharine, Mary, Jackson, Ruth, William, Duncan, Elizabeth and Sarah. Of these Samuel married Martha, daughter of Louis Spirey. She bore him seven children: Basil, Louis (killed at Gettysburg July 2, 1863), Levina, Samuel, William, John A. and A. Jackson. With the exception of Basil the family have been members of the Disciples church. Samuel Swearingen died Dec. 3, 1880, aged seventy-four years, and his widow is still living. John A. was born on the old homestead, and was reared a farmer. He owns the farm where he resides, containing seventy-five acres, and one of ninety-five acres in Greene township. He was married to Melissa J., daughter of James Miller. They have one child, Albert Myron. Mr. Swearingen is a Republican.

JOHN VAN SWEARINGEN, farmer, P. O. Poe, was born Nov. 4, 1816, above Cumberland, W. Va., where he resided until he was six years old. His grandfather, Samuel Swearingen, was born near Bladensburg, Md.; was married there and came to this township in 1779, and settled on the farm now owned by our subject. He took up 400 acres, which was divided among his heirs in 1841, and died at the age of eighty-eight years. His children were William, John V., Thomas, Zachariah, Basil, Samuel and Mrs. Mary Colvin. Of these John V. was seven years old when he came here. He died in 1846, aged seventy-four years. His wife Martha, daughter of George C. Chapman, died Jan. 4, 1861, aged eighty-one years and eight months. They had thirteen children: George C., Samuel V., Hugh, John V., William V., Catharine, Anna, Jane, Betsey, Lena, Martha, Sarah and Mary. Our subject was married, Jan. 19, 1865, to Sarah, daughter of David Beal. She died Sept. 6, 1873, leaving three children: James H., Hugh E. and Thomas B. James H. married Mary H. Cruikshank, and has one daughter Vernah. Mr. Swearingen owns 138 acres of land, and many of the family are buried on the farm. Politically he is a Republican.

CAPTAIN WILLIAM H. SWEARINGEN, farmer, P. O. Harshaville, is a son of Zachariah and Malinda Swearingen, who died on the farm where the Captain now resides. Mrs. Swearingen was a daughter of Thomas Swearingen, of Ohio. They had seven children: Leonard, Basil, Mary, John, William H., Henry C. and Reason W. William

H. and Henry were soldiers in the Civil War. The latter enlisted in the sixty-days' service, in the Pennsylvania militia, and died soon after reaching home. The Captain was born Sept. 5, 1841, on the farm which he now owns, and which contains 230 acres. He was reared and educated in Beaver county, and taught school four winters. He enlisted Aug. 9, 1862, as a private in Company F, 140th Regiment. He participated in the battles of Chancellorsville and Gettysburg; he was wounded at the latter, and was taken sick and conveyed to Chestnut Hill, Philadelphia, Pa. After his recovery he was commissioned first lieutenant of Company E, 32d Regiment United States colored troops, was promoted to captain, and served until Aug. 22, 1865. He was married, Dec. 17, 1868, to Mattie, daughter of James Nelson, and they have four sons: James N., Homer H., John J. and Ernest D. C. Captain and Mrs. Swearingen are members of the United Presbyterian church at Hanover. In politics he is a Republican, and has held several township offices.

EDWARD P. SWEET, cooper, P. O. Water Cure, was born in Scotland, Windham county, Conn., Jan. 9, 1831. His grandfather, James Sweet, who was born in Connecticut of English parents, was a soldier in the War of 1812. David D. Sweet, father of Edward P., has been a farmer, and is yet living; his wife, Alma S. Freeman, died in 1861, aged sixty-one years. Edward P. enlisted in May, 1861, in Company B, 5th Connecticut Volunteers, for three years. January 3, 1863, he was discharged for disability. He then drove an ambulance for the 2d Eastern Shore Maryland, until after the battle of Gettysburg, and was then transferred to Frederick City, Md. There he married Sophia E., daughter of John Richardson. She is the mother of nine children: Charles D., Fannie A., Mollie A., Maggie, John M., Willie R., George R., Day and Nellie. Mr. Sweet learned his trade in Maryland, and followed it there for some time. In May, 1871, he moved to Pittsburgh, and in October of the same year came to Phillipsburg. He is foreman in the cooper department of the Phœnix Glass Works. He is a Republican in politics; a member of the G. A. R. and both himself and Mrs. Sweet are members of the Presbyterian church.

ZACHARIAH SWERINGEN, farmer, P. O. Poe, was born Jan. 13, 1828; he married Rachel, daugh'er of David A. Gilliland, who was killed at the great explosion of the Pittsburgh garrison in 1862, being foreman of the cartridge factory. Four children have been born to this couple: Errett V., Charles G., Sarah L. and Mary L. Mr. and Mrs. Sweringen are members of the United Presbyterian church of Frankfort Springs. He owns a farm of 160 acres, and is a stock raiser. On this farm, A. D. 1790, occurred the bloody Indian tragedy, which resulted in the killing of his aunt, Mrs. Colvin, and her child, and the wounding of her husband. Mr. Sweringen takes a deep interest in both local and national affairs, but is no politician.

REV. WILLIAM G. TAYLOR, D. D., was born in Pittsburgh, Pa., March 3, 1820, of pious Scotch-Irish parents, James and Margaret Taylor. He had nine brothers, six of whom died in infancy, and the others lived to advanced age. One of the three survivors (a half brother) was the distinguished author, Rev. J. B. Walker, D. D., and the remaining two were merchants and manufacturers in Pittsburgh for over forty years. The three sisters lived to advanced age. Dr. Taylor's father was one of the Irish patriots of 1798; was a druggist in Pittsburgh, and, designing William for his own business, commenced to train him while yet in childhood. His father died in August, 1827, leaving the training and education of the boy to his mother, a woman of the common education of that day, but of very vigorous natural mind, and good common sense, devoted piety and implicit trust in God. She was a strict disciplinarian; her rules were obedience, and industry, work, study, and play, and no idleness; these rules developed into *fixed habits* the untiring industry and unconquerable energy that characterized Dr. Taylor in his manhood. A prominent physician said of him, "He loves to undertake things others are afraid to touch, and then with pluck, tact, labor, patience and perseverance, succeeds."

Personal Characteristics. Dr. O. S. Fowler, of New York, in writing of Dr. Taylor says:

"He has one of the best organizations, heads, and temperaments that come under my hand; his intellectual faculties are uncommonly clear, cogent, forcible and powerful, reasoning clearly and right to the point, making deep thought so plain that even the unlettered think them simple truths. He is preëminently adapted to reason on moral and religious subjects; he is a natural theologian, minister, Sabbath-school and Bible-class teacher, and expounder of moral truth; and is peculiarly happy in illustration, and a natural educator of the young. His strongest sentiments are justice, benevolence and the controlling power of conscience; he is not a natural bargain driver, but is capable of prompt and instant comprehension and action in business matters of any kind, and is most likely to succeed. He is a good judge of human nature, and knows just how to take men; he can lay plans and think for others, can attend to a great variety of business at the same time, and in short order, and without confusion. He values money for its use and not for its wealth; he will succeed in any missionary or benevolent work."

He was at home alike in the pulpit, school room or in active business.

Literary, Industrial and Business Education. We have spoken of his industrial home training and habits. During the period between school he was kept in some business house from the time he was nine years old, and always in such houses found ready employment for his school, college and seminary vacations. Hence the confirming of his habits of industry and his business training. He graduated at Jefferson College in 1847, and at the Western Theological Seminary in 1849. He was licensed to preach by the Presbytery of Pittsburgh, in April, 1848, and ordained by the same Presbytery in April, 1849, as an Evangelist, as he designed to devote himself to missionary work among the feeble churches. He was married, April 15, 1849, to Miss Charlotte Thompson, daughter of John and Mary Thompson, of Allegheny City, Pa., who has been his valuable companion and helper. They had six children, all living, viz: Mary M., Charlotte E., James W., Ellen S., John T. and Harry J.

Work. Before graduating at the seminary he was invited to become the assistant editor of the Prairie Herald Publishing Company, Chicago; he declined till through seminary. Accepting, he soon became editor-in-chief. This company then had the only power press in Chicago. They published two religious weeklies, and worked off on their small power press two dailies, one monthly, and two quarterly journals. In connection with this company was a bookstore, and in addition Dr. Taylor assisted the pastor of the Third church, who was in feeble health. This intense labor and chill-fever broke down his health, and he sought rest in preaching to a small New England congregation, but the chill-fever compelled his reurn to Pittsburgh.

Ministerial Work Proper. On his return he commenced work on unbroken ground on Mt. Washington, on the hill above S. Pittsburgh in April, 1851. Here was a good Sabbath-school established, and the foundation laid for the now flourishing church. The Presbyterian church of Beaver having declined from 196 to 42 members, he was invited for half term, but gave them all time, as that was necessary to success, as a neighboring church of 360 members, all active and zealous Christian workers, were gathering into their fold all possible members and hearers. Even under these odds, a reäction took place in favor of the old church; it was handsomely repaired, and in four years increased its communion, and the congregation one-half, with a good Sabbath-school and large catechetical classes.

The church at Tarentum had been in trouble for several years and needed special labor. There was want of harmony and difficulty in raising the salary for half time, the Bull Creek church raising the other half. They made a unanimous call for Dr. Taylor, which was accepted and he entered upon his work. Soon harmony was restored, and a missionary point, at Natrona, added to this field. In four and one-half years both of these churches were able to call a pastor all time, and Bull Creek to build a parsonage and Tarentum kept Natrona mission. This closed his labors on this field.

Dr. Taylor's next field of labor was Mt. Carmel, Beaver county. This church had been without a pastor for *twenty years*, and lacked harmony and ability to support a pastor half the time. He received a unanimous call for half time, but felt all time was necessary if the church prospered, and therefore gave them whole time, commencing in May, 1861. Harmony was restored and the church soon in better condition. In 1865, the pastor of North Branch church leaving, he took that for extra service. He moderated a call for Rev. P. J. Cummings, salary $1,000, in the united churches; soon Mt. Carmel called him all time at the same salary, and were able to build a fine new church edifice.

PHILLIPSBURGH SOLDIERS' ORPHAN SCHOOL. A new and different field opened for the labors of Dr. Taylor. The county superintendents of Beaver, Allegheny, and Washington, and Col.. Quay recommended his appointment as principal to open the first and exclusively soldiers' orphan school in Western Pennsylvania. Many friends of the orphans, knowing his fitness for the work, urged him to accept the appointment that had been made. There were serious difficulties in the way: (1) The State would not provide grounds, building, and furniture. (2) The uncertainty of the continuation of the appropriation. (3) It would require $20,000 cash for thirty acres of ground, buildings, furniture for house and schoolroom, and books and apparatus. (4) The small amount allowed for each orphan ($115, under ten years of age, and $150.00 over ten to sixteen years of age) for boarding, clothing, schooling, books, doctor and medicines, and all expenses. The work for 150 orphans would require twenty assistants to be paid out of this small amount, and these obstacles made considerable *risk* in the undertaking. Dr. Taylor took the risk, and *succeeded*. It was difficult to get a suitable location in this congressional district. At last he bought the former Water Cure, but latterly a summer resort, repaired and furnished it and added a dwelling 34x44, four stories. An additional schoolroom, 27x44, chapel, boys' hall, 24x41, and girls' hall, 20x41, and 210 acres of ground, the whole costing $48,000. All this expense was borne by Dr. Taylor. The next difficulty was to train teachers and help for this new and peculiar work. All the buildings were handsomely and tastefully furnished, as taste is essential to culture, the girls' parlor and music rooms being furnished with Brussels carpet, chairs, piano and organ.

Education. The State prescribed eight grades as the extent of the educational course. To this Dr. Taylor found he could add four grades of a mathematical and scientific course, and one-fourth of the orphans were able to finish these four grades. The average annual progress of the school was one and five-eighths grades, while one-third made two grades. No one was promoted unless their standing was at least seventy-five. The State examination conducted by State Supt. Dr. Wickersham, and Mrs. Nutter, State inspectress, July, 1874, indicated the *average standing of the school* to be ninety-three, for several years they reached ninety-five, while a large number were 100. Probably this is the highest average and progress ever reached by any school so far as known. For six years Prof. S. H. Piersol greatly aided in these results.

Hygiene. The laws of health and life were practically understood and carried out by Dr. Taylor, as the results show. Food was given for bone making, muscle, nerve and brain. All clothing fitted and adapted, perfect cleanliness of body, house, school rooms, wash and out houses, light in abundance, thorough ventilation, nine hours regular sleep, ten hours moderate but diligent work on fixed details, boys one hour regular military drill, play morning, noon, evening and recess, unless on a necessary and indispensable detail duty; clean, warm, feet, good shoes fitted by Dr. Taylor personally, always long enough and with "commonsense heels," guarding against all violent passions. Six hundred and seventeen orphans were thus cared for, over two hundred of whom required medical attention on being received.

Industry. With the aid of his excellent and educated wife, his constant and efficient helper, and who enjoyed a most remarkable home-training in all domestic work and housekeeping, they were able to originate a system of industrial details of labor, to recite daily, in classes, for thirty days, under competent teachers in each department, by which every girl in the Institution (without losing a recitation in school) acquired an intelligent, systematic and practical knowledge of domestic work, in classes in scrubbing, washing, ironing, housecleaning, dining-room work (four classes), dishwashing, cooking, all kinds of baking, mending, darning, plain family sewing, dressmaking, bonnet trimming, house keeping, sweeping, bed making, arranging rooms and parlors, all of which was subject to the daily inspection of Mrs. and Dr. Taylor. Every room, kitchens, and wash-rooms, were open for the inspection of visitors, under the guidance of a member of the Institution, every day but Sabbath, from 8 A. M. till 5 P. M.. All the surroundings and trainings in this work were designed to *form and conform habits of systematic industry*, refine the taste and manners, and give *beauty* and ease to the person, which can not be done without regular habits of industry. The results of this culture and training showed itself everywhere, in private, public and in church.

Moral, Religious and General Instruction. Dr. Taylor had a Bible class of all the scholars, employes (no one was employed in the Institution who declined to attend the Sabbath services), and all of his own family. He preached Sabbath afternoon, and generally lectured in the evening on religious biography, Bible history and archæology. He also during the week gave each day two table talks, of about ten minutes, on some subject, historical, moral, economical, on society, secrets of success and failures, on government, or comments on passing events or incidents that occurred in the school. In addition teachers read on an average per year seventy-five volumes; thus intelligence was increased and the conscience educated to become the guiding and controlling power of their life and conduct.

From boyhood Dr. Taylor took strong ground on the temperance and anti-slavery questions. He felt a deep interest in the late war, and immediately on the firing on Ft. Sumter commenced recruiting for the conflict.

He was deeply interested in the great work of "The Christian Commission" (of which Mr. George H. Stewart, of Philadelphia, was president), at home and on the field. The Beaver County Commission, of whom Judge Agnew was chairman, placed Dr. Taylor in charge of the work in Beaver county. Dr. Boardman, the United States Secretary, said Beaver county was the banner county of the United States in proportion to its population and amount raised. The labor was entirely gratuitous.

The enterprise, public spirit, courage and foresight of the Doctor prepared him to take the risk of progress and improvement. He was one of the seven who met at the call of Mr. Nelson to originate the Beaver County Agricultural Society. He was one of the parties who organized the Beaver Female Seminary, now College. With Prof. Bliss, he was the first to publicly advocate the necessity for a County Superintendent of Common Schools, and conducted the first Teachers' Institute for Hon. Thos. Nicholson, County Superintendent. He earnestly pressed the necessity for and the claims of the Pittsburgh & Lake Erie Railroad, when securing the right of way and stock subscriptions. He was one of the originators of the street railway from Freedom to Beaver. He has also helped young men to start in life, and older men to get homes for their families. He was also one of the advocates for a Presbyterian church at Rochester and at Phillipsburgh.

Dr. Taylor is regarded as a man of wealth, all of which has been made in a legitimate business way, and not by speculation; principally by foresight in investments in real estate, which he commenced in 1847. He saw causes for increase in values and waited patiently for from five to twenty years, generally realizing more than his expectations; hence his present means and the time he has had for the work before noted. His economy always gave him means for any good investment that offered. As a true business man he minded his own business, and kept his own counsel. For thirty-six years Dr. Taylor has been an active participant in the interests of Beaver county, and especially in the vicinity of his home.

REV. M. S. TELFORD, P. O. Harshaville, is of Scotch ancestry. His grandfather, John Telford, came to America when nine years old, and died in May, 1812, at the age of forty-eight. His wife, neé Sarah Beamer, of Irish descent, died April 7, 1840, aged seventy years. Stephen Telford, father of our subject, was born in Washington county, N. Y., June 20, 1795. He was a thrifty farmer, and died at the age of fifty-two years. His wife was Mary, daughter of Rev. John Cree. The latter was born in Perth, Scotland, in 1754; was graduated at Glasgow, and studied theology in the Theological Hall of the General Assembly Synod; was licensed in 1786, and came to America in 1790. He supplied the Associate church in New York City for a year, and was ordained and installed pastor in 1792. He preached in Rockbridge, Va., until 1803, then in Fairfield and Donegal, Westmoreland county, Pa., where he died April 1; 1806. His life was one of useful and earnest labor. Mrs. Mary Telford was nearly seventy years old when she died, and was the mother of eight children: Agnes, George, Mary J., Sarah, Margaret, Morrison S., David and John. The last named is a United Presbyterian minister. Morrison S. Telford was born July 3, 1834; was educated at Westminster College, graduating in 1861; studied theology in Xenia, Ohio, and Allegheny City Pa., graduating at the latter place in 1864. He was licensed to preach in 1863; and had charge of a congregation in Indiana county, Pa. for nine years. He afterward officiated nine years in Jefferson county, and at Beaver Run and Cherry Run, where he did good work, and gained the esteem of his people. Since 1882 he has been located at Hanover, this county. He was married, July 8, 1863, to Anna Barr, who was born Feb. 1, 1839, in Huntingdon county, Pa. She is a daughter of Robert and Jane (McMinn) Barr, and is the mother of three children: Maggie, M. David and Herbert M. Mr. Telford has been a successful minister, and is a strong advocate of the Prohibition party.

J. C. TEMPLE, physician, P. O. Water Cure, is a son of Robert Temple, of Hopewell township, and a descendant of one of the pioneer families of the county, both of his grandfathers having resided here prior to and being soldiers in the War of 1812. He received his primary education in his native county, and read medicine with Drs. Langfitt, of Allegheny City, and J. W. Craig, of Mansfield, Ohio; he attended lectures at the Western Reserve Medical College of Cleveland, and at the Eclectic Medical College of Cincinnati, graduating from the latter institution in 1878. He again attended the Cleveland College, and graduated there also. Obtaining the necessary endorsements from the faculty of the University of Pennsylvania, he settled in Phillipsburg, and soon built up a good practice. He spent some time traveling, and then returned to Phillipsburg, where he continues practice. He was married, in Washington, D. C., Oct. 19, 1876, to Anna M., daughter of Paul J. Hinkle, a member of a prominent family in Wetzlar, Germany. They have two children: Edith Emma and Archie Robert, aged respectively six and four years. The Doctor is a member of the Masonic fraternity, of the E. A. U. and K. of P., and formerly of the State Medical Society of Pennsylvania, and also State Medical Society of Ohio. He is assistant surgeon of the P. & L. E. railroad. He is also a prominent member of the Presbyterian church. A. B. Temple, also a son of Robert Temple, read medicine with his elder brother, and is a graduate of the Cleveland Medical College in the class of 1883. He located in Phillipsburg, and afterward spent a short time in Allegheny City. Then he settled in a thriving town in Eastern Kansas about three years ago, where he has since acquired an extensive practice.

JOHN T. TEMPLE, farmer, P. O. Hookstown, was born in Bullitt county, Ky., Dec. 25, 1816. His grandfather Temple was an Englishman. William Temple, father of John T., was born in Nelson county, Ky., was a farmer, and died in Daviess county, Ky., aged seventy-five years. He was married to Jane Trimble, a native of Ireland, and died in Bullitt county, Ky. She had three children: John T., William and Mary J., of whom only John T. is living. In early life he was a farmer and miller. In 1835 he came to Hookstown, and lived with his uncle, James Trimble. He followed carpentering several years and then bought a farm of seventy-five acres. He married Jane, daughter of John and Rachel (Whitehill) Ewing. Mr. and Mrs. Ewing are active members of the Mill Creek church, of which he is a member of Session. In politics he is a Republican. Mrs. Temple's grandfather, James Ewing, was one of the old pioneers of Beaver county, settling in Greene township, where his descendants yet reside. He was an Indian scout.

HON. ALEXANDER R. THOMSON, farmer, P. O. Seventy-Six, is a native of Independence township, and was born Feb. 29, 1820. He is a great-grandson of Alexander, the progenitor of the old Thomson family from Scotland, and whose sons, William and John, were Revolutionary soldiers. Alexander Thomson, grandson of the pioneer, and father of our subject, came to Beaver county in 1800, and settled permanently in 1804, first living in Hopewell township, and moving a few years later to Independence township, where he died. He was a sickle maker, and followed that trade till modern inventions and methods rendered it unprofitable. He was a major of militia, and his popularity was repeatedly attested by his election to various official positions, including that of county commissioner. He was the only man in Beaver county, as the record will show, who voted for Adams in 1824. He died July 8, 1846, aged sixty-five years. His wife was Jane, daughter of George and Martha (Stringer) McElhaney. She died in the fall of 1867, aged nearly eighty years. Their children were Elizabeth, Martha, Fannie, William, Jane, Margaret. Alexander R., Nancy, Cynthia (died at the age of eighteen), Lucinda and Louisa. Alexander R. was educated in this county, and at Jefferson College. He studied medicine with Dr. Pollock, then of Clinton, now of Pittsburgh. After practicing seven years, he abandoned the profession on account of ill health, and engaged in farming. He afterward studied law with Samuel B. Wilson, Esq., of Beaver, and was admitted to the bar in 1858. His principal business has been farming, and he owns 300 acres. He married Hannah, daughter of John and Elizabeth (Cheney) Charles, of an old pioneer family of Allegheny county. She died, leaving four sons John, William, Alexander F. and William H. S. The latter was named for Secretary Seward, and is now a lawyer in Beaver. Alexander F. is an attorney in Pittsburgh, and John is a farmer in Oregon. William died in Dakota, Jan. 9, 1886. Mr. Thomson's present wife, Ellen Scott, has one son, Jeremiah Morgan. The old Thomson family were Covenanters. Mr. Thomson has held positions of trust and honor. He was elected prothonotary in December, 1854, and held that position until April, 1856, when he resigned on account of ill health. A staunch adherent of Jeffersonian democracy, he was never a blind follower of party. When the question of slavery was thrust upon the people for solution, he raised his voice in public speech against it. He believed that under the Declaration of Independence, the proposition was self-evident—that the American slave was entitled to his freedom. Nature endowed him with rare gifts as a public speaker. With an oratorical diction and temperament, a mind clear, logical and incisive, an accurate knowledge of national politics and the history of political parties, and with a courage that bid him speak the truth as light was given him to see it, he became at once a political speaker of rare force and power. In 1882, he was elected a member of the legislature. During the extra session of that body, convened for the purpose of apportioning the state, as required by the constitution, his speeches made in furtherance of the constitutional provision, and for the strict enforcement of the organic law, attracted attention throughout the state. He has since been living in quiet seclusion on his farm, a condition at once conducive to health, and agreeable to a mind naturally diffident and retiring.

. WILLIAM A. THOMSON (deceased) was born on the old Thomson homestead in Independence township. He was educated in this county, studied under Dr. Kelly, and became a surveyor, which occupation he followed for thirty years. He was an energetic and ambitious man, and injured his health in the discharge of his duty. Among his many good qualities, not the least was that of hospitality. He was a justice of the peace for three terms. Previous to his marriage he bought a farm of 160 acres, where he lived until his demise. On the farm are ten oil wells, for which his widow received $16,000. He was a son of Alexander Thomson, a sickle maker, who at one time lived in Harrisburg. William A. was married, Jan. 24, 1856, to Matilda B., daughter of Nathaniel and Elizabeth (Boyd) Neely. Her grandfather, Samuel Neely, came from Ireland at the age of ten years. He made much money with packhorses in the mountains of Southeastern Pennsylvania, and finally settled in Robinson township, Allegheny county; afterward he purchased 800 acres of land at $1.25 an acre, in Moon township, where he died. His son, Nathaniel, was born in Adams county, Pa., and died in Allegheny county at the age of eighty-two years. He had eight children, of whom five are living.

WILLIAM B. THORNBURG, farmer, P. O. Holt, was born in Raccoon township,

Beaver county, Pa., in 1844. The original pioneer of the Thornburg family emigrated from Ireland to these shores in an early day, and settled in Allegheny county, Pa., where he carried on farming, accumulating considerable wealth; then came to this county, and bought land on Chartier's creek. He married a French lady, who bore him fourteen children, seven of whom grew to maturity; and on the death of their father each of these seven inherited a farm. James, one of the youngest, was born in Allegheny county, and in early life followed blacksmithing, but subsequently abandoned it for farm life. He married, in 1808, Agnes, daughter of Elisha Vesey, and by this union were six daughters and four sons. Elisha, the eldest son, also a farmer, married Nancy, daughter of William Brunton, and by her had twelve children, William B., being second son. He was born and reared in Raccoon township, and remained at home until 1862, in which year he enlisted in Company H, 140th P. V. I., and for three years he was actively engaged. He participated in nearly all the battles of the Army of the Potomac, among which were Gettysburg, Chancellorsville and Spottsylvania. He was wounded at the last engagement, also at Cold Harbor, and was honorably discharged in 1865. Seventy-two acres of his present farm of ninety-five he purchased in 1868, and in 1870 he married Mary F., daughter of James Scott, formerly of Allegheny, now of this, county. One daughter (deceased) was born to them. Mr. Thornburg is a member of the G. A. R., United Presbyterian church; in politics he is a Republican.

WILLIAM L. and JAMES TODD, farmers, P. O. Green Garden. The original spelling of this family name was Tod. Our subject's grandfather, James Tod, emigrated from Scotland, and soon after his arrival located at Pittsburgh, Pa., where for some time he followed the business of carpenter and architect. As early as 1788 he came to Beaver county, and purchased several tracts of land, one of which contains 400 and another 200 acres. He married Kate Forbes, who bore him five sons and two daughters, James being the second son, born in Moon township in 1796. The latter and his sister Susan, on the death of their father, inherited the 400-acre tract of land. James, Jr., married Mary, daughter of William L. Littell, of this county, and five children were born to this union.

William L. Todd, the eldest of this family, was born in 1825, received a common-school education, and has always followed farm life. He married, in 1858, Rachel, daughter of Robert and Mary (Davis) Temple, and eight sons and one daughter have been born to them: James F., Robert H., William R., Mary Lizzie, Temple S., Roscoe A., Eddie L., Wallace Preston and Louis Elmer. For several years Mr. Todd lived on the old homestead, but in 1867 he purchased and removed to his present farm of 200 acres. He and family are members of the United Presbyterian church; in politics he is a Republican.

James Todd, the second son of James and Mary (Littell) Todd, was born on the old homestead, in Raccoon township, in 1828, and in early life learned the trade of tanner and currier, which he followed until 1871. He then purchased 200 acres of land from the heirs of his aunt, Susan Todd Harvey, 120 of which are highly cultivated. He married, in 1851, Mary, daughter of Amasa Brown, and by this union were eleven children, six sons and two daughters now living: Dr. A. W., in Minneapolis; Samuel B., a graduate of Ann Arbor University. Mich., now principal of the Public Schools of Sterling, Kan.; James Walker and Joseph L., farmers and stock raisers, of Ipswich, Dakota; and Sharp. John C., Alice M. and Maggie. Mr. Todd was appointed jury commissioner in 1883, for two years, to fill the vacancy caused by the death of Mr. Christy. Mr. Todd was elected county commissioner in 1887 for a term of three years, by the Republican party, of which party he has been a life-long member. He has also filled many township offices with credit. He and the family are members of the United Presbyterian church.

WILLIAM M. TODD, farmer, P. O. New Sheffield, was born Feb. 3, 1841, in Hopewell township. His grandfather, James Todd, was married, April 10, 1788, to Katie Forbes, and they were among the early settlers of Beaver county, where they also died, he, July 14, 1846, aged eighty-six years, and she June 26, 1843, aged seventy-eight years.

They had seven children, viz.: George, Susan, Janet, James, William, Thomas and John. Of these, John was a United Presbyterian minister. William, the father of our subject, was born Oct. 16, 1798, and died where his son now resides, Feb. 27, 1868. He married Jane G. McCune, who became the mother of seven children, of whom Mrs. Nancy Harvey, John, William M. and Thomas are now living, and James, Margaret and Catherine are deceased. Our subject has been a farmer, and on his farm of seventy acres has a fine gas well. He married Adelaide S., daughter of David and Isabelle (Harvey) Searight. This union was blessed with one son, Walter David Todd. In religious belief, Mr. and Mrs. Todd have remained members of the old church to which their parents belonged—the United Presbyterian church. Politically Mr. Todd votes the Republican ticket.

THOMAS H. TODD, farmer, P. O. New Sheffield, was born Oct. 11, 1844, in Hopewell township, a son of William Todd. [See preceding sketch.] He was educated in his native county, where he has been a farmer nearly all his life, and owns a farm of eighty-three acres, on which there is a gas well. Mr. Todd was married to Sarah E., daughter of Thomas and Eliza (Spaulding) Todd. The following named children have blessed their union: Gilbert, Charlie P., Fred L., Orlando H., Sidney V., and Henry R. In religion Mr. and Mrs. Todd are Presbyterians.

JOHN D. TORRENCE, farmer and miller, P. O. Harshaville, is a grandson of James Torrence, who was a blacksmith at Stevenson's Mill, in Allegheny county. He married Margaret Watson, and had seven children: James, Nancy, Mary, Matilda, Albert, William and Eliza. The parents of these children died in Hanover township. James, father of John D., was a farmer and miller. He bought the James Miller mill, and carried on business there until his death, which occurred in 1874, at the age of seventy-seven years. He and his wife were members of the United Presbyterian church of Hanover, of which he was an elder. He married Elizabeth, daughter of John and Elizabeth (Shafer) Deaver, of German descent. She died June 20, 1873, aged sixty-nine years. She had ten children: John D., James, William, Margaret A., Eliza, Cynthia, Albert, Nancy, Mary J. and Samuel. John D. married Esther, daughter of John and Agnes Boyd. Her father died April 2, 1870, in his eighty-eighth year. Her mother died Aug. 13, 1869, aged seventy-nine years, seven months and twenty-eight days. They were parents of twelve children: Thomas, Martha, Margaret, Mary, Samuel, Sarah, Eliza, John, Ellen, Aaron, Nancy, and Esther. Mr. and Mrs. Torrence have eight children: George A., Nancy A., Aaron B., John G., William F., Eliza J., James S. and Cynthia E. The parents are members of the United Presbyterian church. Mr. Torrence is a Republican.

GILBERT TRUMPETER, gardener, P. O. Water Cure, was born Aug. 4, 1833. His father, John Trumpeter, was born in Würtemberg, Germany, and in 1805, being then five years of age, he came to this country with his father, John Trumpeter, Sr. The latter did not have money enough to pay his passage, and was sent to prison for one year. There he worked at the shoemaker's trade, his wife selling the shoes until the debt was paid. He eventually came west and became a successful farmer. In 1813 he was persuaded to sell his farm and deposit the proceeds with the Economy Society, at Harmony, Butler county. The society was then under the leadership of George Rapp, and afterward removed to Indiana, and in 1827 returned to Pennsylvania and located at Economy. John Trumpeter, Jr., came to Phillipsburgh in 1832 under Count Leon, and died here in 1871, aged seventy-one years. Some time previous to his death he received from the Economy Society his share, a part of the land on which Gilbert Trumpeter now resides. After he seceded from the society he married Miss Agatha Walfort, who had left the society the same time. Their union was blessed with four children. Gilbert was only one year old when his mother died. His father married a second time, and one son of this marriage is living, William. Gilbert assisted his father in paying for his land, to which he has added from time to time until he now owns twenty-three acres in the town.

MILOW TWYFORD, farmer, P. O. Seventy-Six, was born Jan. 8, 1829, in Allegheny county, Pa. His father, Emanuel Twyford, of Scotch descent, settled eventually on the farm now owned by Milow. He married Nancy, daughter of John Cain of Beaver county, and both died in the house now occupied by the subject of this sketch, he at the age of eighty-six and she at the age of seventy-seven years. They had sixteen children. Milow married Eleanor, daughter of Daniel McCallister. They have seven children living: Daniel, register and recorder of Beaver county; James, Jane, Agnes, Emma, George and Margaret. Mr. Twyford is identified with the Democratic party, and has been supervisor of Independence township. He owns the farm of 115 acres where he lives, and another in Hopewell township.

ELISHA VEAZEY came to this county from Maryland and was of English descent. He married Sarah Rutter, and their children were John, Elijah, James, Sarah, Betsey and Julia. Of these Elijah married Margaret McClelland, and their children were Frances, Elizabeth, Elisha, Ellen, Margaret, John, James and Maria. Elijah Veazey died in his sixty-seventh year. Of his children, Elisha was a wagon maker by trade, and followed that business many years. He married Eliza, daughter of Henry and Jane (McCandless) Reed. Mr. Veazey died June 15, 1865, aged sixty years. He was a member of the United Presbyterian church. Mrs. Veazy has been a member of the church fifty years. Her children were Margaret, Henry, James (killed in the army), John and William (twins—John is a United Presbyterian minister at Chase City, Va.), Alexander Mc. (a physician near Louisville, Ky.), Thomas, Jennie (wife of A. L. Scott) and T. Reed (a physician near Louisville, Ky.) Mr. Veazey has a farm of fifty-seven acres, on which is a gas well.

JOHN D. VOGT, farmer, P. O. Water Cure, was born in Wenterbach, Würtemberg, Germany, Dec. 19, 1835, and is a son of Daniel Vogt, a native of the above mentioned place. The latter came to America when John D. was ten years old, with his wife, Catharine Schnabel, who is now eighty-two years old. They settled in Phillipsburg, but soon moved into Moon township, where the father died in 1857, aged fifty-five years. He was an officer in the German Evangelical church. John D. was married in this county to Barbara Hartenbach, by whom he has six children now living: Adam D. (married to Lizzie Merz, and has two children, Bertha and John), Daniel F., Katie F. (married to James A. Cochran, and has one child, Rosa), Rosa, Henry and Emil. Mr. and Mrs. Vogt are members of the German Evangelical church, of which he has been a trustee and treasurer. He owns a farm of 171 acres. He is a Democrat, and has held the office of supervisor.

ISRAEL WAGNER, farmer, P. O. Water Cure, was born in Phillipsburg May 20, 1842, and is a son of Jacob Wagner. He was educated in Beaver and Allegheny counties; resided in Allegheny county about thirteen years, and for six or seven years was in the wholesale dry goods business. He was also for some time in the oil business, a member of the firm of Wagner, Leech & Co. Since 1874 he has been a resident of Moon township, engaged in farming and stock raising. He has 141 acres of land, a part of the old farm owned by his father, and makes a specialty of raising horses. He married Miss Melvina MacTaggart, and has four children: Helen C., Emma M., Leah M., and Mildreth Israella. Mr. Wagner is a Democrat, and holds the offices of supervisor and school director.

WILLIAM WAGNER, blacksmith, P. O. Water Cure, was born in Shelby county, Mo., Aug. 26, 1848. His grandfather, George Wagner, was born in Würtemberg, Germany, was a member of the Economy Society, and died at Powhatan Point, Va. His son, David, was one of the seceders who came to Phillipsburg, removed to Shelby county, Mo., and from there, in the fall of 1862, he went to Oregon, where he farmed until his death in 1874. His wife, Catharine Zuntle, also an Economite, died there in 1883. She had seven children: Emma, Jonathan, Catharine, David, Johannah, Louisa and William. The latter was educated in Missouri and Oregon, and learned his trade with his father. He returned to Phillipsburg in August, 1874, and has followed his trade here ever since. He was married here to Wilhelmina, daughter of Christian Fisher. She is the mother of three children now living: Jonathan D., Emma L. and Anna B.

The parents are members of the Lutheran church, of which Mr. Wagner is trustee. He is a Republican, has been councilman, and is now a member of the school board. He is a partner in a hardware and farm implement store conducted by his brother-in-law, Christian Fisher.

JOSEPH WALLACE, farmer, P. O. Shousetown, was born Dec. 24, 1808. There is a family tradition that the Wallace family is of the same ancestry as Sir William Wallace, the noble hero and patriot of Scotland. It is certain, at least, that their forefathers were natives of Scotland. James Wallace, the grandfather of Joseph Wallace, was born in Scotland. When he was a young man he moved to Ireland, and married Miss Mary Fulton, and to them were born seven children. William, the eldest, married a Miss McClelland, in Ireland; Samuel married a lady of German descent, in Lancaster county, Pa.; Mary married James Prentice, and Sarah married Hugh Morrow. Most of their descendants now live in Beaver county. James Wallace, the father of Joseph Wallace, was born in County Antrim, Ireland, in 1774. He came to America near the close of the last century, and settled in Lancaster county, Pa. About 1800 he married Miss Agnes Ann DeYarmond, and about the year 1804 they moved to Logstown, Beaver county, Pa. About a year afterward they settled on a farm on Squirrel Hill, near New Sheffield. After remaining here several years they exchanged this farm for the one now owned by Alexander Morrow and occupied by Alexander Kennedy. Mrs. Wallace died there in 1820. Two years later Mr. Wallace married Miss Mary Logan. He died in 1834 at the age of sixty years. He was a member of the Old Seceder's church at Scottsville.

Joseph, our subject, was a year old when his parents moved to Logstown. He first went to school in an old log school house, near the present location of Raccoon U. P. church. Among his schoolmates were Thomas McKee, John R. McCune, the Todds, the Johnstons, William Taylor and James Warnock. He also attended school at an old log school-house that stood somewhere between the Morrow farm and the old McCullough farms, all traces of which have long disappeared. He is said to have been an industrious youth, spending his time, when not at school, in clearing away the brush and timber, and turning the wilderness into fruitful fields. In 1824 he went to Rochester, which at that time contained only about half a dozen houses. Here he learned the business of keel boat building. He proved himself capable and reliable, and was soon promoted to the position of foreman. He next engaged in the business of building steamboats, and helped to construct the first steamboat built at Shousetown. He worked at this business in Pittsburgh, Steubenville, Brownsville and Mongahela City. Here he met Miss Rachel Spence, to whom he was married Sept. 20, 1832. She was born in County Antrim, Ireland, Dec. 29, 1808. James Spence, her father, was a silversmith. He married Mary Donnelly, and they came to New York in 1809, afterward settling in Monongahela City. Mr. Spence was drowned in the Monongahela at the age of thirty-six years. His widow died at the home of Joseph Wallace, Jan. 29, 1861. Soon after their marriage they settled on the farm where they still reside. Mr. Wallace has been an active member of the New Bethlehem U. P. church ever since its organization. He has three sons ministers: James M., pastor of the Eighth U. P. church, Pittsburgh; Washington, pastor of the North Branch U. P. church, Jewell county, Kan.; Joseph R., pastor of the U. P. church at Jamestown, Pa. His other children were Mrs. Mary Reed (deceased wife of John C. Reed, of Independence); Mrs. Rachel Asdale (deceased wife of Dr. Asdale, of Pittsburgh); Elizabeth, wife of William M. Calvert, of New Sheffield, and Nancy and John S., who are still at home. Mr. Wallace has been an economical and industrious man, and now has considerable property. The discovery of oil on his land in later years has also added materially to his income.

JOHN B. WEIGEL, farmer, P. O. Water Cure, was born June 8, 1835, on the old homestead in Moon township, where his great-grandfather, John Weigel, settled. The latter bought 400 acres of land, which had been taken up by one Bousman. His son John lived and died on the farm, leaving a wife, Barbara, who died at the age of eighty years, and six daughters and one son. The son, also named John, married Margaret

906   HISTORY OF BEAVER COUNTY.

Baker, who died in 1857, aged fifty-two years. She had five children who reached maturity: Daniel B., John B., James Ray, Margaret (Mrs. Smith) and Nancy. The father helped to build the North Branch Presbyterian church, of which he and his wife and daughters were members. John B. Weigel had been a farmer all his life and owns a farm of sixty-seven acres. He married Catherine, daughter of Robert Moffitt, and has seven children: James, John, Robert, Henry, Graham, Frederick and Thomas. From 1860 to 1872 Mr. Weigel lived in Raccoon township. He is a Democrat, and has been auditor for a number of years.

JOSEPH M. WHITEHILL, farmer, P.O. Kendall, was born on the Whitehill homestead, Dec. 22, 1840. His grandfather, James Whitehill, was born in Lancaster county, Pa., came to this county at an early day, and died here. He married Deborah Stephens, and had a large family of children. Of these James was born April 14, 1804, and died Feb. 10, 1858. He was a successful farmer, and owned 400 acres. He was married Feb. 10, 1825, to Martha, daughter of James and Jane (McLaughlin) Ewing. They were members of the Mill Creek Presbyterian church, of which he was clerk and chorister for many years. Mrs. Whitehill is still living, and is the mother of eight children: James, John, Robert, Martha J., Deborah, Joseph M., David R. and William. David R. was a member of Company H, 140th P. V., was taken prisoner at the second day's battle at Gettysburg, and taken to Richmond; was in Libby prison and on Belle Isle three months, was paroled, sent to Annapolis, Maryland, and returned home, where he remained a short time. He then went back to his regiment; was mortally wounded Dec. 9, and died Dec. 10, 1864. His remains were brought home and buried in Mill Creek cemetery, Jan. 1, 1865. Joseph M. was reared and educated in this county, and has always been a farmer. He owns 100 acres of land. He married Marv E., daughter of Andrew T. Kerr, a native of Belfast, Ireland. She was born in Washington county, Pa., Feb. 15, 1845, and has three children: Minnie L., John T. and Thomas E. Mr. and Mrs. Whitehill are members of the United Presbyterian church of Tomlinson's Run, and he is treasurer and trustee. He is a school director; in politics a Republican.

JAMES WHITHAM, farmer, P. O. Murdocksville, is a son of John Whitham, a native of England, who was born within four miles of Sheffield. His ancestors were of an old family. He was educated in England, learned the trade of a sickle-maker, and shipped to America as a laborer, as mechanics were not permitted to leave the kingdom. He came to Fayette county, Pa., when a young man, and worked at his trade. He married Mary, daughter of Enoch and Elizabeth (Wheatley) Tilton, who were the parents of thirteen children, eleven of whom reached maturity. John and Mary Whitham came to Beaver county about 1830, and bought 100 acres of land in Hanover township, where he followed his trade for many years. He died at the age of fifty-four years. His widow is living, aged eighty-two years. She has two children: Elizabeth (Mrs. Dugan) and James. The latter was born April 25, 1831, in Hanover township, received a common-school education, and has taught school in the county for thirty years. He was associate principal of the Hookstown academy from 1874 to 1880. He also served as county superintendent, filling the vacancy caused by the resignation of J. I. Reed. For the last seven years he has devoted all his time to farming. He and his mother and sister are members of the Baptist church. In politics Mr. Whitham is a Republican.

·JONATHAN T. WILCOXON, farmer, P. O. Poe, was born in this county, Nov. 19, 1839. His grandfather, John Wilcoxon, a native of Maryland, lived in Hancock county, Va., where he died. His wife was Elizabeth Wilcoxon, and they were members of the Church of England. They had about twelve children. Mrs. Wilcoxon's parents owned ninety-nine slaves in Maryland, but she took gold instead of slaves for her marriage dower. Of their children, Reason was born in Virginia, and at the age of sixteen went to Washington county, where he learned the blacksmith's trade. At the age of twenty-one he came to Hanover township and set up a blacksmith shop near Poe postoffice. Several years later he purchased an adjoining farm of about sixty acres, to which he afterward added more land. He was a strong and industrious man; held several township offices, and was a Democrat. His wife, Eleanor, born in Washington county, March 8, 1805, was a daughter of Jonathan and Margaret (Wright) Tucker. They had four children that lived to mature age: Mrs. Margaret McConnel, Mrs. Eleanor Mayhew, Mrs. Catherine Peterson and Jonathan T. The latter was reared in this county, and chose the business of farming. He now owns 362 acres. He married Elizabeth, daughter of Robert and Eleanor McCloud, of West Virginia. They have five children: Oscar S., Ida M., Lou E., Reason R. and Pearl L. Mr. Wilcoxon is identified with the Democratic party.

HUGH R. WILSON, farmer, P. O. Frankfort Springs, was born in North Fayette township, Allegheny county, Pa., Nov. 12, 1835. His grandfather, Hugh Wilson, one of the pioneers of that county, was killed by the upsetting of a load of hay. His son, Thomas Wilson, a farmer by occupation, who was born in the above mentioned township, was run over and killed by an express train at McDonald Station. His wife, Mary Elliott, of an old and respected family, was born on Montour's Run, and died on the old homestead. She had seven children, who reached maturity: Jane, Hugh R., Mary, William, Matilda, Rebecca, Agnes and Alice. Hugh R. was reared and educated in his native county. He became a farmer, and in 1883 bought 200 acres of J. M. Bigger. He married Elizabeth Buchanan, and they have five children: Ella, William, Mary, Thomas and John. Mr. Wilson and his wife are members of the Presbyterian church. He has always been an advocate of the principles of the Republican party.

PATRICK H. WISEMAN, shade maker, P. O. Water Cure, is a son of William and Mary (Murphy) Wiseman. His great uncle was Cardinal Wiseman. William Wiseman was born in Cork, Ireland, immigrated to America and settled in Pittsburgh, where he yet resides. He is a stone mason by trade. His wife died in Bridgewater, aged sixty-eight years. They had eight children, of whom only Patrick H. resides in this county. The latter was educated in Pittsburgh, and at an early age began working in the glass house of Curling, Robinson & Co. He afterward worked in other factories, and in 1880 came to Phillipsburg, and was one of the stockholders of the Phœnix Glass Company. He is now employed in the shade department of the company's works. He was married in Pittsburgh to Kate M., daughter of Levi and Elizabeth (Leslie) Springer, and they have four children: Walter H., William E., Bessie M. and Ethel M. Mr. Wiseman is a member of the E. A. U., of which he has been auxiliary. He is independent in politics, voting for the best candidate, regardless of party.

JOHN S. WITHROW, farmer P. O. Service, was born July 13, 1842. His grandfather, Robert Withrow, a native of Maryland, and of Scotch descent, lived for many years in Washington county, Pa., but subsequently moved to Ohio, where he died. His son, William, born in Washington county, was a miller and followed his trade in various places. He died at Bocktown, Beaver county, at the age of sixty-seven years. Politically he was a Democrat. His wife was Elizabeth Smith, who died in Clinton, Allegheny county, aged seventy-three years. Mr. and Mrs. Withrow were members of the Presbyterian church. They had nine children. John S., our subject, who was in early life a miller, became a tiller of the soil about six years ago, and about two years ago bought the R. Anderson farm of 136 acres, on which he has two fine gas wells, from which he secures a good income, and has his buildings heated and lighted. He has been successful both as a miller and farmer. He married Harriet A. McNary, of Washington county, and their children are Lizzie R., Clara B., Maggie J., Lee McNary and Rhoda Ella. Mr. and Mrs. Withrow are members of the United Presbyterian church. Politically he is a Democrat.

JOHN B. ZITZMAN, glass worker, P. O. Water Cure, is a son of George Zitzman, who died in Germany. His widow, Elizabeth (Rosenberg) Zitzman, immigrated to America with five children, and settled in Pittsburgh, where she reared the family. In 1872 they removed to Moon township, Beaver county, where they farmed, Mrs. Zitzman having previously been married to Michael Keber. John B. Zitzman was educated in Pittsburgh, and at an early age began working in a glass house. He worked at his trade in Bellaire, Ohio, until 1880, when he became a stockholder in the

Phœnix Glass Company, of Phillipsburg, being one of the founders of the company. He was married to Maggie, daughter of George Vogel, and by her has four children: Eva, Alice, Jennie and George. Mr. Zitzman has one child, Mary E., by a former marriage with Mary A. Kever, who died in Bellaire, Ohio. In politics Mr. Zitzman is a Republican.

www.ingramcontent.com/pod-product-compliance
Lightning Source LLC
Chambersburg PA
CBHW050625300426
44112CB00012B/1660